CW01024525

STRONG EXPERIENCES WITH MUSIC

STRONG EXPERIENCES WITH MUSIC

MUSIC IS MUCH MORE THAN JUST MUSIC

ALF GABRIELSSON

Professor Emeritus,
Department of Psychology,
Uppsala University, Sweden

Translated by
ROD BRADBURY

OXFORD
UNIVERSITY PRESS

OXFORD

UNIVERSITY PRESS

Great Clarendon Street, Oxford ox2 6DP

Oxford University Press is a department of the University of Oxford.
It furthers the University's objective of excellence in research, scholarship,
and education by publishing worldwide in

Oxford New York

Athens Auckland Bangkok Bogotá Buenos Aires Cape-Town
Chennai Dar-es-Salaam Delhi Florence Hong-Kong Istanbul Karachi
Kolkata Kuala-Lumpur Madrid Melbourne Mexico-City Mumbai Nairobi
Paris São-Paulo Shanghai Singapore Taipei Tokyo Toronto Warsaw

with associated companies in Berlin Ibadan

Oxford is a registered trade mark of Oxford University Press
in the UK and in certain other countries

Published in the United States
by Oxford University Press Inc., New York

© Oxford University Press, 2011

The moral rights of the author have been asserted

Database right Oxford University Press (maker)

First published 2011
Published in Swedish as Starka musikupplevelser by Gidlunds Förlag in 2008.

All rights reserved. No part of this publication may be reproduced,
stored in a retrieval system, or transmitted, in any form or by any means,
without the prior permission in writing of Oxford University Press,
or as expressly permitted by law, or under terms agreed with the appropriate
reprographics rights organization. Enquiries concerning reproduction
outside the scope of the above should be sent to the Rights Department,
Oxford University Press, at the address above

You must not circulate this book in any other binding or cover
and you must impose the same condition on any acquirer

British Library Cataloguing in Publication Data
Data available

Library of Congress Cataloging in Publication Data
Gabrielsson, Alf.
[Starka musikupplevelser. English]
Strong experiences with music: music is much more than just
music/Alf Gabrielsson; translated by Rod Bradbury.
   p. cm.
Includes bibliographical references and index.
ISBN 978-0-19-969522-5
1. Music—Psychological aspects. 2. Musical perception.
3. Music appreciation. 4. Cognition. I. Bradbury, Rod. II. Title.
ML3830.G23S7313 2011
781'.11—dc23
                                              2011024655

Typeset in Minion by Glyph International, Bangalore, India
Printed in Great Britain
on acid-free paper by
CPI Group (UK) Ltd, Croydon, CR0 4YY

ISBN 978–0–19–969522–5

1 3 5 7 9 10 8 6 4 2

Whilst every effort has been made to ensure that the contents of this book are as complete,
accurate and up-to-date as possible at the date of writing, Oxford University Press is
not able to give any guarantee or assurance that such is the case.

Preface to the swedish edition

Recently I understood that music is something much greater and more important for me than just a lot of sounds.

These experiences have given me some kind of insight that is hard to define in words. Music is something more than just music.

My view of music's great importance and strength in many different situations was further confirmed and strengthened by my experiences in connection with childbirth. Music is probably something much greater than just music.

Now I understand what a musical experience is. I have heard and read about it many times but never thought of it as something other than that one finds the music beautiful. It was something quite different.

The experience has made me better understand what an enormous resource and asset music is—it is not only something for entertainment but there is something else there that can hardly be explained.

The above quotations come from some accounts of strong experiences with music and gave me the idea for the somewhat puzzling subtitle, *Music is much more than just music*. The individuals quoted are saying that these occasions have given them experiences and insights that go far beyond what is usually associated with music. Such experiences may not appear very often, but on the other hand they stay in their memories for a long time, maybe even for the rest of their lives. They represent significant events and may lead to quite another view of music, of oneself, and of life in general.

The accounts have been gathered in a research project on strong experiences with music. They come from almost 1,000 persons. We have accounts from women and men, young and old, musicians and non-musicians, from people with different backgrounds, and with different tastes and preferences regarding music. Each account is unique, but little by little one begins to notice certain recurring features. Altogether the accounts show the enormously rich spectrum of experiences that can be elicited by and through music—a spectrum so comprehensive that one can hardly imagine it, much less expect to experience its entire breadth.

To take part in many people's experiences in this way also puts one's own ideas of music and people on trial. There may be accounts that correspond to one's own experiences, whereas other experiences may seem strange or hard to understand. One can learn much about music, about oneself, and about others from these accounts. Moreover, as they extend over most of the twentieth century, they also reflect which music was prevalent during different parts of the century and how it was received. Indirectly, the accounts also deal with other questions such as views on children, upbringing, social conventions, and the overall atmosphere of society.

The book addresses itself to all who have an interest in music and what music can mean. It should be possible to read without special prior knowledge. I have avoided the technical language of music and psychology as much as possible. Some technical questions appear only towards the end of the book or in special notes to be read at will.

This book, however, is not suitable to be read at one stretch. The material is extensive, and many accounts are of such character and intensity that one should stop now and then and take time to digest them and relate them to one's own experiences. One can also read the chapters in a different order from that presented in the book—look at the chapter titles in the Contents pages and choose according to your own interest. In a way this book can be regarded as a reference work. It presents a variety of strong experiences with music for you to choose from—in listeners and performers, with different music, and in different situations. The large number of accounts offers rich material for reflection and discussion, and it may, therefore, also be suitable for study groups and for discussion about how we are affected by music.

The framework is music psychology, the discipline that studies how we experience and react to music. There are only a few similar investigations, and they are of considerably smaller scope than the one presented here. Nor has academic psychology demonstrated any special interest in the arts. In spite of the fact that almost every person is exposed to some form of the arts every day (music, dance, fiction, theatre, film, pictorial art, architecture, etc.), there is usually not a single word about this in the usual psychology textbooks. It is as though the arts do not exist or do not play any role in the life of human beings. Such questions have been treated more widely in professions outside academic psychology. I hope that this book will encourage colleagues in psychology to pay attention to what different forms of art mean in human development, well-being, and health, and how they make life richer. Of course, this wish is not addressed only to psychologists but to all who may be concerned, not the least people who have influence on education and cultural policy in our country.

Uppsala, November 2007
Alf Gabrielsson

PREFACE TO THE ENGLISH EDITION

I am pleased that my most comprehensive report on people's strong experiences with music is now also being published in English, thanks to a generous grant by 'Riksbankens Jubileumsfond' (earlier 'The Bank of Sweden Tercentenary Foundation') for translation.

I am most grateful to Rod Bradbury for his excellent work of translating hundreds of individually differing accounts into adequate English while still retaining the particular linguistic character of each single account. I have really enjoyed our weekly discussions on translation problems and learned a lot from them.

My thanks also go to Martin Baum and Abigail Stanley at OUP for constructive discussions regarding the layout of the book.

This translation has the same structure as the original Swedish edition. However, some thirty accounts have been omitted because they presuppose special knowledge of Swedish/Scandinavian environments and customs in order to be fully understood. There are still more than 500 accounts to be read at will. Furthermore some of my commentaries have been shortened. There are, on the other hand, several updates in the Notes reflecting literature that has appeared after the publication of the Swedish book in 2008.

Please read the preface to the Swedish edition for a general background and for suggestions about how to read and treat the book.

Many pieces of music mentioned in the accounts may be heard on various Internet sites. But remember that they may be performed in quite other ways or with other artistes or ensembles than those featuring in the book. Remember, too, that the experience may also depend on your own attitude to music of various kinds, on your expectations, and on the actual situation that you find yourself in when meeting the music, as listener or performer.

Uppsala, May 2011
Alf Gabrielsson

Acknowledgements

Postscript to the Swedish Edition

This project would obviously not have been possible without the participation of many others.

First and foremost, a big thank you to all the people across the country who have so generously shared their strong music experiences. Your accounts have been the very basis for the project! It has not been possible to quote all of them in this book, but they have all contributed to the result in its totality. You have made a great contribution to research about what music can mean for mankind.

Siv Lindström Wik has been my enthusiastic colleague for the greater part of the project. Siv carried out the first interviews and wrote the first paper in the project. She has co-authored many publications and has also written a licentiate's dissertation focusing on religious aspects of SEM. Together, we have racked our brains for how one should analyse and achieve some structure in the mass of text that came into our hands. There was much trial and error in the beginning, but gradually things became clearer and a draft version of a descriptive system was born, which was later progressively revised to become what is shown in Appendix A (which, in turn, will certainly be the object of further revision). Thank you, Siv, for all your work and good comradeship, a big hug!

And thank you, all you others who have helped to collect accounts and write papers within the project: Gunilla Antonsson, Susanna Berggren, Hans Boman, Märtha Grill, Anna Karin Gullberg, Ingela Jansson, Marianne Lundahl, AnnCatharine Löfstedt, Kenneth Nilsson, Johanna Ray, Ingrid Sanner, and Maria Tchotoklieva. You have contributed to increasing the width as well as the depth of the project, and it has been a great pleasure to be your supervisor and to discuss with you.

My particular thanks to Johanna Ray who carried out a partly similar study in Swedish-speaking Finland and contributed to further examination of the applicability of the SEM scheme.

I am grateful for good suggestions and opinions I have received from Harald Bohlin, Jan Fagius, Antoon Geels, Björn Merker, Maria Sandgren, Björn Stenberg, and Emma Tranströmer.

A big thank you also to Krister Gidlund and Sven Lagerström for very constructive discussions and proposals concerning the structure of the book. I suspect that your great interest in music has been a contributing factor in this.

Naturally, I would like to express my gratitude to the Bank of Sweden Tercentenary Foundation and the Swedish Royal Academy of Music for supporting the project and the publication of this book.

Behind me there is always the fixed point in life, my family: Barbro and the children—Håkan, Ingela, and Anneli—with their families, including seven delightful grandchildren.

Finally: If you, dear reader, would like to tell of your own experience, or comment upon, discuss, or criticize anything in this book, you are welcome to contact me, by email at Alf.Gabrielsson@psyk.uu.se, or by ordinary mail at The Department of Psychology, Uppsala University, Box 1225, SE–751 42, Uppsala. I cannot promise to answer personally, but am grateful for all reactions after many years of partly solitary work with the project.

I hope that this book will come to inspire continued research on the importance of music for mankind, in theory as well as in practice. As Nietzsche said, 'Without music, life would be a mistake.'

Contents

1. Introduction   1
   1.1 General background   1
   1.2 Strong experiences with music (SEM)   2
   1.3 Some previous studies   3
   1.4 Perception and reaction   5
   1.5 Structure of the book   6

2. How the investigation was carried out   7
   2.1 Tasks and participants   7
   2.2 Analysis of the accounts   9
   2.3 Questionnaire   9

3. General points about the accounts   11

4. Experiences during childhood   13
   4.1 Security/safety and closeness   13
   4.2 Absorbed, moved, in wonderment, struck, overwhelmed   18
   4.3 Music for the first time   22
   4.4 Listening over and over again   25
   4.5 Strong experiences with music on special days   27
   4.6 Singing or playing music oneself   30
   4.7 Other special childhood experiences   33
   4.8 Commentary   35

5. Experiences during one's teenage years   36
   5.1 Meeting one's idols   37
   5.2 Encountering new, unknown music   45
   5.3 Music as consolation, support, and therapy
        during one's teens   56
   5.4 Performing music during one's teens   61
   5.5 Commentary   65

6. When music takes over   67
    6.1 In everyday situations   67
    6.2 Certain music takes over   72

7. Merging with the music   77
    7.1 Special receptivity   77
    7.2 Being drawn into the music   79
    7.3 Alone with the music   81
    7.4 Identifying with the music   83
    7.5 Being led/governed by the music   86

8. Feeling light, floating, leaving one's body   91
    8.1 Feeling light, weightless, taking off, being lifted, floating   91
    8.2 Leaving one's body, out-of-body experiences   93
    8.3 Commentary   97

9. Inner music   99
    9.1 Music that just comes into one's head   99
    9.2 Composing music   103
    9.3 Inner music afterwards   107

10. Inner images   110
    10.1 Images with a background in earlier experiences   110
    10.2 Images in connection with programme music   113
    10.3 Images of a religious character   116
    10.4 Commentary   118

11. Feelings/Emotion   120
    11.1 Strong, intense feelings   121
    11.2 Positive feelings   122
    11.3 Negative feelings   129
        11.3.1 Negative experiences due to other circumstances   130
        11.3.2 Negative experiences ascribed to the music itself   134
    11.4 Mixed, contradictory, changed feelings   140
    11.5 Using music to influence feelings   144

12. Music and existence   149
    12.1 The content and meaning of life   149

12.2 Presence in life, ultimate moments   153

12.3 Changed view of oneself and one's life   155

13. Music and transcendence   159

13.1 Magical, supernatural, mysterious, spiritual experiences   159

13.2 Ecstasy, trance   161

13.3 Cosmic experiences, merging into something greater,
       dissolution of one's ego   162

13.4 Experiences of other worlds, other realities   165

14. Music and religious experiences   171

14.1 Visions of heaven, paradise, eternity   172

14.2 Spiritual peace, holy atmosphere, Christian community   176

14.3 Music conveys a religious message and contact
       with divinity   178

14.4 Meeting the divine, God   182

15. New insights, new possibilities   190

15.1 Making contact with one's innermost self:
       new perspectives   190

15.2 Music opens up new possibilities in negative states   194

16. Confirmation through music   199

16.1 Music reflects me, my feelings, and thoughts   200

16.2 Feeling selected, personally addressed   203

16.3 Self-confidence is strengthened   205

17. Music as therapy   209

17.1 Relief of physical pain   209

17.2 Music in stress, uneasiness, anxiety, and depression   213

17.3 Summarizing comments   220

18. When performing music oneself   222

18.1 Feelings and thoughts while performing music   222

18.2 Getting to play with advanced musicians   234

18.3 Improvisation   235

18.4 Nervousness or performance anxiety, and the
       feelings when it passes   237

18.5 When feelings take over   239

18.6 When everything fits and works: magical moments   242

18.7 Commentary   248

19. Singing in a choir   250

19.1 Choir singing during childhood and adolescence   250

19.2 Singing in large choirs   253

19.3 Choir singing in church/religious contexts   255

19.4 Choir singing in other, unusual surroundings   259

19.5 Commentary   263

20. Music in love: happy and unhappy   264

21. Music in connection with illness and death   272

22. Music at funerals   278

23. Music in nature   283

24. Music from and in other cultures   293

25. Music at concerts: classical music   305

25.1 Experiences of the compositions   305

25.2 Experiences of particular artistes   322

26. Music at concerts: jazz   336

27. Music at concerts: pop and rock   346

28. Metaphors and similes   355

28.1 Descriptions of the music or the performance   355

28.2 Descriptions of both the music and the experience   357

28.3 Listeners' descriptions of the experience   358

28.4 Performers' and composers' descriptions of
       the experience   365

28.5 Summary   367

28.5.1 The music   367

28.5.2 The experience   368

29. Survey of all reactions   373

29.1 General characteristics   374

29.2 Physical reactions and behaviours   374

29.2.1 Physiological reactions   374

29.2.2 Behaviours, actions, activity   376

29.2.3 Quasi-physical reactions   376

29.3 Perception   377

29.3.1 Auditory perception   377

29.3.2 Tactile perception   378

29.3.3 Visual perception   379

29.3.4 Multimodal perception   379

29.3.5 Other senses   380

29.3.6 Synaesthetic perception   380

29.3.7 Intensified perception   381

29.3.8 Musical perception-cognition   381

29.4 Cognition   381

29.4.1 Expectations, receptivity, absorption   382

29.4.2 Altered experience of situation, body–mind,
        time–space, parts–wholeness   382

29.4.3 Lose control, be surprised, moved, struck,
        overwhelmed   383

29.4.4 Special relation to the music   383

29.4.5 Associations, memories, thoughts   384

29.4.6 Inner images, inner music   384

29.4.7 Musical cognition-emotion   385

29.5 Feelings, emotion   385

29.5.1 Strong, intense feelings   385

29.5.2 Positive feelings   386

29.5.3 Negative feelings   387

29.5.4 Mixed, contradictory, changed feelings   388

29.6 Existential and transcendental aspects   389

29.6.1 Existential aspects   389

29.6.2 Transcendental aspects   390

29.6.3 Religious experiences   390

29.7 Personal and social aspects   391

29.7.1 New insights, new possibilities   391

29.7.2 New insights, new possibilities, and new needs
        concerning music   392

29.7.3 Confirmation, self-actualization 393

29.7.4 Community 394

29.8 Answers to other questions 395

29.8.1 Gender and age 395

29.8.2 Listeners and performers 397

29.8.3 Where, when, and in what social situation did SEM occur? 398

29.8.4 Live or reproduced music? 399

29.8.5 The first time? 399

29.8.6 The same strong experience next time? 400

29.8.7 How often does SEM occur? 401

29.8.8 Results of the questionnaire 401

30. Music in SEM 403

30.1 Division into categories 403

30.2 Distribution across different categories 405

30.3 Examples of music in SEM 410

30.3.1 Art music, classical music 410

30.3.2 Artistes and ensembles within art music 410

30.3.3 Religious music 415

30.3.4 Folk music 416

30.3.5 Jazz 416

30.3.6 Rock, pop, other popular music 417

30.3.7 Songs, tunes 417

30.3.8 Entertainment music, dance music 418

30.3.9 Instruments, voices 418

30.4 Connection between categories and reactions? 419

31. What in the music elicited the reactions? 422

31.1 Emotional expression 422

31.2 Special elements in the music 423

31.3 Certain parts or portions of the music 428

31.4 The importance of text (lyrics, libretto) 432

31.5 Commentary 435

32. Causes, consequences, and importance 436

32.1 Causes 436

32.1.1 Music   437

32.1.2 Person   438

32.1.3 Situation   439

32.1.4 Interplay: music–person–situation   441

32.2 Consequences   441

32.2.1 Directly afterwards   441

32.2.2 Long-term perspective   442

32.3 What music can mean: quotations   444

33. Overview, comparisons, questions, outlooks   449

33.1 Brief overview/summary   449

33.2 Comparisons with earlier studies   451

33.3 Similarities with other strong experiences   452

33.4 Can one trust memory and language?   455

33.5 Some outlooks and relations to other topics   457

33.6 Personal final comments   460

Appendix A: A descriptive system for strong experiences
             with music   462

Appendix B: An example of analysis of an account   469

Notes   471

Index   487

CHAPTER 1

INTRODUCTION

1.1 GENERAL BACKGROUND

MUSIC is found in all cultures across the world. It takes on many different forms and is forever developing in new directions. These simple facts are the best proof of the importance of music for mankind.

Nowadays we can be with music as often as we like and in whatever manner we wish. Never before has the scope of what is available been so great and multifaceted. The mass media and Internet give us unlimited possibilities to find our way into the endless world of music. This is a context in which one really can talk of globalization.

Just as music is varied and endless, so are our reactions to music. The very same piece of music can generate totally different reactions in different people, and a person can react quite differently to the same piece of music on different occasions. Individual factors—how you are feeling, how accustomed you are to listening to music, what your tastes are in music, what type of personality you are, and much more besides—can play a major, sometimes completely decisive, role in how you react. Similarly, the experience can be affected by the specific situation: for example, where and when you hear the music (at home, in your car, at a concert, in the daytime, at night), whether or not the acoustics are good, and whether you are on your own or together with others. The experience is thus determined by an interplay of factors in the music, in the individual, and in the situation.

These questions—how we experience and react to music—belong to the science that is called music psychology. The field of music psychology is very large; essentially it embraces everything that concerns our experiences and behaviour in connection with music. It stretches from the study of particular elements in music (pitch, mode, tempo, rhythm, etc.), through comprehensive questions about how music is created, performed, and experienced, to how we make use of music and the importance of music in our lives. The common factor in all these questions is the *experience* of music, how we are affected by music. However, because our experiences do vary so much—on account of qualities in the music itself, of our own personal qualities, and the specific situation—they seem almost inaccessible to any form of systematic classification. Research within music psychology has, understandably, been wary of this complexity and rather directed its attention to more limited questions, such as how particular musical factors (pitch, mode, timbre, rhythm, etc.) affect the experience.[1]

The above facts are the extremely brief background to the study of strong experiences with music (SEM) that is presented in this book. The strongest driving forces behind the study have been a general dissatisfaction with the state of research, and the hope of being able to reach greater clarity as to what musical experiences can mean. In parallel, people's spontaneous accounts and questions about music experiences have urged me on. And, of course, my own lifelong experiences of listening to music and playing music are there in the background.

1.2 STRONG EXPERIENCES WITH MUSIC (SEM)

The experience of music is an endlessly large field and can be studied from different starting points. One such can be the personal commitment in the experience. Sometimes, music is just 'sound wallpaper' in the background while you are doing something completely different. On other occasions, the degree of commitment—of active interest—is total; the music is all that matters and everything else takes a back seat. And there are many different points between these two extremes. When you are at a concert, or listening to a record, your commitment can vary significantly. Sometimes you listen with great concentration, sometimes a little half-heartedly, sometimes your thoughts might be far away.

Investigations carried out recently show, not surprisingly, that music is often just in the background of other activities—for example, when you clean your home, wash the dishes, carry out repairs, read the newspaper, drive your car, or simply take things easy.[2] Such situations are hardly the most suitable if one wishes to penetrate deeper into questions of what a music experience can comprise and what it can mean for the individual. One should rather examine such situations where the music occupies all of the person's attention, as in particularly strong experiences with music. Over a hundred years ago, philosopher and psychologist William James maintained that 'we learn most about a thing when we view it . . . in its most exaggerated form'. His studies concerned strong religious experiences, but the principle is general.[3]

I have therefore chosen to study particularly strong experiences in connection with music. My colleagues and I have asked people to give a completely free account of their strongest experiences with music, when and where these occurred, what they experienced, and how they reacted. We have subsequently collected and analysed their accounts to ascertain what such experiences can consist of, what lies behind them, and what importance they can have. This is described in more detail in the next chapter.

But is it possible to describe strong experiences with music in words? Many people say that it is hard to find words for what they experienced; the experience shuns expression in language, it seems to be 'indescribable'. This is not unique for experiences with music, but is just as applicable to strong experiences in other contexts such as religion, love, nature, and art. One must have had such an experience oneself to 'really' understand what it can mean.

Today, with increasingly sophisticated methods of studying what happens in the body and brain, one might perhaps wonder whether it would be better to examine experiences of music through 'objective' measurements—for example, of heart activity, breathing, muscle activity, or what happens in various parts of the brain. There are a number of such studies, and they can in themselves be of great value. But they can never provide more than rough indications of the person's own 'subjective' experience. So they can complement, but never replace, the person's own description of the experience. And even though language has its limitations, it is nevertheless the best—and quite inescapable—means we have (so far) at our disposal for studying the experience of music in a comparatively thorough manner; and I believe it will continue to be so.

1.3 SOME PREVIOUS STUDIES

It is, of course, nothing new to say that music can provide strong experiences. But there are only a few investigations that touch on questions of strong experiences with music. Leading American psychologist, Abraham Maslow, active in the field of so-called humanistic psychology, published investigations of 'peak experiences' in the 1960s and 1970s. He asked people to describe: 'The most wonderful experience of your life; happiest moments, ecstatic moments, moments of rapture, perhaps from being in love, or from listening to music, or suddenly "being hit" by a book or a painting, or from some great creative moment.'[4] He thus cited listening to music as a possible example of peak experience, and from the accounts of approximately two hundred people, he came to the conclusion that 'the two easiest ways of getting peak experiences . . . are through music and through sex' (music included dance as well).[5] Classical music in particular was what could trigger peak experiences.

Unfortunately, one cannot find any concrete individual descriptions of peak experiences in Maslow's writings. He did, however, provide several characteristics of peak experiences: for example, that one becomes totally absorbed by the phenomenon in question, one forgets time and space, and experiences a special contact or fusion with the phenomenon; all this in combination with strong feelings. The experience is described as completely unique, unforgettable, perhaps as a holy moment in life.[6] It is so wonderful that one wishes to be able to experience it again, and one feels more ready to believe that life is worth living. Maslow also claimed that music and art can do service as psychotherapy and lead to the individual acquiring another view of himself, of other people, and of life in general. Music, rhythm, and dance can be excellent ways of discovering one's own identity, for which reason these subjects must be a part of all teaching.[7]

Robert Panzarella, another American psychologist, was inspired by Maslow's work and advertised for people who were willing to describe 'intense joyous experience of listening to music or looking at visual art'. He collated such descriptions from 103 people in all, 51 of which concerned music and 52 visual art. His analysis of the accounts, some of which he quoted directly, led to four aspects of the experience:

'Renewal ecstasy': a changed view of the world; the world is better and much more beautiful than one thought before.

'Motor-sensory ecstasy': various physical reactions such as shivers, palpitations of the heart, changed breathing, changed posture, various movements, and even so-called quasi-physical reactions such as feeling 'high' and 'floating' sensations.

'Withdrawal ecstasy': one loses contact with one's surroundings and becomes totally absorbed by the music or work of art.

'Fusion-emotional ecstasy': one merges together with the music or work of art.[8]

The experience also means an increased appreciation of music or art, increased aesthetic sensibility, a changed view of oneself, of other people, and of life and the world in general, as well as long-lasting effects on mood. The music was for the greater part classical music, but there were also some examples from folk music and rock and roll. As can be seen, there are several similarities between Maslow's and Panzarella's findings.

Another, earlier, work (1961) was a study by Marghanita Laski who asked sixty or so people if they had had any experience of 'transcendent ecstasy'.[9] She also analysed descriptions of such experiences in literature and texts about religious experiences. Like Maslow, she found that such experiences were mainly triggered by classical music but also by poetry, literature, drama, ballet, and film. She described four categories of experiences: 'ineffability' (in which the experience is beyond words, indescribable), 'quasi-physical experiences' (for example, the sensation of being lifted, of floating), 'feelings of loss' (for example, losing the feeling of time and space and of oneself), and 'feelings of gain' (for example, that one feels/gains relief, happiness, perfection, new knowledge.)

Psychologist John Sloboda asked people to describe musical experiences that had taken place during their childhood. He obtained accounts from about seventy people, some of which he quoted directly.[10] Among other things, he found that positive experiences as a rule occurred in informal situations, where achievement was not a concern, when the person was a listener and in the company of people he liked. Negative experiences were associated with nervousness, humiliation, and criticism from others in situations where music was performed. Positive experiences increased the likelihood that the person would be involved in music in the future, while negative experiences had the opposite effect.

In these investigations, the concern has been mainly with experiences when one listens to music. But strong experiences also occur in connection with one's own making of music, that is, playing or singing, alone or with others. Sometimes the music making goes much better than usual: one surpasses one's own ability, everything seems to happen by itself, one enjoys it enormously and can go on doing it forever.[11] This is an example of what psychologist Gayle Privette has called 'peak performance'.[12] A closely related, and more familiar, term is 'flow', a concept introduced by psychologist Mihaly Csikszentmihalyi. In a state of flow, everything seems to go by itself without any form of exertion at all, and it is a pure delight to keep on with it. Flow can occur in connection with such different activities as mountain climbing, sailing, playing chess, dance, and music making. Here, too, it is a question of being totally absorbed, forgetting time and space, merging together with the phenomenon, losing awareness of oneself.[13]

There are, thus, a few investigations of strong experiences in connection with music.[14] The number of people who have supplied accounts is, however, rather small (for example, about fifty in Panzarella's study; it is not clear how many there were in Maslow's), and the background to the experiences and the situations around them are for the main part not described at all. Furthermore, one may wonder whether strong experiences of music are associated only with 'major' works of classical music, as would seem to be the case in the investigations named above. And can one automatically assume that strong experiences in connection with music are always entirely positive? Both Maslow and Panzarella have expressly described positive experiences. However, experience tells us that one can sometimes have negative experiences in connection with music, perhaps because of the very character of the music or due to other circumstances, for example that the music stirs up unpleasant memories.

Questions such as these provided further motivation for the decision to carry out a more comprehensive investigation of strong experiences in connection with music.

1.4 PERCEPTION AND REACTION

Before we move on, it is necessary to make an important distinction that is not always observed in investigations about experiences with music. One should distinguish between how people perceive music and how they react to it.

How we *perceive* a piece of music can be a matter of various qualities in the form of the piece, or its expression: for example, that the piece has a fast tempo, is in the major mode, is in triple time, is lively and jolly, feels vivacious and energetic, etc. Music is an object 'outside us', that we can observe and describe without necessarily being particularly involved; one can be completely 'neutral'.

By contrast, in the second case, how we *react* to music, we are not neutral observers; rather, we are affected by the music, it enters us or we enter it. Music absorbs us, it sets off thoughts, feelings, movements, perhaps makes us forget time and space, become at one with the music.

Naturally, these are simplified descriptions of two different attitudes. They can be seen as opposing poles with many positions in between. One often goes back and forth between them: sometimes as more of an observer, unaffected and mainly 'outside'— but then something happens which causes us to react and start to live within the music. Or the opposite: one is at first directly 'struck' by the music but after a while perhaps the absorption fades, one becomes more of an observer than a participant.

Our investigation concerns the participants' own *reactions* to music. Sometimes it can be difficult to ascertain if the description is about the music itself or how one reacted to it. 'The music was so beautiful' sounds like a description of the music, but can as readily mean that the person felt delight, pleasure. 'Weird music' can refer to the expression in the music but it could also mean that the person really did get a weird feeling listening to it. Often, both will be present—the description of the expression in the music agrees with how the person reacts, the music is perceived as beautiful and triggers pleasure.

One often assumes that the reaction has the same character as the expression in the music: happy music makes one happy, sad music makes one sad, angry music makes one aggressive, and so on. Experience tells us that such unambiguous connections do not apply at all. The situation and circumstances can have considerable influence. Of course, happy music might make us feel happy, but by no means always. Perhaps one feels stressed, doesn't have time to be happy just now, can feel even more stressed from hearing the happy song, or now is just not a suitable time. Perhaps the happy song is associated with a romantic relationship that broke up; in this case, what will the reaction be? It might also be the case that whatever expression the music has, it doesn't change anything in our mood at the time; the music makes no impression at all. These are just a few examples of how different the connection between perception and reaction can be.[15]

1.5 STRUCTURE OF THE BOOK

Chapter 2 describes how the investigation was carried out. Chapters 3 to 27 give accounts of strong experiences with music of varying character and in different situations (these are detailed in the Contents). The final chapters concern metaphors and similes (Chapter 28), a survey of the reactions provided in the accounts (Chapter 29), the music in the accounts (Chapters 30 and 31), causes and consequences (Chapter 32), and an overview and discussion (Chapter 33).

CHAPTER 2

HOW THE INVESTIGATION WAS CARRIED OUT

THE purpose of the investigation was to gain an overview of reactions that can occur in strong experiences with music. We were, naturally, also keen to examine—as far as was possible—which factors lie behind such experiences, and what importance they can come to have.

2.1 TASKS AND PARTICIPANTS

We gave people of both genders, of different ages, and with different musical preferences, the following task: 'Describe in your own words the strongest (most intense, most profound) experience with music you have ever had. Try to revive it in your mind and describe your experience and reactions in as much detail as you can.' The task was formulated in a completely open manner, that is, without any indication at all as to what the reactions might be, or what sort of music this might concern. In addition, some supplementary questions were asked: for example, whether the person was a listener or took part him/herself as a music maker, whether they reacted in the same way to earlier or later encounters with the same music, how often they had such experiences, what they thought was the reason for the strong experience, what the experience had meant in a longer perspective, and if they had had similar experiences in situations other than with music.

The project started on a small scale at the end of the 1980s and continued—sometimes with long interruptions—throughout the 1990s and into the present century. Most of the answers came in during the first half of the 1990s. Initially, eight selected persons were interviewed, women and men, of different ages and with different musical experiences and preferences. We then turned to students in various study programmes in music (music psychology, music education, and music therapy), the greater part of whom were mostly interested in classical music. We continued with investigations directed towards people with preferences for folk music, jazz, and rock music, then to special groups such as members of choirs, senior secondary school students, and pensioners. Articles and announcements about the project in the daily press, weekly press, radio, and television resulted in several hundred answers. In addition, I have received accounts of strong experiences with music in connection with tasks in study courses that I have held, and other people have sent letters with descriptions of strong experiences.[1]

In all, about 965 people participated in the study. About 250 recount two or more strong experiences with music. The number of stories is thus much greater—about 1,350—than the number of participants. The majority (62%) of the participants are women. Ages of the participants range from 13 years to 91, with a fairly even distribution (between 116 and 176 persons) over successive ten-year stages (ages 10–19, 20–29, etc., up to 60–69). Just over 80 persons are older than 70. Just over half of the participants (56%) describe themselves as amateur musicians, a fifth (20%) as professional musicians, while almost a quarter (24%) say they do not make any music themselves, but listen to music. The musical preferences of the participants range across most types of music: classical music, opera, musicals, folk music, jazz, pop/rock, ballads, religious music, and others.

There is also considerable variation in the educational level of the participants and in their occupations. The youngest participants, up to 20 years of age, were almost all students at senior secondary school, and those between 20 and 30 were partly students following various study programmes and partly people working in various fields. In all, the students numbered about 200.

The middle-aged participants (30–59 years) comprised professional musicians (music teachers, musicians, music therapists, a few composers), about 80 teachers in secondary and senior secondary schools, about 30 academics, about 75 individuals from the healthcare sector (mainly nurses, but also doctors, psychologists, therapists, children's nurses, clerics), about 25 engineers and technicians, about 30 self-employed and in business, about 40 with office jobs (primarily secretaries), about 20 working in libraries and publishing, about 20 artists (including architects, cultural workers), 5 farmers, a number of housewives, and about 25 different occupations such as air hostess, telephonist, car mechanic, maintenance worker, accountant, police officer, naprapath, joiner, programmer, designer, meteorologist, some general labourers and some unemployed people.

Among the older participants (60 years and older) many described themselves as pensioners or housewives, but many of the occupations mentioned for middle-aged participants were also represented.

For approximately 175 participants, there is no information on occupation.

The participants thus represent a wide selection with regard to gender, age, education, occupation, musical experience, and musical preferences. It is therefore likely that there is a high degree of representativeness with regard to the multitude of possible strong experiences with music. However, the selection cannot, of course, be said to be a statistically representative sample of the entire population of Sweden, and participation in the study was for the greater part on a voluntary basis. For example, it is of particular note that women participated to a greater degree than men.

2.2 ANALYSIS OF THE ACCOUNTS

Most participants (90%) described their experiences in written form, the rest (10%) orally in individual interviews. The descriptions vary a great deal in length, language, and content. The shortest descriptions contain only a few sentences, the longest comprise five to ten pages, and the transcribed interviews can be even longer.

Since there was little guidance to be gained from earlier research, the analysis of the accounts had to start from scratch. This meant first making notes of all the reactions mentioned in the accounts and then trying to place them in different categories. Throughout, we have striven to retain the participants' own words and as far as possible avoided further interpretations of their statements. Every account has been read several times on different occasions. Often the rereading leads to the discovery of further reactions and circumstances not noticed on a previous read-through, and this work should perhaps never be seen as completely finished. A great deal of effort, time, and patience has gone into analysing more than 1,300 accounts.

Almost all the accounts (92%) have been analysed by two readers independently of each other, who then compared their analyses and, when necessary, discussed and modified different interpretations. The agreement between different analysts is usually very good.[2] As the analyses have gradually become more refined, the reactions described have been ordered in a descriptive system with three different levels. This is presented in full in Chapter 29 and Appendix A after the survey of the accounts that makes up the greater part of the book. It may be a good idea to turn to Appendix A now, in order to get a sense of the richness of reactions involved in strong experiences with music.

2.3 QUESTIONNAIRE

After the participants had described their strong experience in their own words, most of them (approximately 580 persons, or 60%) were also asked to complete a questionnaire. The questionnaire was in a special envelope that was not to be opened until after the participant had finished their own description of the experience. It contained a large number of statements (60 to 90) about strong experiences with music that we had constructed on the basis of the introductory interviews and other suggestions. For each statement, the participant had to judge how well it agreed with their own experiences, on a scale from 0 ('Does not agree at all') to 10 ('Agrees exactly'), with several stages in between. These values were then analysed with conventional statistical techniques, including factor analysis, for the purpose of determining a number of fundamental dimensions in the experiences that the participants described.

In summary, the investigation thus comprised both a qualitative aspect—the participants' own descriptions of their experiences—and a quantitative aspect, with the ratings of the statements in the questionnaire. In this book, the emphasis is entirely upon the qualitative part. The results from the quantitative part are briefly described in Chapter 29, section 29.8.8; generally they accord well with the qualitative findings.

CHAPTER 3

GENERAL POINTS ABOUT THE ACCOUNTS

THE participants in the project were assured of complete anonymity. For each account, note was made of the person's gender and one of three age categories: young (under 30 years), middle-aged (30–59 years), or old (60 years and over). The decade of life in which the experience took place was also noted. (In a few accounts, however, there is no information about gender, or about age, or about the decade in which the experience occurred.) Any information that could identify specific individuals was excluded.

Most of the accounts were provided in written form. If the account was given during an interview, that is, in oral form, this is noted specifically. The language in the accounts is the participants' own; we have corrected only a number of spelling errors and other minor mistakes. Virtually all the accounts are abbreviated to some extent by the removal of peripheral or irrelevant material.

The accounts comprise strong experiences with music that took place during a period of almost 100 years: the earliest in 1908, the latest in 2004. Of the more than 1,300 experiences, approximately 13% took place before 1950 and just over 42% before 1980. Thus more than half of the experiences took place after 1980, most of them during the 1980s; a large part of these were, of course, among the youngest participants.

In terms of the age of the participants, almost half of all of the experiences took place during the previous ten years of their life, and about 75% during the previous 30 years. About 25% are thus more than 30 years previously; approximately 6% more than 60 years previously. The very longest previously, 82 years, was the short account of an 86-year-old woman of how her mother sang for her when she was four years old. Our oldest participant, then 91 years old, described an experience that was 70 years in the past.

In general, it can be said that every account has a unique content and a unique character. In a few instances, there are accounts from two different participants of the same or almost the same occasion with the same music, but even in these cases there are differences in how the experience is described.

My comments on the accounts are for the main part short. They are intended to explain and provide the reasoning for how the accounts were divided into different groups and to point out and summarize shared features in different accounts. Occasionally, providing slightly longer comments to certain accounts was unavoidable, and these comments may to some degree reflect my own opinions and impressions. On the whole, however, the accounts speak for themselves and do not need unnecessary comment, nor should this be provided. At the same time, I am sure that every reader will have their own comments and reflections upon the various accounts, and see them in relation to their own experiences.

The book contains more than 500 accounts. They have been selected specifically to reflect: (a) experiences of people of different genders and ages; (b) experiences of listeners and music makers; (c) experiences associated with various types of music; (d) experiences in various physical and social situations; and (e) experiences at different times. In addition, they should of course illustrate most of the aspects of experiences that we have found in our analyses. A particular account can sometimes illustrate two or more of these aspects. For that reason, an account may be found in more than one place: in its complete form for the aspect it illustrates best, and in abbreviated form for another aspect that it might also illustrate.

The basic arrangement of the accounts is as follows. Chapters 4 and 5 are about strong experiences with music during childhood and adolescence. Chapters 6 to 17 deal with different aspects of strong experience—such as how 'the music takes over', how one can be 'totally absorbed by the music', experiences of 'inner' music, inner images, emotions of various types, experiences of existential, transcendental, and religious character, as well as a chapter about the therapeutic effects of strong experiences with music. Chapters 18 to 27 contain accounts of strong experiences in different situations, for example when the person is involved in making the music (Chapters 18 and 19), experiences in connection with love, illness, funerals, in nature, in another culture, and at concerts of different types.

Since the experiences extend over almost 100 years (1908–2004), there are also interesting pictures of musical life in Sweden during different parts of the twentieth century with regard to what sort of music could be heard and what attitudes people had to different types of music. Indirectly, the reader is also given contemporary pictures of other issues, such as, for example, children, child-rearing, social conventions, the mood in society (for example, during the Second World War), impressions during visits in countries behind the Iron Curtain, and glimpses into other environments of various types that hardly exist any longer.

CHAPTER 4

EXPERIENCES DURING CHILDHOOD

APPROXIMATELY 135 accounts, 10% of all the accounts, concern experiences during childhood, which is here defined as up to 13 years of age. Just over a third of these concern experiences up to seven years of age, a few of which are from an age of three or four years. Thus most of the accounts are about experiences during the latter part of childhood (8–12 years).

Most accounts (70%) are from women, particularly middle-aged and older women. In just over half of the cases, the experience took place more than 40 years ago, and in 15% of the cases more than 60 years ago. About half took place before 1950, about 75% before 1970, and a total of 86% before 1980. The number of experiences that took place more recently (after 1980) is thus rather small. As we shall see in the next chapter, the opposite applies when it comes to experiences during teenage years.

The accounts illustrate different aspects of early strong experiences with music and what these came to mean. They have been grouped together under the following themes: security/safety and closeness (4.1); absorbed, moved, in wonderment, struck, overwhelmed (4.2); music for the first time (4.3); listening over and over again (4.4); strong experiences with music on special days (4.5); singing or playing music oneself (4.6); other special childhood experiences (4.7).

4.1 SECURITY/SAFETY AND CLOSENESS

The effect of music in early years of life is often associated with a safe and familiar environment where mother, father, or other close relatives or carers are nearby as security and support. The experiences are as a rule characterized by great joy and happiness. They remain in the person's memory and can be of major importance for their attitude towards music, and even result in a decision to devote oneself to music in the future.

(4.1A) Woman, middle-aged, 1950s

We had just bought a piano—I was four years old. My father had been able to learn to play the piano and had a couple of 'showpieces' in his repertoire which he sometimes played, and then I listened too. Sometimes, I woke up in the evening, after having slept for an hour or two, from hearing father playing. I had my own room. It was dark except for a thin sliver of light that shone through the little gap in the door, which wasn't completely closed, and the sound of the music came through too. It was warm, comfortable, cosy, and safe in my little bed and the sound of the piano had an enormous effect. I was happy—felt as if I swelled with happiness—most of all when father played a waltz by Brahms. I almost burst with joy and desperately tried to stay awake so I wouldn't fade away into sleep from this that was so wonderful, which I always did and woke up in the morning and noted in disappointment that I had missed a lot in any case.

I have a feeling that it was the Brahms waltz that made me absolutely want to start to play the piano—me too—and also that it ended with a classical emphasis. Despite my nagging, they didn't find a teacher for me until a year later, but I have played since then and even chosen it as a profession.

I still get a very special feeling just hearing the Brahms waltz and then I want to have peace and quiet around me so that I can listen properly, and not just hear it passively. It isn't the same bubbling feeling of joy any more, but it moves me in the roots of my heart in some way.

A similar example in another environment:

(4.1B) Woman, young, 1980s

I remember when I was five or six years old. Every summer a big gang of Mum and Dad's friends with their children travelled out to a peninsula where we had a campfire, grilled sausages, etc. Me and my little brother sat huddled up on a blue trailer that we had been transported in. The grown-ups sat beside the fire and drank beer, played the guitar, and sang. These times with singing made an enormous impression on me, a lot depending I think on the mood being so jolly, the songs happy, and so much laughter. It felt happy and I wanted to hear more. Me and my little brother eventually fell asleep, wrapped in blankets, with the music and the campfire in the background.

Meant something in the long term? Absolutely! Among other things, it resulted in my going to a renowned school of music.

When two positive factors, music and the safe environment, combine, the experience becomes even stronger. And if one hears the same music later in life, this stirs the memory of that particular context and the feelings one had then.

Presumably, the darkness of the evening—the darkness in the children's bedroom and the darkness around the campfire—contributed to the experience. Darkness cuts out other stimuli so that one's attention is focused. But in the darkness there was also a little light—the gap in the door, the campfire—which creates a feeling of security. A similar situation is described in some other accounts about how Mum turned down the lights in the evening and sang or played her children to sleep.

But, of course, strong experiences with music can occur with Dad or Mum in many different contexts, as in the following two examples.

(4.1C) Woman, middle-aged, 1950s

It must have been a Christmas in the 1950s. There was a big and beautiful radio gramophone in the room with records (old 78 records). Dad took out a record and put it on. Then he sat down in the big armchair and I got up onto his knee. And together we listened to the overture of *The Thieving Magpie* by Rossini. While the orchestra played, Dad told me a sort of little story to the music, where the different instruments played with each other and for fun chased the magpie (which was the flutes), where the finale ended with the magpie getting away from the 'dangerous strings', which had to stay on the ground crestfallen while the magpie flew up into a tree and laughed at them. So all the excitement in the music ended in happiness, and that made me happy too.

When I listen to it now, sometimes I feel the same sense of security and happiness in my tummy as when I was little and sat on Dad's knee. Thanks to a dad who listened to and loved music, who wanted and knew how to pass this feeling for music on to me, this joy in music and curiosity about music have followed me through life.

In the following case, the experience was preceded by a little accident.

(4.1D) Woman, old, 1930s

In the 1930s. Me eight years old. The time is a few minutes before 12. Mum has got time off from the shop, is in a hurry to hear *Today's Poem* on the radio and then Smetana's *Moldau*. As usual I am on the trapeze (set up between two pines). When Mum comes to the gate, I call out 'Look, Mum!' and am going to do a new movement. The result? Flopped onto Mother Earth with grazes on my knees and elbows. After having checked nothing broken, full speed into the kitchen. Me sitting on the kitchen sink. Mum getting out iodine and gauze bandage.

Then *Moldau* starts. To get me quiet, Mum says in a whisper 'Shut your eyes!' and describes the stream that grows and turns into a river, everything that happens on the shores, hunting, wedding, moonshine that glistens in the water, the whirlpool—she got everything in. I listen so intensely that I don't notice the iodine which must have stung quite a lot. When the piece is over I have four nice bandages with bows.

On that occasion Mum gave me the greatest experience of music that has since then followed me through all my life. I have always had nature in my mind when I hear classical music.

In both these cases, the music can be said to be so-called programme music, music that is intended to describe situations and events. An early example is Vivaldi's well-known violin concertos 'The Four Seasons', which came into being in the Baroque period. The great age of programme music occurred in the nineteenth century, and Smetana's *Moldau* crops up in several other accounts later in the book. Programme music can be a pleasing way of 'concretizing' music for children as well as adults, and thereby create motivation for active listening and searching for more music. (But of course, one can also listen to programme music without knowing about the programme in question.)

The security factor can also be in terms of someone from an older generation—Grandma, Grandpa—as in the next account. Perhaps one could also say that this has a little programme music in it.

(4.1E) Man, middle-aged, 1970s

When I was little I spent my summer holidays at Granny and Grandpa's in Härjedalen [a region towards the north of Sweden]. Granny loved to sing when she was doing her household chores; her lovely voice filled the house. Grandpa used to sing when he was outside in his boat on the way to some fishing ground or when we drove in the car through the forests to see if we could see an elk or a bear.

During a car trip we ended up in a place called Sveg, and Granny knew that a musician was going to perform in a park. He was a local talent who did his act with singing and an accordion. Just as we reached the park he started to sing a song that since then has always been in my mind: '*Härliga Härjedalen*' ['Lovely Härjedalen']. It started with the words: 'Go with me to Norrland, lovely Härjedalen is waiting for me!' This was fantastic. A person who sang about my beloved Härjedalen. Wow! Overjoyed. This is the best I've ever heard. I can't remember the other songs but I had this song ringing in my ears, and when we drove home I sang it as loud and as well as I could. Now Grandpa and me had a shared favourite song that we used to sing at least once on every car trip through the big forests. Since we didn't know all the words of the song, we thought up our own words, and when we managed to rhyme we felt particularly proud.

Sometimes the older generation might allow something that the parents normally wouldn't go along with. This gives the experience a very special meaning.

(4.1F) Woman, old, 1930s

Once, when I was about eight years old, Grandma woke me up in the evening so that I would be able to listen to a beautiful sonata by Beethoven on the radio. It was an unusual situation—my rather strict parents were away and I was allowed to be up so late and share Grandma's experience! All my life, that sonata has meant a lot to me.

To feel particularly privileged in this way is a central theme in the following account.

(4.1G) Woman, middle-aged, 1950s

I was perhaps seven or eight. In our town there was a music club (for adults!) and four times a year it was visited by famous artistes.

It was a weekday. Everyone at school had gone to bed, everybody except me—I was sitting in the hall and listening to the world-famous pianist Julius Katchen. What an honour. My mum had fetched me so that I could be there, and I sat close to her. She had her arm round me, and I felt safe, harmonious, and indescribably happy. Mum wanted to accustom me to culture and a richer life. She introduced it to me in a loving way and showed me respect—she took me to a 'grown-up' concert. She believed in my ability to profit by it—I was the only child in the entire hall! I had started playing the piano myself when I was six years old, but I had never heard a pianist 'live'.

I have saved the programme, so I can read that Beethoven's Sonata No. 32 in C minor was performed, then Brahms's Variations and Fugue on a theme by Handel, and after the break five pieces by Chopin: Fantasy in F minor, Op. 49, Grande valse brillante in E-flat major, Op. 18, Scherzo No. 3, Berceuse in D-flat major, Polonaise in A-flat major.

But the highlight came when I had applauded a long time, after the final piece, and the pianist came onto the stage and looked down at me and said that an extra piece would be dedicated to the youngest member of the audience. My joy was complete! He played a

Chopin waltz—I can't remember which one—and I heard the music inside me long, long after that evening.

The experience still remains with me to this day. I became even more determined to continue and work hard with music, to be able to play like him—or at least come close to his music.

The most important component in her experience was probably the feeling of being specially chosen, both by Mum and by the pianist, and being trusted in being able to profit from the music. Moreover, it must be rather rare for a seven-year-old to save a concert programme. That alone bears witness to it being a very strong experience.

In the following account, too, the experience led to a decision about choosing music as a path in life. And here, as well, it is the parents who take the initiative. But this time they are actually overshadowed, and the music takes over completely.

(4.1H) Man, middle-aged, 1940s

I have chosen to describe one of the early experiences with music that I know was emotionally extremely strong and that has been decisive for my choice of later career as a musician. I have often thought back to this occasion and wondered over the strong, and, for me, decisive experience.

I am six years old and my parents want me to go with them to an organ concert in the church. Helmut Walcha played (know this from later reference). I know that I was very much against going with them; I know this through reflections and conversations with my parents afterwards. It was in the evening, autumnal and dark, I was tired and grumpy. Once we got to the church, I fell asleep while waiting for the concert to begin. I gradually woke up during the organ music, found myself in a sort of drowsy state, my senses presumably in a condition between consciousness and unconsciousness, perhaps a liberated position where the experience can speak entirely for itself. Felt that I was resting in a large space, almost floated weightless in the hall. This could be because of the—for a child—so tangibly architectonic space; but the feeling of time and space also came just as tangibly from the flow of the music. I know from later reference that it was Bach's Trio Sonata No. 1 in E-flat major that I listened to.

I experienced an absolute clarity, in a free endless space, where points, lines, small signs played with each other in the air: a sort of kaleidoscopic three-dimensional composition of movements that I followed intensely for at least 20 minutes. My parents have later told me that I was completely captivated by the experience during this composition; they had tried to talk to me and almost been afraid about my absence.

The reason that I myself remember this concert so well is that from now I really want to play the piano myself. My parents observe my interest and I can soon have lessons.

After a few years I also play the organ and have a try at the *Trio* sonatas and remember again the experience of the concert when I was little. I can actually still recall the experience from this early concert. Can feel how my little child body was completely relaxed, can feel the light warmth in my body, the weightless state, the clarity and movement of the sound in the large endless space. Also a feeling of the tones moving me physically, almost like caresses, like material, like light, colour, etc. Now, looking back, I would like to describe it as a unique meeting of experience of time and space. It is difficult to describe the experience verbally in more detail, but I can still feel the condition inside me when I think back to the concert.

I became different as a child after that concert, something fundamental happened to me—my parents clearly noticed a change, they have told me later.

Thus: A little child who has fallen asleep in the autumn darkness and then slowly comes to his senses in an unfamiliar, large, and dimly lit room, where music with timbres he has never heard before is coming from somewhere and spreading out in the space in a polyphonic flow and appears like 'points, lines, small signs' that play in the air and that seem to touch the little relaxed child body that floats weightless in space . . . It is not so hard to imagine his experience if one knows or can listen to the Trio Sonata in E-flat major by Bach. No wonder he was totally absorbed by the experience and inaccessible to his parents' attempts to contact him.

4.2 ABSORBED, MOVED, IN WONDERMENT, STRUCK, OVERWHELMED

Being completely absorbed—'devoured'—is a typical reaction in connection with strong experiences. It is described as being captivated, touched, thrilled or—even stronger—struck, shaken, or totally overwhelmed by the music. Sometimes, the experience is characterized by amazement or surprise at what one is feeling. The music gives rise to previously unknown feelings and leads to thoughts about what music can mean, perhaps even to a desire to devote oneself to music.

Here is a selection of childhood experiences that illustrate such aspects and the individuals' reflections in association with them—reflections that, of course, have come about much later when the person has acquired a perspective on the experience. The accounts are arranged in order of increasing age at the time of the experience, from three years upwards. The experiences have taken place during many different parts of the twentieth century and the music comes from many different genres, but nevertheless there are similarities in the individuals'—children's—reactions.

(4.2A) Woman, middle-aged, 1960s

I can't have been more than three years old when I was struck by passion. A melody (the slow movement from Bruch's Violin Concerto) was coming from a room in the flat. My memory of it is that I am literally pulled into the room and see the tape recorder where the wonderful sound is coming from. I looked for a long time at the revolving tapes in amazement that they could produce something so beautiful. I remember nothing more of the circumstances around this, for example how many times I heard the same piece. But the fact remains that the melody opened the door to a totally new emotional world for me.

(4.2B) Woman, young, 1980s

When I was about five years old, me and my parents were at a concert with the cellist Frans Helmersson. I was incredibly impressed by this large violin that he put down [on the floor] to play. My parents have told me several times how I sat as if I had turned into stone and listened intensely to the music. After that evening I decided that 'when I am grown up I shall start to play the cello', which I did some years later. I think this is my first real experience with music that I can remember.

(4.2C) Woman, young, 1970s

My first strong experience with music took place when I was about five years old, when I sat playing with an old gramophone at home. When I put on Mozart's *Eine kleine Nachtmusik*, it just 'clicked'. I listened over and over again to the first movement and what captivated me the most was the transition from the first theme to the second theme, and the reverse. This was really fantastic, like finding yourself in the music somehow.

In this way I thus became a great Mozart fan and in the long term it has brought with it a lot of things, such as my choice of main instrument and profession. Music is also something I regard as a friend when you are sad and nobody can console you. That is absolutely vital!

(4.2D) Woman, young, 1970s

Bach's Toccata and Fugue in D minor has always had an effect on me. The first time I heard it, I was six years old and sitting in church at an ordinary service. I thought it was a bit boring and sat there thinking about other things. Suddenly, the cantor started to play the postludium. It was the Toccata and Fugue in D minor. My entire being was filled with the magnificent music. What I remember most is when note after note is added to a single large chord. Afterwards, I felt completely empty. It was as if the music had blown away all my thoughts. I no longer had any worries, but nor did I feel any joy. The only thing that filled me was a magnificent feeling.

Every time I hear this melody I feel the same. Even when I play it myself. Perhaps even more then. When you're alone in the church and only hear these strong magnificent notes. Sometimes it is as if it isn't me who is playing. My fingers just go by themselves.

(4.2E) Man, old, 1920s

I was probably about seven years old. A violinist was playing a piece by Handel at a Christmas prayer. Of course I was expectant about everything that was going to happen on Christmas Eve, but this music aroused strange feelings in me, this was incredibly beautiful to me. Everything else suddenly disappeared and I was happy. 'To think that there is something so delightful as this music.'

(4.2F) Woman, middle-aged, 1960s

I was nine years old and was with my dad at a Frank Zappa concert in Stockholm. It was extremely big and we couldn't sit next to each other, so I had to sit on my own. It was the first time I was at a big concert with high volume, spotlights, etc. The stage bathed in different colours and lights that changed, while the volume was high but not uncomfortable.

The music, Zappa himself (who had long, dark, wavy hair), and the lighting made a strong, positive impression on me. It was absolutely fantastic. I felt happy and in high spirits, in another world.

(4.2G) Woman, young, 1980s

[She was ten or 11 years old and had gone to the musical *Cats* in London, where she listened particularly to the melody 'Memory', sung by Elaine Page.] It was an unbelievable atmosphere. Lots of people. High volume. The music was fantastic. The tears flowed, the world around disappeared—suddenly there was only my hearing and the music, nothing else. What was around me sort of didn't exist. It was unbelievable, as if I had been able to fly in the air inside there. I had a feeling that if I got up, went forward to the railing, and threw myself out, then the music would have carried me—I wouldn't have fallen.

Afterwards I was a real pain and completely bonkers. When the feeling from the actual performance had relaxed its hold, I became all bouncy, talked far too much, giggled, and so on—in fact, I became hyperactive. I was sort of forced to hop and jump it all off. I sang when I went away. The others thought I was a bother.

(4.2H) Woman, young, 1980s

When I was at school, in the music class, in the fifth or sixth year [i.e. about 12 years old], we got a new music teacher. I think it is largely thanks to him that I have kept on with music. I'll never forget the first lesson we were going to have with him. When we went into the classroom he was sitting at the piano playing for himself, and seemed completely unaware of our existence. His eyes were looking into the air, sort of unseeing, while he listened to his piano playing and enjoyed the tones that came out of the piano. He was completely enveloped in himself and I remember that I, in my childishness, thought he looked like Jesus. Without directly teaching me, he did nevertheless convey such a love of music that I understood that music could be something spiritual, an experience for the soul.

(4.2I) Woman, middle-aged, 1940s

Sometime in the 1940s, when I was between ten and 12 years old, I was 'struck' by Beethoven: Adagio from 'Moonlight' Sonata, Op. 27, No. 2. This wonderful music poured out of our radio and I was completely charmed. It was my first experience of classical music, and I had never heard anything so wonderful before. That moment was a 'shining star' in my musical life. Have had many experiences of music later in life, but this stands at the centre; it just is there with nothing round about.

(4.2J) Woman, old, 1930s

I'm choosing an experience that came to be of great importance for the rest of my life: the first time I heard classical music. I might have been 11, or 12 at the most, and what happened was quite simply that the school treated us to music in the assembly hall: a pianist played Beethoven's *Appassionata*. It struck the poor, musical child who had neither a radio nor a gramophone at home.

How can I describe the experience? New worlds opened up, or the old one suddenly became rich and beautiful. Somebody interpreted my emotions, somebody offered a possibility to express something that was richer than anything I had come across so far. The pride, the defiance, the passion, the beauty. Somebody spoke a language I understood.

Beethoven was gradually joined by many others, of course, but I think I still have a special place for Beethoven.

(4.2K) Man, old, 1940s

Poor and orphaned, but at the children's home I had been moved to after my parents' illness and death I was nevertheless allowed to learn to play the piano. Looking back, I don't understand how I managed to get the money for the admission ticket to a piano evening at the Gothenburg Concert Hall with the pianist Annie Fischer. I was 11 years old and it was the first time I was at a concert at all and the programme with Beethoven sonatas had made me very expectant.

Several probable reasons for why this became a musical experience that I still remember 50 years later are as follows:

Being able to sit and listen without interruption to what I had previously only heard from the bad loudspeakers of a radio.

The acoustic space that caused the music to 'hover' as if it was separated from the rest of the room.

Sitting among a lot of unknown people who were interested in and enjoying the same music as me, which I hadn't experienced before.

Being able to hear how pieces should be played that I knew.

Being able to hear 'live' a master from the group of pianists who hadn't made virtuosity an end in itself.

In a dreadful situation being able to hear a giant, Beethoven, struggle against hard fate, as in the Sonata, Op. 111 that was played.

In all the above accounts, the experiences have been positive in character. But to be overwhelmed by music as a child can also be a shocking experience.

(4.2L) Woman, old, 1920s

I was five or six years old, had to go with Father and Mother to church. We sat quite a long way towards the back. It must have been something special because the church was full.

Then in the midst of the gloominess something happened. A voice from the gallery just above us. A mezzo-soprano perhaps, poured out and filled the room, a really powerful vibrato. What an experience, I was completely astounded, looked at my parents, couldn't see any reaction. Perhaps they were just as struck? Nobody was talking about the woman who sang 'How amiable are thy tabernacles, O LORD of hosts!' [Book of Psalms, No. 84]. Though I don't think the words touched me. If I hadn't been brought up not to misbehave, I would probably have thrown myself to the floor, perhaps with cramps. Felt how tight it was in my chest and throat, and didn't know how I should breathe and survive.

Hearing that woman sing in the church shocked me almost to death. Ought to have been able to talk about it then. Will never forget it.

Some parents or siblings have told of strong reactions to music that they have observed in their children or younger siblings.

(4.2M)

When my brother was little and Mum was breastfeeding him she was very fond of a group called Wasa Music. Every time Mum was going to feed him, she sat on the sofa and listened to a record by this group. A few years later, we found this record and put it on again and my little brother lit up and said: 'Oh, that!' He recognized the music and was so pleased. Then he would listen to this record all the time, just all the time. He tried to sing along and dance and loved to listen to the music.

(4.2N)

We were at a concert in a school assembly hall. We had our two boys with us. The youngest was two or three years old. We sat in the front row. The music was very strong with fast rhythms. At one point one of the girls sang a very quiet lullaby. She hadn't sung many notes before our youngest boy started to cry uncontrollably on his mother's knee. It was obvious that the music had gone straight into him. A warm smile appeared on the face of the girl who was singing, and tears ran down her cheeks while she sang. There wasn't a sound in the hall.

(4.2O)

My little daughter was with me in school. I had a lesson with a class and was playing the introduction to Stravinsky's *Rite of Spring*. After just a few bars she came running up to me. 'Mum, I'm scared.' I felt very clearly that it was the music that had affected her.

Besides the reactions mentioned in the introduction to this section (absorbed, moved, in wonderment, struck, overwhelmed) even in these childhood experiences we come across many other familiar reactions: tears, the surrounding world disappears, it feels like being able to float, one feels at home in the music, the music interprets one's feelings, one enjoys the beauty and magnificence of the music and feels great joy. There are also examples of conditioning, such as when certain music is associated with an emotionally positive situation and thus gives rise to positive feelings when heard on later occasions. In general, the experience is firmly anchored in the person's memory even though it took place a very long time ago.

4.3 MUSIC FOR THE FIRST TIME

For the older participants, the experiences have often taken place during what they regard as their first real contact with music. Sometimes this happened via radio (perhaps a crystal receiver), a horn record player, or a similar apparatus. For young people today who are used to an unlimited choice of music, it might be hard to understand what a revolutionary experience these meetings with music meant.

(4.3A) Woman, old, 1910s

My first and most powerful experience of music took place in the 1910s. I was ten years old. There was a meeting of the Lecture Society in a school. The school hall was beautifully decorated. The Swedish flag was nicely hung in a corner of the hall. On a little table in front of this, something had been placed that us kids in our backwater had never seen before. It was a fancy horn gramophone. Then, when the lecture was over, this apparatus was started up, which gave me this memory of song and music that I have never forgotten. The singer was Sven Olof Sandberg, who sang '*Barndomshemmet*' ['Childhood home'] to music. A tear came to many an eye from the emotion that this performance caused. I have the same warm feeling for the song that I have for my childhood home, which is still there and where I first saw the light of day.

(4.3B) Man, old, 1920s

When I was four or five years old, the later part of the 1920s, I got to experience music on the radio, probably my first experience with music. It was a crystal receiver with earphones and I can still see before me my grandfather's mother who was still alive then. Her amazed expression when [her face] lit up in wonderment on hearing the sound. It was the changing of the guard at the royal castle, which turned into an indelible memory for me. I would later experience it in reality in Stockholm, where we lived for several years. I have been told that it was the trumpets that especially captivated me, and it is said that I had tears in my eyes on that occasion.

(4.3C) Woman, old, 1920s

Our family had rented a gardener's cottage for the summer. I was the youngest of three girls, four years old. One Sunday, Papa had a large black box with him, and with that in his hand and a square packet under his arm he called out to us all to come down to the bower. We were extremely curious and we climbed up onto the benches around the bower's rough table to see what was inside the box. Papa turned the shiny lock, lifted the lid, and put one of the black records from the packet onto the deep red round plate. He pulled a little golden container out of his pocket. It had a picture of a dog on the lid, a white dog in front of a box. Papa tinkered with something that shone in the sun, like the record did. Then he pushed a silver arm forward and back and . . . suddenly music poured out into the bower!

We were absolutely enchanted! I was filled with a feeling of such great delight and joy that I felt my chest expand as if it was going to explode.

That is my strongest memory of how music came into my life. The first records were violin pieces played by Kreisler—his own *Schön Rosmarin*, *The Spring* by Grieg, Schubert's *Ständchen*, and so on.

(4.3D) Man, old, 1920s

It was in the 1920s in the old school in S. I was five years old and had been allowed to go with my father to the cinema. It was a silent film! But the projectionist had a gramophone that he played a lyrical piece of music on at the same time [as the film was running]. Of course, I didn't know then it was lyrical, but it made a powerful impression on me. The part of the film and the music I remember best was the dark fir trees swaying rhythmically with their branches. I remember that I longed for my mother and wished that she too had been able to experience the same as me.

I am fairly certain that this was the first time I heard any music at all. We didn't have a radio then, and no gramophone or any instrument at home, and we lived a bit out of the way in the forest, a kilometre from the nearest neighbour.

(4.3E) Woman, old, 1930s

My first experience of music. Now, at 60, I remember it as if it was yesterday when, five years old, I heard 'In a Persian market' by Albert Ketelbey for the first time. It was on an old gramophone. When I heard the music I was terrified and hid under the dining table, where I sat and listened and for some reason I could see before me Indians on horses who were charging. I never got enough of this record, it both frightened and fascinated me.

(4.3F) Man, middle-aged, 1950s

The first musical memory is from the 1950s and I remember it very well. It was spring or early summer and we, the children in the yard, played with trolleys. And from a window you could hear 'Sugartime', sung by Alice Babs. We stopped and we sang along, as well as we could, and then I had the melody in my head quite a while. We had fun when we played and it was even more fun when we sang the melody. At about the same time, during the summer, we got our first gramophone and the tunes we listened to then are still in my head even today, and they marked my musical taste for a long time.

In the following accounts, it is instead a first meeting with a symphony orchestra on tour out in the country that is the subject. The local church was the best available setting for the concert. It was an overwhelming encounter—acoustically, musically, and psychologically—that opened paths to another world of music and left impressions for life. Both accounts could also have been included in the previous section on absorption: the narrators were totally absorbed by Schubert's 'Unfinished' and Sibelius's *Finlandia* respectively.

(4.3G) Man, old, 1930s

Gävleborg County Orchestra Society was going to visit H Church for the first time. My father told me that the man who led the orchestra was the son of a Norwegian minister. It sounded exciting. Somewhat perplexing in the newspaper advert was another foreign name too: Schubert. Schubert's unfinished symphony, it said. How could it be called that? And what did a symphony actually sound like?

I wasn't unfamiliar with vocal, string, or organ music in the Mission Covenant Church, but having so many musicians gathered together in the large eighteenth-century church was a new and fascinating experience. And what a sound. Louder and more beautiful than I'd ever heard.

Well, but the music that wasn't finished? Someone from the orchestra had the kindness to give the audience a little introduction to the works that were to be played. This helped to clear up my concerns fairly well. And the other works? I must have been completely absorbed by the 'Unfinished'—I don't have any recollection of the other works. What did I find in Schubert that was so strong that the rest that was played can't fit at all in my memory?

That evening, some sort of opening appeared into a world that I had had no idea of. The opening gradually widened and led to a new existence that I experience more richly every year. And the 'Unfinished' is directly connected to that church, regardless of whether I listen to it in the concert hall or at home on the radio.

(4.3H) Woman, old, 1930s

The experience took place in a church at the end of the 1930s. I was then 11 or 12 years old. I was there together with my classmates and teacher. We cycled to the church from the village school we went to. I am sure I had no expectations of anything.

Gävleborg County Orchestra Society was probably on a tour and one of the works they performed was Jean Sibelius's *Finlandia*. For me, the experience of listening to *Finlandia* was completely revolutionary. I had never heard it before on account of the fact that we didn't yet have a radio in my parents' home. To listen to music at all, I used to go to one family or another in the village where they had a radio, but only at the times accordion music was being played. The villagers liked that music, and they had to economize with the expensive electricity.

When I heard *Finlandia*, paths were opened to experiences that I hitherto hadn't known about. I was pulled along as in ecstasy by the magnificent part that makes up the heart of the piece, and I sat there as though bewitched.

I don't know if the tears ran down my cheeks even then when I heard it. Because that is what happens now, when I hear it performed on the radio or TV. Over the years, *Finlandia* has been my favourite piece. When I hear the piece, I am in some way lifted up to higher areas, my chest expands, I lift my arms and press my hands against my neck, my eyes widen, and I become almost unaware of the surroundings.

In later years, I have tried to understand the meaning of the music. Then what I see in front of me are wild and untamed masses of water that are thrown over a precipice and are washed up on the shores. They are also a dangerous attraction. Gradually the music becomes calmer, milder, and then I can imagine the wild falls having turned into calm rivers. Sometimes, however, I can even imagine that Sibelius is portraying his home country's war history, for example. Perhaps he is describing wild battles . . . which gradually turn into a peaceful cultivation of Mother Earth.

The experience has in the long term meant an incredible amount to me. It opened up the path to classical music for me.

Besides the reactions mentioned previously, in this account there is also a description of how the music gave rise to inner images, notions, in this instance of landscape. There was also a short example of this in the account of the experience of 'In a Persian market'. Many more examples of inner images come later in Chapter 10.

4.4 LISTENING OVER AND OVER AGAIN

Perhaps it wasn't the very first meeting with music. But it was at any rate an early contact with music that the person immediately embraced and couldn't get enough of.

(4.4A) Woman, middle-aged, 1940s

At the beginning of the 1940s, my father had been called up and was in the army, but he had been granted leave on one occasion and he had bought three 78s for us three daughters. I was six years old. My oldest sister got a Hawaiian tune, my other sister got 'It's been a long, long time'. The Hawaiian music was fun, the popular song was really lovely, we danced to it. I got *Ständchen* by Schubert, with Jussi Björling.

We had a wind-up gramophone and we played our records all day long. I *loved* my record most and played it so much that it got very scratched. What a wonderful melody and what a voice. I didn't know *who* was singing, but I enjoyed it immensely. Perhaps I liked *my* record so much because I had got it from my papa whom I missed so much and who of course soon went off again. When I hear *Ständchen* today, I always feel so *delightfully* weepy like you do when it is beautiful and a bit sad at the same time.

(4.4B) Man, middle-aged, 1960s

One of my first strong experiences of music was at about six or seven years of age when I borrowed my sister's portable gramophone and listened to the Beatles song 'Come Together'. I thought it was a really good tune, a bit tough and full of action. I thought too that the record itself was extremely attractive, with a nice apple on the label that revolved at just the right speed. I think I learnt all the lyrics off by heart and I played the record every day. I listened rather intensely and wished that I could play as well as the people on the record. I'm pretty sure I felt a bit grown-up because I listened to and liked 'grown-up music'.

(4.4C) Woman, middle-aged, 1960s

If there is anything that I remember particularly well, then it's the first record of my own that I bought together with my brother, the Beatles album *Sergeant Pepper's Lonely Hearts Club Band*. That record would be my earliest really strong experience with music. I was then 12 years old and he was ten. We must have played the record hundreds of times, learnt the lyrics off by heart, and sang along with the music. We had a sort of portable gramophone of grey hard plastic that we carried around and I have no memory of having any other records. We trained our little sister to turn the record over. I loved the tunes and I still know them off by heart. We had an enormous amount of fun to the music, danced, and rushed around. We really did sit and listen, concentrated, and read the record cover to learn everything off by heart. I don't think I had listened to music like that before. I remember too, extremely clearly, the room where we sat and listened. Had that record for several years. I had a lot of pleasure from it.

(4.4D) Woman, middle-aged, 1960s

My first real emotional memories of music were with the music I had chosen personally. It was when I was about eight or nine years old when I started to become interested in the pop music of the day: Beatles, Kinks, Hollies, etc. That was when I started to form my personality. Before that, it wasn't *me* who chose the music. At the same age I got a transistor radio; I lay for hours in the dark and listened to Radio Luxembourg's broadcasts (with the radio under my pillow).

My strongest emotional memory of music was not until I was about ten or 11 years old. In the summer we used to lie in a tent or be up in the attic at a friend's in the evening and night and play music (Kinks were the favourite). These experiences feel the strongest; I float off, go into another state, things around me change, there is magic, I float around in some space or other. I go inwards at the same time that I expand. All feelings are mixed together.

(4.4E) Man, middle-aged, 1960s

I was about eight to ten years old. The piece I heard was the overture to the third act of *Lohengrin* by Richard Wagner. This took place in my childhood home on a Philips radiogram of the old type with a valve amplifier, lots of bass, and a gentle, mellow sound. It was an old 78 rpm record.

The experience was something of a shock. It suddenly felt as if there were lizards running up and down my back. My heart was squeezed together and then swelled out by turns. The piece of music was in three parts with a euphoric introduction which was repeated at the end. The middle movement was gentle and melancholic. I think it was mainly the introductory fanfares with their violent outbursts, the heady triplets in the violin parts, and the overwhelming sound that caused the powerful sensations (that is what I remember). But the gentle middle movement in the piece caused me to be moved to tears and then to be yet again flung up to the heights by the repeat of the A-part.

I played the record over and over again and became more and more enchanted by the piece of music which had so much of happiness, joy, melancholia, and sadness in it. This must be my first really intense experience of music and love of music. It was as if the music came alive for me that time 35 years ago. It was love at 'first hearing'. I went through an emotional catharsis. I'll never forget it.

Nowadays I tend to find the romantic repertory a bit turgid sometimes, but for the child that I was, Wagner just gobbled me up completely and the music became an exciting living being.

In the two last accounts above, many different reactions are described: physical (tears, shudders, 'lizards . . . up and down my back'), quasi-physical (floating around, heart/body shrinking or expanding), many other strong, mixed, and changing emotions, elements of transcendence (entering into another state, magic), emotional release (catharsis), and immediate love of music.

4.5 Strong experiences with music on special days

Sometimes, the experiences took place on days that have a special significance in Sweden, such as Walpurgis Night (30 April), Advent Sunday, or Christmas. There is then a very special association between the music and the actual situation. When coming across the same music later in life, the whole of the original situation is recalled, as well as the emotions—a typical example of conditioning.

(4.5A) Man, old, 1930s

We children always played without supervision in those days in the countryside. There were no dangers, after all. There were no cars, and all you might meet was a gentle horse who knew the children very well. On one occasion, my mother came and looked for me and informed me in surprising terms that I should go home with her, because we were going to go somewhere together when it got dark and the stars come out, as she explained. But first I must sleep so that I'd manage to go out in the evening.

I have no memories of what then happened, but I can see before me now the burning tar barrels, the fires, and an enormous bonfire that throws its flames up towards the dark-blue spring sky. In the light of these flames, the shadows of people moving among the trees and bushes take on grotesque forms. Then I see a giant snake of fire that twists and turns in among the people and forms into a square next to the big bonfire. The snake is in actual fact the members of a choir who have come to the celebration site holding lit torches. What I am seeing is my first Walpurgis Night and now the choir is singing '*Vintern rasat ut*' ['Winter is gone']. I am sitting on my father's arm and am perhaps five or six years old, but this memory never fades. For me it is absolutely unthinkable to meet the spring without listening to this delightful spring song.

But the song gives rise to such strong feelings that I can't listen to it more than once a year; and this happens on Walpurgis Night itself every year.

That music can give rise to such strong feelings that one is unable—or doesn't dare—to listen to it so often, or at all, is also described in several other accounts.

Advent Sunday, Christmas Eve and the early service on Christmas Day feature in several accounts.

(4.5B) Woman, young, 1960s

Where I come from, for many years they have held a Santa Claus parade on Advent Sunday. Everybody goes to the town centre to listen to bands and watch a long parade of people dressed up as Santa Claus and Saint Lucia. I was six years old the first time I experienced something in connection with this. I remember that as soon as Mum and Dad told me that we would go to the Santa Claus parade I got a funny feeling in my tummy. My little sister was left at home and only me and Mum and Dad were going to go, and that alone made it a big event.

It snowed outside and in town we had to jostle with thousands of people. To see any-thing at all, we were forced to push our way towards the front and when we had got quite far Dad lifted me up onto his shoulders. Then we had to wait, wait, wait. I should think I asked ten times if the parade was going to come soon.

I shall never forget the moment when it did eventually come. I couldn't see anything, but I could certainly hear. To start with, you could only hear the bass drum and that banged right through me. As the parade got closer, you could hear more and more instruments and the most beautiful of all was the glockenspiel. I was so amazed that the man who played it could know where he ought to hit so that it would sound so beautiful.

Then everything went so incredibly quickly and the parade disappeared just as quickly as it had arrived. The difference was that I could still feel the bass drum in my tummy.

The mood that remained in the air when people went their way is indescribable. I can still feel it to this day just by shutting my eyes and thinking of the music, 'The Brownies' guard parade' [by Kurt Noack].

(4.5C) Woman, young, 1980s

It was a tradition at home that early on Christmas Eve somebody would play a record with 'Jul, jul, strålande jul' ['Christmas, glorious Christmas'] and after that we would get up. So I was lying in my bed and waiting for it to be played. When it came, the melody resounded throughout the house. I thought it was the absolutely most wonderful song in the whole world. It starts faintly and gently with something that sounds like delicate bells and with a flute, then the song grows quietly and heartily. I rushed up out of my bed and into our big room. It was completely dark outside but through the window I could still just see the trees weighed down with snow. And when you heard 'Jul, jul, strålande jul', then I knew that it really was Christmas Eve.

I felt so indescribably happy, I had butterflies in my tummy, and I just embraced the music, the smell of the Christmas tree and the beautiful winter landscape all at the same time. But without the tune it would never have been the same, I thought. That moment in the morning was one of the best for the whole of Christmas Eve.

(4.5D) Woman, old, 1930s

I am five years old and sitting with my parents and brothers and sisters in the church. It is the early church service on Christmas Day, with fir branches in front of the altar rails and lighted candles everywhere. The vicar has just finished his sermon, and the cantor plays and sings 'O holy night' by Adolphe Adam. The buzz from the organ, this wonderful tune, the beautiful powerful voice, were such a dizzying experience, the candles that fluttered and warmed. It was as if I was lifted up at the same time as I felt a sense of security and a strong fellowship with everybody who took part in the holy service. 'Fall on your knees! O, hear the angel voices!' and so on—those magnificent words and the magnificent melody grabbed hold of me. 'Oh, let him sing for a long, long time, this beauty must not come to an end,' I thought. And what wonderful joy: 'One more verse! I'll be able to enjoy this beauty one more time!'

As recently as last Christmas, when I heard a young man sing 'O holy night' in church, I was suddenly five years old, seeing and experiencing in my soul the candles, the warmth, the beautiful altarpiece in my childhood church.

(4.5E) Woman, old, 1930s

When Christmas Eve had calmed down, we children had parked ourselves in our beds. For some reason, we hadn't lowered the blinds in the children's room. From my bed in the room where the lights were switched off, I could look at the fantastic deep-blue night sky, which had always had an incredible effect on me, and in the hall outside our room the radio was playing Schubert's entr'acte music for *Rosamunda*.

In some way I evidently experienced the child's awestruck littleness in the face of the majestic endlessness of the firmament coupled with a sense of complete security in experiencing myself as an infinitely little part of this whole, as well as the association with Schubert's music. It surprises me, really, that I experienced the music just then as so positive, because it has its parts where the minor key dominates, and I tend rather to be made sad by music in a minor key. But the joyful and cosy mood evidently caused a strong positive association.

In fact, it is only a very small part of the music that I clearly remember, the very beginning:

Fig 4.1 The beginning of Schubert's entr'acte music for *Rosamunda*.

This is an early example of what one might call a cosmic experience: feeling that one is a tiny part of a greater whole, merging with 'the majestic endlessness of the firmament', the cosmos.

4.6 SINGING OR PLAYING MUSIC ONESELF

Several accounts are about how the person at a young age discovers that they can play an instrument and the amazement, joy, and fascination that follow this discovery.

(4.6A) Woman, old, 1930s

The first experience was when I was only a few years old. We had a little organ at home, I stood on the pedals and stretched my arms up over my head so I could reach the keys without being able to see them, and played C, D, E, F, G, F, E, D, C slowly and listened for a long time to every tone. It was wonderful.

Just a couple of sentences, but nevertheless so telling: one can see the little girl, how she stands on the pedals with her arms held up high so that those tiny fingers could reach the keys. Slowly and with concentration, she manages to play scales: first up and then down again—a fundamental and wonderful discovery of different pitches and how they relate to each other, a discovery that she literally made with her own hands.

Similar amazing discoveries on a slightly more advanced level are to be found in the following accounts. Again, it is an organ (presumably a harmonium) that is the agent of the discovery.

(4.6B) Woman, old, 1930s

When I was eight years old in the 1930s, my father came home with an old organ. This is probably my most important memory of music. Because that was when I discovered that I was musical. I didn't know that was what you called it, but my amazement was great when I discovered that I could produce melodies on the organ. It turned out that of all of us brothers and sisters, there were only two who could do it. That I could feel exactly how far my fingers should be stretched to hit the right note was a sensation for me. I think I was rather cocky about it.

(4.6C) Woman, old, 1930s

I am five or six years old this particular summer. As so often when I have tired of playing outside, I sneak in to Auntie. She is always pleased when I come. We sing together. Auntie plays the guitar and she has a black organ too. She plays that when we sing 'Why are her cheeks so pale?' That's a very sad song. When we get to 'In this world I stand alone, my mother's coffin there at home,' then I feel my throat tightening and I can hardly sing. But Auntie sings. Nobody has as beautiful a vibrato voice as hers. She pushes the pedals, plays with both hands. As for me, I can only play with one finger.

One day, Auntie shows me the keys where 'Why are her cheeks so pale?' starts. I press them, push the pedal, hum, push down five times, then at 'chee(ks)' two steps up, and at '(chee)ks' one key down. Soon I have played the whole verse, it isn't difficult at all.

But it sounds better when Auntie plays, probably because she plays with more fingers. I try: middle finger on the keys I already know, testing with my thumb on the keys below, listen . . . Now I get it, it really is quite simple, you just put your thumb on the second key below the middle-finger key. It sounds exactly right!

But at the last word it sounds as if the melody isn't finished. Perhaps the rule 'every second key' doesn't always apply? I try with other thumb keys. And there it is! On the last word I must jump over *two* keys!

I play the whole verse again every second key up to the last word, then I jump over two keys. It sounds wonderful, completely right. I can play!

What a discovery, what a feeling!

The next person has already learnt how to play but has never played in front of her schoolmates. It was a strong experience.

(4.6D) Woman, young, 1990s

This happened in a music lesson when I was at school [about ten to 12 years of age]. I had taken piano lessons for a couple of years and one of the pieces I had learnt was a song that we had sung earlier in the music lessons, 'The wolf howls', a lullaby that is in the film *Ronia, the Robber's Daughter*. In this lesson the pupils expressed a desire to sing the song. My music teacher was a kind lady and she wanted to fulfil that desire, but there was a problem: she didn't have the score with her, so she couldn't play it.

Then I think a classmate said that I knew it. I had been quite shy over the years and hardly said anything spontaneously in the class. I can only guess how she could know that I could play it. Probably I had dared go up to a piano that had been somewhere public and played the song. Anyhow, I *did* know it off by heart, I who nowadays prefer to play using a score, and I sat down and started to play. Ooh, what a sensation as the others sang when I played. The feeling is hard to describe, my fingers seemed to fly across the keys as if they had never done anything else. I felt as if I was at one with the piano and the music.

Here we see a description of the actual playing (the fingers) seeming to go by itself and of how the individual feels unified with the instrument and the music. A similar description is to be found in the account 4.2D and it crops up in several performers' accounts in Chapter 18.

Singing together with other children is fun, and creates a feeling of fellowship. Everybody focuses on the same task—it feels easy to sing, all shyness disappears, and one feels the power that one can generate together. It is particularly exciting if the choir can perform for others; one is nervous and proud at the same time.

(4.6E) Woman, old, 1940s

Finding a music teacher with a passionate interest in choir singing for children in a country town must be a rare occurrence. But there was one! It was in the 1940s. We were children, aged nine to 12, who had the privilege of being able to sing in a choir during school, learn some singing skills, and sing in parts. The climax was a meeting of children singing where different groups of children during a few weekdays performed together at several places in the county. We were proud, happy, and a bit afraid, but above all completely absorbed by our task. Just imagine, nine years old and being able to fill a whole sports hall with music! I'll never forget it!

(4.6F) Woman, young, 1980s

When I was ten years old, I started in the music class. It was rather exciting to start in a new sort of school, but I could never have imagined the feeling I had the first time all of us in the class sang together!

The longed-for day arrived, and our teacher entered the classroom and introduced himself and talked to us. I liked him straight away. He sat down at the piano, gave us a key, and asked us to sing 'Twinkle, twinkle, little star'. Everybody in the class, shy ten-year-olds who hardly knew each other, was probably just as expectant as I was.

When we started to sing it was as if something snapped! The mood became so happy and everyone seemed a bit surprised. We all sang the same notes, and it felt so easy to sing! All eyes sparkled, and we glanced at each other with a happy look on our faces. The sensation was indescribable!

Afterwards, of course, we talked with everybody, even at home, about what our first music lesson had been like. In some way it felt too as if the entire class had a world fellowship.

There are many accounts of children and singing in choirs in Chapter 19, section 19.1.

Dance and music are, of course, closely associated with each other. One young girl felt how the music and dance fused together as one, and she felt herself to be in a totally different world.

(4.6G) Woman, old, 1930s

It was in the 1930s. I was seven years old and I had been going to dance school for two years and had learnt the basics of classic ballet. The five positions, pirouettes, and other dance steps were a must to be able to do classic dance at all. We practised individual bits which finally became a dance to Tchaikovsky's Piano Concerto No. 1 in B-flat minor. I was chosen to stand at the front of the group at the start of the presentation.

We were going to have a big dance performance at the theatre. I was extremely nervous and when the performance was about to begin I really didn't want to be in it. But the music started, loud and magnificent. Suddenly I thought that two strong arms lifted me and put me in front of the dance group. All my fear disappeared. The music seized all my attention and the dance steps matched with the music and vice versa. A feeling of joy and happiness swept through me. I was in a completely different world. It was so fantastic that music and dance fused together to one unit.

Even the smell on the stage and from the auditorium was special: make-up, dust, floor polish, and a certain shut-in smell. The sensation of this smell and the dance steps are still there in my brain and return when I hear Tchaikovsky's piano concerto. That special sensation returns very intensely.

Finally, in this section, an account of how a young boy one lovely midsummer evening gets the chance to play for the first time together with 'real' musicians and in front of an audience. Initial nervousness turns to great joy.

(4.6H) Man, middle-aged, 1950s

Midsummer Eve, a warm and light summer evening, the smell of the archipelago and the sound of the occasional fishing boat. As we approach the place, the accordion music is mixed with the voices and laughter of happy people celebrating midsummer in the park with the outdoor stage. I have taken my cornet with me because they have promised that I can join in with them and play one or two tunes.

The dance floor is packed and up on the little stage my friend is sitting and playing the guitar in a quartet that besides the guitar also has an accordion, bass and drums. The musicians joke with each other and are having a good time. I am very nervous when I get out my cornet and go up onto the stage. My friend suggests 'All of me', because he knows it is one of the tunes where I have learnt the melody and the harmonies. The big guys in the orchestra notice that I am nervous and do their best to support me.

After a four-bar introduction, I play the melody with some small extensions. The stable and swingish accompaniment feels as if it is carrying all of me. After the melody, the guitar and accordion come in with improvised solos, and then my friend signals to me that it's my turn now. With the melody somewhere at the back of my mind, I walk through the harmonies. In the second bar, I put on a minor ninth in the E7 chord—I've heard Louis Armstrong do that! It is the first time I get to play with other musicians and in front of an audience too! The feeling of creating something together with other musicians is incredibly strong. Afterwards my back is patted by friendly fellow musicians, and one of my greatest experiences with music has happened. During the evening there are more opportunities, and tunes like 'I can't give you anything but love' are mixed with blues of various forms.

A bit after midnight, a happy 12-year-old walks down the path towards the water together with the rest of his family and with a cornet under his arm. The sea is completely calm and out in the bay the first fishing boats are already chugging homewards with tired midsummer revellers.

4.7 OTHER SPECIAL CHILDHOOD EXPERIENCES

We end this chapter with a couple of accounts that, each in their own way, represent a unique and unforgettable association between a particular piece of music and particular circumstances. They are examples of many reactions in strong experiences with music that have already been mentioned—as well as some that have not yet been described.

(4.7A) Woman, young, 1970s

I was sitting in a corridor in the children's wards at the infirmary. I had been there for observation for two weeks and now I was sitting waiting for Mum and Dad to come and fetch me. I remember that I was a bit angry with them because they had agreed to my stay at the infirmary, but at the same time I was burning with eagerness to come home. In the sitting room the radio was playing pop tunes but the one that stuck with me forever was Mary Chapin Carpenter's 'Top of the world'. It wasn't the actual verse, the refrain, or the instruments, but rather her voice, the softness of her voice when she starts with 'Such a feeling's coming over me.'

I was too little then (eight years) to understand all the words in the lyrics, but the voice enchanted me. I remember how it filled me with joy, how it worked as a sort of cleansing filter so that all my feelings became stronger/purer. The 'I am going home' feeling took the upper hand, and I can swear that a ray of sun found its way into the corridor, although my memory says there weren't any windows there.

I have heard the tune several times since then. Dad bought the record. Every time, I am filled with a mixture of melancholy, nostalgia, and happiness that gives me gooseflesh, it's sort of a symbol for a time gone by, carrying all my childhood memories. But still none of all those times have fastened in me like the time in the corridor.

(4.7B) Woman, middle-aged, 1940s

My very first and deepest experience of music happened during the Second World War. I must have been about seven years old. That experience has been engraved so strongly that I can still see the picture and hear the music in my head.

My uncle had a building firm in Norway. When the Germans invaded Norway, they could decide about the firm and the rest of the family, but they couldn't do anything about my uncle—he was Swedish. So in the midst of all the terrible things that happened, my uncle could visit my parental home. He came a few times a year to eat properly and put on weight. He told us sadly about the dreadful situation in Norway. Everything was so tragic and depressing.

My uncle could play the violin. And that is what I can remember. He sat on my parents' bed. And I sat on my little chair, diagonally to the right. He played several different melodies, but the one I remember is *Säterjäntans söndag* ['The herdmaiden's Sunday'] by Ole Bull.

My uncle played a verse and sang one, by turns. I remember both what he sang and what he only played. It is hard to say what etched itself in my mind most, but the light, clear, calming, harmonic tones have penetrated deep into my soul and to this day I can hardly hear them without being moved, especially the bit about the sun rising over the mountain top and the church bells ringing in the valley.

When my uncle played this bit it became sort of so still and quiet around both him and me. The shadows under his eyes disappeared—I thought. There was no war, no problems, no hunger, just light and peace. His face lit up and it was as if it radiated something, and it infected me too, I sort of entered the lit-up landscape. I, who have never ever been up in the mountains, am standing on a mountain top in the brilliant summer weather and looking down into the valley. Just hearing the tones of 'I know that the bells will ring in the valley' makes everything still, in harmony. No evil, no troubles, no discord, just peace and calm.

When he had finished playing, it was all quiet, as if we had been in church, both of us, and I remember that later I asked him to play this tune when he picked up the violin. I waited for the light, sunny tones about the sun rising, and calming ones about the bells ringing in the valley.

It is hard to say what it was that gave me such a strong experience of music in my childhood. I think that the influence of the music on my uncle was so strong that it enveloped me too, because it was as if we were inside an undisturbable harmony, enveloped by it, so that everything else was shut out.

For example, I can't remember if there were any other people in the room when he played. And I can't remember the whole room either. When I see the scene before me, this is all I can see, like I said: the foot of my parents' bed, the violin, me, and my chair. I can't remember any other furniture, mats, or anything like that. No walls in the room, no ceiling. And I can't hear any other sounds, just the violin. That's why I think my uncle's experience was conveyed so strongly to me, that I was sucked into it, so to speak.

That was the first time I heard '*Säterjäntans söndag*' played. I haven't heard it very often since my childhood, but every time I do hear it I am moved to the bottom of my heart and the 'landscape' around me becomes open and lit up by the sun. In the long term, this experience meant that I know there are benevolent oases in the midst of all the dreadful things. An oasis where one's mind is cleansed from insistent trials.

This is one of many accounts with a connection to the situation in Sweden's neighbouring countries during the Second World War. '*Säterjäntans söndag*' by Ole Bull is like a symbol for Norway and it would have felt particularly important during the period when the country was occupied.

The little girl and her uncle are enveloped by harmony, as it were, and everything else is shut out; they are totally absorbed. Her memory of the room includes only the very most central parts of the experience—the violin, her uncle and herself, and where they sat. Nothing else is relevant. At the same time, in her mind she can sometimes be somewhere else, up on a mountain top looking down into the valley. Even much later in life, the music gives rise to similar feelings and can have a therapeutic effect.

4.8 COMMENTARY

Strong experiences with music during one's childhood show many of the reactions that we shall come to meet later in this book: tears, shivers, it feels as if one is floating in mid-air, one is totally absorbed by the music, touched, amazed, affected, overwhelmed, filled with strong emotions, happiness, joy, beauty, and love of the music, sometimes mixed and changing feelings. One can recognize something in the music—it interprets one's feelings—and feel specially chosen, privileged, to be able to hear it. Some accounts describe cosmic feelings, to feel oneself as an infinitesimally small part of the cosmos, to be merged with another state.

The music is often associated with feelings of security and closeness to parents and other close relatives. Sometimes it is associated with certain days, for example Christmas Eve. For older participants, the experience may have meant the first real meeting with music. As a young practitioner, one can make the fantastic discovery of how notes go together with each other, and how one plays an instrument. One can play/sing together with others, feel the fellowship of this, and be both nervous and proud when performing before an audience. In general, the experience opens up an entirely new world and can lead to a desire to devote oneself to music in the future.

One must, of course, remember that these accounts are written by adults long after the time when the experience took place. We do know, however, that events of a strong emotional character and considerable importance result in memories that are very detailed, easy to retrieve, and very resistant to forgetfulness (see further discussion of this in Chapter 33, section 33.4).

CHAPTER 5

EXPERIENCES DURING ONE'S TEENAGE YEARS

About 25% of all the accounts concern experiences during the teenage years (age 13–20). Of these, 63% are from women and 37% from men, almost exactly the same proportions as for the material as a whole (see Chapter 2, section 2.1). More than half of the teenage accounts (57%) come from young participants, the next largest group from middle-aged (26%), and the least from old (17%). This distribution is thus the opposite of that for childhood experiences, where there was a predominance of accounts from middle-aged and old participants, women in particular.

The large number of young participants also means that just over half (54%) of all teenage experiences have taken place during the last ten years of the participants' lives, that is, on the whole after 1980. The rest is fairly evenly distributed across successive ten-year intervals (10 to 19 years previously, 20 to 29 years, and so on), and a small number were more than 60 years in the past. For the childhood experiences, however, just over half were more than 40 years in the past, that is, roughly before 1950.

In the investigation as a whole there are more accounts of strong experiences during the teenage years than during childhood. This predominance of teenage experiences over childhood experiences is especially marked among the younger participants in our study (under 30 years of age, thus born after 1960). This can reflect the generally increased focus on the teenage period that has come about since the middle of the twentieth century, not least in the field of music. Before 1950 in Sweden, not much music was aimed specifically at young people, with the exception of jazz (which in any case was condemned by many music authorities). This position changed radically when rock and pop music made their breakthrough during the following decades, since which time they have dominated the musical choice of young people, together with many other genres of popular music. This question is further discussed in Chapter 30, section 30.3.

Here is a selection of accounts that illustrate different aspects of strong experiences of music during the teenage years. They are divided into the following themes: meeting one's idols (5.1); encountering new, unknown music (5.2); music as consolation, support, and therapy during one's teens (5.3); performing music during one's teens (5.4).

5.1 MEETING ONE'S IDOLS

Several teenage experiences involved meetings with various idols, often a certain artiste or a certain group within the field of popular music. Listeners had often learned the lyrics off by heart and could sing along with their favourite tunes. They had waited for the possibility of seeing and hearing the artistes 'for real' and there were great expectations.

In the first example, the narrator was just about to enter her teens.

(5.1A) Woman, young, 1980s

I was 12 years old, and it was the first artiste's concert that I had been to. Carola [Häggkvist] was my idol. I thought it would be terribly exciting. There were really lots of people there and the atmosphere got better and better while we waited for her to come. When the show eventually began, I thought that everything was absolutely wonderful. I thought that Carola was so clever at singing and dancing. I felt extremely happy and in high spirits. My body was trembling with excitement. I sang and wanted to dance. I could follow along, sort of, with the music. I felt as if I was inside it in some way. I fenced off everything around me. It was only what was on the stage that mattered. I would have liked to have been up there. It was dreadfully exciting and absolutely fantastic.

Afterwards, I worshipped her. I wanted it to have lasted longer. It was a pity that it was over, empty in some way. Didn't want to go home and would rather have stayed behind and absorbed the impressions. When I came home, I wrote her a letter and told her how good I thought she was.

Absorption, admiration, trembling with excitement, singing and wanting to dance, feeling at one with the music, feeling in high spirits, everything is 'absolutely fantastic': the same features recur in several of the following accounts. But directly afterwards, one can feel a bit sad—admittedly happy to have had such an experience, yet at the same time disappointed that it was already over.

The meeting with their idols often takes place at large concerts with thousands or perhaps tens of thousands of listeners. There is a great feeling of fellowship, everybody has come there for the same thing and they incite each other to an increasingly wound-up mood, a 'mass psychosis', which culminates when the artiste/group finally appears—as at this concert with a well-known synth-pop band.

(5.1B) Woman, young, 1990s

Me and some of my best friends, we had got hold of tickets for Depeche Mode, my greatest idols of all time, and we were in seventh heaven. We prepared ourselves by listening to all the music they had done and we learnt virtually all their lyrics. On the train to the concert, there was a great deal of singing.

And then the concert finally started. And what a concert! When they came onto the stage, tears actually started to come to my eyes and I got goosepimply all over. I was transformed into one of those hysterical girls that I had always scorned, but the whole thing was an indescribable experience. A wave of joy passed through my entire body and I wasn't myself any longer. The concert exceeded all my expectations. Me and my friends knew all the lyrics and we could sing along with all the songs.

It is an enormous feeling, to be at a gigantic concert with your idols. Everybody who is there really loves what they are listening to, and there is an enormous sense of fellowship.

Even though there was often a degree of antagonism between the synth-pop fans and the hard rockers, the reactions are similar.

(5.1C) Woman, young, 1990s

I was going to go to the first big rock concert of my life. I had been longing for ages to see my big idols, the hard rockers Guns N' Roses. When it was time, I was in a haze. I remember that I walked around smiling several days before. I was very nervous too, partly because perhaps we would miss everything if the train wasn't there in time, partly because perhaps the concert wouldn't be up to my very high expectations.

It was crammed jammed with people. Everybody was happy and it was like a big party. Although I had travelled from quite a long way away and there were 32,000 people there, I saw several people I knew from home. We got to the arena quite late, so there was a huge crowd in front of us. I was very focused on what was to come.

It was still light when the group came onto the stage. I thought it was a pity because you would have seen them better if it had been dark around them. When the guitarist Slash (my favourite) came onto the stage it was like a shock. He became the centre of my focus and everything else was blurred. I felt dizzy and the others who were with me laughed at me because I looked simply terrified. According to them I shed some tears, but that's nothing I'll admit to.

The music started and I just couldn't move. I couldn't jump up and down, and 'dig' like everybody around me was doing. My concentration demanded all my energy to be on the stage. The volume was dreadfully high and I thought that the bass drum had a horrid crack that broke through the sound image. It was unreal, but at the same time this was what I had always wanted to see and hear. Everything they played was very familiar. The entire concert was a confirmation that what I had heard only on records did actually exist in reality. For me it wasn't cool or tough to finally be able to see my idols, it was just pleasure.

After the concert we went up to the front to look at the stage close up and I remember that it wasn't until then that I felt happy about having seen them. It was as if I could relax after quite a long period of tension and I felt calm and collected. I went around with a permanent smile.

I had been looking forward to this and had prepared for it for a long time. I had heard the music on records so I knew it off by heart. It was in my head every day for a long time and then being able to see and hear it for real was fantastic. The music itself I think I experienced like before, but the total impression has a completely different quality.

A large part of my identity and self-image was built upon my worship of just this particular music. The concert was a confirmation.

> This experience was the climax of my idol worship. After it I could move on but at the same time carry with me this fantastic feeling of how music can move you so deeply.

Before the concert, she was worried that perhaps it might not meet up to her considerable expectations. Afterwards the tension relaxes, the concert feels like a confirmation of her identity and self-image that she has built upon this music. This is a theme that explicitly or implicitly occurs in many similar accounts.

In the following example, the narrator meets one of the greatest figures of rock music, Bruce Springsteen.

(5.1D) Man, middle-aged, 1980s

> Bruce Springsteen and the E Street Band played at an outdoor arena in Gothenburg in front of 64,000 people. The previous evening, a brief excerpt from Friday's concert had been shown on the news and I already felt at that stage that something special was happening. I read a review too. The concert was apparently really fantastic. This meant that I started to have rather high expectations for the concert . . .
>
> The concert really was magical. After the first set, which lasted one and a half hours, I was convinced: this was the best concert I'd seen and it had still barely begun. When the second set started, it had become a bit dark outside. The moments I remember best were when Springsteen sat down on the edge of the stage and told a story about his sister and his brother-in-law. It sounded as if he would start crying at any moment. I was struck dumb by this and just stood there and shivered, and everybody else must have been doing the same because the arena was deadly quiet. After the monologue he played the song 'The River', which is a fantastically beautiful song about dreams that don't always come true. It is one of the few songs I know where you can't distinguish between the music and the lyrics; you really must listen to the lyrics when you hear the song.
>
> The other moment is the complete opposite. Springsteen played 'Cadillac Ranch', a tune that is like a steamroller that just flattens you. As I was in the stands diagonally in front of the stage I could see the entire audience, like a sea with rolling waves. I stood and jumped in time with the music and when I stopped I felt how the concrete rocked, I didn't think it was true but it really was! What was almost even worse was when I looked at the spotlight masts and saw how they swayed, not just a bit but clearly and distinctly. That ought really to have felt unpleasant but I just thought it was fantastic and wonderful. After the Springsteen concerts they did indeed discover cracks in the concrete foundations, and they had to renovate the stands and didn't have concerts there for several years.
>
> When I left the arena I was exhausted, felt empty inside in some strange way. I remember slowly shaking my head and thinking: 'Now I've seen it all, I'll never get to see a better concert.' And I haven't done either.

It is indeed not just one's hearing that is involved at such concerts. The sight (of the artiste and his performance on stage, the swaying masts, etc.) and tactile sensation (the concrete rocking) are absolutely a part of the experience. More and more emphasis is placed on the artiste's clothes (or fancy dress), hair style, movements and body language, accessories such as light and colour and other spectacular effects, stimuli intended to make a visual impression. And because vision usually dominates other senses, the total impression is often formulated not in terms of hearing but more along the lines of: 'Now I've seen it all, I'll never get to see a better concert.'

Similar references to visual impressions often occur in spontaneous accounts as well as in reviews.

Here are some more typical examples. One artiste who has used many different kinds of imagery during his career is Prince.

(5.1E) Man, young, 1980s (edited interview)

After several years' admiration, to finally be able to see and hear and feel a concert with Prince, you can't put that feeling into words. Waiting for hours, waiting . . . waiting. Until the atmosphere is so charged that you could almost touch it. Your nerves completely open.

Then suddenly the lights are turned off in the whole hall. You know it is only a matter of minutes before the whole thing explodes. Suddenly there is the roar of a car engine somewhere. A couple of car headlights light up the stage. The bass drum rolls out the rhythm. Everyone is shouting as loud as they can. There's mass psychosis for a moment. Then he climbs out of a car and into the field of a red spotlight. It is ecstatic. It's him, it's him!

The feeling of ecstasy soon turns into enormous joy. It is like the greatest bloody party in the world! You don't want it ever to come to an end. You are sort of in a totally different world. Standing and screaming, jumping and clapping your hands and singing along. The entire hall was boiling with feeling. The volume was high. It was full of people. You were friends with everybody. I was so inside the music that I didn't notice my mates while the music was playing.

I was pretty jiggered afterwards; it was hard to sleep that evening. My mates and me were entirely agreed about how great it had been, so we could share the experience.

Here is another description of a Prince concert, which also contains reflections about how much the audience's participation means for the experience.

(5.1F) Woman, young, 1980s

My strongest experience with music I think must have been when I was at a Prince concert. I have always liked Prince's music a lot and was already extremely excited on the way there. We had to stand and wait about an hour before it exploded. The music started before the curtain went up and we stood there sort of half paralysed, and just screamed.

It is so hard to explain, because at the same time that nothing except the music exists for you, you are also totally aware of everything going on around you. I mean, it feels as if nothing except the music counts, but if I was standing there all by myself and looking at Prince then it wouldn't be the same thing at all. Everyone in the audience eggs each other on until you're almost up there at a climax and then when the artiste eventually comes on stage he only has to say 'Hello' for you to reach climax.

To a great extent it is the atmosphere among the audience that gives you the actual concert feeling. You feel free in some way. At concerts you dance, jump about, scream and sing as much as you want. It's like you are a part of it all, not just a spectator. Through the entire concert the audience was in complete ecstasy. There was only one thing that counted: the music!

You are filled with that lovely feeling that now everything is good. That you are living only for what is happening right now. It is like you are drunk with joy. If you shut your eyes, then suddenly it's you yourself who is standing there playing. You concentrate 100% on the person on the stage and their music. You don't think about what you're doing. You do what you feel like doing, without even thinking about it.

Prince's music can change my mood in all sorts of ways. Just like at the concert, I cried and laughed, one after the other. Though I listened to his music every day, it was the first time I had heard it live. I think, and thought before the concert too, that his music really is absolutely wonderful. It is different. There are many others who try to get the same sound in their music, but nobody has even come close.

The actual concert feeling goes away quickly when the lights are turned on. Then everything stops, not everything, but the actual mood among the audience. There's nothing worse than when the lights are turned on and the music has silenced. Me and my mates had the jitters right until we got home. The concert was the only thing we talked about for the next two weeks.

Beside everything else, this account also gives us an example of an intense feeling of presence and living in the here and now: 'That you are living only for what is happening right now.' Similar descriptions occur in many other accounts of strong experiences of music.

Another artiste who was just as controversial a public figure was the late Michael Jackson, often called the King of Pop. It felt almost unreal to finally get to meet him.

(5.1G) Man, young, 1980s

It was in Gothenburg, at a Michael Jackson concert. I had waited for this moment for many years and finally I experienced it: Michael Jackson's dancing and music! I'd had the jitters quite a lot during the day, and inside the arena the atmosphere was simply incredible.

It was a bit unreal to see him on stage; the situation was a little dreamlike. It was a stage show that was absolutely incredible. I was probably in a sort of trance. Everything I saw and heard was Michael Jackson, my childhood idol. No thoughts passed through my head. I only heard the music. It possessed me!

After all the waiting, the first song was a sort of discharge. I jumped up and down, sang along, danced and skipped throughout the concert, felt how the whole earth vibrated. I felt only joy, didn't think about the others but just looked at the stage. I was totally absorbed by it. Felt a feeling of joy and inside that feeling I could do anything at all, I thought. My mate said afterwards that he had shouted at me, but I didn't hear him. He had tugged me, but I hadn't felt it.

I felt a bit of melancholia when the concert came to an end. Thought that, well, I'm never going to see him again. The time had gone incredibly quickly. It was a pity that it was over, but I wasn't exactly sad about it. I mean, I was really exhausted and tired and . . . happy. I went and talked with everybody and everybody thought it was good. I was in seventh heaven.

The person in the following account was at the same Michael Jackson concert. But for her it was an encounter with music that was previously almost unknown.

(5.1H) Woman, young, 1980s

A hot summer day, me and 60,000 other expectant people stood in Gothenburg and waited for the world-famous artiste Michael Jackson. For three hours before the start of the concert I waited in front of the stage. The stage lay in a hollow with high stands all around. Down on the grass in front of the stage where I was standing it was extremely hot. The organizers had to spray water over the entire audience to try to reduce the heat a little. Already three hours before the concert the atmosphere was great, you could already feel how squashed it was and I wondered how much worse it could get.

Suddenly everything happened quickly. He was on stage. At first there was silence, everybody had to try to understand that it really was him. And when that had been established there was a roar and the mood was absolutely tip top. The music blared out of the enormously large loudspeaker banks. I didn't have a chance to sit still but was pulled along by the music.

The show was performed in an incredibly professional manner. He had about ten musicians and he also had dancers with him. He filled his hours on stage really well, the time just ran away.

But there was one song that all of us in the audience were waiting for, namely the hit 'Bad'. It came as the final number, and wow, the entire audience really exploded, everybody rocked along with it. It was just unbelievable, what a feeling.

The music filled all of me, and after that song I was completely exhausted and so it seemed were the people round me. After having stood and listened to this man for just over two hours I was fairly tired, but extremely elated and happy.

For me this was an unusual experience as I almost never listen to such music. I'm doing the music study programme at school and devote most of my time to classical music. Classical music and Michael Jackson are so different that you can't compare them. Michael Jackson's concert and its atmosphere were so good that I never regretted going there.

The final comments provide food for thought. Experiencing classical music and experiencing Michael Jackson's music are described as incomparable phenomena. This leads to many reflections as to what the difference consists of. It is obvious that it is not just a question of the music itself; it is just as much the attitude towards the music, the attitude of the artistes as well as of the listeners.

Another well-known artiste is the singer Whitney Houston. Her voice surpassed many others.

(5.1I) Woman, young, 1980s

It was a Whitney Houston concert abroad. I had very great expectations and was in a good mood. There were lots of people, enormous vibes, a delightful atmosphere. We had fantastic seats and we saw and heard everything really well. She was so personal, didn't put on a false front, no changes of clothes. She was completely ordinary. The music was so delightful because she had quiet songs as well as songs with a lot of life in them.

It was wonderful, lovely, really great. Just actually *seeing* her—she was right there in front of us. Her voice penetrated right into my soul. It was so nice that you almost started crying. I got the shivers—the hair all over my body stood on end. I got the creeps in my legs. Wanted to jump up and dance. Everybody in the entire arena got up and started to clap their hands, we all knew the lyrics and could sing along. You felt brave in some way, as if you wanted and could do something. Felt a sense of fellowship with everyone round about you.

The time passed quickly and I didn't want the concert to end. It was a disappointment when she stopped. I talked to my mate afterwards and she thought it had been just as good. The feeling from the concert stayed with me a long time.

Meeting an idol can sometimes take place in a somewhat smaller and calmer setting. And having personal direct contact with the idol can make it an especially memorable occasion.

(5.1J) Man, middle-aged, 1960s

My strongest experience of music so far was when as a 15-year-old I had the opportunity to hear Josh White, the American blues singer. For several years we had listened to and taped songs from his gramophone records, so we were very familiar with his repertoire that evening when we had the opportunity to hear him live. This was the first time I was allowed to go out and listen to music, live at an evening performance in an inn. I had great expectations of the evening.

After the usual food and drink, it turned 23.00 and out of the kitchen door came a dark-skinned singer with a steel-stringed guitar. Being interested in guitars, I remember the colour, form, and appearance of his guitar, including that he hadn't cut off the strings at the pegs but that they stuck out a bit.

He started by lighting a cigarette and he used the bit of the string over the peg as a cigarette holder. Then he started playing a couple of songs that were very familiar to us. We sat on the floor, three metres in front of Josh, my friend that I played music with and me. We just completely drank it in, all the music. Everything stayed with me. I can still to this day hear his voice, how it sounded when he sang and the laughter in his voice when he spoke to us in the audience. And I'd still recognize the sound today, a bit sharp but clear and pure, from his guitar. The bass player also made a great impression where he stood to the left of Josh. Josh stood there with his left leg over the back of a chair. I can still see the picture very clearly before me. The wholeness of the evening was total. Everybody in our gang felt a part of it when Josh joked and talked to the audience.

The performance was getting near the end and that's when it happened. My friend and me who were sitting right at the front started to sing along with the song 'Irene, goodnight'. Josh noticed this and stopped playing his instrument (the bass player kept on playing), took two steps forward, and held out his hand to us. Without our realizing what had happened, we were standing there and singing along with one of our greatest idols. There was nothing in the way, no worry, nervousness, we just sang. I had a microphone in front of me for the first time and we stood there and sang.

We started with the chorus. When that was over, Josh gave us a gentle glance that he'd sing the verse himself. During the verse we had time to get our bearings (probably unconsciously) as to what we were doing, but we didn't feel any of the nervousness that you usually get on stage. When we came to the chorus again, Josh gave a big smile and we felt that we dared to sing out. It even turned into a three-voice chorus and everything felt just perfect. One more verse and chorus before it was over. There was cheering and Josh hugged us. The feeling could well be described as elated, joyful.

Deep in my heart I was proud and happy. Now when I'm sitting here writing this, I can feel a lot of what I felt then, the warmth in my chest. OK, I've had other strong experiences in connection with music after this, but I still think that the experience with Josh lives on inside me as the strongest experience I have ever had with music. And, of course, after a live experience with Josh I wanted an autograph, and on the card he wrote to me it says: 'Good luck and happiness from your friend, Josh White.'

Another special encounter is described in the following example. The idol was the famous French singer Edith Piaf, who died in 1963. The encounter was one that took the form of reading about Edith Piaf and listening to her songs. It led to both positive and negative feelings.

(5.1K) Woman, young, 1980s

I was going to give a talk about Edith Piaf at school. During the spring I had also read the book about Piaf written by her sister, a book that really moved me and meant that I understood her and her music better than ever.

During the entire talk, I felt that something special was happening. I wasn't nervous because I was used to facing an audience, but there was something special in the air. At the end of the talk I played 'Exodus' and '*Je ne regrette rien*' and that was when I felt it right through my body! All of me was filled with music, but it was sad. She was leaving me now! Me and Edith who had worked together all spring, now we would be separated! Just before the talk, I had finished reading the book, which has a very tragic ending, but I didn't understand what it meant until Edith's fantastic singing voice announced that it was over. She was no longer with us.

Afterwards, I cried hysterically, and not even my friends could comfort me. It felt as if a friend had died. It meant that even to this day, almost a year after the experience, I can't listen to Edith Piaf without crying and the painful memory comes back—so all my records and album collection remain untouched on the record shelf.

The previous examples are mainly about artistes who performed during the last decades of the twentieth century. Worship of idols also features in accounts of experiences further back in time, but the atmosphere, the reactions, and the language used to describe them feel very different.

(5.1L) Woman, old, 1930s

It was 1934 or 1935, a concert in a church in Falun. The black American contralto Marian Anderson was soloist and was accompanied by a male pianist. The programme included Schubert's 'Ave Maria' and '*Erlkönig*', Beethoven's 'Adelaide', some negro spirituals, also some music with Swedish lyrics, and songs by Sibelius. The highlight was her interpretation of 'Ave Maria'. I was there together with my sister that unforgettable evening.

The rather heavy, solid brick church has an interior with benches and wall panelling painted in local Dala blue, and there are many gilded carved wooden details and other fancy fittings. And there she stood, Marian Anderson, just to the left in front of the altar rail. In a champagne-coloured lace dress with a simple cut, full-length, with long arms, a shawl or collar arrangement around her shoulders. In her hand, a large but dainty handkerchief in the same colour. She stood there relaxed, still, confident in herself. Simply opened her mouth and her strong, mellow yet gentle voice filled all of the huge room. The tones merged together with her remarkable charisma—her brown skin soft as velvet, her large mouth with its full lips, her large but deep-set black eyes, her black hair in gentle waves framing her face.

We had arrived for the concert in good time. We knew that she would draw a large audience and it was a question of getting close enough to get a good view of the object of our idolatry. We sat almost at the front. The church was full of people but it was solely for me she was singing. I was completely wrapped up in the music. It was an effort for me to try to control myself. The tears flowed and I didn't have a hanky with me.

To show appreciation by clapping in church was unthinkable in those days. On the way home, we tried to talk to each other about the wonderful thing we had experienced— but how could we find words for it? I only know that we held each other tightly arm in arm. And now I could borrow my sister's hanky and at last blow my nose properly. The great expectations we had of both seeing and hearing Marian Anderson had been fulfilled.

And despite the technology (radio, gramophone) being often far from perfect, it has always been more than a pleasure to listen to her voice.

Experiencing a singer who can fill a church with her voice without any amplification whatsoever, the narrator felt herself to be wrapped up in the music. And not only that, but, despite the church being full of people, she was, so to speak, special: 'it was solely for me she was singing'. This is a type of confirmation that is also described in several other accounts (see Chapter 16, section 16.2)

5.2 ENCOUNTERING NEW, UNKNOWN MUSIC

The music of their idols is something that people have often listened to before. But often one's teens are a time when one also meets new, unknown music. Such an experience can be decisive in influencing which music one chooses afterwards, perhaps for the rest of one's life. A common theme in the following accounts is that one is especially susceptible to new impressions during one's teenage years.

Here follows a long cavalcade of accounts about decisive encounters with unknown music. They are arranged according to when they occurred during the twentieth century, from the 1920s to the 1990s. They thus give a picture of the music, the culture, attitudes, and living conditions in Sweden during various periods of the century. The accounts lead us to reflect upon the way we are influenced by music in various stages of our lives. They can speak for themselves without further commentary.

(5.2A) Man, old, 1920s

Sometime during 1929, my father took me to a piano concert at the Grand Hotel in our town. Because of my age and certain other external circumstances I might have been particularly susceptible just then. I was 15 years old, and was having a difficult time (puberty, problems at school, my mother had recently died), so I was probably a bit depressed before the concert.

It was just a solo concert. The pianist, Simon Barere, was Russian. I can't remember the programme. What made an impression on me was the encore he played, namely one of Chopin's études. I was absolutely enthralled and I got the shivers when I heard the music, and found it very hard to get to sleep that evening. The tones and harmonies pursued me. It wasn't the pianist's technical skill that I admired (if I had known the word 'interpretation' at the time, that was the talent that characterized the pianist). Most of all it was the composer and the composition that delighted and enchanted me. Up until then, I had hardly heard of Chopin and now he became my favourite. And it should be noted that it wasn't a melody that fascinated me, but the harmony.

Looking back, I can see that the setting for the concert was classic: a hall-like room with ordinary chairs, crystal chandeliers, and the pianist at his piano almost in the middle of the audience. The concert setting may have strengthened my susceptibility. In the long term, the experience meant that I prefer to listen to romantic piano music.

(5.2B) Man, old, 1930s

In 1934 I turned the radio on out of curiosity. I was 15 years old, but had followed the debate that raged about jazz and how dangerous it was. I was rather inexperienced as a jazz listener. The then head of music on Swedish Radio had forbidden it during the *Gramophone Hour*. But for God knows what reason they broadcast a part of Louis Armstrong's concert in Stockholm. It was like a revelation. The rhythm crept along my backbone. The variations of the theme shook up the inside of my head. I fell for jazz completely, and started to try to play jazz—or 'hot' as it was called then—on the piano that my mother had first let me play when I was eight years old. The passion that Satchmo was the midwife for meant that not long afterwards I became the pianist in a newly formed dance band and developed a lifelong devotion to jazz.

The strength of the experience remained until I was called up in 1940 and completely cut off from the possibility of listening to jazz. They didn't even have a radio in the barracks in those days, not to mention the long months we were 'out in the bushes'. When I was finally discharged, in 1945, the strength of the experience had faded a little. But it is still there, still today.

(5.2C) Woman, old, 1930s

My life's musical experience took place on a Sunday in the 1930s. I was then 19 years old. Expectant and happy, as always before a concert, I went to a cinema auditorium where the Malmö Symphony Orchestra held their concerts. There wasn't a concert hall in Malmö at the time.

That was the first time in my life that I got to hear Tchaikovsky's sixth symphony, *Pathétique*. It moved me from the very first note. I felt as if I was lifted up into another world. Time and space disappeared; perhaps that is what eternity is like. An indescribable feeling of painful joy and bliss filled me. There was a recurrent melancholic theme that I felt that Tchaikovsky had written with the blood of his heart. His pain in these beautiful notes spoke directly to me. I have heard this symphony many times since then and it still moves me today, but never like it did that time. Perhaps you have to be young and filled with *Weltschmerz*.

I had gone to the concert alone and I was glad about that. Didn't want to talk to anybody, nor go home immediately. The experience of having been able to look into another world was so incredible.

(5.2D) Woman, old, 1930s

My first consciously deep experience with music took place in my teens in the 1930s. It was during the school year and I was in that sensitive teenage period. For some reason, my father had got some complementary tickets for the premier of the film about Franz Schubert. And for some reason I got to go along with him instead of my mother. We were going to the big, fancy Palladium, specially invited among other specially invited guests, and I was there as my father's lady. Everything was exciting but also a little frightening, because I was very shy and not used to being among so many unknown people.

I was completely absorbed by the film and by Schubert's life, when he was a teacher, as a friend glad to be among friends, his misfortune and sorrow when he couldn't finish his symphony. And all the time the lovely music that was heard all through the film, the 'Marche militaire', the most agreeable in the world, 'Ave Maria', '*Heidenröslein*', '*Erlkönig*',

'*Die Forelle*', songs and chamber music, and the 'Unfinished', the one the thoughtless girl laughed to bits.

After the end of the film I was still absorbed by it for a long time, filled by the joyful as well as the sad parts. I was hit by the realization of another time and another way to live, that the artistic life was something totally separated from my life, even though it was romanticized in the film. So I was very susceptible to the sorrow and joy that the film expressed. It was the first time that I became aware of Schubert's music; the pieces in the film particularly always touch the strings of my heart.

(5.2E) Man, old, 1940s

In the village where I'm living there was no electricity back then. We had a wireless that ran on batteries but listening time was rationed because of the high running costs. It was mainly news and weather forecasts, and now and then, on some more solemn occasion, something else, for example music. Otherwise hardly any music, perhaps a gramophone record on a portable record player.

Then the experience with music. It was New Year's Eve. My father and mother went to a chapel to see in the New Year. I was alone at home reading a book. When I had finished it, I lit a candle and switched on the radio. It was just past 23.00 and the Gothenburg Radio Orchestra conducted by Sten Frykberg played Franz Schubert's Symphony No. 8 in B minor (the 'Unfinished'). It was a fantastic experience. Everything else around me disappeared. Left were just the music, the candle, the smell of the Christmas tree. I only have a faint memory of what came after, the bell ringing and speeches—but the music, I'll never forget that.

I had never before listened to so-called classical music, and even though I would probably have found my way to serious music without this experience with music, it probably helped to speed up the process. I can neither sing nor play an instrument myself. I only listen to the radio, and preferably to serious music, the most beautiful I know being the Lacrimosa movement from Mozart's *Requiem*.

(5.2F) Man, old, 1940s

In 1939–40 during the Finnish Winter War, there were lots of activities arranged to support Finland under the motto 'We share Finland's cause.' One evening there was a concert where the child prodigy Heimo Haitto, then 13 years old, was going to play virtuoso violin pieces. The main item at the concert was going to be Paganini's Violin Concerto No.1 in D major, which I probably heard for the first time in my life.

That evening's concert meant an experience that was decisive for the rest of my life. I was then 15 years old and had played the violin since I was about ten. My father wanted his son to learn to play the violin. My interest at the time was playing football, and against my will I was made to practise the violin so that, if possible, I could learn to play. The stipulated practice time was 30 minutes every day and I remember very well how I tried to get out of it with all manner of tricks. For example, I became very thirsty from all the practising and had to go into the kitchen to drink water several times during my practice session. This trick was, of course, discovered and I had to take a jug of water with me into the practice room.

When my father told me that we were going to go to the Heimo Haitto concert, I didn't show any particular interest in going, but was nevertheless curious as to how such a young boy could play such difficult things as the posters promised.

The concert was an unprecedented experience for me—it was as though a curtain had been pulled away and the entire world of music opened up before me. The reason for the experience was probably that I was impressed by the soloist's knowledge, which in turn opened the door to the essence of music and gave me such a strong experience.

I then became fanatically interested in violin playing and violin music—above all, that of Fritz Kreisler and his repertoire and the whole list of phenomenal violinists with Jascha Heifetz at the top. I practised seriously and diligently and soon surpassed my father's knowledge, got a place at the Academy of Music, eventually ended up in one of our great orchestras, and was there for many years.

(5.2G) Man, old, 1940s

I have had many strong experiences with music over the years, for example in the 1940s when I heard the trumpeter Bunny Berigan play 'I can't get started' for the first time. After playing the 78 record twice, I followed my dad's summons to mow the lawns. With the music still ringing in my ears, I drove right through borders, the strawberry patch, etc. without being aware of the havoc. The experience with the music was still so total that everything else was wiped out of my consciousness for hours afterwards.

(5.2H) Man, old, 1940s

In my parental home they didn't listen to classical music. We sang songs and ballads, and my sisters played brief well-known pieces on the piano. I liked march music best, and popular songs and some dance tunes. But then classical music came into my life.

I had just started at senior secondary school when a girl asked me to accompany her to a concert at the church. Church music didn't feel very tempting, so I didn't have the slightest desire to go. But whatever—I gave in and we went to the concert together. The orchestra played a couple of pieces and I didn't think it sounded particularly good. Then the orchestra had a break and a man in clerical dress started to speak.

Then the orchestra came back and the lights in the church were dimmed and it became completely silent. Quietly, gently as a warm summer breeze, the music reached me and went right in. I sat there without moving a muscle, leaning forward, and just sort of swallowed it. I had never heard anything so indescribably beautiful. And every bit of me was filled with divine harmony and I was aware that tears were starting to run down my cheeks, but I didn't care about that and I wasn't ashamed even though the girl saw it.

After much too short a time the music withdrew and there was silence. The lights went up, the murmur of the audience came back; I didn't want to talk to anybody, just keep the new, incredible experience to myself. I made up some sort of excuse and left the church and the girl, and walked alone for more than an hour humming and trying to recall what I had heard and experienced. My mood switched in some weird way between joy, amazement, and melancholy.

I didn't think about it then, but later I understood that Mozart's 'Ave verum corpus' that evening opened the door for me to a completely new world within music, a world of unbelievable riches—and inexhaustible too. I am eternally grateful and pleased about that.

Here is an especially long and amusing account of music, opera, teenage infatuations, and home environments in Stockholm around the middle of the century. One of the main characters was a famous opera singer.

(5.2I) Woman, old, 1940s

My strongest experience with music was in Stockholm after the mid-1940s. I was about 17 years old. Music hadn't meant anything at all for me during my childhood. My parents had a large flat and there was a well-polished Steinway grand piano in the drawing room. Nobody in the family could play. It was purely a status decoration. It was very common in those days that young girls in 'good families' should have a number of qualities. Look love-able, be calm, well groomed, and adaptable. Be able to draw and possibly even paint in water colours, embroider, crochet, knit, arrange flowers in a vase, and play the piano. They made me start piano school. How I *detested* those piano lessons. No—riding and rushing around on my pony, that was my big interest.

But then came puberty. I still struggled with my piano lessons. In those days you did what your parents wanted. But when I was 15 I had reached the 'dance age' and discovered jazz and rhythm. And became extremely fond of so-called classic jazz and started to buy gramophone records with my pocket money. Louis Armstrong, Benny Goodman, Glenn Miller, Thore Ehrling, Vera Lynn, and so on. My parents hated that music.

Now and then, both my parents went to the opera, my mother with a new hairdo and a long dress, my father in tails. Once, my father told *Lohengrin* to me as a fairy tale, a legend from the Middle Ages, and that appealed to my romantic frame of mind. Knights and fair maidens—delightful.

When I was 17, I started to 'go steady' with a boy from the neighbouring block. He was extremely interested in music and especially opera music and above all Wagner. He thought my interest in jazz was banal and shallow and he often spoke of Wagnerian leitmotifs and Tannhäuser's love life. Then one day he had two tickets for a completely new and modern opera, which was called *Peter Grimes*, and he nagged me that I must go along with him.

With great reluctance—what won't one do for love?—I promised to go with him. We sat at the back of the third balcony, but we had a pair of binoculars to share. I didn't under-stand a note of the music, but everything was exciting and fascinating and was apparently about an unfortunate lonely seaman who had an apprentice, a little boy, whom he made walk down dark wooden steps to the boats. The boy fell and was killed. It was a dreadful pity about Peter Grimes. He was so handsome with big blue eyes and a blue sailor blouse and he sang so strongly and beautifully, so it felt really good. This opera thing was actually not bad at all. My boyfriend and I held hands when I wasn't using the binoculars.

Of course, I told my best friend about the visit to the opera, and she was just as uninter-ested as I had been. And besides, she had never liked that strange boy I was going out with. 'Don't bother about the boy,' I said. 'It's Peter Grimes I'm interested in.' I showed her the programme and he was called Set Svanholm in reality and was even more handsome on the photo in the programme. 'This Svanholm is going to sing in *Lohengrin* next week and my dad has talked so much about that, it's meant to be extremely delightful, and you simply must see this Svanholm.'

This was the era of the film idols. We had been in love with Errol Flynn, Tyrone Power, Leslie Howard, and so on. And, miracle of all miracles, my best friend promised she'd go with me, and off we went to *Lohengrin*. Stocked with sweets and our mothers' theatre bin-oculars, we took our side seats on the second balcony and then the heavenly music began. Is that what it sounded like! We stared at the red velvet curtain, sniffed the theatre scent of newly ironed clothes, perfume, make-up, and dust, and I sort of sank down in the half-dark and started to hover. It felt as if I rose from the seat and was up there under the ceiling murals and dancing round the big crystal chandelier—it was unreal and wonderful and I hardly dared breathe.

And then the curtain went up. The poor Elsa, princess and everything, in a white full-length dress and thick long golden yellow hair complained so heartbreakingly and, oh dear, one felt so sorry for Elsa, who was accused of having murdered her little brother. Then Elsa went down on her knees and sang a prayer, so heartrending and heartfelt, and it made my hands all sweaty and I felt butterflies in my tummy.

And *then* it happened: along comes a swan on the water, pulling a shell after it on a chain, and *he* is standing in the shell. The beautiful Svanholm in light-blue velvet with silver boots, a silver sword, shield, and shining helmet over curly blond hair, and eyes as blue as cornflowers. My heart beat and thumped and was somewhere up in my throat, so I could neither swallow nor breathe. That music— that knight! And his farewell to the swan. The tears started to fall, the binoculars got misted over and I got my handkerchief out. Sniffles and palpitations.

Of course, I'd cried at the cinema and worshipped film stars, but the melting together of a delightful singer, a romantic knight, the fairy-tale atmosphere, and the unbelievably beautiful singing and music were a total experience that absolutely shook me. When the first act was over and the lights went up, I was dizzy and thought that the light stung my eyes and most of all I just wished that they could have gone on playing straight away. When it was all over, we would have liked to have wandered about on the streets and just feel what it was like. Surrounded by darkness and the music and the stage scenes. We sighed and with the help of banal words tried to explain how we felt. We were dreamy teenagers and my romantic heart immediately embraced the Wagnerian music and the great, heavy voice. But nobody else understood us. When we tried to tell people at school the next day about the experience, we met with incomprehension or scornful laughter. Opera mad. To be honest, I was teased for my suddenly acquired Wagner enthusiasm.

And there was more Wagner. My pocket money was spent on sheet music, records, and opera tickets, and some of it on flowers for the singers. The side seats on the second balcony became our regular places. It was suddenly fun to play the piano. The piano teacher and the grand piano had to suffer 'The pilgrims' chorus' and 'The arrival of the guests at the Wartburg'. I got some of the libretto and I sang all the parts and plonked away at the piano at the same time. My German became unexpectedly good and I improved my grades. You learnt so much strange vocabulary in Wagner, *Quelle*, *Karfreitag* and *Wonnemond*.

Still to this day I feel the same devoted self-absorption in the prelude to *Lohengrin*, I cry and tremble with Brünnhilde's departure and Wotan's departure and Hans Sach's monologues—I can go on for ever.

Here is another similarly overwhelming experience from about the same time with Jean Sibelius as the main character.

(5.2J) Man, middle-aged, 1940s

In those most sensitive teenage years I often listened in peace and quiet in my room to music, indeed to the radio in general. They were years of deeply penetrating experiences with music. From Bach to Bartók, from W.C. Handy to Dizzy Gillespie and Parker. They were thin-skinned teenage years when with the help of a radio apparatus (which would now be a museum piece) you could venture into uncharted musical territory and make incredible discoveries. Virtually all new experiences of music came via crackling radio. Long before stereo and hi-fi even existed as concepts. During the fateful 1940s.

Sometime around 1948–9 on an early spring Sunday, I had made myself comfortable in my basket chair, all ears and eagerly waiting to hear more of Jean Sibelius, whose *Finlandia* had of course made a very strong impression on me during the war years on the radio programme where listeners' favourites were played. This Sunday the gramophone concert at ten o'clock was giving us a whole symphony by Sibelius. But I would hardly manage all of that anyway, me a jazz digger above all! But you could always try to follow along for a little while. One or two movements. There were four in the symphony, Jean Sibelius's Symphony No. 2.

I still hadn't had my first real experience of falling in love. Which ought to be a total experience to surpass all other total experiences. One would expect this to happen at about 17 years of age. (This, I must again point out, is about a past time: 17 years old in the 1940s was not 17 years old in 1990. I know that only too well.)

Now Sibelius's Symphony No. 2 crackled from the loudspeakers. And it was a total experience just as strong as first love. I remember how the music absolutely drilled its way right through my consciousness. How I gradually lost contact with the ground and experienced an intoxication of the senses. Yes, it wasn't just one's ears that got a treat! When the immense intensification in the finale started up, I cried. I remember that my face was completely wet and that I had this feeling of happiness that I later understood could be matched only by what you feel when you fully and completely love another person.

So totally moved and happy that I simply *had to* sit down and write a letter to this fellow human being, Jean Sibelius, and thank him for giving me and many others this incredible thing, this music, which seemed to purify you from the inside and out, physically as well as spiritually. So I wrote a letter of a couple of pages to my fellow human being Jean Sibelius! Absolutely without restraint and without the slightest hesitation. I just *had to* do it. Whether it reached Järvenpää or not, at the end of the 1940s, I have no idea. But I do know that I went directly out into the forest and thanked God because something so unbelievably beautiful had been created by human hand.

The fact that music, both this particular music and then a lot of other music, could make such a thorough impression and move me so strongly I would assume is because I was young and strong, susceptible. Not middle-aged and blasé, and with my head full of other thoughts of a more or less practical character, as of course an adult head is most of the time. Split by thoughts of work, family, money, sport, and heaven knows what! *Then.* Then my senses were extremely susceptible and a bit of medium-wave crackling in the radio didn't disrupt the experience.

Sibelius's No. 2 led to a serious opening up of the great world of music for me. I suddenly realized that you could just ignore all that difficult caboodle. Behind those cold figures and opus numbers, which have certainly resulted in many people never even *beginning* to listen, there were—and are—of course, hidden oceans of beautiful tones! The restraint I had felt with classical music disappeared in a flash and I started to write down a record of my experiences with music!

Now we have reached the middle of the twentieth century. It is still classical music and a little popular music that dominate the accounts.

(5.2K) Woman, middle-aged, 1950s

Being born in the 1930s in a boring little village meant there were few opportunities to experience music. Together with my mother and siblings I sang the soprano voice in our family choir. Very nice and it was often pointed out that 'singing gives rise to noble feelings'.

In 1950 (I think it was), my conception of the world was partly changed. This was because I managed to tune into a foreign radio programme which every day played Perry Como, Rosemary Clooney, and so on—so fantastically modern and different. I was filled with this music, with lyrics I didn't understand, and, despite that, learnt some songs off by heart. Teenage anguish, ennui and gloominess disappeared, when I 'thought' this music or could listen to it. Little did I care about father's 'Turn off that rubbish!' Of course, you had to obey your father in those days, but I had at least for a few moments found myself 'in the climes of the blessed'. The joy, however, was to be decidedly short-lived, because I used the tuning dial so much that it broke. After it was repaired, I didn't dare touch the radio—however, the music was still within me as an intense feeling of consolation in moments of sorrow and powerlessness.

And imagine how this has helped me to understand my own teenagers when they constantly wanted to play the music of their own era. I can still get a lot out of listening to the *Tracks* list [the tunes voted most popular by listeners on Swedish Radio 3] on the radio, and feel when I do so that new music is being created that helps make life easier.

(5.2L) Woman, middle-aged, 1950s

I had just had my seventeenth birthday, was standing at the sink washing the dishes, all the others were having a nap after the meal. It was summer. The only music I had heard for quite a while was accordion music. I was way out in the archipelago staying with relatives for the summer. They still didn't have electricity on the islands, so the radio was battery powered.

Everything was calm and peaceful. I turned the radio on and out poured classical music from a big orchestra. I felt how I sucked in the music, I drank it, swallowed it, was being filled by it. Like a dry sponge which is reacquiring its shape.

Then in comes the grandmother of the house and turns off the radio with the words 'You don't need to run down the batteries for such a racket.' It was as if she had tried to suffocate me; I was completely frustrated. I remember it as a dreadful event, that she turned off the radio. But I remember too just how fantastic it was to be filled with music. I have often found myself thinking that it is a need—a nourishment. I don't experience it intellectually or that the music then gave me emotional experiences. It was like when somebody who is very thirsty is able to drink some water.

Several years later, I listened to David Attenborough on British TV. He was asked what he missed most on his long journeys of discovery. He answered: 'Before the day of the cassette recorder it was classical music.' He couldn't stand three months without classical music. He must have felt much like I did that time out in the archipelago. You don't long for classical music—you yearn for it.

(5.2M) Woman, middle-aged, 1950s

I have decided upon an experience from my teens, when a friend and I got to travel to Vienna, the musical city above all others. The journey was under the auspices of the Jeunnesses Musicales, so we were lots of young people from all over the world who met there.

A musician whom I have admired a lot over the years is the conductor Herbert von Karajan and now at last I was going to have the chance to hear him 'live'. So I felt quite excited and expectant. It didn't look good when we arrived in the city and found that all the tickets to Bach's Mass in B minor were sold out. But for enthusiasts that wasn't a reason to give up. We simply took two little stools and sat where we could watch the ticket-office cashier in the Musikverein in case anybody returned their tickets—and indeed, luck was with us, one standing ticket and one ticket on the first balcony became ours.

I got the standing ticket. The big day arrived; I dashed up the stairs with other enthusiasts to get as close to the rail as possible, but ended up in the middle of the group. But, so what, that didn't matter. I have rarely stood so happily for so long as on that occasion. As soon as the choir and orchestra started on their Kyrie it felt as if my legs were filled with a fizzy drink and I was lifted up to a higher sphere. If there is a heaven after this life, I have already visited it. My experience is similar to that which near-death patients describe: a journey towards light and happiness. I was especially struck by passages such as Aria No. 5, with the violin solo in the introduction and the violin's duet with the soprano. Rhythms such as those in, for example, bar 3, really turn me on, as does the intensification heightening as in bars 5–6. Also, rhythms as in bars 8, 9, 10 make me twitch, my legs and all my body. It really swings, Bach, and it makes you want to move, nice to dance to, and, of course, it is so pleasurable.

Aria No. 9 provides another experience, perhaps more in depth, a feeling of hope, everything will be OK, worries disappear, it gives strength to deal with all sorts of difficulties, it builds you up inside, gives you power. In general, Bach's music lets me see the totality, not to get bogged down in details. Of course, he is a master at writing major works that stick together.

Immediately after Bach's Mass in B minor I drifted out into Vienna's streets intoxicated with joy. The experience has been with me all these years, and now and then comes to the surface and gives me fresh boost and a zest for life.

(5.2N) Woman, middle-aged, 1960s

I was 18 or 19 years old and my dad was going to come along with me to a concert. The Gothenburg Symphony Orchestra played and the main item was Tchaikovsky's sixth symphony, *Pathétique*. I don't remember what I was like beforehand, but I must have been very expectant and looked forward to the evening. I was a very shy teenager and I would never have taken the initiative to go to a concert alone, even though I have loved music as long as I remember. I didn't have a friend who was as interested in music as I was.

I absorbed the music from the beginning, but when the third movement was over I was almost in ecstasy and couldn't hold back the tears, I found it so beautiful. That it became such a strong experience was probably because I really went in for it, and because Tchaikovsky's music is so powerful and the music came so close to me. Afterwards, I felt extremely happy but at the same time sad because, of course, this symphony comes to an end extremely slowly.

This experience meant that I felt much more self-confident, and from that day on I decided that 'Henceforth this is going to be my melody,' that is, nothing would be allowed to stop me from going to concerts in the future, even if I had to go on my own.

(5.2O) Man, middle-aged, 1960s

I am 18 years old and am taking part in a summer course to prepare for my entrance to the College of Music. Perhaps this experience contributed to my choice of career. The Fresk Quartet came to visit one of the evening music arrangements. They perform for us on the course in an intimate setting, with coffee cups on the tables and a relaxed and happy mood. They give an oral presentation of Shostakovich's String Quartet No. 8, for me completely new and unknown. My view of more modern music than Sibelius was very conservative and at the time I still had a 'wait and see' attitude, so my hopes were somewhat dampened.

But then the music hits me! The entire dramatic course in this quartet shows itself with all the clarity one could ask for, and Shostakovich's effects, which the 'Fresks' make the most of, influence me to the fullest, which must be the intention and which is freshest at a first hearing, and on top of that at an age when you are particularly sensitive for experiences! The second movement's reckless fury gives me goosepimples down my back, even now when I write this. When the bombs and the rattle of machine guns (subsequent knowledge! I didn't know this at the time!) are conjured up in the next-to-last movement, fortissimo chords against an immovable pedal point in pianissimo, and the pessimistic calm of the last movement makes its appearance, I completely dissolved into tears and feel greatly agitated.

It feels extremely embarrassing to be among all your mates with this very personal experience, even though everyone is deeply moved. The applause after the final pianissimo chord, an empty fifth, takes a long time to come, but then it breaks out in full. That too is an experience, but I suddenly want to be alone, despite all the good friends and the sense of fellowship on the course.

It is an experience of something dramatically negative (the war and the 1945 bombing of Dresden), but the experience gives me something positively pleasing, because I feel the unfathomable power in the music that has been able to convey this to me, quite unknowingly.

Now, when I write about this, I am inspired to hear it again. I still feel the physical reactions (goosepimples, shudders down my back, tears in the corners of my eyes, warmth) just from thinking about certain parts in the quartet.

In the following accounts, from the 1970s to the 1990s, other musical genres come into the picture.

(5.2P) Man, middle-aged, 1970s

The time of this event was when I was in secondary school. Uninspired and uninterested, we went to a concert in the school hall where some Africans were going to play and dance. We sat right at the front so as to be able to show our lack of interest. They came in and played and danced on drums and other rhythm instruments. I don't think I had ever been to anything other than boring school concerts. For the first time I heard music played live by someone other than teachers. The rhythm and dance were mixed with voices in a simple yet nevertheless complicated manner. The experience swept away all my preconceived expectations and meant that I started to participate with movements in my chair.

The music they played was traditional African music. The lights were turned off and the whole hall was dark, the only light was on the stage. Time and space ceased to exist and I felt a part of it. The situation made it unnecessary to distinguish between artistes and audience. They expressed themselves from the starting point of their culture and through it. They were true. They were in the room and they both danced and sang. Everything was whole. For me the experience was total. In other words, beyond cognitive assessment.

It has inspired me to look for simple music. During the time it remained in my life, it meant lightness and exhilaration. A flow as if I was being reminded of my own pulse.

(5.2Q) Woman, young, 1980s

It was like a stroke of lightning. Already, after a few bars, I felt that this was 'my music', that is, music that I wouldn't tire of. The music engaged me, suited me. It was music that made me feel good, regardless of whether I was sad or happy. The surprise was positive. It was love at first sight.

It was . . . some mates of mine who suggested we should go down to the pub and 'have a couple of beers and listen to some decent music'. First I was a bit hesitant, but it wasn't so hard to convince me, I was curious. We went. At first I wasn't so impressed. The pub was small and the tables were worn, wooden benches and chairs, there weren't so many people there either. It was pleasantly cool in any case, quite cosy really. We sat down at a table right next to the stage, ordered a beer each, started to talk. It was nice, all five of us were in a good mood. Meanwhile the pub filled with people, it wasn't half empty any longer. I liked it!

All of a sudden the taped background music became silent, and right away people were standing on the stage. Then lightning struck. It was an electric guitar that had exploded in front of my eyes and ears. It was loud volume and the music was stirring. The artiste with the reverberating electric guitar was Roffe Wikström with the Hjärtslag [Heartbeat] band, and that band got my heart beating for sure. I was totally fascinated by all the tones that whined out of that guitar. The guy must have been born with a guitar in his hands, I thought. The faces he made when he played were fascinating too.

After the concert I felt rather empty. I must have been pretty tired. If I'd had the energy I'd have wished they could play for a couple more hours (the concert was only three hours long, after all). What an evening. I had danced because I was happy, full of energy, but sometimes I sat down and felt almost melancholy when they played some really complaining and tragic blues. I had had an outlet for a load of feelings. The love is still there, OK, I listen to a lot of other music in various styles, but blues is closest to my heart, I reckon.

(5.2R) Woman, young, 1990s

I've been through a strong experience with music that has to do with punk. I remember it very clearly. It was just before my sixteenth birthday, and us in the band we had slept at the bassist's place and in the morning I was looking for a cassette tape to listen to just to have something to listen to in general. I'm sitting in her room on a mattress and in front of me is a tape recorder with a cassette tape in it. So I reckon I'll listen to the band that's on the tape. Push down the play button and out pours Swedish punk from the beginning of the eighties, it's [a group called] Asta Kask. I'm absolutely flabbergasted! This is like nothing I've ever heard before. Whatever is it? It takes me a while, but then I realize what punk music is. Fascination and the shivers fill all of me and evidently I'm not exactly contactable, according to the others in the band. I remember that I was *absolutely fascinated*.

It's music that roars and tells a story at the same time. Somebody sings in Swedish, which in itself feels pretty new and unusual to me, but above all it's the guitars, because I play the guitar myself, they are what catch me. I've no idea how long this goes on, it could be two seconds or just as easily more like half an hour. The music has my total attention. At the same moment, however long it is, that I am just swept away by this punk band I simply make up my mind—we're going to play punk and it's going to be bloody good!

(5.2S) Woman, young, 1990s

(My first meeting with techno music). Far away you could hear a rhythmic pounding of the bass and I tried to keep time as I walked. The further I got up the slope, the clearer the pounding of the bass became, and I was eager to get there. Now I was standing at the top of the slope. There stood a large circus tent. I started to walk towards the tent. The closer I got, the louder the sound, and the music felt incredibly tempting. When I reached the entrance I was met with sound waves, strong ones. It was like stepping into a new world. It's hard to describe the feeling that I got, but it was as if the music was alive. It gave me welcome thumps on my back with beats in the same rhythm that my heart was beating. My body started to move to the music without my thinking about it. I was captivated by the situation and it was as if time and space stopped. The music was so tempting and everything else all around was so different.

I started to slowly and curiously move around inside the tent. On the walls there were film screens with projected coloured patterns and there were enormous light effects on the dance floor. Deep inside the tent there was a raised stage the DJ played on and round about me there were happy people who danced to the monotone bass and the playful sound loops. Here and there were some small stages that people stood dancing on. I climbed up onto one to be able to see the DJ better and stayed up there a while. Felt a lot of respect for him, don't know why, but perhaps because he showed me a new music that I had been looking for but not known about, until now.

My legs started to make themselves felt and I went out to get a breath of air, so I thought, but the exit was an entrance to a smaller tent. Here you could hear very calm and pleasant music and the sound level was much lower here. The whole [inside of the] tent was covered with hay. I climbed up and lay down in the hay. In here, too, were film screens with coloured patterns and the centre pole was decorated with roses, red roses. Now my mate came and we lay there a while and listened to the music. He wondered why I was so quiet and I said that I was simply happy and that I was pleased he had shown me all this.

That July night was the start of my passionate interest in this musical genre. I also came to learn more about myself that night. Because I felt I was in such an ecstatic mood and this was without the influence of anything other than the music and what I could see, I realized what an effect music has on you, that music can make you laugh with joy. I don't know how many times I've discovered that I'm smiling all over my face when I hear such music. That night was the start of a journey of discovery in the world of techno and I'm still travelling.

The accounts in this long section confirm the impression that the music one encounters during one's teens is often decisive for how one continues to interact with music. As we saw in the previous chapter, this can even apply to strong experiences with music during childhood. It is to be hoped, however, that this doesn't cloud one's vision for types of music other than the music one heard then. The world of music is unending, and it invites one to make ever-new discoveries.

5.3 MUSIC AS CONSOLATION, SUPPORT, AND THERAPY DURING ONE'S TEENS

The period of one's teenage years/puberty is a critical time in many respects. One is no longer a child, but is not yet an adult either. One is increasingly subjected to influences and pressure from many sides—parents, school, mates, mass media,

advertising, etc. To form one's identity under such conditions can be a difficult process associated with thoughts about one's own existence, switches between different
emotional states, often considerable vulnerability, feelings of insecurity, perhaps
depression, or something even worse.

   In such situations, one is especially sensitive to various impressions, and music can
come to mean a lot as consolation, support, and confirmation—as in the following
examples where music lifts the narrators out of a state of melancholy or depression.

(5.3A) Woman, middle-aged, 1950s

I was an only child and had a relatively strict upbringing, had many friends but was nevertheless often alone together with my parents. At the end of my teens, I suffered quite a lot
because, unlike my friends, I didn't have any boyfriends and couldn't go to dances and parties like an adult. I also had a horrible feeling that there was something wrong with me—
that I wasn't good enough.

   On Midsummer Eve we were at our simple cottage, way out on its own in the countryside, and I sat in the boat on the lake and watched the sun setting and felt black inside. After
a while I started to row back to the cottage and went inside to get ready for bed in a little
newly renovated outhouse where I hung out. First, I went into my parents' room and borrowed the radio to have something to amuse myself with. There was a smell of paint in the
outhouse, which contained only a bunk bed and a chair.

   On short wave I tuned into a recording of Mendelssohn's *A Midsummer Night's Dream*.
The sound quality was awful and there was a lot of fading, which meant that the sound
disappeared completely, but I knew the piece well from before and mentally filled in the
gaps. A peaceful feeling crept over me and I pushed away the feeling of loneliness—felt as if
I had a happy secret that made me strong and independent. The music was so valuable that
it replaced everything else. Throughout my life I have been surrounded by books and read
a great deal, above all 'read my way out' of my worries. On this occasion, I fled into the
music. (Strange though it may seem, I always catch the smell of paint when I hear that
music again.)

(5.3B) Woman, young, 1980s

I had my strongest experience with music when I was in the USA as an exchange student.
After having big problems adjusting to the new life and difficulties with identifying myself
and getting into contact with people in the new surroundings, I was sent a tape featuring
Marie Fredriksson from Sweden.

   It was an amazing experience—I heard Swedish again, I was extremely happy. For so
long I had tried to express myself in English, but I hadn't mastered the different nuances of
the language, and my thoughts and feelings didn't come out the way I wanted. But when I
heard Marie sing, it was like a best friend. She took me back to Sweden. It might sound
strange, but I got this feeling of being in love, got the butterflies, was happy . . . yes, my body
wanted to explode with happiness . . . and love for everything . . . life, I think.

   I listened to the tape, I should think, two or three times a day. It was like a feeling
of security amid all the chaos and misunderstandings. When one of my American friends
listened to the tape and showed that they didn't like it, I was terribly angry! It was like
an insult, as if it was me they were directing their dislike at.

Marie and her singing . . . yes, I shared my worries with her voice, so yet again when people don't understand what I went through, I find consolation in her voice. Strange that music can improve your mood so incredibly!

In both the two accounts above, the music has been reproduced electronically. The next account is about live music, with all that means of visual impressions such as, for example, a committed artiste.

(5.3C) Man, young, 1980s (from an edited interview)

I had a strong experience with music when I was at a Styx concert. I had felt really down for several weeks before. Then I went to this concert with a mate. This group isn't just any old group that simply stands up on the stage and plays. They talk an incredible amount with the audience, they're incredibly sensible. The singer stood talking to the audience a very long time, it sounded exactly as if he himself had felt down a very long time, but had started to lift himself up out of the shit . . . [he was saying] that there was no point feeling down, that you should take one day at a time, etc., the usual talk really, but incredibly more genuine . . . I mean, he had experienced everything he sang about, at least that was the impression you got when he talked to the audience, he'd been heavily into drugs and such stuff.

The first song made an incredible impression. Go in and sing alone in front of 10,000 people—just him and nobody else—what a lot of goosepimples, all over my body. He starts to sing 'Tonight is the night we'll make history' . . . he sings for a minute, then the curtain goes up . . . if he had stopped singing then and somebody had dropped a pin at that moment, you'd have heard it. It was just as if God came out onto the stage, sort of. There are 10,000 people standing and staring and there isn't a sound. I was so moved that it was so incredibly nice and beautiful and then when he does it, well, it sounds twice as good. When you've heard the lyrics, then you know what it stands for in some way. If somebody else had come out and sung just as well, he wouldn't have been able to captivate everybody like that. At other concerts you sat there and talked between the songs—'Wonder if they'll do this song now . . .'—but I don't think we said a word during the entire concert.

99% of all the rock groups you go to see, they play their music, talk a bit between the songs and then there isn't any more. But Styx, they seemed to try to get you to feel much better when you left, to have a brighter life in some way. It made me happy. He radiated so incredibly much when he sang. Happiness. I had exactly the same feeling during the entire concert. I think that there were many who experienced it in the same way as me because there was such a response from the audience, the others were quiet just like I was quiet, exactly as if you had got to decide yourself, everything was so perfect in some way.

If I read the lyrics of a song that I'd never heard, then it wouldn't really say much to me, you wouldn't be able to take any of it in. But on the other hand, if it is good and lovely music in just the right mood, then that has quite another effect. It can be as simple as a guy who just stands there straight off and sings with a bass in the background.

After the concert I felt so incredibly good when I left the place, it had been a long time since I'd done that, but afterwards everything got better, everything just went perfectly.

Although the lyrics do have a big part to play in this and many other accounts of strong experiences with music, this narrator thinks that it is not until the lyrics are combined with 'good and lovely music' that they achieve full effect.

In the accounts so far, music has come as a rescue and escape without the person having directly expected or planned it. In other cases, the choice of music can be very deliberate, and the person knows exactly which music is needed.

(5.3D) Woman, young, 1980s

My strongest experience of music took place in the autumn one day when I was at home in my room. I was sad and down and felt that the only thing that could help me was music. So I lowered the venetian blinds, turned off all the lights and put on one of my best records. It is the *Trio* album with my absolute favourite singer Dolly Parton and the two country singers Linda Ronstadt and Emmylou Harris (the whole record is absolutely wonderful, you can't really pick out any special bit, well, perhaps 'My dear companion').

I sat there with my eyes shut in the middle of the floor and felt the music, while I myself sang Dolly's part, the highest. We sang together in such harmony that I've never experienced anything like it before. It felt as if I was hovering and was lifted higher and higher up on the wings of music! All my problems disappeared and my entire body was dissolved in tones. (I want to add that if I can choose, then this is how I want to die sometime in the future, because I've never had it as wonderful as this!)

When the record came to an end it felt as if I had slept for 24 hours solid. I felt so rested! This has meant that I use the record when I'm feeling down. It gives me some sort of inner cleansing, but only in connection with darkness and high volume (but not so loud that my own voice can't be heard, because I must sing too if it is going to help). Also, I prefer to sit with my knees under my chin, hunched up, with my arms around my legs, swaying in time with the music.

Finally in this section, a harrowing account of how life was questioned but was saved thanks to music. The narrator's description of the situation, her thoughts on life and existence, and her love of music are moving and absorbing for every reader, regardless of age and musical taste.

(5.3E) Woman, young, 1980s

I'm a girl and am one of those people who always listen to music. I soak up music as if I were a dustrag, all music, whatever it is, classical, rock, and pop, yeah, everything, and all music is wonderful, if there hadn't been any music, then I'd probably have invented it. I listen to all sorts of music, it depends entirely on how I feel. The music changes with my mood, but most of all I listen to hard rock, and the drum beat in the new rap and acid is simply divine. All music tells its own story, I think, but sometimes it becomes an extra-strong experience and the lyrics stick in your head, that happens often.

It was a perfectly ordinary, boring, grey autumn day and I was feeling really rough, life felt like the dumps, and every day a special thought cropped up inside my head: Why am I alive? What am I doing here? Just think if I were to . . . and I just hardly dare think the rest, but life wasn't exactly a dance on roses and I just wanted to die.

The tape recorder was on, pretty loud. I was listening to a tape with the hard rock group KISS. I know those songs almost by heart. There I sat on a wooden chair beside my desk and was busy thinking about how you could kill yourself in the most painless way, when the sound of 'Detroit Rock City' started to roar from the loudspeakers. The bass, the drums, they exploded in my brain, 'I feel all tired on a Saturday night . . .' (and yeah, sure, I am tired). At the end of the song came the most frightening part. The words are:

I feel so good, I'm so alive
I hear my song playin' on the radio
It goes, get up, everybody gonna move their feet
Get down, everybody gonna leave their seat
12 o'clock I gotta rock
There's a truck on hand, the light's staring at my eyes
Oh, my God, no time to turn
I gotta laugh 'cause I know I'm gonna die. *Why?**

Every word was repeated time after time, long after the song was finished and I thought: It sounds different. So I rewound the cassette and listened again and then I had a vision.

Paul Stanley was standing in front of me with sad eyes and was repeating the question '*Why?*' I opened my eyes, shut them again, and I still saw Paul with that question: '*Why?*' and at that same moment I started to cry and I couldn't stop. I thought about all the people who had died unnecessarily in car accidents, of drugs and of illnesses, of all the starvation and poverty and misery in the world, and here I sat and was thinking about killing myself. What on earth was I doing?

When I eventually could stop crying, I felt so empty. I didn't feel sorrow or joy, just anguish. And a dreadful question: What if I had done it? Now there wasn't a moment's doubt about whether life was worth living or not. I am happy that I have it as good as I do. There are millions of people who have it a thousand times worse than me.

I have asked myself many times why it happened just then and how. The song actually saved my life. Every time I hear the song I am filled with a feeling of joy. The joy of being able to sit here, alive, for real, and listen to my favourite songs. I have been selected to live, I think that 'someone' saved me. Not God or any other divine power. But this 'someone' whom I can't place, they are just there. They are there like a big shadow, not only for me, deep inside, but in the whole of history, the whole history of life. I can only describe it by saying that it frightens me, but it makes me curious. It is magnificent and absolutely unique, but terrible and indestructible.

You probably think that here's a completely crazy girl who ought to be writing some sick horror story, don't you? But I promise and swear that it is like a shadow that protects me. I have been completely down many times, but somebody sort of gives me a hand and makes sure I pull myself together, and I've noticed that certain songs often go deep inside me and they help me. Mostly it's old KISS songs that give me an insight and give me the creeps about various things I've done or thought about doing. Still to this day it's KISS and their music that means the most for me. Even if they torture me and throw me onto a fire, I can't deny that I worship KISS, they guide me, but not like some god; rather it is the music!

As soon as you say to an adult, yeah, 35- to 40-year-olds and older, that you listen to hard rock, heavy metal and that KISS is the greatest ever since Elvis, they just give you a snooty look and accuse you of being devil worshippers and satanists in turn and 'Everybody knows that KISS are Nazis,' they say. Then I get so angry. How the hell can they be satanists and Nazis when all four (or all eight that have been in KISS in their history) were born Jews? Then they just go away and say that they don't want to have anything to do with us young people because everyone knows what rotten types they are! They refuse to listen, but if they would only think back to their own youth and the music then. The adults then said their music was forbidden too, it was sinful and dangerous for your brain. Today the adults say the same about our music. I could go on writing for ever about this and about my experiences of music and if only I could play, then I would have done, but I write songs instead, and poems.

Music is my life—without it I'll die!

Several other accounts of the healing effects of music are to be found in Chapter 17.

5.4 Performing music during one's teens

One's teenage years are the period when many make their first performance in public, as soloists or as members of an ensemble. It is exciting but often associated with considerable nervousness before the performance. When one has finally got started and everything turns out to be going well, the nervousness eases up and one can enter into a trance-like state where everything goes better than it has ever done before. Afterwards, all that one feels is great satisfaction, happiness and joy, not least if one has been entrusted with performing alongside 'real' musicians/artistes to show what one is capable of. The response of the audience and their reactions also mean a great deal. The experience strengthens one's self-confidence and serves as an inspiration to continued practice and new performances, perhaps even to a decision to devote oneself to this for the rest of one's life.

There now follows a selection of accounts of performing during one's teenage period. They represent several different musical genres with all what that implies with respect to attitudes and conventions—but the experiences are very similar regardless of genre.

(5.4A) Man, old, 1940s

I got a violin from my dad and some lessons in violin playing. They didn't go too well, I didn't practise enough, and football and friends were more important. But I didn't really want to stop either.

One day, the music teacher asked me if I could step in and play an easy part in the piece called 'In the monastery garden' at a concert with the school orchestra. Without thinking, I answered yes, was given the score and had two days to learn my part. How my parents, brothers and sisters and neighbours put up with those two days I don't understand. I screeched and groaned, scraped and cursed until long into the evening. A few hours before the rehearsal, I was determined to take to my bed, sick. But suddenly it sounded reasonably decent, so I went off to the rehearsal. It turned out comparatively OK, I thought.

And then a few hours later I sat behind a music stand in the gym hall, nervous but with a bit more self-confidence than before. Then the music teacher raised his baton and we played. And I heard my own part and how it flowed together with the others, but everything became a whole and the music became alive, expressive, and beautiful, and I felt so indescribably happy, proud and absolutely joyful. The noise of the applause after the final notes gave me the shivers all down my spine.

When I went home that evening, the violin was my friend. Thanks to it, I had been able to experience something that was completely new to me: the feeling of being able with others to create or recreate live, real music. I'll never forget that feeling.

(5.4B) Man, young, 1970s

When I was 12, 13 years old, me and my brother we went to Jokkmokk's winter market in northern Sweden. In those days, lots of people who were involved in folk music gathered there. I particularly remember one evening when there was a dance in a cottage and where a mishmash of groups was playing; they were the hottest there were at the time. It was really super cool there and I stood in a corner with my little violin case right next to where they were playing. And I thought, this is simply fantastic, this is what I'd like to do. The entire situation was extremely exciting for a young boy.

My sister knew one of the guys who was playing and he recognized me, so when they had played some tunes he came up to me, ruffled my hair and asked whether I could play a tune, if I could join them in a tune. Well, yes, I did know 'The Jokkmokk waltz'. Right, then we'll do 'The Jokkmokk waltz', he said, and talked to the others.

So we played it, so I could join in and play this tune with these guys who were the hottest you could imagine. I played my little three-quarters violin the best I could and it was a fantastic feeling. This was the best kick in the world. I couldn't have anything better than this. It was delightful to be taken seriously even though you were a kid. That you could do something together with these people who were idols. It was extremely exciting that I could be with those important people. It was also an insight into the adult world that was extremely exciting. It felt as if I'd taken the first step on the way to becoming like them.

When I later travelled home from the market I had sort of decided that this was what I was going to do. I had started as a beginner at the music school but it wasn't until now that I got this direct connection. This is what I'm learning, this is what it can lead to. I hadn't been able to imagine that when I was with the teacher at school. I sometimes think that it would be fun if I met a little boy that I could give something similar to, now that I'm an adult and fairly well established in these circles.

(5.4C) Woman, young, 1980s

I was one of 300 singers in a concert with classic rock songs arranged for symphony orchestra and choir, particularly 'Sailing', 'She's out of my life', 'Hey Jude'. An absolutely fantastic experience! I was totally absorbed by the music, enjoyed every single note, made an effort, sang, laughed, jumped. The rhythm section was standing right in front of our row and they were clowning about and acting up all the time. Every time we came in, we were nervous because we hadn't heard the music before. But the conductor clearly indicated when we should begin, so I don't think we came in late more than once.

When we sang 'Sailing', about a hundred people in the audience lit their cigarette lighters and let the flames wave in the air in time with the music. We stood there, in the strong lighting, singing, and got an enormous response when we saw these tiny flames hovering back and forth in the pitch black. And in 'She's out of my life' the conductor turned round and faced the audience, let the orchestra look after itself, and played the pan flute with a wonderfully beautiful, tremblingly fragile tone.

The encore, 'Hey Jude', was repeated three times! The choir was more or less jumping on the stage and the rhythm section went at it so that the entire stage construction rocked plus certainly half of the girls in the choir fell a bit in love with the incredibly charming and humorous conductor. We were 13–16 years of age.

Afterwards, I was ecstatic, happy, 'on little pink clouds', later sad that it was already over. I didn't want it ever to end. I lived on the memory for months. Can still feel a shiver of joy and expectant tension when I listen to these pieces. Remember the performance with pride, happiness but also with melancholy and longing.

(5.4D) Woman, young, 1980s

Where I come from, every year they have a soloist concert so that those who are thinking of applying to music college will have a chance to perform their pieces in front of an audience. I play classical piano and had prepared for this for more than six months. Before the concert I was extremely nervous. I always am when I'm going to play in front of an audience.

This particular evening I was going to play two difficult pieces. I started with a Chopin étude. It didn't go very well and afterwards I felt depressed. The next piece was the first movement from Brahms's Piano Sonata No. 3. Then something amazing happened. I played as if I was in a trance, and I promise I have never played better. This was an incredible feeling, it was as if time and space disappeared. There was only me and the music, nothing else existed.

When I had finished playing, the applause was like an ovation and the audience stood up in the rows. Several people came up to me afterwards and said that this was the highlight of the concert. I got a lot of praise and felt extremely satisfied. It took a while to grasp what had really happened. Six months' hard work had given a fantastic result.

(5.4E) Woman, young, 1980s

I play the bassoon and have done so for four, almost five, years. During that time I have been taking things at a steady pace and done my home exercises and practised, but never put all my energy into the playing. To put it plainly, it has all always been just so-so, never too much. I have perhaps never really felt joy in playing.

One day I was asked if I wanted to play a solo in concert, with the symphony orchestra as my 'backing orchestra'. Of course, I was both nervous and happy and also got an enormous lift from the idea of it, so I got to work and practised, properly this time.

Despite the fact that the final week before the concert I was so nervous that my fingers couldn't play, I knew that I had mastered my piece. Now there were still the rehearsals with the orchestra and that was almost the worst part. I'd be standing in front of pro musicians who'd played for many years, and I'd be the star and only have them as help. I hardly dared think about how it would go, but I took some comfort from the fact that at least I had some experience from school with the orchestra and would know most of them. My nervousness in front of the orchestra soon faded, because they were wonderful to me. From the first moment, they looked after me, supported, and encouraged me, and it helped. Every time we went through the piece, it just got better.

Eventually, D-Day arrived. I went around in a daze all day and at the final rehearsal I was partly as nervous as could be, and partly had my thoughts in other places. Suddenly it was time. It was now that whether I really could manage the piece would be seen. When I went out together with the conductor onto the podium and acknowledged the warm applause of the audience and the orchestra, it was as if everything inside me dissolved, it was as if I wasn't there, it wasn't me that it was about. I played as never before, not a single error, and everything went smoothly. Everything around me didn't exist. My parents were worried that the crying of small children would disturb me, but I didn't even notice any. And when the piece was finished and people applauded for several minutes, I didn't notice that either—I was so immersed in what I had done that I didn't hear anything else. Well, I heard when the conductor and the orchestra thanked me, I heard when the flower girl said congratulations and gave me the flowers, and I still heard within me the echo of the concert.

It wasn't until afterwards, long afterwards, when I listened to the recording of the concert, that I noticed how much I had missed of what happened afterwards, but my feelings just then, after the concert, the enervation, the joy and all the emotions mixed together to something I can't explain, that was the most important, and it's something I want to experience again.

(5.4F) Man, middle-aged, 1980s

At last it was time for my band to do something big. We were going to take part in the Swedish Rock Championship. We rehearsed two or three times a week and during our first two years were pretty close to each other, musically as well as socially. After we had recorded some demo tapes, we sent the most recent to the selection committee for the Rock Championship. This jury sieved through about 2,000 tapes that had been submitted, and only 50 bands would be able to play in the competition. We were one of them!

When we'd understood that we actually would be playing our songs in front of a jury on a big stage before lots of members of the public, we began to select songs and to do some really serious rehearsing. During the period between the notification and the competition day, I was walking on clouds and everything around me seemed unimportant. I mean, I was the drummer in a band that had gone past almost 2,000 bands in the selection process. I felt a great joy.

The longed-for day had finally arrived. I had a few butterflies in my stomach all that day, which otherwise felt as though it would never end. Usually when we performed with the band, we'd have to pack stuff and set up all the gear, but not this time. Just like the big musicians, we could go to a stage where everything was already in place, all we had to do was plug in our guitars and get on with it. I now realized that I wouldn't be playing on my own familiar drum set, but would be playing on another drum set that was completely unknown to me. This made me a little nervous and the butterflies got more active in my stomach.

People started to pour into the park and fairly soon there was a large crowd in front of the stage. Our turn came along, and the MC introduced us and it was time to ascend this big stage. We were only 17 years old. I sat at the drums and felt how I had the shudders all over, looked out at the audience, which stretched out as far as I could see. I couldn't focus on anything; I had a sort of tunnel vision. After a few seconds I only saw my mates in the band, and it was time to count in the first song. I felt completely rigid, paralysed and without control. It tickled all over my body, along my arms, legs, and stomach. A sort of intoxication that is hard to describe.

When we had got through the first half of the song, things eased up a bit and I thought it was easier to control my arms and legs. Suddenly I heard my own drum playing, I could probably have heard it all the time but I had other things to think about, my body wasn't working like it usually did. The drums had a lot of mikes, and when I trod on the bass drum I got a shock of shivers right through me. What an incredible sound! At last, my drum playing could really be heard. When I did something on the kettle drum it went right out into the audience and every roll of the drumsticks had a purpose. We got through the performance without any hitches at all, I don't know if that had ever happened before.

We finished the last song and I was going to leave this really great drum set. I got up slowly and checked that my legs moved as I wanted them to. It went OK, but not so fast.

When I got back on solid ground outside the actual stage, I felt a sense of joy that was very strong. We in the band just wanted to giggle and laugh. Not until we had talked with family members who were in the audience did we understand that it had gone off fantastically well.

This experience was something that I lived on for ages afterwards. It meant that my interest in making music increased considerably. Knowing that you could get a kick like that again means that you never want to stop playing.

(5.4G) Woman, young, 1990s

Six years ago I was in a rock orchestra. There were about 70 of us and we played rock music as a symphony orchestra. That year's great event was that we were going to have the musician called E-type as guest artiste. We practised for almost eight months before it was time to do it. It really was blood, sweat, and tears before the great day came along. Of course, everybody was nervous. Me and my mates were curious about E-type too, not just as an artiste but even as a person.

During the concert there were about 3,500 people sitting in the audience. The orchestra started the evening itself and the audience remained calm. It was still a bit jittery but once we have got going the whole orchestra usually calms down. I remember that I thought that it couldn't get much better than this, but oh boy, how wrong I was.

When E-type came out onto the stage, the audience woke up. There were teenage girls standing at the very front who just screamed. They tried to get hold of him. They were crying, they were half crazy. I've seen pictures from when the Beatles were popular, and these girls behaved in just the same way, although there weren't more than about ten of them. The rest of the audience remained a bit calmer but they shouted, whistled, sang along, etc. This was an absolutely fantastic feeling. We young people were there playing first and foremost with a famous artiste and then in front of so many people. You could at least deceive yourself that they came for our sake, and not just for E-type. It didn't matter who the audience came for. You felt so incredibly great! The best of all was that E-type was a nice person off stage too.

It was the whole thing, the entire situation that meant that I got an enormous kick. An experience that means that I'll never stop making music.

Many of the experiences and reactions described in these accounts turn up later in the more comprehensive chapter about SEM in musical performances (Chapter 18).

5.5 COMMENTARY

To summarize: Strong experiences with music during one's teens can mean encountering music that one is already very familiar with, for example at big concerts when one at last gets to meet idols that one has previously only heard on records or seen on TV. Other experiences, however, mean encounters with new, unknown music that can be totally revolutionary and leave its traces for a long time to come, perhaps even for the rest of one's life. The teenage period is generally characterized by great sensitivity and vulnerability, and music can then come to function as confirmation, support, consolation, and therapy. During one's teens, one might perhaps also perform in front of an audience with all what that can mean, with, on the one hand, nervousness (before) and, on the other hand, elation, pride, and strengthened self-confidence (after), an experience that can spur one on to continue making music.

Strong experiences with music during childhood and adolescence make up approximately 35% of all the accounts in our material. Some such accounts are also reproduced in later chapters, but the greater part of the content hereafter concerns experiences at an adult age, including old age.

Chapters 6 to 17 provide examples of various reactions in strong experiences with music, for example that one can be overpowered by the music, have inner pictures of the music, that the music gives rise to feelings of many different types as well as experiences that are existential, transcendental, and religious in character. The music can give new insights, confirm one's own identity, and function as therapy. There is a certain degree of overlap between the chapters. Their order is partly arbitrary, and the reader may choose to read them in a different order or in a personal selection.

* 'Detroit Rock City' Words & Music by Paul Stanley & Bob Ezrin © Copyright 1976 Hori Productions America Incorporated/Cafe Americana, USA. Universal Music Publishing Limited. All rights in Germany administered by Universal Music Publ. GmbH. All Rights Reserved. International Copyright Secured.
Used by permission of Music Sales Limited.

CHAPTER 6

WHEN MUSIC TAKES OVER

A typical feature in strong experiences with music is that the music completely dominates one's attention and shuts out everything else. The world around one disappears, time stands still, the only thing that counts is music and oneself, here and now. Sometimes this comes about 'to order', so to speak, for example at a concert with an artiste that one has waited a long time to hear and who fulfils one's every expectation. There were several examples of this in the previous chapter. In other cases, it can be exactly the opposite. One is not at all prepared for something special to happen, but suddenly the music takes over and everything else is pushed to the background. This can happen in all sorts of places—at home, at work, in the car, on the bus, in the crowd on the street, out in the countryside, and when one is busy doing completely different things.

6.1 IN EVERYDAY SITUATIONS

Sometimes people are busy with chores at home when music suddenly causes them immediately to break off what they are doing. First, here are a couple of brief examples.

(6.1A) Woman, middle-aged, 1950s

It was music from the radio. I was sitting sewing, but had to go and stand in front of the radio as if in front of the orchestra. It was incredible music. Powerful: the dissonances and then the violin music, which was so fantastic that I don't think I stood on the floor— I floated up. It was Bela Bartók's Violin Concerto. New for me. Afterwards I feel satisfied, elated, happy, filled with wonder.

(6.1B) Woman, middle-aged, 1970s

On one occasion, I suppose I must have been in my late teens, I had been asked to clean our TV room. I left the TV turned on and Staffan Scheja was playing a piano concerto by Sergei Rachmaninov. I hadn't heard it before, and when the second movement started I was totally overcome by a feeling that washed all over me. I got goosepimples all over my body and the creeps down my back, and I started to cry. It was so unbelievably beautiful and the music sort of came in waves roughly like a swell out at sea. I stopped cleaning and sat down on the sofa and listened to the rest of the concerto. The cleaning took a long time on that occasion.

In the following accounts, the reactions are described more thoroughly, as well as what it was in the music that made a particular impression.

(6.1C) Woman, middle-aged, 1990s

I like sitting up late and working when the rest of the family has gone to bed. I sit on my own at the kitchen table with some paperwork. Then I usually listen to the music channel on the radio. I like the volume to be fairly low, the music is more like company or a light sound background on these occasions, particularly if I'm working with something complicated. At this time of day, I feel more effective and can think clearly.

The music channel offered a mix of goodies and suddenly I heard the introduction of what was for me a well-known and beloved introduction, the cello in the beginning of the overture to *William Tell* by Rossini. This is one of my absolute favourites, I feel as though I know every note, I get the shivers even before harmonies I especially like, simply because I know what's going to come. I particularly like the melancholy solo for oboe, no, English horn it must be. Not to mention the trumpets, when their fanfares lead the entire orchestra at a wild gallop towards the finale.

Pen and paper were now left untouched and I turned up the volume as much as the circumstances allowed. The shivers chased across my body. That's what it was like! No particular factors influenced the situation, my beloved music just came out of the radio, free, unexpected! I could indulge myself a while, and then go back to work, refreshed and happy to have experienced something like that.

(6.1D) Man, young, 1990s

It was on the radio that I heard Sinéad O'Connor's 'Nothing compares 2 U'. I was busy with something in the kitchen and had the radio on. Before the song I felt like I usually do, but when the song had been playing for about a minute, I thought it sounded so good that I turned up the volume a whole lot and took a kitchen chair and sat in front of the loudspeakers to listen intently. What I heard was so nice that I cried, all the way through the song. The song sounded a bit melancholy but I didn't feel sad because of that, rather I had a sense of reaching an inner harmony. The song somehow found its way straight down into my emotional core. Time and space didn't exist, and it also felt as if life/reality in some diffuse way manifested itself in the experience: a lot is pain, injustice, sad—but all the time there is satisfaction, joy, warmth, and you can feel a strong sense of confidence, hope, and trust.

What affected me were exclusively the music and the voice, not the lyrics. The ballad is extremely calm with a very passionate violin and a choir that strengthens the harmonic aspect of the experience. The most characteristic [feature] is the singing voice. Sinéad really uses it as an instrument and 'plays' with it by in turn making it soft and hard and suddenly and unerringly going up in falsetto. The song goes in 'waves' with gentle switches of intensity and emotion. The delicate song is so beautiful!

(6.1E) Woman, middle-aged, 1970s

It was an ordinary day, in the middle of the day, at home in my kitchen. Before the experience, everything was like it usually is, kitchen chores and my thoughts far away, a bit absent-minded and uncommitted.

Suddenly amid the non-stop muzak on the radio I heard a melody, played on saxophones, which went right inside me. All that mattered was to *hear* it. There was a place that was so beautiful that you can't explain it. First there was an ordinary bit, neatly done with wind instruments, with swing, but then came a piece in the middle that was a bit different and was really superb.

I crept closer to the radio, took a pen and paper on the way and just *enjoyed* it. It was as if everything stopped, I only heard music, it almost hurt. I forgot to breathe and my heart was beating hard. I was afraid that I wouldn't be able to hear what the tune was, where the music came from. I just had to hear it again!

It was Ingmar Nordström, who was playing the Beatles' 'Let It Be'. It was an arrangement with saxophones and with a really superb intermezzo between the verses, but no singing! It was so beautiful, a bit sentimental, it had swing, was original.

After the experience I was tired, shaken, surprised, disconcerted that the music ended, disappointed with the music that was played afterwards.

For several years I followed different recordings of 'Let It Be', but found that it was actually Ingmar Nordström who sounded best. I'm still so affected by it that I don't dare play it when I'm driving a car. No other music has been able to surpass this experience, and it suffices to have been able to experience it once in life.

Just imagine if such strong experiences were to happen often, *goodness, how dreadful.*

Yes, what would happen then? Several of our participants say that strong experiences of music don't occur so often, perhaps once or twice a year; some say a little more often than that, while others say that it has happened only once or twice in their whole life (see Chapter 29, section 29.8.7)

The accounts above have described shivers, palpitations, difficulty in breathing, tears, peace, harmony, beauty, delight, joy, invigoration, hope, confidence, thoughts about life and existence—all this when music unexpectedly turns up in the midst of everyday comings and goings. Afterwards, the individuals have felt at peace, satisfied, happy, elated, and refreshed. But sometimes the experience demands so much energy that one feels completely empty afterwards, tired and shaken—or tired and happy at the same time.

The woman in the last account used to play music in the car but didn't dare play the particular music that she described; it would have been far too risky. Other participants have told of unexpectedly strong experiences with music while driving.

(6.1F) Woman, middle-aged, 1990s

On a busy day after work on my way home by car on small roads, where I know every bend and drive fairly fast, I was listening to the car radio. It was somebody who introduced music that had been newly released on CD. I was in a hurry, a thousand thoughts running through my head as I planned everything I would have to get done.

Then the programme presenter says a nice intro and concludes with the words: 'Welcome to paradise'. That catches my attention, and a wonderfully calm and very romantic piece is played, in complete contrast to my inner emotional world just then. I started to drive more slowly so that I would be able to hear the whole piece before I got home. I remember the place where I was when the music faded to silence; there was peace. What I had ahead of me was suddenly no longer so important, *now* was all that counted. Most of all I would like that feeling never to come to an end. Having been tense, I relaxed, the corners of my mouth lifted in a smile and my wrinkles were smoothed out. Everything felt so much easier.

This was my very own experience that nobody could experience like I did just then. That is what is so unique about music. When writing, words, speech are unable to express what we people what to convey; that is when we can use music to help us.

(6.1G) Man, middle-aged, 2000–10

I am driving on the way to rehearse with my fellow musician. As usual I listen to the car radio. They are playing a mix of music. A group and a piece with names that are unknown to me are introduced. Perhaps with South American origins. The music is complex as Latin American music often is. Various rhythms arc played at the same time and make up a weave. Sometimes a guitar or a harp, for a few bars, makes a gliding journey from one rhythm to another. Guitars, a folk harp and some other instruments. All acoustic. The ensemble consists of five to seven people.

The tune is generous and playfully flowery and it hits me completely open and naked. For me it is joyful music and I just exist, just am there. The tears come and immediately I have to stop to listen in peace. All the time I'm crying and I am grateful that there is music that moves me in such a way and that I can be moved in such a way. I cry from the memory now, when I write this.

When the piece comes to an end and they say what it was, I try desperately to catch the name of the musicians and the tune—but no, it's too quick and too hard to hear. I would have to treat it like a shooting star. I turn the radio off. Finish crying and wait until I feel ready to drive again. When I arrive, I tell my fellow musician, who understands me completely and shares my feeling.

Passengers can also be affected by music and suddenly find themselves in another world. In the following account, this in turn led to an extension of the journey.

(6.1H) Man, young, 1980s

I was sitting in the bus on the way home, about 10.00 p.m. Since I had quite a long journey home, more than an hour on the bus, I used to listen to my Walkman. Earlier in the day I had bought a tape with Beethoven. The first side had Concerto for violin and orchestra in D major. The other side contained Concerto for piano and orchestra No. 5 ('Emperor').

I sat on my own, right at the back of the bus. I was fairly tired and even a bit down; during that same evening I had heard that a very close acquaintance was going to move. I listened to the first side of the tape and thought about various things and problems just to pass the time. Somewhere at the beginning of the other side of the tape, something strange happened: first like a creeping sensation along my backbone, time and space disappeared, I didn't see the world around me, just heard the music and felt an enormous sense of well-being. In some way it felt as if I was in another world, I even saw certain things, clouds and a mysterious landscape: at the same time I felt completely at home in the music, joined in and played the piano.

I don't know how long this state lasted, but judging by how far the bus had travelled, I would estimate it at about ten minutes.

Because of this, I had missed my bus stop by about three kilometres and had to walk home. This wasn't a problem, the experience lived on within me a while, I just walked and listened to the same piece again and experienced the same thing, but weaker. Later in the night, I dreamed that I was a pianist and was going to play this particular piece.

In the midst of the hectic bustle of a big city, music can be heard that brings to life what music really is, what music is about.

(6.1I) Man, young, 1980s

I commuted by train to Stockholm and back every day. I even had to spend half an hour on the underground too. So every day I travelled through what must be one of the liveliest and noisiest places in Stockholm, T-Centralen [the hub station of the underground system] and the culverts to the main railway station.

When I had been commuting a couple of months, I'd seen everything and ignored everything. Then one day I was jolted from this state. I was in the middle of the culvert on my way home. It's the beat that I remember. It went right through me. Just imagine that you are air and something goes right through you, is in you. I just walked on, it didn't occur to me to stop and listen. What I saw as I passed was Indians dressed in traditional blankets, with drums, small guitars, and flutes with lots of tubes, pan flutes. The Indians were also wearing those black hats.

It isn't possible to explain what I felt. What I thought was that these people, all men, weren't playing. They used something that exists deep inside. As if they translated something into music. As if they were receivers that let us hear through the music. What I thought about was God. It feels silly to say so, but that was what I thought when I was trying to explain something big to myself. Something which affected me whether I wanted it to or not.

I saw them once more on a later occasion. Then I stopped and listened, but this time there was nothing of what I experienced the first time.

What it has meant for me is probably that I want to see more. I want to see other cultures because it is not only about music, it's about emotions, deep emotions. I have had many strong experiences with music. But this was more than an experience.

In the next narrator's account, music that was heard in the midst of the street bustle gave rise to such strong feelings that it almost hurt.

(6.1J) Woman, middle-aged, 1980s

I was on my way towards the exit from a shopping centre; I was pretty tired after having run around shopping. Suddenly there was somebody who announced singing with four soprano voices; it was beautiful and I was curious as to which shop tried to attract customers in this way.

It turned out that it was four boys about ten years old who sang a four-part arrangement of our most beautiful summer ballads. They sang with an intensity and enthusiasm that only well brought-up boys eager for money can manage; the music went right through me, my critical, well-trained ear for music couldn't find a false tone, a weak voice, an uninspired expression. They looked like cupids and their voices were like arrows of love aimed at the large number of people that had gathered.

My impassive face fought a very tough battle; slowly, slowly, my defences were breached and I cried openly. It was as if my chest was blocked, I felt an intense pain about my lungs. God, it was beautiful! 'They are so sweet, I'll die! It really does hurt?!'

I still can't understand how I could be so moved, as I can usually control myself, but that wasn't possible, I was forced to go away so that my sniffles wouldn't disturb the experience of the others.

I believe that it was on account of my always having loved soprano voices and even sweet little boys with beautiful skin, as well as the fact that they sang faultlessly. There was nothing to criticize, it was perfect. Their facial expressions revealed a genuine and deep feeling for the music and words. It was so good. I'll never forget this.

Now we go from the crowds in the streets out to isolation in the countryside, with the radio as our sole companion.

(6.1K) Man, middle-aged, 1950s

A hot summer in the 1950s. I have a summer job, working on my own for several days, clearing weeds from a forest plantation of tiny saplings. I live in a simple hut and work just close to it. To alleviate the boredom, I put my radio in an open window facing the plantation.

It happened one day. I don't hear the introduction, just when the music starts: first fumblingly and weak, then all the stronger and more powerful. The structure is very clear and the power and magic invade me completely. I just stand still, leaning on my hoe, listening and filled with the magical atmosphere.

In my numbed state, I hear the programme host say that it was Ravel's *Bolero*. It took me all afternoon to get back to full consciousness again. This event is for me almost as strong at the assassinations of John F. Kennedy and Olof Palme.

Sometimes I try to listen to *Bolero* again, but nowadays it feels hopelessly banal and pompous.

6.2 CERTAIN MUSIC TAKES OVER

Also in situations where one is occupied with music listening, playing, singing, it can come about that certain music attracts all one's attention, resulting in other music ending up in the background. And it doesn't have to be the technically most perfect music.

(6.2A) Woman, middle-aged, 1990s

It was an ordinary afternoon during Advent with a couple of music services at the hospital. When everybody had settled in their places, we started the meeting with one of the Advent hymns. In the hospital bed closest to me where I was sitting at the piano, I suddenly heard a voice that was so touchingly beautiful. An old woman sang with all her soul and with an insight that would make any professional singer jealous. Her voice was, of course, cracked and she didn't sing in pure tones, but that wasn't of importance in the context. It was something in her singing that really got to me, an angel's voice in the true sense of the word.

The goosepimples spread out, and I was moved by hearing her sing, I just had time to glance in her direction and caught a glimpse of something fantastic. A little woman marked by illness, who at first sight didn't look as if she could make much of an impression at all, she it was who sang with such power and such an expression that her eyes really glowed! The thought that came to me then was that here was an angel singing.

After the service, I had a little chat with her and she told me how much she had played and sung when she was younger. How much music had meant to her, and that she had often played and sung for herself. She could certainly have told me much more—I only got a few glimpses—because her eagerness when she told me this couldn't be mistaken.

(6.2B) Woman, middle-aged, 1990s

I took part in a cello course. We were about 20 cellists from various parts of Scandinavia. In the teaching room, there sat many polished musicians and ambitious students who took turns to play and receive feedback/criticism from the teacher. It was interesting at first, but after a few days it did actually start to feel a bit repetitive.

Then I heard of a young talent who was going to be given the opportunity to play for the teacher. It was a girl, little in stature, who had just finished school. She walked with uncertain steps up onto the stage and took up position with her cello beside the grand piano. I was sitting right at the back of the room and had intended to sneak out and get a cup of coffee, when the first notes from Shostakovich's cello sonata attracted my attention. Technically speaking, it wasn't particularly advanced; the shifts of position were a bit clumsy, the bow slid hither and thither over the strings, and the tone was shaky and weak *but* there was nevertheless something there which made me stay behind and listen. The other people in the room seemed to share the view that something new and exciting had happened, because I suddenly felt a 'gathered concentration'. People who had been whispering and sitting restlessly were now completely still with their ears pricked. In the teacher, too, you could see a new enthusiasm; he now became even more committed.

I have reflected a lot on what it was that happened, what she actually did that afternoon. The music, despite nervousness, was performed with softness. She formed the phrases in a natural manner despite the lack of technique, and there was a presence but also a sensitivity in her performance. I remember that I thought: Oh, so *beautiful!*

Mentally I started to compare all that I had heard over the previous days and noted that nothing came anywhere near the experience I was having then. Her technical skill was not great and I also doubt whether she had a well thought-out representation of the music. I can't conclude other than that her presence in the music in combination with the simplicity and the naturalness of her playing is the explanation. The simplicity that comes from an unadorned/naked playing, liberated from conceptions of which ideals you should follow, and which therefore approaches something personal.

It was this lesson that gave me the most inspiration during the entire course. The experience was extremely stimulating and gave me a lot to think about. Perhaps it acquired an extra glow because I hadn't expected anything at all.

Indeed, what actually is it that can make a performance so convincing, despite technical shortcomings? Some of the explanation must lie in the music itself, how it is composed (by Shostakovich in this case), but there must in some way be a special concordance between the music and the person performing it—a presence in and empathy with the music, sensitivity, some sort of natural simplicity, and self-evidence, and yet with a personal expression, as the narrator says. But on such occasions, words like these still feel inadequate to do justice to what one spontaneously experiences as 'natural' and 'genuine'.

One may also ask oneself what role the visual impression of the girl and her performance had for the experience. Would one have gained the same impression if she had been sitting hidden behind a screen while she played? One can only speculate about this, as also about what the narrator's preconceptions (or lack of expectations) can have meant for the experience.

In the next account, originally written in English, it is a particular piece of music which totally unexpectedly and in a dramatic manner affects the narrator and brings with it a total revolution in his attitude to music and what it can mean.

(6.2C) Man, middle-aged, 1950s

As a child I was brought up in an environment where music played a major role in our everyday life. There was special music for putting children to sleep, music for death, burial, religion, work, entertainment, etc. Among all these different forms of music was one type which was portrayed as music for the chosen few. These chosen few were classified as intellectuals and aesthetes. Even though this music was often heard on the radio, for me it had always played an insignificant part in my life and never influenced my conscious listening.

In the 1950s I decided to travel from my country of birth to the USA and then on to England. On the ocean liner Queen Mary I met an English jazz musician who had an orchestra that was performing on the ship. We became close friends. After I had been in England for a while, my English friend started trying to persuade me to listen to jazz and classical music. He soon realized that my interest in classical music was zero. He neverthe-less continued trying.

In September 1956, my friend gave me a set of classical records for my birthday. I jok-ingly promised him that I would never play them. The following day I decided to experi-ment by seeing how many jazz LPs I could play non-stop from 9 o'clock in the morning until 9 o'clock in the evening. After about six hours of playing and listening, I consciously began thinking about my English friend and the classical records he had given me as a present. I began thinking that in his honour and to please him I could afford the sacrifice of being bored for a few minutes by listening to at least one of the records he had bought me. I went over to the box of classical records and took one out. I was not careful in my choice, and it was not until after my great emotional experience that I examined the record and found that the label read 'Tchaikovsky Symphony No. 6, Op. 74, Pathétique'.

But before this, I placed the record on the turntable, ready to be bored and expecting that after a few bars I would return to my experiment with the jazz records. Only a few bars of music of the symphony had been played when suddenly I felt a chilly sensation at the back of my neck, the hair at the back of my head seemed to begin growing, the chilly sensation began travelling through my whole body. There was a thick lump in my stomach that slowly seemed to expand, the pain became so intense that I had to fold both my arms around my abdomen, in an effort to prevent what appeared to be heading towards an internal explosion. My breathing became difficult, I started to cry; and the more I did so, the less became the pain in my stomach. One moment I felt like an abandoned child, lost and lonely, the next moment I was like a child in its most carefree moment. I began laughing and found myself doing a sensual dance to Tchaikovsky Symphony No. 6, Op. 74, *Pathétique.*

Suddenly a terrible feeling of confusion came upon me. In what I believe was only a few seconds, a whole series of conflicting thoughts began rushing around in my mind. These thoughts progressed into a series of conflicting emotions: fright, sorrow, hate, love, anger, and, finally, an internal peace that words cannot describe.

All through my growing up, I had been influenced by the belief that certain kinds of music were reserved exclusively for certain kinds of people. The question was: How could the white man's music (Russian at that) have such a strong psychological effect on me? Frightening thoughts coupled with expressed emotion of sadness! Was I acquiring the mentality of the white man? Would I never be able to appreciate fully any more the music of my own race? I screamed God's name loudly as I ran over to the shelves where I kept my jazz records. I pulled out the LP on which Oscar Peterson plays Erroll Garner's 'Tenderly'. The effect was sheer happiness, and the fright disappeared.

Thought coupled with emotion of anger and hate: What kind of mind was it that had created such destructive propaganda, saying that one kind of art was so superior that only the chosen few could understand it? For a moment I was angry at them, and hated them. Thought coupled with love and warmth: Wasn't it the insistency of my English friend that opened a whole new world for me? And wasn't he white? Thought and internal peace were united. Now I believe I felt I understood music in its entirety. For 32 years from that day of my most powerful emotional experience, art has become my personal witch doctor. Through the years I have developed a certain control of my musical experience, and now use it for personal therapy.

This is one of the most dramatic accounts in all of our material. The experience is exactly dated to a certain day, a certain year, at a particular time of day (some details have been left out here), although the account was written 32 years later. Strongly negative expectations of the music (Tchaikovsky) were turned into intensive physical reactions (shivering, hairs on one's neck standing, a thick lump in one's stomach, breathing difficulties, crying) and were followed by ideas and emotions filled with conflict that gradually were reconciled. The narrator developed a new view of music and learned how to use music for personal therapy.

The following account also describes how an entirely unexpected meeting with a particular piece of music affects the person concerned and leads to a total revolution in his world of music. It is a very personal and humorous account, much too long to be printed in full.

The experience starts in an empty room, dealing with mail at a national institution. The narrator has just handed in a letter for posting. It is just after 12 noon, the radio is on and they are playing music after *Poem of the Day*. He is on his way out of the room, when the music stops him.

(6.2D) Man, old, 1960s (excerpt from a long account)

How beautiful! . . . How incredibly beautiful! What are they playing?! God, so . . . but what on earth *is* it? I was sort of touched by the fairy's wand and disappeared under a spell. I stood stock still, gone, in another world.

But what was it? In again, and phone the radio! 'It's about the music after the *Poem of the Day*. What was it?' 'It was . . . I'll just check . . . Beethoven. A movement from Serenade Op. 8 in D major. With Jascha Heifetz. And William Primrose. And Gregor Piatigorsky.'

He rushed off to the nearest record shop and bought the record featuring these musicians. And that wasn't all.

Before *a single* week had passed, I had bought 3,000 crowns' worth of classical music. A large sum, that, in the 1960s. Spent by somebody who *never* before in his life had purchased a single record in that category. The next few days, and weeks, I played records at home as I had never done before. All classical music. Bought and played. Bought more and played. It was beautiful! All of it! Lovely! More, more!

Opus 8 came to function as a key to a door that had previously been closed to me, and opened it wide. I remember what it was like one evening, when I suddenly heard—*heard!*—the delightfully beautiful flower wind its way up as if out of an incense holder in front of me, a bit into the slow movement in Beethoven's ninth. A symphony that I must have played 20 times by then, without really embracing it. Now, afterwards, I don't understand how these wonderfully beautiful tones could have passed by unnoticed. The most beautiful in the entire symphony!

Many a time, I have reflected on how an enormous, new spectrum of beauty suddenly was opened wide for me. Nowadays, it has the feel of my memories from the Physics lessons at school long, long ago. The iron filings lying there on the lab benches, poured out and spread around in a random pile between the magnets. Then the magnets get close—and hey presto!—as if a wand had been waved, the filings sort themselves out, get into order among themselves and between the poles, in strict lines and formations. Opus 8 was the work that happened to come to serve as some sort of 'magnet configuration' in my brain. The time was finally ripe.

I regard myself as a musical illiterate. I don't know what a single note looks like written down. Don't know what a C sounds like, have no idea what a triad is. Still don't know what the difference is between the white and the black keys on a piano. Except the colour. I understand the words of music, but can't read or write its characters or even distinguish and name a single one of them in an auditory confrontation. A complete illiterate, in other words.

But every time I happen to hear a certain string trio played on the radio, a big smile spreads across my face. And I can say: 'Thank you, Opus 8! You were the one that did it!'

CHAPTER 7

MERGING WITH THE MUSIC

When music takes over, the surrounding world disappears. Time stands still, all that counts is the music and me, here and now. We find similar descriptions in this chapter that will illuminate the concordance between the person and the music in strong experiences with music. The boundary between this and the previous chapter is thus fluid; they can be seen as varieties of the same theme of total absorption.

While one often has a certain distance from music—it is something outside oneself—when it comes to strong experiences, there is often a form of 'bonding' with the music. It is described in various terms: one lives the music, is embraced by the music, is embedded in the music, possessed by the music, one identifies oneself with the music, the music and oneself are on the same wavelength. Sometimes, it is described as a special understanding of the music, the music feels self-evident, it is already there and one knows how it is going to continue.

There are many accounts of this type. They have been divided into five groups (7.1–7.5), but there is a degree of overlap between them.

7.1 SPECIAL RECEPTIVITY

Sometimes, the circumstances around the experience seem to be particularly favourable for the person to merge with the music. In some way, the music acquires a special clarity and one is totally inside the music.

(7.1A) Man, middle-aged, 1990s

It was a concert featuring Beethoven's ninth symphony. Almost from the very first chord I had a lovely feeling in my body. I felt calm and happy, and in particular during the slow third movement I felt a wave of almost extraterrestrial joy go through me, more or less the same feeling as being head over heels in love. When I closed my eyes, the tears started to fall. The music somehow flooded directly into me, and my senses were wide open. Most of the time when I listen, I can only follow the theme when it wanders between the different parts and the instruments, and the rest becomes like a carpet of tones in the background. This time, I could distinguish all the details, there was a blast from the trumpets, there was something contrapuntal in the cello part, while the theme lay with the violas, and so on.

Afterwards, I realized that I had been sitting absolutely still all the time, almost one and a half hours. That is most unusual when I am at a concert. We met some of our friends who stood chatting, but I wasn't really present. The music was still inside me, and I was inside the music.

In the following accounts, relaxation, tiredness, and a state between wakefulness and sleep seem to prepare the way for a total immersion in the music.

(7.1B) Woman, middle-aged, 1960s

It was a Sunday evening and I had come home from my Sunday service. I lived in central Stockholm and was on my own that evening. I lay down on the bed without turning the lamp on, but I did turn on the radio. I didn't know what they were going to play, but just as I turned it on, they were introducing Bach's Partita in D minor for violin (the one with the ciaccona). It was David Oistrakh who was playing. I was a bit tired, I was on my own, it was half-dark in the room, I lay on my bed and was totally unprepared for what was going to be played. All this, I think, contributed to my mood being the right one for the experience with the music to be so strong. I was completely numbed by the music. I forgot time and space. My body vanished from my consciousness. I was totally immersed in the music.

(7.1C) Man, middle-aged, 1960s

The experience took place sometime between 11 and 12 one spring evening. I lay in bed and was listening to the radio. I was very close to falling asleep when suddenly Dietrich Fischer-Dieskau sang 'Der Erlkönig' by Franz Schubert. I myself had previously had quite a lot to do with that piece and now—on the boundary between sleep and wakefulness— I really experienced this song in all its facets in an extremely tangible manner. All the variations in the lyrics and music seemed to me to be completely logical and clear and I realized (perhaps for the first time) how music could go right to your heart and mind.

This experience has subsequently come back to me many times, and has influenced me to a great degree in my own music making. 'Der Erlkönig' is, of course, a most admirable example of strong musical drama in miniature and I am fairly certain that my experience that evening (a sort of Aha! experience) has, in a very tangible way, contributed to forming my own interpretations of many compositions with music and lyrics.

I believe that the experience in the first instance was connected with my state of relaxation and sleepiness. I had heard the song several times before and liked it, but never felt it so deeply. And afterwards, too, I have both played and listened to 'Der Erlkönig' (even Dieskau's version), but I have never again had a similar experience.

7.2 BEING DRAWN INTO THE MUSIC

There are many ways of describing an absorption by the music. A common expression is that one is inescapably sucked in by the music, drawn into it. This can take place in many varied contexts.

(7.2A) Woman, middle-aged, 1970s

It was a wonderfully beautiful August evening in Visby [on the Swedish island of Gotland]. As we walked past the ruins of Saint Nicholas's Church, people were starting to arrive for the evening's performance of the musical drama *Petrus de Dacia* (a Dominican monk in the thirteenth century) with music by Friedrich Mehler. I really wanted to see the performance. Edith Thallaug had one of the main roles and I was very curious about her.

At first, everything was just like any other performance, but suddenly I was in some inexplicable way sucked into the music. It felt as if I was somehow lifted up from my seat and sort of floated in the room while at the same time being filled with serenity and inner harmony, in raptures. There was a fantastically beautiful sunset which spread its light over the 'stage', incredibly magnificent music and singing, together with the beautiful church setting. An incredible total experience.

Although I have been to Gotland many times since then, I have never been to the ruins drama again. Perhaps I want to retain the incredible experience I had on that occasion.

The sensation of being lifted up from one's seat and hovering in the room is also described by other narrators. Such experiences are dealt with in more detail in Chapter 8.

In both the next two accounts, it is a particular part of the music with repetitions of the same theme up to a resolution that pulls the listener into the course of events. If one has heard these works (by Shostakovich and Sibelius, respectively) it is not hard to recognize the descriptions.

(7.2B) Woman, middle-aged, 1980s

I heard the Stockholm Philharmonic performing Shostakovich's seventh symphony, the so-called 'Leningrad' Symphony. Yuri Ahronovitch conducted. Went to the Concert Hall, expectant, but I can't remember what I expected it would be like. I only knew that this symphony was special. It is always exciting to go in and sit down and know that the orchestra is going to perform something you really want to hear and have been looking forward to.

What I remember from this symphony, something really particular, is the first movement, the march, the percussion instruments that were right at the front on the left. After a few minutes, this monotonous march started, at first extremely quiet, the same theme, again and again, while the music gets louder and louder. You think you can see, and above all hear, soldiers coming closer and closer. The music increased in intensity and becomes all the more creepy, and the grey apparitions just keep on marching. At the same time as feeling that the music is cruel, you can't help but be fascinated by it. You're sitting on tenterhooks and waiting, because you know that soon the whole orchestra will explode and it feels as if something terrible is happening.

In some way, time and space disappear. You sit there breathless and listen and think that you are a part of the music in some way.

(7.2C) Man, middle-aged, 1950s

The place was the main auditorium at the Stockholm Concert Hall, the music was Jean Sibelius's Symphony No. 2, especially the fourth movement. I was in a good mood, but didn't have any special expectations for the concert. In fact, I'd gone there primarily for another item on the programme. In general, in those days I thought that Sibelius's music was a bit muddy, also thick in texture, and hard to follow. However, I hadn't previously heard the second symphony.

The finale did, however, prove to be extremely easy to follow. I was drawn into the endless repetitions of a sad and melancholy D-minor theme, and got intoxicating kicks from the two surprising major resolutions: the first somewhere in the direction of a relative key, and the other, just before the end, with the parallel key, D major, which, of course, is a stronger effect. The surprises, well prepared via repetitions, can in their way be associated with Ravel's *Bolero*. When the symphony finished, I felt shaken and happy, a feeling almost like being newly in love.

The next narrator merged with the music to such a degree that he knew precisely how the music would continue, and everything felt perfect; he wanted to remain there.

(7.2D) Man, middle-aged, 1970s

It was a summer in the 1970s, and me and a mate we drove out to a glade in the forest after a party. It was early morning and we pulled the loudspeakers out of the car and put a tape on. It was Led Zeppelin's 'Stairway to heaven' that played.

In the mood that I was in that morning, the gentle beginning of the song was just perfect. It was like I belonged to the music, melted in with the notes, one note leading to the other, it was so obvious how it should sound and they did sound like that too. The music crawled inside me; or was it me that crawled inside the music? In some way that was all that existed.

The music in 'Stairway to heaven' starts gently and gets slowly stronger and more majestic the further you get in the tune. I was carried along by the music as it intensified in power and majesty almost to a climax at the end. It was as absolutely perfect as it ever could be.

When the music finished I was in such high spirits and full of it that everything stood still, like holding your breath for something and only wanting to stay on there like that.

In all these accounts, a merging with the music is united with strong emotions. It can become especially strong if somebody takes part personally in the expression of emotions.

(7.2E) Man, young, 1980s

The choir I was in did a concert featuring African Sanctus by David Fanshawe. It's a mix of Catholic mass (the choir's task) and recordings of authentic African people in various situations. For example, there was the call of an Imam at prayer time in Egypt (which was mixed with the Kyrie movement), a wedding party, a dirge, a play and a dance, at various ceremonies that were contrasted with the equivalent expressions in the Catholic mass. War drums, crucifixions and so on.

The fact that the recordings were authentic and directly from the people in Africa gave it all an intimate feeling and made it so much more poignant. I followed or was pulled in by all the emotions, from immediate joy to the deepest sorrow and the fear/terror that war brings. Just becoming so emotionally engaged and also being able to express the feeling meant that the feeling/insight became even stronger. It gave an almost unlimited feeling of sympathy, and nothing else existed or could be more important just then. The sudden switches between the extremes of emotion (happiness–sorrow, heaviness–lightness, consolation–joy) gave the feelings even more content. All of this was emphasized by the music, which in its joyfulness almost became bombastic and euphoric. Everything and everyone (the music recordings from Africa, the choir, the instrumentalists, and the audience) felt like a single whole, as if everyone shared this great feeling of importance and unity.

'What a pity not everyone could be here to experience this' was my first thought afterwards. I felt incredibly sensitized and easily moved. Gradually, there came a feeling of great joy and gratitude that I had been able to experience this—such moments are rare and, in relation to life, rather short.

7.3 ALONE WITH THE MUSIC

Absorption can be experienced as being alone with the music, embraced by the music—nothing else exists despite the fact that one is surrounded by other people.

(7.3A) Woman, old, 1920s

I had come to Stockholm a couple of months earlier, having just qualified to become an elementary school teacher. And now I was sitting at the opera, the side of the third balcony, the seat closest to the centre. On my own. Twenty-two years old. And this was my first visit to an opera. They were going to perform *Samson and Delilah* by Saint-Saëns. The stage scenery was by Isaac Grünewald.

The lights went down. They started to play the overture. Behind the dropped curtain, the choir started to sing. Soon you could faintly make out the singers, who were sitting under the very stylized palms all around the stage. Sound and light become all the more penetrating.

And that was when it happened. The miracle.

It seemed as though I was sitting in an enormous globe of light, filled with music. All the earthly things around me had completely vanished. The rustling of paper, the coughs and scrapings were gone. I was alone with the music, filled with joy, unaware of everything else around me.

The experience lasted perhaps ten minutes. Then I came to my senses again, but still filled with joy and shimmering light.

If I shut my eyes, I can still, after 70 years, feel the same great joy and the same great open space around me as then.

The rest of the performance almost just passed me by. But I have carried the joy with me, all my life.

'But I have carried the joy with me, all my life': a long life. She was the oldest participant in our investigation, 91 years old when she told about this experience—a 'miracle' that lasted perhaps ten minutes but which etched itself into her long-term memory for ever.

Despite the darkness in the auditorium, she feels as if she is enclosed in a 'globe of light' and 'filled with joy and shimmering light'. Using 'light' as a metaphor for happiness and similar emotions is fairly common, but here it is presumably a matter of an actual experience of light. Similar phenomena of light are described in some other accounts and are discussed later in Chapter 29, section 29.3.6.

Another strange experience is described in the next account, this time in a well-known French cathedral. Despite the crush of the crowd there, the narrator feels on his own with the music, becomes one with it, and at the same time experiences a paradoxical synthesis between incompatible impressions from the senses of sight and hearing.

(7.3B) Man, young, 1980s

The experience that I intend to describe is the only one of its kind I've ever had. I had it one November evening in Paris. We were out walking around in the Latin Quarter. The air was warm, there were lots of people on the streets and I felt unusually harmonious and happy. One of those evenings that live up a little to the romantically naïve picture people have of the mythical Paris.

After a while, we crossed the Seine and came to Notre Dame. It was about nine o'clock and outside the illuminated façade of the cathedral there were hordes of people. We went in, and inside it was jammed full. The interior was completely illuminated and at the front by the altar some sort of mass was going on. A group of priests stood in a semi-circle, one of them saying mass. On either side of him, there were two choir boys who devoutly swung two incense holders. At the same time, the entire church building was filled with some sort of experimental organ music, the like of which I'd never heard before. I was separated from my two friends and I ploughed my way through the crowd to be able to see better. Finally, I reached a barrier that I leaned against, looking at the theatre between the railings.

What was fascinating was the tension that arose between the visual element and the music: what you heard didn't merge with what you saw. The religious ritual in front of the altar and the unstructured, unsyntactical music that boomed out from the organ pipes created a strange effect of contrast. You got the impression that it was music that built upon dissonances instead of harmonies, and it sounded as if it was improvised on the spot. It was very far from solemnity, and sort of broke out of the framework for the exterior context.

Suddenly I found myself entirely absorbed by the music. The background murmur sort of faded away, and the music was 'lifted up'. I felt as if I was alone with the music, as if I met it halfway. At the same time as feeling that I was outside the music, I felt myself possessed by it. To use a cliché: I felt at one with the booming of the organ, which was beautiful and apocalyptic at the same time. It was in a sort of dialectic relationship to what was happening in the visual space, and together both sensations formed a magnificent synthesis which I consider virtually indefinable.

When the concert was over, I found my friends again and apologized for having sneaked away for a while. But it turned out I had been gone only ten minutes and not half an hour, which was what I thought. I felt stunned and happy, almost euphoric. It took a while before I was aware that I had been through a thoroughly special experience.

I don't know anything about the music other than that it was a French twentieth-century composer who wrote it; it sounded like impromptu music, as if Quasimodo himself had taken over the cantor's job for a while.

If one has heard the magnificent organ in Notre Dame in situ, then it isn't hard to imagine how the 'booming' of the organ sounded—that organ can give rise to strong experiences, in a metaphorical as well as a literal sense.

Here a performer describes how he feels alone with the music.

(7.3C) Man, young (from an edited interview)

[Musician in a rock band] Playing is tension. You work with your whole body when you play. Every note is from top to toe. It's enormous concentration. It ought to be! Otherwise people can tell. When I get to this sort of level, then I don't experience tension or anything. It's an enormously relaxed feeling, an enormous lightness. It feels physically light. You don't reflect on what you are playing any longer. You just play. In such moments you are there by yourself with the music! There isn't any audience, there are no fellow musicians there either. On an occasion like that it is just music. Then everything stops . . .

Similar descriptions of 'relaxed concentration' in performers come later in Chapter 18, particularly in section 18.6.

7.4 IDENTIFYING WITH THE MUSIC

Merging with the music can be experienced and described as a form of identification.

(7.4A) Woman, old, 1970s

I was listening to Brahms's Symphony No. 3 in F major, the third movement, poco allegretto, at the Concert Hall in Stockholm. During the second movement I had felt a little tired on account of an early journey to Stockholm. Then the third movement started, and the experience was gigantic, I felt myself a part of the music and I knew exactly how it would continue. A quiet ecstasy.

When the last movement started, I was a 'normal' listener again. After this experience I can conjure up the strains of the music and listen and let them sing within me whenever I want, indeed still after 17 years. This particular third movement gives me consolation, strength, joy—it is me, myself.

The listener can identify with a role.

(7.4B) Woman, middle-aged

My most intense experiences with music have always been in connection with vocal music, opera, oratorios, etc. My reactions are of a purely physical nature: the hair on my body stands on end, I get goosepimples, in my chest I get an almost ecstatic feeling of space, my eyes start to moisten. When I was as young as five years old, and loved Puccini's *Madame Butterfly*, I remember that I felt these reactions.

At an opera performance, or when I listen to a record, I can be affected so totally by the work that I react along with the main character. For example, I can mention the last act of *Rigoletto*, where Rigoletto sings his triumph over the death of the duke and is just going to throw the sack with what he thinks is the duke's body into the river—when you suddenly hear the duke in the background sing a bit of '*La donna è mobile*'. The horror and shock that Rigoletto expresses at that point, I share totally, and however many times I hear the work, I am paralysed with horror for a second or two when I hear the first bars of '*La donna*' in the last act.

Identification may apply to a real-life person, for example the person who is making the music.

(7.4C) Man, middle-aged, 1960s

One late night, I was sitting listening to records. While I was listening to a typical tenor saxophonist from the 1930s or 1940s—it might have been Coleman Hawkins—I gradually came to so totally identify with the expression in his playing that I had an experience of completely having crept into his personality. This sort of music can, of course, be a little sentimental and melancholy, and is often so directly oriented towards emotions that you can mime facial expressions and gestures along with it. And now I had become to such a degree tuned into the music that it felt as if I was this stocky, powdered, and slightly showy elegant black man. I could almost smell the scent of his eau de cologne and the pressure of his good-quality white shirt with tie and tiepin. It was a very strange feeling because at the same time I was aware of the enormous difference between us: that my personality type was of quite another sort and that our respective social backgrounds and experiences were so totally different. Yet I was very present in this guest appearance in another person's personality, made possible through his music!

When I compare my strong experiences with music, I think that there is a shared factor that I believe is of decisive importance, and it has to do with identification. Common to all the experiences has been that I have reached a state of very strong identification with music that I have listened to, so strong that I completely co-live with the development of events of the music and am at one with it.

On a couple of occasions, I have thought in terms of 'being in tune with the music', and that probably covers what I mean best. I can see before me the radio metaphor: to be tuned in on the right wavelength.

The concepts of 'tuning' and 'being in tune with', which the narrator finds useful for describing his experience of identification, are used by psychologist Daniel Stern to describe the communication between infants and mothers/carers as a mutual 'tuning in' to the same affective state. It is an example of 'vitality affects' or 'forms of vitality' that are basic phenomena in interpersonal relationships, in the experience of music and other temporal arts, in psychotherapy and other areas.[1]

The next narrator describes the music as 'the most perfect melody together with the most perfect voice, this was *me*, but in the form of music'.

(7.4D) Woman, young, 1980s

A girlfriend and me, we had been at the theatre that evening but we left after the first act. Before going home, I took a notion to go into a record shop and there I found a record which caused me to whoop for joy. I just shouted out. It was the only copy in the entire shop and probably the only and first one in Sweden at the time. Basia, *Time and Tide*, those were the name of the artiste and the title of the album. Before Basia made this solo album, she was one of the three members of British band Matt Bianco that I really, really like, an awful lot. So my expectations for this album were enormous.

I went home, went into my room and put the record on. What happened next, I remember as if it was yesterday. I was kneeling in front of the stereo. The first thing I hear is her voice, nothing else, brilliantly clear, jazzy, then a slow intro, rhythmical, Latin, that grows slowly in the instrumentation and tempo, everything is just woven together, the song and the music for the refrain come along, that's where the climax was.

My knees came up into the air, I came up and was several inches from the floor, it was such a kick—I had tears in my eyes, I was absolutely happy, it made me dizzy, like going on the steepest part of a big dipper, my head felt like it would explode. This was the most perfect melody together with the most perfect voice, this was *me*, but in the form of music. The song was called 'Promises'. The expectations that I'd had were massively fulfilled, this was more than I'd dared dream of, almost too much joy at once. The rest of the record is just as good, but after 'Promises' I could hardly cope with hearing more, it was too much. I can listen to that song thousands of times without ever tiring, but never as strongly, as frighteningly intensely as the first time I heard it, when me and the song were one.

The next narrator also describes how she and the music came to merge together. But in contrast to the previous narrator, she wasn't at all in the mood to listen to music and was sceptical as to the possibilities of art to offer consolation and therapy. Nevertheless, she came to feel all the more how each and every note corresponded directly with her own frame of mind, that every part of the music became a part of her.

(7.4E) Woman, middle-aged, 1980s

I had been involved in something that made me sad several days afterwards. So I wasn't at all in the mood to listen to music. Most of the time I do that when I'm in a good mood or feel harmonious. A few days earlier, I had recorded a live broadcast from the Berwald Concert Hall—Beethoven's Piano Concerto No. 3 in C minor with Greta Erikson as the soloist together with the Radio Symphony Orchestra conducted by Yuri Ahronovitch. It was a rather poor recording, technically speaking, that I put on one afternoon.

What happened when I started to listen didn't feel like a separate physical or mental sensation, more like that every single tone corresponded directly with my own state of mind. Starting from the beginning of the first movement, it felt as if I sank all the deeper into a great and universal concentration. All my senses were directed in towards the music. I was completely plugged into it, body and soul, and nothing could disturb the wholeness that the music and me consisted of. I didn't feel consoled, rather it felt as if I got this deep experience despite the mood I was in. Nor do I think that art offers, or can offer, consolation, or that it can be used for therapy. At any rate, that has never worked for me.

Nevertheless, then and there, every part of the music that reached my ears became a part of me, and the first and second movements as a whole—that was me just then. No feeling of time, just a now, a point. I was inside the music, and the music was inside me. It wasn't possible to distinguish one from the other. All the time the music was playing, I was incapable of moving.

It was the first time I heard the performance. The expression that Greta Erikson conveyed in her interpretation was sorrow, being lost in one's own thoughts, maturity, and a sort of endurance. It was an expression of what I felt then, and couldn't express myself.

In the next account, a performer describes how one identifies with what one is expected to create in the performance.

(7.4F) Man, middle-aged

I have always been of the opinion that music must express something; that all music is programmatic even though composers themselves often deny this. The background of a work of music influences me when I play.

I did Brahms's Piano Quartet in C minor, Shostakovich's Piano Trio in E minor and Franck's Sonata for Violin and Piano at the very same concert. All of these works have a background, sometimes more mythical than true. Brahms is said to have been asked whether the front endpaper should be decorated on the edition of the published piano quartet. According to tradition, he is said to have answered: 'Illustrate it with a pistol! For that is what it felt like when I wrote it; a pistol pointing at me!' Shostakovich wrote his trio after a visit to the dreaded concentration camp, Treblinka. That affected him greatly and came to expression in his music, which is full of Jewish musical idioms and all the musical means one can imagine to express the Jewish fate during the Second World War: jarring dissonances, helpless crystal-clear flageolets, ironic rhythms, heavy implacable sighing chords in a low register, scale fragments like wisps of smoke that disappear into infinity. César Franck's sonata, on the other hand, is traditionally regarded as describing his own marriage: passion, the first stormy years, the solemn devotion, and finally the elderly couple looking back at the life that has passed.

All these thoughts inevitably fly around when you're sitting at the grand piano and are about to play. Every note gains a meaning, every chord a message, a story. And it is a fact that you become identified with what you create. You put yourself in the situation and compare with your own experiences or other similar ones. The first chords in the Brahms quartet give me the creeps and I get goosepimples. The solitary introductory octaves become the imagined pistol shots that Brahms is said to have had in mind. In Shostakovich's trio, I didn't think that the concert grand managed to convey enough of what I wanted to express. I moved down a few octaves during one of the trio's 'danses macabres' to try to express the extreme pain and abandonment by using the extreme settings of the instrument.

After the concert I was incredibly tired, not so much on account of the physical exertion but on account of the emotional one.

7.5 BEING LED/GOVERNED BY THE MUSIC

The sensation of merging with the music can feel as if one's body is completely governed by the music. A variety of this is to merge with the music through bodily movements, dance.

(7.5A) Woman, middle-aged, 1980s

It was a Friday evening at the pub. A band called Smithereens was going to play 'garage rock with its roots in the 1960s'. When I heard the first bars, there was only one thing to do: rush up to get as close to the stage and the band as possible and start dancing. There was a hell of a pace from the very beginning and it never stopped. I jumped and danced like crazy with all the others right next to the stage, shouted and applauded.

I think they played a couple of hours at a stretch without a break—simple, direct, fast, wild, melodious guitar rock—and after about half an hour I was already dead tired, sweaty, and thirsty but I just couldn't stop dancing and walk away. The music and the rhythm forced my body to move, my feet to dance, and my arms to flap by themselves, I couldn't help it. I was just twitching all the time.

Afterwards I was absolutely exhausted, and incredibly happy. In seventh heaven. All my senses were numbed but it felt lovely. Like some sort of cleansing bath, perhaps?

Why was it so great? Perhaps because everything was just right. The right sort of pleasantly small and intimate place with an enthusiastic/ecstatic audience that stood only a couple of feet from the guys who were playing and who take part all the time. A band that plays as though they were possessed and who seem to love their music. It felt as if the band and the audience were on exactly the same wavelength and whipped each other into an ecstasy and got energy from each other. It was a collective experience. In some way I felt almost as active and participating in the music and what was going on as the band itself. And I hate sitting nice and calm and listening to musicians who stand somewhere far away and poke at their instrument with an introverted expression on their faces.

Here, too, the metaphor of 'being on the same wavelength' is used. The concordance is both on an individual level, that is, between the narrator and the music, and on a collective level between the band and the audience. In both cases, this leads to an intensification of the experience and behaviour of the respective parties. The visual impressions of the musicians' commitment and joy of playing were also of considerable importance. The intense physical expression of feelings felt like a cleansing bath, a catharsis.

Another example, which could possibly be seen as even more striking, of totally merging with the music through physical exercise and dance, is in the following account by a young man of a party where African male villagers played drums.

(7.5B) Man, young, 1980s

I am invited to dance, and start to do so. At first I am somewhat tense but after a few tunes I relax and enter the music. I start to play with the rhythm, the beat and my own feet . . . The beat sort of drove me into it all. I was inside it, merged into one with it. You were their hands pattering over the drums. It was, of course, the village men who played . . . but I was a part of it. I was completely captivated and I totally went in for it. All that existed was beat and rhythm . . . There was such a raging tempo, you just kept going. I didn't think at all about what I was doing. Everything felt so natural . . . My limbs moved without my being able to control them . . . The beat accelerated all the time, at the final bit almost ecstatic, hectic, so fast that I just shook. I could feel that now it was the climax, it would come to an end and then *Bang!* Have taken the correct steps and am standing in a particular way with my arms out and legs apart. I have marked the end together with the drummers and one other person, a village man whom I don't notice until now . . . Afterwards I was terribly tired, exhausted . . . but I was as happy as could be.

The whole of this account is to be found in Chapter 24 (account 24G). That section also includes other accounts of how one's body can be totally controlled by African rhythms.

Merging with the music can, of course, be just as pronounced if one is involved personally and producing the rhythms.

(7.5C) Woman, middle-aged, 1980s

The strongest experience with music for me took place on a course in Latin-American rhythms. We were playing from morning to late evening. One evening we were going to have night rumba. We started about 10 p.m. and were going to play as long as it felt OK. First we went through the rhythms, a basic rhythm on the rumba and another one on the conga. We sat close to each other. Then we turned off the lights and started to play; nobody was allowed to talk. The feeling of time disappeared fairly quickly and also the tension in your arms and shoulders. It wasn't until then that I could have short experiences of the rhythms somehow taking off and flowing by themselves. This experience only lasted short periods at first. In between, I heard us as separate individuals. Later I had a long experience of this taking off again; the rhythms flowed, it felt as if they came from a shared body. It was a fantastic experience. I wasn't aware of myself and what I was doing. I didn't feel anything physical. It was a very strong emotional experience and I don't know how long it lasted because time disappeared. When we finally turned the lights on, we had played for two and a half hours.

The next narrator felt 'as if the reggae rhythms were my pulsating blood and my heartbeats'. He is affected physically by the music, rocks with the rhythms, at the same time that his body paradoxically almost disappears from his consciousness.

(7.5D) Man, middle-aged, 1970s

I had gone and bought two LPs, Bob Marley's *Exodus* and *Kaya*. I had heard reggae several times on the radio and its swinging rhythms appealed to me. That evening I played them for the first time. I was alone in the house, so I could play as loud as I wanted.

I put *Exodus* on first and the idea was that I would sort of vaguely listen to it while I wrote a letter. I rocked my way through the first tunes, but there wasn't much letter writing done because I was somehow sucked into the music. Everything around me disappeared, there was only here and now. I became aware of my body in another way. It felt light, sometimes I didn't feel it at all. Sometimes I actually had to look at my fingers to see if they were still there. I was aware of everything around me, and yet not. It was a bit unreal.

This pleasant existence was broken off when the record came to the end and the music stopped. I came to my senses after a while. I turned the record over. The room felt warm and I opened the window out into the cold January night. It was snowing, and I love snow, so I stood in the window and let the snow lash my face while I continued to listen to the music. Yet again, I slipped in somewhere between time and space, but now it wasn't really the same as before. This time I was only aware of the pulsating rhythm of the music, Bob Marley's words in the lyrics and the forces of nature round me. I felt little as far as nature was concerned, but at the same time I felt as one with it. It was as if the reggae rhythms were my pulsating blood and my heartbeats. I felt nothing of my body in any way, and didn't care about that either, rather everything could be as it was.

This existence was broken off again when the music stopped. When my brain registered that the music had now stopped, I became extremely sad and started to cry. I felt as if a close friend had left me. At the same time, I registered that I couldn't remember what I had been thinking about that whole time. I've gone through these sorts of experiences several times and each time I feel that I'm not thinking at all but only feeling with every fibre of my body.

A merging together, not only with the music but also with nature, in a pleasant state of just being, without thoughts, here and now.

Another experience of merging with music is described in the next example. But while the preceding four accounts have concerned tangible physical movements to music, now it is the exact opposite.

(7.5E) Man, middle-aged, 1980s

Want to contribute with what for me was a unique experience with music, which established a fact and boundary beyond what I had previously experienced. The experience dates from a concert with Adolf Fredrik's Bach Choir. The programme included movements from works by Bach and Handel.

And what did this experience consist of? Well, what was unique for me was that every part of my body, every muscle, successively felt all the more heavy, and that bit by bit I perceived the existence of every joint yet without this feeling uncomfortable, but it did feel like a completely new acquaintance. After the concert, it felt as if the normal unconscious control of the function of staying upright had been disconnected; what was now needed was a conscious control of the most automated movements. My muscles were definitely weakened, the concept of relaxation had been taken to the boundary of what was total. That these bodily sensations were experienced at the same time as a deep spiritual calmness can be seen as more self-evident, a typical ingredient in at any rate my experiences of similar sorts of music. What was new was the physical sensation.

I felt gratitude for having been able to experience that my sphere of experiences had been so strikingly extended. I did, of course, feel great joy and great wonder at the power of music.

It can be added that the narrator was familiar with physiology, which is indeed reflected somewhat in the description of the experience.

In the final example, the merging with music feels almost compulsive. The narrator is listening to a well-known piece of music, the expression of which governs her physical and mental reactions in a way she is unable to control.

(7.5F) Woman, middle-aged

Barber's Adagio for Strings: The solitary note at the beginning creates the sad mood which I suspect is the basis for the rest of the piece. I follow the various melodies that grow into each other but feel that I have steady contact with the ground via the bass. Every time there is dissonance I have to hold my breath and then afterwards relax and breathe out when the dissonance is dissolved. My body reacts in a way that I can't control. The expressive melody rises to divine heights, but now the deep bass notes are absent. The tone, the melody, and the crescendo increase the tension in my body, more and more muscles become stretched and I don't breathe out. I shut my eyes and screw up the whole of my face while my left hand plays 'air violin' and I add a lot of extra vibrato with tense fingers. The harmony (dissonance) pierces deep into my heart like a knife and the tears start to run. After this climax (about five and a half minutes), my body has a chance to recover during some short breaks and I can breathe out and my shoulders are lowered a little. The simple melody returns and I feel a great sense of loss, pain, and longing. Although the piece ends with a prominent major third, I feel totally alone, deeply sad, and exhausted.

CHAPTER 8

FEELING LIGHT, FLOATING, LEAVING ONE'S BODY

In accounts of strong experiences with music, many bodily/physical reactions are mentioned. Some of them are well-known physiological reactions such as tears, shivers, goosepimples, palpitations, sweating, and feeling dizzy. Other reactions include behaviours such as moving to the music, jumping, dancing, shouting, laughing, etc., and also the direct opposite such as becoming totally immobile, dead still, 'sitting as though petrified'. Reactions such as these have been described in many earlier accounts, and they are also covered in detail in Chapter 29, section 29.2.

The subject for this chapter is certain other, more remarkable, experiences affecting one's body: feeling lighter than usual or even weightless, taking off from the ground, hovering or floating above the surroundings, feeling as if one leaves one's body and observes oneself from outside: out-of-body experiences. Such reactions may be called *quasi-physical* (Latin: *quasi* = as if); it is as if one's body functions differently than usual, as if one finds oneself in a completely different place from usual. In a strictly physical sense, the body is, of course, in its usual place—on the ground, on the floor, in a chair, etc.—but nevertheless it can feel as if one takes off, hovers, or leaves one's body. These experiences are on the whole fairly short-lived.

8.1 Feeling light, weightless, taking off, being lifted, floating

Examples of experiences of lightness, weightlessness, and floating up in the air have occurred in some earlier accounts, for example in Chapter 4, account 4.1H ('I gradually woke up during the organ music . . . Felt that I was resting in a large space, almost floated weightless in the hall'); in Chapter 7, account 7.2A ('It felt as if I was somehow lifted up from my seat and sort of floated in the room'); and also in Chapter 7, where, in addition to the description provided in account 7.5D, the narrator adds: 'I became aware of my body in another way. It felt light, sometimes I didn't feel it at all. Sometimes I actually had to look at my fingers to see if they were still there.'

We begin with some short descriptions of how listeners experience a feeling of lightness, weightlessness, such as taking off or being lifted from the ground.

(8.1A) Woman, old, 1930s

Lumbye's 'Champagne Galop' gave me a feeling of ecstasy, all my body was part of it, I wanted to move to the music, but it wasn't appropriate. I always felt happy when the piece was played and in some way I was lifted up, I felt light.

(8.1B) Woman, middle-aged, 1960s (from Chapter 25, account 25.1E)

[Listening to the St Matthew Passion] It was as if I was no longer sitting in the pew but rather had risen high above it . . . the experience of being completely lifted from the pew where I sat was really great.

(8.1C) Woman, young, 1980s (from Chapter 25, account 25.1F)

[Listening to Verdi's Requiem] I think it was at Dies Irae that I got close contact with the music . . . I got the creeps from my head down along my backbone, and I felt how I lifted from the pew in time with the music, exploding in a fantastic climax.

In the following examples, there are descriptions of the experience of floating/hovering above one's surroundings. The boundary against the experience of weightlessness and lightness is fluid.

(8.1D) Woman, middle-aged, 1950s

It was Advent. I went with my mother to church. I was sort of hit by the organ's pompous introduction to Gunnar Wennerberg's 'Gören portarna höga' [the Swedish version of 'Macht hoch die Tür, die Tor macht weit', a German Advent song]. A singer sang this hymn in such a totally enchanting way that I came to feel as if I was floating up under the ceiling, I couldn't feel the pew I was sitting on. I have never experienced anything like it, and when the song finished I landed again and felt that I had sort of 'just arrived'.

(8.1E) Woman, old, 1950s (from Chapter 24, account 24A)

[In the Metropolitan Cathedral of Athens] Then we came into the light, wonderfully beautiful church, where the mass had already started. A male choir . . . sang with ethereal beauty. Suddenly, everything round about me became sunny, golden yellow. We walked slowly towards the front of the church, but I couldn't feel the floor, I just sort of floated in this sunny gold, enveloped by the singing and a strong feeling of joy.

Regrettably, the singing soon finished, and I was again standing on the floor.

(8.1F) Man, young, 1980s (from Chapter 27, account 27B)

[At a Mike Oldfield concert] The first notes almost made me faint. It was 'Platinum'! I felt that I disappeared for a moment and then woke up as if in a dream, but all the time aware of the music. In some way I was floating above the audience, which simply was there but I couldn't hear them and they didn't disturb me. It was like a dream, I was floating and the group was playing only for me . . . I was totally gone—my friends noticed as they had tried to make contact with me during the number but failed. I came back to my senses again because of somebody hitting me on my shoulder several times and calling my name and wondering what was happening.

(8.1G) Man, young, 1980s (from Chapter 25, account 25.1M)

[A choral concert] The highlight of the concert was a piece by an American composer. The piece was built up like a sort of canon of 30 voices over the word 'Hallelujah' where the choristers spread themselves out, two by two, throughout the church and sang facing the walls! Here I experienced something that my verbal ability is not enough to give a just description of—but in any case I experienced a weightless state where I floated around unaware of time and space in some sort of dimension of eternity where I was totally surrounded by a wonderful weave of tones and nothing else existed.

8.2 LEAVING ONE'S BODY, OUT-OF-BODY EXPERIENCES

The most spectacular examples of a totally different experience of one's body are to be found in descriptions of how one leaves one's body and sometimes can even observe one's body from somewhere else.

(8.2A) Woman, middle-aged, 1950s (from Chapter 19, account 19.1A)

[A school choir] We sang a song for three voices . . . I remember to this day the bliss I felt when I stood there and sang my part and heard the other voices around me. I could never have imagined such joy. It was as if you left your own body and merged totally with the music.

(8.2B) Woman, middle-aged, 1970s (from Chapter 25, account 25.2H)

[At the opera *Tristan and Isolde*] The great experience took place when Birgit Nilsson sang her final aria, Isolde's '*Liebestod*'. The light was on her face alone, and her voice was all there was. The best word for this experience is 'transcendental'. It really was as if I went outside myself. It was extremely intense and wonderful. I have never experienced anything like it, either before or after that.

(8.2C) Woman, middle-aged, 1960s

[Listening to Beethoven's fifth piano concerto, which she had never heard before] The first movement—beautiful, beautiful, magnificent, powerful. The second movement—still beautiful. Slow, of course, and it was certainly beautiful too, calming, but I found myself dozing off—and then it came! The exciting transition between the second and the third.

And the passage from the dreamlike to the incredible, definitely joyful. That is my strongest experience with music. I was flying! I was suddenly outside myself! Happiness! Joy!

(8.2D) Woman, young, 1980s

We visited the Glyptotek Museum in Copenhagen and had walked around and looked at all the fine exhibits. They also have a beautiful winter garden. Just as we were entering the winter garden, they started to play some sort of music. I think it was some sort of computer music. You got the feeling that it was extraterrestrial music. My body was filled with a strange sensation. It felt as if I was floating outside my own body. As if I wasn't present but floated out into space. It was a rather creepy sensation, but it felt nice at the same time.

I often think about that occasion. I wonder what sort of music it was, and what it was that I experienced. I have never felt anything like it, before or after.

In other examples, even more explicit in their out-of-body character, the narrators describe how they could observe themselves from outside and how they 'came back into' their body.

An elderly woman describes two out-of-body experiences when she was listening to music during concerts with music by Wagner and Beethoven, respectively. The first experience took place in the Wagnerian Festspielhaus in Bayreuth and was preceded by a meeting with none other than Wagner's widow, Cosima Wagner.

(8.2E) Woman, old, 1920s and 1930s

One autumn in the 1920s I was in Germany for the first time. I was invited to visit relatives, particularly one of my father's cousins who was a fairly popular artist but also especially keen on music. As soon as he found out that there was going to be a good concert, he would forget his painting and off we went. For example, we went one day to Bayreuth—visited Cosima Wagner, whom he knew from the past. We placed some flowers on Richard Wagner's grave. Our goal was, of course, to go to the Festspielhaus and enjoy the Wagner concert.

It wasn't the first time I had heard Wagner's music, but I had never previously enjoyed it. I didn't understand it, found it boring, and longed for it to come to an end as quickly as possible. But this time it was completely different!

I can't remember which of Wagner's works we heard, or who it was who played and sang. But it was like a stroke of lightning. It all felt so dramatic, intoxicating, unearthly, and the strange thing was that I sort of vanished from my body and floated away, upwards. It's impossible to find words that can describe what it felt like. I don't know how long it lasted, but I sort of hovered, and it was wonderful. It felt so weird when I came back to my body, which at first felt too stiff and sluggish, but gradually loosened up.

In the 1930s I had the same experience during a concert featuring Beethoven's ninth symphony. I left my body—the weird thing was that I saw my own body, and for a few seconds felt ashamed to be sitting there gaping. But that was only a moment, then the earthly context disappeared and I experienced light. Harmony, bliss. It isn't possible to describe what it felt like, and I hadn't told anybody else either until I became friends with a Finnish woman who herself told me that she had seen her own body lying on the operating table after she had been pronounced dead.

When we asked this narrator if she had had similar strong experiences in situations other than with music, she said:

> Yes, once, probably in the 1950s. Strindberg's *A Dream Play* with Inga Tidblad in the main role. The same experience! But there I wasn't alone. An older girlfriend sat by my side. I understood from what she said that she had been afraid, had almost believed that I was dead for a moment. Of course, I didn't tell her about my experience.

Very explicit out-of-body descriptions come from musicians who, while playing, have suddenly found that they were outside themselves.

(8.2F) Man, middle-aged, 1970s

We were playing in a wind quintet at the county governor's residence. Everything so solemn. Beautiful clothes, an elegant style and artificiality, that is, everyone was putting on a show and behaving properly. The music was the right sort for the context, and everybody in that situation was being correct. However, this is not the point. The point is that in the midst of the 'reverential' situation, I got a sort of double ego or exterior ego, that is, when we played I became two. The person everyone saw and heard was me as a physical person and a musician with an instrument, the other ego (the experience?!) was me without a body—naturally—who was observing the players and, above all, what was happening. This was clear to me. I was about one and a half metres above myself and the other players, and about two metres away. Coldly and clinically, I observed myself and my ego (= other self?), my own playing in relation to the others, and found that it seemed to work fine that I just kept on playing (I knew the piece, after all).

The experience did undoubtedly include comical moments, as I was also aware of the surroundings and of the way my fellow musicians and my physical (playing?) self were all dressed up. Crazy? Perhaps so. Analyse it as best you can. I have had such experiences before and afterwards, but never so clearly.

(8.2G) Man, middle-aged, 1960s

The first, spontaneous, strong experience with music that comes to mind is this. I was almost 30 years old, and had joined a balalaika orchestra to play balalaika bass. A year or so later, we were going to have a concert in the old church in the town. The town's chamber orchestra would be there too.

The evening arrived. Our positions in the church were important for my experience. The choir stood on two or three steps right at the back. The balalaikas in front of them. And I thus came to be sitting virtually right in the midst of all the sounds. So I was sitting there playing, carrying a lot of the other music with the bass, and heard everything else loud and clear from all sides! I was surrounded by sounds from both sides, from above, from below, right in the middle!

The music was magnificent, irresistible, beautiful, it carried us all away! It acquired an especially magnificent dimension through the combination of choir and the expressiveness of the balalaika music, and through the acoustics in the stone church with its high arches. The whole thing was something of an experience, a feeling. But even my thoughts wanted to get involved. They said: 'Don't think too much about how the others sing and play, don't let it tempt you to play wrongly, to forget yourself!' But the worry turned out to be unnecessary.

Suddenly I discovered that I found myself a little bit above myself! There I 'sat', hanging in mid-air, confident that I (the one who was sitting just under me and who was me) would certainly not lose the thread, and I could still take in the fantastic whole! Yes, it was a question of in part the experience of the beauty of the sound (much better than four-channel stereo), in part a personal elevating of consciousness that completely wiped out all fears. Tremendous!

(8.2H) Woman, old, 1970s

The experience took place in a church during a midnight concert on an evening in May. The music was Fauré's *Requiem* and I was one of the soloists. Every last seat in the church was filled. Somewhere in the midst of the flow of music a sort of total peace and calm came about. I had a sense of everyone having the same feeling at the same time: the choir, the orchestra, the conductor, we soloists, and the listeners. I was fully occupied with my own singing but was sort of moved out of my body. Any possible difficulties were gone. Everything flowed easily and self-evidently. I observed everything from above and was completely weightless.

You don't tell just anybody about things like that, but I have sometimes met musicians and ordinary everyday people who have had similar experiences. Once you've felt that, you just have to experience it again, but you can never ask for, or expect, the feeling to come about. I personally am very grateful to have had that feeling and I've come close to the same experience on a few other occasions in connection with music.

In the preceding accounts, the musicians observe themselves and find that everything is going well. In the following example, however, the narrator feels considerable unease on account of uncertainty about how she really managed her performance. Afterwards, she thus doesn't dare enter into the music as much as before.

(8.2I) Woman, middle-aged, 1990s

I want to share a strong experience with music that I had during a concert last year, even though it is impossible to describe this horrible experience in words. I was singing in one of Bach's passions and was going to sing a little solo of about 12 bars in the second part. The first part passed and I enjoyed the wonderful music and the fantastic soloists.

As soon as I turned to the page where my solo was, I felt that I took off from the ground and started to look at and listen to everybody from above. I floated lightly among the shining stars. It was so beautiful out in space! 'Who is the little girl who's singing?' I wondered. 'Gosh, is it me? Then I must get back there and concentrate!' I think that I sang correctly when my soul flew back into my body, but I could be wrong—worst of all is that I don't have any idea what happened here on Earth during my solo! It was the most unpleasant sensation I've ever had. I was disappointed and angry at myself when I stood in the choir and went on singing—I just wanted to get away because I thought I'd made a complete fool of myself.

I have a loss of memory of what happened on Earth from the second I turned the page until we sat down and a girl in the choir behind me pinched my bottom! Anything whatsoever could have happened—it is so embarrassing that I couldn't be present and 'all there' in body and soul when the entire church looked at me. I didn't want to talk to anybody afterwards, I just wanted to get away as quickly as possible and sit at home and cry over my failure. It was like a near-death experience.

Did somebody drug me? I have never tried drugs but I can imagine that it's a similar feeling—I was really on a high! My high lasted perhaps two minutes and the depression afterwards for several hours, and really it is still there because I often wonder how it actually sounded at the concert and how other people experienced it. I would really very much like to see or listen to a recording of that concert so that I could have proper proof that it went off as well as everybody claims.

After this event it is even more important for me to try to turn off a part of the emotional side and to sing/play more 'clinically' or unmoved. That's a pity, but I don't dare enter into the music as much now because I'm afraid that something similar will happen.

8.3 COMMENTARY

Out-of-body experiences are examples of quasi-physical reactions but can also be regarded as transcendental experiences, for which reason they are also briefly mentioned in Chapter 13 and in Chapter 29, section 29.6.2. It is noteworthy that almost all out-of-body experiences took place in connection with live music and when the narrator was together with others, never alone.

To the best of my knowledge, there have been no descriptions in scientific publications of out-of-body experiences in connection with music. Such experiences could very well occur in individuals who do not, however, mention them to anyone else, perhaps because they might be regarded as a bit 'weird'. One of our informants (see account 8.2H above) says that 'You don't tell just anybody about things like that', another (see account 8.2E above) says that she 'of course . . . didn't tell' her friend beside her about the experience.

There are, however, many descriptions of out-of-body experiences in other contexts. People in various extreme states, such as when their life is in danger (e.g. in traffic accidents), when in a drugged state (e.g. in connection with surgery), or during a brief episode of heart failure or close to brain death, have had dramatic experiences of both finding themselves outside their bodies and moving outside their bodies, and of being conscious in this normally 'impossible' state.

Researchers are now beginning to gain insight into which parts of the brain are involved in out-of-body experiences. As early as the 1940s, neurologist Wilder Penfield reported out-of-body experiences as a result of electric stimulation of certain areas of the right side of the brain in a patient suffering from epilepsy. Recently, Swiss neurologists have carried out detailed studies of such experiences in six patients. One of these, prior to an epilepsy operation, was given electric stimulation in a certain area of the right side of the brain, and the patient described feelings of lightness and of floating near the ceiling, and that she could look down from above and see herself lying in bed.[1]

In our examples of out-of-body experiences related to music, there is no suggestion of a connection to epilepsy or other pathological states. To which degree the results of the examinations of epilepsy patients can have any relevance to out-of-body experiences related to music is thus a completely open question. Since the number of such experiences in our material is fairly small (about ten or so), it ought to be a matter of very special cases of interaction between factors in the music (when listening or making music), factors in the person, and in the situation. At present, one can only speculate as to what this could mean.

CHAPTER 9

INNER MUSIC

ONE can think of a piece of music and 'hear' it inside one's head. Several of our participants mention, for example, that they sometimes think back to the strong experience and imagine how the music sounded. Trained musicians can study notes for a piece of music and gain an impression—a 'mental representation' in academic terminology—of what it should sound like, and use this as the basis for their performance.

Now and then, music can also spontaneously turn up in one's head without one actually having particularly thought about it. It can be music one has heard recently, but it can also be music that one has not heard for a long time and that for some (incomprehensible) reason turns up just then. Sometimes a tune can stick in one's mind and just go round and round in a loop—one just can't get rid of it.

These are fairly well-known phenomena. Not nearly as well known is the phenomenon that is dealt with here, namely strong experience with 'inner', imagined music.

9.1 MUSIC THAT JUST COMES INTO ONE'S HEAD

In the first account, there is a description of an experience with inner music that took place just over 30 years ago when the narrator was still a teenager.

(9.1A) Man, middle-aged, 1960s

At the time I am 19 years old. It is a clear night in September and I am on the bridge of a ship somewhere in the Mediterranean. I have the night watch, from 24.00 to 04.00 hours.

Out at sea, a positive change comes about. There is time to be on your own and to devote yourself to ideas about the future, and also to look back. On either side of the ship, dolphins were circling; it is fascinating to see their bodies lit up in the dark night. The wind is only a slight breeze. All your senses are wide open and all you have to do is breathe in all the impressions.

Suddenly I hear music. At first I think I'm dreaming. Can you be standing up and sleeping? I *am* awake and try to concentrate on hearing what it is. It is a concert waltz with variations. I recognize the music but can't remember what it is called. While I'm listening I try to convince myself that it's in my imagination but I realize that, in that case, it doesn't really matter, so I decide to listen to the end. I know I am the only person who can hear this, and there is no explanation. It happens somewhere inside my subconscious mind. I relax and try to concentrate on listening.

I don't know how long this goes on, but after a while a disturbing sound can be heard from outside. I suspect that somebody is calling my name, and of course I don't want to answer but finally do so. Somebody is standing next to me, it is the third mate. The music has vanished and I am back in reality. I know that I was completely awake all the time, it was only sounds that didn't belong to the music that I had turned off, otherwise I could see everything around me. My first inclination was to apologize but I soon realize that the mate hasn't heard what I have heard. This doesn't need explaining. The third mate fancies a cup of coffee and I mumble a hardly audible OK and think that it'll probably be possible to return to the listening.

I remember that during the time that I heard this, the thought occurred to me: 'What a pity that I can't record this, nobody's going to believe me when I tell them about it.'

After the interruption it is impossible to return to what happened. I can't even remember how the tune went. The next night is a completely ordinary night, not even the dolphins are there now, the mystery is no longer there.

Afterwards, I realize that this is the greatest experience with music I've had and feel incredibly happy, chosen, to have been able to experience this miracle. Explaining what happened in words—you just can't do that.

At the beginning of the account, some of the conditions for the experience are possibly hinted at: the stillness out at sea in the darkness of the night; he is alone on watch; there is time for reflection; all his senses are wide open for impressions. But nevertheless: this sudden appearance of a particular tune, why and from where does it come? He does, however, recognize the music, can even be exact as to its form, 'a concert waltz with variations', and it is evidently stored 'somewhere inside my subconscious mind'.

Stillness, silence, and time for reflection are also to be found in the next two accounts, where the experience takes place in church. But the narrators don't recognize the music, only its type.

(9.1B) Woman, middle-aged, 1980s

A friend of mine was visiting me. She was a bit down, because a dear relative of hers had passed away and was to be buried in Germany. My friend had no opportunity to travel there. We sat at the kitchen table, and suddenly she looked at the clock and said: 'The funeral starts in a quarter of an hour.' She looked so desperate. It suddenly occurred to me that we could go down to the local church and light a candle for the deceased. In that way we would still be at his funeral. And we did that.

The church was completely empty, because it was midweek. We each lit a candle and sat down at the front beside the candle holders. We both sat in silence with our thoughts. Although I had never met the deceased, I thought that I knew him; I had, after all, heard so many good things about him.

Then suddenly I can hear a choir singing, like a church choir with an organ and violin in the background. It was so beautiful; there aren't words to describe it. 'Listen,' I whispered to my friend. She looked at me and nodded, a slightly surprised look on her face. I was enchanted by the music, had never heard anything so beautiful.

I don't know how long it lasted. But suddenly my friend whispered that now the funeral was over, and we got up to leave. Then it suddenly struck me that the church was empty. There was no choir there. And to my considerable surprise, my friend hadn't heard any music at all. We nevertheless looked through the church to see if anybody was there, but there was nobody. We checked the radio programme times too, in case it could have been a radio, but nothing fitted. Nor had there been any choir practice that day. But I still have the experience inside me even though my friend heard nothing.

So I can't give any information as to who played and sang, or what it was. I've never heard such beautiful choir singing before. I have heard several church choirs sing, but not like this. It went right inside you.

A similar experience of 'inner singing' in a church is to be found in the following excerpt from a much longer account in the chapter on religious experiences, Chapter 14.

(9.1C) Woman, middle-aged, 1990s (from Chapter 14, account 14.4F)

[She has just entered the church.] The sound of a very faint yet distinguishable melody catches my attention. I raise my head to hear better. Am I hearing a melody or is it an illusion? Am I imagining that I hear somebody singing? I look around to see if anybody else is also standing there listening, but nothing seems to suggest that. I look up at the ceiling. Is the singing coming from high above? Despite my uncertainty, I am sure that I can hear a song. The melody catches my attention totally. Despite the weak sound, it penetrates my body and envelopes me with a glorious melody that I in no way can tear myself away from. I am totally enchanted. I have never heard anything so wonderfully beautiful. I am totally surrounded by the melody, it completely fills my body. I even hold my breath to hear better.

I establish that it is a male choir that is humming a fairly simple melody. I don't know what they are humming, but I guess it is some sort of Gregorian chant. I try to see where these men could be standing but I can't discover anyone. I try to work out where the sound is coming from. The weak melody is concentrated right at the very top of the church, just under the cupola. I stand completely still and look up towards this fascinating singing which in some way is at one with the church. It is extremely hard to explain, but it sort of fits in really perfectly with the church. The cathedral and the singing belong together! The singing merges with the walls . . . I establish that it is a choir of monks that I hear. I don't know where I get that knowledge from, I simply establish that this is the case.

. . . I start to walk further into the church. The melody pursues me all the time, now I can hear it loud and clear. It is so unbelievably beautiful. It is both sad and consoling at the same time. It settles like cotton wool around my heart. I find myself in a very strange state. I am both sad and safe. The monks' choir is singing a message to me, but I don't understand its content. I again look around to discover who is singing but can't see anybody. Nor can

I explain why I experience that it is a monks' choir that is singing. I simply feel that it is monks who are singing.

[Afterwards] What did I hear? Who was it who was singing? What did this experience want to tell me? Why did I react as I did? Since I couldn't discover a male choir, I asked myself whether they played the singing via a loudspeaker. I decided to ask one of the staff from the church about this the next time I went to the church. I talked to a woman who works in the office at the church. She maintained most decisively that there had not been any male choir or any rehearsal for a male choir. Nor is there ever any loudspeaker music at all in the cathedral, and never has been.

Both women describe the music as the most beautiful they have ever heard. They feel enchanted by the music and are confused to find that there is no 'real' music there. The experience remains incomprehensible—and unforgettable. Both experiences have a religious connection, in the first case to a church ceremony (funeral), in the second case to a strongly religious experience that is evident in the complete account (see Chapter 14, account 14.4F).

The next account of inner music also takes place in a church and has a religious content.

(9.1D) Man, middle-aged, 1970s

For the greatest part of my lifetime I have been condemned to loneliness, so music has always been a channel to the Most High to be able to give me help and redress, before myself and Him.

It was on an occasion of sheer mental exhaustion that I instinctively sought out an old stone church from the thirteenth century to again seek peace and consolation before the Most High. I closed my eyes and in my inner vision could see a procession of monks in the same sanctuary where I was sitting. One corridor of the sanctuary was lit up by burning torches along the walls. They met in two lines in groups standing opposite each other. During all the time that this took place they were singing Gregorian music.

The music, or rather the singing, made me relax completely. When I say completely, I really do mean completely. I felt tensions such as I had never experienced before dissolve. My inner self, which had previously been something that had to the very greatest degree been abstract, suddenly became tangible, for I could really feel how things moved when the knots were loosened.

The following short excerpt from a longer account is yet another example of inner singing in connection with a religious experience.

(9.1E) Woman, young, 1980s (from Chapter 14, account 14.4E)

Another little thing that I'd like to mention is a little glimpse that I had when I had just recently become a Christian. I so very much wanted to have some sort of 'picture' of Jesus, so that it would be easier for me to think about him when I prayed. So I prayed for this. The sudden stroke of lightning in my inner mind that then happened completely astounded me. What I felt was a Jesus who *sang*! I sing songs for him—and he sings songs for me! Is that why I have found such spiritual fellowship in music?

A dramatic and strongly negative example of inner music in connection with a potentially fatal event is to be found in Chapter 11, account 11.3S.

9.2 COMPOSING MUSIC

In the accounts above, the narrators have been passive receivers of music. In the following examples, the narrators think they have a certain control over the inner music, that they can govern it.

(9.2A) Man, middle-aged, 1960s

The strongest experience with music that I ever had took place when I was in my car driving over a bridge in Stockholm on the way to the place where I was completing my military service. The music that I heard was inside me and was produced by a complete symphony orchestra, which followed all my compositional ideas and thoughts about instrumentation. It was all for my benefit, the composing and the listening. The setting was pleasing, with an unusually beautiful play of colours in the sky and the branches of the trees decorated with glowing autumn leaves.

My physical and mental state can be described as 'the calm after the storm', with parallel demanding music studies and hard work in music pedagogy abruptly broken off for an uneventful existence as a battalion staff driver and an eternal relief that at last this hated military service would be over once and for all. I was on my own in the car, didn't even have a car radio.

After this experience, I could—within myself—compose and produce music for a large orchestra whenever I wanted. And being able to create and produce already instrumented music at exactly the same moment was of course an absolutely staggering now-experience. The music wasn't diffuse and short term but could be made to sound clearly and with the biggest variations imaginable for a period of several minutes. I never experienced this sudden ability as oppressive or as pathologically caused; rather, I enjoyed it and still do to this day, despite the fact that the ability is no longer anywhere near the same calibre as it was that first time.

(9.2B) Man, middle-aged

This is about music that I can hear inside me. The first time I had this happen was during my childhood, I must have been about ten years old. I went to the local music school and played quite a lot but not enough to be able to write down the music I experienced inside me.

The music comes to me on occasions when I am relatively relaxed, often when I am lying down, half asleep. The course of the music can be governed by me, myself. The music is complex with many diffuse instruments that are evident more as tones/colours than as real, physical instruments. The music is everything from very complex to simpler but always extremely self-evident. It contains rhythms and often singing with lyrics that develop in a way that for me is surprising and interesting. With regard to form, the music is complex, with many parts that develop on the basis of each other. Dynamically, they are very varied with almost overwhelmingly surprising switches—it would take months of full-time work to write down and arrange just one of these pieces. They give me an almost euphoric feeling. For me they form the ultimate music. In terms of expression, the music feels to me to be entirely honest, by that I mean that it doesn't directly copy any music that I've heard.

Both of these narrators are musically active, a fact that sheds light on why they can govern the music themselves. It thus borders on their composing in some form.

The accounts also have in common that the narrators are on their own, are relieved/relaxed, and have time for their own 'inner' activity—conditions that are reminiscent of the situations of the narrators of the earlier accounts.

There are also some accounts of strong experiences in connection with deliberate composing of music. The inspiration often comes suddenly after a period of fruitless attempts.

(9.2C) Man, young, 1980s

It was last summer, the rain was pouring down and in the midst of my personal difficulties I had my most self-evident experience with music ever. I had been asked to compose a piece of music for a church service with music. The work with this was going very slowly, or not at all. A lot of tension and some mysterious events led to a sharpening of my situation, and suddenly, creeping out from nowhere, it was there in my ears. It was as if you had ten holes in the ground around you, took ten balls, threw them at random up in the air, and found that every ball had found its way to its own hole. And as if that wasn't enough, it all happened quite naturally and self-evidently. The Latin text met my purpose and fitted in perfectly with the melodic idea that had matured during difficult moments. Everything fitted into place self-evidently: leading notes, phrases, accents, words, text, harmonies. I got to experience what a teacher told me: 'Music writes itself, the composer is just an amanuensis who writes it down.'

I could explain everything, every little note, it was absolutely crystal clear, it was as if I was at one with the music. Of course, I changed a little here and there, experimented with a few details, the self-evidence gave room for that without changing strength or character. The form demanded a more technical, contrapuntal interlude and an introduction that created atmosphere, and they were just as obvious.

Now came the difficult bit. Everything was so completely clear in my head, but it would all have to go down on paper. It is extremely frustrating to see your hand labouring so slowly when really everything is ready.

The performance didn't give me the same ecstatic experience as the composing did, it was more like a confirmation of what had been in my head, or rather what had always been somewhere and which found its way out through my head and was given form. But the great thing was being able to share your experiences with others in various forms. This experience is always there in some way. The experience has given me a faith in music that I don't have for anything else.

His description of how everything suddenly fits into place and how 'music writes itself' reminds one of statements by musicians who talk of occasions when everything is just right, all the pieces fall into place, it feels as if one is being played by somebody else (see Chapter 18, section 18.6)

Similar Aha! experiences—sudden inspiration, a creative intoxication—are described in the following accounts that come from composers in completely different genres. One also gains interesting insights into how they think and work.

(9.2D) Man, young

There are certain very strong experiences when creating music. I have access to a four-channel portable recording studio, drum machine, synth, guitars, etc. that I use a lot when

I create my own music. Particularly on occasions such as these, it has happened innumerable times that I'm sitting and working, working in a disciplined way without being satisfied with what I'm trying to create. It simply doesn't work at all, and then, bang, it happens just when I've given up, or when I'm not thinking at all about what I've been trying to do. What happens is simply that a melody pops up, a harmonic progression like a flash of lightning from a clear sky. I can do a piece in 15 minutes, compared with certain other ideas that I might work intensely with for a whole week and that don't end up as anything at all.

Now I don't want to claim that it's always like this; rather, most of the time you produce something after having worked with an idea for a long time. But the strange thing is that the strongest experience of joy at having created something is when something comes like a flash of lightning. The pieces that have been created in this way are the ones that are dearest to me. For me they express a lot more, they quite simply say much more to me than the other pieces.

(9.2E) Man, middle-aged, 1980s

Sometimes I go for a walk to get some musical ideas (incidentally, it always feels as if the music 'comes' to me). It is pleasurable; I do it particularly when I'm going to start a composition. I am convinced that I remember the best ideas for years, the poorer ones just fall away.

I choose just such an old experience. It was probably in the autumn. A grey, overcast day. I felt—as usual—a certain expectation as I approached my objective, the walk. I know that it always works, that I'll always hear music.

Once I'd got there, the music came to me. It came in an interplay with thoughts of how it would 'be'. I remember that I could modify and sharpen the ideas, and time after time hear the piece all the way through with increasingly sharp contours. I could listen to the music again and again. I was in the sort of creative intoxication that is called inspiration.

At a later stage, I started to make observations concerning how it sounded and what made it sound like it did. This is a balancing act: if you were to switch on the analysis apparatus fully, then I think the music would disappear. The music was rhythmically very intense, a sort of structured noise. There was no fixed complement of instruments, but an expression and a form that could be used for, say, a symphony orchestra with a lot of percussion instruments, or electro-acoustic music with percussion instruments.

What is typical of such an inner hearing experience is that I think I can hear the entire piece—say it is ten minutes—in one minute. Together with the memory of the music, there is a visual memory. Much later I used this memory as the starting point for a movement in an orchestral piece.

I usually think of a strong experience with music as meaning that all brain cells, all nerves, are brought about by an outside force to bear in the same direction, like when a magnet arranges iron filings in a simple physics experiment.

(9.2F) Man, middle-aged

In connection with pieces I have composed, at an early stage (long before the ideas have reached the music paper) it has felt like after a walk in a long tunnel suddenly to be standing before a majestic crystal hall, filled with previously unheard music. This euphoric feeling has come in connection with compositions for big bands, particularly while carving out the theme and the sounds during long night-time walks. A little detail or momentary image in this overwhelming sensation has then followed along and left its mark on the whole composition—right up to the first rehearsal. There, it's blown away and taken time to find again.

I like to think that certain music on certain occasions fulfils extremely deeply felt, yet hard to express, needs. The need of confirmation or participation. In the examples mentioned above, there is a genuine experience of standing in a 'creative flow' which pours forth, but it isn't a passive stance. The strong feeling has acted like an incentive to work towards a finished result. These memories are strongly linked to the feeling that my personality was carved out—not as a composer's personality but with regard to 'my musical colours'.

(9.2G) Man, middle-aged (from an edited interview)

When we talk about commercial music, then somewhere at the back of my mind it says there is a form of technique in building up such a tune. It should be three minutes long, there should be something logical about when the strings come in, what they should play— should it be distinct things or just a carpet of strings?—in combination with 'wind things'. There is yet another point before you begin: the instruments that are there in the ensemble which somebody else has determined . . . they say that there are 28 strings, four trumpets, four trombones and five saxophones, two guitarists, those synths, this bass, etc. Usually I have complete freedom to decide the tempo for a tune, and even the length. But in a pop song even the tempo is a given, because you can't fit the tune into three minutes if you start constructing too much. So you know the rules of the game.

I sit down. At first it's really boring, filling in all the signatures, etc. Often, when it's that type of music, I write the drums first. And that's more a question of craftsmanship. Then I write down the first idea I get . . . suddenly you hear that this is how it should be . . . it's simply there and it's something emotional . . . then you hear that 'there the strings go up and do this and that, and then the glockenspiel comes in here . . .'

And you just write it down. I can't explain it. But the kick, the joy in this job is when you—in an Aha! experience—suddenly hear something that you've never heard before, in here, in your head. You become—aaah!—happy, simply because you happened to have written a string line that nobody thought of before. Mind you, perhaps there's nobody else who experiences it . . .

(9.2H) Man, young

Creating is a way for me to express myself. When I create music I most often feel a great elation or tension. Although it can be a lot of work, it is incredibly good fun in a way that you can hardly compare with anything else. To sometimes lose track of time and space, well, for me as a musician that is a self-evident thing but it can be hard to explain to an outsider, someone who's not a musician/artiste. On good occasions it is a sensation of total inspiration and joy. I just go on working without feeling hungry or tired, and without my noticing that several hours have passed—and me thinking I've only just begun! Girlfriends or neighbours who get mad at you when you suddenly have to play an idea in the middle of the night. Or wonder how you can sit inside your summer cottage and play hour after hour while the sun's shining. But it's inspiration, that's what I've got, why don't they understand?

The last account is a bit different from the earlier ones, but here too it is a question of creating something quickly, 'straight off'.

(9.2I) Woman, young (from an edited interview)

After the party I came home and was almost unconscious, I was just so bloody tired, but I couldn't refrain from playing. I sat in the armchair or on the floor and just played. But I was nevertheless aware that I was so bloody tired that I couldn't remember what I was doing the next day, so I turned the tape recorder on. I sat and played for a while and then I went to bed.

The next day, I realized that I'd probably thought up something the previous evening. I turned on the tape recorder and . . . well, it was totally different from all the other tunes I'd done earlier. Earlier I'd done ballads, rock, and pop songs, but this was more sort of boogie-ish and wasn't like any other tune I've done, not in the least.

I can't remember anything. I had no idea what I'd done the previous evening. I can't remember what I'd been thinking, and I've no idea how I felt except that I was tired. I just sat there and played. I have the feeling that I did it pretty quickly, straight off. It wasn't like normal when you test, try out, and experiment, that's what it's usually like. It was just straight off, just like that!

It's a weird feeling when you've done things that later are still there when you don't know about them. That tune I made in an unconscious state.

The creative moment comes along often after a time of testing and fruitless attempts. When it does finally come, often suddenly and unexpectedly, then things can move quickly, everything seems to sort itself out, one just has to follow along. One of the composers describes how he thinks he can hear the whole of the long piece in a single minute—a compressed vision of a long event. One finds oneself in a 'creative intoxication', a euphoric state of simultaneous strong concentration and relaxation (even 'unconsciousness'), a seemingly paradoxical combination typical of what Csikszentmihalyi calls 'flow' (see Chapter 1, section 1.3). This is followed by a more 'craftsman-like' phase with polishing of details and writing to get the vision down on music paper (if it's a question of writing musical notation).

Altogether, this fits in well with a well-known attempt to describe the creative process in four stages: preparation; incubation (unconscious processing of the material during a period with other activities); illumination (the sudden solution); and verification (the working-out of the final product).[1]

9.3 INNER MUSIC AFTERWARDS

When one has had a strong experience with music, it is not unusual for the music to stick in your mind for quite a long time afterwards; for example: 'for three or four days after the concert it was as if I was walking on a springy heather moor instead of on asphalt. There was singing inside my whole body from the choir and orchestra.' Here are some other short quotes of the same type.

(9.3A) Man, young

Chopin's Op. 66, I think it's called *Fantaisie-Impromptu* . . . I listened three or four times to this piece within two or three days and the time I remember, the last of these, the music went in deeply. For two days, small passages and phrases slid around in my head. In the end I was really tired of the situation. But luckily the activity faded away. There was no way of controlling this 'inner music'.

(9.3B) Man, old

When I hear a piece of music played in what I think is an appealing way, both classical and jazz, the piece usually sticks in my mind and can stay there for several days. I never cease to be surprised how you can think you are hearing an entire orchestra in your head although there is physical silence all around you.

Inner music afterwards can sometimes lead to undesired consequences, as in Chapter 5, account 5.2G, where the person concerned, after having heard a jazz trumpeter on a record, drove the lawnmower 'right through borders, the strawberry patch, etc. without being aware of the havoc'.

In both the following accounts, there is a fuller description of how a concrete experience of music later came to show itself in the form of an inner representation of the music. The inner music seems to be just as tangible, 'concrete', as the outer music—or perhaps even more so.

(9.3C) Man, old, 1940s

The experience took place at the end of the 1940s when the Stockholm Concert Society orchestra conducted by Carl Garaguly performed Sibelius's Symphony No. 4. A year or so earlier, I had read an introductory article about this symphony, which gave an advance experience of something absolutely outstanding. The performance confirmed this, perhaps not first and foremost through the quality of the playing, but rather by virtue of the fact that it was the first time ever I heard this music.

My conception of music was anchored in a listener experience. During this period I spent a lot of time at the library to prepare for an essay, but perhaps didn't get so much done because the music echoed in my head. The experience totally dominated my entire existence.

What then was it that sounded inside my head? Long, drawn-out tones always orchestrated in different ways. Endless tremolos, short woodwind fragments. Great contrasts between high and low, between starting up and braking to a halt. Perhaps above all the emotional quality of desolation with strings of warmth, grey-brownness with reddish-yellow features (autumn colours!), the ascetic, unadorned, with oases of lushness (though that doesn't mean that the music is a desert!). Moving in a large space.

(9.3D) Woman, young, 1970s/1980s

The first strong experience with music happened twice. The first time must have been after 1970 when Simon and Garfunkel's 'Bridge over Troubled Water' was often played on the radio. I was three or four years old or a little bit older. And I carried that song within me for many years afterwards. I didn't know it properly, but could remember bits of it; it sort of reminded me of its presence now and then. I remember clearly how I often tried to retain the melody loops that bubbled up, so that I could remember the entire song, but it wouldn't work.

The second experience didn't come until the 1980s with Simon and Garfunkel's *Central Park* album, which I sat down to listen to with a completely open mind. Bang—there it was . . . What happens? Well, I think about the music all the time, in as much as I can remember it. It takes over my brain and recreates itself there as soon as I am not distracted by anything. In fact, the risk is greater that I am distracted from more practical activities to instead sit and listen. And it can go on for a long time. In the case of 'Bridge' it must have been a year.

'Bridge' troubled me. It was so beautiful that it hurt, really hurt. What is it in that song that had such power? Partly it was surely the song itself, partly the lyrics, but above all the melody, which is like jubilant sorrow or sorrowful jubilation, or something like that.

Finally, some participants made spontaneous comments about always having music inside oneself. Here is an example.

(9.3E) Woman, middle-aged (original in English)

I also have a strong experience of having a nearly constant 'internal' musical world, that I am living in sound and rhythmic patterns inside myself. Often dream in music (hear/compose music in my dreams).

Regardless of all other comparisons, her description reminds one of how several composers describe that they always hear music inside them; they entirely live in music.

CHAPTER 10

INNER IMAGES

Music can conjure up images, notions, of various sorts. They can be of people, events, situations, or settings that have been associated with a certain piece of music. They are thus images with a background in the person's earlier experiences.

There are also images that seem to be new creations, products of the imagination, which in some way have been prompted by music. But these, too, may be assumed to have been influenced by different factors related to the person or the particular situation. Exactly how can be hard to analyse, but now and then some clues are to be found in the accounts.

In some instances, the music has been so-called programme music, that is, the composer has described what the music is intended to represent, for example, a particular person, event, or situation. The question is whether a listener without any knowledge of the programme can apprehend what the composer wanted to describe. This is usually not especially successful, but occasionally the impression the listener gains may be close to what is intended.

'Images' refer here primarily to visual notions. But the accounts also contain several examples of notions within other senses, such as hearing and smell.

10.1 IMAGES WITH A BACKGROUND IN EARLIER EXPERIENCES

First, some examples of inner images that undoubtedly have their background in the person's earlier experiences.

(10.1A) Woman, young, after 2000

The experience took place one Sunday in church. Before the experience I felt rather lost; I had just come home from a year in Africa that had changed me rather a lot and when I came home so much was the same, but so much was also changed.

During the meeting we sang, as usual, a couple of songs and suddenly they start on the song '*Jesus, Du är kung*' ['Jesus, You are king']. I had never sung that before in Sweden, but in Africa we often sang it. So when they start singing it here at home it is like being transported in time and space. I was back in Africa in the midst of all the missionaries who had come to mean so much to me during the year. I could even almost feel the special smell and hear the goats bleating outside.

Directly afterwards, I felt rather overwhelmed, this was not something I had expected to meet with, which is probably why it made such a strong impression. But, as I say, I felt lost before, and being back in Africa for a few moments gave me strength to carry on a while longer despite the uncertainty.

(10.1B) Man, middle-aged, 1960s (from Chapter 25, account 25.1I)

[The first time he heard Shostakovich's String Quartet No. 8 was in the 1960s.] I could read a little bit about the quartet just before the performance and also hear a short description of the content of the music. I already knew something about the victims of war, I had read about it in school, seen it in cinemas, and besides, as a child I had myself experienced air-raid sirens and a bomb shelter . . . I became absorbed in the music, and felt as if I was being carried along on waves. The musical language was new, but in some way familiar at the same time. It was extremely close, as if it was my own. Then memories started to surface. Experiences from the bomb shelter, the darkness, the dampness of wet steam and the body heat of someone who sat right next to me in the bomb shelter. I recognized the smell, the temperature, the fear.

Shostakovich's eighth string quartet was written shortly after the composer visited Dresden in the then GDR (East Germany), a city that for the greater part had been bombed into ruins during the Second World War. The music, together with the description of its content that the narrator had obtained, evoked memories/images of his own experiences during the war, those of being in the bomb shelter.

There are also images that seem to be new creations, pure products of the imagination. But these, too, may to some extent have their background in earlier experiences.

(10.1C) Man, old, 1960s

It was a grey, raw and chilly winter morning about 30 years ago. In the birch grove close to the house you could still see one or two bright patches of white snow. I was sitting at the kitchen table eating breakfast and now and then just glancing out towards the slope. As usual, I was listening to gramophone music [on the radio]. Then out of the blue I heard the notes of the piece of music entitled '*Fiolen min*' ['My violin'] by the divinely gifted violinist Erik Öst. I stopped eating and listened, listened intently.

Suddenly the room I was in disappeared and I found myself on the edge of a green meadow framed by birch trees, the meadow sloped down towards a little lake, the surface of which rippled in a weak breeze. The music sounded in my ears, and in my gaze the beautiful summer landscape shimmered.

The image came just as the violinists went into the somewhat gentler refrain and then lasted for the whole of the piece. When the music ended, it felt as if a warmth had spread throughout my body. And the remarkable thing was that the vision came back again several times during the day, as did the sensation of warmth, and the music resonating in my ears.

Neither before nor later have I had that sort of feeling. One explanation could be the violinists' brilliant interpretation of the piece of music. I've heard it several times, enjoyed it—but not had that same strong feeling.

Perhaps his image has its origins in visual impressions of folk musician violinists on a Swedish summer meadow. In the next account, there are images of nature in another part of the world, and associated with a road that is the stuff of legends.

(10.1D) Man, middle-aged, 1970s

This took place in the home of a good friend who had just bought a new stereo system for quite a lot of money. It was the album *Silk Road, Part I* by Japanese musician Kitaro. I was a bit excited and curious just before we were going to listen, because I knew that as regards the quality of the sound this was going to be something out of the ordinary. That is important for me, but the reason that it turned into a really special experience was the combination of superb sound and this fabulous music. The closeness and realism that this conveyed was amazing. In the dark room it was possible to be at one with the music, so to speak. I saw before me caravans, sunsets in the desert, dawn breaking in a mountain landscape. It was so clear!

This music conveys a very positive outlook on life. It was composed for a TV series called *The Silk Road* that described the trading route from China via Mongolia to somewhere in Turkey.

Afterwards, I felt as if I had been drilled right through with happiness. The words 'happiness' and perhaps 'harmony' and 'joy' cover so well what his music conveys and what I felt after this hearing.

Even though the inner images here perhaps don't have their origins in direct visual impression, one may assume that they have been influenced by images and stories about the legendary Silk Road. The next narrator speculates as to the background of his notions.

(10.1E) Man, middle-aged

A tune that I have a sort of love–hatred of, or perhaps one could say a sort of love–horror of, is from the Italian LP featuring the Italian bagpipes and called *La zampogna in Italia e le launeddas*. When I hear that piece, it really grabs me. The music takes a vice-like hold on me. I can't turn it off. I put it on, again and again. I can listen to it several times in a row and all the time have the same inexplicable experience:

I feel an oppressive Mediterranean heat. I 'feel' the sound of the cicadas. I smell the fragrance of fresh figs and various flowers and spices and herbs, but also—and this frightens me—the smell of manure and human excrement. I am warm, no, I am hot. And sticky. In the music there is something that makes me feel as if I have heard it before. That I might even have lived before and heard the piece then. As if the piece was a link between another time and the present time, between another country and our country, between another body and my body.

And I wonder: Why? Why do I feel like that about this piece? How come that it makes me so spellbound?

10.2 IMAGES IN CONNECTION WITH PROGRAMME MUSIC

One of the best-known examples of programme music is the symphonic poem about the Moldau River by Bedřich Smetana. In the following account, the listener seems to have an idea of what the music is intended to describe, without having heard about the programme behind the music.

(10.2A) Woman, old, 1930s

When I was about 13 or 14 years old I heard *Moldau* for the first time. I was totally captivated. I assume it was broadcast during the *Gramophone Hour* on the wireless. In any case, there was no introduction at all of the content of the piece, and I had never heard of it before. I am almost certain that I didn't even associate it with the river of the same name.

But later!—or, more correctly, almost immediately—I saw: 'Trickles of water dripping from an icy mountainside, collecting together and swelling into a stream which throws itself over precipices and ripples fast through calm alpine valleys. Young people dance in colourful costumes, the dance music fades away. A still alpine lake with gentle waves lapping the shores, the sun shining. The wind starts to rise, the stream has grown into a river and leaves the lake, flowing on towards the great sea whose waves await it. In the far distance, the tune of the little stream is mixed with the roaring of the great sea.'

I wrote the above immediately (might even have been while the music was still playing) the first time I heard Smetana's *Moldau*.

It must have been 10 to 15 years later that I could confirm that I had seen/heard more or less right. Thus it was genuine interplay between the composer and the listener. The credit, of course, should go to the former.

Sibelius's symphonic poem *Finlandia* can, perhaps, to some degree be regarded as programme music, though without a clearly described programme and thus essentially subject to more interpretations. Here are a couple of examples of images that *Finlandia* has created in listeners.

(10.2B) Woman, old, 1940s

I am Swiss by birth. I was extremely receptive as a child and have many intense memories from my childhood. I experienced the war years intensely, partly through the commitment of my relatives, partly through the very nationalistic spirit that the whole of Switzerland's will to defend itself was built on, and I was very frightened by all the talk of war.

When, sometime around 1940, I heard Sibelius's symphonic poem *Finlandia*, it moved me very strongly. I saw pictures: Finland's waterfalls, silent forests, creeping people, machine guns rattling, soldiers skiing through the snow . . . From that day on, Scandinavia had a place on my map.

These images didn't come from the narrator's own experiences of Finland but from what the then young girl had seen and heard people saying about Finland and the war there.

Finlandia features also in the following extract from an account by a woman who heard *Finlandia* for the first time when she was 11 to 12 years old, and described it as a revolutionary experience. It has become her favourite piece and she describes the images the music gives rise to.

(10.2C) Woman, old, 1930s (from Chapter 4, account 4.3H)

In later years, I have tried to understand the meaning of the music. Then what I see in front of me are wild and untamed masses of water that are thrown over a precipice and are washed up on the shores. They are also a dangerous attraction. Gradually the music becomes calmer, milder, and then I can imagine the wild falls having turned into calm rivers. Sometimes, however, I can even imagine that Sibelius is portraying his home country's war history, for example. Perhaps he is describing wild battles (which account for the fierce rhythm) which gradually turn into a peaceful cultivation of Mother Earth.

Vivaldi's well-known 'The Four Seasons' has of course a clearly formulated programme for each of the seasons of the year. Knowledge of them can naturally be expected to give rise to such images as those described in the following account.

(10.2D) Man, middle-aged, 1980s

It was at the beginning of the 1980s. I had one holiday week left to take. A week in Bonn appealed to me. I sent off for the concert programme, chose three concerts and ordered tickets. All three concerts became unforgettable memories. But it was I Musici di Roma that made the greatest impression. My expectations from this star ensemble were great. I had previously experienced them only via gramophone. Of course, the concert was sold out, an audience of about 2,000. These skilful musicians were in a class of their own. They spread such a sense of cosiness and warmth from the stage that the great hall sort of shrank to a little intimate salon.

Vivaldi's 'The Four Seasons' was the highlight for me. The feeling of sitting in a concert venue completely disappeared. I was transported to Italy. The delightful spring when everything is born again, birdsong and the beginning of warmer weather, but even setbacks in temperature. The summer with oppressive heat, thunderstorms and downpours, you search out shade and feel a bit indolent. The autumn when everything comes to maturity, nature darkens and you prepare for winter. Winter is cold and sparkling, everything feels chilly.

I had heard the same work on gramophone records, but never experienced it so intensely as then. After the concert, I felt happy and exalted, I had really been through something out of the ordinary.

Another well-known work, *Rite of Spring* by Stravinsky, has a programme that is suggested by the very title and in more detail in the various movements of the work, for example Ritual of abduction, Dance of the earth, Glorification of the chosen one, Ritual action of the ancestors, and Sacrificial dance. Two participants describe images brought to mind by the music.

(10.2E) Man, young, 1980s

I was taking part in an orchestra festival and played in the cello section. The absolute highlight of the musical experience came during the first movement of Stravinsky's *Rite of Spring.* I had never heard this fantastic piece before, and was incredibly moved by Stravinsky's unconventional style of music. I remember that during this piece I was totally devoured by the music and I can still feel how I shivered all over. I sort of disappeared from the concert hall: what was particularly moving was the part of the piece when we in the cello section had an extremely marked bass line. It felt as if I found myself in a large, dark, fantastic fairy-tale forest. The experience was so powerful that I really was devoured by the music but nevertheless managed to stay sufficiently concentrated on my cello playing.

At the beginning of the next long and almost poetically written account of images there is a suggestion of a link between what had recently happened to the listener and which images she then saw during the changing course of the music. It should be noted that she wrote down her impressions directly after the experience.

(10.2F) Woman, old, 1950s

This event took place in the spring. I was still in education and the boy I was so passionately in love with had got engaged to another girl. I'd read in the newspaper that they were going to play [on the radio] *Rite of Spring* by Stravinsky. I'd never heard that music before, but thought that the title [the Swedish title of the work is *Spring Sacrifice*] suited me and my situation.

When the magical moment arrived, I lit a candle and lay down in a comfortable position to listen. Closed my eyes. It was such a fantastic experience, was so strong and created such intense images within me that when it was all over I just had to write it down. I enclose a copy of exactly what I wrote then, when I was 21 or 22 years old.

Already on hearing the first strains, the immediate present is erased. I see colours and images: 'I find myself walking in a giant garden. Strange birds flew between fairy-tale trees full of flowers in the colours of the rainbow. Beautiful large butterflies fluttered slowly above fountains with deep blue water. The sun played in thin threads of spider webs. The high grass waved dreamlike in the breeze of early summer. The entire garden seemed to be enveloped in music—where the tones neatly formed my thoughts into stars and hung them up in the enormous trees. The whole space was filled with music like a celebration, and your picture was there in every note. A second of blinding white obliteration. Breathless, I stood still—afraid to disturb for a single moment this which seemed to be infinitely undestroyed.

But then all of a sudden an ice-cold wind blows through my garden. The sky darkened and with a scornful grimace reality broke over me. The notes of space were ripped into a thousand pieces and thrown up into the air. The flowers were trampled into the quaking ground. The birds hid in terror in their nests. The water in the fountains stopped playing. The spiders' webs fell to bits. All except one. The web of hope—the strongest of them all—challenged the reality it didn't believe in. Persevere, persevere, it sang . . .

Through hope, I was brought to the land of loneliness. A land with high mountains dripping with anguish. With horrific intertwined trees of despair. The ground was loose and muddy, with each step it wanted to pull me downwards. Towards the empty nothingness.

But hope showed me a path to firm ground—but that path split into two. Which one should I choose? Which would lead to the reality of the dream? The shells on the ground whispered to my naked foot. What did they whisper? Far away I caught a glimpse of a figure shrouded in veils of dew and the half light of dawn. I called out—but my mouth was dumb.

I stretched out my hands to touch it, but it slipped away on the notes and wasn't dazzled by the light of my eyes . . .

Here it all became a complete confusion of notes and thoughts, and visual images disappeared but I still lay there and continued to listen . . . suddenly I saw myself knocked to the ground. Round about me, beside the flames of fires, misfortune and all the siblings of loneliness sharpened their poison arrows. They joined forces and started a grotesque dance. I closed my eyes and thought: Now it is over. The hope that had followed me all the way was now hardly discernible on its thread.

Then, far away, I heard somebody coming. I stretched out my hands and tried to keep hope there—but she flared up and was out of sight. I screamed when I saw the knives being raised and then they were slowly stabbed into my heart and, bleeding, it ran out into white sand, my certainty about the difficulty of loving without being loved in return . . .'

Thus can dream and reality and music be mixed with each other to a cascade of colour and emotional images.

Her images were certainly linked to her feelings about the stranded passion. The music is interpreted in a way that corresponded with her own situation, rather than with the 'programme' in Stravinsky's *Rite of Spring* (but the final sacrifice is, however, included). Music generally offers many interpretations, and in her situation these images were of course completely adequate, genuine.

10.3　IMAGES OF A RELIGIOUS CHARACTER

The images in the next two accounts have an obvious connection to notions and experiences of a religious character.

(10.3A)　Woman, middle-aged, 1980s

We went to church on Christmas Eve to listen to Christmas music and sing along with the hymns. Now we were sitting in the church pew together with lots of others. Candles were lit. The motet choir was singing and we were going to listen to some soloists, including a music student, Erik Lindman, who was going to perform an improvisation with his singing voice. The singing came from the balcony.

I felt that Erik Lindman's song took me along to Bethlehem, to the stable 2,000 years ago, yet at the same time I experienced everything in the here and now. Soon, the Prince of Peace would arrive. It was so still. The animals chewed calmly on their hay. What stillness. Peace and calm were with me too.

His voice gives me a presentiment of trouble and evil, paralleling this peace. How can there be so much misery, destruction, envy, injustice, and abuse of other people? I am not to be allowed to be left untouched with my peace and harmony, it is disturbed in some way and yet I still have it at the same time. The child has come. What am I disturbed by? Don't the people around me understand that this is deadly serious? They sometimes even sound as if they are about to laugh.

When the singing improvisation is over, I cry silently. I cry over what once has been, and what is now. Nothing has really changed. The experience was very strong. It felt as if I had been present at a very hard job: giving birth and at the same time feeling joy, worry, and anguish.

The singing gave rise to an image of peace and calm but something in it also led to contradictory thoughts and emotions. She finds herself in the peace in Bethlehem—back then, long ago—but is here too, right now, with her worrying thoughts and people around her who don't understand. The image from then collides with the reality now.

The final account is long and full of images. It arose from an organ piece which the narrator was hearing for the first time. The impressions were so vivid and strong that she spoke of them to some people close to her, and wrote them down a couple of days later.

(10.3B) Woman, middle-aged, 1980s

I had my greatest experience with music in the cathedral in Uppsala. I was listening to Work for Organ in E-flat major Op. 8 by Swante Edlund (born 1946). The movements were: Introduction, Fugue, and Finale. Organ music always creates images and moods in me. I remember how I have waded in music with a feeling of lukewarm water around me. I have followed the strains of a flute up a high mountain. I have travelled in enormously high carriages. But this time, I had a long continuous fantasy experience of an unusual type. I felt tears of emotion and joy when the music came to an end. Directly afterwards, I told my husband about the experience to help me remember. A good friend also got to hear it. Two days later, I wrote down the experience. It was the first time I heard this music and I haven't heard it again.

A daydream to music:

'The music started forcefully. I see the Earth breaking up before me and a deep ravine opens up. Some planks are laid across as a footbridge. But I don't think I dare cross over, afraid of heights as I am.

Then angels come from the other side and stand along both sides of the makeshift bridge. They turn their backs on the chasm. Now I walk across. I am aware that several people cross over but I don't look at their faces; rather, I am alone with my experience, although it is shared.

I am now walking on a winding path ascending a steep mountain. The path is only a narrow mountain shelf, but angels stand at the most dangerous spots as protection against the chasm. The music leads me up and up. The path climbs in a spiral round the fairly small mountain peak. I wonder what will be at the very top.

Up there, a beautiful wooden terrace has been built. It covers the whole of the top of the mountain, is square, perhaps 125 square metres altogether. There are many decorative details in the woodwork, it is painted white, with railings in a pale-green colour. A roof in the form of a cupola is supported on corner posts.

Now I walk up to the railings and look down. I am so high up that it feels as if you are looking down out of the window of an aeroplane. Large, silver-coloured birds fly through the air. They come and sit on the railings. Now it feels completely right to get onto the back of a bird like a Nils Holgersson [a boy who flies over Sweden on the necks of wild geese in a well-known book by Selma Lagerlöf]. Now the bird is landing. The Earth approaches. We are above a forest, and the bird lands in a treetop.

I sit there at the top of a tree, as high as the spires of the cathedral in Uppsala. The heart-shaped leaves of the tree are of gold and silver. The tree trunk is a deep violet and around it is a slide made of silver which conveniently takes me down from the tree. Now I am no longer afraid of heights. I am certain that the tree has large juicy lilac-coloured fruits without pips, but I don't have time to eat any.

Once down on the ground, I find myself in a meadow with thick, very thick, soft, short grass. The grass is white. A man in a red cape is standing in the middle of the meadow. A lot of people are there. Beautiful roe deer come up and start to dance around the man in the red cape. I just stand at the edge of the meadow and watch. The middle of the meadow, where the man and the roe deer are, starts to rise up like a top, but I feel that I can't follow along there.

Instead, I see the altar in the church in Åmål before me. It is vivid and real with its many long steps up to the heavenly gates and all the purple clouds round about. It feels completely natural to go onto the altar and start to climb the steps. The music makes my steps easy, and almost dancing, up and up. I feel expectant as to what is going to happen at the very top.

Out of the gates, a man comes to meet me. He is dressed in a grey suit with a waistcoat. He looks pleased. It is my own papa.'

The music stops just then. The climax has been reached. The dream brought to completion. Tears well up behind my eyelids. I sit there enchanted. Happy. A rich experience has been granted me.

In this account, a number of religious motifs are touched upon: catastrophe, the Earth splitting open, threatening chasm; guardian angels during a risk-filled journey; pastoral/paradise-like idyll with silver birds, beautiful dancing roe deer, man in a red mantle; climbing long steps up to the heavenly gates and the meeting with papa/the Father. Similar images—a staircase leading up to heaven, a meadow with 'flowers so beautiful that I have never seen their like', a sort of aura around the flowers—appear in the chapter of religious experiences (see Chapter 14, account 14.2).

10.4 COMMENTARY

In our material as a whole, it is not particularly common to come across accounts that include inner images of some sort; they are mentioned by about 10% of the narrators. In general, there seems to be considerable variation between people as regards the tendency to experience images/notions to music. Some experience this often and completely naturally, and can sometimes almost seem to have a need to 'translate' music into images. Others can experience images now and then; and for yet others, images to music are something that is very unusual, even alien.

In this context, one can mention that a familiar method of music therapy, Guided imagery with music (GIM), developed by Helen Bonny, builds upon the description and interpretation of the images that come to mind to a client when he/she, in a state of relaxation, listens to specially selected music.[1]

Many participants make deliberate use of images/metaphors or similes in their accounts. But then it is not a question of directly experienced images as in this chapter, but rather images/similes that one takes from somewhere else to try to describe the experience: 'It was as if . . .' Such images and similes are dealt with in Chapter 28.

CHAPTER 11

FEELINGS/EMOTION

MUSIC is to a great extent associated with emotions. The accounts in our material, too, leave no doubt that such is the case. It is a question of both 'simple', fundamental emotions like happiness, sorrow, anger, and fear, and more 'complex' and modulated emotions, such as security, reverence, gratitude, feelings of magnificence, tension, and many others. The narrators also point to emotions for which one doesn't have a language—the words do not suffice to describe what one 'really' experiences, the feeling is indescribable and can only be understood in the direct encounter with the music. One interviewee expressed it thus: 'Music has the ability to go beyond my intellect and my verbal ability, it is about something completely different . . . It includes things that verbally I can but touch upon.' Similar statements have been made by many philosophers, musicians, and theorists of music from antiquity to the present day.

Nevertheless, a common way to try to describe the character of the experience is to make use of images or similes, that is, the experience is compared with, or likened to, other phenomena. Many participants have done that, and there is a list of their suggestions in Chapter 28. But, ultimately, one cannot escape the fact that music—just like every other art form—has some inherent, unique qualities that will not allow themselves to be moved over to some other medium, but are only evident in the encounter itself with the music.

With all these reservations in mind, we have nevertheless attempted to collect and categorize the emotional reactions that are described in the accounts. This analysis has resulted in a division into four groups:

a) Strong, intense feelings in general

b) positive feelings

c) negative feelings

d) mixed, contradictory, changed feelings.

11.1 Strong, intense feelings

Many narrators generally say that music aroused strong feelings in them. 'It was an enormous emotional experience', 'Great and majestic feelings', 'My feelings overflowed everywhere', and similar expressions. Usually they don't mention a particular feeling, but rather it is the intensity of the feeling that is emphasized. Here are three examples from different parts of the twentieth century, and with music from different genres.

(11.1A) Man, middle-aged, 1980s

While we were on an Inter-rail holiday and were in Ireland we bought tickets to a concert starring rock group Thin Lizzy. I was pretty high even before the concert started. It is fairly rare for me to sit and listen to a concert without taking part in it, emotionally I mean.

What I remember is that I sang very loudly and as well as I could, these songs that I knew well, danced all over the place with an Irish guy, and the next moment was rolling around in the high grass. The guitar playing was what mostly got me to fly in the air. All my emotions and bodily movements followed the rhythm of the music exactly. They were overwhelming waves of feelings that simply poured out as a reaction to the music, and my body just followed along. I was absolutely unable to control the eruption of emotions. That's what it felt like, so *absolute* and so *impossible* to do anything about it.

That eruption of emotions found its outer expression in singing and wild dancing. In the next account, it shows itself in the form of tears.

(11.1B) Woman, old, 1930s

My very greatest experience in the world of music came the year we had married and had bought our first wireless. I remember how I would try to tune into different wavelengths virtually every evening in the hope of getting music from other countries. One evening I tuned into music that really delighted me, it intoxicated me, I just wanted to cry. Quite a long time passed before I got to know what this wonderful piece of music was called. It was Smetana's *Moldau*, you could hear it now and then on the radio and it always moved me in the same way, which never stopped. I was ashamed that I found it so hard to control myself, but the emotions were so strong.

Then I had a birthday that I'll never forget. My husband is up and busy doing something—I wake up—and what do I hear and where is the music coming from? It is the strains of *Moldau*, my emotions overflow and the tears run down my cheeks while I snuggle down and hide myself under the covers. My dear husband knew how obsessed I was by this piece, so he had bought a gramophone and the record with *Moldau*, which he had hidden in a wardrobe, and that's where the music was coming from.

In the next example, the strong feelings are expressed in shared singing together with a charismatic musician. In the background there is a politically charged situation.

(11.1C) Woman, middle-aged, 1970s

We were listening to Theodorakis performing his own music in Stockholm. It was at the time of the Greek junta and his music was forbidden in Greece. One of the women singers had become ill, so Theodorakis himself sang, which alone was a very strong experience, because he is a very intense music maker and he sings with body and soul.

After the ordinary concert programme, the Greeks in the auditorium stood up and sang together with the orchestra and Theodorakis, they sang his songs for about an hour. They went on and on singing, and didn't want to stop. It felt as if they were singing all their long-ing for Greece, about how they were missing their loved ones in Greece. An emotional charge that was making them and us ready to explode. It was an experience that became more and more intense, almost becoming unbearable, and the memory has not faded after 20 years.

11.2 POSITIVE FEELINGS

Positive feelings are, as expected, the dominating group; some sort of positive feelings are described by more than 70% of the participants. The feelings most often men-tioned are happiness and joy, then come enjoyment, pleasure, delight, and beauty. These are all so close to each other in meaning that they are often mentioned together in various combinations.

Then come two groups of feelings that can be seen as each other's opposite. One of the groups comprises feelings such as calmness, serenity, stillness, harmony, security/consolation, and warmth, that is, feelings with a low level of activation. The other group comprises feelings with high activation such as elation, agitation, excitement, enthusiasm, euphoria, intoxication, dizziness, and rapture.

Other feelings mentioned are: satisfaction, contentment, gratitude, perfection, love, feeling of magnificence, pride, solemnity, wonder, humility, reverence, respect, admiration, patriotism, and feelings about sex.

There is thus a wide spectrum of positive feelings. The accounts in this chapter represent a limited selection from this manifold array.

First, a couple of accounts of joy. Not the unbounded, gushing, and openly expressed joy that is described so often otherwise, but a quiet inner joy in unpretentious contexts.

(11.2A) Woman, old, 1960s (from an edited interview)

This took place when I was at 'Music for the family' as it was called, at a community college. They have a week for the whole family. It was beautiful weather, it was pleasant, we made music and the children could join in as much as they wanted and had the energy for. We practised playing together, strings and flutes. Then we had this little orchestra which sat and played in a classroom.

We played Handel's 'Water Music', arranged simply for beginner music makers. We weren't playing because it was going to be performed in some special way, rather we played for each other, mainly to experience the music. There isn't much more to say than that I have a memory of being filled with such a strong feeling of joy. I thought: to think that you can be so happy from such simple little music! To think that music is like this! That I can join in and make music and can listen and my children can listen. We were a group who experienced the same thing in such an incredibly simple context. I felt totally in tune with what we were doing, and with life in general, with my children, and with people that I had just got to know, with the summer, with the light. I had a strong feeling that the others were just as happy as I was.

I have felt similar things, of course, later when I was working with a youth choir, and so on. I know that it isn't perfect and that it can't be compared with the big achievements. But I thought it was an experience, that you could feel so happy with a little flute in your hand and a little simple piece of music and an ordinary human environment.

Similar feelings and reflections on the joy of little events in everyday life are to be found in the next account. The encounter with music is likened to a meeting with a dear friend.

(11.2B) Woman, middle-aged, 1980s

This event took place in Canada. One Sunday morning I'd got up and brewed coffee and had just snuggled down into bed again to enjoy it. I was listening to my favourite radio station, CBC. At the time I was studying very intensely, I felt a bit tired and overworked. I did feel a certain contentedness, nevertheless, because I had a free day to enjoy.

Then a tune was played which filled my heart with an incredible warmth and joy. It was a tango that was played on a guitar. I experienced it as 'unpredictable' and 'mischievous', restrained but also beautiful, happy, and wild. It was gentle at the same time as being rhythmic and having lots of nuances. The feeling I got was like when you meet a dear friend whom you haven't seen for a long time; you look carefully at each other, your eyes light up, you hug each other, and your hearts are filled with a feeling of togetherness and secret joy. There's also that lovely smell of skin and the sensation of soft hairs on their neck that tickle your nose.

I grabbed pen and paper to note down the name of the tune. 'Charlie Bird on guitar, a tango', I wrote. A month or so later, I visited Vancouver. My joy was unbelievable when, in a record shop, I found a cassette tape with Charlie Bird and Laurindo Almeido called *Tango*. When I turned the package over, I saw that this was it: '*Tanguero*'. What a feeling! The road from Vancouver home took about five hours to drive and during that time I could play this tape many times.

This tango blew new life into me! It lifted me out of a state that I'd been in for a while. Had been feeling melancholic and worn out, although without being depressed. The music strengthened, in a way that can't be explained, my understanding that joy is the little events in life if only you allow yourself time to notice them by making use of all your senses.

Since moving back to Sweden I've heard '*Tanguero*' on the radio at home only once. It felt like meeting somebody in secret—indescribable and lovely.

A quiet happiness and joy go often hand in hand with feelings of serenity, calm, and harmony, as in the following accounts.

(11.2C) Woman, young, 1980s

I usually leave the radio on at low volume at night. One night I woke up to the shrieking of seagulls. In the background you could hear the gentle lapping of waves and a weak, calm melody. The shrieking of the gulls was played on an electric guitar. Soon it merged with the melody. Several tones were added and the melody became more intense. At about the middle of the tune it exploded and what had been calm and cosy now became dramatic yet still calming. Now I was wide awake and an incredible calmness descended on me. A feeling of joy that I didn't think was possible for a piece of music overwhelmed me.

The next day, I phoned the information desk at Swedish Radio. In the list of music that had been played, they could read that it had come from Micke Andersson's LP *Efter elden* [*After the fire*].

But I haven't dared look for it. The fear that it won't make the same impression on me now as then has prevented me.

(11.2D) Man, 1980s

My strongest experience with music. Yes, that's the heading I want to use for my experience of the recording of *Missa Criolla* in a TV broadcast. What I could hear was a fantastic performance which moved me incredibly. During the entire recording, I just sat there and enjoyed the extremely good performance of both the soloist and the choir, as well as the various orchestral instruments. After the programme I sat quietly for a long time and felt a great serenity within me that I've never experienced before.

(11.2E) Woman, middle-aged, 1980s

A few years ago I saw the opera *A Masked Ball*. Erik Saedén played the role of Count Holberg. In Act II, Holberg sings a very beautiful aria about his love for his wife. Although I had heard this many times, I was so moved by it that I started to cry and I had to go out in the middle of the performance.

After such an experience I feel very calm, almost resting on a cloud of calmness and harmony, and most of all want to be alone and to enjoy the aftertaste of the experience without talking it to bits.

Of course, the situation and surroundings also play a major role for such experiences.

(11.2F) Woman, old, 1980s

I was on an art trip to Florence. The highlight of the trip was a visit to the Piazzale Michelangelo. The view over Florence in blue mist. The Arno glittering with silver. The wind soft as velvet. And the visit to San Mineate al Monte. The sensation which filled me when I saw the beauty of the cathedral and the atmosphere and I heard the sound of the organ, sometimes gentle and sometimes majestic like a divine waterfall: Bach! What I experienced then, I shall always retain it like a jewel in my box of memories! I felt a total serenity.

The church setting is in itself often associated with quiet, serenity, and reflection. Music can further strengthen this.

(11.2G) Woman, old, 1980s

I was showing the church of my childhood to a friend. We were lucky in that the cantor was practising just then in preparation for an event, and we wondered if we could hear a little sample. The cantor, who is a good friend, promised to play if I would agree to relax. Music came—I don't know what—but I sank down into the most wonderful quiet, lovely condition—I thought mainly about my parents, their life, and what they had thought on their visits to the church. The tears gradually blotted out my surroundings, what serenity. So lovely!

I have always visited churches when we travel around. Is there something that pulls me to them? Radiation—force fields!? Psychotherapy, I'd call it. The setting is better than valium.

(11.2H) Man, young, 1980s (from Chapter 19, account 19.4D)

[At a choir concert in church] . . . I experienced a stillness beyond compare. Time had stopped and everything else felt of no consequence. Worries, plans for the future, dreams were somewhere far away. What was important was to be there in the here and now and the stillness that at the same time felt eternal. Several seconds after the final notes had faded away and been caught by the cold stone wall, stillness was alive. No one in the audience could even think of turning around or scratching an itch. The serenity that I felt then I have occasionally also been able to feel for a few moments in other contexts. It is something you carry with you once you've first touched it.

From these serene feelings, we switch abruptly to the exact opposite, with feelings such as euphoria, agitation, enthusiasm, and rapture. First, a very special example with a connection to a dramatic and decisive event in twentieth-century history.

(11.2I) Man, old, 1945

The year is 1945. It is night-time and I am lying there listening to a foreign radio station which broadcasts only music. Listening on short wave with reception reports for the stations was starting to be a sport. Home-made radio receivers were common.

The station that I'd tuned into was playing 'Ciribiribin'. Suddenly the sound is muffled and an announcer says 'Hitler ist tot.' After a short pause the announcer literally shouts out for joy: 'Hitler ist tot' several times. After yet another short pause, he gathers together what is left of his senses and reads a short announcement about what has happened. This is the strongest experience with music that I have had. Hitler's death and 'Ciribiribin' together after 45 years. Stuck together as if they had been glued. Which other experience of music has such vitality?

I was so relaxed, almost half asleep at that late hour, it was 01.30, and then to get such joyful news. We listened all the time to the coded broadcasts of the Norwegian Resistance. We were there in spirit with the Resistance. Gave refugees sanctuary, and later they returned to continue the struggle. Very shaken, I woke up two other short-wave listeners I knew and told them about the news. This is 'Ciribiribin' for me.

This is also an instructive example of how a particular piece of music by pure chance comes to be associated with a particular event and the emotions caused by it. In the following accounts, however, it is a question of feelings triggered in typical musical situations.

(11.2J) Woman, old, 1960s

We were a large group who travelled to Vienna and Salzburg to enjoy the spring and good music. Our guide had already told us that he had unfortunately not been able to get hold of any tickets for Herbert von Karajan's production of Bizet's *Carmen* and that made us all disappointed. But one morning he came to the hotel room and said that he had got a few tickets to one of the rehearsals at 11 o'clock. We hurried to the opera in Salzburg, where we were. The audience were smartly dressed and there was an expectant murmur. It felt so unusual to be at the opera so early in the day, but it was exciting.

Then von Karajan went up onto the conductor's stand, dressed in a white polo jumper and black trousers. You could have heard a pin drop. Then he raised his baton and beat in the overture to *Carmen*. I was in such raptures that I think I almost had a heart attack when the music flared up, and my mother is said to have muttered to herself: 'Now she's dying!' And that's what I almost did. It was an enchanting musical experience! Carmen was played by a black actress by the name of Grace Bumbry and she was temperamental and brilliant. In the ensemble scenes, an enormous dance group from South America danced, and, of course, I have never seen or heard anything like it.

(11.2K) Woman, middle-aged, 1980s (from Chapter 25, account 25.2J)

[During a concert with two singers] After Pergolesi's Stabat Mater, the audience broke into wild cheering and after a while I discovered that I had got up and stood there calling out, with the palms of my hands burning hot. I don't know what I called out, it might not have been more than 'Bravo!' but I do still remember the sensation of not really being able to control my voice. It was as if only half was my real voice, and the rest was emotion.

The duet from Bellini's *Norma* came as an encore, and now I hardly knew what to do with all the excitement I felt. They gave us a coloratura bravura which was stunning. It was like going to the circus and I remember the feeling that 'this isn't true, I'm dreaming, you just can't do this'. I had the same butterflies in my tummy as when I'm waiting at the dentist's, a tension that makes you almost lose your breath. What was fascinating was that despite the breakneck singing tricks, the singers conveyed great sensitivity and insight. I know that I found it hard to get back to reality afterwards, and that I sort of bounced along all the way home.

(11.2L) Woman, middle-aged, 1980s

This concert is the most special experience with music I have had. I had heard of Gunnar Idenstam and was all keyed-up to hear him improvise, hopefully. Towards the end of the concert, it came, what I had been waiting for, the improvisation, I've no idea upon what, the reviewer the next day said that for example a theme from one of Bach's Brandenburg concertos had sneaked past, but that wasn't anything I noticed.

I was totally taken by surprise by all this fascinating sound that streamed towards me. How could he possibly manage to do it? I had never heard the like. The darkness and heat embraced me and I found myself in a vacuum where there was only me present together with these strains that were sent out from the concert grand piano by this miracle of a musician. I was in raptures, bewitched and totally absorbed by this phenomenon. A heavy, joyful warmth that was intoxicating spread right through my body. I should think that I wasn't contactable at that moment.

Afterwards I can only find one explanation for this experience, namely that I fell in love. Not with the person, but with his music, which in turn was very tangibly, in effect, a person in the moments when it was about improvisation.

(11.2M) Woman, young, 1990s

I stand there listening to and looking at Joakim Thåström, the rock singer. It is the 'new' Thåström who doesn't work with punk but with another type of music that I find difficult to classify. I'm standing there feeling completely indifferent and thinking that yes, well, here is Thåström . . . ha, ha, yes, yes. But then suddenly I wake up as the concert ends and the entire audience wants him to come back and play some more.

That's when it happens. He does two old punk tunes as encores. From having stood right at the back and thinking 'Won't it soon be over?' sort of, I don't know how it happens, but I find myself in the midst of the crush of people and jumping, and I am as incredibly bubbly happy as can be. At this particular moment I can do absolutely anything whatsoever. Grab the moon—no problem.

I sing along with the lyrics. I have never felt myself specially struck by them and don't now for that matter, but I sing automatically because I happen to remember them.

At just that moment, my world consists of all people and Thåström but above all of the music. I am completely gone, but still completely inside it. I don't know where my mates are and I'm not worried about getting squashed by the mass of people, it is only when I lose my breath once that I wonder a little what I'm doing but I don't bother about it. This is perfect. I am happy, happy, happy! Elated! I lose all my inhibitions and there is only me in my world, with lots of punk music.

In such euphoric states, one can feel omnipotent: 'At this particular moment I can do absolutely anything whatsoever. Grab the moon—no problem.' As a musician, one can experience similar feelings of complete control, power and perfection when everything goes as it should. Here are a couple of introductory examples of this.

(11.2N) Woman, middle-aged, 1980s

My strongest experience of music so far was when I took my cantor's exam in the cathedral in Uppsala. I had then been taking organ lessons for three years and discovered that the church organ is the most fantastic instrument you can play! Before the exam I had prepared Edward Elgar's *Carillon*, a piece where you hear church bells ringing with varying intensity in the organ manuals. During the course, the students were meant to take part in an evening concert in the cathedral and some of us played our exam pieces. I was one of the chosen ones.

Now came the big moment when my practising in secret would reward itself and I could show what I could do on an organ that is wonderful to play on and has stops that can do justice to this piece. It felt overwhelming to be able to fill the whole church, every corner and every ear with tones, let the music gush out to a big crescendo. 'Now we're flying,' said one of the people who was helping me with the registration before I started to play and it felt like an airplane flight.

(11.2O) Man, young, 1980s (from an edited interview)

[He is taking part in a performance of modern classical music in a church, with many musicians and a large choir.] It was so magnificent. So great. Just the feeling that you're involved in creating something that is really magnificent, which is bloody big . . . then you're happy! There were about 13 minutes' reverberation in the church, I mean, that was *Wow!* And it gave you that feeling of power, sort of. You felt like the Hulk! It was a great feeling. You felt like a part of the cosmos.

It was really cool! A hell of a kick! When you experience this you think that synths with choir and strings aren't so great really. It's a bit special with classical music, there's that feeling of magnificence. That big feeling. Take Stravinsky's *Rite of Spring*, for example . . . that's hard-rock without electricity! So bloody big and powerful. There's such energy in it.

It is worth noting that both these experiences take place in large churches with a long reverberation (although 13 minutes is something of an exaggeration . . .). The acoustics play an important role. The feeling of being able to fill the enormous space with sound/music and that the walls 'answer'—give feedback to—one's own playing can easily give an intoxicating feeling of being all-powerful; it feels as if one can achieve anything whatsoever (I know this from my own experience . . .). Similar examples of this in other contexts are to be found in Chapter 18.

An experience of perfection can also be glimpsed in the previous accounts. Here are a couple of other examples of experiences of perfection.

(11.2P) Woman, 1980s

I have had many strong experiences with music, but the highest point might be said to have come when I was able to attend a performance of *Aida* in the arena in Verona. It wasn't only the suggestive setting, the warm night soft as velvet, and all the 10,000 people who had gathered on the antique steps, and all the candles that were suddenly lit when the performance was to begin. The audience were able to buy candles which they lit at a certain moment and which then lit up and shimmered like a starry sky in the entire arena.

The whole of the performance was just one long delight, it was so perfect that it wouldn't be possible to make it more perfect. The trumpeters stood in different groups on the steps and responded to each other during the triumphal march, and when the dancers came in wave after wave . . . and horses and donkeys were there too on the enormous stage.

The performance started at 21.30 and was over sometime before 2 o'clock in the morning. It's something that everybody should see.

(11.2Q) Man, middle-aged, 1990s (from Chapter 25, account 25.1L)

[A concert with a Finnish children's choir, the Tapiola Choir] They started the concert with an English madrigal for five voices. They sang that difficult choral piece as easy as anything . . . It was as clear as a bell! The phrasing was wonderful, every phrase was alive. Every note was tenderly cared for. I think it was the first time I have heard a perfect performance of an English madrigal . . . During the 60 minutes the concert lasted, the children's choir managed to sing in eight different languages and in every imaginable style, from Palestrina to Morthenson. All of it as clear as a bell! The intonation was perfect! The phrasing was wonderful! Never before have I experienced anything like it. The music was music. That it was a children's choir that was singing, I didn't think about that at all. I just experienced the music, it was everywhere . . . everything was perfect music! No striving for effects, all they did on stage was to convey the self-evident message of the music . . . It was as if the music had always been there and that it always would be there.

Of course, the experience of beauty is a component of many accounts, often together with expressions for perfection. This can be exemplified with only a few short excerpts.

(11.2R) Man, old, 1980s (from Chapter 25, account 25.2L)

Brahms's *Ein deutsches Requiem* was on the programme . . . Out came Barbara Hendricks, a little, dainty, dark-skinned creature . . . Then came the first tones, and everything became like it was enchanted. Immediately, all comparisons regarding beauty of tone just evaporated . . . now Barbara Hendricks's singing is the most beautiful I experience of music in all categories . . . I feel something of the blessedness of musicians when she sings!

(11.2S) Woman, middle-aged, 1980s (from Chapter 12, account 12.3E)

[While listening to Mozart's *Requiem*] The whole room, the whole universe is present here in perfect harmony . . . I seem to be experiencing directly and have no words to capture this state (not feeling) of bliss, harmony, meaningless beauty. I am totally a part of it all . . . The whole world (there is no world) is dancing before my eyes—I am calm, tears run down my cheeks, I have no idea why . . . That pure existence and nothing else could be so beautiful! Satisfaction. Ecstasy.

There are many similar examples in other accounts in various places in this book. In general, the accounts in this section represent only a small selection of the large number of positive feelings. A systematic compilation of all the positive feelings mentioned is to be found in Chapter 29, section 29.5.2.

11.3 NEGATIVE FEELINGS

Not all feelings in connection with strong experiences with music are positive; there are also many examples of negative feelings. As we shall see, however, some of them are not particularly serious, and often they are not brought about by the music either, but by other conditions and factors.

The most often mentioned negative feelings are tiredness, exhaustion, and 'emptiness', above all in the final phase of the experience. For listeners, the impressions of the music can be so overwhelming that, afterwards, they can feel completely drained and need time to recover. Musicians who have put their soul into their performance are totally exhausted afterwards. But for listeners as well as performers, the tiredness is often a natural consequence of the strong commitment, and they are tired and happy at the same time.

Other feelings mentioned fairly often are sorrow, depression, sadness, and melancholia, and (to a somewhat lesser degree) worry, nervousness, and confusion. Yet it is often not the music that is the primary cause, but other circumstances. The music can give rise to sorrow because it is associated with a negative event, for example a broken romance, an accident, illness, or death. The examples of nervousness are above all associated with music makers who are worried about a forthcoming performance. Worry or nervousness can also occur in listeners, for example if one is afraid that one's expectations of the music or the performance won't be fulfilled. For the same reasons, one perhaps might not dare listen again to music that has provided a strong experience—one doesn't wish to jeopardize the original experience.

Other negative experiences are longing/regret, embarrassment/shame, jealousy/envy, and feelings of loneliness/abandonment. It is often a question of fairly mild varieties of these feelings, and they are usually caused by different circumstances in the particular situation—one feels longing for a situation or person previously associated with the music; one is embarrassed about not being able to hide one's strong feelings from those around one; one feels jealousy because the music is associated with earlier romantic rivalry, and so on.

Stronger negative feelings are disappointment/frustration, discomfort, fear, anguish, pain, despair, anger, hatred, horror, and panic. Fortunately, these occur in only a few cases, and even then they are also mainly dependent upon circumstances other than the music.

The accounts in the following section are divided into two groups. In the first group are examples of how negative feelings are triggered by various non-musical circumstances, while the accounts in the second group illustrate negative feelings triggered by the music itself.

11.3.1 Negative experiences due to other circumstances

First, some short accounts that show how the music has come to be associated with something unpleasant, and thereby led to a negative reaction.

(11.3A) Woman, middle-aged (written in English)

My emotional reactions can last for years. I prefer not to hear Beethoven's third symphony because I heard this music which was used as background music in a film about circulation of blood. Now this music makes me feel bad.

(11.3B) Woman, young, 2000–10

I recently had an experience with music that conveyed feelings of discomfort above all caused by associations. I was sitting in the car and having a sleep when I woke to an organ piece by Philip Glass on the radio and was suddenly affected by strong feelings of discomfort because the mood in this piece and its form directly coincided with the form and the atmosphere in a recurring nightmare that I had as a little child more than 20 years ago. It was a very strange sensation to re-experience the exact same feeling, albeit in a milder version. Evidently this feeling was caused by my own associations because the man who was driving the car didn't feel anything similar, but really appreciated the music!

(11.3C) Woman, middle-aged, 1990s

The sun was shining and it was hot. Lots of people out walking, eating or listening to music in the park. I sat and listened to an Australian guy who was very clever on the didgeridoo. The instrument's warm, suggestive, and rumbling tones swept across the lawn. I shut my eyes and enjoyed it, and for a moment I was on the other side of the globe.

After the last piece, something very strange happened. The final note. Applause. And then it became completely silent! The birds stopped singing and within two minutes there was a full storm in the area! The rain beat down on the lawns and the paths, food tents floated away, mothers ran off with their screaming children in search of shelter. There was enormous chaos! I myself became very scared and made my way indoors. My pulse was extremely high and I was breathing heavily. The weird thing was that the last piece he played on the didgeridoo was about calling forth the Gods of Weather! Many others besides me were very affected, and still to this day I feel a mixture of delight and horror when I hear the didgeridoo.

In the following example, it is presumably a question of interplay of certain qualities in the music and an uncomfortable situation.

(11.3D) Woman, middle-aged, 1950s

My family lived in a large and spacious house in the grounds of a hospital, which can seem very desolate when you are at home alone, which I was one evening in the dark season of the year. I probably wasn't doing anything in particular, perhaps I was reading with the wireless on, when suddenly without any warning the start of Stravinsky's *Rite of Spring* bursts out. I almost panicked, and it felt extremely uncomfortable, and I had to turn the wireless off.

In both of the following accounts, an association has come about between experiences of war and a well-known piece of music, *Finlandia* by Sibelius.

(11.3E) Woman, middle-aged, 1950s

Stockholm's Philharmonic Orchestra, conducted by Carl Garaguly, was playing *Finlandia* by Jean Sibelius. The then aged composer, who was visiting Sweden, sat on an armchair not far from the orchestra. This was the autumn of 1950.

I had extremely mixed feelings—not to mention that I was in a sort of chaos which wouldn't release its grip. The reason was that the announcer stated that the work portrayed Finland's varied nature and barren landscape, wind and storm and so on—and nothing else.

The first time I heard *Finlandia* was on the *Gramophone Hour* in the radio in 1940, while the war was raging. I was a child and was living with my grandmother in Sweden, separated from my parents and not knowing when I'd see them again. I was very frightened by the piece, because I immediately interpreted the trumpet blasts as machine guns, heard bomb explosions and so on. I felt anguish.

Both of these experiences of the same concert piece are still there and more or less keep me reminded. Regrettably, I can't listen to *Finlandia* with anything but mixed feelings— fright and great wonder. I won't say it is exactly pleasurable.

(11.3F) Woman, old, 1940s

The anguish and fear that the suggestive introduction of *Finlandia* still, after 50 years, gives me must have their origins in experiences from the Finnish Winter War of 1939. I grew up by the Västerbotten coast [in northern Sweden], and we were very committed to Finland's cause. We had friends in the hell at the battle front, and we always listened to Finnish radio. And the war reports were very often followed by *Finlandia*; for me it became linked with the horrors of war. So it wasn't on one particular occasion that this anguish arose, rather it grew up and became deeper during all the war years, and it sticks. I experience the same anguish when hearing these rising and falling tones as when I hear an ambulance, the terror comes then. I have never been in an accident where an ambulance was involved and which could be behind this feeling, it is the sound. This has definitely destroyed Sibelius for me; composers such as Mozart, Bach, and Carl Nielsen, I enjoy so much that words can't describe it, but not Sibelius.

Music that has come to be associated with a broken romance can bring forth strong negative reactions. In Chapter 20, concerning music in love—happy and unhappy— there are accounts of the sorrow, emptiness, loss, and pain that one feels when the music concerned stirs up the memory of the broken romance.

There are some accounts of strong negative reactions that stem from the intolerance or the lack of understanding of those around one. Here are two tragic examples.

(11.3G) Woman, old, 1940s

My experience of music is strongly negative, but I choose to write about it nevertheless, because it has constantly recurred during the course of my life. But I have never done anything constructive about it, ever. I have wondered about that sometimes: why I have allowed myself, and still allow myself, to be invaded by my mother's irritation when I sat there at the piano and practised and thought it was fun.

I loved 'An der schönen, blauen Donau' ['The Blue Danube'] and was happy when I could play it. I imagined learning to play other pieces when I got older and could handle the piano like Mother did.

Mother played classical music, nothing else was good enough. I thought that 'An der schönen, blauen Donau' belonged there. And I often sat at the piano when I had come home from school. One day Mother said to me in her sharp, strict voice, in rough tones: 'Be quiet, I can't stand it, stop tinkling on the piano!' I was so sad and angry that she didn't see how much fun it was for me that I stopped playing once and for all, and I still remember how I thought that I wouldn't care about anything to do with music in my life.

And that's how it is. I don't have any gramophone records at home, no stereo system, I never listen to music on the radio, never go to concerts. I become worried and afraid at the thought that I perhaps won't understand, and I am afraid that what I feel is wrong, afraid that my taste isn't good enough, that I am weird. There are a lot of things that I don't understand because I'm ignorant, quite simply. I can feel sad and bad about having missed grand experiences of music. But the choice was mine. That's how deeply I was affected that day I was seven years old.

Now, afterwards, I regret that I have allowed myself to be affected to such a degree that I won't permit myself to have a lot of what is first rate. About everything else in life, I think that it is never too late to start again, but when it comes to music it feels difficult. I haven't started, not yet!

(11.3H) Woman, young, 1980s

Together with a few older girls, my mate's big sister had started to play the piano, and when I saw them play I decided to start playing the piano too. But I was too little to start at the music school, so I had to have private lessons. I remember that I was proud that I would start to play the piano. When I had to practise at home I wasn't so interested and often was told I hadn't done it properly. At school I liked to show people what I knew and was proud to be able to say that I really did have private piano lessons!

Then I came to the point that would be the beginning of a turning point for my pleasure as regards playing the piano. I was in the school choir and we practised for an assembly of the whole school. My choir leader asked me if I wanted to play something that day. If I wanted! I was so happy about this. I could choose two tunes all by myself. On the way home that day, I was probably thinking how proudly I would go up to the piano on the day and play. Everybody would be at the assembly, all the pupils and all the staff. Besides, my very first love would also be there . . . The time up to the Day—with a capital D—was spent practising the piano and my two tunes. I had never practised so well with any homework before. When the day came, I knew my tunes off by heart.

So at last it was time. The choir was in place, my class was sitting in its place, and of course *he* was sitting there. My choir leader finally called upon me to come up and asked me to announce my two tunes myself. Proudly, with my very first, red, piano book under my arm, I say: 'Yes, I can. I shall play '*Önskevisan*' ['Wishing ballad'] and . . . (I can't remember the other tune). Then my choir leader says in a loud and very clear voice while looking down at me and at the same time looking embarrassedly at the audience: 'No, dear, weren't they . . .' and then says the name of two completely different tunes.

Just imagine the situation for this little (eight-year-old) girl. Here she has practised and practised like never before and is standing for the first time in her life in front of so many people who also include her first love. Then along comes a big and dreadful schoolmistress and says they are the wrong tunes that this girl has been practising, although this little girl could choose her tunes by herself!

I can't remember how quickly I answered her, but in the end I did say very quietly: 'Yes, those were the ones.' I didn't dare speak against her in front of all the people. With those words I walked up to the piano and opened the piano book with the music for the tune that she in front of all the audience had said I would play. After that, my memories are extremely fragmentary. I remember the image of the notes fairly well but most of all how I press key after key on the piano and not a note is right! I feel the panic rising, start sweating, tears and still not a note right! I remember that I ran home and my mother has told me that I was completely hysterical when I came home. I just cried and cried and my mother could do no more than try to calm me until I could tell her what had happened.

I can't remember any more. But that is enough for me, that day destroyed so much for me. To this day I get palpitations and break into a cold sweat when I get a note wrong. It doesn't matter if it's in front of close relatives or friends or completely unknown people, because, believe me, I have tried. I didn't stop playing the piano after this. Nor did I stop playing in front of the class. When I started in the music school, my piano teacher got me to play in shops, at lunchtime in restaurants, etc. But then she had to bribe me and

I remember that I was extremely afraid of playing wrong. I even get palpitations from writing this and the tears are welling up.

I have forgotten the name of one of the tunes I had practised, and whether that is connected with some sort of repression I don't know, but I do remember 'Önskevisan'. What I've never thought about until today is that I can't remember ever having played or even heard that tune since then. Nor do I know how I would react if I got to hear that tune or was forced to play it. What I do know is that on several occasions after that I put myself in the same situation—but this time playing the right tunes—and on all those occasions I got palpitations and started sweating if I thought I'd done anything the slightest bit wrong.

What I ask myself to this day is: What would it have mattered if I had played those two tunes I wanted to play? Why did she have to correct me, this little girl who was so proud of her piano playing, in front of all those people? I hope that I shall always remember this clearly, so that I can treat those children I meet in a far better and more respectful way.

These accounts can serve as a reminder for all of us who concern ourselves with music. Negative treatment can rapidly destroy the desire to play or sing. Many people, both children and adults, have, for example, been told that their singing voice is not good enough, that they can't be in the choir, that they can skip the music lessons—experiences that have not uncommonly caused severe traumas for a long time to come, just as in the accounts above and in the following one.

(11.3I) Woman, middle-aged

I was the only child of old parents in a home without music or singing. My father considered them an unnecessary luxury. My female schoolteacher regarded me as completely unmusical and I was told only to move my lips. Once every semester our singing would be graded, marked, you had to stand up and sing solo, everybody giggled. The result: music was my horror. I don't perform any music at all, don't even sing in the bathroom. My childhood experiences put a definitive stop to that.

11.3.2 Negative experiences ascribed to the music itself

The accounts in this section bear witness that the negative reaction must above all be ascribed to qualities in the music itself or in its performance. At the same time, it would also seem that other factors—in the person or the situation—contribute to the experience. As always, it is an interplay between music, the person, and the situation, in these cases with music as the foremost agent.

First, an example from childhood.

(11.3J) Woman, old, 1910s

I was born at the beginning of the twentieth century and at that time the operetta *The Merry Widow* was quite new. We sang and played theatre a lot in my childhood home. Every time the so-called 'Widows' waltz' was played, I was seized by a strong feeling of melancholia bordering on sorrow, and the tears started to run. At that time I was about six or seven years old. Later in life, I have often seen that operetta both here and abroad with the foremost opera artistes. I certainly haven't reacted like in my childhood but a little, little bit of melancholia nevertheless—perhaps the memory from the child's experience with the music.

Another example is the shocking experience of the five-year-old girl the first time she heard 'In a Persian market', a well-known piece of salon music—see Chapter 4, account 4.3E. In both these cases, nothing is explicitly said of what it is in the music that caused the negative feeling.

The following accounts concern experiences at an adult age and also, as a rule, contain reflections about what it was in the music that provoked the negative reactions. But apart from the music, there are also other circumstances to consider.

In the first case, 'devilish music' is said to be the reason for reacting in horror. The darkness in the auditorium and other factors may also have played a part.

(11.3K) Woman, middle-aged, 1980s

The strongest experience with music that I had was when I saw *The Phantom of the Opera* at a theatre in Stockholm. I was there together with colleagues from work. I can't remember what I felt like before, but I like going to the theatre, so I was certainly looking forward to it.

It was during the overture that I had my strongest experience. The auditorium was dark and when the music started I felt a sort of growing panic. I think I tried to hold onto something, perhaps the arm of the seat, or the seat itself, and I know that I looked around me to see if it was only me who felt this uneasiness about the music. My heart was racing and I was about to cry. Most of all I would have liked to have run off, away from all the blackness around me. I didn't experience the music as bad or badly played, but as very strong, dark—well, I don't know what words I should use but 'devilish' comes to mind. I remember that something hung from the ceiling, a crystal chandelier, that almost fell down onto the audience.

After the performance, I talked with the others about what I had felt, but none of them had had such a strong experience as I had. Then I still felt affected by what had happened. Perhaps I had built up a picture around the phantom and ghosts and together with the excitement of going to the theatre this made me especially susceptible for emotions. It was the first time I heard that particular music.

As soon as anyone mentions *Phantom of the Opera*, I think about the experience. If Andrew Lloyd Webber wanted to convey horror, then he has really succeeded with me.

In the next example, it is an individual element in the music, a certain chord, that sets off a reaction of horror.

(11.3L) Man, middle-aged, 1970s

It was an evening in the late summer. A few days earlier, my grandmother—who has meant a lot to me—had been buried. The sorrow and the longing were heavy to bear, even though she was more than 93 when she died.

We were sitting in the living room. Outside, there was the sound of the water lapping in the bay, and the big window was deep black. Mahler's tenth symphony was on the gramophone turntable. It was Rafael Kubelik conducting and I had hardly heard the piece before. The greatest part of this symphony is divine typical Mahler stuff. A super romantic (like early Schönberg) winding between different keys where the marked absence of beginning and end produces a somewhat hypnotic effect not unlike the feeling you experience when you lie in a boat moored by an island in the archipelago.

But then it happened. A chord so heart-rending and hair-raising, such as I'd never experienced before. A single sound (trumpet, if I remember rightly) which is then built up with a large number of other instruments from the orchestra, not unlike an enormous organ where you've pulled out all the stops at random, a dissonance which pierces right into the very marrow of your bones. My brother and I reacted in the same way: we were both filled with a horror so elementary and almost primeval that neither of us could utter a word. We both looked at the big black window next to us and we both seemed to see the face of Death himself staring in at us from outside. A face about two metres in diameter.

It was not until five years had passed that I dared to listen to the piece again. The very thought of this chord gives me the creeps and a sort of atavistic horror even to this day, many years later. Neither before nor afterwards have I felt anything like on that evening late in the summer many years ago. The only spiritual experience that I could possibly compare it with is the elemental fear I felt once when as a teenager I was present during an earthquake that lasted about 20 seconds.

The dissonant, heart-rending chord was what set off the reaction of horror. But it took place in a situation where other conditions worked in a negative direction: the narrator mourning and greatly missing his grandmother, the presence of death in the setting, and its staring face in the big black window.

A similar reaction of horror from hearing the same chord is described in another account of this Mahler symphony.

(11.3M) Woman, middle-aged, 1980s (from Chapter 25, account 25.1P)

Towards the end of the first movement, the entire orchestra gathers together in a large, dreadful organ-like sound—a scream of pain and horror. It came as a shock after a fairly drawn-out pianissimo bit. I was completely overwhelmed by the violence in this horror when facing death. I started sweating and could hardly breathe. For once, I thought, I had been knocked to the ground by something that was so great and so strong that it obliterated all the thoughts that can otherwise flutter past when you listen without giving your full concentration.

In both cases, the narrators make reference to death. Both, too, liken the dissonant chord to the sound from a loud organ ('where you've pulled out all the stops at random'). There is no organ in the orchestra, but the sound is built up successively by all the instruments in the large orchestra with close intervals, which, in combination with the loud volume, produces the horrifying dissonance.[1]

In some accounts, there are negative reactions to unknown and radically different music.

(11.3N) Woman, old, 1960s

This is about when I heard electronic music for the first time. I had heard about such music and was rather curious about it. Then I saw in the radio programme listings that they were going to have such music one evening. I can't remember what the pieces were called. I do, however, remember that the music made me feel very uneasy, and I was thinking of turning the radio off, but couldn't—I was going to listen to the end.

I can't say that I liked it, and afterwards I slept very uneasily and felt as if I had a temperature. And I did too—39.6! To calm myself, I boiled some milk and drank that, something that usually helps when I feel worried.

In the morning my temperature was back to normal, and I have no other explanation for the feverish night but that there was something in the music that made me react like that. I suppose I still feel a bit worried when I hear electronic music, but at least I can put up with it a bit better now. The other day, for example, I did hear such music and thought that it was sometimes quite nice.

In the next account, one comes across one of the most famous avant-garde composers from the last century, John Cage (the man who wished everybody 'Happy New Ears').

(11.3O) Woman, middle-aged, 1970s

A strong experience with music happened to me during my studies in Basel. John Cage was on the programme and everybody was going to listen. The event was to be listened to in the foyer in the new theatre that was still covered in cement dust and was completely unfinished. The listeners could sit wherever they wanted. Cage sat in the middle of the room beside a large control table; around us and high up, large loudspeakers had been set up— very avant-garde for the time!

Now the 'concert' got under way. Cage began to work the switches on his control table and all hell broke loose! With a smile, Cage looked at the listeners; the noise—recordings of street noise and compressors in various combinations—was let out and it pounced onto us defenceless listeners. The crashing and the din—it wasn't music—was so deafening that the mass of people started to get up and walk about. I couldn't stand listening to it. Aggressiveness in everybody increased, people started to bang on the walls and construction barriers with umbrellas, the din increased. Cage liked to control the auditorium.

After one hour's 'happening', there was a break. Outside was pelting rain, inside there was spiritual chaos for many people. Several went home, many tried to stick it out for the second part. People weren't even in a condition to start conversations, they were tired and had had enough, but me, being stubborn, I listened to the second part too. That was roughly just as violent, with new varieties of recorded sounds: waterfalls, cannon shots, etc. Cage's concert was a matter of him interpreting the reaction of the audience and playing and experimenting with it.

After the final noise in this boring setting, the audience stumbled out, tired, sad, depressed, and a remarkable experience 'richer'. For a long time I had this dreadful feeling inside me of how you could attack people with sound—extreme sound—and oppress them. Of course, afterwards I felt that it was pretty tough of me to stick it! Because it *was* an interesting experience! But it wasn't in any way accompanied by anything nice, beautiful, such as colours or light, everything was just grey.

The sound resources of an organ can sometimes be too much for listeners, indeed even terrifying in combination with compact dissonances.

(11.3P) Woman, middle-aged, 1980s

[During an organ concert in a church] The second half of the concert consisted mainly of organ music. These organ pieces became more and more intense and dramatic. Sometimes it sounded as if the person playing laid his arms along the entire keyboard and his feet sideways across all the pedals—resulting in a roaring and a vibrating in the entire cathedral. The volume of the organ was very high and strong. The pieces that were played were mainly very modern compositions.

This music and way of playing made me feel all the more ill. I got feelings of anguish that just got stronger and stronger and I felt that most of all I'd like to run away from it all. The concert was getting near the end and all the time I was thinking that I must try to stick it just a little longer. I was sitting some way in on the church pew and thought at the same time that it would be impolite to leave the concert now that there were so few organ pieces left. But for me it seemed as though it would never end! I felt panic and said to my sister-in-law: 'I'm leaving now, I can't stand listening any longer,' but hesitated anyway out of consideration to the concert performers.

The last piece was played with even more drama and roaring. I experienced it as if all the evil powers in the nether world had got loose and wanted to destroy me. I tried to sink into myself to get away from these dreadful feelings of anguish that I had, and suddenly it became silent and the applause exploded! I threw myself out of the pew and rushed out onto the church steps and more or less gasped for breath. My pulse was very fast by then, there was a throbbing in my head and I felt completely exhausted! I felt persecuted and thought that I had escaped by the skin of my teeth!

The next moment I felt how the anger started to build up inside me! How could they treat an instrument in that way? To my mind it was pure assault! I also felt a very strong need to talk about my anguish and worry with somebody else, which I did out there on the church steps.

Finally I felt a bit calmer and we could be on our way home, but I still felt agitated and full of anguish, sad and angry in turn, and disappointed!

There is nothing I hate as much as extreme modern disharmonic music! I wasn't prepared for them to play that type of music. I was more or less forced to listen to the sort of music I didn't like and I couldn't get out of it as I thought it was embarrassing and impolite to leave the concert premises!

In the account about John Cage as well as in this account, the listeners feel oppressed, attacked, and persecuted by the unusual, extreme music/sound.

Similar negative reactions to certain musical elements—very high sound level, shrill tones, dissonances—including a desire to flee the situation, can also occur in other musical genres such as jazz and rock music.

(11.3Q) Woman, middle-aged, 1950s

I remember once when we had tickets to John Coltrane at the Concert Hall. Can't remember if Miles Davis was there too, I didn't like him then and don't even now, but anyhow it was John Coltrane, tenor sax, who was the main cause of the problem. And, Jesus Christ, it was so terrible. This tone, shrill and nasal at the same time, cut right through me and straight into my stomach nerves. I had often heard Coltrane on the gramophone and always reacted negatively, but it had been bearable. Now it was unbearable. After two and a half tunes I left, feeling extremely nauseous.

(11.3R) Man, young, 1980s

We were a gang who were listening to a rock gala outdoors. After a while they announced a Berlin band with girls, Malaria they were called, symptomatically. They played a hard, heavy fateful synth rock at top volume.

We had been sitting quite close but it was soon unbearable. The bass boomed out a heavy, numbing carpet of sound, monotonous, which penetrated your body. The drummer too played with heavy and tired hits. Added to that was a howling saxophone that screamed in anguish, completely lacking melody and a definite key. The girl on the saxophone was accompanied by a girl singer who sang completely freely the most monotonous and howling song I've heard. They had heavy black make-up and pale skin, all of them in the band, black clothes and the style that has become quite widespread since then, but this was my first contact with it.

This naked and ghastly death music that poured out and drowned us from the loudspeakers made me feel nauseous. Intuitively, I just wanted to get away from the music and got up to go. At the same time, whole groups of young boys and girls dressed in black poured towards the stage and the loudspeakers. They all looked so pale and listless, lifeless. I tried to keep standing in the howling but felt that it only evoked a destructive nauseous feeling. 'After listening to this you'd want to smash concrete!' I thought.

I thought that Malaria and the audience, with their open anguish about the future and life, allied themselves with death and destruction in a totally ghastly way. They used their clothes and their own skin to signal their terror and their surrender, yet not in revolt against the dark, but through identification and alliance with the blackness. It was a deeply negative experience, powerful and ghastly.

In this case it is obvious that the negative reaction to the music became even stronger from the visual impressions of the appearance, clothing, and behaviour of the musicians.

Finally, an extreme example of a horrible experience after a suicide attempt, an experience which in a state of mortal dread becomes a misinterpretation of what is happening in the surroundings and to the narrator. Music is there in the process, but it is (only) imagined and is a part of the horrible experience while also further worsening it.

(11.3S) Man, middle-aged, 1980s

The origin of the experience was a suicide attempt. The physical injuries I inflicted upon myself were extremely severe. I don't want to go into detail about those. The first period at the hospital, I lived in a sort of dream state where my feeling of terror that the staff would kill me was extremely real. I really felt terror like what I think the Jews must have felt outside the gas chambers. Anyway, this is the setting.

I was wheeled along to what was probably an X-ray examination, but that I thought was the end of my life, the waiting room of death, the place where they were going to kill me. On the way to the X-ray theatre I thought I saw some people in prison clothes. They were trying to trick me by going in the lift, wheeling me along corridors, etc. However, I knew that *everyone* was deceiving me: that they all knew and wanted to see what a person's last moments in life would look like. I knew that this was going to be recorded on video and then be shown to the medical students. Everybody mocked me on my way to the death room except one girl who was crying.

Then when I was wheeled into the X-ray room (I saw stretchers with human bodies covered with white sheets), they started to swap name labels with each other, first guys with guys, girls with girls, then even between guys and girls. Bags of blood (?) and a drip that hung over my bed were swapped with new colours, a trick to delay things, so to speak.

They made fun again of my mother and now I was convinced that they would saw my foot off. When the moment of death was supposed to come, they swapped the oxygen tube for a thinner one which in that way would give me less oxygen and suffocate me. I cried out to my Lord, to my mother and father, to the devil, to anyone that could save me.

Then there was the orchestra: this music of the devil, this music that welcomed me to hell. It consisted of violins that were being played on the nut, resulting in a hysterical and horrible sound. The tones were in a D minor mode (D, E, F, G, A). There were also the shrill screams of a saxophone in an inhumanly high pitch. Now the end was very close; I saw the tunnel and the light, not the light to the kingdom of heaven, but the light to hell. The orchestra was now playing together with an enormous gong-gong, a sound that was the last thing I was aware of.

Since that experience I have found it very hard to listen to Mahler. This music is in some way so incredibly close to this experience of music, has a power of suggestion that can be compared with Mahler. I can sometimes have associations that are of an unpleasant type, for example a lift that is pressed against the lift shaft so that a screeching metallic sound is produced.

In Chapter 29, section 29.5.3, there is a systematic listing of all the negative feelings mentioned in the accounts.

11.4 MIXED, CONTRADICTORY, CHANGED FEELINGS

Feelings can change during the course of the experience. Different feelings can follow each other, positive and negative feelings can be mixed together, negative feelings can be succeeded by positive feelings—all of this in a very varied manner for every individual.

Swinging between positive and negative feelings occurs in many different ways. With children, it can be a confusing discovery.

(11.4A) Man, old, 1920s

I had my first strong experience with music when I was 11 or 12 years old. I was lying in my bed in the evening, the door was open to another room, when I heard my mother sing a hymn which really gripped me thoroughly. The words were 'Here pours a fountain, blessed who will find her, it is deep but clear, hidden but obvious' [free translation of the Swedish original]. Perhaps it was the mysterious words that moved me so strongly, but the music certainly strengthened the impression a lot. I became worried, melancholia and anguish gripped me, but I also felt some form of joy. I had never felt anything like that before, it was as if I had come to a completely unknown area of my life. And this impression is evidently very deep, it is suddenly there (perhaps once or twice a year), and makes me feel happy and unhappy at the same time.

The next narrator became almost hysterical from switching between contradictory feelings, perhaps also from the attempts to hide them from others, whatever the cost. The account also mirrors a little of the spirit of the time in question regarding musical taste and the upbringing of children.

(11.4B) Woman, middle-aged, 1940s

I was 11 years old. We were visiting my uncle. He was stern and strict (I thought) and I was told to 'behave properly' (you said that to children in those days). Above all, I was not to say that I liked 'negro music' and Alice Babs.

It was obvious that my uncle would play for us. I wasn't particularly interested but suddenly I was completely overwhelmed. As early as the first bars of *Fantaisie-Impromptu*, Chopin!!

I can't describe in words the strong experience that suddenly affected me and which lasted right to the end of the piece. It was something really extra special. A mixture of despair and joy—the desire to run away somewhere, almost hysterical! That was the start of a great love of Chopin's music.

I revealed absolutely nothing of how overwhelmed I felt—at least not in any positive way. On the journey home, I was told off for appearing grumpy and uninterested. Presumably I didn't want to lose face in front of relatives and show my sensitivity and vulnerability. I was meant to behave properly and you don't launch into uncontrolled expressions of joy.

The following experience took place much later during a large and well-known event in the 1980s that was broadcast on television over large parts of the world. The music was combined with humanitarian and economic commitment. The narrator swings between joy at being able to see her favourite group and sorrow over the situation that had led to the concert.

(11.4C) Woman, young, 1980s

It was at the Live Aid concert in Wembley Stadium in London. I was both happy and sad, happy about all the money that would come in for the starving, and sad for their sake, but since Duran Duran was then my favourite group, one of their songs, 'Save a prayer', became a special memory. That made an extremely strong impression.

I got an enormous feeling of togetherness with all the people who were there and I remember that my friend cried; there were a lot of people who did. When Bob Geldof was on the stage and talked about Ethiopia and the starving people, it made you sad, but after a while he went up again and said how much money had come in, and that made you happy.

I had a bad conscience about having it so good, but above all I felt joy from being there and being able to experience this.

In the next account, too, there is a mixed experience of beauty, joy, and sadness.

(11.4D) Woman, young, 1990s

I lay in my bed and tried to get to sleep, but I couldn't. My mate that I was living with was out somewhere and I must have felt a bit lonely. Besides, I was busy trying to push a boy away from my thoughts. In any case, I got up and chose a record. It was late, so I wanted to hear something calm and soothing. I found one of my mate's classical records that would do nicely. The music was beautiful, but I didn't think much about it at first, rather I just lay there brooding.

But suddenly there was a piece that I started to listen particularly to. I had heard it several times before without thinking much about it. But now it was so wonderfully beautiful that tears came to my eyes. I felt sad and happy at the same time, you could say. The piece was 'Barcarolle' by Offenbach. Particularly in a couple of places in the piece it is specially beautiful, when the sounds sort of 'split up' and are played in parts, that was when tears came to my eyes.

I think it was a combination of the time, the lighting, and my mental state, and of course this wonderful music that made me experience this occasion so strongly.

In nostalgia, a melancholic longing is joined by simultaneous pleasure.

(11.4E) Woman, middle-aged, 1980s

A popular TV programme with Jacob Dahlin was broadcast late on Saturday evenings. At the end you can see a picture of Stockholm in the dark, where you can only see the silhouettes of towers and pinnacles, house roofs, and cupolas. The neon lights of the city light up here and there, as do the beams of vehicles sweeping along down on the streets. There are flashes of light, there are reflections from the water surfaces, a church bell rings, you can hear a car siren, the sounds of the night are mixed with weak voices. And sort of from nowhere, above all this you can hear, weakly but clearly distinguishable, Zarah Leander sing 'Stockholm is Stockholm . . .' It is only the first verse and it gradually fades down.

When I see and hear this, a strong and inexplicable feeling of melancholia comes over me. It's as if the sounds of the city together with Zarah's voice symbolize past times and remind me of people and voices that fell silent long ago; only a quiet murmur remains over the city, a Stockholm that has changed. Nothing is like it used to be. That is painful, but I enjoy it at the same time. It gives me the creeps, but I don't cry. Afterwards, I try to retain that feeling and mood as long as possible.

All the way through the programme I wait for the finale to come. I have wondered why I become so fascinated; I know that I react the same way every time, and this never ceases to surprise me.

In the next account, the music and setting create an atmosphere of absolute stillness, sincerity, and beauty, but there is also a touch of melancholy because of the fickleness of life.

(11.4F) Woman, middle-aged, 1980s

Our family was visiting good old friends, Aunt Karin and Uncle Ruben, wonderful people. We sat one evening in their lovely living room and looked out over the river. Uncle Ruben thought we should listen to music before we went to bed. He put a gramophone record on. It was Schubert's String Quintet in C major. It was the first time I heard it. I was totally unprepared for it being so beautiful and sincere. It was a perfect expression of the atmosphere in the room. It was a summer evening, it was dusk, it was absolutely still and quiet. The room was so beautiful, Aunt Karin had wild flowers in a silver vase on the table. And the music, the music was so delightful. I remembered every single tone afterwards.

I thought about life, its fickleness. Our old friends, both of them a bit over 80. Would they be alive next year, will we get to meet them one more time? It was so bittersweet and melancholic. And the music, the music moved us to tears. We sat completely still. It was as if you never wanted to move again.

The next narrator had learnt from his very childhood that classical music was not for him. When he unwillingly listens for the first time to Tchaikovsky's *Pathétique* symphony he is struck by the emotional expressions in this music and by conflict-ridden thoughts and feelings.

(11.4G) Man, middle-aged, 1950s (from Chapter 6, account 6.2C)

Suddenly a terrible feeling of confusion came upon me. In what I believe was only a few seconds, a whole series of conflicting thoughts began rushing around in my mind. These thoughts progressed into a series of conflicting emotions: fright, sorrow, hate, love, anger, and, finally, an internal peace that words cannot describe.

All through my growing up, I had been influenced by the belief that certain kinds of music were reserved exclusively for certain kinds of people. The question was: How could the white man's music (Russian at that) have such a strong psychological effect on me? Frightening thoughts coupled with expressed emotion of sadness! Was I acquiring the mentality of the white man? Would I never be able to appreciate fully any more the music of my own race? I screamed God's name loudly as I ran over to the shelves where I kept my jazz records. I pulled out the LP on which Oscar Peterson plays Erroll Garner's 'Tenderly'. The effect was sheer happiness, and the fright disappeared.

Thought coupled with emotion of anger and hate: What kind of mind was it that had created such destructive propaganda, saying that one kind of art was so superior that only the chosen few could understand it? For a moment I was angry at them, and hated them. Thought coupled with love and warmth: Wasn't it the insistency of my English friend that opened a whole new world for me? And wasn't he white?

Many examples of mixed and contradictory feelings are also to be found in accounts of unhappy love and broken relationships; see Chapter 20. Here is an introductory, rather special, example.

(11.4H) Woman, middle-aged, 1980s

I was depressed, my most committed love affair had come to an end amid great disappointment that I couldn't deal with. It was evening. I can't remember if I had already cried, but I turned the radio on—the music channel—and out poured the strains of one of my favourite pieces, Schubert's posthumous string quintet. I sat at the kitchen table and my little cat sat on it and sought my attention. When I heard the music I just laid my head on my arms on the table. The tears ran, it was painful and pleasant at the same time.

When the quintet faded out, I raised my head and saw that my cat lay on its back completely relaxed with its eyes shut. I was very moved. Thought that I had got confirmation of what I had noticed earlier, that this cat was the most musical I'd had. Perhaps it was a feeling of sharing with the cat that strengthened the experience of the marvellous music.

A common theme in many accounts is a shift from negative feelings to positive ones. Sometimes, this is described in very few—yet telling—words, as in the following case.

(11.4I) Man, middle-aged, 1970s

Dolly Parton, song. I was listening. Before: ill, alone, afraid, tired. Afterwards: free, grateful.

The next narrator describes how feelings of anguish were replaced by security and calm. The course of the feelings was governed entirely by the intensity and harmonic structure of the music.

(11.4J) Man, middle-aged, 1980s (excerpt)

It was a choral concert with the Radio Choir. The piece was *Agnus Dei* by Sven-David Sandström. I had to close my eyes because it was such an enormous emotional experience, I almost became part of the piece. It almost created a feeling of anxiety, a sort of pressure in my chest, because it was so intense and extremely strong. You only had to lean back, you started to almost breathe heavily from the pressure you felt. It was a 16-part piece, atonal, without the common chords of three or four notes but still a bit romantic, sometimes with familiar chords. The piece ended in a long, weak 'pure' chord. The pressure relaxed, the feeling of security returned, and it became calm, and ended in the safe, pure F major chord.

In the last account in this section, a profound change of emotional state is described. The music is a Swedish symphony known for its strong personal expression.

(11.4K) Man, middle-aged, 1980s

The most profound experience with music can best be described as a form of *unio mystica*. In other words, a state where one completely transforms an extremely complicated structure to a total unit where even the instruments cease to exist as a concept. There are no thought processes at all; everything is experienced as pure tone, a tone that has its residence inside me.

This experience took place for the first time in 1987. The work that was being played was Allan Pettersson's Symphony No. 7. I took part as a listener. Before the experience, I was depressed.

Afterwards, it felt as if I in some respect had been through a concentrated grieving process, an active grieving that had led to reconciliation. Catharsis. Pure harmony and empathy.

This account could also have been quoted in Chapter 7 about how one merges with the music ('a form of *unio mystica*'), as well as later in Chapter 16 on confirmation, on recognizing oneself in the music. Many other examples of how negative emotional states have been turned into positive ones through music are to be found in Chapter 17 on music as therapy, in Chapter 22 on music at funerals and in Chapter 18, section 18.4, on performers who have mastered nervousness.

11.5 USING MUSIC TO INFLUENCE FEELINGS

Many participants tell of how their strong experience with music has meant that even afterwards they try to influence their mood with the help of the same music.

(11.5A) Woman, old

During periods when it has been possible, in my daily schedule I have included a short music-listening interlude in the morning before work. During one period I used parts of Dvořák's symphony 'From the New World'. This meant that I became very familiar with both Dvořák and the symphony. This was extremely important. I heard the tones, the orchestra, and the solo instruments inside me for the rest of the day. I was confronted with intense people during my entire working day, and I felt that I gained a reserve of energy and balance which removed the risk of becoming worn down in everyday life.

(11.5B) Woman, old

I saw a film where Smetana's *Moldau* was played throughout the film. The entire music is so nice. When the piece begins, it goes up, is stormy, calms down to a quieter level, and becomes delightful. All of this beautiful piece of music was with me. It 'played' for me afterwards too. During all the years that have passed since I heard *Moldau* the first time, I've been able to hear it without it being played in actuality. It was still there inside me in some way.

When life is tough and you are sad, this music is a consolation. I think that it's the storm that is heard in the music, then it quietens down a bit. It is like saying: 'Now it is difficult, it can get better, then calmer.' The music can cry with me, it can laugh with me, it can make me happy, it can make me sad, and it can console me if I am sad.

(11.5C) Woman, young, 1990s (from Chapter 25, account 25.10)

[Schubert's Fantasy for piano in F minor] is the most loved record in my collection . . . If I feel sad for some reason or other, I often choose to listen to this music, but sometimes when I'm very happy and jolly I can also feel a strong need to hear this fantasy. In the first case I think I am looking for (and get) consolation from the music; in the second, it usually simply feels so nice to hear the music—I am not really certain why this is. It is interesting that I can never let this piece of music serve as background music for other activities such as reading books or writing letters—regardless of my mood, Schubert's Fantasy demands too much of my attention and any other activities would simply suffer.

To use music in these ways to influence one's mood is fairly common, to judge by several recent investigations.[2] This is evident in our material too. Without our actually having directly asked about this, about 100 people (just over 10% of the participants) have spontaneously described how they make use of music to influence—confirm, strengthen, change—their mood. (If we had asked a direct question, we would certainly have got even more descriptions.)

Below are some more examples of such accounts. First a few descriptions of the principle.

(11.5D) Woman, young

You look for music that either suits your own mood or something that can bring about a change of your mood. For example, I like to listen to calm and sad music when I'm sad. Sometimes, however, you can't be in a bad mood, perhaps you're invited to a party or something else that requires you to be in a good mood. Then I force myself to listen to really happy and light music, with a lot of regular rhythm in it, for example a happy pop, soul, or jazz tune that you can sing along with. For me, it is important that you can sing along with the tune, that usually makes me happy after a while.

(11.5E) Man, young

For me music is also an emotional catalyst and a mood creator that can be used to strengthen the feeling that I have at a particular time or counter it. Like a sort of do-it-yourself music therapy. Maybe it's not so unusual, but it's probably something that most people don't think about. If I'm happy or in a party mood, then I want to listen to certain records that strengthen that feeling. It's the same if I'm angry or sad, then there are other records where the music and even the lyrics express the feeling I have. My girlfriends have all had a certain tune that I've associated with them in particular, and that I've listened to when I've missed them.

(11.5F) Woman, young

We have probably all experienced how music has helped us spontaneously to give full expression to various emotions. It's probably a common situation when, for example, we come home after a day at work and put a record on to help us relax and feel good. On these occasions, I don't think you reflect so much about why you put that particular record on, but I think we unconsciously choose the music that expresses the feeling we have inside us. What I find so fantastic about this is that without being fully aware of exactly what I'm feeling, without reflecting especially on it, I can choose music that makes me feel good. Music is quite simply a fantastic aid to achieving a sort of mental balance.

(11.5G) Woman, young (from an edited interview)

It's a strange thing with music . . . it helps me in my life. Sometimes I want to confirm or emphasize a feeling—for example, if I'm feeling a bit down in the dumps, sad, or melancholy—then I might want to play such music. By now, I know roughly which songs contain this, which touch upon the feeling. Then I want to confirm it . . . Or if I come home and am in a really great mood, what I do then is pull out a stirring song which simply makes everything even better.

At the same time, I can do the opposite—change my mood with the help of music. I can be on the way to feeling a bit low. Then I can decide: 'No, now I must put such-and-such on so that it'll cheer me up a little, and make me happier and I'll get a little confidence again.' And it really works, like snapping your fingers.

I am so incredibly influenced by music—it's easy to see that! It's good, it is like therapy, a resource.

(11.5H) Woman, young

Singing is a part of me. By singing, I can deal with emotions and impressions but also convey what is important to me or my mood to those who are listening. Through song and music I have the possibility to express what I feel, think, my imagination, and my longing—a way of communicating with myself, with my heart. The older I get, the more I notice how singing and music are like a tool for me. Something that helps me on my path in life. When I listen actively to music, I can't remain unmoved. I get either totally absorbed, positive, happy, or simply euphoric, or I become frustrated, angry, or furious. My reaction depends on whether the music or the songs are in agreement with my emotions/values or not.

Now I can't imagine a life without music. Music is forever taking me on new journeys, sometimes on my own, sometimes together with others. Music, but above all singing, gives me experiences or little kicks that help me get by for a while. These small grains of music settle in my consciousness and I feel that I grow as a person.

Finally, a couple of very detailed accounts of how one can systematically make use of music to influence mood.

(11.5I) Woman, middle-aged

I often use music to help me change moods. I know exactly which tracks in my CD rack arouse me and which ones lead to a pleasant relaxation and easing of tension. Music medicine must, however, be taken in well-balanced doses. Sometimes I have to confirm the mood that I am already in (for example, in high spirits, stressed), before successively easing up. Depending on my original mood, a certain tune can also work in different ways. A calm tune makes me relax if I am stressed, but if I feel a tinge of sorrow then it can also trigger those feelings. Of course, sometimes you can want to get rid of, say, all the sorrow you feel and then you can use music to provoke tears, which leads to catharsis. In the same way, a mechanically intense techno tune on one occasion (if I am rested) can feel delightful and give me energy, but on another occasion (if I've been working too hard) bring associations of something manic, lifeless, and mechanical.

Another example is that music has been my salvation during many hours of essay writing on my computer. Then it's music that is my locomotive when I don't feel I can manage it. It gives me energy and keeps me on track. A super cure in crisis situations is to have my CD player on low volume all night long (using the repeat function) with some sort of extremely persistent (dull, gentle, continuous bass), meditative, instrumental tune. In the morning I wake up a new person.

Music is of enormous importance to me. I can be fantastically powerfully moved in both body and soul. I think it is probably the closest I come to a religious or spiritual experience.

(11.5J) Woman, young

I always think about how I'm feeling before I put on a record or play/sing for myself, because I feel that I am strongly influenced by what I hear, passively as well as actively. A lot of music that I find good and beautiful is sad, depressing, or at any rate not happy. That means that it is often difficult to choose music because I often feel happy or neutral and don't want to 'destroy' that good mood by letting myself be influenced by sad music.

Sometimes, when I only want to be completely pure and good in my thoughts, then I put on, say, a record of one of Mozart's violin concertos, or play one myself. A favourite among the happy tunes is the first track on the record by that wonderful clarinettist Giora Feidman, 'Magic of the klezmer'. For many years, that tune has managed to match my happiest mood, but it also has an ability to match my angry mood. How can that be? How can a tune 'work' when I'm angry as well as when I'm happy? Presumably because it is so passionate, expressive, and full of vigour and energy, which is something that happy and angry feelings have in common.

When I feel really desperate and sad, then I can always rely on Zoltán Kodály's Sonata for solo cello, Op. 8. It conveys a broad register of emotions in a very expressive way. As opposed to my angry/happy music, this music is rather complex and complicated.

When I am angry or feel a bubbling happiness, then what satisfies me is music that is 'direct', while music that is too complicated just feels difficult to cope with. When I am angry, I most often prefer non-complex and expressive music like the klezmer tune I describe above, but often I want it to be aggressive like a really furious hard rock tune, for example by Nirvana—or I can sit down at the piano and fire off Rachmaninov's Prelude in C-sharp minor with a purely physical experience by hammering at the piano. I then achieve a catharsis effect by living through my anger so that I can feel calmer afterwards.

When I feel melancholy, sad, or down, I like to listen to music that feels like that, although it doesn't perhaps always succeed in giving me the same catharsis effect as in the case with the angry music. Often, I only feel even sadder after having listened to the low-spirited music, but I enjoy wallowing in my misery. The catharsis effect is perhaps delayed, or doesn't come at all. If I'm unhappily in love, then I might choose to listen to 'our tune' or something similar.

In the different cases I have described so far, I have chosen music that in one way or another is similar to, or emphasizes, the mood I'm in and the emotions I'm feeling. When I'm feeling worried and stressed, I often do the opposite, but not always. It can feel better just then to listen to monotonous, stressed music. I have to force myself to put on calm, meditative music, which feels like a pain right up until I notice how it has had an effect and made me calmer. It is often Gregorian music.

Another little aspect to consider when I use music therapeutically is to adjust the volume. For example, I get extremely stressed if it is too loud when I'm eating. If I listen to a hard rock tune I have to have it really, really loud to feel the effect.

I enjoy music, like to be in the company of music, in lots of other different ways too, and when I write that I 'use music therapeutically', I do it more or less consciously. But more and more often unconsciously. The danger with being too aware of how music affects you is that I can find a situation insufferable if I can't choose the music and the volume myself.

Further examples of systematic use of music to influence one's frame of mind are to be found in Chapter 15, New insights, new possibilities, and Chapter 17, Music as therapy. The border between the contents of this chapter and those two is fluid.

CHAPTER 12

MUSIC AND EXISTENCE

STRONG experiences of music can embrace thoughts and reflections on life and existence. Music can be perceived as mirroring what it means to be a human being, the conditions for life in its various phases, what life can offer, and how one ought/can take advantage of its possibilities. The experience can lead to a changed view of oneself, of one's relation to other people and of existence in general. Some people point out the almost paradoxical fact that a few minutes of music radically altered their entire life.

Under this heading, we are also dealing with intensive experiences of 'presence in life'—rare occasions when the only essential thing is to 'just be', to let everything else sink away, quite simply to be there and experience the world and life in all their richness and beauty.

Some experiences are of such a unique and overwhelming character that one cannot expect to go through anything similar ever again. They are described as 'unrivalled', 'ultimate', or 'holy' moments in life.

Existential aspects such as these sometimes border upon transcendental and religious aspects that are treated in Chapters 13 and 14.

12.1 THE CONTENT AND MEANING OF LIFE

In the accounts below, the music is of very varying character and from different genres (rock, classical, electronic, flamenco) but what is important and common about them in this context is which emotions and thoughts the music gives rise to about life—the content and meaning of life, its richness, magnificence, and transitory nature, what it means to be a human being and to feel presence in life.

(12.1A) Man, young, 1980s

The strongest experience of music was a Bruce Springsteen concert. I had made up my mind not to listen to him. Didn't want to believe all the extolling articles even though I had listened a bit to his music and thought it was OK. Talked to a mate who isn't usually one to lavish praise on music of this type and she was in raptures about it. This mate had a strong influence on me when she said it had been incredibly good.

I went to Stockholm and the experience was extremely strong. For me, the concert was an expression of what it means to be human. The difficulties, love, joy, drivel, playing, seriousness, guilt, hopelessness. All of this was incorporated in the concert in a way that moved me extremely strongly. It was a bit like a church service, or a lot like a church service as it could be when it is at its best. A drama that fills all of life, all those parts that make up what it means to be human.

It was both an experience that what was said, sung, and expressed in the music affects me especially and an experience of fellowship with the other 8,000 people who were in the hall. Really, the effect of the music experience wasn't at its greatest during the actual concert but afterwards when the impressions reverberate again and lines from the songs are suddenly filled with blood, life, and concern me.

The reason? Presumably I was longing for a person or people who could captivate me and give words and music to what I, and many with me, felt just then. The experience has lived on inside me since then, and is still there. It was a sort of paradigm change in my way of meeting life.

In the following account, music was the decisive turning point in a situation when the narrator's own existence was at risk.

(12.1B) Woman, young, 1980s (from Chapter 5, account 5.3E)

It was a perfectly ordinary, boring, grey autumn day and I was feeling really rough, life felt like the dumps, and every day a special thought cropped up inside my head: Why am I alive? What am I doing here? Just think if I were to . . . and I just hardly dare think the rest, but life wasn't exactly a dance on roses and I just wanted to die.

The tape recorder was on, pretty loud. I was listening to a tape with the hard rock group KISS. I know those songs almost by heart. There I sat on a wooden chair beside my desk and was busy thinking about how you could kill yourself in the most painless way, when the sound of 'Detroit Rock City' started to roar from the loudspeakers. The bass, the drums, they exploded in my brain, 'I feel all tired on a Saturday night . . .' (and, yeah, sure, I am tired). At the end of the song came the most frightening part. The words are:

I feel so good, I'm so alive
I hear my song playin' on the radio
It goes, get up, everybody gonna move their feet
Get down, everybody gonna leave their seat
12 o'clock I gotta rock
There's a truck on hand, the light's staring at my eyes
Oh, my God, no time to turn
I gotta laugh 'cause I know I'm gonna die. *Why?*

. . . I rewound the cassette and listened again and then I had a vision.

Paul Stanley was standing in front of me with sad eyes and was repeating the question: 'Why?' I opened my eyes, shut them again, and I still saw Paul with that question: 'Why?' and at that same moment I started to cry and I couldn't stop. I thought about all the people who had died unnecessarily in car accidents, of drugs and of illnesses, of all the starvation and poverty and misery in the world, and here I sat and was thinking about killing myself. What on earth was I doing?

When I eventually could stop crying, I felt so empty. I didn't feel sorrow or joy, just anguish. And a dreadful question. What if I had done it? Now there wasn't a moment's doubt about whether life was worth living or not. I am happy that I have it as good as I do. There are millions of people who have it a thousand times worse than me.

I have asked myself many times why it happened just then and how. The song actually saved my life. Every time I hear the song I am filled with a feeling of joy. The joy of being able to sit here, alive, for real, and listen to my favourite songs. I have been selected to live, I think that 'someone' saved me. Not God or any other divine power. But this 'someone' whom I can't place, they are just there. They are there like a big shadow, not only for me, deep inside, but in the whole of history, the whole history of life. I can only describe it by saying that it frightens me, but it makes me curious. It is magnificent and absolutely unique, but terrible and indestructible.

In the next example, the music is Gustav Mahler's immense eighth symphony *Sinfonie der Tausend*, the second (i.e. last) movement of which is based on the end of Goethe's *Faust* with its lofty spiritual character and homage to the liberating force of love.

(12.1C) Woman, middle-aged, 1980s

About 20 years ago, I had a very strong music experience that meant a change in my life. I had a ticket to Gustav Mahler's Symphony No. 8. The Stockholm Philharmonic Orchestra and choir conducted by Yuri Ahronovitch. It was one of his last concerts as chief conductor. However, I was hesitant if I should really go to the concert. I had no close relation to Mahler except for the well-known Adagietto in his fifth symphony and I have heard that so many times that I was pretty tired of it.

But already when I came to the concert hall I felt that there was such an expectant atmosphere there, everybody seemed full of expectation when they walked in to find their seats. And then when all the musicians began to come in, I was fascinated by how many they were, the stage was just full of them. It felt like a sort of vibration in the air: 'Soon, soon . . .'

And then the symphony begins with 'Veni creator spiritus' in impetuous fortissimo chords, it is an incredible start all at once, and I got sort of a physical blow from these very first chords. I got so captivated by the music that I tried reading in the programme notes what the music was about, I wanted to know what Mahler was telling me about, what was it? But I could only read some fragments here and there.

Then, in the last movement, when the choir started to sing, in a barely audible pianissimo, the Chorus mysticus, '*Alles Vergängliche ist nur ein Gleichnis*' ['All that is transitory is but a symbol'], it just creeps into my mind that life is transitory, this is your moment in life, the moment for you to come to a decision. And when the choir 'pulls along' the orchestra and soloists in a crescendo that accelerates right up to the last notes where the concert hall's magnificent organ joins them in a fortissimo, I am no longer in a concert hall, I am on Mount Tabor! Everything around me has disappeared, the music has lifted me up from my seat and into a light where an unbelievable feeling of the greatness of life, but also its transitory nature, fills me . . . The last tones fade away and everything lands in a breathless silence which lasts a long, long time.

When Ahronovitch finally turns towards the audience and receives the applause, I look around and see that my cheeks are not the only ones shining with tears. Then the conductor does something that is very rare. He orders the orchestra and choir to repeat the entire last movement. The seriousness in his face convinces me that this is not just to flatter the audience, rather it is a strong awareness that all of us, performers as well as listeners, have just shared such a unique experience that we simply must be able to work through it again before we go our separate ways.

I was very moved by the conductor's powerful radiance of energy and warmth which resulted in an unusually devoted commitment from the musicians. A very important part of this was the feeling that the music united us all in a wordless understanding that all of us had been part of a unique *shared experience*. All of this together meant that it was an unforgettably powerful emotional experience.

Besides a sort of experience of falling in love with Mahler's musical language, the music conveyed a clear message, the tones as well as the words, that gave rise to thoughts and associations around the existential issues that were extremely topical for me just then. It was as if things were suddenly put in order in my life: Yes, this is how it should be. It was a kind of purification, catharsis, as if all dross had been weeded out and I didn't give a damn—this is how I should go on, what I should focus upon. It was an experience of decisive importance for my life.

In the next account, existential issues are portrayed in dance to romantic and electronic music.

(12.1D) Man, middle-aged, 1980s

[An experience of Carlotta Ikeda, a virtuoso of Buto dance in the expressive and singular solo piece *Utt*. The music was partly contemporary electronic music, partly romantic from Fauré's *Requiem*, 'Pie Jesu'.]

You have to go back to your youth to recall the artistic impressions that brought forth tears and such a harrowing emotional experience as Ikeda's total performance. Her insight into this world of notes and colours, light and darkness, and her ability to project drama and energy out of all this, cutting right through all our emotional defences, was unique. Her dance is about existential issues, birth, childhood, old age, and death. With her enormous metamorphic ability, she leads us through the life cycle and strikes the resonance within us that we can easily identify with, as it is universal.

Such an experience is of great importance for an understanding of how different forms of artistic expression—when they are in the hands of a great artist who has considerable experience of life—can raise us above an everyday level.

In the following examples, the narrators are captivated by strong and convincing expressions for a belief in life, what life can consist of, and offer. There is an intense feeling of presence.

(12.1E) Man, young, 1980s (from Chapter 27, account 27J, edited interview)

[A rock concert with a well-known American rock band] It was just such a hell of a force, such energy, such power in the performance. Such happiness, such intensity, such honesty.

It felt so simple, so honest. It went right into your heart . . . I think the artiste means every bloody word he says, there is such conviction in the words . . . It fills you with joy and a belief in life . . . Concerts like this are necessary. It isn't just a concert but a lifestyle, how you think. I suppose it's a sort of belief in something that the artiste is helping you to verbalize. If you have some dreams, perhaps you might believe in them a little longer. It becomes easier to live for a while!

(12.1F) Woman, young, 1980s (see also Chapter 16, account 16.1I)

[About flamenco] The guitarist Eva Möller comes to the school once a year and tells us about flamenco music. She has enormous charisma, and she is so good at telling about things. She is poetic, reads poems. It was amazing when she talked to us, what she sang, and how she played the guitar. It made you want to cry afterwards. It was simply fantastic. The entire class was there and I remember that something really did happen in that room for all the people there, I am certain that everyone felt it, because the whole atmosphere was simply vibrating. There was such an incredibly strong sensation, from the music and from what she told us. It is something that affects you deeply, something that is important inside me, it feels . . . well, it's to do with existence itself, with life.

You feel more than usually present in life in some way—an enhanced feeling of existing, just now, just here. You get such a strong feeling of life, of living a life. It is everything, life, death, existing as a human being. All the pain, sorrow, passion, joy. It is exactly as if everything is compressed into that music . . . it affects you in an incredibly strong way. On that occasion, I started crying, I remember.

12.2 PRESENCE IN LIFE, ULTIMATE MOMENTS

The feeling of presence in life, here and now, is also reflected in the following short extracts from other accounts.

(12.2A) Man, middle-aged, 1950s (from Chapter 23, account 23G)

A summer night. The house lay beside a lake with not a ripple on the surface. It was about 3 or 4 in the morning . . . I pulled out the record with music by Johnny Mandel . . . Bang. There it was, the agreement between what I saw . . . and what I heard . . . everything just 'was'. To experience the beauty, the stillness, and existence without relation to knowledge and references, to just be there in this, was an overwhelming experience.

(12.2B) Woman, middle-aged (from Chapter 23, account 23H)

One year some Maasai came to visit the Falu Folk Music Festival. At one point they were in an outdoor concert that consisted of a walk around a mere in the woods . . . The sun started to rise, there were patches of mist over the lake . . . We who were left stood in a ring around the Maasai who themselves danced in a ring inside ours . . . After a while, they took us into the ring and we danced together with them . . . There was a fantastic atmosphere, meditative in some sense. It all connected into a total experience: the smells, the dance, the singing, the sandy beach, the drum on the other side of the lake, the mist, and the sunrise. It was an intense experience of being present, or of just 'being'.

From these descriptions of intense presence, it is not a big step to description of 'ultimate' moments in life—experiences of such a unique and overwhelming character that one can't expect to experience anything like it ever again. At that moment, it seems as if one has experienced the best and the high spot of what life can offer; now one might just as well die . . .

(12.2C) Woman, middle-aged, 1960s

I was in my early thirties. I was listening to the radio, to '*Förklädd Gud*' ['God in disguise'] by Lars-Erik Larsson. Who was singing and who was playing, that I don't know, but it was a strong experience and afterwards I thought that there was nothing more to wish for. I could just as well be dead and they could carry me off.

(12.2D) Man, middle-aged, 1980s (excerpt)

Bruce Springsteen and the E Street Band were playing in Gothenburg in front of 64,000 people . . . When I went home afterwards I was exhausted, felt empty in some strange way. I remember that I shook my head and thought: 'Now I have seen everything, I'm never going to see a better concert.' And I haven't done either.

(12.2E) Woman, young, 1980s (from Chapter 26, account 26K)

[She is listening to four well-known jazz musicians.] My highest expectations were fulfilled as to what I thought it could be like, and more besides! The best that I had heard from every musician in various contexts now merged together into something . . . really great! . . . I thought that this is the best I've heard. I might never get to experience this again. This is the total, the ultimate! Music can't get better than this.

Straight afterwards, it felt empty . . . I was tired in my soul, my head, everywhere, because you feel so much. It is a bit like being in love. It makes life bigger and gives a deeper picture of life. It's important. That life can be like this!

(12.2F) Woman, middle-aged (from Chapter 19, account 19.4B)

[At the end of a choral concert abroad] The audience was so moved that they stayed in their seats. There was no applause. After the concert, we walked out slowly and walked along the aisles around where the audience was sitting while we sang 'Alta trinita beata'. The audience looked at us and there was such a charged feeling between us. The singing sounded so delightful that it gave me the creeps, and in the end we disappeared along a staircase at the far end of the monastery. As I walked along, I remember that I thought: Let this moment never end. It was a heavenly feeling and I don't think I'll ever get to feel anything so strong again.

(12.2G) Woman, old, 1980s (from Chapter 23, account 23N)

[She happened to listen to music performed by three musicians during what was at times a frightening ride in a lift car in the Alps.] They stood there with their instruments pointed straight up towards the sky . . . and played . . . Austrian folk tunes—sadly, passionately, lovingly . . . They played out their love of the music, their pride in being able to play, and their debt of gratitude to this beautiful fairy-tale-like landscape.

I felt how the tears dropped down my cheeks; I felt as if I was right in the middle of a *holy moment in life*. It couldn't get any better than this! . . . I have been present at a number of music events . . . but nothing has managed to captivate all of my being like this simple music conveyed as a gift of love during a 22-minute journey through the air.

(12.2H) Woman, young, 1980s

We took part in three performances of '*En Vintersaga*' ['A Winter's Tale'] by Lars-Erik Larsson. The music was so simple, so vivid, so pure! I was ready to cry—it was so beautiful that it hurt. For those few minutes I lived with an intensity that I have felt only a few times in my life. Already after the end of the first movement, I was longing for the next concert, when I would be able to hear all of it again.

Afterwards, I was breathless, silent, wanted time to stop—play it again and again! The feeling that music as good as this must be found in Heaven! Felt that when I die, I want to be enveloped by the music, be a part of it!

A very good metaphor is the legend of the thorn bird which sings only once in its life, namely when it impales itself against a thorn and sings more beautifully than any other bird while it is dying. Just then, on these three occasions, for me the music was just so intense, so beautiful, so painfully wonderful. In a way I wanted to fall down dead, just like that, in the middle of this fantastic music, to be absorbed by the music, to become a whole with it and just float there in the music for ever and ever.

12.3 CHANGED VIEW OF ONESELF AND ONE'S LIFE

Some experiences can lead to decisive changes in the person's attitudes, in their view of themselves or others or of various aspects of existence. In Chapter 4, account 4.1H, there was a description of a six-year-old's strong experience in a church of a piece for organ by Bach. It led to the outcome that 'I became different as a child after that concert, something fundamental happened to me—my parents clearly noticed a change, they have told me later.' A woman who listened to *Pastoralsviten* [Pastoral suite] by Lars-Erik Larsson found that 'The music had opened my eyes. Suddenly I saw nature in a different way. The music experience had opened a door into the very core of my emotional life. Since then, I am very sensitive to charged, sensual, and powerful music' (from Chapter 23, account 23J). Another woman who one summer's day sang in a church 'was filled with an intense feeling of happiness . . . I wanted to embrace the entire world. Everything was suddenly so extremely beautiful. The music, the calm in the church, the sun, and the dust that could be seen in the rays of sunshine—all joined together in a great joy and a certainty that everything was all right' (from Chapter 19, account 19.1E).

Here are a few more examples. Strangely, the first two are both associated with the same music.

(12.3A) Woman, middle-aged, 1950s

In 1951, I was 'struck' by classical music. I had been told to varnish a kitchen floor. The only channel on the wireless played Bruch's Violin Concerto. At first unwillingly, then all the more fascinated, I listened to this concert. I felt a bliss without bounds and 'floated', so it seemed to me, several metres above the floor. I had a vision of another, better, life—a feeling of there being unimagined possibilities even for me.

It was probably this strong experience that stirred up the decision to abandon the little village and go to the big city. As soon as I could afford to, I bought a record player and I must have played this concerto a couple of hundred times. I hummed and whistled all the concerto, or felt it. I carried it within me like a gift that gave me inspiration and joy whenever I wanted it (of course, I knew it by heart).

If I hear this concerto today, I don't feel any more than 'Aha, yes, that was it . . .' Nowadays I experience it as the little starter that aroused my appetite for the musical menu with all that it can offer.

(12.3B) Woman, middle-aged, 1980s

Bruch's Violin Concerto No. 1, Op. 26 is my strongest experience with music. The first time I heard it was on a course abroad. For a long time I had been wrestling with questions such as 'Who am I, what am I doing here, what is the meaning of it all?' During these intense weeks on the course, these questions came to the surface in an increasingly strong light. One day, during lunch, I was walking by myself in the mountains and thinking; I felt rather sad and unhappy.

That day's afternoon session ended with music, and it was Bruch's violin concerto. Suddenly it was as if all of me was filled with music and a light warmth. It filled my entire body and I 'grew', I expanded and filled the whole room. It felt as if my head 'bumped' into the ceiling. It's hard to describe the feeling with ordinary words. The tears ran down my cheeks, but I wasn't sad, rather it was a happiness I felt which brought with it calm, confidence, and a feeling for my own ability. I can do what I want to do. After the music had finished, it still felt as if I had a great calmness inside me.

(12.3C) Man, young, 1970s

I was 13 years old. The music that actually changed my life was a little piece on the album *The lamb lies down on Broadway* by Genesis. The track is called 'Silent sorrow in empty boats'. Before this experience I was a fairly ordinary lad. I listened a lot to music, but only to pop/rock, everything else was too complicated.

What did I feel like after this experience? Well, it is extremely difficult to describe. I suppose you could say that my mind was completely blank but was all the more full of emotions. Melancholy in a liberating way. Melancholy on the edge of being ready to cry, but nevertheless relieved. A bit afraid because I had allowed something so trifling as a 'bit of music' to captivate me to such an amazing degree.

I had actually busied myself a bit with music before this happened, but after this event I listened as well as played on a much deeper level, which has led to my becoming deeper as a person and unfortunately fairly introverted and something of a lone wolf. I do fully believe that this is on account of that little event (it is really rather crazy when I think about it, three minutes that changed my entire life).

(12.3D) Woman, young (from Chapter 20, account 20E)

[She is listening to a pop ballad with her new-found partner.] It was in the beginning, when you are a bit shy about saying what you think, and those lyrics said *everything* in some way. We didn't have to say anything. The music sort of said what we were thinking, and because of that it became so strong for us. No words were needed. It spoke for us instead . . .

I have had lots of music experiences in many different ways, but I never thought that I would have one that meant so much in a positive sense . . . For me, it meant an end to ten years of battling with myself and all the others and everyone around me. The end of ten years of acting and not daring to be yourself, of being super-nervous and a bit nuts. Ah, I found my way home!

Finally, here is a longer account that illustrates many different aspects of a strong experience with music, and could thus be quoted in several different places in this book. It starts in a very sombre mood, but when the narrator puts on some music by Mozart she becomes totally absorbed by it, sinks into it, loses awareness of time, space, and body. Her perception changes—everything seems to radiate perfection, beauty, and harmony. She feels a sense of security, she feels warmth and love, and gains a totally new awareness of life.

(12.3E) Woman, middle-aged, 1980s

[Written in English] November, mid afternoon in a sitting room filled with flat IKEA furniture. Grey, grey, grey—the first snow, grey sky, cold. So tired, so alone, so isolated, alone for days now, only the TV and the Swedish–English dictionary. I don't dare go outside because the thermometer shows it's below freezing. Grey, grey, grey—I am dead. Nobody would know if I was to die but even that luxury is not allowed. I am dead anyway—there is no life here in this life I have now.

For some reason I put on Mozart's *Requiem* (I am not aware of logically thinking in any way about this act). Back to the grey IKEA sofa. I read the sleeve notes and sink, sink, sink deeper—no time—only the sounds enveloping me in a world aside of this sinking deeper beyond words, beyond thoughts, only the waterfall of sound cascading around and through me.

There is no division, there is no music, there is no me. My head is gone, body too, and yet I am here. The grey four-square table leg is exquisite in its perfection—vibrant beyond meaning, in the intensity of its greyness, displays a perfection that defies description in words such as elegance, balance, and other such aesthetic valuations.

It simply is what it is, nothing more or less—the whole room, the whole universe is present here in perfect harmony. All colours are vivid beyond description, I see. I simply see. I seem to be experiencing directly and have no words to capture this state (not feeling) of bliss, harmony, meaningless beauty. I am totally a part of it all, the dirty carpet, the four-square table, the patterns on the wooden floor—how could they be so perfect? The whole world (there is no world) is dancing before my eyes—I am calm, tears run down my cheeks, I have no idea why.

There is no pain—pain is only resistance to the way it is. I remember thinking so. I am not happy, I am not sad, am not anything in particular, yet feel the potential for anything to pass through me. My tummy is soft and relaxed, no knots. Melted butter but not floppy—secure and warm and full of love. I want to kiss the postman, ring the whole world and tell it 'It's okay, it's all okay, there's no need to fight.'

I recognize the source of thoughts now emerging, solidifying an unexplainable profundity in words and descriptions. But the total qualitative shift in my relating to the world, universe, whatever you can now call it, remains.

That pure existence and nothing else could be so beautiful! Satisfaction. Ecstasy.

What this experience has meant to me: An awareness of the possibility of breakthrough in everyday life. That what we see in a normal state of waking consciousness is but a small percentage of what is available. That by letting go we have it all. A desire to make available to all mankind—not least myself!—such experience. An awareness that the problems of mankind are of his own making and therein lies the key. A much deepened and deepening respect to sound and music and to life in general. A personal commitment to quality in life, a strong drive to express myself through music.

The entire experience could well be described as a revelation. The grey existence is transformed into a world full of beauty and perfection: 'bliss, harmony, meaningless beauty . . . That pure existence and nothing else could be so beautiful! Satisfaction. Ecstasy.' And it is all there if only we will allow it to come to us, 'by letting go we have it all'.

Her impressionistic description includes contradictions that might irritate a logician—'There is no division, there is no music, there is no me. My head is gone, body too, and yet I am here'—but in the moment of the experience they are completely natural and self-evident. Her perception is more intense than usual ('All colours are vivid beyond description'), direct and without words ('I simply see. I seem to be experiencing directly and have no words to capture this state'), and she is absorbed by something bigger ('I am totally a part of it all . . . The whole world . . . is dancing before my eyes'). In all there is a 'total qualitative shift in my relating to the world . . . A much deepened . . . respect to sound and music and to life in general . . . A desire to make available to all mankind . . . such experience'.

She clothed this in similar terms in another account about music and love:

> Again this transformation of the world and all it contains, deep harmony, beauty, vibrancy in every living and non-living thing, sense of non-self, non-existence as an individual unit. Oneness. Ecstasy. Same bright colours, perfection, ease, and grace. The world is at peace.

These last accounts also contain elements of transcendental character and thus border on the following chapter about music and transcendence.

CHAPTER 13

MUSIC AND TRANSCENDENCE

In accounts of strong experiences with music, the experience is sometimes described with words such as 'magical', 'mysterious', 'supernatural', 'extraterrestrial' or similar expressions. The narrator feels as if he/she is put in a trance or ecstasy, there may be a feeling of totally merging with something bigger and of glimpsing other worlds or existences. These are examples of transcendental experiences (from the Latin *transcendere* = to exceed, surpass), that is, experiences that go beyond what is considered as ordinary perception and experience.

Here is a selection of accounts that can illustrate such transcendental experiences in connection with music. It is, of course, self-evident that these are hard to put into words. Often, such descriptions are restricted to one or several expressions of the type above, perhaps with the addition of an image or a metaphor.

One can also count so-called 'out-of-body experiences' as transcendental experiences. These, however, have already been dealt with in Chapter 8. Another, distinct, group of transcendental experiences comprises religious experiences. These are treated separately in Chapter 14.

13.1 MAGICAL, SUPERNATURAL, MYSTERIOUS, SPIRITUAL EXPERIENCES

Expressions of this kind occur as elements in many accounts from listeners as well as performers.

A singer describes a mysterious experience when he was rehearsing '*Mondnacht*' by Robert Schumann.

(13.1A) Man, middle-aged, 1970s (from Chapter 18, account 18.1C)

> Very suddenly . . . I was 'inside' the song. It was almost like a mystical experience. It felt as if the ceiling in the practice room disintegrated, and I was standing there under the stars in the moonlight and living in the song—not singing it. And every note meant something very special, and I understood what every note meant. And she and I were not singer and pianist, but had some sort of joint revelation. It was like an enchantment.

Another musician describes a partly similar experience he had as a listener at a jazz concert.

(13.1B) Man, old, 1980s (from Chapter 26, account 26J)

> After a while, when they played a tune it felt suddenly exactly as if the premises had disappeared, the surrounding almost disappeared like in a hallucination, the walls disappeared, it was sort of like in a dream. I could almost see how the ceiling opened up above the orchestra like when there are thunder clouds and there is a hole, an opening where the light comes through, the sun can be seen, that's exactly how I saw it, as if it was open up above and the orchestra sort of was raised up a bit in that hole. An incredible experience, afterwards I had to shake my head and I didn't understand what had happened.

A man who listened to a concert with the band Pink Floyd described a part of his experience like this.

(13.1C) Man, middle-aged, 1990s (from Chapter 27, account 27E)

> In the middle of the concert, I experience the entire situation with this gigantic lightshow and the magnificent music from the stage as almost unreal. I feel as though I have been moved to another planet and I suddenly have a distinct feeling of communication. Almost as if I have something supernatural before me that is desperately trying to catch my attention and make me understand something.

A similar sensation was experienced by a woman on a visit to the Glyptotek Museum in Copenhagen who heard 'extraterrestrial music' and thought that she was floating out into space (see Chapter 8, account 8.2D).

Some narrators describe their experiences as 'spiritual' experiences. Spirituality is, of course, often associated with religious experiences, but the next narrator characterizes the experience as spiritual without having religious elements.

(13.1D) Man, young, 1970s (from an edited interview)

> I was 13 years old. I was in a large church with lots of candles, it was such a solemn atmosphere. The music that was played was by Bach. That was an enormous kick too. It penetrated right into your pores everywhere. It was a spiritual experience without having anything to do with religion. Something just comes over you . . . *yeah*, you are just there. It's hard to explain how. It makes you devout. Makes you respect the music. It's so powerful.

With the next narrator, there is an emphasis on the experience of the spirit as opposed to body and matter.

(13.1E) Man, young, 1980s

[The experience took place during a musical play in a church ruin.] Roughly in the middle of the concert, an angel comes forth and I have a sort of revelation. Everything was so beautiful! I forgot about the existence of myself and others. I was right in the midst of the play and the music, was sort of there where it was happening. I had no distance from the play or the performance. I was right in the middle of it. It became reality. I was absorbed.

I consisted solely of spirit. The idea of body and matter wasn't there. I wasn't aware of my body at all, it was a floating, weightless feeling. It was only my soul or spirit that was there. It was so incredibly beautiful. I was moved and happy.

It all lasted for about one minute. Afterwards, I felt happy and melancholy. It was an incredibly delightful feeling or condition, a pity that I couldn't stay in it.

His body didn't exist any longer; he felt himself to consist only of spirit. He thought he floated freely, which of course has a natural connection to the feeling of incorporeity: the spirit is free from the body and can float freely. In that respect, the account has some similarities to the theme of Chapter 8. Another aspect of the experience is the total absorption: he feels as if he is in the midst of the play and the music, thus providing a further example of what was covered in Chapter 7, about merging with the music.

The next account could perhaps also be placed in Chapter 14 about religious experiences (the concept 'eternity' often has a religious content), or indeed also in the previous chapter on existential experiences. The borders between these are really fluid.

(13.1F) Woman, middle-aged, 1970s

I was alone at my parents' home and watching a TV programme about one of my favourite artists, Kathleen Ferrier. The programme ended with her singing the final part of '*Der Abschied*' from Mahler's *Das Lied von der Erde*. I had heard the recording a couple of times before, but now it struck me in a different way. Particularly the end, where she repeats '*Ewig, ewig*', time after time. I had a sensation of eternity. I remember how that evening I felt open and susceptible. Now, when I think about that experience, tears come to my eyes!

A special group of experiences comprises what musicians describe as 'magical moments', that is, when everything works perfectly without them having to make any effort at all: everything works by itself. When one plays together with others, it sometimes feels as if everybody is on the same wavelength, they all know exactly what is going to happen the next moment, nothing can go wrong. Accounts of this type come later in Chapter 18, especially in section 18.6.

13.2 ECSTASY, TRANCE

Ecstasy and trance are two well-known examples of transcendental phenomena. In the accounts, they are as a rule described with the use of one of these words; for example: 'One was in total ecstasy,' 'Everybody was pulled along in the ecstasy of the dance and the music,' 'The continually repeated rhythmic pattern carried me into some sort of trance.' The meanings of the terms 'ecstasy' and 'trance', respectively, are as a rule taken for granted, but in fact both terms are used rather indiscriminately and in different ways by different people, even among experts in the field.[1]

Here are a couple of examples, first from a listener, and then from a performer.

(13.2A) Woman, 1970s

It was a symphony concert and the first item on the programme was Bruch's Violin Concerto No. 1. The piece itself is delightful, and the soloist, the Korean Kyung-Wha Chung, played with such fervour, temperament, and empathy that she captivated the entire audience. I don't think that I have ever, before or since, felt so strongly after an experience of music or any experience at all. After the concerto there was an interval, and my cousin and me, we both walked out of the auditorium as if in a trance. We didn't say anything for a few minutes, and the few words that came after that showed that we were both just as moved by the experience. Almost with one voice we then said: 'Let's leave! Everything after this is just going to be wrong!' We were very quiet in the car. I have never driven so slowly on the road. Indeed, I would sometimes notice how the speed lessened and sometimes I wasn't driving faster than 50 kph. It was as if I was in a complete trance.

(13.2B) Man, young, 1980s

I was going to take part in a concert in a church and play a piece for guitar, the first prelude by Villa-Lobos. The item before me was a girl who played a solo piece for violin by J. S. Bach. The superb acoustics of the thirteenth-century church gave life to the sound of the violin and it was extremely beautiful. In fact, it was so beautiful that I forgot everything else and just merged myself totally with the music.

Then when it was my turn to play, it was as if I was in a trance. I don't remember that I walked out and sat there; rather, I was suddenly just sitting there and the music flowed. I wasn't aware that I myself was playing, but I just listened to the music and enjoyed it. At the same time, I felt that it was I who formed the tones, I had achieved total concentration.

Afterwards, it was like waking up; I hardly knew where I was. Since that time, I have worked at trying to recreate that total concentration but I have only partly succeeded. One of the reasons why it was so special on just that particular occasion was probably the excellent acoustics in the church.

Other musicians also mention trance-like conditions in connection with especially memorable performances (see the accounts in Chapter 18).

13.3 Cosmic experiences,
merging into something greater,
dissolution of one's ego

Examples of cosmic experiences can be that one has a feeling of timelessness or eternity, that one's ego is dissolved and that one merges into something greater, something that is outside, and one feels at one with the universe. Often, the experience includes an incorporeal floating.

Expressions such as 'eternity' and 'merging into something greater' tend to steer one's thoughts to religious experiences, and the border with religious experiences is fluid. In the accounts quoted below, there is as a rule no connection (or only a vaguely implied one) to religious experience.

Occasionally, such expressions as 'total experience' also occur. It is not entirely easy to interpret the content of this. In certain cases, it seems to mean some form of fusion of experiences in several different dimensions, in other cases that the experience embraces 'everything' (there is nothing besides this) or that the experience is completely overwhelming, or a combination of all these alternatives.

The following accounts exemplify one or several of the above aspects of cosmic experiences.

(13.3A) Woman, old, 1930s

When there was a choir rehearsal at the church, the cantor and I both happened to come too early. He said to me: 'Now you're going to hear something lovely,' and then he played for me Bach's Toccata and Fugue in C major on the organ. I sat there in the gloom in the empty church hall and it felt as if my heart would burst because I was in such raptures. I myself and the church hall expanded in some way and merged in a larger context—a part of the universe, perhaps.

This was a turning point for me—from then on, music was 'my room'; this is where I was safe and happy.

(13.3B) Woman, old, 1940s

In the concert hall they performed Brahms's *Requiem*, conducted by Wilhelm Furtwängler. I sang the soprano voice in the choir. This work was a first-time experience for me. Suddenly the experience of the sound of the orchestra and choir together with the content of the text became so powerful that I was sort of lifted up out of myself. Perhaps it could be expressed in terms of 'falling to bits'. I don't know how long this sensation lasted, but it was a comparatively short moment.

I have sung the solo part of this work and then I've felt a sort of inspiration from long ago. It feels as if you are united with something that is outside you.

(13.3C) Man, middle-aged, 1970s

I was 12 years old, had been singing in the boys' choir and played the piano for a couple of years. I was at school and had cycled home during the lunch break. There was only my mum and me at home. In those days Swedish Radio broadcasted entertainment music and at home a little radio was on. My mum was busy doing things, the gas cooker was hissing, and suddenly I was struck. In my home, there was no so-called classical music, it was mostly jazz or my mum played old pop tunes on the piano. So perhaps it is a bit strange that it was Beethoven's Leonora Overture No. 3 that grabbed me, so that I disappeared completely.

The music was suddenly there round about me, as if it comprised a transparent but evidently impenetrable wall. I thought that it told me something, and I listened and answered, and when the music/story went on, I felt a joy that was so enormous that I experienced it as being almost cosmic. The condition that the story led me into was plastic—almost as if I was floating around or hovering inside the transparent wall. Nothing, nobody, could reach me. It was like a salvation, but without religious elements, and the warmth and joy and the calm that I experienced and heard long followed me. The experience influenced me for a long time after that in a deep and distinct manner.

(13.3D) Man, middle-aged, 1980s

It was in Oslo at the Edvard Munch Museum. The morning, not many people inside the museum. It was quiet for a long time; I looked at the works of art. Then in comes the pianist who is going to practise. They were going to have a concert in the evening, and he played Chopin, one of his mazurkas I think it was.

I was walking around looking at these works of art, and then when he started to play it was a sort of . . . well, it is very difficult to be precise about what sort of experience it was . . . It was a strong experience, that's the first thing I'd say. It felt to me almost like when you merge into something that is bigger, to express it in almost religious terms.

It was in the minor mode. It was partly connected to the atmosphere in the room and perhaps how I was feeling myself. That was perhaps why it struck me as powerfully as it did, that experience, partly that minor key, partly that it was quiet round about me and that everything together gave an enormous connection—of melancholy but at the same time of joy, euphoria, or exhilaration in some strange way . . . it is terribly hard for me to distinguish that this is a special musical experience, rather, for me the music is interwoven, in this case with art, an experience with Edvard Munch's paintings. It isn't a purely musical experience, I think it is a total experience in some strange way—that it happens at the same time.

In this description, the narrator emphasized a certain factor in the music—the minor mode—as an important element in the experience. The narrator in the following example is, however, of the opinion that the experience in part was dependent upon her not being able to structure the musical course.

(13.3E) Woman, young, 1980s

The music was *Das Rheingold* by Wagner, the first time for me. I don't think I was in any special physical or mental condition—my mood was fairly neutral.

The experience came gradually—started as a sort of charge or tension in the atmosphere, which gradually became all the more intense—roughly like a scent which you first get a hint of, rather than really feel, before it washes over you, inebriates you and takes you over. It was a feeling of intense expectation with all my senses on full alert, wide open and susceptible, sucking in every note. This feeling was mixed successively with a sort of elation which grew all the bigger—filled me up—until it seemed to overflow, and I felt a sensation of incorporeal floating, a total merging with the music, or quite simply with something bigger—God or the universe, perhaps—where the experience of me, myself, was completely annihilated. I think of it as that the experience at this stage is very like a religious salvation experience or being high on drugs.

Externally, I'm sure that no reaction could be seen in me. But I did, however, experience the light and the applause afterwards as irritating, almost painful, a feeling that was almost exactly like when you are rudely awakened by an alarm clock. I would have liked to sit there, still, alone, in silence and contemplation and gradually let the experience lift like a mist. Applause and cries of bravo seemed to be more like sacrilege in the true sense of the word.

That the music was by Wagner does perhaps explain some of it (*unendliche Melodie*, the harmonic progressions, the instrumentation, etc.). Since I hadn't heard the music before, and in those days had very little knowledge of music theory, I couldn't structure the musical course at all, which presumably made the experience so direct and purely emotional.

The feeling stayed with me in a vague and indefinable way, like the memory of a pleasant dream after you wake up, before it gradually fades away and disappears. This experience, together with other similar ones, made me opt for music as a profession.

There are several examples in other places in this book. One woman described an experience as a child when one Christmas Eve she lay in her bed and looked at the deep blue night sky while she heard music by Schubert.

(13.3F) Woman, old (from Chapter 4, account 4.5E)

In some way I evidently experienced the child's awestruck littleness in the face of the majestic endlessness of the firmament coupled with a sense of complete security in experiencing myself as an infinitely little part of this whole . . .

Another woman recalls her experience at an outdoor concert featuring Pink Floyd.

(13.3G) Woman, young, 1980S (from account 27F)

And then they played the good old tunes mixed with new but just as good ones, and I knew them so well and could stand there and sway and sing along. I felt at one with the music . . . After the break, darkness had settled over the stadium and they had good use for the light effects which included laser beams that 'went out into the universe'. Yes, that is actually what it felt like, everything became so infinite and I was one with it . . . Borders are erased. I am at one with the universe.

13.4 EXPERIENCES OF OTHER WORLDS, OTHER REALITIES

Experiences of other worlds, other realities, are mentioned in several accounts. One feels that one has been moved to another world beyond time and space. Sometimes this is united with a sensation of being lifted up, of floating in mid-air or of travelling, as well as feelings of great beauty and joy. In some accounts, the 'other world' could perhaps be interpreted in a religious sense, as when a narrator says (in connection with music by Mozart) 'it was heaven, it was paradise, it was everything that was beautiful, pure, and most loving', or when another narrator speaks of 'a death that was also a birth into something that was liberatingly light'. Neither of them, however, refers directly to a religious experience.

The music that is mentioned in the accounts is of different types, but in some cases there is an indication of what qualities in the music may have contributed to the experience, as well as other circumstances behind the experience.

(13.4A) Woman, middle-aged

I've had a number of strong experiences of music together with other people by listening and dancing to shaman drums. At the sound of the drum 'I see the crack between worlds' and in an altered state of consciousness I journey to high and light places or to deep and gloomy worlds and many places in between.

(13.4B) Woman, old, 1950s

I was sitting in a full church to listen to '*Förklädd Gud*' ['God in disguise'] by Lars-Erik Larsson. As soon as I sat down in the pew, I had a feeling of peace and calm in my soul and everything outside the here and now disappeared. And when the music and singing started, I followed along to another world. It felt as if the music, the singing, the poetry filled me and I became jubilantly happy. The music took me with it to dizzy heights.

(13.4C) Woman, old, 1970s

At an evening concert by Anders Wadenberg I got to hear Schubert and Beethoven sonatas interpreted in such a way that I was in raptures. After the last notes of the last sonata, I felt as if I was in another world, floating up high. I was up there until the applause broke out. Applause that totally smashed my musical experience.

(13.4D) Woman, old (from Chapter 5, account 5.2C)

That was the first time in my life that I got to hear Tchaikovsky's sixth symphony . . . It moved me from the very first note. I felt as if I was lifted up into another world. Time and space disappeared, perhaps that is what eternity is like. An indescribable feeling of painful joy and bliss filled me. There was a recurrent melancholic theme that I felt that Tchaikovsky had written with the blood of his heart. His pain in these beautiful notes spoke directly to me . . . I had gone to the concert alone and I was glad about that. Didn't want to talk to anybody, nor go home immediately. The experience of having been able to look into another world was so incredible.

(13.4E) Woman, old, 1940s

I was studying at university and had many friends there who were interested in music. I understood from them that Mozart was something quite exceptional, but I couldn't find anything in his music; just thought that it made a confused and disparate impression.

One evening in the summer, I went with two friends to a midnight concert at the Nationalmuseum [Stockholm]. I experienced harmony between us, I enjoyed the beautiful museum and the art. Then they played Mozart's Symphony No. 40. A new and wonderful world was opened up for me. It was heaven; it was paradise; it was everything that was beautiful, pure, and deeply loving. Since that day, I have enjoyed Mozart.

It wasn't until the tenth tone that I was, so to say, aroused. Don't know how I can explain this without a score, but the symphony starts one–two–three, one–two–three, one–two–three–four, which I found so brilliant:

Fig 13.1 The beginning of Mozart's Symphony No. 40 in G minor.

(13.4F) Man, old, 1980s

I was listening to a TV broadcast of a concert. There is an item with the title '*Mio Gesù*'. The piece is sung by a soprano and a boy soprano together with some choir singers, accompanied by an organ. The final part with a baritone's safe voice 'embraced' the work in a gentle, calming way. The soprano and boy soprano duet ending with the baritone was unforgettable. The music carried me into another world. I was enchanted, to put it mildly. I turned down the volume on the TV afterwards, didn't want to listen to anything else straight away. Silence and reflection seemed necessary. It was the first time I heard Lloyd Webber's *Requiem* with '*Mio Gesù*' ('*Pie Jesu*').

(13.4G) Woman, old, 1970s

I was on an opera visit to Verona, where they were performing Puccini's *Madame Butterfly*. It was the first time I was in an amphitheatre. It was a wonderfully beautiful evening. As it was an open-air theatre, that evening you could see a velvet-blue sky and a large shining moon above us. We had bought small candle stumps at the entrance, and we lit these in the darkness when the performance started. What an atmosphere!

Despite the hard stone bench which I was sitting on, my joy was indescribable. And then came the highlight of the evening: 'The humming chorus', which made my heart melt. Neither before nor since have I experienced anything like it. At first I felt a shiver in my body. I closed my eyes and found myself in another world. I was so moved by the wonderful music that I wanted to cry.

When we left the theatre, I didn't want to talk to anybody, I wanted to stay on in the world that gave me such a feeling of joy.

(13.4H) Woman, middle-aged, 1980s

The composer Ralph Lundsten said in a radio programme by way of introduction: 'You don't have to understand music to be able to enjoy music. We humans don't understand love, for example, but nevertheless we are blissful when it affects us.' It was like an Aha experience and I started to listen. To his programme. To his music. To other music. To sounds. Ralph's programme and his music have since then been a door, a gateway, to a completely new world. Since then I haven't cared about what I do or don't know. Like I said, I don't need to know about notes in a score, or how to play an instrument, or music history, or to be able to sing or dance. It is enough to listen, to take in, experience, and let something inside me—my body, soul, or subconscious—receive, register, and give back.

I had the opportunity to make an educational visit to Ralph Lundsten's studio, Andromeda. The environment in his studio is absolutely unique and totally stunning. I can't remember exactly what they were playing when I came—it might have been pieces from his 'Paradise' Symphony. After that we could hear music from A Midwinter Saga—Nordic Nature Symphony No. 3. It was the first time I heard that music. The music flowed out of his exclusive loudspeakers, all of his science-fiction-like studio with mixer table, tape recorders of various sizes and sorts, synths of all different types, special lighting, everything vibrated—and into your entire consciousness goes the most delightful, most powerful, most caressing lyrical nature music. You see the stars, you see the snow and can smell it, you enjoy the peace, you shiver in the cold, and are swept along by enormous waves. I felt as if I was transferred in time and space, as if I was in another world.

When I left the studio, it felt as if I had been on a fantastic journey, a cosmic voyage, where the landing, the touchdown, in my own reality was slow and friendly—nice and gently I found myself in my own world again a few hours later. But even so, never again would my world be the same, because now there were the sounds, the music, and never again would I be alone because there were music and sounds to experience, to venture further into. I felt that I was sort of chosen to experience this, humble and grateful that I had had the privilege.

(13.41) Woman, middle-aged

When an experience is strong, it goes beyond the barrier where we have made use of words to describe and tell about things. So I am fumbling for words.

The music that I have experienced so strongly on one occasion, it is difficult to find words for. The closest I can come is a cosmic total experience beyond time and space. My body and the music became a whole where I knew I was dead, but it was a death that was a birth into something that was liberatingly light. A light that didn't exist in this life. I even vanished from this life, so I can't remember anything of my surroundings. Everything that happened wasn't connected to this world.

I remember the words: '*Es ist vollbracht*' and the singer Dietrich Fischer-Dieskau. And also a wind instrument (oboe?) that sounded heavenly. Probably a movement from a Bach cantata.

I always carry this experience within me, which means that I 'see' another life and think that much of our earthly striving is unimportant.

Here is a suitable point to go outside our research and quote what film director Ingmar Bergman said about his view of music in an interview broadcast on TV.[2]

> Music . . . for me it is messages about there being other realities. Outside our reality there are other realities, and it is only music that can give us proof that those realities exist. And I think that the messages that we can sometimes get are so tremendous. And it isn't that you are just imagining it, but it strikes you right in your emotional core where the most difficult questions, the biggest questions, where they are and sort all this out and suddenly make everything self-evident and natural. And just like I think that it is the case that suddenly one day when you perhaps are dead without knowing it, perhaps you think like this: Well now, was it really that simple! And that is what music time after time tells me.'

The same ideas were repeated in Ingmar Bergman's radio programme when he presented his choice of music (18 July, 2004, Swedish Radio Broadcasting, programme 1). At the end, he asked the question 'Where does music come from?' and went on: 'I personally have an understanding that we have been given music as a gift. I am not a religious believer, but nevertheless I do think that we have been given music as a gift to let us have an idea about realities and worlds outside the world we live in.'

To conclude this chapter, there are a couple of accounts that are related to each other in that they both touch upon several of the transcendental experiences that have previously been mentioned. They could also be quoted in the chapter on existential aspects as they provide examples of how the experience affects the narrator's understanding of the surrounding world. Objects and people seem to be 'animated', given a special role and purpose in the universe, 'everything is marked by being something

universal and comprehensive'. Both these narrators also analyse which musical structures seem to trigger such experiences: slow, peaceful, repetitive, and meditative
instrumental music. It also requires that you give yourself the time to really listen.

(13.4J) Man, young, 1990s

I bought an album by Brian Eno called *Ambient 1: Music for Airports*. Eno has used eight
different tape loops of varying lengths. On these he has recorded various tracks and intervals. What happens is that the loops continually shift in time in relation to each other, and
thus an ever-changing musical course is produced. The music is very slow. The first times
I played it, I didn't feel so much except that I thought it was wonderful music.

However, this changed one day when I was walking in the Old Town in Stockholm with
Music for Airports in my Walkman earphones. Suddenly, everything was 'animated'. Every
screw, building, car, person. Everything had a meaning and a role in the great universe. It
felt like a music video but for real. I thought that everything can't really be just as important, but whatever I chose to look at, it was the same all the time. It didn't matter if it was a
grumpy-looking old lady, a torn bit of paper, or a poster advertising hair spray. Everything
had a history and a soul. This has actually made me see big things in trifles, like feeling
empathy with insensitive objects such as the discarded advertising flyer which was simply
forgotten and thrown away without fulfilling its function.

After this remarkable and strong experience for about 45 minutes (the length of the
record), I had some other music of a similar ambient character but that didn't give me
anything like the feeling that I'd had before.

I thought that this particular record's ability to bring forth emotions was unique.
It didn't take long before I discovered that such was not the case. I was at a friend's place
where I had been lots of times before, so I knew all the things and pictures he has in his
home. He had bought an album by the composer Arvo Pärt. On it there was a number
called 'Spiegel im Spiegel'. He played this and suddenly the feeling was there again. All the
objects in the room had a soul. For example, an old picture postcard that we'd laughed at
because a man in the picture looks like a friend of ours. This man was suddenly an important part of the world and sort of had a meaning as he was hiking in the mountains. I'd seen
that card hundreds of time without feeling like that.

I said that I'd had experienced the same thing with Eno's record, and as my friend had
that, we tried listening to it. Now it really did get charged with emotion. If 'Spiegel im
Spiegel' had got us feeling like that, *Music for Airports* was an overdose of the same thing.
I got so many impressions and emotions from the album that I thought I'd go crazy. In the
end, we had to turn it off and, so to speak, come back to reality with other music.

(13.4K) Man, young, 1990s

A magical power is inherent in certain music and it feels as if this can affect the environment around you. So what sort of strains of music possess this remarkable ability to give an
extra dimension, for example to a view of nature? In the first place, instrumental music
appears to be most effective. The meditative condition seems to be disturbed if there
is singing. For my part, music should have distinct elements of melancholy, a feeling of
longing, humility, and reflection. Tranquillity and silence are important.

On certain occasions, the feeling has been particularly evident and this has been characterized by everything acquiring a stamp of something universal and comprehensive. It is as if the

tones show meanings that are not noticeable in everyday situations. But once you've sat down to listen and to give yourself time, these secrets are revealed. The condition that I rather clumsily am trying to describe has mainly affected me when I haven't tried to achieve it to order.

For example, on one occasion when a friend and I were sitting at my table. That time, Arvo Pärt's 'Spiegel im Spiegel' was coming from the stereo. That piece contains all that I've already mentioned: simplicity, calm, melancholy, etc. And it is instrumental too, which means that the music can speak for itself and is, so to speak, neutral. Thus you're free to make your own interpretation. 'Spiegel im Spiegel' has a repetitive character. That contributes to your being put into the 'visionary' meditative condition. Repetition is evidently an ingredient in the recipe. While the piece of music was playing, my ability to concentrate increased, and the seemingly inanimate objects that lay placed where they were in my room sort of acquired a character of their own, each one of them. An object that perhaps isn't used so often, or that quite simply isn't as practicable as another one, acquired in this rare moment a purpose, a meaning.

This phenomenon doesn't apply only to things; rather, the same feeling can come if you are out walking, with headphones over your ears, and watch people as they come and go. All your irritation, all your fixed ideas and prejudices, etc., that you now and then carry with you, they just sink away. For a moment, existence gets a shimmering glow, and becomes a little warmer, lighter, and simpler.

The weird, almost religious—or at any rate mysterious—feeling that you sometimes have the privilege to experience, where does it come from? What is it in music that opens the door slightly to something much stranger than that which you are normally aware of?

The final words without doubt remind us of Ingmar Bergman's understanding that music is 'messages about there being other realities'.

Using the accounts in this section (13.4) as a starting point, if one tries to see which factors can lie behind experiences of other worlds/existences, one gains a fairly complex picture. The music has been of many different types. In accounts 13.4J and 13.4K, there is an emphasis on the importance of the music (by Brian Eno and Arvo Pärt, respectively) being slow, tranquil, repetitive, and purely instrumental. It is also characterized as meditative, and one of the narrators even mentioned other elements in the music like melancholy, a feeling of longing, humility, and reflection; these qualities, however, are rather to be seen as different elements in the experience of the music than as inherent to the music itself. Rhythms on shaman drums (account 13.4A) are also repetitive and instrumental (but hardly slow and peaceful), and are often named as a means of bringing forth a trance condition. Ralph Lundsten's electro-acoustic music often seems to be intended to arouse feelings of space and eternity.

In other accounts, the music is completely different, for example the main theme in Mozart's 40th symphony, a theme in Tchaikovsky's *Pathétique* symphony, vocal music in Lloyd Webber's *Requiem* and Puccini's opera *Madame Butterfly* and in a Bach cantata (together with an oboe).

A shared factor may be the beauty of the music pieces in question, but the musical factors behind the experience of beauty are nevertheless very dissimilar in the various works. Other non-musical factors to be considered, may be, for example, that the music was listened to in a special setting, such as the amphitheatre in Verona (account 13.4G) or Ralph Lundsten's studio, Andromeda (13.4H).

CHAPTER 14

MUSIC AND RELIGIOUS EXPERIENCES

RELIGION and music have always been closely associated. Regardless of which religion, music is an important part of rites and cult activities, sometimes even dance. Within Christianity, the examples stretch all the way from early Gregorian chant, and the vocal polyphony that developed out of that, to major works such as cantatas, masses, passions, and oratorios, many of which are considered masterpieces in the Western art of music and are often performed in a concert setting. Other examples are, of course, hymns and spiritual songs, in more recent times also gospel and Christian rock and pop songs.

So it is not surprising that in our material there are many examples of strong experiences with music in connection with religious experiences. There are also several examples of people making comparisons—they think they find similarities—between experiences of music and religious experiences.

The narrators' attitudes to Christianity vary. Some of them are explicit religious believers, others haven't taken a stance; some describe themselves as atheists and others don't mention anything at all about this (nor was it in any way a part of the purpose of the research).

The accounts vary considerably in both length and depth. Some of the accounts are very short and general, such as: 'It was (like) a religious experience.' As they don't say anything more about the content of the experience, these are not taken up here.

The accounts have been divided into different groups according to content or theme. A first group of accounts is about how music gave rise to visions of heaven, life to come, paradise, or eternity.

The accounts in the second group provide examples of how music is associated with experiences of spiritual peace, holiness, and Christian fellowship.

The theme in the third group could be said to be religious communication. On the one hand, music and the text/lyrics can convey a religious message to the listener—the listener is reached by a Christian address. On the other hand, music can be used to search for contact with the Godhead, for example through hymns and songs of praise. These two aspects sometimes merge with each other.

The culmination of religious experience in connection with music can be found in descriptions of religious conversion and experiencing the presence of (or a meeting with) God, Jesus Christ, or the Holy Ghost. Accounts with such content make up the fourth and final group.

As usual, there is a certain degree of overlap between these different aspects. Even if an account has been placed under a particular heading, it can at the same time also illustrate other aspects.

The music in the accounts belongs in most instances to what can be characterized as religious music, but there are also examples of 'worldly' music.

14.1 VISIONS OF HEAVEN, PARADISE, ETERNITY

In several accounts, music is described as having given rise to visions of heaven, paradise, and eternity. The music in question comes from several different sources. Not unexpectedly, there is music here from the great Baroque masters, Bach and Handel.

(14.1A) Woman, middle-aged, 1940s

It was after my 15th birthday. On Good Friday I got to follow along with the family to listen to the *St Matthew Passion* by J. S. Bach. You sat on hard church pews in a cold church, completely full. The *Passion* lasts four hours. In a longish break you can get some fresh air in the churchyard and eat a sandwich you've brought with you. This is during the hard times in the post-war period in Germany.

The experience of the music is incredible: the orchestra's swaying, heavy pull in the introduction (this was long before Harnoncourt's swinging Baroque style), a full choir, the evangelist who sings the well-known gospel with great empathy, the role of Jesus sung by a well-known bass singer, arias, extremely sorrowful. Everybody was dressed in black, we knew the alto soloist personally . . . that they could sing so beautifully!

I remember the shivers right through my body, the tears and then in the final chorale 'Ruhe sanfte, sanfte Ruh': this must go on forever, keep on, keep on. And thought or said: this must be what it sounds like in heaven.

(14.1B) Woman, middle-aged, 1960s

It was a Saturday, and I was out walking about in town. Was a student and curious about most of the music life on offer in the big city. Concerts, opera!

Caught sight of a poster this same Saturday. They were performing Bach's *St Matthew Passion* in Engelbrekt Church, foreign artistes, members of the Swedish Radio Symphony Orchestra! That was something to go to! So, in good time before 15.00 hours (it was the dress rehearsal) I went there, there was a long queue and when I finally got a ticket it was a standing ticket up in the balcony.

It turned three o'clock, I was standing there in the squash on the balcony, the church was packed with people, the music started and the choir stood up, I couldn't see that much, but I could hear. Heard heavenly beautiful violin music, and there was breathless silence among this listening crowd and I was in the middle of them. And the music continued sometimes so painfully, sometimes so beautifully, so consolingly. It felt as if the music grabbed my soul and took it up to heavenly spheres.

The work takes just over three hours. But I felt that the music held me captive. The time? I didn't notice it.

(14.1C) Woman, young, 1980s

The choir at school sings the Hallelujah chorus from Handel's *Messiah* at the end of term before the Christmas holiday. The feeling is the same every time and probably will be the same every time I sing that song. There is something great, everybody sings 'Hallelujah' together first and then it embroiders itself into a never-ending song of praise to God. It feels as if you are in heaven and there are lots of angels singing. Yes, it feels like a foretaste of eternity.

When we practised, we practised a bit at a time, but we could never stop. It felt like a victory manifestation to sing like that, I was filled with a bubbling joy and a longing to praise God. I don't know how I can explain it, but my soul strove to reach God in some way.

The music in the next account has its origins in the early Christian era, but at the time of the experience this was completely unknown to the narrator (as it was for many others at the same time).

(14.1D) Man, old, 1930s

I was an elementary school teacher and a church organist. But now it was the summer holidays and I was at home. I had read an advertisement for a church concert in a nearby town one summer's evening. I wasn't spoiled for such events, so it tempted me.

From the balcony, the choir sang some hymns by composers of the time, Wennerberg, Nordqvist, Nyvall. It was done well, of course, but it was nothing that was especially striking. This was followed by an organ solo. And during this the choir left the balcony, they walked down the centre aisle in a procession up to the altar, where they split into men and women each on their own side of the chancel.

And then something began that I had never heard before or been able to imagine. It resounded like nothing I had ever heard before. It was plainsong, chanting. A type of tone language that was totally new to me. Neither major nor minor. This singing in unison, plainsong, antiphonal, responsorial—it was all unknown to me. Long afterwards I understood that they were canonical hours. I assume that they were either vespers or completorium, probably the former.

I was absolutely enchanted, shocked. In a way that I shall never forget. More than 50 years have passed since that time. I remember how I thought then—and always when I have thought about it later—that *if* any worldly song could give a vision of heavenly song, this was it.

My experience is indescribable. During my long life I have of course had the time to have many experiences of music, positive as well as negative. But no experience came anywhere near this. I cycled home. With this new resounding singing in my ears, heart, soul. It is *impossible* to describe this in words, but I can still recall the impressions that evening gave me.

In the following account, the vision is aroused by communal singing of a well-known hymn.

(14.1E) Woman, middle-aged, 1980s

For me, experiences of music go hand in hand with my Christian faith, so you might also call this a spiritual experience but through music. I was at a conference in Germany. At the conference, there were young people from all over Europe, and even from the USA and South America. At the meetings in the enormous sports hall we were all gathered together, about 5,000 of us, and we sang mainly in English, somebody taught us, there were prayers, dance and drama.

One evening I was sitting almost right at the top of one of the balconies in the hall, with a view out over the mass of people. We sang as usual that evening, but something special happened. Everybody sang the old Swedish song 'O store Gud' [literally: 'Oh great God'; the Swedish version of 'How great Thou art'], which has been translated into many languages the world over. But instead of everyone singing the song together in English, you could hear 'O store Gud' being sung in lots of languages in the hall. I was absolutely overcome. Stood still, closed my eyes, was myself silent for a moment, listened to the people who were singing around me, looked out over the gathering and sang along in this choir. In my mind's eye I could see that this was what it was going to be like in heaven, all these language groups collected together, people singing communally each in their own language and it sounds out, just beautiful and in harmony.

Despite the fact that I left home alone, I didn't feel alone; my voice and me, we were important. It was with joy that I left this gathering and I have with me an experience in life, an experience that I won't forget. When I hear 'O store Gud' being sung, I can recall that summer's evening in Germany, there on the balcony when I got a foretaste of heaven.

The music in the following accounts is considerably more recent, namely gospel. Gospel is also mentioned in several other accounts in the book.

(14.1F) Man, middle-aged, 1990s

We had the privilege of participating in a course arranged by the Stockholm Gospel Choir Festival for choir leaders, music teachers, and others who were interested. The programme included a banquet at which several of the instructors performed. It was when one of the lady soloists sang a song about heaven that I experienced something out of the ordinary. It felt as if she took us there with her. I think it was her feeling that moved me. I can't remember which song she sang, except that it was a gospel ballad. What I do remember is that it was about heaven and that she got me to feel as if I was there. The tears started to flow with some of us. We suddenly felt a different depth in our being together and in the conversation.

Of course, it wasn't entirely comfortable to expose your feelings in front of completely new acquaintances. But the experience was worth more than the feeling of embarrassment.

(14.1G) Woman, young, 1980s

It was a choir that sang songs of praise to God and gospel songs in turn. We were sitting so that I couldn't see when the trumpeter Phil Driscoll stepped forward and started to play together with the choir, in the middle of a song that was about God's glory and purity ('We are standing on holy ground'). The heavenly strains of the trumpet moved me so that the tears just ran. I was surprised that something can sound like I have only guessed what it would sound like in heaven.

Straight afterwards, I felt glad and exhilarated about God being so glorious and magnificent. To think that He can use music to convey his glory to me!

The Adagietto movement in Gustav Mahler's fifth symphony is music that occurs in several accounts in our material. In the following account, it gives rise to a religious vision.

(14.1H) Man, young, 1980s

I have had several experiences that you could perhaps count as strong and intensive. A piece of music that has given such an experience is the Adagietto from Mahler's fifth symphony. The recording is by the Chicago Symphony Orchestra, conducted by Georg Solti. The day it 'happened' I was on my own at home, probably after school at about three or four o'clock. My physical condition was normal. Mentally, I was gloomy and reflective like I usually am.

Mahler's fifth symphony and especially the Adagietto is one of my favourite pieces in general. The music fills you with a sort of intoxication, or shivers where every chord goes through you like waves. You lose grasp of time and to a certain extent of space too, in the sense that the whole room I am lying in starts to revolve. In the fortissimo on the dominant in the last bars, it is like a light passes over my closed eyes, fading out more and more in the following diminuendo.

Afterwards, I stay lying there a few minutes and let the music sink away and back. The moment after is probably the only time I feel calm and satisfied with myself and the world around. Your own problems and the burden of your own personality disappear at the same time that it feels as if you have found yourself!

Always when I listen to music I try to translate my experiences or the composer's message into words or ideas—little words that I meditate upon. In the Adagietto, my thoughts and feelings revolve around longing—death—God—salvation. The music and my feeling make me understand (at least emotionally) the incomprehensible but still elementary. Things that I otherwise doubt appear to me as truths with the power of music. Music becomes a confirmation of my own longing and my doubts and faith. Music also manifests another life, another existence that I hope will be mine. An existence where you are satisfied with yourself, live in harmony with the world around you, and where it is peaceful and love is the spring of life.

In the previous chapter, there were some statements by Ingmar Bergman about music revealing other realities, opening up difficult questions and making everything seem simple and self-evident. The young man in the account above says something similar: 'Music also manifests another life, another existence that I hope will be mine,' as well as 'The music and my feeling make me understand . . . the incomprehensible but still elementary. Things that I otherwise doubt appear to me as truths with the power of music.'

14.2 SPIRITUAL PEACE, HOLY ATMOSPHERE, CHRISTIAN COMMUNITY

In the accounts about visions, feelings of peace and great Christian fellowship were mentioned as well. In the following accounts, music and the surroundings together create an atmosphere of tranquillity, spiritual peace, purity, and holiness. In the first example, this happens in the narrator's solitude and with peaceful nature as a framework for the music.

(14.2A) Woman, 1980s

It was an August evening. It had been raining during the day. But now the sun was shining. And it was as if the evening was enveloped in a glittering veil. A blackbird could be heard warbling. Mysterious and beautiful, the river flowed past the white house where I lived.

I turned the radio on. Music by Scarlatti (a cantata) poured into the room. I lay on the bed and listened. The room was filled with a spiritual purity. In my mind's eye, I saw a staircase that led up to heaven. I went up those stairs and came to a meadow with flowers so beautiful that I have never seen their like. In front of me on the table was a posy of wild flowers. It was as if the flowers sucked in the music. There was a sort of aura around the posy of flowers that I can't describe in words.

My mind became peaceful and calm. And I felt gratitude at being able to experience the music as something holy.

In the following examples, however, the narrator is together with many other people. The experiences take place abroad in various Christian environments.

(14.2B) Woman, old, 1960s

As a group of Swedish tourists, we visited the monastery at Montserrat in Spain. It was a sunny, warm, and pleasant October day. It was a pleasure to sit down in the pews and feel the spiritual peace. We were told that a boys' choir would sing. There wasn't a sound to be heard when the concert was about to start. Yes, then everything was filled with a divine experience, the voices resounded right into my head, in fact in all of my body. It felt like a great loving embrace. A tear tumbled down my cheek and my nose started to run . . . I don't know how long the song lasted, nor what they sang. My everlasting memory is the incredibly beautiful sound of the flow of voices and the very strong emotional commitment.

The experience can, naturally, be especially strong if one is in a place that is associated with particular figures and events in the history of Christianity. Such places are visited by people from radically different countries and with different languages. They can nevertheless feel a great sense of community by virtue of sharing the same faith and expressions of this faith in music and prayer. Assisi is just such a place.

(14.2C) Man, young, 1980s

Our choir made a journey to Assisi to learn more about Francis. We had prepared for this for a long time before we travelled down there by reading about Francis's life and about Assisi. A couple of days later we were sitting in the church where Francis sat when he had received his calling from God. There were about 40 of us and there were about as many again from several different countries. I remember that somebody spoke about something first and then our choir leader started up with '*Thuma mina*' and everybody sang along with the responses.

It was such a radical experience to sit in an old church together with Christians from different countries and sing music from the Christians in Africa. It was as if all the preparations we had made led to this occasion during these few minutes. Like when you have just finished a jigsaw puzzle where every bit has been put in place to form a whole picture.

When we had finished singing, everybody said the Lord's Prayer, each in their own language. It was a wonderful mixture of Swedish, English, German, Italian, and Finnish. But the prayer had the same rhythm and just as many syllables in all the languages and every 'Amen' came at exactly the same time. It was Christendom without borders!

Another such place is, naturally, Jerusalem. The next narrator is there in a particular place and on a particular day, both of them of central importance within Christianity. To be just there, and at just that time, that alone was an overwhelming experience. Then when all the visitors joined together in a song, it felt like a holy meeting with all of humanity.

(14.2D) Woman, middle-aged

Easter Sunday morning beside the empty grave in Jerusalem. It is 7 o'clock. A warm wind with scents that were absolutely enchanting. The grave is embedded in greenery with an exotic vegetation and plants that flowered in all manner of colours. People of all nationalities were sitting everywhere, they spoke quietly beside the lunch baskets they had taken with them. I went around and tried to count all the different languages that were being spoken, but I had to give up, there must have been 20 or so. It was as if I was completely intoxicated by what I saw and heard, and I found a place beside the wall around the grave to be able to see and hear everything. I felt like Zacchaeus who climbed up in a tree to be better able to see Jesus when he came on his way.

Then an orchestra started to play a song that is called '*Han lever*' in Swedish ['He is alive']. Suddenly, the conductor turns round and gets all the audience to sing along. A song where everybody felt fellowship and could take part without any demands and expectations as to quality.

What I experienced then was indescribable, the tears just ran down and I couldn't make a single sound. My breathing felt like an irritating element, time and space didn't exist any longer. I was in a heavenly condition that I didn't want to come to an end. All of me was filled with some holy meeting with all the world's humanity. Here stood little me and listened to about 1,000 people singing the same song in all these languages with a message in the words that stood for the same thing. We were united in a musical fellowship, where there was no feeling of being strangers, all of us were one. All ages, different races, men and women, no difference. The music built a bridge to fellowship. We were all united in the singing.

14.3 MUSIC CONVEYS A RELIGIOUS MESSAGE AND CONTACT WITH DIVINITY

In the following accounts, the main theme is that through music one can be affected by a religious message or through music one can seek contact with divinity. Naturally, the accompanying text is of great importance for the experience, here as in several other accounts. The accounts sometimes also contain elements of previously mentioned aspects such as visions, holy atmosphere, and Christian fellowship.

(14.3A) Woman, old, 1980s

Bach's Christmas Oratorio, about ten years ago. A friend has asked me to go to the church. I don't think I had heard the Christmas Oratorio before. So I sat there, completely unprepared. And the choir called out: '*Jauchzet, frohlocket, auf preiset die Tage*'. It hit me right in the chest, I got goosepimples, the tears ran down my cheeks and I knew everything and I dissolved and I wanted to fall down on my knees and kiss His feet. I who am an atheist. I felt eternity, everlastingness. A sentence came to me: 'Come, for all things are now ready.'

Another experience was just as strong. It was Hector Berlioz's *L'enfance du Christ* that was played. I had heard it before, had recorded it on tape, from the radio, with pretty poor sound. So I recognized most of it, but what a difference hearing it live! The great experience (with the same symptoms as above) came when some angels, sopranos, answered the big choir from infinitely far away: 'Amen, Amen'. It was a three-dimensional experience, a feeling that you were in the middle. Fantastic, unbearably beautiful!

This narrator was struck by the religious message despite the fact that she was an atheist. The following narrators are convinced believers, and their faith is further strengthened through the message in the music and the words, performed by skilful and charismatic musicians.

(14.3B) Man, young, 2000–10

A Christian event was arranged in Stockholm for young people. It lasted for 24 hours with various concerts, seminars, etc. The concert that my experience of music is based on took place on a Saturday. The British group that was playing is called Delirious. They play British rock/pop and as regards style can be compared with bands like U2 and Radiohead. Before the concert I felt extremely expectant, partly because I had some of the group's albums and think their music and the message are extremely good, and partly because I wanted to see them live.

As a Christian, I see a spiritual dimension in the music. I believe that God has created all music and given it to us, mankind. So I am convinced that Jesus can move people through music, and at the same time that we through music can express ourselves to Him and even through our music making show Jesus to other people. I noticed this clearly during the Delirious concert. Their focus wasn't to show themselves but rather through their music to be able to honour Jesus. The group consists of extremely competent musicians and produces good tunes and plays with a lot of feeling. They got the audience with them in an extremely good way and I felt I was a participant in what happened. During the entire concert there was a wonderful atmosphere in the entire concert hall and this was especially obvious during the song 'Intimate Stranger'.

Straight afterwards I felt deeply touched. I was touched by God through the music and God can touch us in all situations. I think the biggest reason for the experience depended on God's presence during the concert.

(14.3C) Woman, middle-aged, 1980s

I spent some months in the USA and came into contact with a worldwide Christian movement that engages young people for pioneering missionary work. I found myself in a wonderful lovely fellowship. I got to live in a shabby old house together with some other girls, and had no difficulty in becoming one of the gang.

Already the first week there was talk that those who wanted to could follow along into New York, to the Salvation Army and go to a rock concert. It was a Christian rock group, Second Chapter of Acts, who were going to play. Rock? Thump, thump, terribly boring music, sounds the same all the time. I had no expectations whatsoever, it was just that it was a chance to be at something different. So I followed along.

We had to wait a while before the group came on, and then it took them some time to get established on the platform too, everything went dark, apart from a few quivering candles that glowed.

And then the music and the well-known hymn: 'Holy, Holy, Holy, Lord God Almighty'. It was beyond all words. The tears simply ran, time and space disappeared and, Oh, if they could go on forever with their fantastic song of praise! Everybody seemed to experience the same thing. Moist eyes, wet cheeks, and there was a slight delay before the thunderous applause broke out.

Never ever, either before or afterwards, have I experienced anything like it. Now and then I happen to sing that hymn in Swedish, then I remember how the song of praise ought to sound, and I can feel a little bit of Heaven on Earth like that time.

How did it come about? What is it in music when it is at its best? I have absolutely no answer, but it was a fantastic experience! And it has helped me to understand better others who often seem to experience music so much stronger than I do. They really experience something, it isn't just make-believe.

In the next account, the message in the lyrics and the music also lead to a release of suppressed feelings, a 'thaw'.

(14.3D) Woman, young, 1980s

At Christmas that year I was in a period where I couldn't cry, it felt as if I didn't have any contact with my emotions—they never came up to the surface. Then I got to hear 'Marias sång' ['Mary's song'] sung by Annika Skoglund on the album of a musical called Vildhonung [Wild honey] by Tomas Boström. The musical is about different women in the Bible, and the song that Annika Skoglund sang expressed Mary Magdalen's pain over the fact that Jesus was dead and was no longer with her. 'How can I live without him?' she sings.

Even though I can't really accept Annika Skoglund's way of singing in every respect, at any rate the lyrics went right into my heart, the hard armour around my emotions was pierced and I could cry and laugh again. They were such extremely good lyrics in 'Mary's song' and the music fitted so well, and I must admit that Annika Skoglund does in fact sing it with much more insight than other singers I have heard subsequently. In Mary Magdalen's cries and pain I could see the cries and pain of all women who have lost their loved one. That is probably mainly what I saw before me—that the song wasn't just an unusually good song but also fulfilled a function. That through this song you could get help to give full expression to your own sorrow, anger, and pain.

After I heard this song, I went around for all of the Christmas holidays and was incredibly sensitive and easily moved, and was also extremely happy that I was able to feel like that. If you want to say it a bit poetically, you could say that the song broke the ice and after that there was a thaw!

A similar release of suppressed emotions is described in the following account. The music is a monumental work in art music, composed with its starting point in a biblical text.

(14.3E) Man, middle-aged, 1960s

The occasion that I often think of is a concert when I was in London. I had taken part in a festival that demanded a great deal of concentration and nerves. To relax, I went to a concert at the Royal Festival Hall one humid hot summer's evening. As a musician and person I am a decidedly romantic, unworldly type, and my experience that evening can be seen against that background!

The lasting memory from that evening was a particular work, *Psalmus Hungaricus* by Zoltán Kodály. The text is a paraphrase of David's 55th Psalm where he cries out to God in his suffering and flees to Him in anguish and despair, and finally finds consolation in Him—a truly human prayer, where each and every one of us will recognize themselves! That evening, that was the music that was waiting for me!

The monumental work with its Hungarian folk tone as a base struck me like a storm, shook me with its power and stirred up things inside me, I cried in my seat, there was something convulsive that had long been in a knot that was now released by the tones of the crying choir, supported by the rich orchestral timbre. It was as if my own voice was there in the prayer to God! I discovered the work that evening (even though I had heard it before!).

The experience of music was strongly emotional, I have since heard the work several times—but never been as agitated as that time in London! It was a unique event in my life, and I sometimes think about how differently music can work. As early as the time of the ancient Greeks, music could speak to one's feelings, I have read. But even in our day, it is a force of nature, sensual, spiritual, gentle, thunderous, simple, and with a complex structure. I think that now it is needed more than ever in a world of 'solitudes', conflicts and anxiety-ridden needs!

Although he was a listener, it was as if his 'own voice was there in the prayer to God'; he was, so to speak, both the receiver (listener) and the sender (in the prayer). In the following accounts, the narrators address themselves to God in songs of praise and invocation. This happens in very different situations and with different backgrounds. In the first example, the experience with music occurs in a place where one wouldn't expect it to happen: a pizzeria. Through the music, which is in itself a song of praise, the pizza in the narrator's reflection acquires a religious content, it becomes a symbol for the bread from heaven. Beethoven's song of praise is succeeded by her own song of praise to the joy of God.

(14.3F) Woman, middle-aged, 1980s

I wanted to take a pizza home with me after I left work. Nipped into a pizzeria close by. The place was empty, the evening rush hadn't begun. Soft music from a stereo filled the room. When I'd decided which pizza I was going to have, and was following with interest the skilful work going on behind the counter, the stereo changed records and out poured the rejoicing chorus from Beethoven's ninth symphony, '*An die Freude, Freude schöner Götterfunken*' ['Joy, beautiful spark of divinity']. The pizza dough was worked to these heavenly strains, and was then put into the oven.

I was left alone with the fantastic rejoicing choir's ecstatic singing. In my mind, I am rejoicing too, the joy is really a God-given spark, the most sublime that can be experienced by the human soul. Man has a need to sing, to give the experience of one's heart a form of expression, let it become a song of praise. It immediately becomes clear to me that the song of praise is what our spirit lives on.

Behind the glass pane of the oven, my solitary pizza is now baking. For me, it is a symbol for this bread from heaven.

I'm standing there totally overwhelmed by the strains of Beethoven with the joyful crying in my throat, happy and relaxed after an arduous day. I am in raptures on the wings of the music and the singing, so unexpectedly here in a banal little pizzeria. I philosophize for myself about the life-giving function of the song of praise in the spiritual life of man. The belief in him who was 'Panis angelicus', the bread from heaven, has created a large number of songs of praise throughout our entire world. We can give expression to our joy in God both through songs like Beethoven's magnificent '*Die Ehre Gottes aus der Natur*' ['The glory of God in nature'] and the chorus '*Mische seinen Jubel ein!*' ['Join in our jubilation!'] of unknown origin.

The singing from the loudspeakers undulates and hisses, is carried along on high waves by the symphony orchestra's irrepressible music. A crescendo to a maximum, a tutti of all the orchestra's resources, a bravura achievement in singing of what human throats can achieve, lift out Schiller's words: '*Brüder! Überm Sternenzelt/Muss ein lieber Vater wohnen*' ['Brothers, above the starry canopy/Must a loving Father dwell'].

The pizza is ready at the same time that the singing and music have gone through all the turns and counter-turns, struggled in the tension of the tones to the final resolution, reached harbour, the goal, peace, satisfaction, perfection, as one often experiences in a piece by Beethoven. I must wake from my rapture, pay and leave.

Once out on the street I feel the heat from the pizza through the carton. I thank God for this solemn moment, and I think I am walking homewards with bread from heaven in my hands. Suddenly, as I'm walking, to my surprise I am singing to myself a simple little chorus: '*Brist nu ut i jubel min själ*' ['Rejoice now, my soul, rejoice!']. But perhaps it wasn't so strange. Isn't it about the same thing?

The next account, too, ends in a song of praise, sung in unison by thousands of people as a finale at a well-known rock group's concert after the group's members have left the stage. There is a tense atmosphere, warm and religious, and the Bic cigarette lighters feel like prayer candles in the darkness.

(14.3G) Man, middle-aged, 1980s

Cold January. Together with 10,000 others we make our way to the arena for the concert. Expectation vibrates in the air.

The accompanying arrangement is discriminating. There is no advanced lighting. No smoke bombs exploding and no laser rays playing above our heads. What makes it work is first and foremost the radiation. The simplicity of the stage scenery is like a sign that the group, U2, trusts in its own charisma and music. The singer Bono has a personal charm and self-evident authority that reaches right out to the last row of seats.

The music is driving, floating. The songs are not primarily entire melodies but rather simple sentences pulled out of their context and repeated time after time, which makes it feel very special and unique. Bono never stands still but moves about over the entire stage, eager to reach us. He climbs around on the speaker scaffolding, stretching out to shake hands with people. We in the audience are all the time on the same wavelength. When Bono starts with call and response (he sings a phrase and the audience responds with the same phrase) it feels as if we could go on forever.

Suddenly the concert changes tempo for a while and everything comes to a standstill. Bono sits on the edge of the stage and sings the gospel classic above all others, 'Amazing grace'. We react reverently and a warm, devout mood settles over all of us in the ice stadium.

During the concert's final song, something strange happens. U2 want us to sing along in the refrain and the arena is transformed into a resounding and rocking community-singing evening. At the same time, the group starts to leave the stage, one after the other. First Bono, then the guitarist. Then, when the bassist puts down his bass, there is just us, 10,000 intoxicated singers and the drummer who keeps time for us. Finally he too leaves the stage and we stand there alone and sing so that the roof rises.

The cigarette lighters shine out like prayer candles in the darkness and the mood is dense, warm, and quite obviously religious. As if the group wanted to say to us in the audience: There you are, you can manage on your own, together you have the power and the strength that will last long after this concert.

So we sing, must have been at least 15 minutes. By ourselves. What we are standing there singing is a song of praise to God, largely taken from the Book of Psalms, number 40:

I waited patiently for the LORD; he turned to me and heard my cry.
He lifted me out of the slimy pit, out of the mud and mire; he set my feet on a rock and gave me
a firm place to stand.
He put a new song in my mouth, a hymn of praise to our God.

A little while later, on the way home on the underground, here and there people were still humming the song. We looked at each other and knew that we had been present at something special; in some carriages singing started up again and could be heard clear and loud right up to the Central Station. Hope and fellowship. For me this was a spiritual experience that stayed for a long, long time.

14.4 MEETING THE DIVINE, GOD

The most detailed descriptions of strong musical and religious experience are in situations where the narrator feels the presence of God or experiences a meeting with somebody from the Christian trinity—God the Father, Jesus Christ, or the Holy Ghost. The experiences can take place in solitude or in company with others. The place or the situation for the experience has a religious connection, for example in churches, at concerts, or religious gatherings. The music is of very varying character, everything from Gregorian chant to rock opera, but belongs to the sphere of religious music or has connection with religious subjects.

The reactions of the narrators include everything from tears and shivers to revolutionary experiences of existential-spiritual-religious character. In the two introductory accounts, powerful and peaceful music in a committed performance is what creates a tranquil calmness and a conviction that God/Christ is present.

(14.4A) Woman, young, 1990s

A strong experience with music was a gospel concert where The Master's Voice from Stockholm performed. The entire evening was characterized by bustle, happiness, loud volume, and general rejoicing. They saved the most magnificent song for the end, however. This song was entirely different from the others. It was calm and was sung in several voices without music. The choir sang with intensity and concentration and really put a meaning behind every syllable they sang.

The concert premises that had previously been happy and merry now became more atmospheric and a peaceful calm settled over the audience. The atmosphere became so apparent that you could physically have touched it. The choir stood at the front of the church and honoured and praised the God that had created them. Every spectator, believer or not, was convinced that the God the choir was singing about was present in the premises. I had the shivers all over and was so moved by the power of God that tears started to run down my cheeks. When the song had faded away, there was a delay of about ten seconds before anybody wanted to break the wonderfully delightful atmosphere with applause. But then what an applause that broke out!

(14.4B) Woman, middle-aged, 1970s

The strongest experience with music that I have had is the rock opera *Jesus Christ Superstar* by Tim Rice and Andrew Lloyd Webber. There was a large stage, a large orchestra, lots of soloists, and several different choirs. I remember the scenes as very realistic and exciting. Since I had myself read the entire story of the passion of Jesus in the Bible, I recognized every part of the opera. The music reinforced the last days of Jesus in an intensive and captivating way. I was totally absorbed by the plot and the musical course. The entire audience seemed to be strongly committed. What gripped me the most was probably how the leading actor interpreted the character of Jesus. Musically, it was a great achievement in which he seemed to give everything.

A few months later, when I listened to the album, I experienced the opera again. At the end of the album is a piece of music that is played only quietly when Jesus hangs on the cross. I sat by myself on the floor in a large room in my school where I was studying at the time. While the music poured out of the speakers, I could see a Jesus figure on the wall. I particularly remember the look in his eyes and the holes in his hands from the nails. I know that I shall never forget the opera and the experience afterwards. I decided then that I would believe in Him forever.

In the following account, the experience of God's presence gives rise to feelings of smallness, broken-heartedness, and dread in the face of his greatness and magnificence. But at the same time there is also the sensation of just now being in a holy moment in life, with the privilege of contact with this higher being, God.

(14.4C) Woman, young, 1980s

I took part in some project days where we were studying the function of music and religious services. The project days were just about to come to an end. A boy sat at the grand piano and played some songs, presumably simple songs of prayer. The rest of us sang along, some improvised voices.

Then the song came to an end and the piano music faded away. A person sitting far down in the hall said a few words as a greeting from the God we had just sung the praises of. The words were: 'Play, my son, play!'

The pianist, who is a professional in his field and a believer himself, but not so used to this mixture of music and prayer, started to play. I had long admired him for his skill at the piano and his personal sensitive style, but now I was almost filled with dread and an enormously great respect (the words sound paltry). I wasn't afraid, but I felt something of the smallness you can feel at the foot of a mountain when nature shows all of its scenery, but this was nevertheless different, much stronger. I automatically bowed my head and did not dare—did not want to and could not—move, and it wasn't the pianist I felt small before, it was God. I felt broken-hearted, not floored but, like I said, extremely small.

I think that if the expression 'holy ground' can be used today, then that is how I experienced it—as holy, saturated moments where I experienced that the centre was moved away from myself and I experienced as suddenly manifest that there was somebody who was greater, of a completely different dimension, close, and I was absolutely present, in the midst of the experience, and moved by this higher being—God.

I think it was God himself who, through the Holy Ghost, was present. God is God and we rarely meet him in the sense of him as a person, but mainly in the sense of our own conditions and concepts. When we do sometimes get a proper meeting with him, we are shaken, shocked by the reality. God's character, which glowed through his presence, was so strong for me that I could hardly handle it, but just had to capitulate before the fact that he is God and that is what he is like (magnificent and warm).

The pianist himself later said that he could choose exactly what he wanted to play, but that he experienced that he played according to divine instruction and that the Holy Ghost touched the music; it was a holy experience for him too.

I have also gained a new respect for the world containing greater realities that what you might think at a quick look, and that a living God cares about how we handle music as well as the world around us.

The following accounts describe how experience with certain music led to religious conversion and a consoling faith in God. The experience may have been preceded by worry, sorrow, feelings of emptiness and loneliness, a search for meaning and purpose with life. The music, and everything associated with it, changes everything all at once. Worry, loneliness, and searching are replaced by relief, liberation, a feeling of having received answers to all questions—'finding one's home'—and of being able to feel calmness, harmony, strength, and security for all the future in a faith in God. Music was the path to this; it can feel as if it came from God himself.

(14.4D) Woman, middle-aged, 1970s

I am young and on my first visit to Stockholm. Have been able to borrow a flat from a good friend. The flat is very close to Oscar Church, which became so important.

On my own in the city, I can still remember the feeling of being able to spread my wings perhaps for the first time. Being interested in art and history, I was going to get my fill this Easter weekend. The days were fully booked with a programme that I'd decided in advance. I would, of course, visit the church, but when? Anyhow, Good Friday night seemed to fit in well. Then they would be presenting something called *Ur Jordens Natt* [*Nox Angustiae, Night of Anguish*] by Torsten Nilsson. I can't remember what I was expecting it to be like, but something nice, easy to digest like it usually is, I suppose. But how did it turn out?

That night changed my life!

A musical experience that penetrated into the depths of my soul, where it has since then marked my life and work. Nothing else has ever affected me like that. The entire Good Friday drama became very much alive thanks to the suggestive music, partly on an organ played by Karl-Erik Welin, whom I admire immensely. Fantastic choir singing, recitations in Latin, which I love to listen to. All the pieces fell into place! I can hardly write this down without shaking, it was just so unbelievable. The passion of Jesus became so evident that it hurt. I remember that inside the church itself it was dark, only five red roses on the altar were lit up. Everything fitted my mood and my longing for knowledge about the Christian faith. I got answers to all my questions, and since then have lived in the secure faith that has carried me through many difficulties. That is how much music can mean.

(14.4E) Woman, young, 1980s

I was 18 years old. There was nothing really special about me, I was a fairly ordinary girl. I was successful in many areas, but my biggest weaknesses were probably in my relations with other people—so I was rather lonely, but I was used to that. Nevertheless, recently I had felt an enormous emptiness in life—what was the point of everything I was doing?

The reason I had started to think like that was that I had a feeling that there was a much greater richness in life which I didn't have. I had started to meet young Christian people who had something I couldn't really grasp—but wanted to. My spiritual longing had awoken. This meant that I was now on the way to Stockholm for some work experience. I wanted to see more but was nevertheless unprepared for what was going to come.

The entire train journey I was alone with my thoughts and questions. Arriving in Stockholm in the evening was an experience in itself. Such estrangement between people. The underground train rattled, empty looks, cold looks . . .

A few steps across the street brought me to the church where I was going to meet my friends. They had already started. The sound of the music met me as soon as I came into the lobby. But when I stepped into the hall itself it simply washed over me and went straight through my heart. So this was what I'd been missing! This was what I had sensed in their eyes! Because the music that I heard wasn't just notes and words. It had a dimension of life, a depth and warmth that made me cry from longing as well as relief. Relief at finally knowing what was going to fill my empty heart. It wasn't the music that I had found, but the source and heart of music; God himself, whom I could come to know through his music.

Since I hadn't yet given my heart to God, I couldn't take part in the singing (that would have been hypocrisy in the highest degree—it felt like that because the singing was so vibrant and had such content). Otherwise they were simple songs with words from the

Bible where everybody sang along in spontaneous part-singing. I can't remember much of what was then said or what happened. I was already 'possessed'.

A few days later when I could be there and join in the singing, something had happened that caused my friend to wonder what had given me my new singing voice. But now the music was alive, of course! It had a receiver and a sender! It was a deep spiritual fellowship. Earlier, I had once heard something similar but then I wasn't ready for it. I drew back a little. Thought it was a bit weird.

Anyhow, since this happened I have been overwhelmed in connection with music on several occasions. You can't really compare the experiences, because each time it has been unique, depending on which situation I have found myself in. But on all these occasions it has been like a liberation of my soul and a glimpse into a much greater reality where I, as tangibly as one can, have 'met' God. This doesn't mean that I haven't been able to meet God in other ways, without music, but the most perfect has been in music.

Since I became a Christian, I have myself also started to play music a lot, and it has come to mean a great deal to me to be able to sit at a piano and sing. Even if this doesn't give any great experiences, it does work as a sort of therapy where I find harmony. To sing *together* with other Christians is most often a much greater experience.

When it feels as if something is lacking in my spiritual life, it has then sometimes been music from the heart of God that has been the breeze of life that I have needed. I can put on a record with a group or a singer who really have a feeling for the music, and then I listen intensely. Then what I do in my solitude is that I let the music live inside me and express it with both body and soul. Then the music becomes so rich! Then my knotted emotions can free themselves. But it is very *important* that the person who is singing has 'the heartbeats of God' in their singing.

Another little thing that I'd like to mention is a little glimpse that I had when I had just recently become a Christian. I so very much wanted to have some sort of 'picture' of Jesus, so that it would be easier for me to think about him when I prayed. So I prayed for this. The sudden stroke of lightning in my mind that then happened completely astounded me. What I felt was a Jesus who *sang*! I sing songs for him—and he sings songs for me! Is that why I have found such spiritual fellowship in music?

In the final account, we can read of a unique experience described in a manner that gives us the possibility to completely follow the narrator's thoughts, emotions, and actions during the fairly short period in which this revolutionary experience takes place.

(14.4F) Woman, middle-aged, 1990s

I walk slowly towards the cathedral. I have been there a few times before as I had discovered that this is the right place for me when I want to gather my thoughts. I discovered that it gave me spiritual peace at the same time as giving me perspective on my studies. At the same time, I have felt a great joy and gratitude for having the chance to visit the cathedral which is historic as well as incredibly beautiful. I have felt the wings of history and been able to dream about lost times.

This particular afternoon I go into the church as usual. I stop just inside the door to take off my backpack and undo my jacket. When I pull down the zip on my jacket, the sound of a very faint yet distinguishable melody catches my attention. I raise my head to hear better. Am I hearing a melody or is it an illusion? Am I imagining that I hear somebody singing?

I look around to see if anybody else is also standing there listening, but nothing seems to suggest that. I look up at the ceiling. Is the singing coming from high above? Despite my uncertainty, I am sure that I can hear a song. The melody catches my attention totally. Despite the weak sound, it penetrates my body and envelopes me with a glorious melody that I in no way can tear myself away from. I am totally enchanted. I have never heard anything so wonderfully beautiful. I am totally surrounded by the melody, it completely fills my body. I even hold my breath to hear better.

I establish that it is a male choir that is humming a fairly simple melody. I don't know what they are humming, but I guess it is some sort of Gregorian chant. I try to see where these men could be standing but I can't discover anyone. I try to work out where the sound is coming from. The weak melody is concentrated right at the very top of the church, just under the cupola. I stand completely still and look up towards this fascinating singing which in some way is at one with the church. It is extremely hard to explain, but it sort of fits in really perfectly with the church. The cathedral and the singing belong together! The singing merges with the walls.

While the sorrow washes over me, I establish that it is a choir of monks that I hear. I don't know where I get that knowledge from, I simply establish that this is the case. I could feel the crying building up in my chest, and I just want to burst into tears. I try to control myself and return to the here and now, to why I came here, but I'm unable to rein in those sorrowful feelings. I think of all the people I have loved and who are now no more. I go up to the globe of candleholders in an attempt to stifle the crying which is still trying to come out. At the same time, I feel that I want to light a candle, not only for those I have loved, but for everyone in the world who has lost somebody they have loved and cared for. I think about the victims of the *Estonia* [ferry disaster in 1994] and their loved ones. I think about all the wars that are being fought in various parts of our world. I know that I am not alone in feeling sorrow.

I don't want to start crying in front of the people who are also standing gathered around the candlelight globe, so I start to walk further into the church. The melody pursues me all the time, now I can hear it loud and clear. It is so unbelievably beautiful. It is both sad and consoling at the same time. It settles like cotton wool around my heart. I find myself in a very strange state. I am both sad and safe. The monks' choir is singing a message to me, but I don't understand its content. I again look around to discover who is singing but can't see anybody. Nor can I explain why I experience that it is a monks' choir that is singing. I simply feel that it is monks who are singing. There is no music accompanying the singing, they are singing a cappella.

When I get further inside the church, there is another set of candle holders. I stop there and now the tears start to run down my cheeks. I light two candles while crying silently, and at the same time say a prayer for my loved ones and all the other people with sorrow. At this moment I feel so dreadfully lonely, so incredibly little and vulnerable, so despairing about the cruelties of life that make it so difficult for us. Apart from the sorrow, now loneliness is what fills my soul. The music guides me all the time. I follow it emotionally. I have no chance of avoiding it or shutting it out. The music governs me.

While the crying abates, a new feeling rises up inside me. I want to kneel down and pray to God to help me to cope, to find, to see what I can do the rest of my life, what I can do with my studies, with my feeling of loneliness, my desire to be able to help others in distress. I become even more confused about myself and my feelings and thoughts. I even feel embarrassed by my strong need to get on my knees and pray to God for help. I try to shake off that feeling, but the music fills me so totally and completely that there isn't room for anything else. I can't escape.

I try to return to my 'usual' condition by continuing down the aisle further into the church. After just a few metres, I discover a little altar with room for one person. It is just beside the aisle. It looks as if it has been put there, as if it knew that I would be coming and in what condition I would be. I stop and look at it, while wrestling with my unwillingness and my uncertainty. I want to get onto my knees and pray but can I, do I dare? Suddenly, I put my bag down, walk up to the altar, get onto my knees and put my hands together. The music convinces me that this is the only right and proper thing. I abandon myself totally to the feeling and the singing. I pray to God for help. The music has peeled all the obstacles off me.

During my prayer, something happens that leaves the most mark on me afterwards. I feel a safe and warm arm being placed around my shoulders. All loneliness and sorrow just ease up and disappear, after which a calmness settles in me which is just as fantastic as the singing which had enchanted me a moment earlier. I am not alone! Somebody is with me! After a fraction of a second, I think: 'Perhaps I never have been alone! Perhaps I have somebody by my side although I've never realized it.' I get up slowly with a completely new feeling of strength and calmness which originates in all of me.

I continue my walk around in the church but with a totally different feeling from when I came in. I enter the part with Gustav Vasa's grave, look at Saint Bridget, after a while sit down and just am. I feel so incredibly calm and harmonious. It feels as if, after years of despair and seeking, I have finally found my 'home' and landed. Not crash-landed like so many times before, but gently and carefully. I feel repaired and whole!

The entire event takes perhaps 15–20 minutes. Afterwards I remain seated for about 40 minutes. On the train home, I have dinner and a glass of red wine to go with it. In the dark train window, I see my own smiling face, which is completely unwrinkled and without a care.

Long after this, I find myself wondering if the music was still there when I left the church or if it became silent after my prayer. I can't answer that. The biggest mystery was, and still is: What did I hear? Who was it who was singing? What did this experience want to tell me? Why did I react as I did? Since I couldn't discover a male choir, I asked myself whether they played the singing via a loudspeaker. I decided to ask one of the staff from the church about this the next time I went to the church. I talked to a woman who works in the office at the church. She maintained most decisively that there had not been any male choir or any rehearsal period for a male choir. Nor is there ever any loudspeaker music at all in the cathedral, and never has been. She wondered whether I had muddled up the time or the day.

What should I believe? What have I experienced? One thing is certain. The music that I heard gave me an experience that altered my faith in God. I got a new faith, a new way of thinking. Somewhere there is a God, for each and every one of us, when we really want and need a God. I have gained a new self-knowledge and self-esteem which I will humbly carry with me the rest of my life.

While I have been writing this account, I have again experienced the singing all the time. It is firmly etched into my soul. Every time I think about the event, I experience a weightless feeling of space at the same time that I seem to be shut inside an enormous soap bubble. I have never before had any strong experience of music of this type.

A wonderfully beautiful melody which merges with the walls in the cathedral, embraces, enchants, and controls her; she can't escape it. It convinces her to abandon herself totally, to go down onto her knees and pray. And everything changes, all previous loneliness and sorrow disappear and are transformed into an entirely new feeling of strength, calmness, and harmony. She feels herself to be 'repaired and whole' and given a new self-knowledge and self-esteem to carry with her the rest of her life.

Where did the music come from? She asks the same question as another woman who had similarly heard wonderful music in her inner ear in connection with an imagined funeral ceremony (see Chapter 9, account 9.1B). At some time, they will presumably have heard something similar in reality—both women know what sort of music it is—and have a representation of that stored somewhere in their long-term memory. Both women say, too, that they have never heard anything so beautiful. Thus, even if they can identify the type of music, it is experienced just now as more beautiful than ever. Here, one can only speculate as to what the actual situation and their mood have meant for the experience.

Long after the experience, the narrator can re-experience the singing and then experiences a weightless feeling of space, and feels as if she is shut inside an enormous soap bubble. Both these phenomena have been described earlier in Chapter 8 (weightlessness) and in Chapter 7, account 7.3A ('as though I was sitting in an enormous globe of light') respectively.

The question of similarities between religious and musical experiences is dealt with separately in Chapter 33, section 33.3.

CHAPTER 15

NEW INSIGHTS, NEW POSSIBILITIES

A strong experience with music often leads to a new view of what music can mean for well-being and quality of life. It makes one want to continue to listen to and to learn more about music; one can be inspired to start playing and creating music oneself, perhaps even to choose music as a career and to spread knowledge of the positive effects of music to other people. This has been evident in many earlier accounts, and is also described later in Chapter 29, section 29.7.2.

The accounts in this chapter provide examples of other positive effects of strong experiences with music. Music can open the door to a completely new world of emotions, something that perhaps applies especially during childhood and youth (see Chapter 5, section 5.2) but, naturally, even later in life. A strong experience with music can also give one insight into thoughts and feelings that one already has, but that one has not been aware of. This is often described as coming into contact with one's innermost self. The experience can further mean that one gets a release of pent-up feelings (catharsis), that one feels liberated, elevated, purified, and healed. During crises, and in other negative states, music can provide relief and consolation, can inspire, give new hope and new strength, and give one the chance to see new possibilities.

One can analyse these questions in many different ways. Here, the subject has been divided into two, partly overlapping, points: how music can give new insights about one's own character and life/reality (15.1), and how music can open up new possibilities in negative situations (15.2).

15.1 MAKING CONTACT WITH ONE'S INNERMOST SELF: NEW PERSPECTIVES

Several participants express themselves in general terms about the importance that music has for self-knowledge and one's understanding of reality. Here are a couple of examples.

(15.1A) Woman, young

There is something special about music which can hardly be explained with words. Often when it comes to strong experiences with music, the thing is that the music in some way expresses and makes situations and emotions clearer. Music can help us to reach into things that we can't reach by ourselves.

(15.1B) Woman, middle-aged

Music, for me, has been an enlarged part of reality, an extension. Through music, I can find myself, my identity, my strength, my soul. It always strengthens me, makes me feel fulfilled, bigger than myself. Gives me calm, peace, harmony, and balance. Without music I am a half-person; for me, music is just as important as the food I eat.

The following accounts provide examples of how music can set off a sort of Aha experience which in a single blow changes the situation. One becomes aware of emotions, thoughts, and attitudes that have been 'hidden and forgotten'. It feels as if the music penetrates into the depths of one's mind, that one comes into contact with one's innermost self. Music reveals and dissolves deadlocks and blockages, provides new perspectives on one's own person and life/reality, provides a feeling of openness, confidence, and liberation.

(15.1C) Man, middle-aged, 1990s

It is at the beginning of October, and I am in Turkey. One day, a trip is arranged up to a little valley up in the mountains. I am going to perform in front of my fellow travellers and some of the locals. An elderly man with a banjo-like instrument is there too.

First we play together, then each by himself. I now experience that the elderly man in his singing carries something great and passionate which makes me feel very good. Despite the not particularly well-tuned banjo and the squeaky voice, I am strongly affected. I feel totally harmonious and free from the usual awareness of myself. A very pleasant sensation spreads across my chest and down to my solar plexus. It feels like fresh air. I feel contact with an inner ego, my soul.

I feel love in the presence of this man. When he sings, it feels so great that everything else is unimportant. These tones accord with my absolute inner self or, more correctly, with his inner self. In some way, I am one with him. It is as if we together find ourselves in a room of our own which doesn't allow any disturbances to come in. After this moment of absolute stillness and wholeness, everything feels good. I could stay here longer.

The music he played was traditional Turkish music. What captivated me most was his voice. The melody and ornamentation also had a great influence. In the latter, it is the special figures, like trills in our folk music, that appeal to me.

In the long term, this experience is going to be a possibility to relive a lovely feeling, a state of total harmony. It also gave me the insight that music influences me very deeply and that I can gain access to a different level inside myself.

(15.1D) Woman, old, 1940s

The place was Salzburg. I was in a group of music teachers and music lovers on a very eventful holiday. One Sunday, the entire group was invited to an anonymous home where there would be '*Hausmusik*'. The hosts were hearty and we made ourselves comfortable in an old-fashioned home with velvet-covered armchairs, dark walls, and heavy curtains.

Then the five string musicians arrived, made themselves comfortable and played Mozart's String Quintet in G minor, K516.

The music immediately got a really strong hold on me. The intensity in the playing, the seriousness and precision, the expression, and above all the music! I recognized the horrors of war, death, and destruction, and my own gloomy thoughts in a strong, distinct, and easy joy. Mozart's ability to rapidly associate from one emotional state to another, to be able to affect our very deepest and most emotionally charged needs of human expression with a seemingly easy shallowness, has later never ceased to amaze me! The intensely tragic motifs that didn't fasten in any form of sentimentality (which I abhor!) but were dissolved in an elegant lightness—a refreshing vitality! And this was conveyed so intimately in this environment—on the same level, so to speak. No podium attitude or critical evaluation of technique and established performance practice. Just a direct music making from one person right into another.

My own mental state at this time of my life was a great hunger for music and to be able to realize myself in a serious manner that would develop into something. I tried to brush away depressive and impatient thoughts—one ought to be happy for what one has—one is so well off in comparison to . . . In this music it was permitted to be depressed, happy, impatient, impetuous, questioning, sparkling, and all of this formed a whole. I think that I became aware of what life consists of: all these emotions at once! And it was permitted! Enjoyable, beautiful, and consoling!

The experience stayed with me a long time! I listened with a new interest to chamber music, bought the record and sheet music and for a long time sang in my head the themes from the G minor quintet. Even before this, the G minor key had had a particularly emotional effect on me, and after this experience the love of G minor stays there! This was the start of my getting seriously involved in playing music again! Later in life, that same quintet has meant consolation and renewed courage in severe crises.

(15.1E) Man, middle-aged, 1980s

The music was Handel: Concerto Grosso, Op. 6, No. 6 (Musette larghetto). Herbert von Karajan, Berliner Symfoniker.

I have been able to borrow a cassette with this music and play it on a Walkman. I'm lying on the bed and looking at the moon and the sea. I notice my usual irritation over the strutting character of classical music. I experience it as dry, affected, and intellectual. I notice that the music doesn't grip me the same way as good rock music.

I think that if it doesn't grip me, could I grip it? I feel that there is something opposing it in the centre of my body. It is as if I don't want to follow, or let myself by led by the music. I think that I ought to be able to follow the music with every part of me. If I drop the opposition that I feel, perhaps I can understand what it is in this music that captivates other people. I try to make myself receptive and soft inside, so that I can follow the music with my 'body's spiritual soft parts'.

Now we come to No. 6 and something lets go inside me. The beauty and depth I feel, they are boundless. It is as if places inside me that many, many years ago stiffened up now become soft and take part in the music. But this doesn't happen passively, there is a definite quality of really following along. There is a total freedom here just now. It is alive now in a place inside me where I have previously been dead. The place that is now alive is the place that gives depth and contact with life. The very zest and taste.

I get up from the bed and look out across the sea. I realize that I normally live shut in, and without this deeper contact with reality. But here it is, fresh and newly born and all the time new. Like it probably was when I was a child. The music is about forgiveness. An old burden lightens and I see that everything I normally wish for is here. And it has always been there right in front of me.

The experience of the content of the music and the meaning I gave it disappeared when the music fell silent. But the openness remained for several days, and to a certain degree is always with me now. It was like a window that opened and this window is now always ajar.

(15.1F) Woman, middle-aged, 1980s

I have taken my seat to see six hours of theatre, *Den stora vreden* [*The big rage*]. It is dark in the auditorium. Only the big, empty open circular stage is slightly illuminated. A solitary woman comes in, some sort of 'first mother' with a magic drum. She starts to beat it, a simple regular rhythm, tam–tam–tam–tam, not particularly fast. The first mother is in the light. The rest of the auditorium is in darkness, but from the gloom her rhythm is added to, the same simple timing, tam–tam–tam–tam, nothing complicated, just more, and more and even more. Other drums, bigger drums with a deeper tone, around the room join in. I can just about see them in the darkness, but most of them are hidden. And the drumming grows, it ceases to be a sound, it finally becomes just *power*, it penetrates inside me, throws aside my everyday blockages, opens rooms inside me that have otherwise (always?) been closed, frightens me, and makes me happy—is all this delightfulness inside me? Help! What shall I do with it? It gets hard to breathe, I burst out crying, don't want it ever to end and yet I want to leave, and the drumming keeps on growing in strength.

Finally, what has already happened inside me also happens in the performance: a built-up wall collapses and a fire-breathing dragon appears. Then the spell is broken and the theatre demands my concentration again, but those drums have changed the image I have of myself. Through them, I found out that in my mind there are places that I never otherwise find, and I was completely shocked by the discovery. I don't know much about what is in them, other than that the feelings are so strong that they presumably can be dangerous. I also believe that it is the temptation to come into contact with these emotional storms that causes people to be attracted to religious organizations where they can feel ecstasy and speak in tongues, as well as to rock concerts where the volume is so high that everything that is irrelevant is washed away in the stream of sound. Perhaps people can achieve this in an intoxication through narcotics. In that case, I can understand what makes drugs so attractive.

The next narrator avoids listening to music in the company of others. A deep contact with the music and his own inner self can only be reached by listening in complete solitude. The experience can hardly be formulated in words, and goes far beyond what musical terminology can convey.

(15.1G) Man, middle-aged

Live music has never given me the very strongest, deepest experience that I shall attempt to explain here, never 'that' feeling. I can only experience that feeling in solitude. I have never been able to feel it in company. People around me disturb me because I can't be certain that they feel the same or understand. Words have never been sufficient.

But, on my own, the pictures are painted before me. I see them as pictures even though I can't say what they represent, in concrete terms. What I do know is that I feel that I am transported into these pictures, landscapes, worlds. The music has touched something deep inside me and tempted forth something original, fundamental. Something timeless and eternal. Something unfathomable. It is hard to find words to use to properly describe the experience, but it is undoubtedly a feeling of beauty. Great beauty and sadness, beauty, and eternity. In fact, it reminds me of how I experience being in love. That, too, gets at you somewhere deep inside and tempts forth states that are otherwise hidden and forgotten. That is the only parallel there is to the deepest experience with music.

The music that gives me this comes from musicians who performed in the 1970s on the edge of what is considered to be the rock scene, for example, Brian Eno's 'Through hollow lands' and 'Spider and I' from the LP *Before and After Science*, David Bowie's and Eno's 'Warzawa' from the LP *Low*, Robert Wyatt's 'Sea song' from the LP *Rock Bottom*. More modern music and new artistes in the same tradition have followed, and in my eyes succeeded: Wim Mertens and Soft Verdict with 'Close cover' from the LP *Struggle for Pleasure*, David Sylvian's 'Camp fire' from the LP *Gone to Earth*.

It's relevant to say that I am not a musician myself. Can hardly sing a note. This has meant that it has been difficult to try to compare and discuss music more thoroughly with other people. I have lacked a language. On the other hand, I have felt strengthened in my feelings for my music when I've experienced that I stand outside the technical language, expert comments, and so on that you can experience as standard practice within a group of specialists. I have been able to trust that my opinion is my own. It doesn't come from anywhere else.

15.2 MUSIC OPENS UP NEW POSSIBILITIES IN NEGATIVE STATES

Music can be of great importance in alleviating, counteracting, and changing negative states such as depression, anxiety, sorrow, or illness. There were telling examples of this in Chapter 5, section 5.3, dealing with music as consolation, support, and therapy during one's teens, and further accounts on the same theme follow here. The narrators describe how music grips them, gives them strength and power, security and peace, a feeling of freedom and inspiration, new joy of life, increased self-confidence, and another perspective on existence. Music becomes a resource to resort to when necessary.

(15.2A) Woman, middle-aged, 1980s

This music affects me greatly inside my body. I can listen to it and feel how the music grabs hold of me and makes me grow and become strong. If I am feeling low, it can make me feel sad but also at the same time make me strong again and full of new energy. The music makes me also feel calm and peaceful. The music can also get my imagination going in some sections. It feels like floating.

The music I am talking about is Dvořák's symphony 'From the New World'. And I mean the theme that recurs several times. This music speaks directly to my feelings, my innermost place. I use it when I need to fill up with energy.

(15.2B) Woman, middle-aged, 1980s

Music can give me strong sensations when I'm feeling happy. I try to listen to music even when I am depressed. Sometimes it goes OK. Then, when I play music in the minor mode, I often cry till it feels better. I cry, too, when I hear something that I find beautiful. But those are tears of joy.

A few years ago, I had some problems with my eyesight (cataracts). I was all revved up before the operation. Then I used music to try to slow down a bit, and when I felt sad and disappointed with the healthcare. I listened a lot to classical music on the gramophone as well as on the radio.

Since then I've kept on listening. Fairly often, I have the radio on quietly during the night. Then I can relax and fall asleep more easily when I hear a voice that I think is talking to me and playing nice music. It feels safe.

(15.2C) Woman, middle-aged, 1950s

For a long time I was in hospital and had to undergo a whole series of operations. After the third operation, the following happened. I lay in bed in my room, by myself, and after a long period under deep anaesthetic was trying to 'get back', I heard music, the bedside radio was turned on and to Felix Mendelssohn's Violin Concerto in E minor I experienced a wonderful vision or dream. I was sitting on a rock on the beach with a wide ocean in front of me; I was filled with the joy of living and started to laugh. The laughter acquired a shape, large and small 'soap bubbles' in every colour imaginable. They all moved to the music. This went on throughout the piece.

The strange thing is that after the next two operations, I experienced exactly the same thing. For some reason, this particular concerto was played on the radio at just these times I was waking up from the anaesthetic. About six months later, I could check whether this music really had been in a radio programme. And it had—the first time they had played the entire concerto, the second and third times just part of it. So Mendelssohn's E minor concerto has become incredibly strong for me and something of a 'last resort' sometimes when my genuine inner joy of life has been seriously challenged. Then I play this music and remember the laughter.

(15.2D) Man, old, 1940s

I was in a severe personal crisis on the verge of despair and was walking around on the streets of Stockholm one late evening. By chance, I went along the street passing the Nationalmuseum and saw that it was lit up, and the doors were open. There was going to be a so-called Midnight Concert. I decided to go in. There were a lot of people there, but I found a seat fairly high up on the stairs [the audience sits on the stairs during these concerts] so that I could see the participating orchestra. Guido Vecchi was the soloist on the viola da gamba. It was music by Corelli and probably Vivaldi too.

For me, in those days, that sort of music was a totally new experience. It was like a wonderful dream. I was lifted up onto a higher level. I suppose you could call it a religious experience, extremely liberating. When I left afterwards there was singing inside me. I decided to take up my cello playing again; I had started when I was in my early teens, but later dropped it. Then, calm and relaxed, I walked home to my little rented room and slept soundly.

The fact is that I am still deeply moved when I think back to that experience. It has meant so much to my entire life. The next day I succeeded in borrowing a cello and also found a cellist who was willing to give me lessons completely free. Since then, the cello has been my permanent companion, and music my foremost hobby.

(15.2E) Woman, middle-aged, 1980s

I was listening to a programme on the radio, early in the morning. I am tired in the morning and listened half-asleep. But then they played a jazz tune which went straight into my consciousness. It made me happy and gave me hope. I forgot my tiredness and my aches and pains. I got some extra energy. The music stirred my imagination. There was so much I wanted to do, so many ideas that I thought were good. A lot of things became clear to me. I had often thought about, and missed, the things that I could no longer do on account of my back. Now I could see clearly what I would manage to be able to do. It was a record by Sidney Bechet. I looked for his records in every single record shop until I found the tune which had etched itself into my memory, namely 'Halle Hallelujah'. Just when he starts his solo, that's the bit that made such a great impression on me and gave me an experience of joy.

On hearing that tune on the radio the first time, I felt elevated. I found myself somewhere above all trivialities. And the music felt pure and clear; it had sort of cleaned out my low-spiritedness and made room for happy, positive thoughts and ideas. Why did the music make such an impression on me? Perhaps because I had come to an insight about my down situation, permanent pain, fact that I had stopped working . . . The feeling of not being able to go to my job any more because I haven't the energy, that is strongest in the morning when people are rushing off to work. Then I feel a bit lower, if only for a while. Perhaps that was why the music lifted me up above all the everyday problems, lifted me up to happiness and joy.

Music has made me realize that I can manage certain things and that I am actually good at them. And being able to feel happiness, that is important.

Music can be a constant companion in various stages of life, a pathfinder to one's very core and a partner in conversation who supports, consoles, soothes, gives hope, strength, and confidence.

(15.2F) Man, old, 1980s and later (excerpt from a longer account)

Ever since my youth, music has been important in my life. Just *how* important, I understood late, but not *too* late. Its true importance wasn't clear to me until I was well into adult age. It wasn't until I was almost 50 that I seriously started to suspect how important music was for me. Certain music could make me light-hearted and decidedly liven me up. For me, however, the most important music was (and still is) that which managed to open my mind totally and give me access to my innermost self. In there were sorrow, despair, and a lot of crying. Then came light, a feeling of consolation and hope. Afterwards came satisfaction and tranquillity. Something that led my thoughts to the consoling touch of a mother's hand. Balm for the soul. In short: catharsis.

I started to actively look for the music that could give me this relief, not just once but often. It happened when I played a record of music by Mikis Theodorakis and Manos Hadzidhakis, with singing by Michael Theodore: *Griechische Lieder von Liebe und Freiheit*. A blow like being hit with a club wrapped in cotton wool. That was how I experienced it. Theodorakis's music has come to mean a lot for me and my mental health. In most cases, his music goes directly into my Holiest of Holies—that is, right to my heart.

The melancholia in our rich treasury of folk music also seems to meet with response inside me. In later times, church music and spiritual music in general have come to be all the more important for me. Stabat Mater by Pergolesi has also given me pleasant emotional night-time moments when sleep doesn't seem to the most important thing.

(15.2G) Woman, middle-aged, 1980s

The Greek composer Mikis Theodorakis's music means a lot to me. I have heard several live concerts with him, the most recent at the Concert Hall in Stockholm. He was there with a Greek orchestra, several Greek singers, and among the musicians particularly a very fine bouzouki player.

I can't pick out particular sections in the music that were more important than others; it was the experience of the concert in its totality. A strong and very inspiring experience. I remember a moment when one of the soloists put a lot of energy into his performance and that moved me greatly, the contact between the conductor Theodorakis and one of the singers, the intensity of the bouzouki player, or when Theodorakis himself towards the end of the concert turned towards the audience and started to sing.

Directly after the concert I felt really elated, with a feeling of joy, happiness, and strength inside me. I felt alive, present in the kernel of life, 'intoxicated by music'. I had been deeply moved in my soul and I felt very inspired. I think that I can say without exaggeration that this music gives me the courage to face life. It gives me strength when I feel that I need it, it brings to life joy and a fighting spirit and inspiration.

(15.2H) Woman

What I want to describe is music as a pathfinder to my inner self. For me, it is an important part of a daily dialogue but here are also colour, form, and many other senses. But now, concretely about music:

When I was close to being destroyed: '*Dödens triumf*' ['The triumph of Death'] by Savage Rose.

Mozart's *The Magic Flute* when I was in therapy.

Theordorakis when my power of resistance was strengthened.

Merit Hemmingson's *Bröllopsmusik* [*Wedding Music*] when my sorrow about my marriage, which was dreadful already from the beginning, started to show itself in its true guise.

My Fair Lady when I started to oppose the man = the oppressor.

Nana Mouskori when my shut-in singing started to come forth.

African drumming when my sexual life started to wake up.

Faroese chain dance to strengthen me in my mortal dread when somebody had tried to kill me.

Aida's death song in *Aida* when I have felt a sense of doom.

Swedish folk music when my zest for life has come back.

The old hymn '*Vår Gud är oss en väldig borg*' ['A mighty fortress is our God'] when I've needed support from outside.

Stravinsky's *Rite of Spring* when I have felt myself hunted like a wild animal.

Music and my life have been woven together. Music has explained, supported, guided, consoled, relieved, helped me in my great despair, horror, distress, joy, hope, consolation.

Most dreadful of all was a period when everything was silent—then too I was dying.

Now I often wake with music—which talks to me and guides me.

Some of the accounts in this chapter could just as easily have been placed in the chapter on music as therapy (Chapter 17), perhaps even in the chapter on existential aspects (Chapter 12). The boundaries between these various aspects of strong experiences with music are very fluid. Other descriptions, too, of what music has meant in difficult situations can be found in accounts of music in connection with illness, death, and funerals (Chapters 21 and 22).

CHAPTER 16

CONFIRMATION THROUGH MUSIC

To feel confirmed—seen, accepted, understood, appreciated, needed, chosen—is a fundamental need in all of us. It is an important base for one to be able to develop good self-esteem, to realize one's ideas and abilities, and build up a stable identity. All of this takes places in an interplay with the people around us. Our self-image and identity are, to a great extent, formed through meetings with others, when we are confronted with their attitudes and reactions towards us.

What role can music play in this process? Music can be seen as a representative for another person, a fellow being and conversation partner who understands my situation, my thoughts, and feelings. Music reflects me, myself, I recognize myself in the music and can identify with it. It can feel as if music speaks directly to me and nobody else, as though I am chosen to receive what the music has to say. One can experience this both in solitude and when one is together with other people.

A further form of confirmation is the appreciation that is accorded musicians when they play, through the positive reactions of the audience (applause, whistling, being called back to the stage, positive reviews, etc.). To perform music is a way to be seen and noticed, which in itself can be an important driving force to devote oneself to music. Performing music can also provide a possibility to test one's boundaries, to dare to do more, and to find ways of expressing what one has inside oneself; in other words, to realize a part of oneself.

One can thus get confirmation both from the music itself and by performing the music. If both these factors should coincide, that is, if one receives appreciation for one's performance of music which at the same time reflects one's own character, then the positive effect for self-confidence and one's own identity is even greater.

16.1 MUSIC REFLECTS ME, MY FEELINGS, AND THOUGHTS

To recognize oneself—one's own thoughts and feelings—in music can mean a very great deal for self-esteem, not least in the stages of life when identity is created, as well as during times of uncertainty and crisis. The following accounts describe such experiences during different periods in life, in different situations, and with different types of music.

First, some accounts from childhood and youth.

(16.1A) Woman, old, 1930s (from Chapter 4, account 4.2J)

The school treated us to music in the assembly hall: a pianist played Beethoven's *Appassionata*. It struck the poor, musical child who had neither a wireless nor a gramophone at home . . . New worlds opened up, or the old one suddenly became rich and beautiful. Somebody interpreted my emotions, somebody offered a possibility to express something that was richer than anything I had come across so far. The pride, the defiance, the passion, the beauty. Somebody spoke a language I understood.

(16.1B) Man, old, 1940s

It was a long time ago, in my youth. Peter Tchaikovsky, sixth symphony, *Pathétique*, the last movement. I got a kick, a euphoric feeling took possession of me. I thought I saw the world and existence in another way. The music really gripped me. The music in that last movement which really drilled right into me. I was perhaps susceptible on this occasion.

It meant that I started to listen to classical music. That, in turn, has resulted in a great richness and joy in my life. Every time I hear this music, it grips me, lifts me.

Why does this piece of music mean so much for me? Not easy to answer that in a few words, but it is presumably the romantic element, united with strong melancholy, which influences one's mood. I think this music has everything: it gives associations to experiences from childhood and youth, rippling spring streams. It reminds me of the happiest and most beautiful moments in my life. But also of the dark times, the dark and heavy moments.

This music reflects my life. It is my life.

(16.1C) Woman, young, 1990s (from Chapter 5, account 5.1C)

I had been longing for ages to see my big idols, the hard rockers Guns N' Roses . . . Everything they played was very familiar. The entire concert was like a confirmation that what I had heard only on records did actually exist in reality . . . I had been looking forward to this and had prepared for it for a long time . . . [The music] was in my head every day for a long time and then being able to see and hear it for real was fantastic . . . A large part of my identity and self-image was built upon my worship of just this particular music. The concert was a confirmation.

By virtue of music reflecting one's own character, it can also give you peace, consolation, happiness, and strength (thus further examples of what was dealt with in the previous chapter, section 15.2).

(16.1D) Woman, young, 1990s

Personally, I have many experiences of how a particular piece has helped me through heavy times in my life. One example is when, a few years ago, I experienced a sort of existential crisis, when a lot of what I had built my life on turned out not to work at all. I simply didn't realize what was happening, but just that I had completely lost my footing. It was a very painful and frightening time. When it was at its worst, I listened to the Largo from Dvořák's ninth symphony. It was as if it said everything that I felt myself, and when I listened to this movement I felt some sort of peace and rest.

(16.1E) Woman, old, 1970s

I listened to Johannes Brahms's Symphony No. 3 played by the Stockholm Philharmonic Orchestra . . . Then the third movement, Poco allegretto, started and it was an enormous experience. I felt as if I was a part of the music and I knew exactly how it would go on. A tranquil ecstasy . . . After that experience I can bring out and listen and let the music sing within me whenever I want, indeed still today after 16 or 17 years. The third movement in particular gives consolation, strength, happiness—it is me, myself.

Next, a couple of examples of how music reflects feelings in connection with broken romances.

(16.1F) Woman, young, 1990s

I sing in a big band and there is a piece that I am always extremely moved by when I sing it, the jazz ballad 'Travelin' light'. It's about a woman who has been abandoned by her beloved. At the time I got the ballad, I had just left a relationship and wasn't especially happy. I identified with the words in the tune, which I experienced as according with my own situation. Every time I sing it, I remember how I experienced that period and I get quite shaky. Towards the end of the song, my face almost always starts to quiver. A lot of people have told me that there is something special when I sing that particular song, that you can feel my pain in some way.

(16.1G) Man, middle-aged, 1980s (from Chapter 20, account 20L)

I had just bought Dire Straits's second album, *Communique*, and everything felt exactly right straight away! This music expressed most of what was inside me! I was in the most intense period of my life, as I was mortally in love with a woman . . . The album spoke just as intensely to me for almost a year until we broke up and I had to go on living knowing that I would never experience a greater love affair. But during all of this period I played it like somebody possessed . . . The music . . . gave me a gentle, strong self-confidence, it gave me self-esteem, an identity, gave me a new and harmonious relation to myself . . . In short, I found music that was like a mirror for me, that worked whatever state I was in, plus it had a basic existential tone that I had been looking for. I loved the record, and it loved me.

In the following two accounts, the feeling of presence in life and the feeling of being understood are united—the music expresses what one is thinking and feeling.

(16.1H) Woman, middle-aged, 1980s

I have been in a silent retreat for three days, which means devotions, prayers, masses, walks, etc. These days were like a cleansing for the soul. I felt more 'present' in my own.

When the retreat is at end, I have time to spare and I go into the town church. Want to retain the silence. There is nobody at all inside the church. I go and sit right at the front and take pleasure in just being there in the church and the tranquillity. I hear that somebody is up on the organ balcony, the cantor is there to practise, and he begins to play. The music helps me in my desire to be in a reflective state.

One of the pieces gave me a special experience. It is modern twentieth-century music. The piece starts in the minor mode, unobtrusively and tentatively. Gradually the door is opened to a section in the major mode in total freedom and dedication. Finally, back to minor, this time more self-evident and with power.

My experience is strong. Early in the piece, I start to cry. Intensely, with the tears streaming down my cheeks. It is as if the language of the music confirms something that I have inside me. The music supports me. Helps me. Emphasizes a feeling I have about life in general—my life! The music and my own life are sort of on the same wavelength. I feel understood. All the time, I am calm. Life feels welcoming. The experience is positive. All the time, it is beautiful.

Her choice of words in the description of the music—an unobtrusive and tentative start in the minor mode, followed by a section in the major mode 'in total freedom and dedication', after which the music returns to a 'self-evident' minor with power—can mean that the course of the music reflects a process that she herself has gone through and which now leads to insight, calm, and confidence.

In the second account, it is the intense expression in the flamenco music that creates a strong feeling of identity with this music—'it expresses what I feel inside, my soul, my feelings'. In that way, the music also becomes a way to get to know oneself better. One finds one's inner self manifested in the expression of the music and can get a strong feeling of special presence 'just now, just here'.

(16.1I) Woman, young, 1970s (from an edited interview)

There's a flamenco guitarist, Eva Möller. The first time I heard her, I was 15–16 years old. She and a flamenco dancer called Carmen Lucena were on a visit and it was an 'Aha thing'— it was so strong, I was so affected by it, I mean deeply moved emotionally. I remember that I arrived late and I almost didn't dare go in at first. Then I was let into the hall. Suddenly you were just there in this room and there was this little person Carmen and Eva Möller who played the guitar . . . and there was this incredible music and it was like entering another dimension! Another world in some way! Everything around us just disappeared completely, nothing else mattered at all.

I had an incredibly strong emotional experience—possessed by something. It felt like . . . it agreed with me exactly, my inner self. I still feel like that with flamenco—it is exactly as if it expresses what I feel inside, my soul, my feelings. Deep inside. True, genuine, like a contact.

This is something that suits me. This agrees with my way of being. Inside. It's a sort of identity. I really do need it, it is a necessity in my life because it expresses my soul and helps me . . . to know myself too, to recognize what is inside and that it finds expression. *Yes!* This is exactly how it is. This is me! I got a feeling of 'Oh, these people, they're playing this just for me, she is singing this just for me and she and I are the only people in this room and we know exactly what this is about, and it is about living.' *And that's it!* You feel more than usually present in life in some way—an enhanced feeling of existing, just now, just here.

I was so terribly fascinated by these people . . . you can see in their faces too that they feel exactly the way I feel and you get a strong feeling of these people knowing . . . yes, we are sisters, we know exactly . . . we function the same. We have never spoken with each other but it was a meeting of souls—a strong contact between people.

I felt that I had found something in me that I wasn't alone with—that there are actually other people who feel the same, who are like me inside. This thing with finding your own identity, which I haven't done until recent years, dance and music were a help in that, a channel.

An intense, convincing description of how music can confirm and contribute to creating a person's identity.

A component in this was the feeling of being specially chosen—'Oh, these people, they're playing this just for me, she is singing this just for me.' That is the theme of the next section.

16.2 FEELING SELECTED, PERSONALLY ADDRESSED

The feeling of being selected, of being chosen to receive the music, that the music is about me personally—this is found in many accounts. Though one may be surrounded by many other people at big concerts, one can experience that the music or the musicians direct themselves especially to me, that it is I who am being addressed.

(16.2A) Woman, old, 1930s (from Chapter 5, account 5.1L)

[A concert in a church in Falun] The black American contralto Marian Anderson was soloist and was accompanied by a male pianist . . . She stood there relaxed, still, confident in herself. Simply opened her mouth and her strong, mellow yet gentle voice filled all of the huge room . . . We sat almost at the front. The church was full of people but it was solely for me she was singing. I was completely wrapped up in the music.

(16.2B) Man, young, 1980s (from Chapter 27, account 27B)

[At a Mike Oldfield concert] In 1976, Mike Oldfield released . . . a number . . . called 'Platinum' which for me is one of the best ever done. It is an old and long . . . tune so I didn't have any expectations of hearing that particular tune . . . The first notes almost made me faint. It was 'Platinum'! I felt that I disappeared for a moment and then woke up as if in a dream, but all the time aware of the music. In some way I was floating above the audience, which simply was there but I couldn't hear them and they didn't disturb me. It was like a dream, I was floating and the group was playing only for me . . . I was totally gone—my friends noticed as they had tried to make contact with me during the number but failed.

(16.2C) Woman, middle-aged, 1980s (from Chapter 25, account 25.1P)

[Listening to a concert performance of Mahler's tenth symphony] It felt as if I had not missed a single note. I have never seen pictures or anything else when I listen to music, and I didn't this time either, but the feeling of having been addressed, strongly and directly, lived inside me . . . It felt as if I had understood a message—from one era to another, from one person to another.

(16.2D) Woman, middle-aged, 1960s (from Chapter 24, account 24C)

[In St Petersburg, then called Leningrad] Just across [from the hotel] stood Leningrad's famous concert hall with its excellent acoustics. We made our way there one evening, and to our joy they had Russian music in the programme [including] Peter Tchaikovsky's Symphony No. 6, *Pathétique*. I've listened to that hundreds of times before, but never ever before like this. It felt like the first time, completely new, interpreted in the correct way, for me as well as for several of my friends. I knew, of course, about Tchaikovsky's tragic life, but here the music reflected more than that. All the melancholia and history of suffering of the Russian people was there in it . . . We sat fairly close to the orchestra; the whole time, the audience was very quiet, the atmosphere was charged. It felt as if the musicians were playing for us alone. I don't think the musicians were unaware of how moved and captivated the little Swedish party was.

In a couple of examples, Nature happens to be the frame around the feeling of the music being addressed to just me, and nobody else.

(16.2E) Woman, old, 1950s (from Chapter 23, account 23K)

One July evening, we were ready to set sail . . . out across the Baltic towards Gotland. It was a wonderful evening . . . After dinner I turned on the wireless and heard court singer Sigurd Björling sing Gustaf Nordqvist's *'Till havs'* ['Out at sea'] with his delightfully warm voice and real insight. The situation was perfect, so I absorbed the music more intensely than before. *It was just for us he was singing!*

(16.2F) Woman, old, 1980s

I had my grandchildren with me on a visit to the Eskilstuna Zoo. We went on the swings, the roundabouts, the adventure playground . . . Finally, the children went for one last go on the climbing frame and I started to walk down the valley. Then I hear it coming towards me where I'm standing under the fir trees all on my own, tired after a day with two lively youngsters—'Amazing grace', coming from the valley, performed by a choir and a brass band with 65 players. Well, I've never experienced anything so wonderful. A blissful feeling, elevating; I stood completely still and let it all pour over me, there was only me there, and

I got everything. The tears simply ran, but from joy. Even today, when I write this down, the tears fall, but out of gratitude for my being given the opportunity to experience this.

On the way home, each of us told what we had done. But I was the only one in our group who had heard this wonderful music which filled the entire valley, and which I had been allowed to receive.

The feeling of being specially selected and that the music addresses just me is something that is also described by people who have found themselves in a crisis. The music reflects their situation and becomes a turning point. Here are a couple of short quotes about this (the complete accounts are in Chapter 17, about music as therapy). A tired mother of young children who wasn't feeling well was in a retreat without the children. Then this happened.

(16.2G) Woman, middle-aged, 1970s (from Chapter 17, account 17.2F)

Entirely absorbed in myself and without the ability to make contact with anybody, suddenly . . . I hear music from a nearby park . . . From the very first moment the music spoke to me and my feelings suddenly came to life again . . . I dared to feel how sad I was about circumstances that I had no control over, but perhaps above all that it was permitted to feel so.

A young woman who was depressed went to a performance of Finnish tango, listened and danced.

(16.2H) Woman, young, 1980s (from Chapter 17, account 17.2L)

I was dancing, whirling, and really gave myself up to the music and the rhythms . . . The music set me free from my sober everyday life . . . All the dramatic sentiment that it conveyed reflected my own situation in life—but in a new way that I liked . . . Afterwards I was bouncy, giggling, lively, and filled with deep joy. It was really about a life-kick . . . It was so bewildering that it almost felt like a salvation. It was as if I was selected to take part in such an experience when I needed it the most.

16.3 SELF-CONFIDENCE IS STRENGTHENED

To feel confirmed, understood, appreciated, selected means that one is strengthened in one's identity; one's self-confidence increases and one dares to do more. This has already been evident in the previous accounts. Other examples of this are to be found in accounts of playing music. A self-evident example is that one receives appreciation for one's performance.

(16.3A) Man, middle-aged, 1970s

I had my strongest experience with music when I made my debut as Radames in the Verdi opera *Aida*. I wasn't nervous, but concentrated, and I knew what I had mastered after months of rehearsals. The applause after the aria in the first act gave me further courage, and in the just over three hours that the performance went on, I was in a pleasantly creative situation which gave stability to all the rest of my life. Afterwards, I felt an extreme relaxation and joy with the applause and the flowers. The knowledge that I had performed one of the greatest works in opera literature felt elevating.

(16.3B) Man, young, 1980s (from edited interview)

I was going to sing a piece from a musical at the end of term. Before the concert, I was in a good mood but extremely nervous. I probably did think that it would go well but I didn't know how it would be received.

There were student caps, white clothing, and atmosphere. Everything went perfectly. Everything went exactly right and it was just those feelings of happiness. When the audience looked pleased, I became all the more sure of myself. I could sing better and better and it felt really good. That happy feeling comes sort of from inside, bubbles up sort of . . . like a big smile.

I thought it was really great to sing for the students. To have been chosen. And then that they thought it was so good. Afterwards, it felt even better and the feeling of happiness stayed with me a long time.

(16.3C) Woman, young, 1990s

I am 17 years old, and there's a rock gala in an ice-hockey rink. We go up onto the stage. After a short presentation, we start off with the first tune. People are jumping up and down like mad, we're used to it, but this is something different from the usual. The stage rocks and the drums fall down after the first tune and it feels really good. It feels, in fact, as if the audience is on the same level as us. They understand us and we understand them and there is so much happiness around us. Now, for me, it is about expression and intensity. I'm not the slightest bit nervous and I'm absolutely enjoying every second on stage, I don't want ever to stop. So here's a great crowd of people of all ages who aren't punks, and it feels as if they understand us, our punk and everything about us.

We played ten tunes and three of them were covers, the rest our own. It felt like our tunes were experienced by the audience as being on the same level as the covers we played. *Everything* was on the same level. A weird feeling, but one that was completely natural in the context. I have never experienced this contact with the audience again.

There are other examples of how self-confidence is strengthened from the appreciation of the listeners in several accounts in Chapter 18, sections 18.1 and 18.4.

To be entrusted with playing with more experienced musicians is also a boost for one's self-confidence.

(16.3D) Man, young, 1970s (from Chapter 5, account 5.4B)

[About playing at the Jokkmokk winter market] My sister knew one of the guys who was playing and he recognized me, so when they had played some tunes he came up to me, ruffled my hair and asked whether I could play a tune, if I could join them in a tune. Well, yes, I did know 'The Jokkmokk waltz'. Right, then we'll do 'The Jokkmokk waltz' he said, and talked to the others.

So we played it, so I could join in and play this tune with these guys who were the hottest you could imagine. I played my little three-quarters violin the best I could and it was a fantastic feeling. This was the best kick in the world. I couldn't have anything better than this. It was delightful to be taken seriously even though you were a kid. That you could do something together with these people who were idols.

Several musicians describe how, before their performances, they have been extremely nervous and most of all would have liked to disappear. As the performance turns out well, one's self-confidence increases, one feels all the more approved, and the response and appreciation of the audience and fellow musicians can lead to an enormous confirmation, and one becomes strengthened in one's identity as a musician. There were several examples of this in Chapter 5, section 5.4, about performances during one's teens, and there will be several more in Chapter 18, section 18.4. Here is a foretaste.

(16.3E) Woman, young, 1980s (from Chapter 18, account 18.4B, interview)

[Prior to the rock band's first performance, she has been nervous for several weeks and wishes she could be ill so she could miss it.] The first tunes I just stood there, I reckon, couldn't think or anything. I just saw that everybody was looking at me . . . I reckon I sang my notes properly and so on, we had of course rehearsed a lot so I had it all in me somewhere, but I stood completely stiff with my hands in my trouser pockets.

But then when I saw that people liked it . . . things loosened up after a while . . . But God, what's happening—it's going well! It was a fantastic sensation to feel the nervousness relax its hold more and more. To feel that you dared, dared to sing out, dared to move. I can do it! I dare! Yes, I dare do it. All my inhibitions vanished and I just sang for all I was worth . . .

Afterwards, I was exhausted but happy. We could have gone on playing for ages and ages . . . I wanted to do it again and again . . . it's a kick for your ego and self-esteem!

To perform music can give one the possibility to test boundaries, to dare to take risks, to find a means to express what one has inside one, to realize a part of oneself.

(16.3F) Woman, young, 1980s

A year or so ago, I started to play the saxophone and now I feel that I have found my instrument. I can express myself on the saxophone. I have started to play in a rock band. It's fun. To dare to stand on stage and play solo. To dare to express yourself—in public—on your instrument. It gives me strong feelings. To dare . . . And, of course, the saxophone is traditionally a male instrument. It feels nice to defy gender stereotypes.

This experience with music is new for me. I am making music! I'm expressing my emotions. I'm using what's inside me. I'm conquering the feeling of 'But I couldn't do that . . .' I experience it as if I am breaching boundaries, my own but also society's gender boundaries.

This experience of being able to make music myself, I think it will mean a lot to me in the long term. I set goals and try to reach them. I haven't done that before to the same degree. Sometimes it actually feels as if the saxophone is my soul.

In the final account, at the end there is an emphatic indication of how the narrator has found his identity as a musician.

(16.3G) Man, middle-aged, 1950s

[Guitarist, describing the first time he played for a dance in school premises] The evening when my first gig was to take place, we musicians got there in good time to get all the dance/jazz arrangements in the right order, tune the instruments and get used to the acoustics. The room seemed to be filled to the brim with notes in such a way that the direction of the sound became unimportant. I experienced that both the tonal mass and the rhythm became all-embracing, a listening situation that you hardly ever get to experience in a concert hall. A feeling of joy started to germinate inside me. What a joy to be able to stand in the midst of a vibrating mass of tone that you can colour yourself, and at the same time get to pulsate rhythmically, like life itself.

When the dance music was about to begin, I felt a sort of eagerness to be able at last to share and really display these wonderfully charming harmonies that I had so covetously developed in the past years. We started to play for the first dance, and, as usual, every dance consisted of two melodies: one slow, one fast. Already in the first melody ('Red sails in the sunset') I experienced a combined feeling of happiness and power. Here, for the first time in my life, I felt what it was like to steer people by remote control with the help of sound waves. In the second, faster, melody ('In the mood'), apart from at the beginning feeling rhythmic happiness, I could also experience what it feels like when the audience guides the musicians with remote control and they almost kill the sense of rhythm by clapping on the wrong beat. Every dance taught me more and more about the interplay of sound and movement, and in general about our understanding of, reaction to, and attitude to music.

After the applause that followed the ecstatic performance of 'Hey, Baberiba', I saw how the cellar roof broke up and a flood of light poured in. At the same moment, I thought—in exactly these words—the following: 'This is my place in life.' The memory of that feeling lives on with such force that hardly a week has gone by during the 40 years that have passed since that experience when I haven't had it in my mind.

Music thus offers several possibilities to build up and reinforce identity.[1]

CHAPTER 17

MUSIC AS THERAPY

In several earlier accounts, there have been glimpses of how strong experiences with music can have therapeutic effect. It is, however, difficult to determine where the border might be said to run between generally positive effects on well-being and health, and 'genuinely' therapeutic effect—it is a question of definitions and of various considerations. In this chapter, I have collected a number of examples of experiences which the narrators themselves have described as decisive moments during a critical condition, something that came to be a turning point in a positive direction. Some narrators also use the word 'therapy' in their description of the experience.

While therapy as a rule assumes the participation of a therapist—and this is true in different kinds of so-called music therapy too—there is no such therapist in these accounts. It is the music itself that is the active agent, the 'therapist'. The music, so to speak, intervenes in the course of events and turns a negative state towards a positive direction. There is a great deal of variation from case to case as to how this happens, which can be seen in the following accounts. They have been grouped into two sections. The first concerns the alleviation of physical pain, the second the alleviation of problems such as stress, uneasiness, anxiety, or depression.

17.1 Relief of physical pain

Some participants have described how music relieved or eliminated sensations of physical pain.

One of our oldest informants, born at the beginning of the twentieth century, has told of three childhood experiences with music. One of them was as follows.

(17.1A) Woman, old, 1910s

In the old days, in my childhood, they didn't usually do any fillings on milk teeth. Anyhow, whatever the reason, I often had toothache. My father came home one day with a gramophone with an enormous horn that I would have liked to crawl into. He had bought a lot of gramophone records too, mainly classical music. But also one or two lighter classics such as H. C. Lumbye's 'Champagne Galop'. When my toothache was at its worst, I wound up the gramophone and played the 'Champagne Galop'. Strange though it may seem, the pain went away. Every time!

It is not so likely that Lumbye's 'Champagne Galop' had a direct physical effect on the reason for the pain, but one can well imagine how the lively expression of Lumbye's well-known piece with its rapid pace could engage the young girl physically as well as mentally and in that way be a distraction from the toothache. That she also thought it was fun to use a horn gramophone—a novelty in that day—could have contributed as well.

In the next case, it is a one-off event, with Mozart coming to the narrator's aid.

(17.1B) Woman, middle-aged, 1970s

On one occasion, music made me well. I was mortally ill with fungus poisoning, but luckily I didn't realize it. I am and was fairly knowledgeable about wild mushrooms and I knew exactly what I was picking. The thing is that I was relying on an out-of-date mushroom book, and the information had later been revised. Being a responsible housewife, I bit into every specimen of the new mushroom that I had just learnt to recognize, and ate it. Later, when I became dreadfully poorly, I asked my husband to throw away all the mushrooms that I had picked. Later, at a mushroom exhibition, I found out that this mushroom is now regarded as decidedly poisonous.

Anyhow, I had a very painful night, vomiting and having cramps. I had the radio turned on. At about five in the morning I was suddenly struck by the thought that my heart might not manage this. Just then, there came a piece by Mozart on the radio; it was delightful. It was God and heaven and all angels, and I felt that now I had reached a turning point. And to the strains of that music I conquered the poisoning.

In this case, too, it is hardly likely that the music had a direct effect on the reason for the pain (the poison). But perhaps the Mozart piece came at a decisive moment in her body's struggle against the poison, and its delightful character thus emphasized—and perhaps even contributed to—the positive turn. The final words do, of course, indicate that it was she herself who conquered the poisoning, accompanied by Mozart's music.

Many people suffer from constant pain. The woman in the next account found a piece of music that always gave her some relief.

(17.1C) Woman, middle-aged, 1990s

A year or so ago I got an invalid's pension because of problems with my backbone. I have continual pain. But when I listen to Chopin's Nocturne No. 1, then things ease up, however dark I might have been feeling just before, and for a moment the pain doesn't reach me. On the whole, I have experienced that music makes me forget, or represses or dulls the aches, so that the sensation of pain is weakened or doesn't reach me at all.

The music distracts attention from the pain so that it is weakened or doesn't reach her at all. But this does not, of course, work with just any music. For her it was Chopin's nocturne in B-flat minor that counted. For both the previous and the following narrators, it is a question of certain pieces of music that in some way suit that particular person in the particular situation they find themselves in. The fact that it suits can be on account of both the expression experienced in the music and the way that it is associated with some positive memory, as in the following account, where the music was Gregorian chant.

(17.1D) Woman, middle-aged, 1980s

The music was Gregorian chant by Benedictine monks from the Solesmes Monastery (Coro dei Monaco Dell'Abbazia Saint Pierre di Solesmes).

I played the music during a period of about ten days. Was in my home. On my own. After an operation and a ten-day hospital stay. Was given morphine at the hospital for stomach spasms. Didn't take any medicine for the pain after I got home.

I'd bought the Gregorian music in Rome a week before the operation as if I'd understood (not consciously) that I would soon come to need this music.

I had a dull pain all the time, but it got worse in attacks and then was almost unbearable. Every time the pain came, I put the music on. Listened for several hours every day. The attacks of pain lasted 20–30 minutes and then turned into a dull pain which was there all the time and disappeared after about two weeks.

The Gregorian music is humming and means consolation. I descend into the ancient church, down into my own archaic places, places where somebody hummed. There is a distinct image. I was one year and ten months old when she died. Ingrid had long white aprons. When she died I almost pined away. The whooping cough that I got afterwards kept on for almost a year. It was a long drawn-out experience, of decisive importance for my life. All the time, I could remember Ingrid's humming and in that way I had consolation within me.

Re-experienced this now. Needed solitude and found it hard to talk to anybody. Felt that I could only get through this by myself. I played Gregorian music and pulled myself through the pain. The outer (the music) and the inner (Ingrid's humming) met. The Gregorian humming activated my old ability to console myself.

Since then, I listen to Gregorian music when I am faced with difficult tasks. I become introverted, concentrated, and feel self-evident when I listen to that music.

A humming voice had been associated with consolation early in life. The similarity between the humming voice and the Gregorian chant meant that the chant too could serve as consolation.

It seems nowadays that music is used at childbirth in some maternity units in Sweden. In the account below, however, it is the mother-to-be who has chosen the music herself.

(17.1E) Woman, middle-aged, 1980s

I shall try to write a little about thoughts and experiences I have with music in connection with pain and the feeling of changed pain. Music as a form of pain relief when I gave birth to my children.

Before the birth of our first child, the preparations were very thorough in many ways, including a readiness for what might be a very long delivery. To fill that time, I put together a tape especially for this occasion, later calling it the 'delivery tape'. A tape with music I like, quite simply. Music of various types that means something special to me, 'pearls' for me, if you like. This delivery tape came to be of much greater importance than I had expected.

The day finally came. When the labour pains had started properly and it was beginning to be unbearably painful, my husband produced the tape, which at that point I had forgotten about completely. I remember that at this particular moment it felt irrelevant and unnecessary to listen to music, as the pain was the only thing I was feeling then.

Despite my feeble protests, the tape was put on and the little, white, unfamiliar delivery room was filled with music. My own music. Almost immediately and in an indescribable and completely new way, my music filled me with energy, courage, and security in such a strong manner that no experience of music has later been able to match it. The intensity of the labour pains paled, it was still there but was subordinated to the music, completely manageable and not as excruciating any longer. All the other medical pain relief that had been started felt entirely unnecessary and was soon curtailed.

Despite the fact that I have had music in me and around me virtually the whole of my life, and in different ways, this experience was utterly new in some way. To have my own music in this alien and completely new situation changed my entire situation. Pain relief of the most effective type, mentally and physically. Another of the strengths and possibilities of music. With the help of which, the birth of my daughter was a very positive event with a great sense of presence, for me, with regard to what actually happens during the delivery, as well as a great deal of joy.

The possibilities of music are many, but nevertheless . . . what was it in the music that affected my experience of the pain? The music itself, its message of security, or the reaction of the body itself, perhaps in the form of relaxation in the encounter with the familiar music? Perhaps there are physiological as well as psychological changes during experiences with music, which possibly in my case, at that particular time, was important for the sensation of pain.

Another idea is that music has the possibility to arouse, perhaps even to confront, emotions and how important would that then have been in my case, as it is about the feelings of pain during labour? A closer look at the choice of music tells me that the emotions that the music conveys to me are to a considerable degree of the same sort: happiness, strength, and some form of hope and vitality. Could it be that the message of the music in these cases quite simply is not compatible with pain, and that the power of the music was so much greater, so that the pain was reduced and was overshadowed? Another thought is that just a personal tape of music was of great importance, as this particular music was of value and importance to me just then.

My understanding of the great importance and strength of music, in many different contexts, was further confirmed and reinforced by my experiences during childbirth. Music is presumably something much greater than just music. Not being able to find answers, being humble in the face of greatness, to let experiences and feelings just happen—I think this too is something that is important for us today. Perhaps music, its importance and manifoldness, is precisely one of those areas where we won't find all answers and where the questions, instead, will become all the more.

Her own analysis of the reasons for the pain relief supplements the preceding analyses. Music that is familiar to her and has been specially selected ('pearls') creates a sense of security and promotes relaxation, and the feelings that the music conveys—'happiness, strength, and some form of hope and vitality'—are incompatible with pain; the pain is overshadowed, attention is diverted. The music as well as what it is associated with, both are important. It is a question of an interplay between music, person, and situation: 'just a personal tape of music was of great importance, as this particular music was of value and importance to me just then'.[1]

The music that is spoken of in the next account was also specially selected and had been sung for the intended listener for two months. The question is whether it thereby became familiar for the little listener and thus conveyed something that perhaps contributed to a decisive turn in a dramatic situation. That is how the narrator experienced it.

(17.1F) Man, middle-aged, 1980s

T. came into the world after a normal delivery. I had been singing '*Byssan lull*' [a traditional lullaby] for him for a couple of months before he was born, and I sang the same song for him shortly after he came out of the womb.

The next morning, the catastrophe happened. T. stopped breathing and was put on a respirator. To make a long story short, and get to the point, the reader must imagine a very dramatic situation where the reality is that life is hanging on a thread. In a room where T.'s heart movements can be followed on a monitor, you can see the struggle taking place. When the senior doctor's look confirms his previous statement that 'only a miracle' can turn this, I get an impulse to go up close and sing '*Byssan lull*' into the incubator.

Then amazing things happen. On the face of the tiny baby you can see small expressions of something other than the terrible cramp attacks, and a powerful feeling of response and contact fills me. I see how all the people in the room start to cry silently.

Later, people said how obvious it had been that the song seemed to be the active influence which at that particular moment changed the situation and was victorious over death. Nobody knows what would have happened if there had been no song . . . Since that traumatic time, T. has carried music within him as an effective life spirit in the struggle to compensate the after-effects of the stroke which caused him to stop breathing . . . Today, his major interest is creating music with his computer. Other people say that his music is soothing, calming, relaxing.

17.2 MUSIC IN STRESS, UNEASINESS, ANXIETY, AND DEPRESSION

There are a number of accounts of the positive influence of music in conditions like those in the above heading. They might relate to music in general, but for the main part they concern a certain piece of music (or several) that can express or arouse feelings that are positive for that particular person in the particular condition at the time.

(17.2A) Woman, old, 1970s

When I was studying for my qualifications, I had to go on sick leave for a couple of weeks because of exhaustion and stress. One day during that sickness period I felt an extreme uneasiness and heart palpitations despite having my loved ones beside me. In the end, my husband put on a piano concerto by Mozart and after I'd heard that I relaxed and a complete sense of calm settled over me. That is the strongest experience I have had, from intense anxiety to complete calmness.

(17.2B) Woman, old, 1950s

About 30 years ago, for two years I lived under extreme mental pressure. During that time, I discovered that music could give relief. I played Beethoven's Sonata in C-sharp minor, Op. 27—the so-called 'Moonlight' Sonata—the first movement, Adagio sostenuto, pianist Wilhelm Backhaus, a 78 record.

Tranquil, soft music that entered me and possessed me totally, untangled all the knots and all the pressure, and left me completely calm and pleasantly relaxed. As soon as everything started to feel too difficult, I played my favourite record which could help me persevere. I know that if I get into difficulties in the future, I shall seek help and relief in lovely music.

(17.2C) Man, young, 1980s

A couple of times, music has succeeded in untangling rather deep anxiety knots (Rachmaninov's Symphonic Dances No.1; Genesis's album *A trick of the tail*). The experience is similar both times—sort of like a door that opens into a flooded bathroom.

I have actually learnt how to make use of this—some music can actually work as a sort of do-it-yourself-therapy! I think that's really nice, because I actually often go around feeling anxiety—performance anxiety mainly because of the sometimes far too high demands I have for myself, and anxiety because of things deeper inside me.

(17.2D) Woman, middle-aged

My son was born just over 20 years ago. He was born slightly prematurely and had something wrong with his lungs so that he couldn't breathe by himself. He was put straight into an incubator and given oxygen. The first four or five days were very critical for him. I had to leave the maternity unit without him and be at home two weeks without my baby.

For some reason, I put on a record with Chopin's waltzes. It was a fantastic experience for me during this wonderful, melancholy music to go and think about my baby and just hope everything would be all right. It turned out that I played this music over and over again, all day long, for about two weeks. Thank you, dear Chopin, for your help in this difficult period which ended so fortunately. Still to this day, when I hear Chopin I am reminded of all of that extremely strongly, as if it was yesterday.

The people in the above accounts may have experienced the music as a form of personal address—calming, liberating, consoling, helping. This is perhaps even more pronounced in the next account.

(17.2E) Woman, middle-aged

About 20 years ago, I met with an event which gave me a deep, personal shock. This resulted in my not being able to get contact with people and life around me. I felt as if I was living in a glass jar completely cut off from life. The only thing that reached into me was music. I lay in a dark room and listened to music on the gramophone. The music could penetrate through the walls and seep into me, and I think it was the music that meant that after a month or so I could start to fumble my way back out into life again.

A very telling image: music that is able to seep into the glass jar, her sealed-off inner world. Only music, nothing else, could reach her. What sort of music it was, and what made the contact with her inner self possible remain unanswered questions from this short account. One of the foundations of music therapy in its different forms, however, is that music can reach out to a person in situations where other means of contact don't work.

This could be said to be a common theme in the following accounts. The circumstances around the experience vary considerably from account to account, but, regardless of that, music opens the way to a sealed-off inner and shows a way out of the depressive condition.

(17.2F) Woman, middle-aged, 1970s

A tired mother of small children at a retreat without her children. On that occasion, I felt mentally rather bad. As a mother I felt great guilt for not being able to cope with my family as I should. Everything in life was just 'ought', 'must', etc., and filled with demands not so much from people around me as from within myself.

Anyhow, entirely absorbed in myself and without the ability to make contact with anybody, suddenly that Sunday afternoon I hear music from a nearby park. There are four young people sitting there and playing a string quartet, I still don't know which one and at that particular time it didn't matter in the slightest. It was absolutely not the best-played concert I have listened to, but from the very first moment the music spoke to me and my feelings suddenly came to life again. While the music flowed, I dared to feel how sad I was about circumstances that I had no control over, but perhaps above all that it was permitted to feel so.

From having been a zombie for several months completely sealed up within myself, these strains from the melancholy tones of a few violins and a cello got me, within the next hour, to both laugh and cry. There was, of course, melancholia in the music, but also variation of high and low notes, and in the tempo, but together it was harmony. It was there that the music started to say to me that life can be just like that too.

I sneaked away somewhat elated, but at the same time with an inner calmness and I just knew that after this experience with the help of music, life would go on. The music had succeeded in both opening the door to my inner being and in having a healing effect.

(17.2G) Woman, middle-aged, 1960s

The most important experience with music took place when I was just over 20 years old. I found myself in a shocking, very harrowing situation, aimlessly wandering around in the centre of Stockholm and not knowing where I should go. Just felt a strong need to be left in peace, to calm down and to sort out all my thoughts.

Then I caught sight of the Church of Jakob and went in. Somebody was playing the organ and I sat down in a pew and felt in what a delightfully salutary way the music affected me. The kindly J. S. Bach helped me to get back into balance, to regain my strength and to free myself from the worst anxiety.

I realized that this was something that helped me and that I needed, so I found out that they usually played music every Saturday, after which I went back there many times. I also kept a lookout for other concerts in the churches, and I went and listened to them. They were masses, oratorios, I went to everything I could, and felt that the music had a calming and edifying effect that was necessary for me.

Since then, I have used music as a lifebuoy during difficult and trying periods. When I have a nervous breakdown or depression, I choose certain pieces that I think help me best. At the present time, these include Beethoven's Triple Concerto, his Violin Concerto, his fourth and seventh symphonies. Up to now, I have experienced Beethoven's music as the best 'medicine'. I experience it as very emotional and that it speaks to me directly, just nicely sentimental without being vulgar, and at the same time powerful, edifyingly positive. It has helped me a lot.

Last year I went through a difficult time, I felt absolutely exhausted mentally after several severe experiences one after the other. To deal with it all, I charged my 'lifebuoy'—music— and recorded several tapes with different pieces: Verdi's *La Traviata*, Mendelssohn's Violin Concerto, Schubert's Trout Quintet, Barbara Hendricks singing spirituals, Beethoven's Piano Concerto No. 3, Albinoni's Adagio, plus the pieces I've already mentioned by Beethoven. Kiri Te Kanawa singing Mozart arias. Ruggero Raimondi singing *Don Carlos*. Can't remember for certain whether I had something by Jussi Björling too.

So I rely more on music than on doctors and pills.

(17.2H) Woman, middle-aged, 1980s

I was on holiday but had no joy in it because I was in a deep depression, everything was black. I knew that music was good for me and, with some effort, I had made myself go to one concert after another without actually getting very much out of them.

This particular day started like all the others. I had considerable difficulty in trying to persuade myself to get out of my hiding place in bed, and to go out into the threatening prospect of the new day before me. I went to the Church of St Clara in Stockholm where the organist, Per Thunarf, was going to play the organ at 12 o'clock as usual. That day he played music by August Söderman, Gustav Hägg, Lars Egebjer, and Erland von Koch.

Somewhere in the piece by Gustav Hägg—'Prayer F major' from Six Original Compositions, Op. 29—something fantastic happened. My mood changed completely, darkness became light and my uneasy mind found peace. After the lunch music ended, I left the church filled with an appetite for life.

Later, I told Per Thunarf about this. He found it interesting. I asked him whether he could possibly play the same programme again, and to my great joy he agreed immediately, and played exactly four years—to the day—after the experience I have described. On this occasion I was in a normal, harmonious state and the music could not, of course, have the same effect on me, but it was nice to listen to, and it gave me a feeling of tranquillity.

Music is vitally important for me. It is an inexhaustible source of strength. I prepare myself with the help of music, I celebrate with music, and I let myself be consoled by music.

During a later bout of depression, music was 'prescribed' for me. I managed to get my doctor to understand my attitude to using medications, namely that medicine seems to dull my senses, but music opens them.

I like to be able to stay behind in an experience with music, for example in the total tranquillity that can be the result, so I often remain seated for a while after a concert has finished. Twice I have been locked inside the concert hall, and been let out through the stage entrance. It is hard to go out into the crowd as if nothing has happened.

In the next two accounts, sexual abuse during childhood is the reason behind the experiences. Music seems to bypass barriers that have been built up as a defence against grave, repressed memories.

(17.2I) Woman

We were at a concert which included a work by Shostakovich. My friend was going through a difficult time. She was in therapy to get over her hard childhood during which she had suffered from very grave experiences of incest. It was extremely difficult for her to get in touch with these memories, which, however, was important to allow her to move on. It was a wonderful concert and I was totally absorbed by the music. Suddenly I feel how my friend takes hold of my hand and grips it firmly while the tears run down her face. We sit like that until the concert is over and then I help her home. Afterwards, she told me that she had been completely possessed by the music, and forgotten both time and space. She had been completely relaxed and absorbed the music. Suddenly, memories from an especially difficult occasion came back. In her therapy, it had been completely impossible to get in touch with these memories. It was as if the music had managed to get past the defences, and allowed and carried the weight of all the pain. The music had such a depth that it could cope with the entire effect.

In the next account, an insecure child created two free zones, away from abuse. To sing and to make up her own songs were one of them; a meadow and a tree to escape to were the other. Singing and her own, clear, beautiful voice created a moment's easing of the tension, gave her courage and security, a freedom quite simply to be a child, to be herself, without fear of abuse.

(17.2J) Woman, young

I was extremely insecure when I was little, and music became my free zone. The insecurity that I felt was because of sexual abuse by an old man who lived nearby. My family and other adults were unable to pick up my signals because I didn't say anything with words. It remained a secret within me that I didn't dare share until I was an adult. I repressed it altogether.

My age at the time was about seven or eight. The memory is that I am standing in a meadow, this is a meadow I was often in. I had measured how quickly I could run and climb up a tree that was at the edge of the meadow. The tree was my great salvation because if I climbed up, then nobody could hurt me. In the tree I was safe and secure and it was my other free zone. I dared to be out in the meadow without being afraid. I could see if anybody was coming and, like a cat, I knew my route of escape to the tree.

Out in the meadow I started to sing and made up my own songs. For me they were beautiful songs—first they were scales in a major key but that changed and there could have been more in a minor key. The songs were about the flowers I picked and about what colour they were and what they looked like. It was the same tune I sang over and over again. Something like 'Here I go, picking my flowers, and they are yellow, white'—the words kept repeating and belonged to some sort of refrain. 'Here's a bumble bee buzzing, he's flying to the red flower' was a verse with it that could vary depending on what I could see.

It surprised me to hear my own voice, so clear and beautiful. I started to dare to sing quite loudly, and really let myself go for it. I knew that the people in the houses could hear me if they were outside or had the windows open. I was so moved that I started to cry when, for the first time, I let out a little of all the terrible things that had happened to me. It was lovely to let some of the tension out through crying, a breathing space. The occasion was an invitation to be free. I felt so safe and could be a child for a moment without lots of pressure on me that something would happen.

I was proud that I had dared to sing so loudly, even though people could hear. I took my friends with me too and we played there and then, too, we sang spontaneous songs. I know that I often used to sit in my favourite tree and sing songs, but then they'd be children's songs I had heard on the radio.

I see the pattern of how music has become my free zone where I can develop, and through it I have been allowed to be myself without a lot of abuse.

Now, back to some further moving accounts of how music became the path out of a deep depression.

(17.2K) Woman, old, 1960s

My strongest—without any comparison—experience with music came when I had just been given a recording of Rachmaninov's Piano Concerto No. 2 in C minor. I could take it with me together with a simple little battery-run plastic gramophone, when I was voluntarily admitted to a psychiatric clinic in a severe state of crisis. Because I had a room of my own, I could play this fantastic music from morning to evening. But I always had the door open so that as many people as possible would be able to let themselves soar and feel all that I felt, which was indescribable. But I was greatly surprised by people's lukewarm reaction.

I was in a deep depression, but as I continued to listen to the music my thoughts gradually became lighter. Everything was so sad and for me the music was so sad, but it got me to feel more and more that life came back. It lit up around me quite markedly. It was as if the sun shone right into my room, into my heart. This process went on for four weeks. Every bar, every note in all of this fantastic piano concerto was so endlessly dear to me, so indescribably beautiful and full of variety. I could hardly fathom that there was something so divinely beautiful. After this, it took 15 years before I could cope with listening to that music again, the associations were so strong.[2]

(17.2L) Woman, young, 1980s

I looked forward with curiosity to my first encounter with a band playing Finnish tango. It was in a pub crowded with people. There was no stage, so the band was standing at the same level as all the others and this gave another kind of community between musicians and audience. The band started and let their instruments whirl in fervent dramatic tango rhythms. Even then I was filled by such a special feeling that the music began to take command of my body. I was charged, in a way. A tremendous feeling of harmony which made me really enjoy the music, and I found it difficult to stand still.

But it was not until the second half of the performance that the mystery and the power really gripped me. I was filled by an enormous warmth and heat. I really swallowed all the notes that were streaming out in the air, not a single note, effect or sequence missed my hungry ears. The music became so distinct. I was captivated by each of the instruments and what they had to offer me. Nothing else existed!

I was dancing, whirling, and really gave myself up to the music and the rhythms, over-joyed—laughing. Tears came into my eyes—however strange that may seem—and it was as a further sign, some kind of liberation. The music set me free from my sober everyday life. Now I could let my body parts dance as freely as they wanted—just let them follow the rhythms and totally lose control.

The music danced around like a whirlwind in the narrow room and all the dramatic sentiment that it conveyed reflected my own situation in life—but in a new way that I liked. I went hand in hand with the music. Afterwards I remained standing flushed with joy, as if intoxicated, and it was a real kick for me. I felt religious—and the music was my god.

Before I was in a very bad state. Depressed. It was during the most critical time ever in my life. I found it hard to get on with people and had to really exert myself to be able to get to grips with things. Afterwards I was bouncy, giggling, lively, and filled with deep joy. It was really about a life kick. There was also a kind of religious feeling. It was so bewildering that it almost felt like a salvation. It was as if I was selected to take part in such an experience when I needed it the most. I was filled by zest for life and suddenly had quite another view of the grey tomorrow.

I think that you are extremely susceptible to strong experiences with music when you feel bad and weak. At least I was. This event became a kind of turning point in my life. During the period after the experience it was very important. It helped to loosen all knots that I had within me so that instead of going even further into my depression I started to climb out of it.

She became totally absorbed—captivated—by the music; it took command of her body, liberated her from the level-headedness of everyday life, while at the same time mirroring her own situation in life. She felt religious, chosen, allowed to have such an experience when she needed it most, and it was music that was her God.

Finally, a deeply thought-provoking account of music as psychotherapy.

(17.2M) Man, old

I was born and brought up in an environment where there wasn't any music. My parents neither sang nor played. Nor was there any singing or music anywhere around me. I can't sing myself or whistle or reproduce music in any way. I could never take part in singing at school, not even in primary school. There was no wireless in my parent's home until the mid 1930s, when I had left home. I lived for a long time as a boarder in a room without a wireless. So I have been starved of music. Now I experience this as a very great loss.

In middle age I was affected by a very deep and long-lasting depression. I lost all my zest for life. I couldn't concentrate on my work. My financial situation suffered. And my family suffered. I couldn't function as a father for my son. My thoughts just circled incessantly around my failure. I was on medication but it didn't give me peace of mind. A few times, I was an in-patient at a hospital for depression.

I don't know what it was that led to my becoming interested in music in this situation. I started to go to concerts. I bought a record player and started to buy records. I suppose most of the music was just temporary relaxation, but certain music got its teeth into me and came to play a decisive role for my path out of the depression. Without this music, I would presumably never have managed to get out of it. That is what I call my great experience with music.

I think that what caught my deepest interest first was music by Bartók (*The Miraculous Mandarin* and Divertimento for strings). This music reproduced a pain and a sorrow that I felt reflected my own situation. But it led to a delivery, which also became a delivery for me. I soon discovered more music of the same type (Honegger's Symphony No. 2 for strings and trumpet, Alban Berg's Violin Concerto, Mendelssohn's string quartet Requiem for Fanny and, much later, Allan Pettersson's Symphonies Nos. 8 and 10 and not least the wonderful Violin Concerto No. 2). Another sort of music also meant a lot—music that, so to speak, 'rocked' me to calmness like a lullaby. The first of this type was a record with music by Terry Riley (Untitled organ, Dorian Reeds) which I came across by chance, and a record with Tibetan monastery music (*The Eternal Voice*). Somewhat later, perhaps also music by Ligeti and Stockhausen, and even later more music by Terry Riley ('In C'), Steve Reich, more Tibetan music, Japanese music, etc. So it isn't a question of music on just a single occasion. Quite the opposite, several records that I played again and again were a great irritation for my family who didn't appreciate the music the same way I did.

The effect of the music was to give me a sense of peace. It absorbed my attention totally, and caused my torments to sink away. The effect was often that I fell asleep, and slept deeply and peacefully, something that I hadn't been able to do before. This must be an effect of music that can't, in general, be seen as desirable but that was wonderful in my situation. In the long term, the music also had a distracting and a relaxing effect. It succeeded where doctors and medicines had failed—not in solving my problems but in reducing their importance and in getting me to return to what was at least a more normal life.

If I were to point out one particular occasion, then it must be the first contact with Bartók's miraculous mandarin and Riley's untitled organ music which must have been the experiences that opened up the way for what followed.

This, then, was my strong and deep-going experience with music—music as psychotherapy. Many more people must have had similar experiences and I believe that correctly chosen music ought to be able to be of far greater importance than now if it is consciously and deliberately used for therapeutic purposes. It wasn't a doctor or psychologist who helped me to find my way to music. Perhaps one could say that it was by chance that I succeeded in getting it right.

17.3 SUMMARIZING COMMENTS

Music can have deep-going therapeutic effects, as has long been shown within various branches of professionally practised music therapy. But what is special with the accounts in this chapter is that the positive effects come about without the participation of a special therapist; it is the music itself that is the 'therapist'. As our last narrator says, a lot of people, like him, must have had similar experiences of music as therapy.

Such experiences, however, remain untold. One doesn't mention them to other people since they can concern extremely private issues, perhaps also because one is afraid of being regarded as a bit 'weird' if one describes one's strong experience. In general, several people in the investigation have explained that this was the first time that they had ever described their strong experience with music; some have added that it felt like a relief finally to get to describe it, and even to be encouraged to do so. Hopefully, all this can tempt forth others to describe similar experiences.

What explanations can there be for these positive effects? From the narrators' own descriptions and attempts at explanation, one can distinguish certain possible factors. In critical situations, well-known and liked—perhaps specially selected—music can have a relaxing and calming effect, provide security and the relief of built-up negative feelings such as worry and anxiety. The music can divert attention from negative feelings and states, physical and/or mental, and cause them, perhaps, not to be eliminated but to be reduced and become subordinate to the music. The music can express and arouse positive feelings such as calmness, security, happiness, strength, vitality, hope, and liberation, feelings that are incompatible with pain. One can flee into the music, into a world other than the possibly painful reality. The music can be associated with some important positive memory that has become relevant in the critical situation. The music can reflect the person's situation, feelings, and thoughts and thus be timely and provide new insights. The music can reach into (repressed) levels in the person's inner that have been inaccessible to other therapeutic techniques.[3]

Instead of thinking of the music as 'just' music, one can regard the music as representing another person, a person who understands and talks to you. Many people experience the music as a personal message, that the music is directed straight at them, that they are chosen, are allowed to share in what the music says.

But this doesn't work with just any music. The expression and course of the music, as well as the content if there are lyrics, must in some way suit the particular person in precisely the situation in which he or she finds themselves. It is always a question of cooperation between factors in the music, in the person, and in the situation.

These attempts at explanation remain nevertheless a rough analysis and give rise to many other questions. In accordance with the character of every experience and the circumstances surrounding them, one can conceive of links to various (psycho)therapeutic specialisms, but such analyses presume considerably more information than is contained in the accounts quoted here.

The content of the chapter is, however, completely clear: music in itself has a great therapeutic potential.

CHAPTER 18

WHEN PERFORMING MUSIC ONESELF

Most of the accounts in our material (81%) are about experiences one has had as listener. But there are also many accounts of strong experiences with music when making music, that is, playing or singing, alone or together with others. They comprise 19% of all the accounts, and have been divided into six groups.

The first group (18.1) contains accounts with feelings and thoughts that musicians have had while making music, as well as before and afterwards. The second group (18.2) is about occasions when one has had the possibility to play together with more advanced musicians. The third group (18.3) is about experiences in connection with improvisation. The fourth and fifth groups concern problems that can arise in connection with performing (stage fright, stage nerves: 18.4), and the fact that the performance can be jeopardized if one becomes too emotionally involved (18.5). The last group (18.6) is about those magical moments when absolutely everything is just perfect and it all goes along by itself, as if one was being played by somebody else.

As usual, there is a certain degree of overlap between the various sections. In addition, there are sometimes references to earlier sections on performing music during childhood (Chapter 4, section 4.6) and one's teens (Chapter 5, section 5.4).

18.1 FEELINGS AND THOUGHTS WHILE PERFORMING MUSIC

It is not often that one is able to find out what happens 'inside' a musician who is in the middle of a performance. It is, of course difficult—almost impossible—to study such experiences during the actual performance, at any rate if one wants verbal descriptions: it would unavoidably interfere with the performance itself. It is thus a question of descriptions afterwards, but they can nevertheless convey vivid pictures of what it feels like when one is in the middle of a performance, as well as what it feels like before and after. Sometimes, there are also reflections on how the music should be interpreted.

In this section, a number of musicians from different genres and on different levels describe their experiences, beginning with some accounts of performances of classical music.

(18.1A) Woman, young

I look for and achieve some sort of catharsis when I play Gavotte in D major by Rameau on the violin. The piece is in A–B–A form with a–b–a form (calm–somewhat livelier–calm) even within the A parts, while the B part hurries along with triplet sequences, which contribute to a certain nervousness as if it just keeps on going without coming to an end. Finally, the A part is repeated, and calm comes back again.

A possible explanation for the strong emotional experience of this simple little gavotte is that it reflects the construction of a powerful emotional experience. It starts weakly and cautiously, and then reaches a high intensity and energy which break out in a climax, catharsis, only to fade away and reflect back to the entire emotional course.

Here a direct parallel is drawn between the structure of the piece and various phases in the emotional experience. The same in the next account.

(18.1B) Woman, middle-aged, 1970s

I have sometimes wondered why I get so 'turned on' by a part of Bach's Mass in B minor, especially the 'Cum sancto spiritu' movement. I am a first soprano and find it easy to sing coloratura roles. This movement contains long coloratura bits or windings that are very melodious. Some parts sound as if the voices are singing in canon. There is such a lively dynamic in the piece. You can feel the music rolling. If you're standing in the middle of this rolling sea, you become really euphoric and you surf along on the music.

It is these windings that make me almost get the shivers down my back. I experience it most intensively when I can look at the sheet music and listen to the music at the same time. It feels more vivid when I see the windings that 'roll up and down' in the sheet music while the music is rolling.

Some bars, which I am more captivated by than others, go from the upbeat to bar 55 until half-bar 60, and the upbeat to bar 86 until half-bar 90. The upbeats start with a syncope feeling, which feels so nice and gentle to start with. It tickles my body gently and wonderfully when I start at these two places. I don't really know why, to be honest, but something in these upbeats makes it feel a bit special every time I sing them.

Now and then, one finds oneself quite suddenly understanding the content of the music that one previously has not got anywhere with.

(18.1C) Man, middle-aged, 1970s

I was studying singing at music college. I was rehearsing Schumann together with my accompanist. We had got as far as the song 'Mondnacht'. We had been working quite a lot with the song, really slogging away at it, you might say. And neither she nor I was satisfied.

But we decided to do it all the way through anyway—even though we were a bit tired and grumpy.

Technically, it is a very difficult song, because it has to be so restrained, piano nuances in quite a high register. It so easily ends up entirely without feeling and intensity. Or it gets too loud and too tense. The lyrics describe a scene from nature. The moon is shining over the silent fields . . .

Anyhow, we started the song . . . and very suddenly—from the first note—I was 'inside' the song. It was almost like a mystical experience. It felt as if the ceiling in the practice room disintegrated, and I was standing there under the stars in the moonlight and living in the song—not singing it. And every note meant something very special, and I understood what every note meant. And she and I were not singer and pianist, but had some sort of joint revelation. It was like an enchantment. And I can still see that particular star-filled sky and the moonlight and feel the nameless insight when I think back to it.

And when we had got to the end of the song, we were completely agreed that we had been in some other very special place in the music, and been there together! There could have been several reasons: after long preparatory work, all the bits finally fell into place—although that happens now and then without it becoming a mysterious experience. Because I can never explain that 'supernatural' feeling. It's a mystery to this day.

He merged with the music and understood what every single note meant. The ceiling disappeared, he was out under the stars in the moonlight that the lyrics tell of. A mysterious, supernatural experience, for which reason it has also been briefly quoted in the chapter on transcendental experiences (Chapter 13, section 13.1).

The next account comes from a member of an orchestra. It also contains elements of a transcendental character, a 'trance-like semi-euphoric state'.

(18.1D) Man, young, 1980s

It's about a symphony orchestra concert that I took part in while I was studying music. The rehearsal work went along fairly smoothly, but nevertheless it wasn't easy music to practise, so everybody was more or less nervous when the evening of the concert arrived. The symphony by Dvořák would be played after the break, and there was a decidedly expectant atmosphere in the auditorium.

Halfway into the first movement, I noticed that I had slipped into the trance-like semi-euphoric state I can sometimes find myself in during performances. This takes place when I am fairly, but not exaggeratedly, nervous and it just happens to settle on exactly the right place in my body, namely such that it disconnects all consciousness about motor activity and all irrelevant information. You simply concentrate on producing the music, not on what you should do to produce it; and you concentrate 100% without actually making an effort. This state, as a rule, ceases when you stop playing. So I was extremely surprised that it didn't cease during the middle movements where I had tacet (didn't play).

The finale started, everything was flowing along nicely. When we got into the variations, I noticed that something started to happen—I noticed in some way an increased tension that at first could seem paradoxical in comparison to the course of the music, which slowly goes down before finally almost coming to a halt before the final discharge. I guessed that more and more of the orchestra members began to feel something similar to my state (I talked to quite a lot of the musicians afterwards and found that my guess was pretty accurate). When the orchestra tutti finally came, it was like a steamroller—a will, an idea multiplied 80 times! (Perhaps it sounds a bit pathetic, but that's what it actually felt like!)

During the coda, I realized that this was actually the same feeling that I had had earlier when I'd played rock and jazz with musicians where we've been on the same wavelength, namely a feeling of total shared concentration; but only so much stronger. It's that feeling that makes you—when you are on a stage with, say, a fusion band—do another round in a tune simply because everyone knows that you should, despite the fact that nobody has in any way communicated either visually or in speech about it.

The coda was completed in a sort of ecstatic berserk fury and the feeling during the final chords was something that I haven't managed to find any satisfactory words for. Need I say that the concert was a success? The conductor was called back four or five times.

Straight afterwards, I felt roughly like a euphoric dishcloth (one that has been wrung out), and pretty pleased with myself, or rather with us, because all the time it had felt like a collective experience.

One 'disconnects all consciousness about motor activity and all irrelevant information. You simply concentrate on producing the music, not on what you should do to produce it; and you concentrate 100% without actually making an effort'— an example of what can be included in the 'flow' phenomenon as it is described by Csikszentmihalyi (see Chapter 1, section 1.3). And it doesn't happen on just an individual but on a collective level: a 'total shared concentration', 'a will, an idea multiplied 80 times'.

One finds similar elements in the account by another orchestra musician, this time in the field of opera. First, however, comes a reflection upon how strong experiences with music are related to a constant state of music.

(18.1E) Woman, middle-aged, 1990s

I am always fascinated by accounts of strong experiences with music . . . then the thought strikes me—that's something I never experience. Music experience described in words becomes so easily reduced to just this particular occasion when the music reached all the way, right inside. Music experience is, for me, rather like the essence of life: something that you can't be without and still feel good at the same time. Perhaps a peak experience doesn't become so pronounced when you live in a continuous state of music, just as unlikely as breakfast becoming a gastronomic surprise every morning.

People have often asked me whether a Wagner opera of almost five hours isn't dreadful to play. And sure, there are evenings when nothing seems to go right, when the music machinery ticks out of time; but then on other evenings you get that deep concentration. The total involvement in the music, the 'now' without anxiety or fear of the difficulties, when your hearing is sharpened, your enjoyment is increased, and above all when time ceases to exist, all that is there in a course of musical events. The closest you can get is to call it a state of trance, but keen and clear as crystal, without any thought of your own ego and your own life's circumstances, the focus is somewhere else, on a general human, or rather universal, plane. It is at just such a moment you could die calmly, without worry or sorrow. Just ascend . . .

So I suppose that is my experience with music, the calm . . . the eye of the hurricane—in the midst of life.

Then yesterday evening I played *Parsifal*, the last of Wagner's operas, the one that heralds and is allied with the great impressionistic works. It had been an extremely long and heavy day, and I and several of my colleagues had been on a selection panel listening to one

Mozart concerto after the other played by musicians auditioning. The mood in the orchestra pit was tired and a little uncommitted.

The lights were turned down, and he made his entrance, the conductor with the heavy facial features and the heavy walk, who had shown only one, or at the most two, smiles during the last two months' rehearsals and performances. The overture, the prelude, begins just as beautifully as usual and exactly the same, but somewhere during the first act a new structure is exposed, the orchestra begins to be like one of those old toasters that we had when I was a child, it glows in the red-hot wires inside, the electricity increases in tension and tiny sounds caused by the heat can begin to be heard.

Suddenly we don't need the chair backs any longer; Parsifal's voice rolls over the edge of the stage, and the professional, blasé faces are transformed with a touch. This particular evening the voice that always sounds so beautiful lifts itself up towards the ceiling's enormous chandelier, and lifts not only itself but also all the tired souls in the orchestra pit, all our colleagues on the deep stage, from the tired old Gurnemanz to Kundry's ill-fated female character. Lifts them all to musical grand achievements that explode after the end of the third act in a roaring applause that never stops. What, then, are five hours in a non-ergonomic playing position? Just a puff of wind.

Some key elements in her description: total involvement in the music, no worry, no time, no ego, trance, collective touch, general human, universal . . . and the conclusion: 'It is at just such a moment you could die calmly, without worry or sorrow. Just ascend . . .'

Now an account from the person in front of the orchestra, the conductor. Even though the conductor's task does, of course, differ from that of the members of the orchestra, there are great similarities in the descriptions of what they experience: total concentration, concordance, time and space disappear, all that matters is the music, transcendence, the joy of the performance, and the audience's reactions. The account also offers an insight into questions of how certain parts in the music should be interpreted.

(18.1F) Man, middle-aged, 1980s

The main item was Schumann's Piano Concerto in A minor. Before the concert, I felt a certain tension and a mainly positive expectation. There had been an intense period with several concerts, so the orchestra was well trimmed-in, and there was a feeling of absolute trust and confidence between me and the soloist. I was, however, aware that there were places where it could go completely wrong . . .

Unfortunately, sometimes during a concert there are certain moments when I might lose concentration. It's not that I don't have control of the course of the music, but still it is some sort of distraction, a feeling of being outside, a sort of vacuum. But during virtually all of this work and in particular in certain passages, it felt as if time and space ceased to exist. There was only *music*.

Of course, the actual final moment was by far the strongest, but it was preceded by some moments that in themselves contributed to the total experience. In those passages in the music, there was an experience of total concordance between the soloist and the orchestra as regards interpretation. This combined with the joy of my own intentions as conductor being realized to a greater degree than I could have imagined before, let alone hoped for.

The special passages were:

Movement I, bars 134–185 and 456 to the end.

Movement II, bar 99 and onwards.

Movement III, bars 165–188 and the equivalent parallel place in bar 561 and onwards. The theme in the strings (à la Brahms) which leads up to the piano's syncope in bars 181–184 and the transition to the augmented triple metre is so refined that it gives me shivers of delight. Because not least with regard to time beating, this place is a dilemma: did Schumann want a tension lying in the change between big triple meters (which to my mind is the only way that sounds right) and ordinary triple meters with one beat in the bar? Or did he want to achieve a tension which consists of everyone experiencing big triple meters while the conductor alone stands and tries to maintain the small triple meter's straitjacket and conformist dictatorship? The latter feels absurd but that is what several conductors claim. Others again regard the first as correct. Anyhow, considering Schumann's fate, perhaps the ambiguity was on purpose. Then there is a transition to the main theme in bar 323 which, in the light of the difficulties described above, seems like a gate to paradise; which in itself comprises that very main theme in bar 327.

I have only rarely experienced such a tangible feeling of a shared experience between the conductor (me), a piano soloist, orchestra, and audience too. I could tangibly feel the extremely dense atmosphere there in the auditorium. It was a feeling of participation by the audience and, as it seemed to me, a gratitude about this. It was such a concrete feeling there between the last chord in the orchestra and the audience's applause. This in particular, this shared experience of 'transcendence' was probably the most fantastic thing I have been through in that style.

When you are conducting—fully occupied with keeping a difficult piece of music together, and with your back to the audience too—just being able to feel such a wave of warmth, gratitude for the privilege of being part of it, and joy over the achievement of the performers that radiated from the audience, well, I didn't think it was possible for that to happen. And it is something that I gratefully carry with me.

After the concert, I felt tired, wrung-out, more or less, but without that feeling of emptiness that can often come after a considerable exertion. Rather, it was a strong feeling of joy and a sense of calmness. Perhaps, too, a portion of gratitude for having been able to experience this. I also asked the soloist and the orchestra if they had experienced anything out of the ordinary. There were more of them who had than I expected. And several members of the audience spontaneously came up and told me of a similar experience.

Of course, something like this makes you grow a little, not least in your self-esteem.

The very last sentence is a little example of what is covered in Chapter 16, section 16.3, about the strengthening of self-confidence.

In the previous accounts, it has been a question of musicians at an advanced level. Here, as a contrast, comes an account of fascinating discoveries by a beginner on the piano in her attempts at playing a minuet by Bach. She describes amazement at how the composition has been made and at how her hands gradually seem to work by themselves, wonder, and an admiration which grows to fascination and an almost transcendental experience.

(18.1G) Woman, middle-aged, 1980s (written in English)

I started to take piano lessons and now sit before a page of black dots and lines supposedly written by J. S. Bach—a minuet. I practise the right hand, the left hand, slowly, and painfully put the two together. How come my brain feels like it's splitting in two? The right hand tune sounds like this. The left hand tune is equally complete and melodic in itself. And now, when I put the two together, a whole new dimension is opened up—the two are still each the same and identifiable as such but something much more is present, not just a third tune, when played together. I notice that while I can consciously focus my attention on what the right-hand fingers are doing, the left hand seems to do its own thing—if I direct my attention to it, it collapses completely. Best to leave it to do its own thing, then.

I play the same minuet over and over and over. As soon as I get to the last bar, there is a natural magnetism drawing me back to the first bar. There is no question of boredom, rather the opposite. It becomes more and more fascinating—how can it be possible, how can he have written such a thing, where did it come from—such simplicity, such nothingness, so rich and complex and exciting, interesting, involving? So many years ago and here now as alive as anything.

Now I notice a new element—there is actually music being made here—I start to hear, really hear, the results of pushing down these black and white things in relation to those black and white patterns on the paper. And now another miracle—I am no longer 'playing the piano'—my hands and fingers are moving up and down, the listening is happening simultaneously. I am suspended in space and time, being lifted higher and higher as if a string is connecting the top of my head to heaven. Where is the sound coming from, where is it going to?

I start to lose my balance on the edge of this pool and fall back momentarily into the mechanics as if my ego had started to admire its handiwork and in that moment destroyed this place of perfect stillness. I regain my balance on the edge of nothingness and try not to get in my own way, enormously excited and yet recognizing that were I to give in to this feeling, I would destroy the whole—like the eye of a hurricane.

And so it goes on a while. But I have to go. I am light, fully aware of my own presence, totally free from any previous worries, the Underground [railway] is fresh, awake, living, all the people seem also to have been transformed into peaceful, happy, loving beings. I feel so totally alive, at ease, unbothered, and somehow watching myself from above and yet fully present inside myself. I feel humbled and small but not in a derogatory sense. Just aware of my insignificance in a huge world. Thank God!

A revolutionary discovery, wonder and fascination as to what can be experienced even in a beginner's first fumbling attempts. And afterwards she feels light, free from worries, totally alive, seeing herself as if from above while at the same time being fully present inside herself. The people and the surroundings, even the metro, seem to be more beautiful and happier than before. Last of all, she expresses a cosmic experience, the feeling of littleness and insignificance in an endless world—but also gratitude. All this in the encounter with a simple minuet by Bach. Is there anything that Bach can't achieve?

The music in the next account can be said to be in a border zone between art music and folk music.

(18.1H) Woman, middle-aged, 1980s (from an edited interview)

This was during a folk music festival. We were doing the first performance of a new piece. I had put a lot of effort into this piece for six months and rehearsed it because it was fairly difficult from a technical point of view. I had really lived with this music and had positive expectations, a sort of conviction that this is going to go well. At the same time, you are always nervous in the face of big things.

Then when we performed this piece, I really did feel that now time is standing still. You are in the music, in what you are doing, there are a lot of herding calls—'kulning', those loud high-pitched calls—it's very physical in some way, strong in the sound itself but also strongly emotional to perform it. The very feeling of the encounter with a full auditorium and this music that is so naked and timid, it is both fun and serious, dreadful and simple and in high spirits. At the same time, it was as if it was a question of life, the feeling that you are exposing yourself totally while at the same time feeling that now I am standing here, and the meeting is here. There is something new coming into being, here. It felt extremely nice.

Afterwards, I was totally exhausted. And everybody cried, the audience cried and we cried. As if we had done some really hard work, not just physically but mentally, although in a positive sense. That is also what was so wonderful with this piece, it ended with this feeling that everything is possible. This open feeling both from the people who were there and from yourself too . . . it took me six months before I could listen to this music again.

Similar elements are to be found in many accounts by performers: one is completely inside the music, time stands still, strong feelings prevail, something is really happening here. But the feelings change, to perform this music for this audience is 'both fun and serious, dreadful and simple and in high spirits'. She exposes herself totally in the encounter with the audience, it's a question of sink or swim. Afterwards, there is a mixture of exhaustion, relief, and joy.

The next example is from a folk music meeting amid Swedish early-summer greenery. To feel total unity in the interplay with another person, to feel both closeness and respect, to give and to take, makes time and one's surroundings disappear; it is quite simply just to 'be', just here, just now.

(18.1I) Woman, middle-aged (from an edited interview)

It was at the folk music assembly in Ransäter [in the province of Värmland in west central Sweden]. The first assembly of the year, you arrive and quickly put up your tent, you are out in God's open air and in the greenery of June. There is nothing complicated, no boundaries, no thresholds, no doors, no nothing, you just have to 'be'.

I played together with a person I've played with for a long time previously, but it was like a new dimension to our playing together. To stand and play together with another person and feel the total unity, it just all fits as well as the conditions permit . . . Yes, it becomes a whole, and in that whole the surroundings are gone. You are so deeply involved in it that you don't notice what is happening round about you, rather it is sort of back-and-forth with the person you are standing there playing with, which gives rise to new ideas and new ways of thinking in the playing. There is so much closeness when you play, and yet there is respect for how the other person expresses himself in the playing and everything. It is, of course, about give and take all the time. Once you're inside such a situation, there is no end to a tune, rather it is like an eternity, you can play for ages and ages because it has come to be of such importance to you that you don't want it to come to an end.

Now, two jazz musicians describe performances they especially remember. Both of them describe a tense atmosphere in the packed premises and a tangible feeling of communication with the audience whose strong response, in turn, inspires the musicians to give all they can.

(18.1J) Man, middle-aged, 1980s

We had a booking at the Stockholm Jazz Days. It was crammed with people. When you began, you immediately felt that there was going to be something magical about this job. Everything quickly became extremely quiet in the room and I thought the music was so good, everybody played so well. It was the first time I could just as well have been sitting and listening as playing—it was just as much fun as being active. It felt as though the entire room was involved, it felt so strong, so magical.

The entire concert was a long curve from fairly quiet music and then there was a tangible increase in both intensity and volume. It got more and more, and in the end it was almost unbearable. For the first time, I had a polyphonic synth, so I could arrange a fantastic end, really fancy, a sound that stayed behind and resounded a long, long time after we had left the stage.

After we had finished, there were enormous reactions from the audience. Some cried. Normally, I find it hard to deal with such strong emotions from the audience, but this particular evening I felt as if we had done something together, all of us.

(18.1K) Man, middle-aged, 1970s

A concert in South America. It was an extremely strange performance; as far as organization was concerned, everything was chaos, but we thought we could go there and check whether there was going to be a concert at all. There were about 2,000 people queuing. We supposed it must be for a rock concert, and thought it might be fun to go to that instead. However, it was the place we were going to play at.

I was suffering a bad stomach illness of some sort, and felt really rough, but we got out all our gear. The place was crammed with people. The band's concept was to see what happens when we get onto the stage, to be as spontaneous as possible, to give ourselves challenges. Sometimes we played certain tunes, sometimes not. It was something of an experience to enter the packed place with such a vague repertory. First, people roared as if they were possessed, then when we came out it was so quiet you could hear a pin drop. It was as if there was a lid on the entire place, a tense atmosphere. We had everything in our hands; I nodded to the other saxophonist and we played a note, any one at all, and then were silent again. A second later, I looked up at the audience, and then they were jumping about a metre above the floor and shouting as loudly as they could. Two seconds later, it was dead quiet again. I was completely shocked, was close to fainting.

We played for several hours, no problem, there was fantastic communication with the audience. They really went wild, cried and laughed. We absolutely wanted to give a lot in this performance but we didn't need to impress. It was a really huge audience and they just got happier and happier while we thought up new moves, just as long as we were genuine, took everything seriously, with love. A remarkable experience, an ideal state. These experiences will never leave me!

Now some accounts from young rock musicians. In the first one, the narrator meets a musician who provides inspiration for his own playing, and achieves relief.

(18.1L) Man, young, 1980s (from an edited interview)

[He has been invited to play in a rock band. He has not been playing for a long time, and yearns intensely to be able to do that.] Just to be able to play together with this guy . . . There was such an incredible energy coming from him. He gave me such a hell of a kick so I couldn't stop myself from going up to him and shouting 'Solo!' right in his ear, so that I could get it out of me. He was so shocked, so he said: 'OK, sure.' Then I hadn't moved an inch for ages so it was one hell of a kick. Just letting everything go . . . I had so much adrenalin that it was unbelievable. Just to let it all out . . . really unbelievable. You just hand out lots of happiness all at once. It is like scooping it out. It just pours out . . . more . . . here you are. Take it! I was unbelievably happy. It is like opening the floodgates, everything just comes out. You could hardly stop me . . .

The same blissful intoxication while playing also occurs in both the following accounts. One is going at high rev—high arousal is the technical term—and the audience's response adds to this.

(18.1M) Man, young, 1980s (from an edited interview)

[The band is playing in their home town.] After four or five tunes, everyone in the audience is standing and shouting at the front by the stage. I'm thinking: This can't be true! It's not us playing! And then you feel all the more elated. It's just a total bloody intoxication. Everything just lets go and sounds really fantastic. You're standing there on the stage and watching 200 people who are having a really great time, shouting like hell, dancing, cheering, and you feel: This is the real thing. There was such an incredible feeling to be standing there in front of 200 bloody happy people who thought it was bloody fun to watch us. That must be the most fortunate feeling I've had. It was a *kick*, it really was.

You get a real surplus of adrenalin. It tingles right out to the ends of your fingernails, you're sparkling, vibrating. You go crazy with all that adrenalin, and would like to run around the room seven or eight times to calm down. Instead, you play harder, sort of float along. You look at people and just smile in a daft feeling of bliss . . . That evening, everything was just perfect. We were happy, the audience was happy, and the right feeling came along.

Afterwards, you are dead tired, completely wiped out. You are pleased, tired, in a daze, and happy as hell. You stand there and grin happily at each other. This is, like, the reason I'm doing this, this feeling. The evening was fantastic. It was a total boost. There's nothing I would swap for that feeling.

(18.1N) Man, young (from an edited interview)

There are lots of occasions when you've stood on the stage and are just thrilled and have thought: This is smashing! It's a religious thing too. A super kick. You're standing there thrilled and feel possessed. It's the biggest kick you can get. To stand on the stage . . . people are looking at me!

You turn into somebody else on stage. You have a different ego, the one who stands on stage. A person you have inside you. You put something on when you go up onto the stage. You are so immersed in the music, it's hard to contact and communicate with me then. You get sort of absorbed and are very concentrated. You get rid of piles of adrenalin.

Afterwards, you're absolutely happy. But even though I feel happy I feel empty, bloody empty. It's like you've given everything in such a short time. It is hard to give so much of yourself, to captivate the audience and try to convey a feeling that should be equally strong for 40 minutes. You miss it as soon as you leave the stage. It's like you want to stay on in that feeling, you want to go on. Then it takes three to four hours before you wind down and are yourself again.

This also emphasizes the role, the other ego, which one adopts when one goes out onto the stage. It is also emphasized by the next narrator who feels it liberating to be able to get away from her usual roles and dare to do things she otherwise wouldn't dare to do.

(18.10) Woman, young (from an edited interview)

[She is a singer in a rock band.] I don't feel that time passes. When we get to the last tune I realize that the time is up and it feels as if only one minute has passed. I don't feel that I'm present. It is as if everything runs on its own. Just as if I don't control my own voice and the singing but that it happens by itself. I don't need to do anything, don't have to make any effort. You just relax and it feels as if someone else looks after everything. There's almost a feeling of it being a bit supernatural. You sort of stop working . . . Your whole body works for exactly the same thing!

I don't think about anything else while it's going on. There are no outside factors that disturb you at all. If there's something you've gone and thought about, then you empty your mind. Everything else disappears and I'm totally concentrated. I remember the audience but not as individuals. I forget that the band is even on the stage. It doesn't affect the result, it is only me standing there!

It's just as if I get some extra adrenalin from somewhere once I'm standing there. That you get strength from somewhere, it just pours out, and all the energy that you get, it's sort of generated in the music . . . It's an enormous feeling of wanting to share this too. When you see people getting happy, you want them to become even happier.

It's really liberating to stand up on stage. All these role systems and who you are meant to be and how you are related to one another, they just disappear when you go up on stage. When you get that feeling, you don't care about how you behave on stage: God, I got onto my knees and sang and did this and that. And you can't fathom that it was me who did it. *Wow!* It doesn't feel as if you are the same person. You dare so much more and you are allowed to do it too. There is nothing to stop you!

When you feel it like this, you could manage without everything else. It is so *crazily* enjoyable! It's worth it, all the hard work. The reward is to be up on stage and you get a kick. It is sort of like a drug!

Afterwards, I feel completely empty and completely exhausted. I often sit on my own for 30–45 minutes afterwards. I don't want to talk with anybody. I don't stay behind in that kick feeling, I just feel completely empty, it's as if I run out of steam.

Her account summarizes a great deal of what has been said by the previous musicians: one is totally focused, unaware of time and one's surroundings, one acquires extra strength in some way, everything looks after itself, the happiness is complete, one is rewarded for all the work one has put in, it is a kick that can be similar to a drug. Afterwards, there is a mixture of happiness, exhaustion, and emptiness. It is hard to wind down and become yourself again.

The language in the accounts by these rock musicians differs quite a lot from the language in most of the other accounts. This reflects some of the character one often associates with rock music but is also because they are spontaneous oral accounts in an interview situation. If the same people had written down their experiences, the language would probably have been different, as it is in some other accounts of rock music not included here.

Finally in this section comes a completely different account. A man—a fairly unschooled singer—describes what he experienced when he sang for a very special listener.[1]

(18.1P) Man, middle-aged, 1980s

I hadn't been particularly interested in singing before. The turning point came when we were expecting our first child. The months before the birth we often sat in the evening and felt the vibrations from small feet that kicked against the stomach. For fun, we'd sing a lullaby for the baby-to-come: 'Byssan lull'. It turned into a routine almost every evening up to the birth.

Finally, the day came we had all been waiting for. The journey into the maternity unit took place in the middle of the night. It was a difficult delivery, but the baby comes in the end, red, slimy and all wrinkled, but oh, how delightful! A daughter!

After a moment on her mother's breast, a quick medical check and a bit of drying, I am allowed to hold the little girl in my arms, wrapped up so that the beautiful little red face is all that you can see of her. She starts crying as loudly as she can. I try to hush her so that she'll stop crying, but to no effect. Then I suddenly remember the lullaby. I don't get further than a couple of lines before—believe it or not—the girl is completely quiet and for the first time opens her eyes and looks, as I experience it, with big warm eyes right at me, and if she hadn't understood that I was her father, then at least she recognized the lullaby and became quiet and calm.

For me, this was an enormous experience. I continued to sing the lullaby time and time again because she continued to lie there completely quiet and look right into my eyes. Was she listening, did she recognize the lullaby? I don't know, but the contact I felt that I got with her at that moment has been a strong and warm memory for me. During her early childhood years, I have often sung the same lullaby for her at bedtime, and even on occasion later when it has been a difficult and uneasy day for her and it has been hard to fall asleep in the evening. She feels, and I feel, a calmness and tranquillity at such moments, which is consoling. Could it be because of our first contact with each other, where I believe the singing contributed to the sense of security and harmony that I, and presumably she too, felt?

I have been convinced that she had heard the lullaby before she was born. Now, when I read in the literature on music about studies where they have established that a foetus's hearing is developing as early as the fifth or sixth month, then it feels like a nice confirmation of my theory about the experience.

The experience meant a turning point for me, as far as singing is concerned. It is, of course, very common that a new parent sings for his or her newborn child, but the response I got from my girl changed my entire attitude to the importance of singing for children and adults.

18.2 GETTING TO PLAY WITH ADVANCED MUSICIANS

Having a chance to play together with 'real', more advanced musicians gives an enormous boost to one's self-confidence. The joy, pride, and inspiration that one then feels has already been illustrated in some accounts from childhood and youth. A 12-year-old could play his cornet in a jazz orchestra one midsummer's eve (Chapter 4, account 4.6H), another played violin in 'The Jokkmokk waltz' (Chapter 5, account 5.4B), and a young girl played in an orchestra together with the artiste E-type (Chapter 5, account 5.4G).

There are similar accounts from experiences at an adult age. Here are a couple of examples. Both happen to be from the field of jazz, and describe what a big step forward and what a release it was to be able to play together with world-class musicians.

(18.2A) Man, middle-aged, 1950s

As an active young jazz musician, I got a chance for the first time to play with experienced American jazz old-timers at the end of the 1950s for a recording. We were going to play with musicians from the Quincy Jones Big Band, which was on tour. There was a charged atmosphere before, during, and after the session. It felt like floating up in a higher sphere of music experience. I was sober and drunk at the same time, and was completely convinced—and probably this was the case too—that the music I created was far above my ability in normal situations. It was fantastic to meet musicians whom I'd regarded as superior to me, but the feeling of that diminished because they were so well disposed to me, so generous, and very positive about the session. They managed to create an atmosphere charged with creative impulses and suddenly it felt as if everything went perfectly and was possible to achieve.

(18.2B) Man, old, 1960s

From many a strong experience of music, I choose a chance session with the late tenor saxophonist Albert Ayler, from the USA. The third musician was my friend T. H. on double bass.

A few weeks earlier, far away across the tables at the Golden Circle jazz restaurant, I had made eye contact with a smiling black man with an especially sparkling charisma. I felt the pull, went over, we started to talk and he mentioned that he played the saxophone. Ayler had been living for some time with a girlfriend in Stockholm but was evidently completely misunderstood and excluded from musical circles here—with one big exception. The enthusiast Bengt 'Frippe' Nordström arranged and documented this—for me quite unforgettable—session with a tape recorder and microphone which he bought in all haste. Afterwards, Albert Ayler almost acquired saintly status and this particular occasion has been marketed as his first recording.

The room we played in was desolately empty, with reverberating acoustics. A few curious people peeped in sometimes, but most of them soon disappeared to another part of the building with music that was easier to listen to, more suited to dancing to. We were really geared up to play, and got on extremely well together. Apart from a short stand-in by Ayler at a gig we had in Stockholm a month before, this was the first and only occasion for us to meet and play along in his highly personal and different tonal world. We played ordinary standards, well known to most jazz musicians of my generation: 8-bar periods, chord sequences, and rhythms that are just there in our musical mind. We now met around this joint musical inheritance, without any sort of earlier planning.

To be able to let yourself go—together with others in a swinging ensemble—to experience the joy of everything going perfectly, well, I have had that privilege in ample measure during my musical life. But now, together with Albert Ayler, it was about completely different journeys. I don't think I have ever experienced so much air under my wings! The whole thing was a dazzling adventure of swim or sink. Can we still touch the ground? The form, will it hold? The periods? The harmonies? And at the same time this relaxed mutuality.

Ayler's playing was physically down to earth, his address direct and powerful. This music was his own language. He conveyed the message with an absolute conviction, appealing and exhorting, cutting right through established patterns, path-finding in new territories. All done with a great and mature, raw, but also glimmering saxophone sound rich in overtones, full of expression like a living being. A passionate sermon? At one and the same time, a challenge and an act of love. Bold phrasing and idiosyncratic division—often with unexpected leaps and time shifts—meant the very form could appear to be broken up, floating. He moved with supreme freedom in a music seemingly without bar lines.

What release and liberation to be able to let yourself go in the midst of all this! Like being lifted high up and being able to discern endless possibilities! A spontaneous and resolute flood of inspiration, conscious and unconscious at the same time. Like a blessed gift from above—it isn't me who is playing—I am letting somebody play me.

But if for a moment I were to ask whether this state is possible, to logically try to grasp how it comes about, then in that very same moment I would lose everything, the totality would be broken . . .

Personally, I am very strongly moved by this music now when I listen to it many years later. How much does this depend on the fact that I as a co-creator can re-experience the charged atmosphere when we played together that time? How is the experience affected by the conviction that just this particular experience came to be of such radical importance for my continued life as a musician?

It was a lift up to a level where both structure and expression gained another content than before—a dizzying adventure but at the same time so relaxed and self-evident that it felt as if one was being played by somebody else. A release, a 'blessed gift from above' which seems to escape all logical description, a magical moment of the type that is described later in section 18.6.

18.3 Improvisation

There are some accounts of experiences while improvising—really free improvisation—together with other musicians. The next two accounts come from musicians within different genres, but there are great similarities in what they describe.

(18.3A) Man, young

The music was quite simply improvised, where you started 'jamming', say, with a rhythmic figure, or an initial harmonic sequence, or quite simply somebody started with a note, and then what happened, well, it simply happened. Such an experience was possible if the chemistry between us musicians was good to start with, plus each one of us was open to listen to what happened, plus you were not inhibited by your possibilities as musicians and that you forgot your well-trodden paths as instrumentalists. You found yourself in a collective musical state of intoxication. You felt that you could play for ever and ever, or to be more exact that you didn't have that idea in your head at all, you didn't think about where you were, and how long it would go on, but you were swept along by a wave that you followed until it faded away.

The instrument wasn't a bit of wood with strings any longer, but everything was me. Completely uninhibited without a thought as to what I was playing and why, without a thought as to the difficulty or the simplicity of what we were trying to achieve, quite simply we didn't think at all about the interaction of instrument–musician, we 'just' played. This 'just' was an experience of inner balance and the music we played was like a sort of train that rushed along at full speed through and past inner stations, somewhere where you've not been able to reach rationally. I would like to point out this particular liberation from analysing thoughts about what I did and why. There was nothing of that, rather you expressed something ad lib, something that came from inner sources that were manifested in notes. And all this was a terribly positive experience, full of bliss.

(18.3B) Man, middle-aged

For several years, I have played together with two other musicians. We have made a type of music that is sometimes called improvisations but which is closer to a sort of instant composition which acquires its tonal form directly in the here and now. All three of us have a background both as musicians and as composers, and have worked together in what you could call workshops, where we have developed structures, form concepts, emotional states, etc. which have been stored in memory and are triggered and built upon further when actually playing. We know each other's attitudes to music, and are familiar with a shared musical language.

We have done a whole series of concerts where we, so to speak, challenge fate. We meet on the occasion of the concert and then, completely without any preconceived notions, get out and walk the tightrope. The music is composed and interpreted directly in the here and now, in front of the audience. For us, this always results in very exciting musical journeys, but sometimes something happens that is really special.

Suddenly there is a feeling of absolute concordance, between us as musicians but also in relation to the musical intention and our own creation. The form becomes clear as crystal, the interpretation, phrasing, agogics, dynamics, etc. are just perfect, down to the microsecond. The music immediately acquires a special meaning, content, function—something happens that is beyond the private, the music is lifted out from the stylistic and cultural aspects, it becomes—so to say—biological or perhaps rather universal, an experience in space, time, and movement which lifts you up into a condition of total preoccupation. You hardly know that you are playing—you simply 'are' in the music. A state where you completely forget yourself, forget all everyday associations and find yourself in a flow of function with the universe. (Saying this at the risk of being regarded as a religious mystic, but that isn't what I mean.)

For me, it has actually become so that the very reason I do these concerts, expose myself to walking the tightrope in front of an audience, is these sometimes very short periods of what I might term 'true music'.

When I listen to a concert, these states of absolute music sometimes arise. There can be a lot of dead time during a concert, but—suddenly, you are 'there'. Perhaps it can all be explained by the fact that there arises an absolute motoric synchronization in the musical structure, but there is also something more, a dimension of musical content.

The prerequisites: that the musicians are very familiar with each other, that one is totally open for what the others do, that one forgets oneself and one's practised tracks as an instrumentalist, drops all the usual questions about how and why, allows oneself to be pulled along in a collective process.

The result: one is totally immersed in the music, devoured by it, 'just' playing as though intoxicated, everyone knows exactly what is going to happen next, everything is clear as crystal, the consensus is total. It can feel as if the music was 'like a sort of train that rushed along at full speed through and past inner stations', or like an absolute, 'true' music free from all external irrelevant references, almost universal.

In summary: narrator A: the expression of something 'ad lib', something that came from 'inner sources', a terribly positive experience, in raptures; narrator B: the music acquires a special 'meaning, content, function' over and above the private, it becomes biological, or rather perhaps universal, 'true music'.

18.4 NERVOUSNESS OR PERFORMANCE ANXIETY, AND THE FEELINGS WHEN IT PASSES

Stage fright—performance anxiety—is unfortunately an all too common problem among musicians. It leads to considerable strain, physical and mental, sometimes to such a degree that musicians are forced to abandon their career.[2]

Among young children, performance anxiety is fortunately rare. But there are signs of it during later childhood, and it can be fully evident during the teenage years, as we have seen in earlier accounts: when a young woman made her debut as a solo bassoonist (Chapter 5, account 5.4E) and when a drummer competed in the Swedish Rock Championship (Chapter 5, account 5.4F). That such events are nevertheless described as strong positive experiences is because the nervousness is successively replaced by relief and great happiness, almost euphoria at the end; one's self-confidence gets a hefty push upwards. That is also what happens in the following accounts.

(18.4A) Man, 1990s (from an edited interview)

We were playing in a pub, folk music from Eastern Europe, and you wouldn't really think that would be successful in a pub. I was nervous and had some nightmares. I was expecting that people would just sit there with their beer and turn their backs on us. I thought that the music wouldn't fit in that setting.

It was a bit uncertain at the beginning, but eventually the whole room was in a state of agitation. And at the end we came to encores. It started with my having an introduction on the bouzouki and people started shouting 'Bouzouki, bouzouki,' and then when I played the first phrase, people started cheering. They were shouting out. And then I played another phrase, and they shouted even louder. It was as if I was being blown up like an enormous balloon and everyone in the place was helping to blow up that balloon. And then when the tune got going, everybody started jumping, dancing, and going wild. It was delightful, a feeling of joy. An extreme confirmation. You feel big and important. They responded and responded and showed that they loved me, all of them. There was no conflict or tension, but only confirmation.

(18.4B) Woman, young, 1980s (from an edited interview).

[Prior to the rock band's first performance, she has been nervous for several weeks and wishes she could be ill so she could miss it.] The first tunes I just stood there, I reckon, couldn't think or anything. I just saw that everybody was looking at me. I didn't really know where I was. I was completely paralysed and totally stiff. I can't remember anything from the beginning. I reckon I sang my notes properly and so on, we had of course rehearsed a lot so I had it all in me somewhere, but I stood completely stiff with my hands in my trouser pockets.

But then when I saw that people liked it, danced, smiled and had fun, things loosened up after a while. It was like an awakening! I heard my own voice somewhere. But God, what's happening—it's going well! It was a fantastic sensation to feel the nervousness relax its hold more and more. To feel that you dared, dared to sing out, dared to move. I can do it! I dare! All my inhibitions vanished and I just played for all I was worth.

It's just so great to see that you can convey such a feeling of high spirits to people. People are going around and are happy. Roaring, rocking, completely letting everything go! It's like playing ping-pong with the audience, you get the ball back all the time; if they really get going, we get going even more. It's lovely. It's like being in raptures, sort of.

Afterwards, I was exhausted but happy. We could have gone on playing for ages and ages. You get a sort of 'now it's over' feeling. I wanted to do it again and again . . . it's a kick for your ego and self-esteem!

(18.4C) Man, young, 1990s (from an edited interview)

[His band plays rock music.] It was the first concert and I was so nervous . . . I can't remember anything from the first three tunes because I was so *dreadfully* nervous. I almost got a sort of stage fright. Everybody standing there and watching when you go out onto the stage. It was a miracle that I got all the cables and plugs in the right sockets so that I got some sound out of this bloody instrument. It is rare that I have been so nervous and when I think back I can still feel how it bites into all of my stomach, how I was almost like paralysed, almost like when somebody's got an iron grip of the upper part of your stomach that you simply can't get out of.

If somebody had said to me, 'Sorry, you can't play,' then I'd probably have turned religious and thanked God that I didn't have to go up onto the stage. Because just then, there was nothing I wanted more than to sneak out the back door and go home. Anything at all, just as long as I wouldn't have to go up there! The audience felt to me like a flock of hungry wolves, who wanted nothing better than to kill me almost.

By the fourth or fifth tune I start to remember a little. The first memory I have is that I'm looking straight at a mate who stood right at the front of the stage. Before that, it's like a sort of black hole. Then when things start to ease up you felt like a mixture between Springsteen and Bowie. You felt like you were the biggest rock star in the world just because some people stood there watching you, and when you'd played quite a lot of tunes it was a real joy to be standing there. Yeah, and that people didn't leave, that you weren't thrown out, that nobody disconnected the electricity!

It was a sort of ordeal. I had no choice. I knew the tunes, they were a part of me. If I'd been forced to think, it wouldn't have worked. I just played, went off somewhere in some way. It was a sort of joy when the nervousness eased up—you'd done it! It works, Jesus, you can feel that it works.

Now I know that it can be done. It works. I could go up onto the stage. I could play. I could leave the stage again without being slaughtered and without falling down dead. I managed the whole thing.

All three accounts above are further examples of what was covered in Chapter 16, section 16.3 about gaining confirmation and reinforcing one's self-confidence.

18.5 WHEN FEELINGS TAKE OVER

Sometimes performers find themselves in a situation where they are unable to maintain sufficient distance from the emotions in the music. One is overpowered by the music and loses control of one's performance. Depending on the rest of the situation it can all be fairly innocent and not cause any real problems. But it can also feel embarrassing, perhaps most of all for experienced professional musicians, to lose face in front of fellow players or an audience; one tries to hide one's reaction as best one can.

Here are a few examples from our material. First, a couple of singers.

(18.5A) WOMAN, YOUNG, 1990S

Through my choir singing I have had some strong experiences. On one occasion we performed Orff's piece *Carmina Burana*. In the last movement, 'O Fortuna', there were several in the choir who afterwards told of how moved they had been. They described how the sounds seemed to fasten in their throats, about sweating and goosepimples. I personally found it almost hard to sing and I was close to tears.

(18.5B) MAN, MIDDLE-AGED

I was singing in a choir in a concert in a church. It was a lovely day early in the summer with lilac blossoms outside the church and rays of sunlight coming in through the church windows.

Above all, there were two pieces of music that affected me so strongly that I couldn't sing but just stood in my place and listened, totally absorbed in the experience. First an opening piece called '*Bliven stilla*' ['Be silent', Psalm 46:11], a short but powerful song. The other one was Malotte's 'Our Father', where the choir spread out in the aisles in the church which formed a cross, the same effect, I couldn't manage to sing.

Afterwards, we stood in two rows outside the church in the summer sunshine and formed an alley along which the concert audience could walk out. Many of the people cried and thanked us in the choir on right and left while they walked out and all the time we sang '*Härlig är jorden*' ['Glorious is the Earth', a well-known Swedish hymn]. After this, I walked about by myself and reflected upon what had happened. I came to the conclusion that it was the most beautiful experience with music I'd ever had.

Below follow two accounts of what happened to musicians while performing in symphony orchestras.

(18.5C) Man, middle-aged, 1970s

During my last years at school I was in a youth symphony orchestra. On this particular occasion, the orchestra was going to play Mahler's third symphony, third movement, and Beethoven's seventh symphony. For the Mahler symphony I ended up in position for fourth bassoon. My notes consisted mainly of pauses with the exception of a C now and then. The entire movement consists of long melody lines which continually run into each other. And what is so typical for late Romantic works: an eternal avoidance of cadences, and if they do come along then they definitely don't reach the tonic. This creates a single long continuo, and in Mahler's hands this becomes a single 20-minute-long striving towards the climax that ends the movement—a booming C major chord (if I remember correctly). The coda is very drawn-out and the intensity very penetrating. Sitting there in the midst of this massed C major became so powerful that I burst into tears.

A day or so later, when we were playing Beethoven's seventh, I burst into tears then too during the second movement. I was overwhelmed by the sadness, the delightfulness, and the celestial calm that comes when A minor suddenly becomes A major, and a clarinet goes on its way with a light and lovely melody: a declaration of light in a dark and uncertain world.

(18.5D) Man, middle-aged

The experience was in connection with a concert where I myself was sitting in the orchestra. We played a work by a contemporary composer, a cantata written for soloists, recitation, mixed choir, children's choir, and symphony orchestra. The work itself didn't at first make much of an impression on me, and the rehearsals were mainly just standard routine. There were a lot of people on the stage, more than 200, and at some strong nuances it even felt tiresome.

But just after such a nuance in forte–fortissimo in the choir and the whole orchestra somewhere in the middle of the piece, there is suddenly a section with the children's choir. For me, this section came as a surprise every time. It was above all the tone that first made me listen. This great contrast in intensity, volume, and timbre, I thought it was a good thing on the composer's part but hardly more than that.

So we did our rehearsals and then came the performance. There are, of course, always things to think about in such a situation. I remember that I paid particular attention to listening to the whole of the text of the recitation, as we had skipped bits in the rehearsals. The text was about our times, and there were several places in it that made me listen and gave me associations. It also had the function that I managed to completely forget the other place right until a few bars before it came, where the sound grew and grew all the time. There was something extra that time, as if everyone had agreed to make the most of the music. I thought that this forte would never end, it was impossible to sit still on account of sounds and vibrations.

And then, nevertheless surprisingly, the sound became as clear as a bell and genuine. I felt how tears suddenly came to my eyes and at the same time got a feeling of becoming light and lulled into a cosy warmth. I was surprised by the reaction and tried to hide my face, I had tremors through my body and I was a bit embarrassed, but at the same time, deep inside I was happy. Would handle all of this, but still I was in some way pleased that I had something only for myself.

I got the same reaction the next evening too, when we repeated the concert. But this time I was better prepared and tried to sink down a bit before it. That was when the first oboist came up to me after the concert and started to talk to me about our reactions to music and said that since it was hard to hide anyway, he had long since decided to stop doing it. He had seen me both times.

In the final example a musician describes one of the most anxiety-ridden experiences with music he had ever had.

(18.5E) Man, middle-aged

Mahler's Adagietto, it must be 15 years since I last heard it, and then I decided that I would never listen to it again. I have consistently turned off the radio if it should happen to come along, and it has been unthinkable to go to a concert where it has been included.

Fifteen years ago I was new as a viola player in one of our larger orchestras. We were going to do a tour in Europe and one of the works we would play was Mahler's fifth symphony. I don't know how it happens that I had never before either heard or played Mahler. I grew up with Bach and Mozart and 'music while you work'. I had played both Brahms and Stravinsky, but could never even in my wildest imagination conceive that there was something like Mahler.

I took the score home to practise. The first movements were extremely demanding, technically speaking. The last movement went OK, and the fourth, Adagietto, was completely ridiculous: only whole notes and half notes as far as you could see. I didn't even play them through.

The first rehearsal was something of a shock. I thought that it was the first time a composer had a message directly for me. Other music consisted of musical factors, but Mahler had an extra musical message that he conveyed just as clearly as if he had said it in words. He said: I have lived and now I know that the world is evil and life is suffering. Even where you think there is jollity and happiness, there, too, fate is grinning at you just under the shiny surface.

I was shocked by this message but nevertheless fully in agreement. You often are when you are about 25 years old. But then came the Adagietto and suddenly I didn't understand anything. What did he mean with this mild caress? It couldn't be true! I wanted to get up and shout across the decades: You are lying, you have just told us how cruel the world is, there is no room here for this humble love!

But you don't get up and shout during a rehearsal. You sit properly still, you follow the up-bows and down-bows and you are completely unprepared. Then what absolutely should not happen at a rehearsal did happen anyway. This numbing beautiful capitulation to life made me start to cry. Tears and snot ran down my face and I couldn't do anything about it. If I'd been able to lie down under my chair and die in peace and quiet, I would have preferred that. I was too tough and blasé and hard-boiled to cope with this completely unexpected reaction.

I came to the next rehearsal with ice-cold resolve. Anything could happen, but there were not going to be any tears here, that I was bloody sure about. And just before the Adagietto I bit the inside of my lip so that it bled. My pulse went up to 200 and I started sweating. But when I was going to start playing, my bow hand began to shake so that I couldn't reach down to the strings any longer.

And it went on like that. I travelled around Europe, but when faced with all these whole notes and half notes that I had so contemptuously dismissed, the entire mechanism just seized up. I had to pretend to play a centimetre or two above the string so as not to disturb the delightful pianissimo of the violas.

Then I left this music, and I thought that if it's only up to me then we would never meet again. Today, I have got it back. The language is still just as clear. Yet it means something else. I parted with a painful capitulation, but I have got back a credo filled with love and confidence.[3]

The Adagietto in Mahler's fifth symphony occurs in several accounts by listeners, while here it is also in a performer's account. The expression in the fourth movement, Adagietto, is of a completely different character from the other movements.

From a professional point of view, one can of course be critical of the 'failures' that occurred in the accounts above. But from a more human point of view, it is hard to feel critical—and the reaction does say a lot about the power of music to influence our senses.

18.6 WHEN EVERYTHING FITS AND WORKS: MAGICAL MOMENTS

Among all the occasions on which one has been involved in performing music, certain stand out in a special light: those times when everything worked perfectly, it all seemed to go by itself without the slightest effort, one could do anything at all, one 'knew' exactly what would happen next, one just had to go ahead, it couldn't go wrong in any way. It felt almost unreal, magical, as if one was being played by somebody else, one's fingers moving of their own accord, one felt more like a listener than a performer.

We have already come across accounts of such experiences earlier in this chapter, for example accounts 18.1M, 18.1O and 18.2B, as well as earlier in the book. Here follow some additional accounts that illustrate what these experiences mean. First, some general descriptions without links to particular occasions.

(18.6A) Man, middle-aged

There is a cliché which describes the proportions between inspiration and transpiration (10% and 90%, respectively). On rare music-making occasions in life, perhaps every fifth year, it happens that time suddenly stands still, the 'here and now' is everything and will-power is taken over by a self-driven accelerating spiral where transpiration makes up 0% and inspiration circa 110%! 'Feeling' takes charge while 'reason' is pushed aside and just stands there and looks on with a gaping mouth. The person who is playing experiences that an autopilot takes over and perhaps even does things that the person concerned really doesn't master as regards technique! One can experience this by oneself or when playing together with others. What happens at this moment cannot be described with language or by the rather clumsy tools of 'reason'. Here we are moving into domains that border upon, or quite simply are, magic.

(18.6B) Woman, old

I often sit at the piano and play. Easy pieces, old well-practised pieces and new ones, sometimes far too difficult for me. On some occasions in my life, the remarkable thing has happened that the difficult pieces with their runs and awkward passages have suddenly become possible. I can just run them off with elegance and without resistance. Afterwards, I sit there astounded and wonder how on earth that happened. It feels as if there is some-body else controlling my hands and I only have to think about what it should sound like. I would be really pleased if I could find out if it would be possible to achieve these condi-tions a little more often. Is it me myself who impedes my playing in normal situations, or is there an extra power that sometimes comes to me from above?

On courses, I have come into contact with musicians from various parts of the country. On the whole, the work together is enjoyable and interesting, but a few times I have expe-rienced something really special: *The day when everything goes just right—when 'I' am not 'me' any longer.* Everyone present becomes a single big unit, where all the music makers seem to merge together into an enormous tonal box. One's entire body is filled with vibrat-ing harmony. It feels like listening to a concert instead of taking part. Everything is just right: the correct tempo, nuances, pausing, phrasing—yes, everything is perfect. This is how one would always like to perform the work.

The following day you try to recreate the same insight and lift, but it doesn't let itself happen so soon. Then you have to devote your time to the everyday analytical game again, and feel your mind filled with wonderful pleasures when thinking about the earlier experience.

(18.6C) Man, young

You are always on the hunt for magic moments, but they don't come to order, rather they come now and then when all the external conditions are suited for something more, over and above the ordinary, to happen. The musicians surprise each other and themselves on the stage, they achieve something they didn't think they could do. That extra-magic moment is when it happens for an entire evening, you feel that you are at your best, what you are aiming for, and want to reach. This music is, of course, like walking the tightrope, sometimes you succeed, sometimes you fall down. When you succeed, it feels twice as good, then you're flying and you can tell from the audience, you can see it in their eyes, you notice more involvement, you see a direct communication between the stage and the audience and then the kick you yourself get from the achievement is doubled, when you get it back too. That's the best that can happen of anything.

It's a feeling that is just as hard to describe as love, too abstract, it just feels right and one adds a lot to oneself, the group, and the members of the audience. I feel like an aerial, a conveyor for something that sometimes reaches all the way to the audience.

(18.6D) Man, young (from an edited interview)

[About playing in a rock band] When you feel that it all fits together, when all five wheels roll together and it's the same speed, and there is a sort of swing together, it turns into some form of crazy swing . . . that is the big kick. All individuals do something together so that it makes everything into a whole—when that happens, then it's really great!

When I get a kick I'm not aware of the world around me. You forget everything for a moment. You are absent, just inside something, but concentrated. You have to be totally concentrated so that you are there all the time. Then when it flows, then you nip into yourself a bit discreetly . . . When you are inside something totally like that, then you only want to give even more in some way. When you pull out everything and try to pull out a little bit more . . . That's when I stop breathing!

(18.6E) Woman, middle-aged

[About herding calls, 'kulning'] When I listen to herding calls I simply shiver with sensual pleasure. It's a signal that reaches beyond everything tangible and acquired. A call that contacts the prehistoric human within me. I listen and want to answer! The call tempts you to communicate.

I have to be in a really special frame of mind to want to sing these calls. When that state comes about, then sky-high tones come out of my throat without effort, seemingly by themselves. I don't think at all about the technique or notes and can experience that I can hear my voice coming from somewhere else. The perception of time partly disappears and I rarely know how long I have been singing. I can't claim that I shut my eyes but anyhow I don't see anything around me, instead I feel the presence of people and it is in part that energy which is used for the herding calls.

After singing the calls I feel good mentally, and experience satisfaction. It feels like some type of cleansing, perhaps healing.

Some accounts follow of special occasions when one has achieved something above the ordinary and when it felt as if one was being played/controlled by somebody else, something else, something greater. One describes it in such terms as ecstatic, magical, occult, extraterrestrial, like a religious experience. The examples come from several different genres.

(18.6F) Man, middle-aged, 1970s

Two Greek friends and me, we were playing (I played bouzouki) one evening at a Latin-American fiesta. Some Greeks came who danced Greek folk dances. I had never before played for dance in this way. The tunes I had learnt had remained 'pieces of music' for me. Suddenly, while the dancing was going on, I noticed that the tempo increased spontaneously in time with the dancers to such a degree that I found myself playing much faster than had been my ambition, and also much faster than I had thought myself capable of. It was quite simply as if it wasn't me who was playing but the dancers who were playing me.

(18.6G) Woman, old, 1970s

After a Lieder course I was invited by a couple of the participants to relive what we had studied during the summer course. They were Lieder of various types, Schumann, Schubert, Brahms, Wolf, and so on. The singer was good but not a star, and most of the time it was me sitting at the grand piano. After playing for several hours, it was time for the last song of the evening. It was Schubert's 'Ave Maria'.

Then that indescribable thing happened. The song acquired a volume and a fullness that I hadn't heard before with the singer. My piano playing became so perfect that I couldn't have wished for better. When the song came to an end, all three of us sank into something resembling devotions. None of us wanted to break the wonderful mood for quite a while. Finally, the girlfriend—who had been listening—whispered: 'That was the most beautiful thing I've ever heard.' All three of us were moved to tears and in the grip of deep feelings. An extraterrestrial feeling of community.

(18.6H) Man, young, 1980s

There are an awful lot of fantastic small experiences but they last only perhaps one or two seconds and then can return several minutes later. The more you play, the more often these moments come along. These moments arise in a situation where all those who are playing have a total communication. Suddenly everything falls into place as if *one* person was playing—not several—for a few seconds.

There was a situation with a trio that I was out with a while ago. It was about timing. The timing of all of us coincided at one point, we were 100% playing together, which is really an impossibility. It's a sort of occult experience. It was a situation where we played a whole series of the same musical figures one after the other for perhaps ten seconds. Later when you heard the tape recording you could hear that all of us came in exactly with each other, not a beat wrong, completely synchronized.

(18.6I) Woman, young, 1980s

It was an assembly for accordion music. From Thursday to Sunday it was music, music, and music. The night between Friday and Saturday, we had been drinking coffee together with two young Norwegian accordionists. After the coffee, we moved to the tent vestibule, got out our accordions and started to play. Some other accordionists came along and wanted to join in. We didn't know each other but the fellowship we felt was so great. We were like one big family.

It was a wonderfully mild summer's night with music everywhere! The hours went by so quickly, and we just kept playing and playing. Somebody started a tune and then we all joined in. It was so simple to find the right buttons, my fingers danced along on the accordion. It felt as if somebody else was controlling my hands. I remember that I got a bit tired, but I didn't want to, or couldn't, stop. I was forced to go on, it was like a craving. To be able to play until it was morning! It was almost that I started to doubt whether it was dream or reality. It felt as if I was in Heaven.

(18.6J) Man, young, 1980s (from an edited interview)

[The band is about to play country rock at a music festival.] We went up on stage at about 23.00. We had been waiting a long time and had almost lost heart . . . At first it felt a bit doubtful but after two or three numbers you could feel that now, damn it, it's really going bloody well! It wouldn't have mattered if a fuse had blown, we'd have gone on playing anyway. It is bloody close to an ecstatic or religious experience. You get so close to the edge that you don't know what you're busy with. You know what you are doing, of course, but have gone over the edge when you don't care whether you make a fool of yourself. You felt that everything worked; something inside my head tells me: Now everything's right!

It's a total feeling. Euphoric! I can't say that it is as if your hair curls or the tears run. It is more of a feeling in your mind, emotional. Total, like. I can imagine that it is like a religious experience . . . You're bloody happy, a happy person! It is then and just at that moment.

It's the attack! You don't play the guitar, you hit the guitar! However hard I hit, I won't break the strings, it'll just be fine. Everyone in the band must feel the same thing. You increase the feeling by hitting harder. You can almost not stand still between the tunes. If somebody broke off after 30 minutes you'd go crazy.

The greatest satisfaction comes exactly when you can leave the stage, are sweaty and know you've done a bloody good thing. Then you've got total satisfaction from what you've done. It's this blissful feeling you have afterwards, you are extremely intoxicated without having drunk anything.

As far as I know, I didn't think anything. I just thought about my having the guitar, what I would sing in the next line and so forth. I had only the lyrics in my head. You didn't have to think much. It just seemed natural. On this particular evening everything fitted in right. The pieces fitted together just like that. Fell into place. Everything worked, the sound, the technique, and me myself altogether. That is what did it. I wondered: Can it be like this once more?

(18.6K) Man, middle-aged, 1970s (from an edited interview)

I was out playing and cut lots of records with a female singer. Sometimes the 'moment' could come when you suddenly feel that you have this total togetherness, you don't have to think, there is some sort of collective thought behind it. She and I found it exceptionally easy to work together, because we didn't need to think, not at all. I just had to sit and listen to what my fingers did together with her! It was fantastic!

I remember one concert particularly well. We started on one tune. OK, we had fooled around a bit lots of times in such a way that in the middle of the tune she suddenly had a feeling for doing something completely different. She could think up lyrics herself, and stand there and talk rubbish. And at that concert we carried on like that with one tune for 20 minutes! We switched keys, everything was a total feeling of belonging together! Fantastic! I remember it so well, it's something I won't forget—then it was as if I wasn't thinking any-thing, it was just a feeling all the time and we were in the same feeling. Whatever I did, she just followed along, or vice versa. It's rather fantastic that it's like that with music!

It's the same when you play together, you are fairly free, not just accompanying. It works perfectly together, you create something in that very second, without having planned it.

Quite suddenly it just works. And really, those particular minutes are the entire reason you go out and play. That's what makes you happy. Total happiness.

Quite suddenly you can play something you've never played before. It can quite suddenly work, with the guitarist, for example. A sort of duel—everything works perfectly. It doesn't need to be anything special technique-wise. Suddenly you can feel that there is a single big driving force behind everything and it's something you can't explain. Quite suddenly you are just washed along by something. It's actually rather delightful. It's like being intoxicated.

Finally, a couple of accounts with very special experiences. In both cases, the experience has strong elements of transcendental character: one feels possessed by another person's spirit or influenced by some invisible external force that governs the playing. The music suddenly seems completely self-evident.

(18.6L) Woman, young, 1980s

I played the piano for a teacher who was totally into Bach. She had given me the task of playing Prelude No. 2 in C minor from *Das Wohltemperierte Klavier I*. I had practised that piece for many years, and since she was very thorough I knew the prelude inside out. After the summer I was going to play a test piece and I chose the prelude plus the fugue afterwards. So I had reason to practise all summer on these pieces. The test went well, and after that I didn't practise the piece for a month.

But one day when I was at school, alone in the big music room, I sat down at the grand piano. I played the prelude and the fugue, and then I was suddenly filled with an incredibly strong feeling that I could feel in both my body and my head. It was as if I was charged with some sort of high voltage, like a strong intoxication. The feeling made me ecstatic, inexplicably elated, everything concentrated to a single now. The music sort of flowed by itself. At that moment it felt to me as if I was filled with Bach's spirit: the music suddenly became so self-evident. There was no doubt any longer as to how it should be played, as if I'd come to the deepest insight and found the genuine, true, and correct expression. The intoxication lasted for the whole piece and afterwards I staggered out.

Two days later, in my diary I wrote: 'On Friday when I was alone in the music room, I sat down and played Prelude and fugue in C minor by Bach, which I'd hardly played since the entrance test, and then all of me was suddenly filled with something that was like an intoxication. Technically perhaps it wasn't so extremely good, but the actual playing of it, the emotional element, that was all through my body and everything suddenly became self-evident. It felt as if just all of me had been filled with the spirit of Bach. What a fantastically happy experience! I could feel right out to the ends of my hair that it sounded fantastic, that everything was fantastic. It isn't possible to describe.'

It still makes me happy when I play the fugue. The music flows along, there is a rocking rhythm that can be felt in your entire body. But I have never, either before or after, felt it so strongly as on the occasion I have described.

(18.6M) Man, middle-aged, 1970s (from an edited interview)

I used to take my violin with me when I went out to the country. It is so good because there you can sit and play all night long. Sat alone in the kitchen one evening. I tried to tune the violin in a way I'd never done before: A–E–A–E. Then I lowered the A to a Baroque A as a G-sharp. I got a strange sort of tuning and tried it a little.

Then, quite simply, there came a tune that was extremely clear straight away. I almost got the feeling that there was a higher power who had given me that tune. It was a strange tune, partly a refrain which came all the time just the same, partly a theme with endless variations. The melody was extremely suggestive because it was so extremely simple. There was nothing complicated in it, rather it went right in.

It was extremely strong. After a while it turned rather nasty. It wasn't just a positive experience, but was extremely tiresome. There was no end. I got extremely intoxicated. I suddenly realized what it was they meant with all those tall stories, the story of the Näcken [a mythical figure in Swedish folklore, considered evil but also musical, playing the violin], that you really can be sucked up by the music so strongly. It just went on and on. I sort of couldn't stop playing, I was intoxicated by the sound that came from the violin. It sounded a different way, responded in a different way.

Then it felt as if somebody was standing behind me and that was a bit worrisome. It was horrid. Didn't dare stop playing because it would be so silent. Have no idea how long I played because I had no sense of time. Then I threw the violin aside.

Became extremely agitated. Turned on an old radio, picked up Radio Luxembourg which I put on because I didn't want to keep that feeling. Tried to get rid of it. But the feeling was that somebody was standing there watching me. It felt as if the music wasn't mine. Here it was just a ready-made package that I played.

It took quite a long time before I had calmed down. I was forced to destroy that experience with music. It was a must, otherwise I wouldn't have been able to stay there.

18.7 COMMENTARY

Strong experiences while playing music oneself are in many ways similar to strong experiences that listeners have, for example that one is totally absorbed by the music, time and space disappear, one merges with the music, is emotionally greatly involved, and might have experiences of transcendence. What is specific to the experience of performers is the actual playing and the contact with fellow players and the audience, to a certain degree also the contact with oneself.

As regards the actual performance, what is particularly emphasized are the 'magical' occasions when everything works perfectly, when one surpasses oneself, when it feels as if one is being played by somebody else, one is in a euphoric, trance-like state. This can happen both when one is playing or singing alone or when one is making music with others. In the latter instance, a special contact arises with the fellow players. In some remarkable way, everybody agrees with each other about timing, form, and expression, everybody 'knows' what is going to happen next, one doesn't have to think, one just has to go on, it can't go wrong. The necessary condition is, as a rule, that the musicians need to know each other well, musically as well as personally, that each is totally open for what the others do and lets oneself be pulled along in a collective process.

Such magical moments do not, as a rule, come especially often but on the other hand are so fantastic that they compensate for all the effort in getting there. One becomes even more motivated to carry on with music, one yearns to experience these moments again, it is the epitome of joy.[4]

Communication with the audience is an important factor. On the one hand, the visual impressions of the musicians playing and commitment mean a lot for the listeners' experience; on the other, the musicians are affected by what they see and notice of the listeners' reactions. Positive reactions by the listeners inspire the musicians to (even) greater commitment, which in turn spurs the listeners to (even) greater response, and so on. One narrator expressed it as being like 'playing ping-pong with the audience, you get the ball back all the time; if they really get going, we get going even more'.

The relationship with the audience includes the feeling that one exposes oneself to their verdict. But it can happen in different ways. One can do it with an active attitude in a strong conviction as to how the music should be interpreted: this is what the music should sound like, you can think what you want, it's a case of sink or swim. One challenges the audience, so to speak. If, however, one is very nervous and uncertain, it easily gives rise to an expectation that the audience is going to react negatively. But if one conquers one's nervousness—thanks to the performance working and the audience being positive—one's self-confidence gets a boost and one is strengthened in one's identity as a musician. Perhaps also in one's identity as an independent individual. Playing music can lead to one becoming aware of one's own feelings and thoughts, and acquiring a means to express them—perhaps to show other sides of oneself—in a way that one hasn't been able to do before. It can thus become a double confirmation, both from outside (from the listeners) and from within oneself.

CHAPTER 19

SINGING IN A CHOIR

SINGING in a choir is something that hundreds of thousands of people in Sweden are involved in. Choirs of all types are to be found throughout the country, even in small communities, ranging from amateur choirs to fully or semi-professional choirs. (In Uppsala alone, the city where this book is being written, there are hundreds of choirs.) Swedish choir singing is thus wide-ranging and can also display choirs that belong to the world elite in their field. Every year, Swedish choirs win prizes in international choir competitions.

So it is no surprise that there are many accounts of experiences in connection with singing in a choir. Here is a selection divided into four sections: choir singing during childhood and adolescence (19.1), singing in large choirs (19.2), choir singing in church/religious contexts (19.3), and choir singing in other, unusual surroundings (19.4).

19.1 CHOIR SINGING DURING CHILDHOOD AND ADOLESCENCE

There have already been accounts of children who have sung in choirs (Chapter 4, section 4.6), for example, proud and happy nine-year-olds who filled an entire sports hall with their singing (Chapter 4, account 4.6E) and ten-year-olds who sang together in a music class for the first time and directly felt a 'world fellowship' (Chapter 4, account 4.6F). In the following accounts, there are descriptions of other typical experiences during choir singing, such as hearing one's own voice merging together with the other voices, feeling the enormous power in the choir, and a mixture of excitement and joy when the choir is going to perform.

(19.1A) Woman, middle-aged, 1950s

I was in the fourth year of elementary school, I think, so I was about ten years old. We had a school choir, and were rehearsing the end of spring-term assembly. It was the first time I sang in voices. We sang a song for three voices. I think it was 'Plocka vill jag skogsviol' ['I want to pick wild violets']. I remember to this day the bliss I felt when I stood there and sang my part and heard the other voices around me. I could never have imagined such joy. It was as if you left your own body and merged totally with the music.

(19.1B) Woman, middle-aged, 1970s

As a child I sang in a choir, and—together with other choirs—we were going to sing Hilding Rosenberg and Hjalmar Gullberg's 'Den heliga natten' ['Holy night']. It required a lot of practice, bit by bit, and for a 12-year-old these were long, concentrated, tiring sessions. It did indeed seem to be going well, but I took it as one performance among others.

But then we stood there, with a temperamental conductor who angrily stamped his foot at us when we sang wrongly, and the church was full to the brim. And then the wonderful music started, with the beautiful alto solo, the song of the Three Wise Men, and Herod's furious bass outburst. And not least the music to the recitatives was wonderful; it increased in light, hopeful tone at 'And then an angel of the Lord stood before them', as well as in 'This is the song about the star'. When we sang the last song about the star, I wasn't standing on the floor any longer. I was flying, or floating, a foot above the floor, surrounded by these wonderful notes that I was helping to produce and then it was over, and all of me said to myself, 'Oh no! It mustn't be over yet!' But it was.

(19.1C) Woman, young, 1980s

I had my very greatest experience with music when I was about ten years old and was singing in a children's choir. We were asked if we wanted to be part of a performance of Carmina Burana (Carl Orff) that other choirs were going to do in a big concert. The children's choir only had a few small sections to sing along in, and on the big stage they had put a raised platform where the choir would sit. In front of the choir was the orchestra and right at the front stood the soloists. The concert was being held on a large stage and you felt so incredibly little, above all when the entire choir of about 300—400 people was gathered, the orchestra and then the enormous audience that you couldn't see anything of but knew it was there even though it was far away.

It happened very suddenly somewhere in the middle of the work, at a place where the children's choir wasn't singing anything, that the whole of the other choir stood up and sang for all they were worth. There was such a force that I felt as if my soul was going to rise high up into the air, I couldn't sit still. I felt totally empty and hot and at the same time so elated. When I write about this, the feeling actually comes back and I long to experience the same thing again. It felt as if I was alone in a sea of an incredible power that wanted to blow up the entire atmosphere. The incredible force of the music depended partly on the volume of a 300-strong choir singing fff [forte fortissimo], partly on the very harmonies of the music.

I started to smile, to smile with all my face, and I couldn't do anything about it. I started to feel a bit ashamed to be just sitting there with a big smile in front of perhaps 1,000 or more people in the audience, but I couldn't stop. The more I tried to stop, the more I smiled. I wanted to get up and dance and sing. I have never experienced such an unbelievable feeling of joy!

Afterwards, I was totally elated and the power and joy lived on inside me, at least for a while. In the long term, this experience has meant that music can be something quite incredible. Above all, that it can make you feel happy and elated.

For me, it was the very first time I'd heard *Carmina Burana* and since then I have only heard it on a record, which isn't the same thing at all. I think that you get the very most out of it by sitting in the choir.

In the accounts above, there is also mention of the feeling of merging with the music (see Chapter 7) and of floating or leaving one's body (see Chapter 8). Another very special experience was had by a young woman when she sang in a very well-known work.

(19.1D) Woman, old, 1940s

I had just had my seventeenth birthday, and had got a place in the solo singing class at the college of music. The students' choir was rehearsing Brahms's *Requiem* for the first time, and when we came to 'Wie lieblich sind deine Wohnungen', bar 66, where the altos and basses sing in unison, I experienced an extremely strong feeling. I thought I was filled with a strong light, as if I became luminous! I don't remember what I felt like before, but I do know that I was afraid my classmates would notice that something special had happened to me. I did everything so that nobody would notice what had happened. (It has to do with the harmonies and the melody in the alto and bass voices in bar 66 and also 68.)

The experience of strong light is something we have come across earlier, for example the woman who experienced that she sat in an enormous globe of light, filled with music (Chapter 7, account 7.3A). There are other examples of similar experiences of light; they are commented upon together in Chapter 29, section 29.3.6.

An experience of light is a component of the next account too, but this time it is about natural sunlight. The light, nature, the colours, and the acoustics in the church, the light girls' voices and the summer hymn—all of these contributed to an experience of beauty, happiness, and joy in being alive.

(19.1E) Woman, young, 1980s

It was spring, the Ascension Day holiday weekend. The youth choir was on a tour on Gotland [island in the Baltic]. The countryside was a mild light green, the flowers had just started to bloom, and the nightingale sang all night long.

One day we were in Visby. Five or six girls, including me, went into the cathedral. The rays of the sun came in through the beautiful glass windows and the church was big, light, and spacious. We went into the chancel and started to sing '*En vänlig grönskas rika dräkt*' [a well-known Swedish summer hymn] in voices. Light girls' voices floated out under the arches and the sun shone a bit extra.

And suddenly I felt how I, who was already calm and happy with the nice journey, was filled with an intense feeling of happiness. I felt warm, calm, rich, and fortunate, wanted to embrace the entire world. Everything was suddenly so extremely beautiful. The music, the calm in the church, the sun, and the dust that could be seen in the rays of sunshine—all joined together in a great joy and a certainty that everything was all right.

The summer hymn has always been of great importance to me, but on that occasion everything that is nice and beautiful melted together into a warm ball of joy in my chest and stomach. When I recall the event, I can remind myself of the lovely feeling I had then, and the joy that I felt in being alive.

19.2 SINGING IN LARGE CHOIRS

There is something special about standing in the middle of a giant choir, being right in the middle of the sea of sound, feeling the force of the choir, and being a part of a process that far exceeds what one can achieve as a single person. Everybody is part of the same fellowship; there are no social barriers here, everybody uplifts one another, the mood is euphoric, and one can hardly stop singing.

(19.2A) Woman, young, 1970s

It was in the concert hall, where they had arranged an open house that was called 'Choir Day'. You could walk around in the various rooms where different sorts of music were being sung by different choirs. The events of the day culminated in a large concert in the big hall where all the singers and all the audience took part. Everybody just joined in without caring about how they sounded or what they looked like; they sang as much as they could manage, and never wanted to stop. The piece—Elgar's 'Pomp and Circumstance' with lyrics in Swedish—was repeated lots of times. Everybody sang so powerfully that in the end it was impossible to hear your own voice. The sound was deafening and at the same time delightful; you were right in the midst of all of it. There were all sorts of people there, and I think that a lot of them, just like me, were a bit surprised at how crazily enjoyable it was. There was a feeling of euphoria and fellowship. Sharing such a delightful experience with people you otherwise wouldn't have had any reason to have contact with.

Directly afterwards, I felt elated and had some sort of need to have contact with people around the hall. Everybody nearby thought: 'Fantastic, wasn't it!' And everyone you could imagine, or even those you couldn't imagine doing so, spoke with each other.

(19.2B) Woman, middle-aged, 1980s

It was a midnight concert in the church. Lots of people from the choir assembly made their way to the church in winding queues. And the singers in the various choirs started singing while we waited to come in. When we got in, the church was soon filled with people already warmed up for singing, who were in high spirits and in the right mood. Once inside the church, I felt blissful, devout, as well as thrilled and expectant.

Then things quietened down and we waited to see what would happen. But then a voice was heard from behind, one from the side, one from the other side, some from in front, singing a song of freedom. Oh, I just felt this shiver of a thrill going right through me, and suddenly it almost felt cold in the church and then it got really hot. Indeed, when the singers came in I really got the shivers and then I started sweating profusely. And then everybody started singing. I sang and completely lost track of time and space. I can't remember how long the concert lasted, I just remember the feeling—it was strong.

When we finally left the church, we hardly knew where we were, where we ought to go. We just walked around and sang and kept on singing until I fell asleep. It was a fantastic experience. It was so total.

(19.2C) Woman, old, 1980s

[In Washington, USA] Every year they arrange a community singing concert, the Messiah Sing Along, in the biggest opera auditorium at the Kennedy Centre. The opera's professional choirs took part with their own conductors and soloists. The audience consisted of lots of amateur choirs and other people who were interested in singing, such as my husband and me. All of us were given booklets with scores.

Then they sang and played Handel's *Messiah,* sometimes with the professional choirs and soloists, sometimes with everybody joining in. Sometimes the opera choirs got to sing first so that we in the auditorium would hear what it ought to sound like. Many of those in the choir audience had very beautiful voices. I could distinguish basses as well as tenors close to me with voices that made me shiver with pleasure. Even though I wasn't a member of a choir or hadn't practised in advance, I tried to follow the score and sing in the forte bits where my singing was drowned among the many beautiful voices. I sang, I listened, in turn, all the time intensely present. It gave me an incredibly strong feeling of fellowship with all the other participants, a share of a great musical achievement. An unforgettable experience.

(19.2D) Man, middle-aged

I was in the Scandinavian Festival Choir with about 1,000 singers from Norway, Sweden, and Denmark. The audience was about 15,000 people, and the event was broadcast on television across all of Europe.

We arrived at Oslo in the morning. At 12.00, the rehearsals started. The acoustics in the arena were sensational. The sound echoed a long time along the walls of the arena. When we began to practise '*Ja, vi elsker detta lannet*' [the Norwegian national anthem] there were a few sunbathers up on the stands. They immediately stood up and remained standing and staring during the entire practice. When the echoes had died out after the final chord, you could hear somebody applauding from up on the stands, to the general amusement of the choir. Many members must have felt shivers down their backs after that practice!

The actual concert was just as much of an experience as the practice. Just seeing the stream of people coming in to listen was fantastic. In brilliant sunshine and 25° Celsius in the shade, we sat there and tried to protect our foreheads and our scalps. Then it was time to start!

Ja, vi elsker . . . the Norwegians on the stand, 15,000 of them, stood up—*every one of them*! We sang as we had never sung before, forte and fortissimo. The cheering that broke out afterwards was indescribable. The storm of applause went on a long, long time. It felt as if time stopped for a while. There was an extremely strong feeling of fellowship in the choir.

After the end of the concert there came a feeling of emptiness, of loss, a sort of longing to have that moment back. It took several hours to get over it.

Another couple of accounts about how special it can be to sing out loud in large choirs are included at the end of the next section, accounts 19.3F and 19.3G.

19.3 CHOIR SINGING IN CHURCH/RELIGIOUS CONTEXTS

Choir singing has a strong position within the church, both within the Swedish Church and various Free Churches. A lot of people consider that this is a major factor behind what is sometimes called 'the Swedish choir miracle'. Here, some choir singers describe their experiences in connection with performances of Christian choir music from various epochs (see, too, earlier accounts in Chapter 14: accounts 14.1C, 14.1E, 14.2C, 14.2D).

For a lot people, singing in one of Bach's Passions has been a radical experience in many ways.

(19.3A) Woman, middle-aged, 1960s

I was working with the *St John Passion* for the first time. I considered it to be an honour that the youth choir was going to join in and sing together with the 'the big ones'. I sing soprano and it can be pretty tough—singing in a high pitch isn't always so easy.

The first concert was in one of the town's churches, and, as is normal, started with a certain tension. Everybody is all tensed up about how it will go, how it will sound. It never feels as if you have had enough time with the orchestra, and . . . well, it feels a bit nervous. Anyhow, the concert went well and it felt as if everybody had done their bit. For the first time, I experienced the soloists' performance from my position in the choir, and that was delightful.

Yes, it all developed into a sort of crescendo and after the final chord of the final chorale had faded away, and the conductor had beaten off, it felt really unbelievably strong. A sort of experience of wholeness, exhaustion, satisfaction, and joy. I remember the seconds after the final cut-off like being in a sort of light, while at the same time I was gasping for breath so that I could begin breathing normally again after a couple of hours concentrating. I had done it! Kept up during the whole work, sung correctly, and been a part of a big unit.

Afterwards, in the general tumult that arises, I just remember a feeling of euphoric happiness and general 'bounciness' in my body. We were a few young people who were there and I remember that we ran through a snowstorm on the way home after the concert. I think that this concert was the kick that later made me a choir singer 'for real'.

In this description, the concern was mainly about having been faced with a challenge—to sing the whole of the *St John Passion* for the first time, and to feel the satisfaction and joy of having carried it off. The same applies to the highest degree also in the following lively account of a choir leader and a particular part of the *St John Passion* which placed 'unreasonable' demands on the choir singers.

(19.3B) Woman, middle-aged, 1980s

I was a member of a church choir. We sang mainly at services and musical services. But suddenly, our choir leader had become obsessed by the idea of our performing the *St John Passion* by J. S. Bach. We were a happy little choir with about 15 'permanent' ladies of different ages and about five 'permanent' men. We used to laugh and have fun at our practices, but with Bach everything became so serious in our choir. Suddenly, it was just hard work and effort, with endless and impossible runs and entrances. The mood got worse, and we were told that the choir would be strengthened with borrowed voices from other choirs for the concert. That didn't feel particularly good either.

We thought it was especially hopeless to get it right with chorale no. 36, 'Kreuzige'! I thought that the voices sounded like racing fire engines that never managed to get their sirens to stop at the same time. 'When is he going to realize that this is too difficult for us?' I and several others in the choir talked about quitting in pure protest, but that too felt as if we were letting the others down.

Anyhow, that was the situation this Wednesday evening. Downheartedly, we opened our scores to yet again suffer this horrible 'Kreuzige'. After the 'sprachen' of the recitative, we got going: we sopranos at a violent G, the tenors and basses and then the altos. We sang and sang, everybody concentrated on their own part. Fingers nimbly followed the notes in the score. Nobody had time to look up to see whether our choir leader was conducting or not.

Goodness, we were approaching the end and were still keeping up! And now the last bars: 'Kreuzige, kreuzige, kreuzige!' Endless silence. We all looked up, at the choir leader, at each other, red in the face from concentration and effort. Good God! We did it! We did end at the same time, the last chords still hung in the air. We did it! Without bringing in expert singers! We laughed when the tension lost its hold, tears falling on some cheeks, and the feeling of joy, pride, and fellowship was incredible.

The feeling afterwards when I came home was three great types of gratitude. Thanks to God—I am not really especially religious but just then I felt that without God this music could not have been created. Thanks that somebody had been able to write something as fantastic as this. Thanks that I had been given a voice to sing with and given a chance to be a part of what happened this evening. To think that I stuck it out!! And that the choir leader believed in us!

The concert with the *St John Passion* was a fantastic experience. The church was full and the applause was long.

In the next account, it is also a matter of a very accomplished performance. Yet, it is other aspects—existential and religious—that are the most central, aspects that are linked to the meaning of the *St Matthew Passion* and which also had a close personal experience as a background. The drama in the *St Matthew Passion* mirrored a self-experienced drama.

(19.3C) Woman, middle-aged, 1980s

I was studying in London and sang in the Bach Choir with David Willcocks as the musical director. Just before Easter, we sang the *St Matthew Passion* at the Royal Festival Hall together with the Philharmonia Orchestra and outstanding soloists. I stood in the choir, which consisted of about 200 singers.

During the concert there was a period of dead silence in the concert hall, while the music went on. It lasted probably a few minutes. It is indescribable, but for me it was as if another dimension extended the space of life and we were standing outside time. At the next rehearsal, David Willcocks said that it was the best performance of the *St Matthew Passion* he had conducted. Everything had gone right, everyone had done their best. He also mentioned that it had been so quiet in the audience.

Some weeks before the concert, one of my best friends had died of cancer after some months of suffering. For me, the whole drama in the *St Matthew Passion* was like his suffering and death, or Christ's suffering and death in him. For the entire concert, I was in this mood and aware of the eternal dimension of life in some way, and I remember that for a while it was really difficult to sing because I wanted to cry.

Anyway, the highlight was the moment when everything was completely calm. Exactly where in the *Passion* it was, I can't remember, but I think it was during a solo aria and continued into a choir section. The strongest moment was there only for a few minutes, but I could feel it in me for at least the rest of the day. Like being touched by something holy.

The experience has been one of my finest memories in life. It strengthens my belief that music is something very valuable and that it speaks to us deep inside our conscious frames.

In the next account, the music is a work from the twentieth century, Hilding Rosenberg's Symphony No. 4, 'The Revelation of St John'.

(19.3D) Woman, middle-aged, 1980s

I sang in the choir in 'The Revelation of St John' by Hilding Rosenberg. It is a great and difficult work. The sound of the orchestra is strong and majestic. The choir has difficult entrances. The sopranos have demanding parts at very high registers. The work has some wonderful texts from the Book of Revelations and by Hjalmar Gullberg, texts that require clear diction. It was the year before Hilding Rosenberg died and we knew that he would be sitting in the church. This contributed to increasing our nervousness as well as our concentration.

To stand there in the full church, as a little member in something so big, to hear the last notes echo away . . . well, it is as if you really feel a part of something that I would like to call divine. You feel so little, but you also feel so big. As if this particular feeling, that you are possessed by just then, becomes so total. I have experienced something similar only while meditating. The strong concentration that you are in during both these states, I feel it as a strong white, almost dazzling light. At the same time, I felt almost unbelievably elated by such a strong feeling of joy. When the tension relaxed, when I started to be able to perceive my surroundings again, the tears just poured down my cheeks.

In the following accounts, it is about quite different forms of contemporary religious singing. It is mainly music with more 'go' and the mood is as might be expected.

(19.3E) Man, young, 1980s

I was out touring with a singing group. There was going to be a choral service in a fairly small church and it didn't feel like a fantastic place for a good concert. Anyhow, it was getting close to the time when the concert was going to start and people were just pouring in! More and more of them. The caretaker fetched chairs, cushions, benches, anything you could sit on, and still it wasn't enough, so the doors out to the big churchyard had to remain open to allow more people to see and hear.

Gosh, it was a real turn-on! Then we did one of our programmes that contained a lot of our own music—Christian ballads, Christian rock (acoustic). There can't have been many who had heard the music before.

But what a response! Already after two tunes there was cheering between the tunes and there was an incredible enthusiasm from the audience that I've never felt before.

Our evenings usually lasted one and a half hours, but this particular evening lasted five hours in which we finally ploughed through all of our sing-along booklet that we had put together ourselves, and did so in an incredible 'jam-session' spirit. All the instruments came out: flutes, trumpet, tuba, trombone, and it would have been hard to beat the enthusiasm that built up. People sang and sang, we sang till our throats almost bled, and played till we lost the feeling in our fingers. This was unbelievable!

Afterwards, we were totally whacked and could hardly manage to get back to our accommodation. We then kept going for a long time on this experience, and got a lot of energy from it. In the long term, it must be one of the strongest experiences that really made me love music.

It seems almost to have been a case of community singing. The joy of singing out loud is also reflected in both the following examples, where the narrators are in choirs with hundreds of members. Everyone is totally focused on the music, the sound level is enormous, and the experience so overwhelming and powerful that tears fall; afterwards, one is totally exhausted, speechless, and needs to be on one's own in order to digest the experience.

(19.3F) Woman, young, 1980s

I had my first strong experience with music when I was at a Christian choir conference. We had been practising for two days, everyone was tired and lacking in concentration, our throats were about to break down. Most of the songs were rather mediocre, typical choir music for Christian youth choirs. Everyone was longing for the moment when we would finish for the day.

Suddenly, the entire accompanying band came in and the choir leader asked us to sing through just one more tune, 'Worship the Lord', modern gospel, one of the tunes with a bit of go in it. The music started up, the conductor waved us in, and when the 300-strong choir started to sing after the signal there was such a force in it that everyone looked pleasantly surprised. I sang as best as my throat could manage, and with all my heart. The music and the song meant that I was transported with joy. I felt elated, happy, and totally at one with the music. Intense joy, without any real awareness of time.

When the last note had faded away, it was completely silent for a while and I dropped down to the ground again. I gasped for breath and sighed happily. I felt very overwhelmed and happy, but at the same time extremely confused, pulled down to the Earth and almost depressed by having to return to reality. I was mentally and physically exhausted. I was totally whacked and not capable of doing anything sensible, and absolutely incapable of saying anything sensible. In other words, I was silent.

Everybody wanted us to sing again, the same song. I was transported with joy again. After this time I was so exhausted and happy that some tears flowed. Absolutely exhausted and silent, I left the practice after this and was completely satisfied with just being by myself for a little while.

It is fantastic to sing in a giant choir—there is such a force in it. The experience was no doubt strengthened by our being so tired and fed up with practising, so that it became wonderful when we got to sing 'for real'.

The experience has given me more joy in music. It has inspired me when I've been feeling low. The experience also meant that I developed a slightly different relationship with God—it wasn't just boring, plodding, and full of toil to be Christian, there was life in it all too.

(19.3G) Woman, young, 2000–10

It was a gospel festival and we were going to be there in the enormous choir that had gathered together singers from the entire county. I didn't have any great expectations, in fact I didn't think it would be any good at all, but already on the Friday when we arrived to start the practice, I felt that it was going to be something really special. What an atmosphere there was! We carried on all of Saturday with the rehearsals and now that the orchestra was there too it just got better. It was wonderful to sing together, so many of us, and I was really looking forward to the big concert.

When it was finally time for the concert on the Sunday evening, everything was just complete chaos until we all knew how we should walk and stand. I was totally exhausted by the time the concert was about to begin and everybody was in place. The entire first act went fantastically well and both the soloist and the choir were pleased. But the real test was to come. We were going to sing 'Kumbayah' a cappella and I was so nervous. How would 200 singers be able to keep in tune without losing the pitch?

When the second act was about to begin, it was dead quiet in the concert hall. The pianist gave us a key. Silence again, so long that I almost wondered if the conductor had completely lost it. Then she raises her hands and beats us into a forte fortissimo: 'Kumbayah, my Lord! Kumbayah!' The sound was enormous from all these voices and perfectly arranged parts. I'd thought it had sounded good when we had practised before, but now it was fabulous! My legs could hardly support me! I'm not the slightest bit religious but I'd call this an enormous spiritual experience. It literally felt as if I'd been saved for a short moment. I think that every single hair on my body stood on end. After this, there was nothing to stop me. I stood there afterwards, all of the second act, and the tears just poured down my cheeks.

It's an enormous experience to sing in a choir and to experience the music together with other people. After the concert, I didn't say a word for quite a while. I think that an experience as strong as this must have time to sink in.

19.4 CHOIR SINGING IN OTHER, UNUSUAL SURROUNDINGS

Tours are often the highlights of a choir's activities. Everyone is keen to show what the choir can do, and being so close together and working intensely on many concerts in a short time welds the choir together even more. Every day one meets a new audience and new settings—new impressions to digest while one must remain entirely focused on one's task, the singing.

The first two accounts describe experiences in countries behind the Iron Curtain (now no longer there).

(19.4A) Man, young, 1980s

My strongest experience with music took place one spring afternoon in a square in Poland. After having performed a concert on the theme of peace and freedom, the choir that I was singing in walked out from the concert area while singing. Experience in Sweden told us that this was a good way to end as people could go off on their way home with the singing still ringing in their ears.

But now people didn't walk away as we had expected, but stayed behind in the entrance to the concert area and kept on listening. After a while, we went out into the street and the square outside the building. There, even more people came. People poured in from all sides and, when we finally sang, all of us together, the hymn 'Dona nobis pacem' with the Polish words—which mean 'Give us peace and freedom'—I think I got my strongest (greatest, happiest, most overwhelming) experience ever.

Commitment against oppression, war, lack of freedom, etc. here at home can often be like something that is just an afterthought. In Poland, I found people who really longed for the freedom that I myself am so spoilt with. When the people in the over-full square sang, they did so with a feeling that my choir often lacks. I think that music, like other art forms, when it is created is really an expression of man's thoughts and innermost feelings. When we learn a song or piece of music, it falls flat if we don't also put some personal feeling of interpretation into the performance. In Poland, in the fellowship in that totally foreign square, that feeling was there and it was expressed with a depth that I didn't believe existed but which on that occasion I could not only see and listen to passively, but also actively become a part of.

(19.4B) Woman, middle-aged

One of my strongest experiences with music was on a journey to East Germany. In Dresden, we met a youth orchestra that was going to play Roman's Swedish Mass together with us. They were extremely good and ambitious and we got to know them a little better each day. We did a concert in Dresden and were then going to travel to some other towns before returning and doing two final concerts together.

When we met again, we were made really welcome and they did everything they could to make us comfortable and give us a good time. In those days, everything was rationed and the food was dreadfully poor. They always let us help ourselves first, even though they hadn't seen meat for several months. We didn't realize that until later.

Before the last concert, expectations increased enormously. Partly, everyone knew it was the last evening, partly we had got to know the young people so well that we knew that there was nothing they wanted more than to be able to travel away from the GDR, but it wasn't allowed. This last evening they played with all their heart and with an intensity that was fantastic. The soloists were delightful too, especially the soprano soloist, who was such a warm person and sang divinely. This last concert took place in a monastery, where the acoustics were fantastic. Everything sounded twice as good, whatever we did, and that, of course, gave the choir a lift. It was an evening when everything went just right, and we gave a concert that I don't think anyone will ever forget because everybody did their utmost and you could tell. Everything fitted perfectly and during the entire concert it felt as if I was floating in a higher sphere. It is hard to describe but if I was ever to say that I was high, it would have been then. Everybody—the orchestra, the soloists, our conductor and the choir—we were one, and we performed Roman with all the feeling we could muster.

The audience was so moved that they stayed in their seats. There was no applause. After the concert, we walked out slowly and walked along the aisles around where the audience was sitting while we sang 'Alta trinita beata'. The audience looked at us and there was such a charged feeling between us. The singing sounded so delightful that it gave me the creeps, and in the end we disappeared along a staircase at the far end of the monastery. As I walked along, I remember that I thought: Let this moment never end. It was a heavenly feeling and I don't think I'll ever get to feel anything so strong again.

The evening there in the GDR ended, of course, with a lovely party with lots of singing and many speeches about how we would meet again, which unfortunately never became a reality. But the music gave rise to really strong feelings, so if we'd been able to, the orchestra would have followed us home straight away. They came and waved us off the next day, even though we started at the crack of dawn, and many tears were shed.

In the next account, the choir is indeed on tour in Sweden, but what they are singing is about what happened during the Nazi period in Germany. We are confronted with one of the greatest traumas of the twentieth century.

(19.4C) Woman, young, 1990s

When I was 17, our choir rehearsed the piece *RUT#1946* together with three actors and two dancers. *RUT* was based on Agneta Pleijel's book with the same name, which in turn was based on the Book of Ruth in the Bible. Our director had used the manuscript in Pleijel's book but set in the period after the Second World War, and those who took part were to portray Jews who had survived the concentration camps. We members of the choir had minor parts and with our singing we were responsible for the atmosphere and mood. The music was demanding in many ways, it was 'Amen' and the suite of songs, *Szeroka Woda*, by the Polish composer Henryk Mikołaj Górecki, and we were to sing the songs in the original Polish.

It wasn't really until after Christmas that the rehearsals got going properly. It was then that I started to feel so strongly about what we were working with. All the late rehearsals, the weekends that we spent practising the songs and learning the words, meeting and rehearsing with the choir—for me there was nothing better. Some of the preparations meant trying to understand the situation of the Jews. We were visited by Emerich Roth, a man who was a survivor from the concentration camps, and we got to see a film with his story and later also discuss the events with him. Then we tried to recreate those feelings during the performances . . . many a time, I and many others were so moved that the performances ended in tears for those taking part.

On the tour we travelled on, the choir's unity was strengthened, and with that also the emotional expression in our music. I experienced very strongly that the music and the emotional content of the performance had now become one and couldn't be separated. The strange thing was that we never talked about what we experienced during our performances—it was almost as if it was too personal to discuss. Anyway, it was quite obvious that the music strengthened the feelings we tried to project during the performances.

During the intensive period when we performed *RUT*, I lived as if I was in another world. Despite my being only one in the group of all the escaping Jews that we were to portray, it felt as if just my contribution was decisive. The music we sang influenced me enormously. I felt that my voice developed to a great degree and my self-confidence grew as regards my voice. I wasn't acting in the performance, I *was* in the performance, lived in it.

I didn't want to be anywhere else than the church where we were performing, just be with the people who were taking part and never listen to anything other than Górecki and the songs we sang. There wasn't a world outside with school and studies, there was only the music and Ruth's fate that held me in an incredible grip.

All of us wanted to do our utmost in all respects and as far as our musical achievement was concerned, there was no question of anything other than the absolute best. Personally, I felt that it was my duty, in order to honour Jews and dissidents who were exterminated during the Second World War, to put my soul into the performances, and the only way I could do that was by forming the music in such a way that made these feelings reach out.

RUT went on for four months and is still going on in some ways. After the tour, when we read all the reviews we'd been given, it felt as if you'd won a huge fortune on the lottery. There was line after line of superlatives and suggestions that what we had performed ought to be set up everywhere and receive attention in the world. It was wonderful to read that everything we'd felt and wanted to convey really had reached out to the audience!

Last, an account about singing German choir music in just the sort of setting in which it had originally been created.

(19.4D) Man, young, 1980s

The experience is from a journey in Germany with a chamber choir. To sing German choir music in its home country and in cathedrals, churches, and concert premises that were already there when the music was written is an experience. It feels as if walls, ceilings, and paintings—perhaps even the dust—are delighted by the music. The music in question is, of course, also written for the acoustics of these premises and also for the traditions that have been there.

The choir consisted of music students, all of whom were good singers. The feeling of safety that this led to also characterized the time outside the concert premises. It was heightened by the fact that our conductor is the very personification of calm, security, and experience. What you don't notice until you know him well is the sense of fun and the rather tongue-in-cheek attitude that is always there under the surface. This you find infectious. A journey with such people can hardly be monotonous.

My experience is from a concert during this tour. It took place in a fairly ordinary German church setting. A really large audience had come. I think that we sang from some German mass from the seventeenth century. What distinguished this concert from the others we had given earlier in the week was the way we were stood. Partly, we stood 'mixed' (i.e. not grouped in voice parts but altos, tenors, basses, sopranos just any old how). As well as this, on this occasion each of us stood about three to four metres from the next person. In this way, we managed to fill literally the entire podium from corner to corner. From me to the person who stood farthest away, it was about 40 metres.

The piece started quietly—I think it was quieter than ever just this particular day. I had to lean my head to one side to see our conductor. He stood there alone, a bit down the centre aisle. He held his safe, almost blessing, hands at shoulder height. Despite the distance and the fact that he was hard to see, there were no problems in feeling his impulses. The air in the church carried forth what he wished through its caresses. The picture of sound that reached him was quiet but at the same time was an enormous stereo picture that flowed. Every voice in the more than 30-man-strong choir formed the tone in its own special way. Homogeneous and subordinate at the same time as being vigorous and lively. A multiplicity that could be likened to how all the flowers in a meadow or all the trees in a forest create a whole in which every part is unique. To really feel that you are an important part of this is great. The music switched between different nuances and went out in waves between the walls of the church. Slowly, the notes came into full bloom, only to come to rest again just as quickly. The voices took turns to grow, before moving towards quietness altogether.

It might not sound so remarkable. But on that occasion I experienced a stillness beyond compare. Time had stopped and everything else felt of no consequence. Worries, plans for the future, dreams were somewhere far away. What was important was to be there in the here and now and the stillness that at the same time felt eternal. Several seconds after the final chord had faded away and been caught by the cold stone wall, stillness was alive. No one in the audience could even think of turning around or scratching an itch. The serenity that I felt then I have now and then also been able to feel for a few moments in other contexts. It is something you carry with you once you've first touched it.

It is moments like these that are one of the reasons I have music as my profession. The feeling of eternity in connection with experiences with music is something I experience at least a couple of times a week.

19.5 COMMENTARY

In this chapter, we have met choir singing in many different forms, contexts, and settings. The feelings of the narrators stretch all the way from total peace to euphoria. One feels oneself to be enveloped by the music and people, everyone is focused on the same task, and thus they mutually strengthen one another. As regards voice, one gets support and resonance through the voices of the others, one's own voice seems better and stronger than otherwise. Together one can achieve things that go far beyond what every single individual is capable of. One becomes a part of something much greater, a part of the expression and the power that the choir can develop. What the choir manages to achieve thus spills over to the personal level as a form of confirmation and increased self-confidence—perhaps a bit of self-realization—at the same time that one feels a collective pride over the appreciation that the choir has received.

Add to this an attractive outer setting, fantastic acoustics, a concentrated audience, and an important message to perform in expressively sounding form—it can't get much better than that.

An important aspect is the social intercourse that participation in the choir automatically brings with it. It is not just about music but also about meeting and getting to know other people. One has the chance to naturally create a social network which can be of importance far outside the choir activities. A well-functioning choir seems to be something of an ideal for human intercourse.[1]

CHAPTER 20

MUSIC IN LOVE: HAPPY AND UNHAPPY

Love is often connected with music. Music can function as a catalyst in a loving relationship and in maintaining it afterwards—music sets off, interprets, confirms, strengthens, and maintains the feelings. It can arouse associations and memories, inner images and fantasies, and be a refuge in critical situations.

Several accounts in our material bear witness to such questions. They are often about music and the circumstances around the first meeting (actual or imaginary) with the loved one. The experience is stored in one's long-term memory and can now and then turn up spontaneously as an unforgettable moment. Or one might deliberately bring this memory out in order to experience again the strong feelings that then applied—perhaps as a way of influencing one's own mood in a positive direction.

But music can also be the opposite. It can be associated with jealousy, bittersweet love, forbidden love, unhappy love, a lack of love, or with sorrow and pain after a broken relationship.

First come some accounts about incipient love, which music occurred then and what it seemed to express. Subsequently the music always becomes associated with the event.

(20A) Woman, middle-aged, 1960s

One thing I remember was when I was ten years old. I was by myself at home, sitting in the living room and listening to records. I put on 'If I Fell' by the Beatles. I experienced it extremely strongly just then, played it time and time again, discovered more and more in the music. On that occasion I think I was in love for the first time. It was a boy who was in the eighth form and whom I'd only seen at a distance. It was him I was thinking about when I listened to the record. The music expressed what I felt. Afterwards, I was thrilled.

(20B) Woman, young, 1980s

It was Saturday evening and we were in the park to listen to an artiste. After the performance, we were inside the discotheque and he was there too. I had liked him for a year or two by then, but he had been away studying, so I hadn't seen him so often recently. I had almost forgotten about him. But now, when he was there and I had become older and more mature, it struck me that I could ask him to dance just to see what my feelings for him were like.

I heard a slow song starting up and suddenly I was standing in front of him without understanding how I'd got there. I asked cautiously: Shall we dance? Yeah, sure, he answered. And then I realized what I had done. We then danced to 'Maybe we're about to fall in love'. I thought I was dreaming, but nevertheless I felt calm and secure. I didn't get palpitations as I'd thought, and above all I didn't faint.

When the song finished, and we each went our own way, I felt extremely happy that I'd danced with him. The only thing I heard inside my head was 'Maybe we're about to fall in love'. The next day I was totally elated and even now I think about him when I hear this wonderful song. I will presumably always have this memory because he was the first boy I was really in love with.

(20C) Woman, middle-aged, 1960s

I was 18 or 19 years old, just started to study music and was really in love for the first time, in love with the primary in the college orchestra and string quartet. At a big concert in the church, one of the works they were going to perform was Mozart's G minor quintet with my own violinist as the primary. Before the concert, which took place in the month of May, I had had every theme in the quintet explained to me in terms of nature poetry, filtered through my loving ears. My experience of the concert was revolutionary for all of my life, and Mozart's G minor has followed me all my life.

Perhaps this strong experience depended partly on the open mind that being in love means, partly on the fact that this was one of the first concerts of quality in my life for 'the little girl from the country'.

The experience has stayed with me all my life; they are innumerable, the disappointments and worries that I have taken care of with the help of the G minor quintet!

The next account gives an example of how someone can deliberately use music associated with love to affect their mood.

(20D) Man, young, 1990s (from an edited interview)

[About a tune associated with the start of a romance. Every time he hears this particular tune, he re-experiences the feeling of being in love.] I only need to hear the first chords on this tune and I find myself in a special mood. When I feel a bit low or down, I can put it on. It works better than other tricks that people use to get into a good mood. It never fails!

I re-experience the feelings, just this about just having fallen in love. The flowers burst into life and it is summer, even though it is the middle of winter—and you are so terribly happy! Satisfied, fortunate, *shamelessly* fortunate! The feeling of just having fallen in love, shamelessly, childishly . . . *enormously* happy. There are no problems. You see everything through rose-coloured spectacles. It's a really nice feeling, perhaps the best.

Being really happy: I think that means you can be really free too. You are free from problems. No problem is so big that you can't deal with it. You feel like . . . well, perhaps not God, but like an extremely lucky person.

This tune, it became a feeling that will always be there. The tune took on meaning afterwards, just because I was so happy then. Wherever I am when I hear it, that feeling comes back. I feel good, it makes me happy. It works like a healing balm!

In the following accounts, no words were needed; the music interpreted the feelings and led to a catharsis of feelings that had been pent up for a long time.

(20E) Woman, young, 1990s (from an edited interview)

[She is listening to a pop ballad with her new-found partner.] It was in the beginning, when you are a bit shy about saying what you think, and those lyrics said *everything* in some way. We didn't have to say anything. The music sort of said what we were thinking, and because of that it became so strong for us. No words were needed. It spoke for us instead, so we didn't need those unnecessary and embarrassing twists and turns.

We danced in the living room. This was new for me, it was the first time that I dared to admit to myself that I liked somebody. Such a relief, just happiness, it was altogether too much! I felt calm and harmonious and so incredibly happy—blissful. We sat on the sofa and without my noticing it a tear dropped without my feeling ashamed about it. It was completely natural. It was so nice just to be yourself . . . Just this thing that the feelings are so strong that you can't keep them back. It just happens. There's no logic, no fear, no shame, no guilt, because the feelings are so strong.

It becomes so strong too because for many years you have gone and hidden your love and not even dared to admit it to yourself. It gets sort of doubly reinforced. And then when you know it is reciprocated . . . It was sort of everything all mixed together, all the joyful things there are: love, harmony, happiness. To discover something positive in yourself and in another person, to see the world with fresh eyes, sort of.

I have had lots of music experiences in many different ways, but I never thought that I would have one that meant so much in a positive sense . . . so then it becomes so enormously strong! For me, it meant an end to ten years of battling with myself and all the others and everyone around me. The end of ten years of acting and not daring to be myself, of being super-nervous and a bit nuts. Ah, I found my way home!

(20F) Woman, middle-aged, 1980s

At home with my beloved one summer's evening. Timbre music—a minimum of notes, and between every note in–cred–ib–le pauses . . . Raindrop music. 'Raindrops (notes) that quivered, gradually loosening their hold, a leaf, the handlebars of a cycle, the tip of a nose . . .' (song by Harold Budd)

Our relationship was incredibly explosive. We had known each other for two months. I was open and vulnerable and sensitive. Curious and thirsty for love. I felt as if I was going to fall to bits inside me. Just so unprecedented! An enormous feeling of relief! It was a long, long time since I had felt so open, so naked. Without a mask or pretence. Perhaps I was really happy too, just then? I felt ready to take in anything at all!

A year has passed since then; I think up all sorts of excuses so that I can 'avoid' hearing that record again . . . although I so heartily want to! The pain/pleasure progressively increased . . . it became unbearable! Somewhere inside me I wanted to get away, away . . . Just turn off, because this tormented me, driving me crazy—or was it the opposite? I started to cry. Quietly and calmly. I didn't cry like I used to . . . completely different . . . because now I felt (knew!) so intensely why I cried! A bird that has been let out of its cage for the first time in its life! Chaos!? A colossal longing for understanding, warmth . . . mutual understanding flooded over me!! I felt I was needed. 'Little me' felt loved and appreciated for who she was!

And when will I dare to listen again?

Now an account about love that defies language boundaries, and where a particular tune happens to fit in perfectly as an interpretation of feelings at the decisive moment.

(20G) Man, middle-aged, 1980s

It all started when I met a girl on holiday in Hungary. We couldn't talk with each other because she spoke only Hungarian and my knowledge of that language is extremely limited. We met just one single evening. There was no sex. We just looked deeply into each other's eyes and felt an incredibly strong feeling of belonging together. When we separated it was really heartbreaking for both of us. We cried—although we hardly knew each other, let alone could talk.

Six months later I decided to go and look for her in Hungary and see whether the same strong feeling came back. Because I couldn't get it out of my head. I celebrated New Year with her and her friends. We still couldn't talk to each other, but we communicated fairly well with a drawing pad and dictionary. The time passed quickly; it was fun being together.

But the day for my journey home was getting closer. The evening before that, we met, the drawings on the pad formed themselves into questions: What shall we do? Do you want to come with me to Sweden? Can I come with you? What about my job and my friends? When I went to bed that evening, I still didn't know what would happen. My train was leaving at 10.15 in the morning.

In the morning I lay there on the bed half-watching MTV. Suddenly there was a knock on the door. I open it and she's standing there with a suitcase in each hand and a big warm smile on her face. We were united in a long, intense hug and both of us knew that we had now taken the step—now we would share our lives with each other.

While we're standing there hugging each other, MTV is playing Phil Collins's 'Another Day in Paradise'. The music fits so incredibly perfectly with the mood we were feeling. The music touches the same chord in both of us, we look deep, deep into each other's eyes, and tears of joy burst forth. We get goosepimples all over our bodies.

Still, two and a half years later, when we hear that tune, tears come to our eyes and we remember those minutes.

After these accounts of positive feelings when in love, there now follow accounts about music and feelings in love relationships that have broken up or never come about. The feelings are sometimes purely negative, sometimes negative and positive in turn (for example, bittersweet), or negative that for various reasons nevertheless are turned into mainly positive. The music interprets and gives expression to the feelings, brings to life memories of them and of the situation at the time.

(20H) Woman, old, 1930s

One summer, 55 years ago. I experienced first love as strongly as one does at that age. However, he loved another. The Danish tango 'Jalousie' captured exactly my feelings of dreadful jealousy. I thank God that that man did not become my fate, but nevertheless, after all these years, I can't hear the melody without feeling the agony.

(20I) Woman, young, 1980s

It was Orup who sang his ballad 'Alla borde få ha någon, någon gang, någonstans' ['Everybody ought to have somebody, some time, somewhere']. I was lying in my bed and philosophiz-ing about the everyday things of life, when I heard this wonderful tune for the first time. I don't usually listen so closely to the lyrics, but because I wasn't doing anything special

I now listened very carefully to the words. It is about how everybody ought to be allowed to feel real love and to feel that they are loved.

The words moved me so strongly that I was close to crying. The reason was that earlier in the day I had tried to console a girl who told me of her innermost feelings. She had said that she didn't feel loved and that she missed having a friend in whom she could confide. It fitted precisely with the lyrics, she ought to have someone who loved her and someone to whom she could give all the love she carried within her. Every time I hear this tune on the radio, I turn it off. My friend did not, unfortunately, find anybody to love before it was too late.

(20J) Woman, middle-aged, 1980s

A piece that gives me the shivers down my backbone is 'Meditation' from *Thaïs* by Jules Massenet. A violinist and a pianist played. The experience is about something as bittersweet as forbidden love. I was there together with a man who a little earlier had gone back to his wife after very advanced plans to divorce.

The concert was the last one we went to together. We sat there, two middle-aged people, and felt as though we were 14 or 15 years old instead. We didn't say anything. We held each other's hands and simply enjoyed the music in the presence of the other. I think we hoped, both of us, that it wouldn't be our last concert together, but at the same time somewhere there was the fear, and perhaps even the certain knowledge, that it probably was anyway. We have never spoken with each other about this particular experience, but on one occasion a little later we gave each other a recording with this particular 'Meditation'. Neither of us knew that we were going to get it from the other.

Now that I have this experience behind me, the music is still there. Music doesn't abandon a person, even if people do. What would life be like without music? A great deal poorer, in my opinion.

(20K) Woman, young, 1980s

The event took place when we were flying over the Atlantic. We were all extremely nervous before the journey. It was exactly one year after the plane exploded over Lockerbie, when so many people died. There had been threats, so there were lots of extra security arrangements. A week or so before, I had broken up with my boyfriend and said some things that I ought not to have said, and I suppose I had begun to regret that things turned out as they did. He went off on a long journey a few days after the break-up.

When we were in the air, and I was at my most nervous, they handed out earphones to all the passengers. Almost immediately after I had chosen a channel at random, this really wonderful melody came, 'All around the world' by Lisa Stansfield. All I thought was how incredibly well that tune fitted with my life situation at that moment. The song is about a girl who has broken up with her boyfriend and doesn't know where on earth he can be just now, but she is firmly determined to travel all around the world to find him. Just like me, she regrets things she has said and done, but you don't get a sad impression when you hear the song, rather it is filled with energy and the joy of life.

The feeling I got was that everything fitted, I too would travel around the world to find my beloved. It felt as if nothing mattered any longer, things would turn out as they did, but still I had this feeling all the time of an enormous sense of hope that everything would work out for the best. My nervousness disappeared completely, and I could remain calm and relaxed for the rest of the journey.

(20L) Man, middle-aged, 1980s

It was summer, I had just bought Dire Straits's second album, *Communique*, and every-thing felt exactly right straight away! This music expressed most of what was inside me! I was in the most intense period of my life, as I was mortally in love with a woman. I can't give a particular time because the album spoke just as intensely to me for almost a year until we broke up and I had to go on living knowing that I would never experience a greater love affair. But during all of this period I played it like somebody possessed. It worked during the deepest happiness we had. It worked as consolation during the worst despair. I play it just now, but I can't experience more than parts of the feelings it gave me then.

The music had a purely physical effect too, it caressed tensions until they disappeared, it gave me a gentle, strong self-confidence, it gave me self-esteem, an identity, gave me a new and harmonious relation to myself. The tunes worked in slightly different ways, of course, but the basic feeling of the music meant that almost all the record was a single great love.

In short, I found music that was like a mirror for me, that worked whatever state I was in, plus it had a basic existential tone that I had been looking for. I loved the record, and it loved me. It contained warmth, longing, tender sadness, anger, rest, sorrow, happiness, hope, randiness, playfulness, common sense, humanity, social commitment, love, perhaps above all a lot of human love.

The music reflected his feelings in every possible state, and gave him a strong self-confidence, an identity (for which reason the account is also quoted in Chapter 16, section 16.1). The record was a great love and it felt as though it was mutual: 'I loved the record, and it loved me.'

Something similar happened in the following example. The music absorbed the narrator totally, put her into a trance, there was only her and the music, and the unhappy love was replaced by a moment's happy love in the music.

(20M) Woman, young, 1980s

Björn J:son Lindh and Staffan Scheja were going to give a concert featuring *Spirits of Europa I* and *II*. I had listened a lot to these albums, so I knew all the pieces off by heart and used to hum along with the melodies.

During the spring, I had a romance with a man that I knew from before. The problem was that he had a girlfriend that he had broken up with (but without that actually meaning that they had broken up). The entire spring, I was torn between hope and despair. One day I was happy and in love, the next I was unhappy and in love. A couple of days before the concert, I saw him with the 'ex-'girlfriend. I was terribly hurt, disappointed and felt I had been tricked.

On the day of the concert, I had decided not to go. I thought, 'What will I get out of it? I know it already.' So I didn't have any special expectations of the concert, but at the last minute my friend managed to persuade me to go anyway.

The concert started, and, sure, it was good right from the beginning, but it was nothing extraordinary. But gradually my interest and my insight in the music increased, my experi-ence became more and more intense. It started with a general feeling of exhilaration, happiness, but it ended like a trance. So I was one with the music: there was only me and the music. I was forced to pinch the arm of my seat hard so as not to sing aloud. It felt as if I was going to burst from joy. Time and space disappeared. There was nothing except me and the music. Everything was just right. Everything belonged together. Nothing else meant anything. It was almost as if I had left my own physical body, because I can't remember any 'physical' reactions. It was an intoxication. I felt I was in love, in love with the music.

The feeling was strong right up to the last piece, when the applause woke me up. Afterwards, I felt physically tired, but the feeling of happiness stayed with me all evening. I think that my unhappy love might have been the reason for the strong experience. Here I got to experience a moment's happy love. Many of my strongest experiences with music have come in connection with my being emotionally vulnerable in one way or another.

The strong experience scared me a little at first. If I were to listen to the music I would probably be disappointed at not feeling it just as strongly. It wasn't until the following autumn that I listened to the albums again. Then the memory of the experience became stronger at the same time as I felt a regret at having lost someone, and sorrow. It felt as if I had lost a friend. Since that time I haven't listened (haven't wanted to listen) to this music.

In the following accounts, there are descriptions of strong negative reactions, bodily as well as mental, after a broken relationship. The music and lyrics express and agree with the sorrow, emptiness, regret over a loss, and the pain that the narrators feel.

(20N) Woman, middle-aged

I especially remember a song called 'Nothing compares' by Sinéad O'Connor, that was played for me the first time via telephone. It wasn't my musical taste at all, but it really grabbed me in full force because I associated it with my darling. The love story came to an abrupt end, and I felt a pain that I'd never experienced before. The melody was charged with this pain, too, which by that time I experienced as excruciating. As soon as I would happen to hear the introduction on the radio, my sympathetic nervous system reacted and I had palpitations. I quickly changed stations. On one occasion, I forced myself to listen to the entire melody and then measured my pulse. It was way up—far above 100!

(20O) Woman, young, 1980s

I sat on the floor beside my bed and wrote in my diary. My mood was subdued. I busied my thoughts with my ex-boyfriend, we had decided to go our separate ways a few weeks earlier, even though we both loved each other. Inside I still felt like only half a person.

In the next room, Prince's album *Purple Rain* was revolving on the turntable. I love his music, almost fanatically, and just that particular album is one of my favourites. So I had heard it several times before, loved the music, but never reacted so strongly as I did now. Well, I was sort of half-listening, but then suddenly it was there, the start of 'Purple Rain' (the last track on the album with the same name). Seemed to go right into my chest, then came the words [. . .] It felt 'Ouch!'—like a sudden pain in your stomach that makes you lose your breath for a moment. I literally gasped for breath, the music went right into me and clutched my insides. The words went on [. . .] Although I was still sitting on the floor, the volume seemed to increase, all the background sounds disappeared, there was only the voice and the melancholy guitar accompaniment. I started to shake and burst into tears.

The feeling directly afterwards was an enormous feeling of emptiness and loss. That I reacted like I did was, of course, because of breaking up with my boyfriend. I had heard the tune before without reacting so strongly.

Finally in this chapter, an example of how a certain piece of music by pure chance can come to be associated with the course of a love relationship right to its bitter end. The music in itself doesn't reflect these feelings, 'It could have been any music at all', but nevertheless arouses very strong negative reactions as a consequence of the circumstances under which it has occurred.

(20P) Woman, middle-aged, 1980s

The absolutely most intense experience with music that I have had took place in connection with a passionate love affair that came to an end. I was myself very surprised by the force of my reaction, by the feelings that poured out, by how totally impossible it was for me to master and control these feelings. For about eight months I had listened to this music (*After Here Through Midland* by Cock Robin), thought it was nice, not listened especially actively but had the record more as background music. During this time I had also experienced a very intense love affair.

Then came the time for my experience with music. The passion was over, I felt harrowed, rootless, abandoned—angry, hurt, sad . . . I put the record on to listen to something nice. Then it hit me. I lived through the whole course of events again—how we met, all the waiting for telephone calls at night, visits—I saw myself standing on the balcony and smoking and waiting—I felt how the tears came, how enormously happy I had been at the same time as I had experienced the emptiness as a physical pain. I was shaking and I had to turn the music off. I could feel every nuance in the entire course of events, the world around became vague, I felt sick . . . When I had taken the record off, I felt all washed out, empty.

A year later when I played the same music, the experience was still strong, but with time the intensity had become subdued and I could listen to the entire record without being forced to turn it off.

I think that the force of the experience was especially to do with what sort of music it was about. The circumstances meant that it could have been any music at all—I think—because it was music I listened to often, and it was the changed situation that led to the emotional outburst. For me, the entire experience was strange because I am one of those people who listen very little to music—always passively, and who thus never before or after experienced anything similar.

In this chapter, one might perhaps expect something about strong experiences with music in connection with sex. In fact, such accounts are rare, in all only eight accounts in our material. One man hinted that it was 'really erotic' when he played music with a woman, one woman wrote that in general she was prepared for sex in connection with rock music, and a boy wrote that he became aroused because of a pretty singer. In the other accounts, it is not a question of any real experience of sex, but the experience of music is compared in general with sexual intercourse, especially with orgasm, sometimes described as 'spiritual orgasm'.

CHAPTER 21

MUSIC IN CONNECTION WITH ILLNESS AND DEATH

Few events in life are associated with such difficult and strong memories as when one is affected by some serious illness, or when this has happened to a close friend or relation. The situation is even heavier to bear if this has led to the death of the friend, relation, parent, or spouse. The accounts in this chapter show how much music can mean by confirming feelings, distracting from negative thoughts, consoling, creating meaning, and giving strength to go on.

It would feel out of place to make any more comments on these deeply personal accounts. There are therefore only a few short sentences as bridging passages between the different accounts.

To start with, some accounts about what music has meant during stays in hospital.

(21A) Man, old, 1940s

When I was 22, I got TB and was 'locked up' in a sanatorium far from my home. Of course, I suffered severely from worry about the future and whether I would become healthy again. From the time at the sanatorium I remember an aria on the wireless from *The Pearl Fishers* by Bizet, possibly with an Italian tenor. I associated this aria with sunny Pacific Ocean views, waving palms, coral reefs, etc. It was probably an emotional reaction to my vulnerable, abandoned situation during this period of illness that I associated the listening with such a strong effect. It is especially the notes at the beginning of the aria that I remember when I still hear it in my head. The song gave expression to my intense longing for freedom, health, a longing to get away from the restriction, the tiredness, the loneliness.

(21B) Woman, 1990s

They discovered a tumour in my eye. For ten days I was an in-patient at the hospital for investigation. They wanted to be certain that it was a tumour and whether it was malignant. During this period of just waiting, my mood went between hope and pitch-black despair.

It was then that music came in. Because even though in that situation you need to think, there is a risk that you ponder too much. Read—yes, sure. But partly I couldn't manage to read so much because one eye was not functioning, partly there wasn't much to read that could keep my depressing thoughts at bay.

But there was one thing. The music on the radio's classical channel. There was the music that could shut the world out. That entertained and captivated. That demanded so much commitment that my thoughts were caught and didn't go wandering off down forbidden paths. There too was so much calmness that my thoughts didn't need to wander off. The radio and the music there saved many difficult days. Some of the music, it was the first time I heard it, but some other pieces gave me the joy of recognition.

Now I have one eye, but otherwise am in good form. And I listen even more to music. In particular classical. I'd say it gave me a little 'kick'.

(21C) Woman, middle-aged, 1990s (from an edited interview)

It was when I was working at a hospital. A friend and me, at that time we were busy practising a song for a wedding, an old folk song, a love song.

It must have been a perfectly ordinary day at the hospital. I went in to visit a patient I'd never met before and who was dying. I was walking around and humming in his room. Then he says: 'You could sing something for me, couldn't you?' Then I sat beside him and I sang this love ballad and held his hand. It was terribly moving. When I had finished singing, he says: 'Oh, that was the most beautiful thing I've ever heard.' I don't sing terribly well, but nevertheless, it felt so . . . we came close to each other, even though we didn't know each other.

Just after I'd finished singing, it became silent, we were with each other and I sat and held his hand. He fell asleep. I'll never forget it. I don't remember how I got out of the room, or anything afterwards, just that it sort of stopped.

I don't feel as afraid of death any longer. It is actually easier to go in and see a dying patient now.

In the following accounts, there is a description of the music and the thoughts and feelings that are awakened when one has witnessed the suffering of close friends, or lost them.

(21D) Woman, young, 1990s

It was at a discotheque, I was there with my boyfriend. A few months earlier, a very close friend of mine had died in a traffic accident. I had been thinking a lot about death since then. Where was she just now, whether she was doing OK wherever she was. Because it was so unjust that she should die when she was so young, only 17 years old, her life had only just begun and she was not allowed to live. It was so unjust. But life can't simply end, there must be somewhere you go to.

And we were having a good time as usual at the disco, but then they started to play 'Himlen' ['Heaven'] by the band Ratata and very suddenly I felt how the tears fell. Because they were singing about how you'll have it good in heaven and I immediately thought about her. It was so nice to hear it, because it was a proof for me that she has it good where she is just now. It was so terribly nice, to just hear them singing about heaven, and let the tears fall.

(21E) Woman, young, 1980s

The experience that came up first in my memory, I had it in an old monastery church. In this church that evening they were celebrating what is known as a Taizé religious service, with songs from Taizé. They are simple songs with only a couple of verses in each one and you repeat these several times. The church was dark apart from the light that came from the night lights that were everywhere in the church, and on the floor there were blankets laid out to sit on. I sat down in one corner so that I could lean against the wall, felt a bit like sitting inside a lantern or a cave.

What I remember now afterwards isn't anything about how the actual service went, but that at the end there was 'just' singing. Participated in the songs and felt how they sort of embraced me altogether. Relaxed in all my body and sort of flowed into the singing and became a part of it. It felt like showering to get clean, but on the inside. Music can help us to reach into those places that we can't reach by ourselves. All my blocks were breached and I just cried, a quiet crying—a bit like summer rain.

What was I crying about? Well, a few months earlier, one of my best friends was ill and at the end of the period she told me that she was close to taking her own life—had been standing with the pills in one hand and a glass of water in the other. Then we cried together over what could have happened and I was sure I had got over it, but now here in the midst of this music my defences collapsed and I understood in my heart what I had previously understood in my brain—that I could have lost her and been forced to live without her. I just cried and sort of found support and consolation, 'crying help', and perhaps even closeness in the music which embraced me all the time.

When I had finished crying and mourning, I could rest, feel pure and free. Again I participated with my singing in the music.

(21F) Woman, middle-aged, 1970s

One of my women friends died. The cause of death was a brain tumour that had led to a lot of suffering on several levels for several months. I visited her at the hospital. She was beyond reach then. When we drove in the car to the hospital I put the radio on and heard Erna Tauro's composition of Tove Jansson's 'Höstvisa' ['Autumn song']. I don't know if it was the words or the music that moved me the most, I think perhaps it was the words. They include 'Hurry beloved, hurry to love . . . soon the fleeting summer is over.'

I felt so strongly, like at no other time during her illness, that it was all too late for her. I liked 'Autumn song' before, but from this time on it acquired a special meaning for me, and I always remember this car journey and this hospital visit every time I hear it.

Often, the experience is connected to a special person. The thing is that music doesn't abandon the person. Even when the person whom you associate with a particular piece of music isn't anywhere near, you can still get strong feelings from the piece in question. Sometimes the lyrics and the music are intimately connected, and it is hard to know which is the more important, the words or the music.

(21G) Woman, middle-aged, 1980s

My friend was in hospital and she was very poorly. I phoned the hospital every four hours to ask how she was, and the reports got worse each time. Like me, she had cancer. We had got the news—cancer—several times and we shared the feelings and thoughts. Thoughts that only somebody who has been affected can understand. We had both learnt to make use of everything good that life had to offer, and to dismiss unimportant things. We had talked about death and wondered what waited after it.

She died in the night. We were in the car on the way home. It was a clear sky full of stars. Even all the small stars, the ones that are not visible so often, shone brightly. I said to my friends that there was a party up there because my friend had arrived. The sorrow was heavy and new.

I dropped off my passengers and so I was left alone in the car. The hour was late and I had a long way still to drive and had to concentrate and put on a tape. Jerry Williams sang 'Woman'. Then everything gave way. The rock music that I already liked before now took on a completely different meaning. The lyrics were about my friend. I played the tune over and over again, I cried and I looked at the stars—perhaps I would see her, I don't know what I thought.

When I got home and had gone to bed and cried for another hour or so, I suddenly became calm. The lyrics in the tune had in some way made me feel her presence and I fell asleep.

The day she was buried, I was given a tape with lyrics and music by Karin Liungman. The lyrics in four of these tunes are exactly about things that we talked of. One of the songs starts: 'In the middle of the universe on a little blue planet, I look out at the stars and won-der where I am . . .' And I who had looked up at the stars and wondered if she was there . . . I discovered new meanings all the time. Always played these when I was alone. It was in some way as if my friend helped me in my grieving process thanks to our having talked and thought about things in just such terms. It was so typical of her that she should be a support even when she was dead.

I still listen to this music, but I don't need it in the same way. It will always mean some-thing special for me. I am very grateful for this experience because it was something new for me. I didn't feel alone in my grief. I had the music, after all.

I have even said that I want one of these tunes to be played at my funeral. It sounds sad but it isn't at all, and when you have been as close to death as I have, then it isn't frightening at all, but just something natural. Because it isn't until you are familiar with death that you can live your life more richly.

The narrators in the following accounts describe what music has meant for their feelings and thoughts when they lost a parent or a spouse.

(21H) Woman, middle-aged

It was the night after my father died. I sat with him when he died late in the afternoon, and I came home completely shattered. Then I put on the earphones and listened to 'En midvin-tersaga' ['A Midwinter Saga'] by Ralph Lundsten. And I remained sitting there until the morning and listened to his winter saga. It was as if I was lifted up towards the stars and floated up there. And the music went into my heart and healed my wounds, and when morning came I was almost happy.

(21I) Man, middle-aged, 1950s

I had joined a record club and this particular day I had just received the Record of the Month, a Brahms record. In the evening, the pupils' union had a party and I hadn't had time to listen to the record. During the party there was a message via telephone that my father had died that day in an accident. The message took an iron grip of me, and I retired to my room to be alone.

To divert my thoughts, I put the record on. It was after listening for a while that I made the discovery. The state that I entered can perhaps be most likened to a trance. Time and space were dissolved by a feeling where sorrow and despair were relieved. It felt like walking in an isolated hilly landscape on a night with melancholy light.

When the piece of music had ended and I came back again, I looked at the record cover to find out what I had been listening to. It was Brahms's Symphony No. 4 in E minor, Op. 98, the second movement (Frankfurter Operahaus Orchester with Carl Bamberger as conductor) and on the record cover it said: '*In diesem von Wehmut und Resignation durchdrungenden Satz sah Richard Strauss einen Leichenzug, der schweigsam über vom Mond beschienenen Höhen zieht*' ['In this movement, penetrated by melancholy and resignation, Richard Strauss saw a funeral procession that moved silently across hills illuminated by the moon']. That is precisely what I had been through.

It is hardly necessary to add that the experience felt like balm in a difficult moment and it caused tears to fall. After many years it is still hard for me to tell about the experience without that feeling and the tears coming to the fore. The record is still one of my dearest treasures, but the trance experience has never returned. Have often thought about whether music is a direct, but wordless, language from heart to heart.

(21J) Woman, young, 1990s (told by a close member of the family)

[During the grieving process after the death of her father] When she started seeing a therapist, the process of grieving for her father got going. Today she has just been on such a visit and she was just as fragile as I now understand she can be as far as her deceased father is concerned.

After we had finished eating, and quite unaware of what was to come, I put on Bach's 'Air' while I washed the dishes. I suddenly heard how the music was mingling with sobs from the living room. The sobs soon turned into loud crying. I leave the dishes and rush to where she is lying on the sofa with a stream of tears pouring down her cheek. She doesn't stop until the music fades out and then she tells me the reason for her emotional outburst: 'The music, it's the fault of the music!'

Afterwards, both she and I realized that perhaps it wasn't so bad but rather quite nice for her to have this gust of emotion, this close contact with her dead father. What I didn't really understand just then was how and in what way the music can cause a storm of emotions that was more like a torrent in its sudden course and with the cleansing effect that that has. Now it turned out that the music had a very personal and very intimate relation to her and her family. It was her father's favourite piece that the whole family had had to listen to day and night regardless of whether they had wanted to or not. It was also the music that was played at his funeral. Every time she listens to this piece, it is a reminder of her dead father and thus associated with extremely strong feelings. I myself was so moved that now I too have a fairly strong relationship to Bach's 'Air'.

(21K) Woman, old, 1970s

My greatest and most intense experience of music took place when my husband died. I was absolutely desperate and didn't want to live any longer. An event that I'll never get over.

That day I happened to listen to a recording of Tchaikovsky's sixth symphony, *Pathétique*, with the Berlin Philharmonic and Herbert von Karajan. I think that the entire symphony is a desperate cry for help, and I experienced it as such and cried uncontrollably all the time. I have later had confirmation of how unhappy and desperate Tchaikovsky was when he wrote the symphony. I can't say that any part is better than the others, but think that the entire work is a cry for help. An extreme desperation and the fantastic thing is that, afterwards, when everything has quietened down, I get a feeling of being lifted out of the room, up into the sky, where I float, endlessly happy. That state can last a long time.

This wasn't the first time I had heard the music, but it affected me so completely that day—I was ready to understand and to take it in. I often listen to *Pathétique* when I feel sad and that can happen a few times a year. I get the same intense experience and the same consolation.

(21L) Woman, old, 1980s

My husband had cancer. Despite this, we could sing and play for yet another year. He became more and more ill, his voice disappeared and we waited for the end. Our son came home and we helped each other to take care of husband and father.

It was a Sunday morning in the summer. The tension and tiredness plus great sadness felt almost paralysing for me. I was in the sick room upstairs and heard music from the grand piano down in the room. I went downstairs—lay down on the sofa with my eyes closed and heard a fairly new song that our son played. I got the lyrics later. When I listened, big tears fell from my eyes down over my cheeks, but I felt an indescribable relief in my chest as if a burden disappeared when he played:

> Rest in me,
> you will see that all will be
> calm in you,
> through me you can be free.
> I am here with you,
> though the waves are high,
> you can rest,
> rest in me.
>
> [Swedish hymn No. 755]

On the afternoon of that same day, my husband passed away and life has gone on, but I shall never forget the experience.

(21M) Woman, old

[Summarizing a long account] I venture to say as my final words: For me music is also a way of *living* and of going on despite everything. My husband and daughter died of cancer. At first, everything was paralysed! Couldn't hear any music while the grieving process went on. But then music came back: soothing, healing, gave me the courage to face life again. Through it, it became possible to deal with the grief.

CHAPTER 22

MUSIC AT FUNERALS

FUNERALS of close friends or family members are among the most difficult moments in life. Amidst all the dark sorrow at these farewells, music can bring relief, light, consolation, security, and—despite everything—hope for the future.

First, a memory from the large public funeral of one of Sweden's internationally best known and most respected persons.

(22A) Woman, middle-aged, 1961

My greatest, strongest experience of music took place during the funeral of Dag Hammarskjöld in 1961. We who are middle-aged and older remember well the shocking news of Hammarskjöld's death. What grief, shock, horror! What will happen to us, to the world?

Then there was the funeral in the cathedral in Uppsala. The whole world was represented there, mourning, stunned, stony faces, the darkness felt solid.

Then in the bottomless distress, there came an angel sent by God—Elisabeth Söderström—who sang the wonderful aria from Handel's *Messiah*: 'I know that my Redeemer liveth'. The music and the words went straight into my heart, largely thanks to Elisabeth Söderström's heartfelt interpretation. The relief and the light flooded over me like a hot wave, and I understood: 'There is hope!'

I have always been interested in music, loved most of it, and of course I was familiar with the *Messiah,* but after that occasion there has always been a special elevation and consolation in that soprano aria.

Now, two accounts of music that was played at the funerals of close acquaintances and, as in the previous account, gave relief and hope.

(22B) Woman, middle-aged, 1980s

It was in the autumn. Our very best friends' teenage son was going to be buried after being killed in a car accident. My family plus about 400 other people were listeners and participants in a big mourning ceremony. I felt an indescribable grief, grief, grief. I must have heard previously the piece of music that this account is about, but then I hadn't reacted in any way.

An overcast day, with low clouds and rain hanging in the air. It was heavy in many ways. When the funeral service had been going on for perhaps half an hour, a flute started playing (perhaps an organ too, not sure, it is the flute I remember), and after a few bars the sun started to shine in through the different-coloured altar windows, and the entire church became light and you 'take off' in some way and you felt some sort of surprise, relief, consolation. When these different feelings arose, I didn't know that the piece that was playing was called '*Dimman lättar*' ['The mist lifts'] by Carl Nielsen, but I saw this in the programme a little while later. I still felt incredibly sad, but with some sort of feeling of . . . hope?

A very strange experience. An event that I have thought a lot about since then. Perhaps as an attempt to console myself?

A few months later, I experienced exactly the same feelings, grief–surprise–relief, when the same piece was played on the radio. After only two or three notes, I started to cry and had to stop at the side of the road (I was in the car), but the sadness soon passed and everything felt light, consoling.

(22C) Woman, middle-aged, 1970s

It was in the winter. The temperature was minus 6 [Celsius] and a bit of snow had coloured the ground white. This day, nature had dressed itself in white costume and the sun shone from a clear blue sky. The church lay there so serenely and seemed to be waiting. There was going to be a funeral. A popular colleague at work was to go to his final rest. I had never been to a funeral before, and I dreaded it and it was with some apprehension that I went there.

We walked quietly into the church. The family and chief mourners had already arrived. It was so peaceful and beautiful, with beautiful wreaths of flowers and lighted candles surrounding the coffin. There were also candles in front of the sculpture before the sanctuary, Jesus standing there with outstretched hands: 'Come unto me, all ye that labour and are heavy laden, and I will give you rest.'

The stillness, the peace—and yet the grief. All of this made a great impression on me. I felt very moved and a moment of self-examination followed. I had dreaded this moment, but now I felt only serenity and a quiet calmness.

The bells started to ring loudly and urgently. A silent moment. Then the organ music began to fill the church. A music that I had never heard before. It was notes whirling around like snowflakes, weightless. It was like angels playing the flute and the trumpet—notes that filled the room with happiness and hope. The music flooded into me, it felt as if it filled every fibre of my body and I shivered and felt frozen. The tears ran down my cheeks, not from grief, but from an endless happiness and joy. The music proclaimed: 'Life is not over, it goes on, it continues happily. Now is your time on Earth, make use of it, live, live—then come and follow me!'

Now I understand what an experience with music is. I have heard about it many times and read about it, but never thought of it as anything other than that you think the music is beautiful. This was something completely different.

When I came home from the funeral, I couldn't relax until I had phoned the organist and found out what the piece of music was. It turned out that it was by J. S. Bach, *Actus Tragicus*. As soon as I could, I bought the record, but however loud I played it, and wherever I played it, it never again filled me with such a wonderful feeling as that time in the church.

In the following accounts of funerals of relatives or parents, it is singers who by virtue of their performances manage to turn the dark mood into feelings of light, security, and confidence.

(22D) Woman, middle-aged, 1970s

My [maternal] aunt had been ill a long time and now she was dead and was to be buried. We sat in the church, close to the front, my mother, my brother and me. In front of us, up beside the altar, was the coffin and there sat my aunt's siblings on one side and my uncle with his children on the other. What I remember most before the experience was my cousins' faces. The son, 15 years old, was completely petrified and his sister in tears. Life couldn't be more dark and terrible, my brother and I thought. Here there is no way out, here there is only darkness.

I think that was when the cantor started to play again, and my father started to sing 'Långt bortom rymder vida' ['Far beyond the starry sky', Psalm based on Matthew 7:7–8]. Or perhaps 'Den store hvide flok' ['The great white flock']. It was like a door being opened. I remember that I thought: 'The world hasn't stopped after all. Father's voice is there and it is just the same as usual.' It felt so secure. What else happened in the church, I don't really know. I just remember a warm, good security.

That type of music, especially a solitary man's voice but also hymns that I know, as well as men's choirs, has often given me security and a spark to make a fresh effort when life has been heavy and hard.

So I try to teach my children that music like that is important, because even if the world cracks open, it will always be there, and it is important to be able to find something that is old and familiar.

(22E) Woman, middle-aged, 1980s

An occasion when I was colossally moved by music was at my father's funeral. Because he was a musician from the beginning and he appreciated good music, I had said to the funeral director that I wanted somebody of accomplishment who would play or sing—whatever the cost.

The man who arranged the funeral knew my father well, and he sort of knew best, in a way that irritated me a little, but he could get the person he suggested, who was the wife of the vicar at the time. My mother pointed out that 'she sings nicely' and that you can't bypass the local talent, so I said OK without any particular enthusiasm.

Your own father's funeral is quite an arduous business and I sat there in the church pew during the service. Then came the singing. And this vicar's wife does have a wonderful voice. If she hadn't been a vicar's wife she could have been an opera singer, at least that's what I think. I was extremely moved and elevated and quite suddenly it wasn't a funeral any longer but a fellowship of souls, where my father too was certainly with us. That's what it felt like.

Then we came out into the most beautiful sunshine of a June day and walked to the grave and lowered the coffin, with lots of speeches and many beautiful flowers. It some way it wasn't sad but was a very pleasant arrangement. And for that I have the singer to thank.

Sometimes the reactions to the music at a funeral can be a little equivocal, as in the next two accounts.

(22F) Man, middle-aged, 1980s

The experience that I think was probably the most powerful I've had was almost ten years ago. My [maternal] grandfather was to be buried. I was very sad. Tear-filled eyes and a lump in my throat. Everybody round about was very affected and there was a lot of sniffling. Candles. Me and my siblings had all been baptized in this church. Grandma and my father were buried here. Dad and Mum had got married here. So this church was right at the core of the big events of our lives.

The piece was 'Solveig's song' from *Peer Gynt* by Grieg. Played on the church organ and viola. Under normal circumstances I think the piece is beautiful but now it became painfully beautiful. I died there in that church pew. The very combination of organ and viola did an awful lot. You couldn't defend yourself against them. The viola voice went right into my heart. Simply wanted to get up and bawl.

Luckily the piece isn't so long and I survived, but I have an ambivalent relationship with it now. When I hear it today it moves me and makes me happy in a melancholy way, but I'm also afraid of what it can do to me; it hurts.

(22G) Woman, young, 1980s

I'll never forget the situation. A small, very beautiful church. I'm sitting in one of the pews, almost at the very front. In front of me is an erect, serious old lady with a sorrowful expression on her face. She isn't crying. Beside her, with his right arm around her, sits an equally erect, equally serious man, my dad. The little old lady is my grandmother, 87 years old. There are other people in the church, but I don't think about them, don't even know if I see them at all. On the floor in front of the first row lies the coffin, the coffin with my grandfather.

It is so quiet you could hear a pin drop, and I remember that I sat and thought about all the fun we had had, Grandpa and me. I was Grandpa's favourite. Always. It wasn't terrible, everybody dies and Grandpa had reached the admirable age of 90. He had lived his life. A life that hadn't perhaps always been so easy, but nevertheless, he had been able to experience . . .

I remember that up until the music started to pour out of the organ pipes, I thought only about nice things. It was Grandpa and me out walking, it was Grandpa and me who looked after the garden, it was Grandpa and me . . .

Then came the music, Albinoni's Adagio. First there was a laugh inside me, a bubbling laugh that wanted to come out but wasn't allowed to, because we were actually at a funeral. Then the hysterical crying and the grief. It was just as if I had suddenly come to realize that I would never again be able to experience anything at all with Grandpa. My brother held me tightly and stroked my cheek all the time.

The crying turned into laughter again . . . oh, my God! The organist sounds as if she had pressed the high-speed button. The adagio sounded like the theme in a comedy. And as if that wasn't enough, one thing led to another, the word 'comedy' made me think about an amusing scene in a film that made me roar with laughter in my head and all the time with the adagio in the background.

I can imagine that laughter in a situation such as a funeral is a sort of defence mechanism. The funny thing was that as soon as the organ became silent, then the laughter disappeared, and then the grief and the tears came back.

To this day, I still find it hard to listen to the Adagio but I don't stop doing it; on the contrary, at Christmas the same year I got a gift card for an album and went straight out and bought Albinoni's Adagio. I feel that I must put the record on now . . .

Finally, an account of how a singer experienced her participation at a funeral.

(22H) Woman, young, 2000–10

My sister-in-law's grandmother was going to be buried. As the family had heard me sing earlier, they particularly wanted me to sing now too. After thinking it over for a while, I agreed. This was the first and so far only funeral that I have sung at.

We arrived a bit early so that I had time to practise with the cantor. I was going to sing 'Så skimrande var aldrig havet' ['Never did the sea shimmer so'] and 'Där rosor aldrig dör' ['Where roses never die']. When I had tested singing the songs together with the cantor playing, the vicar thought that I should stand right at the front of the church instead of up in the gallery. I wasn't sure about this, but couldn't say no. The vicar explained that this was my gift to them.

The funeral started, and after a while it was my turn to sing. I was nervous but at the same time calm because I thought that this was my gift to them and that they really wanted me to be there even though I didn't know them so well. It felt so wonderful to be able to please them on a sad day. Afterwards, I was happy that I had agreed to sing, because I saw that it meant so much to them.

CHAPTER 23

MUSIC IN NATURE

SEVERAL people describe strong experiences with music out in nature. The natural environment—its beauty, special qualities, stillness, or wildness, associations that it gives rise to—is the frame around the experience of music but at the same time is an important part of the experience in its totality. The music and nature interact, and the result is a stronger experience than would have been the case if only the one—music or nature—had occurred.

The music comes from a solo instrument, from some instruments together or from a whole ensemble. In some cases it is performed live, in other cases it is reproduced (from cassettes, records). Nature varies: in the country, in town, beside water, or out at sea.

The flute is an instrument that is often associated with nature. As long ago as in the mythology of antiquity, the (Pan) flute was the attribute of the god of the forest, Pan. In the first account, the flute actually occurs in a natural scenery with memories from antiquity.

(23A) Woman, old, 1980s

Last spring, my husband and I visited Hierapolis, that wonderfully beautiful place beside Pamukkale (Turkey). We were walking among old Roman ruins up towards an amphitheatre, when we heard the faint sound of a flute. Was it our imagination? No, we heard it again. Further away on the slope, there was a shepherd herding sheep. He was playing!

We had a feeling of being transported far back in time. You couldn't see any modern buildings, only ruins from Roman times, high mountains, meadows, cypresses, cedars . . . An experience I'll never forget!

A similar situation with flute music took place one quiet summer Sunday in the countryside on the island of Gotland [in the Baltic]. Here, too, there was a ruin in the background.

(23B) Woman, middle-aged, 1980s

I was together with the family on a holiday on Gotland. It was Sunday and we decided to make a car trip on the north part of the island. We drove along narrow gravel roads and made our first stop at Hångers Källa, an old spring. When we got out of the car, we were struck by the absolute silence and peace to be found there beside the old abandoned farm. All that you could hear was the larks warbling out there over the meadows. The magnificence of flowers was stunning in the field beside the barn and in the overgrown garden. Far away you could hear the pealing of bells from one of the innumerable churches. It felt solemn and at the same time unreal in some way.

We drove on a bit further and stopped beside a derelict church. The same serenity was to be found there. The field around the ruin was covered in flowering rock roses, and our son sat down in the green grass to draw the church ruin.

Suddenly and like a confirmation that we really were in paradise, you could hear a solitary flute play the second movement from the Piccolo flute concerto in C major by Vivaldi. We looked at each other and thought: This is just too unreal. Close to the ruin was what we thought was a deserted house. But suddenly, there on the steps, a barefoot young man was standing there playing—not on a piccolo flute but on a concert flute—this wonderful piece of music right out into Gotland nature.

Every time I hear that piece, I again experience this wonderful summer's day on Gotland. This piece of music is, of course, played often and I knew it before, but then I hadn't, so to speak, really got going on it.

In the following case, the encounter with the flute took place in an everyday situation, albeit in the silence of the night.

(23C) Woman, middle-aged, 1980s

It was at night. I delivered newspapers and was out working at 3.30 in the morning. Then somebody opened the window and played his flute. It was some classical piece, and included trills. I was in the middle of my delivery round, but when I came out of a building I heard this flute. Before that I was just as usual. But this music in the night was so indescribably beautiful. Even the birds were silent, so I stood there a long time and listened. Would have liked to have stayed and listened even longer, but unfortunately I had to go on working.

But this music as dawn was breaking is something I'll never forget, I just wish I could experience it again. It has sort of become an inner longing. I have heard many people play the flute and always think it is the most beautiful music but this was something unbelievably beautiful.

Why did it turn into such an experience? I suppose it was the time of day, the silence all around, the darkness and the totally unexpected. Who would think that somebody can play something so beautiful at that time of day?

In the following accounts, the setting is the Swedish summer—in the morning, during the daytime, in the evening, or in the light summer night.

(23D) Woman, old, 1940s

The strongest experience with music in my life was a very long time ago. I was about 11 or 12 years old. I'll never forget it. It was a quiet summer morning and so silent out at our summer place in Lake Mälaren. The big bay that separates the island where we lived from the next island was as smooth as a mirror. It was a Sunday because I had my Sunday dress, which was white, and I had been picking flowers.

Suddenly, across the water some wonderful piano music could be heard. I stood completely still so that the crunching of the gravel on the path wouldn't intrude. I remember how happy I was that nobody called out to me to come in and lay the table or something like that. I had heard the music before but only on the radio with the earphones pressed tightly against my ears. But this! I recognized it, Sinding's *'Frühlingsrauschen'* ['The Rustle of spring'].

I am not musical. Can't sing, played the piano a bit in my childhood, don't understand how music is constructed and can't hear in which key the music is written. Anyway, I often go and hear our excellent symphony orchestra. I enjoy it, every bit of me from head to foot. Sometimes when it is really lovely, I remember that peaceful summer morning.

(23E) Woman, young, 1980s

The strongest experience in connection with music was when I finally got to my first folk music assembly. When you walked through the area on some land between birches and red cottages, you were met with an enormous sound like a mish-mash of violins and life. But when you got closer you could distinguish the melodies that were different in every group that sat there on the grass, on the outdoor furniture, in the cottages and on a stage, so you only had to walk around and enjoy every group or sit down on the grass with your picnic basket and go off in your dreams, and listen to the intense, beautiful music.

I went inside one of the cottages and there I was thrilled: it was the group Sågskära, who were sitting there in a ring on old kitchen chairs and with old furniture, a fire blazing in the grate, and old stencilled wallpaper around them, and they were playing so beautifully on their violins and traditional Swedish keyed fiddles so that the air was really glowing in the light from the candles. And they were all of them so fully concentrated and playing with the deepest of feeling, sometimes looking each other in the eye, and there were strong emotionally charged rays between them. It felt as if all of me was completely filled with music and you felt so elated, bubbling like all your body was filled with flowers, when you heard this heart-rending music with its wonderfully positive approach to life. It felt so genuine, something that has always been there, timeless music.

I love nature, so I suppose that has something to do with why I experienced this so strongly, because I have, of course, heard this music before but not live and in such a genuine setting. It's never the same when you're sitting at home; it is best live.

(23F) Woman, middle-aged, 1980s

There were four of us from the country and we were on the loose in Stockholm. On holiday and without the children, we wandered around in the city and enjoyed its pulse and life. *Bompa, bompa, bompa*—there came the parade of the guards and, of course, we went after them and followed the marching soldiers up to the palace and the courtyard. This summer was very hot and later we heard that just this particular day it was the hottest day on record in Stockholm, and you could feel it! We who were thinly dressed delighted in the weather— but how could the soldiers cope? Anyway, we watched their performance in the courtyard with the changing of the guard and everything in the quivering heat of the almost still air.

The programme finally ended with a boy taking two steps forward and playing 'Memory' on solo trumpet and with some slightly muted accompaniment of drums at the end. The whole city stopped, and the goosepimples spread over your skin despite the heat.

It was fantastically beautiful and still to this day I can relive this inside me when I hear that melody played. At the time, we were totally captivated, yes, almost so much so that tears welled in your eyes, and I remembered that I was woken up by some very loud applause that was directed towards the musicians. Wonderful.

(23G) Man, middle-aged, 1950s

A summer night. The house sat beside a lake with not a ripple on the surface. It was about 3 or 4 in the morning. I was unable to get back to sleep, got up and was enchanted by the beauty of the scenery, felt that I needed more contact with this experience that was already strong. Elvis in this early morning pastoral picture? Out of the question.

After some thought, I remembered that I had been given a jazz record with music from the film *I want to live* by a cousin the previous Christmas. At first listening I hadn't really got to like it, but one tune was still in my head, almost hidden. I pulled out the record with music by Johnny Mandel with musicians like Gerry Mulligan, Art Farmer, and Red Mitchell.

Bang. There it was, the concordance between what I saw (the outer as well as the inner) and what I heard. The experience. Everything just 'was'. To experience the beauty, the stillness, and existence without relation to knowledge and references, to just be there in this, was an overwhelming experience.

Being, just existing—to let go of everything else and just be, here and now—is an experience that comes again in the following account from a light summer night.

(23H) Woman, middle-aged

One year some Maasai came to visit the Falu Folk Music Festival. At one point they were in an outdoor concert that consisted of a walk around a mere in the woods where there were different sorts of music with African origins along the path round the mere. I went out there and walked round the lake late in the evening and listened to the different musicians.

After midnight, the crowd started to thin out, and finally there were only about 20 or 30 people left on the shore. The sun started to rise, there were patches of mist over the lake, and you could hear a solitary drum from the other side. We who were left stood in a ring around the Maasai who themselves danced in a ring inside ours. Sometimes, one of them stepped inside the ring and did a solo dance that consisted of a lot of almost unbelievably high jumps with both feet together. We stood behind and breathed in the rhythm, the singing and their special, rather strong smell. After a while, they took us into the ring and we danced together with them. The steps in the ring were not difficult, but it was a rather unusual rhythm, but fairly soon we were just doing it automatically.

There was a fantastic atmosphere, meditative in some sense. It all connected into a total experience: the smells, the dance, the singing, the sandy beach, the drum on the other side of the lake, the mist, and the sunrise. It was an intense experience of being present, or of just 'being', existing. I don't know how long we danced, it must have been for at least half an hour, probably longer. It was sort of an experience beyond time.

(23I) Woman, middle-aged, 1980s

I quite often travel to the 'Music at Lake Siljan' festival. This time we had been to a concert in Rättvik. When it was over, we ran down to the long jetty on the shore of Lake Siljan to be in time for the *Electronic music in the summer night*, music by Ralph Lundsten. I hadn't really been interested in that type of music before, but curiosity has always been an incentive when it comes to seeking out new music.

When we got to the shore, the music was booming out of the loudspeakers. We sat in the sand down by the lake and suddenly I was in the midst of the music. The sun had set, and the sky flared up in the most fantastic colours, red, violet, yellow, orange, turquoise, blue.

The water was like a mirror. We were so far away from the road that the noise of the traffic didn't reach us. All the people sitting on the shore were quiet and still, nothing disturbed the experience. The music on the shore of the lake, the colours, the heat, the mood, all of this turned it into a total experience.

When the music faded away, we walked out to the end of the jetty. We didn't talk much but let the experience sink into our consciousness. To this day, I still get tears in my eyes when I think about that evening.

The sea is the common factor in the following accounts. The view of the sea at sunset, sailing on the open sea in wonderful weather, and music that fits the mood perfectly.

(23J) Woman, middle-aged, 1960s

My experience with music took place one autumn afternoon during a music lesson at a residential college beside the sea. The piece of music was Lars-Erik Larsson's *Pastoralsvit* [Pastoral suite]. The entire class listened. Before the lesson I had thought, music, OK, but I've always followed that with great interest. So, not really thinking so much about it, but curious, I took a seat.

But, goodness, what an experience. The sunset over the sea, with nature round about us in autumn colours, plus this powerful music. It felt as if I was lifted up by the music and floated freely. The surroundings in the classroom just disappeared.

Afterwards, I left the lesson as if in a trance. The music had opened my eyes. Suddenly I saw nature in a different way. The music experience had opened a door into the very core of my emotional life. Since then, I am very sensitive to charged, sensual, and powerful music. Always, when *Pastoralsvit* is played, I see the sea with the sunset before me.

(23K) Woman, old, 1950s

One July evening, we were ready to set sail in our boat out across the Baltic towards Gotland. A lovely sail during the night was waiting for us, it was a wonderful evening and we felt expectant about a whole month's holiday sailing. Our five-year-old son would be able to experience some real long-distance sailing for the first time.

After dinner I turned on the wireless and heard court singer Sigurd Björling singing Gustaf Nordqvist's '*Till havs*' ['Out at sea'] with his delightfully warm voice and real insight. The situation was perfect, so I absorbed the music more intensely than before. *It was just for us he was singing*!

Every time I have heard '*Till havs*' sung since then, but only by Sigurd or Jussi Björling, I have again experienced that delightful July evening with the wonderful array of colours over the sea and the wind playing in the sails. Of course, I had heard this song many times before, but this was the first time I myself was physically out at sea too.

(23L) Man, middle-aged, 1980s

My mates and I usually go sailing in the Baltic for a week or so. Now it was the second or third day of the week, the wind had calmed in the late afternoon and we had adapted ourselves to the calmer tempo and the unbelievably beautiful nature in our archipelago.

No telephones, no unpleasant noise. Nobody said anything. All you could hear was a cassette somebody had brought with them that was playing on the boat's stereo loudspeakers, just loud enough in the cockpit. The music was incredibly harmonious and with a close feeling of nature. What was so nice and made it such a lovely experience was that the music reflected the atmosphere, the beautiful nature, and the mood in which we found ourselves. Half-tired after the sail and in a relaxed holiday mood, I had goosepimples all over my body from the music. It felt like a massage, warm and soft inside. The music was very emotional, sometimes happy and positive, sometimes melancholy and a bit sentimental.

The actual feeling while the music was playing was as if time stood still. As if you lost the concept of time and space. Then when the music came to an end, it felt as if I woke up after having been asleep. For how long, I'd no idea. The music could have been playing for five minutes or six hours, I had no idea.

The music was Andreas Vollenweider on the LPs *Caverna Magica* and *White Winds*. One of the instruments he plays is an electrified harp. It's the changes in the music between optimism and melancholia that I think are so lovely. One part of the title melody 'Caverna magica' starts with a dripping sound that develops into a rhythm which then builds up all of the melodious content of the piece.

The bit that gave and still gives me the strongest feelings is the track 'The glass hall' from the LP *White Winds*. It starts completely quiet and is built up by a simple rhythm like waves that wash up against a shore. After a while, it turns into harp and flute. I can still get goosepimples and feel elated when I hear it.

From the open sea, we return to land. In the open air, the playing of loud wind instruments can be heard far and wide, and can lead to strange experiences. The same applies to the special singing technique called 'kulning', which was originally used to call cattle in from mountain pastures. Nowadays, kulning often occurs in different musical contexts.

(23M) Man, old, 1970s

Then an invitation came to what would become my great experience with music, namely participation in the Falun Folk Music Festival. We horn players, together with local singers who specialized in the difficult art of kulning, were going to perform something that was described in the programme as 'Herding music around Stång mere', the mere being a little lake outside Falun. The herding music consisted of the horn players responding with horn tunes to the girl singers' kulning calls, and we were all rather eager to hear the echo that would be the work's crowning glory. You could say that you are in the unique situation of being just as much a listener as a performer.

And that evening—or more correctly that night, because the performance didn't start until 23.00—you really could listen to what the programme described as 'herding music around a perfectly calm forest mere on a warm June night'. Everything went perfectly in the quiet summer night, with a silent crowd of listeners around the mere and a far from silent echo from the surrounding hills!

It is on such occasions you think that the silence sounds very nice for performers as well as listeners. It is virtually impossible to describe in words such an experience with music in nature's own concert hall—it has to be experienced on the spot! Somebody who wrote in the programme has, however, come quite close to what I want to say about this experience with the following words: 'the tones of the herding songs that rise in a tremble across a forest lake smooth as a mirror, eventually echoing from the distant blue mountain tops on the other side'. You experience in some way that the music had acquired yet another dimension, namely nature's!

There is no doubt that music has acquired yet another dimension—nature's—in the following experience with brass band music in a magnificent alpine setting.

(23N) Woman, old, 1980s

Was with my daughter and a couple of friends on a journey by car in Europe that summer. Tired of the big cities, the driving, museums, and exhaust fumes, we wanted to breathe clean alpine air and go walking on the last three days before our flight home. We arrived in idyllic St Johann in the Tyrol and experienced two wonderful days of hiking with sunshine, fresh air, silence—interrupted only by the sound of the cowbells in the distance. Peace and freedom spread within us and it felt lovely after all the cultural cramming. We breathed freely!

On the last day, a Sunday, the sky was overcast, drizzle hung in the air. We decided to do a walk anyway. From Kitzbühel, we took an extremely steep lift up to Hahnenkamm. It was the steepest we had ever experienced; the cabin hung—literally—between heaven and earth. When we stepped out onto solid ground, we were already getting butterflies in our stomachs at the thought of the journey down again. You were aware of it all the time, although nobody said anything about it. We cheered ourselves up and set off on a long walk in the drizzle. The clouds hovered around us and were like a thick mist between us and the views we knew to be there but couldn't see. Despite the weather, there were lots of people moving around up there.

The hours passed and rather unwillingly we made our way back to the lift. Suddenly we heard the music of brass instruments and its echo. We stopped and listened, surprised. Once we got back to the lift there was a long queue. We slowly moved forward in the queue and then the music was there again, now closer. When we reached the cabin, the doors were closed right in front of our noses. The cabin was full (must have been about 30 people) and it started off. We saw how the cabin passed the pylon at the drop, how it started to sway and then disappeared down the precipice. We felt it in our stomachs, and now had 25 minutes to live with that feeling while waiting for the next cabin.

The queue behind us grew longer, it was one of the last rides down for the day. I was getting the jitters all the more.

When the cabin came, we were squashed in right at the front. It was packed full. I thought that some latecomers arrived at the last moment. The doors were closed and this roomful of people started to move—at first slowly, then more quickly, and then came the *pylon*! Then some idiot pulls down the window on the entry door. You felt like shouting: 'Are you completely mad?' but then came the pylon and the bump and the entire cabin started to sway and weird noises erupted from most throats, a spontaneous expression of that terror in people's stomachs.

At the same moment you could hear a wonderful triad which dissolved into the simplest, but most wonderful melody I've ever heard! As if someone had waved a magic wand, the atmosphere of terror disappeared. After having experienced the terror individually— each standing there like a miserable little person, struggling—we were now transformed into a smiling congregation, and we smiled at each other, feeling safe.

The latecomers turned out to be three musicians and in the squash they had had to open the window to be able to play. They stood there with their instruments pointed straight up towards the sky (a trumpet, a French horn, and a tuba) and played what must have been Austrian folk tunes—sadly, passionately, lovingly. It was as if they found their way to these marvellous triads in mutual understanding, making slow little melodies and ending up with new surprising harmonies. They played out their love of the music, their pride in being able to play, and their debt of gratitude to this beautiful fairy-tale-like landscape.

I felt how the tears dropped down my cheeks; I felt as if I was right in the middle of a *holy moment in life*. It couldn't get any better than this! To be once again suspended in mid-air between heaven and earth and slowly but now wonderfully surely and safely be able to approach our planet. I have been present at a number of music events during my 60 years—from Papa's singing and playing when I was a child, to concerts of world-class level—but nothing has managed to captivate all of my being like this simple music conveyed as a gift of love during a 22-minute journey through the air.

When our cabin approached the ground, we had left the clouds above us and now had a clear view. Then we could see how all the people down there had stopped and were looking upwards, and how they all smiled and swayed in time with the music. Like a fortunate phoenix, our cabin landed so gently and elegantly that I'd never experienced a landing like it. When the four of us found each other again on solid ground, we cried openly and for a long time in a four-person hug, endlessly grateful for this shared final experience in the essence of music.

Two evenings earlier, we had heard the string soloists from the Vienna Philharmonic give a concert, and enjoyed it enormously. That was a first-class musical experience. But these last minutes we ourselves had had the privilege of living in the midst of the music and experiencing the *healing power* of music.

When the tears had stopped falling and I had come to my senses again, the three musicians were gone. It was too late to thank them. The experience was too great, too, to just be frittered away through small talk. But I went up to the station staff and asked them if it was usual to have music on the lift rides. It happened to be 'Music Day' in Kitzbühel, and on that day the town's musicians were divided among the various alpine peaks and played against each other at specified times; those were the 'echoes' we had heard.

Compared with the Vienna Philharmonic's perfect strings, the trumpet, French horn, and tuba were worn, dented, and not properly tuned, but what did it matter, when the soul of music was present? (Sorry, Vienna Philharmonic! We *really* enjoyed your concert! Incidentally, you can't compare them!)

Perhaps it isn't the big orchestras or the most skilful soloists who always give us the strongest musical experiences.

In a couple of accounts, a force of nature—thunder—cooperates with the music. Strangely, in both cases it is Beethoven's fifth symphony, with its motif of fate, which gets further accompaniment.

(230) Man, middle-aged, 1940s

One August evening when I was ten years old, my mother took me to a late-summer concert in the concert hall at Liseberg in Gothenburg. It was the first time that I was at a concert with an entire symphony orchestra, and I was full of expectation about hearing a massive orchestra sound instead of the pathetic sound that came out of our rickety wireless. The concert hall isn't there any longer, but it was built in the style of the Crystal Palace in London: an enormous nave covered with a half cupola—all in a slender construction of thin steel ribs and an enormous amount of window glass. It felt as though you were sitting out in the park, but you were indoors.

This particular evening, the Gothenburg Symphony Orchestra and France Ellegaard were performing Chopin's F minor concert as well as Beethoven's fifth symphony. The conductor was Sixten Ehrling who was then beginning to become a name in the Swedish music world. The Chopin concert passed without making any especially great impression. Ellegaard had a cold and went out and coughed and drank water between the movements.

During the break, I looked out of the windows and saw that a thunderstorm was building up. When we took our seats again to wait for the conductor to come in, the rain started to pour down in floods, as if a waterfall was landing on the roof of the concert hall. There were lightning and thunder in the distance, getting all the closer. At that moment, Ehrling came in to conduct the fifth symphony, a first time for me.

Now the thunderstorm broke right over our heads, and Ehrling waited until the worst peals of thunder had faded away. They he lifted his baton. So I was sitting there almost outdoors, subject to the whim of the forces of nature, as if it was raining on me and as if the lightning struck my head. The excitement was at its maximum. And at exactly the same tenth of a second that the first chord's emphasis came (ta-ta-ta-taaa) an enormous stroke of lightning hit the lightning conductor of the roof of the concert hall, followed by a simultaneous rumbling of thunder worthy of doomsday itself, which made the glass walls rattle. And when phrase number two, one tone step lower, came, the phenomenon was repeated. Here, nature was taking an active part in the music, was emphasized and expanded by the music (or vice versa: the music went outdoors and made use of the forces of nature to become even more charged).

This was something that was completely unparalleled that I have never before nor later experienced. The thunderstorm went on for almost the entire first movement. This 'fate' symphony pierced my very marrow and shook all of my inside. It felt as if my soul left my body and became one with Sister Music and Brother Thunder.

I remember that in the break between the first two movements, I felt I was perspiring all over my body. The thunderstorm moved away during the second movement, just in keeping with that movement's lighter character. I was still paying maximum attention to the music; I don't think that I missed a single note. The third movement's heavy dance got me to slow up and become a bit concert-restless like you do sometimes—stare at neighbours, at the way the conductor keeps time, at the interior decoration, etc. But the music still went right into my brain. And then the fourth movement with its reprises, especially of the first. I sat up dead straight and just sucked in every bar. Still to this day, in my memory I can reproduce the 'Fate' symphony in its entirety as I heard it the first time, with every accent, pause, dynamic shift, and so on.

After the concert I went to the artistes' dressing room to get Ehrling's autograph. I saw large pearls of sweat on his brow, he was chain-smoking, and his hands shook. Nowadays, I know that great musicians usually look like that when they have put their all into a performance, but at that time I thought that his experience was just as great as mine. We shared those feelings, and that belief amplified the overwhelming impression that music had given me.

When we came out from the concert hall, I felt physically as well as mentally loose-limbed and excited. Mum and I talked away as though possessed, continually interrupting each other all the way home. She had had an experience that easily equalled mine—perhaps the same also applied to our fellow listeners, who I thought looked unusually affected afterwards.

That is a version of Beethoven's fifth that one would very much like to have a recording of! One can imagine what Beethoven himself would have thought of this unique coincidence between the Fate symphony and nature/thunder.

We encounter something similar in the following account which, however, took place as far away from Gothenburg as you can get, in Australia.

(23P) Man, young, 1980s

[Written in English] It was autumn in Australia where I lived and nearing the end of the term. I had lots of homework most nights, and the night of this musical experience was no different. It was reasonably late and I had nearly finished my three-hour homework session. I was the only one awake in the house and I had the music on pretty softly. I realized that the piece of music that was on the radio was familiar to me. I wasn't too sure when it began or what exactly it was, but it made me listen and leave the homework desk for a more appropriate place to listen to music—lying on the bed. I wanted to hear more details of the music, so I put on my headphones and turned up the volume.

Outside my window there was an autumn storm. Having the headphones on meant that I could not hear the strong wind blowing through the trees or the rain falling on the roof. I was isolated from the storm and, instead, I was feeling this excitement and energy from the powerful surging music. I identified the music as being somewhere in the middle of Beethoven's masterful fifth symphony.

The idea of going outside and listening to the music was a result of the excitement and high that I felt. I had to do something. I couldn't just lie there and listen. It seems like a strange thing to do, but at the time it was necessary. I had to. So out I went and sat on the stairway that led into our garage, armed with my dad's big golf umbrella and Beethoven's tumult occupying my head. I sat still there for the rest of the piece.

It was magical. The music and storm seemed to be on the same wavelength. The reality of the storm was experienced by my physical body, but I could not hear the storm. That in itself seemed to put me in an unreal situation. I was isolated from reality by the 'unreal' sound in my ears. The music was more than in my ears, it seemed to resonate through my entire body.

I was taken to a greater place. I was experiencing this almost religious experience, something that was hard to comprehend then and just as hard to explain now, yet of great influence to me at that stage of my life. I suppose that I saw the power of music to evoke different emotions and take me away from reality. Playing scales, études, practice rooms, technique and examinations seemed far from this. Music became a feeling, an experience that I wanted to be a part of. It captured my interest in performing music and even awakened an interest in composing music myself. The night seemed to redefine my concept of music. I saw the forest, not just a clump of trees.

The unique combination of music and stormy nature felt magical, almost religious, and at a stroke gave the assiduous student quite new, 'higher' perspectives on what music can mean and achieve.

From the experience of music out in nature, we now turn to strong music experiences in different cultural settings.

CHAPTER 24

MUSIC FROM AND IN OTHER CULTURES

THE accounts in our material are for the greater part about experiences connected with various types of Western music. There are also, however, a number of accounts of unforgettable encounters with unfamiliar music from other countries or cultures. As a rule, it is a question of first-time encounters that have occurred during journeys or stays in other countries. In some cases, they have also taken place on home ground in Sweden.

First, a couple of accounts about music that individuals have come across in other parts of Europe.

(24A) Woman, old, 1950s

My most outstanding experience with music happened during a group visit in Greece. We were staying about 20 km outside Athens. My husband and I had decided to attend the Greek Orthodox mass in the Metropolitan Cathedral in Athens, which would be a new experience for us. It started at eight o'clock. The bus that we were going to travel on didn't come, and eventually we managed to get a black taxi. It was a lovely morning, and I was happy and expectant but also a little nervous since we were somewhat late.

Then we came into the light, wonderfully beautiful church, where the mass had already started. A male choir—were they priests or ordinary lay members?—sang with ethereal beauty. Suddenly, everything round about me became sunny, golden yellow. We walked slowly towards the front of the church, but I couldn't feel the floor, I just sort of floated in this sunny gold, enveloped by the singing and a strong feeling of joy.

Regrettably, the singing soon finished, and I was again standing on the floor. My immediate spontaneous reaction was: it must be like this in heaven, and then came great amazement at what had really happened. I wished that the choir would start singing again, which they eventually did (it is part of the mass), but the intense experience didn't come back.

We have been in Greece several times since then, and each time I go into a church there, somewhere within me I have a silly hope that I will experience the same again, and a certain disappointment that it doesn't happen. But the memory is there forever.

Among the reactions she describes, one notices the feeling of being in a special light, 'sunny, golden yellow'. Similar experiences of special light are also described in other places, for example in Chapter 7, account 7.3A, Chapter 16, account 16.3G, and Chapter19, account 19.1E. They are treated together later in Chapter 29, section 29.3.6.

In both the following accounts, the music was indeed familiar earlier, but it acquired a different character when it was performed and listened to in the country where it had been created. Besides, it was a special setting: the narrators were on a journey behind the former Iron Curtain.

(24B) Man, 1960s

It is a late-summer evening in Hungary, to be more precise in a large tourist hotel beside Lake Balaton. Ten years after the invasion and the country seems entirely paralysed and apathetic. We have been riding in the Hungarian countryside for eight days and got to see and experience the country off the ordinary tourist tracks.

Now it is our last evening in Hungary on this journey. We have just eaten a farewell banquet, and the Swedish group sits and enjoys Tokajer [a wine] to the accompaniment of the big gypsy orchestra's concert. The guests in the dining room are for the greater part high-ranking members of the occupying power, and you can see from the look on the faces of the staff that this is something they are forced to put up with.

It is my evening of my birthday, and I treat all the members of the orchestra to a drink and send over a few dollars as thanks for the excellent music. Then the devil grabs hold of me and I think: This is surely the right place to hear Liszt's Hungarian Rhapsody No. 2, isn't it? At the time, it was taboo to perform this in the country.

No sooner thought than done. I asked Primas to perform it. He gave me a long, slightly questioning look, but then he gave an affirmative nod and the orchestra performed this magnificent work. Among us Swedes, the women as well as the men, the emotions overflowed, and when we applauded raucously you could hear only one or two of the other guests applauding. There were tears in the eyes of many Swedes as well as the serving staff, and I just had to thank the orchestra with another round of Tokajer and a few more dollars.

(24C) Woman, middle-aged, 1960s

An experience that has remained unforgettable was a concert that our little tourist group attended in Leningrad [now St Petersburg]. In those days, trips to the Soviet Union were rather unusual, so it was a big adventure, which was experienced with mixed feelings. We were about 20 enthusiastic young artists, architects, musicians, and academics who wanted to experience something of what Russian culture had to offer.

Just across the street, opposite the old traditional hotel where we were staying, stood Leningrad's famous concert hall with its excellent acoustics. We made our way there one evening, and to our joy they had Russian music in the programme. First, they played a work by a young Russian composer we didn't know, who was present in person and was celebrated by the fairly small audience as best it could.

After the break, they performed Peter Tchaikovsky's Symphony No. 6, *Pathétique*. I've listened to that hundreds of times before, but never ever before like this. It felt like the first time, completely new, interpreted in the correct way, for me as well as for several of my friends. I knew, of course, about Tchaikovsky's tragic life, but here the music reflected more than that. All the melancholia and history of suffering of the Russian people was there in it, by the way also masterly expressed by Shostakovich later on. We sat fairly close to the orchestra; the whole time, the audience was very quiet, the atmosphere was charged. It felt as if the musicians were playing for us alone. I don't think the musicians were unaware of how moved and captivated the little Swedish party was. There was a breathless silence when the last notes of the diminuendo faded away.

We stayed behind a long time and applauded, and when we did finally, totally captivated, leave the hall and went back to the hotel, we couldn't go our separate ways but sat together for several hours and talked about the evening's experience.

The following experiences take place in an African or African-American setting. First an encounter with music that one can often hear even in Sweden, but of which the narrator has a totally different impression when she encounters it in a more genuine environment.

(24D) Woman, 1980s

A rainy September Sunday in New York. We were travelling around in a sightseeing bus with an American guide, chewing away on her chewing gum, who told us how dangerous it was for a white person to go around in Harlem and that we were not allowed to sneak away from her, because then she wouldn't answer for what might happen to us. Then the bus stopped together with many others in front of a large church. For some reason, there were lots of police officers outside, and it was raining heavily. We had been informed that we would be allowed the privilege of going in and that we must come out again quickly so that we didn't disturb the black congregation's religious service.

When we came in, everyone gave us friendly and happy smiles and they squeezed together so that there would be room for all of us. They were all dressed in their Sunday best suits and finest dresses with hats, and everybody sang. The entire church rocked to the most delightful gospel rhythms, in four places there was music—organ, percussion, trumpets and saxophones—and at least three choirs were singing too, the way gospel singers can make their singing appear so improvised. I thought at first that everybody was singing in their own key, but after a while it became so beautiful. Everybody in the congregation was singing as well, each in their own way, and me too. The entire church rocked and I cried, I who otherwise never cry however sad I am, but now I was crying from being in raptures. I could have murdered the guide when she waved to us to go out. I didn't ever want to leave.

After we got home, I said to my choir leader: 'Now I never again want to sing gospel or spirituals or listen to such music performed by Swedish singers.'

In the following account, it is again a matter of religious music, this time in Africa. A mixture of Catholic and African choir singing with a special vocal tone that takes the narrator by surprise and overwhelms her.

(24E) Woman, middle-aged, 1980s

That year, we were living in a little village in northern Zambia. We had been able to listen to lots of lovely African music, that is, singing in several voices with rhythm instruments, during our few weeks. As I sing in a choir myself, I was interested as well as impressed by the Zambian people's self-evident and seemingly natural way of singing in harmonies.

South of our village there was a Catholic boarding school for girls. One Sunday morning we cycled to the village so we could be there for Mass. 'The girls sing so well,' we had heard several Europeans say. Neither of us is religious, but being curious about the singing and the environment, we went there. I didn't have any expectations. Compared to the small huts we were living in, the building was impressive. Brick and glass—simple—but in our eyes big and mighty. A high ceiling, lots of light.

We sit right at the back and in front of us almost 400 Zambian girls sit in yellow cardigans and green skirts. The Catholic priest comes in and I hear one girl sing a verse, another start to drum on a hand drum—there is a muffled echo—and suddenly all the girls are singing. The music completely overwhelms me. The experience is so extremely strong that tears roll down my cheeks. The singing fills the premises. And me.

It is a sort of mixture of Catholic and African choir singing. Now, afterwards, it is difficult to describe the actual music. But I do remember clearly the nuances in the singing. The light, weak tone which intensifies into mighty music. The soloists with shrill voices and the entire choir that responds. The enormous sound of so many girls' voices singing so purely, thinly, lightly, glimmering—but also strong and full all the time as a single sounding body. (I don't know how many parts, at least four). No music sheets, no books. And the rolling of the drums. It is matchless.

But the experience was a 'religious' experience (what is a religious experience?). Filled. Blessed. Peaceful afterwards. I felt as if I was elated, elevated, happy (almost purified), strong.

Another experience in Africa, now in the hot dark African night in a paradise-like setting. Everything—the environment, the people, the music—fitted into the whole, and the young guitarist's insight in the music was total.

(24F) Woman, young, 1980s

I was living in Guinea-Bissau for a year, and during a holiday I was on an island where a Swedish family was living. One evening, we decided to go out for a walk. We enjoyed the hot night. When we had walked a little way, we heard music and decided to follow it. We came to a tree where five or six boys were sitting having a small party. One of the boys had a guitar and he sat there playing it.

He played wonderfully, and even though I didn't know the language especially well I managed to get him to understand that I wanted him to play more—and more. I have *never* seen anybody play so well and with such insight. Everything was just exactly right: the palms, the hot dark night, the smell of the sea, and the huts that you could see in the light from the fire. Even the rusty old iron bed that we sat on fitted into the whole picture! I quickly learned to sing the refrain to one of the tunes, it was a song to celebrate the island and Guinea-Bissau. And all the time I just sat there and watched his fingers that flew across the strings, and his face, which indeed wasn't beautiful but which spoke of how he enjoyed playing.

Afterwards I felt so full of the music and I envied him for his being able to play like that, I was full of admiration and longed for the next evening when he would come to the hotel and play for me, I had asked him in my broken Portuguese to come and he promised. I'll never forget the feeling I had when we sat there, and thinking back to the occasion makes me calm.

I love that island, it is a paradise on Earth. Everything is so basic and you feel that you are alive when you're there. Kids in straw skirts and old people wrinkled with age and very beautiful. And the friendliness!

Something that is especially associated with African music is drum rhythms. The rhythmic energy and the complexity can become completely overwhelming, shut out all other impressions, and inexorably push one's body to a climax, complete exhaustion—and total joy.

(24G) Man, young, 1980s (from an edited interview)

[He was invited to a village party. The music was played on drums by men from the village.] I am invited to dance, and start to do so. At first I am somewhat tense, but after a few tunes I relax and enter the music. I start to play with the rhythm, the beat and my own feet. It was so simple. The beat sort of drove me into it all. I was inside it, merged into one with it. You were their hands pattering the drums. It was, of course, the village men who played . . . but I was a part of it. I was completely captivated and I totally went in for it. All that existed was beat and rhythm.

The music starts calmly, then increases in intensity successively to then end in a special beat, in a sort of climax. There was such a raging tempo, you just kept going. I didn't think at all about what I was doing. Everything felt so natural . . . Sometimes a thought cropped up like: 'God, I'm so tired! Oops, I've splashed sand onto them!' But then it disappeared, was gone. Then you were inside it again.

It was so intense. There were no thoughts of anything else. I felt absent and understood that I had been that when at the end I became aware of the surroundings. I was so dreadfully tired, had lactic acid throughout my whole body. My limbs moved without my being able to control them. My muscles said: We can't manage any more now . . . but my head wanted to go on. My head won, pushed aside the needs of my body. What my body said didn't make any difference. It was a deal between brain, ears, and feet. Sometimes the body's needs came out on top. Then I was slightly aware of them, but the beat soon pulled me back in. My entire body moved to the beat, a pulse. It was the beat I danced with, the dream princess.

The end, especially, was an experience. It was as if you'd rehearsed it 100 times. It went off perfectly. You could feel how it was, what was going to be played in the next beat without 'feeling' the music. The beat accelerated all the time, at the final bit almost ecstatic, hectic, so fast that I just shook. I could feel that now it was the climax, it would come to an end and then *Bang!* Have taken the correct steps and am standing in a particular way with my arms out and legs apart. I have marked the end together with the drummers and one other person, a village man whom I don't notice until now. There was an ecstatic joy between us. We couldn't talk with each other, but knew that we had experienced the same thing. His eyes just sparkled and I too must have shone like a sun.

Afterwards, I was terribly tired, exhausted. My knees quivered, my muscles pulsated in some way, shook. I couldn't get my breath back again for I don't know how long. The dance had been so intense. I was totally worn out but I was as happy as could be. Afterwards it was a sleepless night. I was so affected by what had happened. I have never experienced such joy.

But one doesn't necessarily have to be there in Africa to have similar experiences. They can occur even on one's home ground, as can be seen in the following three accounts.

(24H) Woman, middle-aged, 1980s

[A mission church party with African music in a Swedish town] One of the last evenings, we arranged a party with music. Among the audience were a lot of people with their own experience of Africa, missionaries and foreign-aid workers. And it was a nice mix of different ages, many young people and young families with children.

After an introductory programme of songs and games, everything developed into letting spontaneous ideas take over. What happened was that all of this suddenly caught fire and started to live a life of its own. We just played as a part of something bigger that happened to us all. Songs and marimba music and drums and games and movement—they all just merged with each other. Different people slid in and out as active and as starting up the others. Sometimes it was only me, sometimes somebody else in our group, sometimes somebody from the audience. It wasn't important who it was. And it wasn't about deciding what would come next. It just happened. The border between artistes and audience was completely erased. What I felt was a total consensus and an intense shared pulse that lived through everything we did, even during a moment's break for a salad snack. Then we went on singing again, playing, clapping, and dancing. There was such an atmosphere that it could have gone on forever.

How long it actually did go on and how everything gradually wound down, I don't know, because the duration that was agreed had long since been passed and we were getting close to the forthcoming evening organ concert. We handed over responsibility to others in the group and disappeared into the church close by.

And here comes my second experience with music, totally impossible to remember anything. There was organ music all around me and the organist was said to have played exceedingly well, but it was totally wasted on me. I couldn't take in a single note. African rhythms were still pulsating in my body and were impossible to stop. It is as if I was immunized against all other sounds. It went on for several hours afterwards. I have never ever experienced music as intensely physically as that time, but many later occasions have felt like reminders of that feeling.

(24I) Man, middle-aged, 1990s

[African drum virtuosos playing at a folk music festival] The performance was something of a shock. I knew that my rhythmic ability is one of my strongest musical sides. Here I was standing like an idiot and couldn't even find the downbeat. After a long while, I managed to discern a structure in these rhythmic fireworks. Yes, now I found the downbeat—or, no, not where I had expected, but now—oops! there it was, just before I expected it. Two parallel metres at the same time, one in quadruple time, the other in sextuple time with a shared downbeat. Gorgeous! Now I had the plot for a while.

A drum soloist started up a pattering cascade that pulled my fragile metric base away. I was literally (!) about to lose my balance and fall over! A new soloist took over with the aim of portraying the first as a cowardly beginner. The bass drum rhythm was indeed an ostinato, but an ostinato that all the time sounded like a completely new pattern on account of the extremely complicated structure of the whole. Quite suddenly, I felt almost angry with myself. 'What sort of silly Western office type are you, standing here trying to count beats? You can't even manage that! Give up! Listen and enjoy it instead!'

No sooner said than done. The music became even more complicated and intense. I was filled with an incredible respect and subservient reverence when given the possibility of sharing an artistically highly advanced cultural heritage with a function that perhaps is the equivalent of Shakespeare or even Bach in our culture based on writing. At this stage, I was standing there as if petrified and just receiving. I felt that now the maximum has been achieved of what I emotionally can manage to take in. That's enough now. I can't cope with any more!

Then they increased the tempo.

My vocabulary ends here. It is meaningless to try to describe the feeling I had at that particular moment!

Later I have gone on courses in West African drumming and learnt how to handle and play polymetric phenomena such as 'four against three' and so on . . . but year after year at new courses it is the same story: after less than 10 minutes I'm standing there with my mouth open wide and groping around for a walking frame.

(24J) Woman, middle-aged, 1990s

I registered for a course in West African dance with a teacher and musicians with djembe, doun doun and marimba . . . The tempo was terribly fast and we danced for three hours, so that the sweat was pouring. The rhythms of the drums were so incredibly suggestive, and you simply *could not* disconnect from the music and try to think of anything else. The music really worked its way into my body and although I was so extremely tired I wasn't able to go and sit down and rest. It was a direct physical reaction to the music that I couldn't resist.

Lunch break, and we had a moment's rest. My pulse went up as I lay there and rested, the sweat poured off me and a very unpleasant nausea came over me. Everything just whirled around and my friends could hardly get through to me. In the end, I vomited and cried buckets. It felt as if all the worries in the world simply ran off me. One of the musicians came and asked how I was feeling and then he looked me in the eye and said—'It's magic, don't worry.' I understood nothing! Magic? Yeah, what next!

After I had been given some salt pills and drank lots of water I came to my senses and started to dance again. The days passed and my muscles were aching. The third day was really awful. The entire dance group seemed to have got out of the wrong side of bed, there was just a lot of hassle and most people were in a dreadful mood. I travelled home to my parents and sat there and cried all evening. I didn't know if I'd be able to cope with listening to even one more drum rhythm all my life.

That night, I slept better than ever before, and the next day I was so full of energy that I was almost glowing with it.

There is a totally different character in the setting and the experiences associated with classical Indian music in the following accounts.

(24K) Man, middle-aged, 1970s

An evening concert at a library in London. An Indian sitar master by the name of Imrat Khan is playing. No microphones or loudspeakers. You could have heard a pin drop in the room. The previous day, I had met a sitar player who was going to be my teacher for a short time, after having had a strong listening relationship to Indian classical music for many years without being able to play the sitar myself.

When I came out of the room after the end of the concert, I said to the person I was with that now I could die happy . . . What do I remember of the experience? Imrat Khan's combination of total musical mastery with a self-evident charisma of warmth and humour, that meant he could play on the verge of being inaudibly silent and everything could be heard. Quite simply I was happy. I wonder whether I have ever before met with the combination of virtuosity (in the true sense) and playfulness. I have certainly never afterwards had such an experience in any equivalent context.

(24L) Man, middle-aged, 1980s

It was during a seminar in Stockholm. An Indian sitar player was invited to demonstrate his instrument and its music. For some reason there was talk of the use of the sitar and other instruments in therapeutic contexts. One of the things our guest told us was how Indian music therapists work out a patient's 'personal number' before a treatment session is embarked upon. In Indian tradition, it is very important that these numbers are correctly related to the 'instrument number' that different musical instruments have. Put simply: it is important that the patient's 'oscillation' in is phase with the 'oscillation' of the instruments that they are going to play. Well, anyhow: there was considerable interest in what our guest talked about, and those present listened attentively.

When the seminar was about to end, we asked him to play something for us. He was happy to do so. Everybody made themselves comfortable, our guest tuned his instrument, improvised some note sequences and decided to play an evening raga.

I had never previously heard or seen a sitar in real life, but I particularly noticed the instrument's unusual timbre. In the half-dark room, notes were thrown out like silvered drops of rain. Everything seemed to be pervaded by it. Like carbon dioxide bubbles making their way through the liquid in a bottle of pop. An experience of almost tangibly physical nature: how these notes seemed to penetrate into your pores, expand your skin and then seek out again.

Unceasingly, as long as he played, I had a feeling of being lifted up and in some way purified. A sort of spiritual steam bath. On the way home from school, I carried with me a feeling of having been lifted and purified. And I felt in really good spirits.

(24M) Man, middle-aged, 1980s

It was at Shiv Kumar Sharma's concert in the Berwald Hall, Stockholm. What struck me first was how small Shiv Kumar Sharma looked. I was almost starting to become worried that the santor wouldn't be heard in the large hall. But that worry disappeared when he started to play. I was surprised by how the fairly weak and tinny tone could fill the hall with such force.

After he had finished tuning his instrument, he looked out into the audience and told us that he was going to play raga Kirvani. Then he paused for quite a long time, and it was absolutely silent in the full concert hall. There was a very peaceful and expectant atmosphere. Slowly and tentatively, he started his alap. Bit by bit, he pulled out the notes of the raga. Started to sink down and rummage among the bass notes and then slowly made his way up the scale, finally to end up in the higher regions. In the usual way, created tension by letting the audience wait for a long time for high Sá (the basic note), by staying at the note before (Ni) and by just touching on Sá or even brushing against Ré (the note above Sá). The tension was heightened and finally relieved when he at last reached Sá. The process became even more tangible when the same approach was repeated around the Pá note, which is the most important note in raga Kirvani and is the equivalent of G if the basic note is C.

Then he gradually increased the tempo, and the pulse came into the music, which intensi-fied in a matchless fast tempo and crescendo. What captivated me was how despite the fast tempo you could still distinguish every note. The crystal-clear playing is characteristic of Shiv Kumar Sharma. The tabla playing was also unusually homogeneous and in concordance with the santor playing.

I understood what force there can be in music. That you don't need a loud instrument to produce that force. Rather, the force comes from the music itself and what it conveys. In the mood and feeling that are in the music.

The strange thing is that when I experienced this and sank into the music, it was as if I felt what was going to come just a moment in advance. As if the music was already there. In such a way that Shiv Kumar just pulled the notes down for us, like a sort of intermediary for a world of music that was already there. Or however one ought to express that? Sometimes you get a feeling that the music flows out by itself, without any previous thoughts or planning and that the musician puts himself in a special state to become a part of that flow. Or perhaps musicians put themselves in the state to create the flow.

There was an indescribable elevated clarity in the music. An enormous force despite the weak and tinny tone. At first, I felt calm, relaxed, and elevated, then came melancholy dream images with mountainous landscapes and people who worked in the fields down in the valleys. Towards the end, an absorption into the musical events as if everything hap-pened by itself. Really this is too hard to describe in words. Afterwards, I felt purified, as if my soul had been given nourishment.

All three narrators express their admiration for the masterly musicians and are fasci-nated by the strange tone of the instruments and by how the quiet instruments could still be heard very clearly in all passages, even at a high tempo. The clarity depended, of course, on the skill of the musicians but to a certain degree on the fact that the audience was completely silent, which in turn was certainly caused by the actions and attitude of the musicians. Afterwards, one felt elevated and purified, happy. The last narrator could, by virtue of his previous knowledge, follow how the music was built up. This might be connected with his experience of knowing in advance what would come next—as if the music was already there waiting to be pulled out by the musician, as if everything happened by itself.

These experiences of classical Indian music did, of course, take place outside India, in London and Stockholm respectively. The following accounts are examples of expe-riences that took place during journeys in the country where the music belonged, namely China.

(24N) Woman, middle-aged, 1970s

Chinese music is for the greater part alien to us. Its notes and scales are different, in some degree exciting, in some degree just weird. But there are small, presumably very propagan-distic flute pieces from the 1960s and 1970s that have a special place in my heart, and what I want to describe is the first time I heard such a piece.

One summer in the 1970s, I travelled together with other students on the trans-Siberian railway to China. The journey through the enormous Soviet Union was long and some-times strenuous, and with lots of bureaucratic difficulties. After almost a week on the train we reached the Chinese border and, of course, had to make a long stop for the border formalities and to change to a train suited to the width of the Chinese rail tracks. But it felt as if a lot of other things changed too. Everything opened up and became simpler. Smiling, rosy-cheeked Chinese wanted to help us instead of making everything difficult for us (as we had experienced in the Soviet Union). And I do believe that the sun shone brighter too!

Eventually, our train chugged away, pulled by a powerful steam locomotive. Behind on the platform stood happy, waving Chinese friends and—at last comes the experience with music—from blaring loudspeakers suddenly this for me completely overwhelming flute music pours out. It is happy but with a touch of melancholy, fast and exciting, melodically simple for me as a Westerner to take in and yet in its construction quite distinct as to its country of origin, this is China that pours out to me in the form of music.

I become happy and tears come to my eyes, and I am filled with the harmonies, the notes, long after we have chugged out of hearing. From a technical point of view, the reproduction was a catastrophe, both the recording and the loudspeakers were dreadful, but it doesn't matter the slightest, because, ever since, I carry this music and this moment in a place all of its own in my heart. Flute music like that was played here and there during our journey around China and I bought a record with it to take home. But I don't really need to put it on, the music is within me anyway and it warms me from within.

(240) Man, young, 1980s

During a visit to China, we were invited by an elderly Chinese to a Chinese folk music performance in Chengdu, in Sichuan province. After a walk of about an hour, we came to a tea house where we were invited to sit in a large room with about 200 elderly men dressed in blue. That evening they were performing tasima music, which is named after the main instrument called a tasima. It has a thousand-year history and is reminiscent of our zither. The other instruments were all unknown to me but they stretched from bass to soprano.

The theme for the evening was a well-known musician who had died 55 years ago. They explained to us that this was typical for this type of music, and besides they honoured the person concerned by writing his name and some poems on the wall behind the musicians. We sat expectantly on our wooden chairs and didn't know what was going to happen.

The musicians took their places and sat down. They started to very carefully sound their instruments, while they also joined in the harmony with their voices. Very slowly from a weak beginning, all the instruments and singing voices moved to a powerful ecstatic peak, and then to total silence. The listeners applauded with delight, but we couldn't really understand why.

The evening continued in the same style and for a long time it was hard for us follow the nuances and we didn't understand when we should applaud or cheer with delight. But as the evening progressed, we learnt to appreciate the nuances and the idea behind the musical experience for these people—it was simply basic emotions that were stirred up and this was done very skilfully. And that wasn't surprising, considering that the music had rehearsed for many thousands of years.

After about three hours listening and tea drinking, we left the premises with a very strange feeling of liberation, that is, all this emotional manipulation had made us harmonious and we had a very strong feeling of well-being.

After this experience, I have a completely different view of music, listening as well as performing. Music has acquired a much more distinct place as an international means of communication. We sat there, two Swedes, and understood exactly what the musicians meant even though we spoke completely different languages and had completely different cultural backgrounds.

The following two accounts are connected with South East Asia in various ways. The first is about an encounter with gamelan music from Indonesia.

(24P) Woman, old

It was while I was stationed in Holland. At weekends, I used to travel over to the beautiful old town of Leiden where there is a unique ethnographic museum, filled with treasures that the Dutch had taken with them from Indonesia. You can spend hours there walking around admiring incredibly skilfully made jewellery, costumes, and weapons. For me, the most fascinating was the big gamelan orchestra. If I say that it was a great musical experience, then it wasn't of an immediate one-off character—no, it was necessary for me to return again and again and sort of grow into the music. With extremely small rhythmic and melodic shifts, this music goes on hour after hour—in the end you almost find yourself in a trance and can't tear yourself away.

I came to this music with 'clean ears', so to speak, that is, I had no knowledge of it and no preconceived ideas. So it went right in—there were no barriers. You could say that one's senses expanded. I realized how endlessly multi-faceted and shifting music is. I believe that the experience of Indonesian music has contributed to my now being able to take in contemporary music too, that is, listen totally without any preconceived notions.

The music in the following account is indeed Swedish, but it is performed and listened to in a totally different environment, in Laos. A musical encounter across all borders.

(24Q) Woman, middle-aged, 1990s

It is January. The place is the old capital in Laos, Luang Prabang. Together with my folk music team, I have been in this beautiful country for about a week. We have been able to experience the country's beauty from the inside as well as the outside by looking around in the countryside and meeting different people and singers in the country, and enjoying their generous, friendly, polite way of being. In Laos, they are not rich in money, but rich in life. They are very proud of what they have in all simplicity. Their homes often consist of huts but they are well looked after. The tempo is calm—if you don't have time today, you'll have time tomorrow or another day. It didn't take many days before we, too, melted in, in this easy-going, comfortable tempo—there was no point in hurrying because we wouldn't get more done if we did!

We had visited the town on a couple of days and among other things had a concert and party together with the town's musicians. Our team leader knew a music teacher in the town from before, so his house became a meeting place. This last morning in the town is something I will remember for a long time. We go into the house carefully and quietly—people like to be careful in Laos. We sit down on the floor and are offered some dried fruit.

Our team leader starts to play the [traditional Swedish drinking] song 'Nu alla goda vänners skål!' ['A toast to all good friends!'] on the violin. Mr Ponsay takes his violin and starts to play too. It is otherwise silent in the room, nobody says anything. We others just listen.

After a while, our leader starts to sing the song while Mr Ponsay plays. The atmosphere in the room is enchantingly tense, really magical. The hairs on my arms stood on end. The world suddenly becomes really tiny when you're sitting far away in Asia and listening to an old Swedish song played by a Laotian musician and sung by a Swede. Music really can build bridges!

In itself, this is not a giant musical experience as regards volume, audience, professional musicians, and so on, but for me, a person who quite often both plays and has experiences of music, this is clearly one of the greatest. It really grabbed hold of my soul and got stuck deep inside me. It is many years ago that we were there, but I can still almost smell the odours, the heat—both in the air and that which was spread in the room when the music joined together our two continents. How fortunate one is to have been a part of this!

When they had finished playing, we said goodbye and went to the hotel. I was completely possessed by the music and the feelings it had conveyed. One might well ask how such a simple song could give such an experience. I think it was the entire context. We were far from home and the usual security. We had each other and the music to rely on. That the two musicians played together meant that I felt even more fellowship with the people and the music. I am not sure that it would have been the same experience if the situation had been similar but had taken place in Sweden.

Further examples of strong experiences with music from other countries and cultures are found in an account about Turkish folk music (Chapter 15, account 15.1C) and an account about experience of flamenco music (Chapter 16, account 16.1I). Other accounts that haven't been included concern experiences of Portuguese fado singing, Italian bagpipes (zampogna), launeddas players from Sardinia (launeddas is a sort of triple clarinet), male choirs from Georgia and rhythmically complex Latin American music.

The accounts in this chapter show that unknown music from other cultures can give just as strong experiences as familiar music from one's own cultural circle. With the support of these accounts, one can thus, to a certain degree, speak of music as a way to communicate across cultural and other borders. But, at the same time, in many other cases there are descriptions of uncomprehending reactions in the face of music from another culture, as well as the fact that the music we are familiar with can seem totally alien to people in other cultures.

The question of whether there are general features in all music the world over, so-called universals, is both intricate and controversial. There is, as yet, no clear answer to that question.[1]

CHAPTER 25

MUSIC AT CONCERTS: CLASSICAL MUSIC

As one might expect, many strong experiences with music take place at concerts. There have been several examples of this already in the chapter about experiences during one's teens (Chapter 5, sections 5.1 and 5.2). Hereafter, they are for the greater part the experiences of adults at concerts of classical music (this chapter), jazz (Chapter 26), and pop/rock (Chapter 27).

Concerts of classical music usually take place in concert halls, churches, opera houses, and theatres, sometimes in other settings too. The following accounts most often concern experiences of well-known works within Western art music, but the situations vary a great deal. It might be a matter of a first-time encounter with music that was completely unknown to the narrator, or music that one has heard about and that has aroused curiosity, or music one has heard earlier without it having made much of an impression.

This chapter starts with accounts in which the experience is primarily ascribed to the music itself (section 25.1). These are followed by accounts in which the experience is primarily associated with the artiste who performs the music (section 25.2). Naturally, there is some overlap between these two categories.

25.1 EXPERIENCES OF THE COMPOSITIONS

In this section, there is a series of accounts of strong experiences at concerts. I have grouped them based on similarities regarding which music occurred or based on similarities in the reactions described. But, naturally, the accounts can also be read in a different order if one chooses.

In the introductory accounts, it is above all the power of a large symphony orchestra—the loudness, the volume, the wealth of timbres—that overwhelms the listeners. In the first example, it is primarily the brass section and the timpani that enchant the narrator and give rise to shivers. The visual impression of the orchestra, one of the finest in the world, and the magnificent auditorium add to it all.

(25.1A) Man, middle-aged, 1960s

As a young student on a journey I had stopped in Salzburg during the last week of the festival and managed to get hold of tickets to a matinee with the Vienna Philharmonic in Grosses Festspielhaus. All of this meant that my expectations were highly wound-up. The concert was to be conducted by Georg Solti and the programme contained works by Beethoven and Brahms that I knew well.

The surprise, however, was the introductory item, a piece that was totally unknown to me, *Sinfonietta* by Leoš Janáček. He was an almost unknown name for me then, I only had a vague idea that his music was 'semi-modern'. I read somewhat distractedly in the programme sheet about the sinfonietta and one of the things I noted was that it had nine trumpets. The sight of this huge orchestra, above all the brass section, was impressive, not least in this magnificent hall.

Already the urgent fanfares and the timpani entrances in the first movement of the sinfonietta completely enchanted me. What a timbre! Shivers of sensual pleasure ran down my back in a steady stream. The following three movements, too, are of course full of wonderful music in a delightful orchestral guise and went straight into my heart. The last and fifth movement started with a slightly uneasy and tentative section. Then, suddenly, the trumpet fanfares from the first movement came in again and that music was repeated in its entirety, but besides the brass and the timpani all the other voices in the strings and woodwinds played as well in wonderful big trills to back up the fanfares. Now, a little discreetly, I simply had to lean forward in my seat to leave the way free for the shivers to run down my back.

After the sinfonietta I was completely exhausted. When the next work on the programme started I was still totally captivated by the previous piece. I noted only at an intellectual level that now they were playing Beethoven, but not until well into the first movement did I begin to be able to follow along.

This narrator was evidently very knowledgeable about music; he is precise as to which instruments do what in which passages, and what it sounds like. The next narrator describes the music in rather more general terms: it is majestic, grand, beautiful. He is so moved that he feels 'obliged' to clearly demonstrate his feelings and appreciation.

(25.1B) Man, middle-aged, 1970s

The music was performed in an aircraft hangar where the acoustics were actually extremely good for music. It was Dvořák's 'From the New World' that I was hearing for the first time. The Swedish Radio Symphony Orchestra conducted by Sergiu Celibidache. Went there with open ears and eyes. Time, place, and a live symphony orchestra meant a lot in terms of my expectations.

It was a very strong experience that I perceived with completely 'pure' ears and in which the melodies, the harmonies, the instrumentation, the timbres overwhelmed me. I experienced it with strong and positive emotions that I thought must correspond to what the music gave me. It felt majestic, grand, beautiful, and great. I took it in at once, a completely unconditional listening and perhaps quite simply pleasure in its beauty, its drama. Emotionally, it gave me a lot of positive self-confidence, it moved me very much and obliged me to show a counter reaction. It set forces into motion that meant that when the symphony was over I was absolutely the first to start very enthusiastic applause. I must have managed to get at least half of the audience with me in applauding.

But there was one movement left . . . This meant that the experience of the last movement was different from the previous movements. The concentration and the keenness in the listening were not the same as in the beginning. The experience of the same music changed very quickly and didn't have the same positive power that it had in the beginning.

At concerts of classical music one is indeed generally expected not to applaud until the entire work (symphony in this case) has reached the end. A notable exception is, however, an opera audience, which often rewards a singer with applause after a well-sung aria. At jazz concerts, every soloist gets his or her applause, and at pop/rock concerts there are no limits to reactions of various types.

In the next account, it is the force in the orchestra and the sight of committed musicians which entirely absorb the listeners and even cause them not to start up the applause until after a marked pause.

(25.1C) Man, young, 1980s

To go and listen to classical music wasn't one of my habits at all. The reason that I ended up there was a music course which included a visit for study purposes. The pieces in the first part of the programme, I can't remember at all. I thought it was monotonous and boring.

But it was when the orchestra started to play something by Ravel that things started happening. They started to play with an unusual glow (it was probably a rewarding, lively piece) and their movements became freer and all of them seemed to strive in the same direction. I could see from the musicians' faces that they became moved, eyes wide open, smiles being exchanged. It was like a meltdown, one thing led to another, and the volume of the music must have bordered on a record high in art music contexts.

As for myself, I wasn't thinking at all, in contrast to now when I must find a way to describe this absolutely special liberation in words. My whole body was a part of the music, physical shock waves from the timpani hit me in my midriff, my feet and hands moved in time with the pulse and my eyes sucked in the movements of the musicians and the instruments. It was a joy to do all this. A wholeness that was continually confirmed with every visual impression and was conveyed further to the people sitting on either side of me, who, in turn . . . It was a mass phenomenon, nobody in the hall could have missed being affected in some way.

After the final chord, at first there was complete silence. I myself felt an incredible surprise that it could come to an end, and at the same time I was struck by the insight into the existence of everyday life. Because I had in fact been completely unaware of it for 15 to 20 minutes. The others had probably also had something to think about, but after a marked pause the audience stood up, everybody, and applauded wildly and cheered. The conductor beamed with all of his sweaty face and before long played the last movement again, and there were several encores and endless ovations, bows and calls. It was as if all barriers had been opened, the joy of life that perhaps must be kept under control in everyday situations so as not to create an imbalance now overflowed without hindrance in the orchestra and your neighbours in the seats on either side. You won't meet either of them tomorrow, and thus it entails no responsibility. We are all free in relation to each other, which I believe is an important condition for strong experiences of happiness. Happiness makes the individual extremely vulnerable and provides a weapon for conscious as well as naive combatants. A certain feeling of happiness stayed with me until I fell asleep, but it was blurred with sadness on account of its ethereal origin.

His reactions are described on several different levels: physical (shock waves to his midriff, movement in hands and feet), cognitive (total absorption, no thoughts, no time), emotional (unrestrained happiness/joy, liberated from usual control of one's reactions) and social (mass phenomenon, collective audience reaction). Afterwards, too, a reflection on the preconditions for experiences of happiness.

Several of these reactions also occur in the next account. Committed musicians produce music which grows to an 'ocean' of notes that embrace the listener and culminate in a triumphant final chord. The music fills the narrator with energy, almost lifting her up out of her seat. The feeling of happiness is mixed with wonder at her own reaction.

(25.1D) Woman, middle-aged, 1980s

I was at the Concert Hall to listen to the Philharmonic Orchestra when they performed the symphonic poem '*I pini di Roma*' ['The Pines of Rome'] by Respighi. I had never heard, or heard of, this piece of music.

During the introduction to the concert I was totally absorbed by the person who sat beside me and didn't pay any attention to the music at all. Suddenly the lights were dimmed in the hall. This was the first external sign that attracted my attention. I perceived a vibrating, pulsating, unobtrusive rhythm which slowly increased in loudness. All of a sudden I became expectant and paid attention to the conductor with his large head of curly hair. I noted that he had the classic look of a conductor and thought that I could also sense a deep concentration in him. Suddenly I also saw the musicians on the stage and perceived in them a keenness and an intense eagerness to convey something. The music became all the louder and suddenly I felt an immense joy and wonder, and a joy at feeling so in wonderment! Questions and exclamations like 'Goodness, what is this?' arose within me without my necessarily having any intention of interpreting the reaction. I discovered that I liked the feeling of being surprised.

Suddenly brass instruments could be heard 'as if by magic' in all directions on the balconies around the auditorium, and what had recently seemed to have reached its zenith further increased in force and intensity! The sound effect that arose gave me the feeling of being sucked into a heaving *ocean* of notes/music. I experienced that the will to say something was so strong in the music itself that it became irrepressible for the conductor as well as the musicians and the listeners. While the music further increased in force and intensity, I got goosepimples on my arms and I felt as if a new energy filled me. I remember that I held tightly onto the armrests of the seat as if otherwise something would lift me up out of it.

The music ended in a *triumphant* final chord. After this ending, all of the audience in the full concert hall stood up without hesitation and applauded and cheered (for me, this scene too became a part of the total experience). The conductor came onto the stage several times, shook hands with the musicians, bowed, waved the score high above his head and kissed it time after time.

Certain events in life become engraved in your memory and this was one of those.

The great works of religious music include Bach's Passions, which occur in several accounts. Here is one of them.

(25.1E) Woman, middle-aged, 1960s

It was Easter time and I was going to listen to the *St Matthew Passion* in Engelbrekt Church in Stockholm. It was the Radio Choir under Eric Ericson who were singing and, as usual, Birgit Stenberg sang the alto part. The evangelist was van Kesteren, a really fantastic voice. Erik Saedén sang the Jesus part. I must have been about 16 years old. A teenager who often felt lonely, perhaps because she was so alone in her school form with her interest in music.

I remember the solemn feeling of being there on such an evening. The church pew was hard, but you could feel some sort of peaceful tranquillity. Then when the first bars started with their gentle strings, calmness came—great calmness. Yes, and then I remember the feeling of happiness—how it gushed and bubbled within me. To be able to follow on that 'journey' was a great experience then. I admired Eric Ericson for his safe hands, his movements. This particular evening, my insight was total. I flew along in the wonderfully beautiful choir parts—was pulled into the voices and felt a great joy. It was as if I was no longer sitting in the pew but rather had risen high above it. In the shorter, aggressive choir parts, my body was roused and I suppose my strong teenage urges found expression.

When the solo parts came, well, then came the tears. The serious, wonderfully beautiful alto voice was gold, I thought. Oh, how I admired that voice, but I also understood the joy in singing such a part. Van Kesteren sang with such insight and his strong expression was fascinating—his voice spoke to me in some way.

So I was flying too, enjoying the light voices—like silver—of the boys' choir, and the solos, recitatives, and choir parts were like stations for me, but I kept on flying. The choir parts particularly gave me raptures. I felt the tension and the release, but also the springiness. That evening there was extra 'springiness', I thought, and the experience of being completely lifted from the pew where I sat was really great. When we came to the final choral, the security and calmness came back to me. I had travelled quite far and felt comfortably tired.

When it was all over I had difficulty getting up, leaving my safe place, leaving the incredibly beauty. All the way home, the music was in my body, I didn't want to let go of the experience and thus found it hard to talk afterwards. But both the music and the experience stayed there and even the next day I could feel an incredible happiness. It was a feeling of freedom for me, which led to my wanting to play and learn all about Bach's music.

This account could also have been placed in Chapter 7, Merging with the music. Her insight into the music is total, and her feelings follow the changes in the music. She also describes how it feels being lifted from the pew and flying along in the music (see Chapter 8, section 8.1).

The next narrator also felt how she 'lifted from the pew' listening to Verdi's *Requiem*.

(25.1F) Woman, young, 1980s

It was winter and dark outside. The concert I was going to attend was in the Church of the Holy Trinity and it was Verdi's *Requiem* on the programme. The church was full and there was an atmosphere like at the early service on Christmas morning.

We sat expectantly and waited for the concert to begin. I was bothered as usual by having to sit so close to others in the rather squashed church pew. I forgot this the very second the music started. Slowly but surely a concentration was created with a stillness that spread throughout the church. It was so beautiful and moving.

When the first part turned into the second, I shut my eyes and the music took hold of me. I think it was at Dies Irae that I got close contact with the music. It flowed towards me and it knocked and hit me in a comfortable way. I couldn't distance myself and listen to the music. I remember that I received that feeling calmly and let it take hold of me. I got the creeps from my head down along my backbone, and I felt how I lifted from the pew in time with the music, exploding in a fantastic climax. I got to experience this wonderful and liberating feeling several times during the concert when similar bits were played by the orchestra.

After the concert, I felt purified and deeply moved. I often listened to Verdi's *Requiem* after the concert and felt that the piece was like a purifier for me. The feeling that was released when I listened was a comfortable melancholy and at the same time a feeling of lightness.

During a conversation with a good friend, he mentioned, in passing, occasions when you leave your body. Laughing, I told him about a teacher we had had who claimed that it was possible to fly after several years of studying meditation. At the same time, though with some hesitation, I told him that I remembered hovering in the church and realized that it was possible. It was just too fantastic to be real. After letting go of unimportant intellectual proofs of whether what I experienced was true or not, I feel and remember very clearly what I experienced on the occasion of the concert. I took off!

Verdi's *Requiem* features again in the next account of a concert in the same church on a different occasion. Here too, the enormous power of the music is emphasized, especially in the Dies Irae movement, but also in other parts with stillness and beauty. The music gives feelings of relief and purification.

(25.1G) Man, old, 1970s

Gävleborg Symphony Orchestra gave a concert at the Church of the Holy Trinity with the *Missa da Requiem* by Verdi. Of course, I had heard Verdi's *Requiem* before, but on the radio and without paying special attention. My expectations before the concert were great. We were there in good time to get good seats. I always like to combine listening with visual impressions.

For us and our friends, the concert became an enormous experience—the sound of the orchestra powerful in the church, the soloists in superb form, the choir professionally knowledgeable. Many a time I have been moved by music and performances. But this concert exceeded everything I had experienced up to then. All of my being was affected by an internal revolution. The music, the text, the soloists, the vibrations in the pews, floor, walls of the big church, all of this contributed to an incredibly moving experience.

Afterwards it was off home for us, for some food. There we stood, three grown-up men each at a window, and more or less cried from the musical experience that the memory of the music in our minds still aroused in us.

What was it that achieved this strong emotion, which I can recall still to this day? Certainly I was influenced by the strong entrance of the timpani together with the rest of the orchestra and the choir in the Dies Irae movement. But it was the Rex Tremendae Majestatis movement that was the definite knock-out for me. As a written commentary to the work puts it: 'As the tremendous phrase dies away, each of the soloists, starting with the bass, sings the key phrase of the section to the words 'Salva me, fons pietatis' ('Save me, O fount of mercy'), joined afterwards by the chorus. This fervent prayer reaches a great emotional climax and ends touchingly with a final quiet plea'. Yes, exactly, 'great emotional climax'! And later came the Offertorium, extremely moving and relieving at the same time. For me, the theme 'Save me' in Rex Tremendae and the main theme in the Offertorium lived on in my mind for a long, long time, came and went, always emotionally moving.

We encounter completely different music—calm, meditative, almost still—in the next account. It also contrasts strongly with all the other music that was played in the same context.

(25.1H) Man, middle-aged, 1980s

I was attending a festival for contemporary music. It was incredibly exciting and gave me many ideas. It is of course often specifically from avant-garde music that new movements and musical ideals grow up. I do not, however, think that much of what was played will find a place in music history in exactly the form it was performed there.

I was convinced of that until I went to a concert by Ensemble des XX Jahrhunderts from Vienna. They ended their concert with a 30-minute piece by the Estonian-born composer Arvo Pärt, *Tabula rasa*, which is a concerto for two violins, 'prepared piano' and large orchestra.

Then came the metamorphosis and what gave me one of my very greatest experiences with music. Gone were the shrieking tones, experiments to break all bounds, tonal as well as rhythmical. This was 'pure' music, completely clear and beautiful. At one and the same time, a rare mix of Russian Orthodox church music deriving its origin from centuries ago and contemporary modern tones that one has never heard before. It was music that one has heard many times before, while at the same time never having heard anything like it. All the time, the orchestra played pure and beautiful notes, the string soloists embroidered upon this and it was accompanied by the 'prepared piano' which brought forth sounds that were more like gongs or church bells.

From the very first note, I heard that something new had come. At first, I was surprised and wondered what it was, but then I enjoyed it such as I had rarely done before. I wandered off in dreams when I heard the almost meditative music, and despite the fact that it is very calm and 'static', I could hardly sit still. The music in all its simplicity made me follow along in the rhythmic course with all my body.

As a string player, I always listen to how the string musicians play, what technique they have, how they solve difficult technical passages, and so on. But there was nothing of this now. *I just listened to the music.* No technical reflections, no other shallow thoughts that disturbed the musical experience itself. I think that it is this music's completely new expression, mixed with this very strong support in traditions, that made such a strong impression on me. When the last slow movement had been played, I sat with tears in my eyes and would most of all have liked there not to have been any applause at all. Just silent meditation.

Music that one thinks one has heard many times before but that nevertheless has no comparison. Arvo Pärt's music is like no other.

A professional disease of many musicians is that they often focus on their colleagues' way of performing the music, their technical skill, their way of handling the instrument, phrasing, and so on, to the detriment of their own experience of the music itself. But now and then, as in this case, the music gains the upper hand and absorbs all attention: '*I just listened to the music.*'

The next narrator, another musician, was also aware that the musical craft can stand in the way of the experience. But here, too, the music gained the upper hand, by its own force, its experienced relation, and in combination with the memories it called forth.

(25.1I) Man, middle-aged, 1960s

It was the first time I got to hear Shostakovich's String Quartet No. 8. It happened in a not particularly impressive concert hall one early autumn evening. I didn't know much about Shostakovich's music. I could read a little bit about the quartet just before the performance and also a short description of the content of the music. I already knew something about the victims of war, I had read about it in school, seen it in cinemas, and besides, as a child I had myself experienced air-raid sirens and a bomb shelter.

String music felt close for me since I was a string player myself, but at the same time I had perhaps already begun to be a bit 'destroyed'—my own experience of the actual craft of playing sometimes came between the music and me. For example, I would notice technical details, how to shape each note and, so on, when listening to music, and this could be disturbing and distracting. I was aware of this and before the evening's performance perhaps felt some extra tension.

But I soon forgot all of this. I became absorbed in the music, and felt as if I was being carried along on waves. The musical language was new, but in some way familiar at the same time. It was extremely close, as if it was my own. Then memories started to surface. Experiences from the bomb shelter, the darkness, the dampness of wet steam and the body heat of someone who sat right next to me in the bomb shelter. I recognized the smell, the temperature, the fear.

And it was precisely with the fear that something happened—as if it began to be transformed at the same time. It was—but at the same time, it wasn't. I got over the fear in some way. It acquired a new dimension for me, it didn't frighten me, I felt that I became strong and that it was an intense feeling of liberation.

I don't have any memory of how the concert ended. However, I do know how I walked for hours afterwards on the streets with a feeling of timelessness, fellowship and gratitude. I was on my own, but felt like one of many who wouldn't allow themselves to be affected by fear, that it wouldn't happen again. I was a sort of 'world citizen' who was walking and crying in the rain . . .

The experience went far beyond the moment when the music was heard. The fear was replaced by an intense feeling of liberation—this horror would not happen again—gratitude, and fellowship.

Shostakovich's music is often strongly associated with the situation in the then Soviet Union. One of his symphonies is associated with the German siege of Leningrad during the Second World War. The following narrator knew most things about the symphony in advance and got strong impressions from the intensity in the music and the insight of the conductor. He also experienced that 'this was not just music', but something more: he takes part in the events in the music, had 'travelled along in the music' from one state to another—a form of merging of the type that was treated in Chapter 7.

(25.1J) Man, middle-aged, 1980s

Perhaps the most intensive experience with music that I have been involved in took place when I heard the Stockholm Philharmonic under Yuri Ahronovitch perform Shostakovich's Symphony No. 7. I don't really think this work is among his best. The form in the first movement really demands a different construction of the continuation. In the slow movement and the finale, there are parts that I think are 'empty'. But at the same time, I had a thorough knowledge of the story around the music, I had read about the fantastic performance of the symphony on 20 March 1942 in Leningrad during the dreadful siege. Later, in the Soviet Union, I managed to get hold of a recording with the Leningrad Philharmonic conducted by the same Karl Eliasberg who conducted on this incredible occasion, when the then nine-year-old Yuri stood outside the Philharmonic's building and heard the music pour out of the loudspeakers that had been put up for the day. As a little boy, he endured the horrific Leningrad blockade. I had also analysed the symphony with a score at hand. So I had a thorough knowledge of the construction of the symphony as well as the history of how it came into being.

Before the concert, I took the opportunity to go round the shops. And when the concert started, I was actually rather tired. When the music came to the third movement, I did in fact doze off, to be honest. But when the music came to the finale, in some way I became all the more present: I felt that this was not just music, I had travelled along in the music from one state to another. Perhaps I could describe what happened as that I stepped into a musical process similar to a transformation of a mental condition: a sort of creeping into a musical form built as a symphony.

I started to feel a fellowship with all the others in the audience—I started to think about all the misery that Stalin had unleashed in Eastern Europe, which is what I see as the root of much of Shostakovich's music—I started to feel an even greater fellowship with all these victims of Stalinism. I don't know if I shed a few tears—I probably did. When I was getting my clothes from the cloakroom, suddenly another person that I didn't know at all started to talk with me about our shared experience. It was just as if we had known each other for several years, the sense of community that I had experienced in the concert hall itself was still in the air. I really do think that Shostakovich 'composed' this feeling of community into the music—or perhaps solidarity is a better word? But at the same time, it is a solidarity that can't be described in words. The music says something that you couldn't say in words during this time.

But I think the most important thing is to be present at a live performance, you can experience the sound immediately. For example, such a 'simple' thing as when all the extra brass players make their entry in the coda of the finale and increase the volume of the music means a lot for the increased intensity of the music! But I am also convinced that Ahronovitch's interpretation was fantastic, I perceived him as so insightful and familiar with the music.

The feeling of fellowship that was aroused by the music is reminiscent of what was described in the previous account about the experience of Shostakovich's eighth string quartet. The narrator speculates that Shostakovich has 'composed' this feeling of community into the music. An interesting thought, but the question is whether a listener who doesn't know the background to the symphony would experience the same thing. (There is also another account of this symphony in Chapter 7, focusing on the suggestive, repeated, and all the more intensive march theme that it contains; see account 7.2B.)

There now follow three accounts of experiences at concerts with choir music. In the first of these, the background to the music is the same as in the two previous accounts—war and human suffering. The narrator's initial scepticism with regard to the music is successively transformed into total insight and final catharsis.

(25.1K) Woman, middle-aged, 1980s

It was a Radio Choir concert. The last piece was Poulenc's *Figure Humaine*. I didn't know anything about Poulenc other than that the work was from the post-war period, and that didn't make me look forward to it because I don't care much for modern music. My expectations before this particular item were thus negative. Somebody said a little about the work first; he mentioned the suffering of the Second World War, the concentration camps and prisoners. Some of the text was probably read out in Swedish, even though I don't remember how much, but the phrase 'I write your name, Liberty' must have been mentioned.

My first reaction was 'Pah, it sounds too modern, like I expected,' but fairly soon I began to think the sounds and the harmonies were enjoyable, and the French language, which is so musical, put me in a more amiable mood. The appreciative feeling got all the stronger; I thought that what had been said in the presentation matched the music, and felt a sort of tension in the midst of the notes. I lived the music more and more and everything else disappeared in some way, there were just tonal masses, sorrow, suffering, something that sucked me into the music. In the break before the Liberté movement, I was deeply moved but calm.

But then the Liberté movement started. A great deep crying started to well up within me; I became vaguely aware that I was sitting in a concert hall and couldn't let myself go but must behave properly. But of course it wasn't possible, the music grasped me and it was as if I was crying with all my senses, all the stronger in some sort of parallel with the intensification toward the final released Liberté. I experienced at the same time sorrow and death, suffering, pain, torment, cruelty, inhumanity, and a serene, concentrated, increasing, intense feeling of liberation and relief. I can't describe it in words, but when the music had faded away I felt purified inside; it was a catharsis experience.

I came home, my eyes red from crying, and as soon as I could I borrowed a recording from the music library and found Éluard's poems in the original French and then spent some time finding the right poems and listening again and again until I knew every note.

This evening, I pulled out *Figure Humaine* again, sat down with the text and my stereo earphones and played it again for the first time in six or seven years. Before I put it on, I couldn't remember a single note, but the first bars were of course sufficient for me to feel 'Yes, of course, that's what it sounds like.' I thought that I'd be so used to it now that I could just listen, relaxed—but just think, this time, too, tears and sobs came that I couldn't prevent during the Liberté movement. It still moves me profoundly to this day.

In both the next two instances, the narrators had no expectation of what was going to come. Perhaps this contributed to their being almost shocked by the self-evident and total perfection that the choirs showed. The intonation was clear as a bell, the phrasing and articulation were perfect. The music was everywhere, filled the room and everything that was there, it was as if it had always been there. It also gave rise to experiences of transcendence or religious character.

(25.1L) Man, middle-aged, 1990s

I had bought a ticket to a concert by a children's choir from Finland, the Tapiola Choir. I didn't have any special expectations, I was really rather indifferent. I didn't know anything about the choir or the repertoire.

Then the concert starts and in come a gang of happy Finnish children. There were about 45 of them and they were all dressed the same. They started the concert with an English madrigal for five voices. They sang that difficult choral piece as easy as anything. The conductor wasn't on the stage yet, rather they sang as if it came completely freely, direct from their hearts. The children sort of paired off, two by two, and stood and rocked to the choral piece. It was as clear as a bell! The phrasing was wonderful, every phrase was alive. Every note was tenderly cared for. I think it was the first time I have heard a perfect performance of an English madrigal. There were several others beside me who clapped their hands so hard that it hurt.

Then the conductor comes in and the concert continues. During the 60 minutes the concert lasted, the children's choir managed to sing in eight different languages and in every imaginable style, from Palestrina to Morthenson. All of it as clear as a bell! The intonation was perfect! The phrasing was wonderful! Never before have I experienced anything like it. The music was music. That it was a children's choir that was singing, I didn't think about that at all. I don't think I thought about anything. I just experienced the music, it was everywhere. In me, around me, yes, indeed it filled the room and everything that was there.

It was the first time that a modern piece of music (Morthenson) became just music! Often when I listen to newly written music with new forms of expression such as screams, hissing sounds, or whatever the composer has thought up, then it sounds just like screams or hissing sounds. It is rarely that those ingredients become music in me. Most of the time, I experience them as effects and funny elements in the music. However, this choir did full justice to the composer and the music. They shrieked like seagulls, or soughed like the wind, the waves, or whatever it was. It was just that everything was perfect music! No striving for effects, all they did on stage was to convey the self-evident message of the music. This was the first time such a work appealed to me, I understood the music. It was as if the music had always been there and that it always would be there.

After this first hour with the Tapiola Choir, there was chaos inside me. I saw a conductor in the audience, his face was wet with tears, as was mine. We don't know each other personally, but here in the auditorium there was an accord between us and all the others who had been affected.

In the break, I walked through the crowd of people, all of whom looked so happy, out to the park outside. I had to get away from all the people. Once I was sitting on a park bench, the shock came over me. I started to cry and couldn't stop. Not from sadness, but from joy or whatever the weird feeling was that I had in my body. I felt some sort of great gratitude for what I had been able to be a part of. It seemed like a meeting with God, where I had been able to meet God through the music.

I was uncertain whether I would dare to go in and hear some more, but I did. In this second half of the concert, the choir gave us a very entertaining programme which was characterized by folk music. This part, too, was performed to perfection by the happy and joyful children, they played, danced, and sang. It all seemed so simple. I didn't, however, experience this part of the concert as strongly as the first part. Now I knew that you could perform music in this way. That also meant that it was easier for me to handle the feelings inside me.

(25.1M) Man, young, 1980s

Just once in my life have I had a very strong and unusual experience in connection with music. The experience seems to me to have been extremely remarkable and I have never experienced anything like it, either before or after. I have absolutely no explanation for what happened. I was at the time in excellent health, normally rested and completely without any influence of stimulants. The incident in question took place about one and a half years ago. It was at a concert with a mixed choir from Riga with about 60 members, that took place in a church. The choir was on a visit in an exchange with one of the town's choirs. My expectations before the concert were not really especially high.

The first half of the programme consisted of Baltic composers, after which an American piece followed. The music was now and then extremely advanced in the harmonies (with dense clusters and the second, fourth and fifth intervals as main elements) and often with far more than four voices—a tonal world entirely to my taste.

If my expectations as to the choir had been small, then my surprise was all the greater when the choir started to sing—they sang perfectly in tune from the first note to the last! During the entire concert, I didn't hear the slightest hesitation in the intonation anywhere, and all the time the choir showed an almost unbelievable capability of expression, flexibility (in the dynamics, tempi, and so on), and precision (in the articulation, tempo changes, and so on).

The highlight of the concert was a piece by an American composer. The piece was built up like a sort of canon of 30 voices over the word 'Hallelujah', where the choristers spread themselves out, two by two, throughout the church and sang facing the walls! Here I experienced something that my verbal ability is not enough to give a just description of—but in any case I experienced a weightless state where I floated around unaware of time and space in some sort of dimension of eternity where I was totally surrounded by a wonderful weave of tones and nothing else existed. I was in some way entirely enveloped by a pleasant light that seemed to come from every side and I remember that shortly afterwards I thought: 'If there is a Heaven and if there is singing there—then this is what it sounds like.'

How the concert ended, I have no idea—I just became suddenly aware of everybody starting to applaud, and I began more or less automatically to add my contribution to the racket (that was more like what I perceived it as).

After the concert, I felt completely bewildered, rather absent, and more or less physically exhausted. I nipped out the back door to avoid having to meet and talk with all the people I knew in the audience, and I went on a long walk in the dark before going home and going to bed without having spoken to anybody after the concert.

In the next account, too, the experience is associated with singing, now in a concert version of a familiar opera. Before the concert, the narrator felt she was out of balance and the weather gods were in a bad mood. The preconditions for a great experience seemed to be virtually non-existent.

(25.1N) Woman, middle-aged, 1980s

Nicolai Gedda, Håkan Hagegård, and a couple of women soloists were going to sing Bizet's *The Pearl Fishers* at the Concert Hall in Stockholm. I had an old recording of the work but hadn't really been able to digest this, with the exception of '*Au fond de temple saint*' and '*Je crois encore entendre*'.

When the day came for the performance, I didn't really want to go there at all. For several reasons, I was out of balance physically as well as mentally. It was raining cats and dogs, there was a heavy wind, and I arrived at the Concert Hall frozen, wet, and tired. There were plenty of wet and irritated people there, and there were long queues to the cloakrooms. I was convinced that I wasn't going to get very much out of the performance. At the same time, I knew from before that a good musical experience can be the best medicine for me when I feel out of balance mentally, and I nevertheless felt a need to do something nice.

To my surprise, the music completely gripped me from the very start. The music that I had not previously managed to digest now suddenly streamed through me. When Nicolai Gedda and Håkan Hagegård sang '*Au fond de temple saint*', I got goosepimples all over my body, my face burnt, and I felt *overjoyed*. The audience cheered and I was suddenly in the very best of moods. And my enthusiasm and the audience's became even greater when Nicolai Gedda sang '*Je crois encore entendre*'. The entire audience held their breath. The cheering was enormous. My anxiety disappeared and I felt completely calm and at the same time bubbling with energy. During the intervals, I met several good friends and I felt all the better, didn't long to be at home any more, wanted the performance to go on all night.

After the concert, the applause never seemed to end. I didn't want to leave at all. Wished that the concert could start from the beginning again. The queues to the cloakrooms were suddenly a mere trifle. When I got outside, it was raining heavily, but I didn't want to be squashed together with other people. I felt a strong need to be alone. Despite the heavy rain, I walked, without an umbrella, to the station. The music was ringing in my ears all the time, the tiredness was as if blown away. I felt that I was incredibly strong and I think that I had a blissful smile on my lips. At any rate I got some astonished looks from people that I met. I heard the music all the way home, and right up until I fell asleep. The next morning, I put on my CD and now I suddenly loved *The Pearl Fishers*. I still often listen to it, and then I feel extremely calm and elevated at the same time.

I often need music when I feel I'm in poor mental or physical balance. The music works as some form of safety valve for me, a contrast to the stress and gloominess one meets in everyday life. When most things feel black and difficult, then I take the time to go to the Opera or to a concert, and then I usually feel like a new person afterwards.

She knew what was necessary to improve her mood, and she made use of that knowledge—an example of how one can systematically use music to influence one's mood; see Chapter 11, section 11.5.

In the last three accounts in this section, the music is by Schubert, Mahler, and Tchaikovsky. It is a question of very profound, and at the same time both shocking and extremely happy, experiences. All three narrators give detailed descriptions of their reactions in certain parts of the music. They swing, or are thrown, between different emotions and think that because of the music they can acquaint themselves with the composer's innermost thoughts and feelings, get to know him as a person, receive a message from him.

(25.1O) Woman, young, 1990s

It is a lovely evening early in summer and I am sitting expectantly and waiting for the concert to begin. The piano piece for four hands that is the first piece on the programme will be a new acquaintance for me—Schubert's Fantasy for Piano in F minor. 'You are going to like this!' my father whispers to me while the two pianists walk up to the grand piano and sit down.

I had presumably expected the first piece to be a grand and majestic affair, because already after the first tones of Schubert's Fantasy, I felt how my expectant smile became set. A little frail and extremely beautiful melody voice sought its way in the big church, and without the slightest warning I suddenly felt goosepimples and felt the shivers down my spine. So beautiful, so incredibly beautiful! I wanted to close my eyes and just enjoy it, but for some reason I couldn't even manage to close my eyes—instead I sat there absolutely still and just listened . . . so beautiful, so sorrowful!

All at once, I felt inexplicably sad. In the beautiful melodious voice, I thought I could hear a complaining, unhappy voice. A voice that expressed longing for a beloved, a longing so strong—a love so impossible. Hopelessness! The voice gives expression to its despair, the melodious voice is no longer frail and little—no, now the voice is screaming out all its resignation! But nobody hears, nobody helps. The little frail voice is all that is left. But there is a tiny hope, I can glimpse a little ray of hope behind the big, dark clouds. Will it be all right?

After the music had faded away, I noticed how exhausted I felt. The music really had completely grasped me. In an inexplicable way, I had experienced that I had shared another person's innermost thoughts and feelings (or were they my own?), I really did think that I had felt the hopelessness and worry—but also the hope! To interrupt this enchantment with wild applause felt wrong at first, but very soon I realized what fantastic music and what fantastic musicians I had just had the privilege of meeting, and I too raised my hands and took part in the applause.

After this experience, the hunt started to find a recording of this fantastic music—I felt that I simply must hear it again! Now, the CD with Schubert's Fantasy for piano in F minor with Murray Perahia and Radu Lupu at the piano is the most loved record in my collection. But I can't listen to the record just any time—no, I must feel in a very special mood to be able to listen to this fantastic music, which still takes me away to a fantasy landscape where somebody gives expression to a longing and a loss so strong, and really struggles to be able again to see and be united with their beloved.

If I feel sad for some reason or other, I often choose to listen to this music, but sometimes when I'm very happy and jolly I can also feel a strong need to hear this fantasy. In the first case I think I am looking for (and get) consolation from the music; in the second, it usually simply feels so nice to hear the music—I am not really certain why this is. It is interesting that I can never let this piece of music serve as background music for other activities such as reading books or writing letters—regardless of my mood, Schubert's Fantasy demands too much of my attention and any other activities would simply suffer.

(25.1P) Woman, middle-aged, 1980s

It was in the Berwald Hall in Stockholm. The Philharmonic was making a guest appearance under the English conductor Simon Rattle. I had gone there to hear the Swedish premiere of a work nobody really should get to hear, because it is only a sketch—a sketch for a symphony from 1910.

I remember that before the interval there was a piano concerto by Schumann. The audience applauded enthusiastically afterwards, but I don't myself remember what it sounded like and who the soloist was—I hardly think I heard anything at all. I was just waiting in a frightened mood for what was going to come after the interval. I was afraid. Yes, even much earlier, at home and on the underground travelling into the city, I was afraid. Afraid of being disappointed, afraid that this work that I had wondered about so much would not be the precipice that I had imagined, that it would not be the step to the newer music that I believed. The work was the reconstruction of Gustav Mahler's tenth, unfinished, symphony.

Anyhow, now the interval was over. I don't think I had ever been so full of expectation before. The conductor came in. It became silent. Then he raised his baton and beat in the solitary violin voice. After a few bars with this monotonous, curiously ambiguous song, like doubt, comes the sun. The orchestra breaks out in a warmth that is delightfully painful. I remember that the tears welled up in my eyes. It felt as if I had understood a message—from one era to another, from one person to another. I sat there petrified with my fingers holding tightly onto the armrests. After a while I became completely dizzy. Then I discovered that I had forgotten to breathe.

Towards the end of the first movement, the entire orchestra gathers together in a large, dreadful organ-like sound—a scream of pain and horror. It came as a shock after a fairly drawn-out pianissimo bit. I was completely overwhelmed by the violence in this horror before death. I started sweating and could hardly breathe. For once, I thought, I had been knocked to the ground by something that was so great and so strong that it obliterated all the thoughts that can otherwise flutter past when you listen without giving your full concentration.

But at the same time, I never stopped being afraid that there would be just 'transport bits' or routine stuff. That sounds dreadful, of course. Just as if I was some sort of judge of taste or an omniscient expert. It often turns out later that I haven't understood what I have at first dismissed. Mahler, of course, often balances on the boundary of what seems banal. He plays with waltzes, marches, triumphs, only to break them up, laugh at them, cry with them. It was this ambiguous, sometimes ironic method of expression that I didn't understand, but could sometimes dismiss as 'transport bits' or 'routine stuff'.

The symphony consists of five movements. They are all very different from one another, but still all just strangely macabre. The last movement starts with beats of an enormous wooden club against the very largest bass drum. The effect is horrific. A flute, followed by strings, begins to hesitantly build up a melody, but is suddenly smashed by the blows of the wooden club. I was completely taken by surprise. With every blow of the club, the horror grabbed me. Every time an instrument started to sound, hesitantly, and I predicted that there would be a blow of the club, I grieved. Here, too, I had the feeling of being the recipient of a message.

The symphony ends in a peculiar way. At first, the music seems to thin out, to become weaker, die away. But then, suddenly, the strings, in unison, a double octave upwards, take a step right out into nothingness. And then it is all over.

It felt as if I had not missed a single note. I have never seen pictures or anything else when I listen to music, and I didn't this time either, but the feeling of having been addressed, strongly and directly, lived inside me. Perhaps it was because I knew that the music was not a finished composition, had not been adorned, that it was so naked—an uncensored document about a state swaying between the deepest fear of death and attraction towards the darkness.

When the orchestra had silenced, we in the audience sat quietly a long while. How long, I don't know. Perhaps it was just a few moments. I believe that there were a lot of people like me who thought that we had been allowed to look into a soul, and thus felt joy. Then the applause broke out. And it didn't want to end. The path through the symphony had been difficult and frightening and even shocking, but it was a great joy—indeed, almost an honour—to have been allowed to be a part of this. I flew home, weightless. In fact, I would have liked to have run to the underground station. And I was pleased that I had gone to the concert on my own, because now all words seemed superfluous—even my own. My thoughts had nothing to do with words.

When I left the Berwald Hall, I was actually a different person from when I went there. I felt that I had been allowed to be a part of something extremely important, that I had been able to look into a soul and its secret. That feeling has not left me afterwards, when I re-experience this music with my inner ear, I feel just the same.[1]

(25.1Q) Woman, middle-aged, 1980s

The musical experience that I want to describe concerns Tchaikovsky's *Pathétique*, that is, his sixth symphony. I heard it together with good friends on two different occasions with one or two years between them. My experience was similar both times, but perhaps most overwhelming the first time—the second time, I was, of course, prepared.

I was familiar with classical music before this, with *Pathétique* too, but I don't think that the experience can be really great until it is in a concert hall setting: it is live music, the acoustics are the best possible, and above all you are so totally concentrated on this one thing, on listening to the music.

I have had similar experiences with other music, but nothing so fantastically profound as *Pathétique*. In some passages, it brings forth sobs and I feel totally broken-hearted—my listening is totally concentrated, the rest of the world sort of disappears and I merge with the music, or it merges with me, it possesses me totally. I also have physical reactions, wet eyes, my breathing becomes sobbing at certain passages, and a feeling of wanting to cry in my throat and chest. If I should try to put words to the actual emotions, I would want to use words like broken-hearted, shocked, tragedy, perhaps death, merging, but also tenderness, longing, desire (vain), will to live, prayer. The entire experience also has the character of a total cessation, a sort of meditative rest, a last definite and absolute final point after which nothing else can follow.

There is another thing that made me particularly interested. It is something that happened only with *Pathétique* and not with any other piece of music at all. It is that I think I am meeting the composer! I think he communicates directly with me, and I think that I know him personally. I know who he is. After the second occasion, this led to my looking him up in a book I have, and what I read there made me think, rather shocked: 'But I already knew that!' I was astounded that the music alone had been able to convey the information so exactly. For example, it said: 'In Peter Tchaikovsky's (1840–93) sixth symphony, *Pathétique*, where the composer—through music—confesses his tragic fate, the painful content has taken command of the usual symphonic form. And when Hector Berlioz (1803–69), Franz Liszt (1811–86), and Richard Strauss (1864–1949) write symphonic music, the classical Viennese musical forms are blown to bits. What these composers wanted was, with the help of music, to tell something to the listener, just like when you tell something with words.'

What I reacted to in this text was the wording: 'where the composer—through music—confesses his tragic fate, the painful content has taken command of the usual symphonic form'; and also 'What these composers wanted was, with the help of music, to tell something to the listener, just like when you tell something with words.' The last phrase, of course, referred primarily to Berlioz, Liszt, and Strauss, but I thought it fitted Tchaikovsky too. What I read in the text, and what I thought that I 'already knew', was that Tchaikovsky's fate was so tragic, that it is this he is telling about, that he has an unusual perspicacity about the darker sides of life and, finally, that he exposes himself completely. He doesn't hold back anything. Emotion has the absolutely highest priority—then all the form dogmatists can pack up and go home. There is nothing more to add.

And at that point Tchaikovsky is so totally defenceless that one can only yield to him, the defencelessness and how he exposes himself are a part of the profundity of the experience I have of him. And I also think that in his desire to find expression for what he feels, he gets it so terribly right, it is just spot on. He really does succeed in conveying what he wants to, and that means an exceptional originality and a personal address.

After the experience of the music I am sort of absent—the people in the foyer and their murmuring are sort of at a distance, like a side scene in a theatre more than something real. I find it hard to talk with them, hard to get going and return to ordinary reality. Hardest of all is to talk about the actual experience of the music, I can do that only afterwards when it has subsided a little. On several occasions, what has happened is that we just stand there and shake our heads and look down at the floor, nobody finds any words, you can't add anything to what the music has already said. We go and get our coats from the cloakroom as if in a trance.

And, finally, about which parts that move me particularly strongly. I have a memory of descending strings: they go down (in pitch), in melancholy, but also caressing sequences, between every sequence there is a breathless and emotionally charged little rest. The tone of the strings is yearning, longing. Then starts the descent: the entire string sound is moved step by step (sequence by sequence) further down into lower and lower pitch, the rhythm slows down a little—and keeping time with this change the seriousness increases, the caressing and longing, perhaps cautiously hopeful, diminishes, more and more. What is now growing up is a dreadful picture, a tragedy—and just when you think that he (Tchaikovsky) has reached the bottom, then he adds another tone . . . It just finishes you off. I believe that this last tone is a semitone down, and I also think that it, in contrast to all the others in the descending series, stays there a while. It is an extremely deep bass tone. It is at the end of the first movement, just before the main theme (what I perceive as the main theme) returns for the last time.

Other parts that also move me are precisely the main theme in the first movement as well as the theme that introduces the fourth movement. I also like the 'clarified' parts that Tchaikovsky has put in sometimes, for example at the end of the first movement and somewhere in the middle of the fourth movement. It is often wind instruments, and often an almost sacral tone. For me, they stand as an ultimate reconciliation where no reconciliation, in fact, is possible: 'beyond everything'.

The second and third movements affect me less directly or deeply, but I listen to them against the background of the first movement, which gives them a special depth. For me, the second movement stands for beauty and harmony. The third movement is strutting, almost humorous—it is the unconscious optimist who naively but proudly goes on and on.

If we try to briefly summarize the reactions that have been described in this section, we find the following:

Physical reactions, behaviours:
  Shivers, goosepimples, tears, sweating, 'face burning', changed breathing, one moves to the music or is absolutely still.

Quasi-physical reactions:
  Feeling weightless, feeling as if one is lifted up, takes off, hovers.

Perceptual phenomena:
  High sound level, special timbre, feeling enveloped by the sound/music; tactile sensations (the music is felt in one's body); strong visual impressions of musicians' appearance and commitment; experiences of special light without physical equivalents.

Cognitive phenomena/processes:
  Total absorption, no sense of time, no thoughts/analyses; one is moved, affected, surprised, shocked, overwhelmed; the music arouses associations, memories; one feels filled with music, merges with the music, understands the music, thinks that one is receiving a message.

Feelings/emotions:
  Pleasure, joy, happiness, enthusiasm, perfection; calm, beauty, wonder, longing, tenderness, gratitude; sorrow, fear, feeling exhausted, broken-hearted, shock, dread; switching between different feelings.

Transcendental/religious aspects:
  Visions of heaven, feeling of eternity.

Personal and social aspects:
  Feeling alert/exhilarated, feeling relief, alleviation, liberation, purifying, catharsis, affinity, fellowship.
There is a thorough survey of all these aspects in Chapter 29.

25.2 EXPERIENCES OF PARTICULAR ARTISTES

In many accounts, it is artistes who stand at the centre of the description rather than the music they perform. Many are singers. One of them—naturally—is Jussi Björling. An old woman described a meeting with the young Jussi Björling.

(25.2A) Woman, old, 1920s

One evening there was an assembly in the hall and we were going to hear a promising young singer. It was Jussi Björling, then the same age as me, 18 years old. I can't remember what he sang, but I do remember the feeling in my body. It was as if the ceiling was going to lift up, the hall seemed too little for his fantastic voice.

In the summertime, Jussi Björling often performed at Gröna Lund or Solliden in Stockholm.

(25.2B) Woman, middle-aged, 1950s

There were lots of us young people there, noisy youths, but even the rowdy people became perfectly quiet when Jussi started to sing. Hardly an eye was dry after he had finished singing. It was an extremely strong experience—I would say that we all felt affinity in some way.

One of Jussi Björling's showpieces was 'Till havs' ['Out at sea'] by Gustav Nordqvist. His song brought forth inner visions in the listeners and perhaps even influenced their choice of career.

(25.2C) Woman, middle-aged, 1940s

I was ten years old at the time. The event took place on a weekday and I had come home from school. Now I was going to listen to gramophone records . . . But goodness, what wonderful music! 'Till havs' by Jussi Björling, who sings so delightfully, the high pure tones lift me up—out at sea! I am a little disharmonic, but the music causes me, in my mind, to be the eagle who is flying there, out at sea! Jussi's wonderful voice and the pure tones carried away my inner me. To this day, I can still recall the feeling of the little girl who listened to the radio gramophone. Just think, if I had been a female Jussi!

(25.2D) Woman, middle-aged, 1950s

When Jussi Björling sang 'Till havs', I thought it was the most beautiful thing I'd ever heard, I was out at sea, far away, I think.

(25.2E) Woman, middle-aged, 1950s

Jussi Björling sang 'Till havs', with the result that later in life I became a ship's officer. I usually stand and look out of the porthole when there is a storm, and then I hear Jussi singing the sea, an incredible experience.

Another showpiece was 'Land, du välsignade' ['Thou blessed country', a patriotic Swedish song] by Ragnar Althén. Jussi sang that as an encore at a large concert in the USA the year he died.

(25.2F) Woman, middle-aged, 1960

It was a Tuesday evening in April, 1960. The concert was going to begin at 8 p.m. In the enormous car park outside Pasadena Civic Auditorium in California, thousands of cars were parked. People streamed up the stairs to the many different entrances. The auditorium had 3,000 seats and all the tickets had been sold out in advance very quickly. The soloist was clearly featured. The newspapers had pictures of him, and radio and TV told about the event. He was in truth welcome, waited for, longed for—the world-famous tenor Jussi Bjoerling from Sweden.

Together with an American audience of all ages sat most of the Swedish-Americans from the Los Angeles area. And that's where we were, a young Swedish couple, who were now in the last month of our stay in the USA. We took our seats and started to read the programme. 'Jussi Bjoerling sings for you on RCA Victor Records,' it said on the inside of the cover, together with a photograph of him. On the next-to-last page it announced: 'Tonight's artiste: Jussi Bjoerling, leading tenor with the world's most notable opera companies. At the piano, Frederick Schauwecker'.

The bells in the foyer rang when two minutes remained before the concert. The lights in the many crystal chandeliers were dimmed slowly, the curtain went up. The first item was Tamino's aria from *The Magic Flute* by Mozart, 'sung in Swedish'. Then songs by Brahms, Liszt, Hugo Wolf, Richard Strauss, Flotow, Rimsky-Korsakov, and Borodin, and there were also many of the greatest works in opera. As a finale came the libretto from *Andrea Chénier* by Giordano. The ovations were enormous. Jussi was celebrated as the greatest tenor in the world. He was showered with flowers and cheered, and was called back to the stage innumerable times. I had extremely poor knowledge of the world of opera, and therefore certainly couldn't sufficiently appreciate each and every one of the great works in the concert. But now I understood how great he was.

Then came the very last encore by request. The *great* little Jussi Björling stood beside the grand piano, surrounded by the most fantastic bouquets of flowers. It was dead quiet in the whole of the large auditorium. Schauwecker struck up and Jussi began. Softly, calmly, but firmly and convincingly. Erect, with his chest high and filled with music. Head high and proud, looking far out over the audience. '*Land du välsignade, tag min sång . . .*' ['Thou blessed country, take my song . . .']. Every syllable was sung slowly, clearly, and full of expression. Every word was filled with solemnity, reverence, grandeur. All the 3,000 people stood up and remained standing for the whole song. Deeply moved, enchanted, overwhelmed.

And I cried. *Cried!* Not from sorrow or a longing for home. From love and admiration. I cried, and before the song was over the tears were running down the cheeks of every single person in the audience. The blessed country of which he sang was Sweden. In the great country in the west, he sang of the little country in Scandinavia!

We had been able to experience six fantastic months in America. Experienced only the very best and finest. But we knew that Sweden was and would remain our home country. In just a few weeks, we would journey *home* again to Sweden. I have sometimes thought that, deep in their hearts, more than one of the wonderful Swedish-Americans we met there would have liked to follow us. Despite everything being so fantastic. Despite everything being so grand. Despite that.

Just a few months later, Jussi Björling was dead . . . But with what pride I remembered that he was Swedish! And still do to this day!

Magnificent singing and great patriotism in union. The patriotism was probably particularly strong because she found herself in a foreign country. One often feels more Swedish abroad, than one does at home . . .

Another singer who also turns up in several accounts is Birgit Nilsson. Her voice was heard above everything else.

(25.2G) Woman, old, 1960s

About 25 years ago, I saw and heard Birgit Nilsson at the Opera in I don't know what. Up until then, big orchestras had just been cacophony for me, but from that day on, well, goodness . . . Even though every single instrument in the whole orchestra sounded at its loudest, you could hear Birgit's voice, clear and wonderful, above it all. I got goosepimples, I shuddered with delight, and shivered with cold, and sort of was lifted out of my seat. From that evening on, I have loved classical music.

Birgit Nilsson was best known as a Wagner singer.

(25.2H) Woman, middle-aged, 1970s

I had quite unexpectedly been invited to a performance of Wagner's *Tristan and Isolde* at the Opera, featuring Birgit Nilsson. I had only been to opera a few times. I didn't know this particular music, but I did at any rate have a positive preconceived idea of opera music as such. I had heard Birgit Nilsson on the radio without thinking any more about it. I had never understood what it was that was so special about her.

I had the opportunity to read the programme and the libretto in advance. I skimmed through it all. It also told about the music and various themes that are repeated and the philosophical ideas behind it. I thought that all of it was interesting, and it spoke to me in a special way. I was in the middle of a divorce crisis, and during this period was very introspective and had a lot of deep emotional and spiritual experiences. The way had thus been paved, one might say, for a strong musical experience and it isn't particularly surprising that the theme of love and death especially appealed to me!

The performance as a whole, I found rather poor. The man who played Tristan was wooden and stiff, Birgit Nilsson was probably more lively, and neither the direction nor the stage setting made much of an impression. I can't remember, either, how I experienced the music, but I presume I liked it and was involved emotionally.

The great experience took place when Birgit Nilsson sang her final aria, Isolde's '*Liebestod*'. The light was on her face alone, and her voice was all there was. The best word for this experience is 'transcendental'. It really was as if I went outside myself. It was extremely intense and wonderful. I have never experienced anything like it, either before or after that.

Afterwards, it was really nice to be able to applaud, of course there were ovations and the very experience was such a tension, there was so much energy which had to find expression. I have never applauded like that before either. I talked with my friends afterwards, and of course they thought it had been good, but none of them had had such an experience as mine. As for me, now I understood how great Birgit Nilsson was! Much later, I recorded this aria from the radio and I still think it is very beautiful, but the same experience, no, it is never that.

The experience meant that I really began to notice opera. I think opera is primarily emotional music, there is hardly any other music that expresses feelings in that way. And I suppose that was why it worked; the music expressed my own feelings and experiences, things that can't be entirely expressed in words.

The divorce crisis that the narrator was going through was the background to the experience; the opera is about the unhappy love between Tristan and Isolde.

The opera's content and music reflected her own situation. I have also heard other people describe as unforgettable the final scene with the light on Birgit Nilsson's face. Here, the experience is described as transcendental, 'as if I went outside myself'.

Another of Birgit Nilsson's star roles was Brünnhilde in Wagner's opera *The Valkyrie*.

(25.2I) Woman, middle-aged, 1950s

The first time I heard Wagner's *The Valkyrie* was at the Stockholm Opera. The entire opera deeply affected me, but most of all I was moved by the long final scene when Wotan puts Brünnhilde into deep sleep, surrounded by flames. It was Birgit Nilsson who was singing, and it was the first time I had heard her 'live'. That, of course, also contributed to the highest degree to the experience. Ever since then, she has been the greatest of singers, in my opinion.

I felt hesitant before the performance. A friend who was a great Wagnerian had been trying to persuade me for weeks. I was very reluctant but, to bring her nagging to an end, I finally bought a ticket.

Afterwards, I was completely bewildered. I sat on the bench and cried, from joy and an emotional outburst. And I was the more enthusiastic of the two of us afterwards, and we both stood outside the stage door to get Birgit Nilsson's autograph.

In the long term, it came to be infinitely important for me. It was what opened the door for me to Wagner, Verdi, and so on. I also went to concerts and started to buy records, listened to opera and classical music on the radio, and so on. Precisely because I was partly well prepared and expecting to have to suffer several hours, partly was so totally unprepared for what it was really about, the experience became so strong.

Swedish singers are also found in the following accounts. In the first, the narrator is pushed to an almost ecstatic state by two female singers who combine virtuosity with feeling and insight.

(25.2J) Woman, middle-aged, 1980s

[A summer concert in the Palace Chapel, Stockholm] I had read a long time before that there would be a concert but not yet bought tickets. Then I read that day's papers with reviews of the performance—only standing ovations and roses. The same concert was to be given three evenings in a row, and I managed to get tickets. So I was excited and already in high spirits when we took our seats. The Palace Chapel is not known for its comfort, but we sat right at the front and at least had a clear view . . .

Then finally it came, what I had been waiting most for, Pergolesi's Stabat Mater, with Britt Marie Aruhn and Doris Soffel as soloists. What then followed was an experience that carried me far away, upwards, out . . . I don't know where. I sat bolt upright almost all the time, and with a lovely smile on my lips. Afterwards, I had backache and a bit of a stiff neck, but I didn't notice anything of this during the concert. I wasn't aware of my body, rather I experienced that all of my being melted together with the music.

Above all, I thought that Britt Marie Arhun's singing was ethereally beautiful. Her beautiful but unaffected appearance did everything for the music to really come alive. Seemingly without effort, she took me with her and I experienced how the music filled the entire chapel and embraced me. Doris Soffel was a sparkling complement, and not just in her appearance. Her amazingly great voice sent out messages, each more charged than the one before. She described the suffering and sorrow of the Holy Mother so that I could feel it physically. My husband told me that he had been irritated by somebody coughing very close to us—I hadn't noticed that more than just once.

After Pergolesi, the audience broke into wild cheering and after a while I discovered that I had got up and stood there calling out, with the palms of my hands burning hot. I don't know what I called out, it might not have been more than 'Bravo!' but I do still remember the sensation of not really being able to control my voice. It was as if only half was my real voice, and the rest was emotion.

The duet from Bellini's *Norma* came as an encore, and now I hardly knew what to do with all the excitement I felt. They gave us a coloratura bravura which was stunning. It was like going to the circus and I remember the feeling that 'this isn't true, I'm dreaming, you just can't do this'. I had the same butterflies in my tummy as when I'm waiting at the dentist's, a tension that makes you almost lose your breath. What was fascinating was that despite the breakneck singing tricks, the singers conveyed great sensitivity and insight. I know that I found it hard to get back to reality afterwards, and that I sort of bounced along all the way home.

In the next account, the music and the mood are completely different. The artiste's voice and interpretation of the music bring the listener to a state of total concentration, silence, and serenity. Nobody wants to break the mood with applause.

(25.2K) Woman, old, 1980s

My greatest musical experience in a class of its own is Håkan Hagegård's interpretation of Fröding-Rangström's '*Kung Eriks visor*' ['King Erik's songs']. A large concert with the main focus on [Swedish poet] Gustaf Fröding. The auditorium was packed. Håkan came out wearing tails, and you could feel the concentration. Not a sound to be heard. Then he started to sing.

Already after the first bars of the ballad of '*Welam Welamsson*' I stopped breathing, I think. The tragedy behind the 'amusing things' was apparent in the interpretation. The song can, of course, be done with purely bravura singing and chest tones, but that wasn't the case here. The climax was reached with '*En visa till Karin ur fängelset*' ['A song to Karin from the prison']. 'Hair-raising' is not the right phrase, but the fact is that my heart felt completely squeezed inside my chest.

When Håkan ended with 'King Erik's last song', I was completely whacked. I could have sworn that I hadn't breathed once during the entire cycle of songs. The alto who was sitting beside me collapsed totally and said that now she could die, because there was no more. The soprano on my other side had completely red eyes and said: 'It is not until now that I understand how tragic Erik XIV's life was.' At that point I was crying too, and I don't know what I said, or if I said anything at all. Nobody dared to applaud for quite a while. It would have been like swearing in church.

Why these reactions? I think it was because of the interpretation of the lyrics and music. Håkan knows what he is singing about, every word and tone is well thought-out, and the humility confronted by the music shines through. His voice is not of this world, all the work he has put into this is hidden—he just opens his mouth and it sounds so natural and beautiful—it is absolutely unique.

A female singer with links to Sweden is Barbara Hendricks. The narrator is enchanted by her appearance and singing.

(25.2L) Man, old, 1980s

It was in the Gothenburg Concert Hall. I have listened to the standard symphonic repertoire many times over. I would claim that I am an experienced and good listener.

But then the great miracle took place! Brahms's *Ein deutsches Requiem* was on the programme—a composition that I had heard several times before. Out came Barbara Hendricks, a little, dainty, dark-skinned creature. Without any movement, she was waiting for her entrance in front of the hundred-man orchestra. Then came the first tones, and everything became like it was enchanted. Immediately, all comparisons regarding beauty of tone just evaporated. Up until then, the mellow vibrating violin tone from a noble instrument had been my ideal, but now Barbara Hendricks's singing is the most beautiful I experience of music in all categories.

My experience of that beauty is still just as strong. I never miss an opportunity to listen to her and I have all her LPs. The experience of her singing is so incredibly strong that I can't allow myself to follow in the lyrics so that I won't miss any of her pure, fabulously beautiful singing. I feel something of the blessedness of musicians when she sings!

In the next two examples, the narrators have the opportunity to hear their favourite singer, and it is an experience of intense joy. The first narrator also describes a paradoxical feeling of both being isolated in her experience and at the same time still being a part of what is happening, something she wishes that more people could experience.

(25.2M) Woman, middle-aged, 1980s

It was a performance of Mozart's opera *Idomeneo* at the Metropolitan in New York. I knew that my great favourite among singers, Fredrica von Stade, was going to sing at the Metropolitan just then. Before the performance the excitement was intense, a mixture of joy and happiness to be able to experience this. Her voice and delivery always reach into my innermost feelings.

This became a performance that for me was an experience of total joy. At certain points, among them the duet in the first act between Idamante and Ilia, it felt as if you reached another level where you are isolated in your experience, but at the same time are still a part of what is happening, and you wonder if others feel the same way at the same moment. This, really, is totally unimportant, but you wish that more people could experience the same thing. Physically, it feels as if I completely relax, and this particularly applies to the muscles in my face where I otherwise can feel tension and irritation, but on this occasion I was completely relaxed. The experience opened an entirely new dimension within me on account of the music and its content.

Afterwards, I walked to the hotel, very elevated and filled with a feeling of total joy. In tense situations where I need to relax or to calm down, I bring out that feeling of complete joy and this quickly helps me to come into balance.

The artiste in the next account is one of those who are usually called 'The Three Tenors'.

(25.2N) Woman, old, 1990s

It was a romance evening with José Carreras, an event that I had been really looking forward to. He had been very ill, and everyone thought he was going to die of leukaemia. But the great miracle happened, and he recovered and just over a year after the outbreak of the illness, this great man was back on the stage.

He had a generous programme of songs by such composers as Stradella, Tosti, Massenet, and Puccini. The stage was completely empty except for a concert grand, no flowers or other decorations. And then when this man (he is very small) came in with his Italian pianist, minutes of applause and I felt that everybody here loved him and we were happy that he was back. I was very moved the whole time, and when he sang Tosti's '*Ideale*' in a way I'd never heard before, with the most delightful pianissimos—then I knew that he wasn't just back with his voice, but he was also singing more beautifully, with greater feeling than he had ever done before.

Besides having a spectacular voice he has a stage presence and a charisma that mean that you completely merge with the music and are hardly aware that lots of people are sitting around you. But you do, of course, become aware of this when the thunders of applause came after every piece. I felt so strengthened and so happy, and I felt that I was sitting among people who felt the same. When he finished with 'Granada' as his final encore, neither the audience nor I could contain our joy.

I left the concert hall with tears running down my cheeks, not of sorrow but of joy, gratitude, and great emotion from having seen my great idol, that he was healthy again, and that his voice was at its absolute peak. Luckily, the concert was broadcast on the radio a few weeks later, so I have it on tape and it is so wonderful to sit in peace and quiet at home and go through song after song and just remember.

The next narrator is completely enchanted with and obsessed by—in love with—a voice that came to him on a record he had just acquired. He describes the music and the female singer's performance in lyrical terms and with great expert knowledge. Her voice seems almost ethereal, heavenly beautiful. Here is a much abbreviated version of his very long account.

(25.2O) Man, old, 1980s

My interest in Mozart was further strengthened by the film *Amadeus*, and it is in that context that my greatest experience with music came. I saw the film a couple of times before I bought the record—the album with four sides of soundtrack from *Amadeus*. It was Saturday evening but I wasn't prepared for any once-in-a-lifetime experience other than that I was keen to sit down in my favourite armchair for a couple of hours' relaxed listening. I knew that this would be a really enjoyable occasion, but I had no idea just how much.

Then something really special came on side 2, the Kyrie Eleison from the C minor mass (K 427). Already the powerful opening choir gives a strongly poignant touch, but then after some introductory downward bow movements in the accompaniment comes a soprano solo where the tone foundation of the strings becomes like a catapult for the exultant flight of the solo voice, as if lifted by invisible wings towards the heights. A light, silver-glimmering voice that throws itself in dizzying intervals from low tones right up into the stratosphere. Everything is so light and fantastically beautifully sung, already the singer's very timbre is so fascinating and extremely personal. The solo voice is most of all reminiscent of the movements of a bird up and down in the air. I must play the piece again. And what is this fantastic singer called? Felicity Lott! Have never heard of that name . . .

In the introductory track on the fourth side comes the very greatest experience, the graceful aria '*Ruhe sanft*' from the unfinished opera *Zaide*, again with Felicity Lott as the soloist. I was completely overwhelmed, I had never heard anything as beautiful. The strangely delightful melody with its floating and slightly 'swingy' theme, the sucking minuet rhythm, the easily recognizable and recurring main melody, the singer's way of phrasing, her exquisite diction, and her outstanding pianissimo. During more than 30 years' listening to opera and other classical singing, I have never heard a more beautiful voice. In '*Ruhe sanft*', Felicity Lott exposes her gentle and flexible voice throughout the entire aria and when she reaches the peaks (an A in the fourth and fifth bars repeated in the twelfth and thirteenth), the pianissimo comes without effort like a veil that thinly covers the tone and gives it its silver gleam. This A isn't really so typically pianissimo, because the tone is in itself not so much softer than the surrounding ones, her typical pianissimo— almost inaudible—is perhaps more noticeable in other songs, but she opens this tone in pianissimo almost straight without vibrato, and with a sort of light sigh, which should not be confused with the loud 'sobbing' of the Italians. It reminds me of the singers of the Golden Age or the young Elisabeth Schwarzkopf.

I became obsessed by this voice, it came so unexpectedly straight into my earphones and pierced right into my soul. I had to play the aria over and over again. I couldn't hold the tears back, and then when this was followed by *Requiem* with 'Lacrimosa' and all, the tears gushed.

Afterwards, I felt completely drained. Everything was so bewildering. How could a completely unknown singer sing so ravishingly? I felt almost ecstatic and found it hard to go to bed. I walked around for hours and thought that a miracle had taken place, that an angel from the heavenly Lord had materialized and settled in the singer's chest. Because surely an ordinary mortal couldn't sing with such celestial beauty? When I played '*Ruhe sanft*' and the Kyrie again, I said to myself: I have fallen in love with a voice!

After this, the narrator took every opportunity to hear the singer live and on recordings. He also had the opportunity to meet and interview her personally.

The next narrator was also enchanted by a voice, this time a male voice.

(25.2P) Woman, middle-aged, 1970s

My strongest experience with music came on a New Year's Eve when I was 20 years old. I had sat down to watch a New Year's programme with a concert from London. As always on New Year's Eve, I was a little melancholy but also a little expectant. So there I am sitting and enjoying the music on TV, they change to a new item, a symphony orchestra starts to play an English folk tune and a male voice begins to sing 'The streams of lovely Nancy'.

I was completely thrilled, it felt as if a point in my midriff started to glow and spread heat throughout my body, together with an indescribable feeling of joy. I was absolutely enchanted, I felt every note in my body and the longer the melody went on, the higher I was floating up in the sky. I didn't want it to come to an end.

The feeling of joy after the music was enormous. The melody and the voice stayed inside me, I only had to think about it and it came back. Now I had also got to know that the voice belonged to an Englishman by the name of Martin Best. At the same time, I felt a loss—it was over and I wanted to hear more—this was my music. I had probably been unconsciously looking for music that suited me, and now it suddenly came to me.

I think it was mainly the voice that I reacted to, Martin Best's voice moved me in a way that nobody else has been able to do. I had that particular melody, 'The streams of lovely Nancy', left in my head just over a year without hearing it again. Whenever I wanted to, I could sense the music, the voice, and the feeling again, which I can still do 17 years later, and feel the same warmth and joy. On another occasion in a concert he sang '*Så skimrande var aldrig havet*' ['Never did the sea shimmer so'] so that you almost cried.

I had personal contact with him a year later, and met him. Hearing him live for the first time, further strengthened my feeling of his *voice*. That voice can completely enchant me.

After these testimonies, and also those of many others, of how enormously powerfully moved one can be by a singing voice—the instrument that is in the body itself—one might wonder if any other instrument can match the singing voice in this respect. I leave this question open . . .

The following accounts feature musicians with other instruments. Pianist Clara Haskil (1895–1960) is mentioned in several accounts. They are entirely unanimous in their descriptions.

(25.2Q) Woman, middle-aged, 1950s

A piano evening with Clara Haskil. I knew she was a great pianist but I didn't know she was so fragile as a person. The big concert hall was filled to the point of bursting. She was going to play Mozart, her favourite composer. She came in, black, hunch-backed, and started to play. The entire world was transformed, everything disappeared. She, the great Clara, disappeared, there were just notes, timbre, enthusiasm, beauty, joy in the hall. I, then a teenager, went home that evening as if I had wings. And I can pull these wings out any time at all as a living, resounding memory, it's a reality, I am elevated, get new energy and strength.

(25.2R) Man, old, 1960

In Italy on one occasion, in Florence, I saw a poster saying that a certain Clara Haskil would be giving a concert. Had no idea about her then. In came a black, severely hunch-backed woman, aged between 50 and 60, I would estimate. Then the surrounding world disappeared!

(25.2S) Man, old, 1950s

As usual, I am sitting in the concert hall and waiting for the soloist to make her entrance. In comes an old, hunch-backed lady. It seemed to me that it was with some effort she made her way to the piano. And then she struck the first chords. Time and space ceased to exist. It was Clara Haskil.

A unique experience was to get to hear a great composer perform one of his best-known works.

(25.2T) Woman, old, 1930s

One of the greatest musical experiences was when Sergei Rachmaninov honoured Stockholm. One spring evening in 1935, he played in the large auditorium at the Stockholm

Concert Hall, and I and my husband had great expectations for this concert. During my young years, I had got to play his 'Melody' and the Prelude in C-sharp minor and now hoped to hear the prelude.

I remember that the programme didn't contain any Rachmaninov at all, but the concert was brilliant and the applause never seemed to end. Then came the much longed-for C-sharp minor prelude. To hear it played by the composer himself was the blessed moment of the evening. I listened carefully to his own interpretation, the slow introduction, followed by a dizzy agitato and then the heavy, drawn-out ending, which fades away in soft, hardly audible chords.

The skill and insight of a pianist from a much later time got the next narrator to sit absolutely still, as if she was part of the seat, and feel as if she experienced the music with every fibre of her body.

(25.2U) Woman, young, 1980s

A pianist by the name of Vladimir Ashkenazy was going to play Bach's Piano Concerto in D minor. I was reading the programme notes and the orchestra members were tuning their instruments. The conductor came in, and then Ashkenazy. He sat down at the piano and I looked at his hands, since I myself had played the piano a long time and I think it is nice to see the dexterity of a skilful pianist. I had never heard the piece before, nor this pianist. Then he started to play.

Never in all my life have I heard a piece that has affected me so strongly. Especially in the beginning of the piece, I experienced some parts as entirely matchless. He, too, is a matchless pianist, Ashkenazy, he moves so much when he plays and really seems to live the music to one hundred per cent. I experienced the allegro in the beginning very strongly, and even the faster parts in the second movement. I sat there as if I was a part of the seat, as if I'd been glued to it. I simply couldn't move a muscle, it was so beautiful. Throughout the piece, I sat there as if petrified. The music flowed and I felt that I experienced it with every tiny fibre in my body. Like when you drink or eat, it seemed to merge with my thoughts and feelings.

I personally experienced that it affected me so strongly because it was in the minor mode. I was absolutely not melancholy or sad that day, on the contrary, happy and satisfied. But sometimes I have noticed that the pieces in the minor mode can affect me emotionally on a deeper level than the ones in the major mode. Otherwise, I might have experienced them as being equally beautiful.

Directly after the concert I felt as if I had been through a tough training session at the gym, spiritually. I grabbed hold of my boyfriend's arm and explained to him how fantastic I thought the music had been. I was completely intoxicated by the music for a long while afterwards, went and hummed bits of the first movement, and thought: I must hear this piece again. Every time I hear this piece, it feels absolutely fantastic. I get pleasant goosepimples all over, and can really relax. As soon as I feel I'm exhausted when I come home from work, or generally out of sorts, I put this record on or something by Chopin.

I have bought the music and the score of the piece and happened to mention to my music teacher that I had the score even though I couldn't play it. She laughed and said: 'If you practise and play enough for a few years it is not an impossibility that you will be able to play bits of this piece.' That evening I just had to run all the way to the bus (only two kilometres, but even so . . .) to have an outlet for all the happiness, energy, and playing enthusiasm that I felt. A joy that was indescribable. Just the very thought that some time, even if it be in tens of years, I'd be able to play this, it felt fantastic.

How enormously inspired one can be when one has heard a great musician! One wants nothing more than to try to learn to play just as well.

Her notion about the how the minor mode seems to affect her on a deeper level than the major mode occurs in other accounts too, for example in Chapter 13, account 13.3D.

Now some accounts of eminent string musicians. In the first example, the narrator is spellbound by the charisma of the artists, the beauty of the timbre, and the perfection of the performance.

(25.2V) Man, middle-aged, 1980s

It was a superb spring evening and a concert in Gothenburg's magnificent concert hall, Ludwig van Beethoven's Violin Concerto in D major with the brilliant young instrumentalist Anne-Sophie Mutter as soloist. Despite her youth, she was already a renowned world artiste, whom I would now for the first time encounter directly in a concert setting.

After the break, the evening's soloist makes her entrance. At a fast tempo and wearing an exquisite green long dress. Already here in her striking entrance, a very charismatic figure.

Now the first absolute silence after the welcoming applause. Then the orchestra's pompous and powerful introduction in the march-like theme of the first movement, with timpani, for some very effective minutes. Then the solitary violin on the same theme, in dazzling virtuoso tones, performed with absolute perfection. I sat there in the box, with my legs stretched out, completely still! Spellbound by the music out there on the strongly illuminated stage, with the solo violinist radiating total concentration, all performed in perfect concord with the orchestra and conductor. The music's alternately tinny and strong silver-gleaming tones, from this solitary violin, in an almost unspeakable and unfathomable beauty, which gave me such strong sensations of joy that I literally felt shivers and had tear-filled eyes. Particularly evident in the gleaming, pure, and frail tones of the andante movement. But also in the second movement's antiphon-like 'singing' between the violin soloist and the orchestra. The latter is of a really high class under the direction of Neeme Järvi! Then the end, and the loud ovations that I almost mechanically joined in on account of my pronounced feeling of joy.

Afterwards, I couldn't talk about the experience. But I had to wind down, by walking slowly down the avenue that lovely spring evening.

A Swedish cellist and the interplay between him and committed musicians filled the next narrator to the brim and strengthened her to face all her everyday worries.

(25.2W) Woman, middle-aged, 1990s

It was the Umeå Sinfonietta who were playing with Frans Helmersson as soloist and conductor in Haydn's Cello Concerto in C major. There was an interplay between this fantastic musician and the sinfonietta's musicians that made the concert unforgettable. There sits Frans in relaxed concentration, making music. The cello is a part of him, himself. The orchestra is with him in every crescendo, in every little move. They create *music* and give us of all they have. You could clearly see how orchestra musicians and soloist/conductor liked to be together and showed this by really playing with joy and commitment for themselves and for us. I sat there and let myself be filled to the brim and a bit more.

Afterwards, a strong feeling of light and happiness. I felt strong, or rather perhaps strengthened, elevated, ready to meet the trivialities of everyday life. Afterwards I thought: If I wasn't able to experience music in this way, I would die! Or at any rate slowly fade away!

The same total mastery of instruments and perfection in the interplay in a string quartet meant that the music affected the narrator directly and without any distracting thoughts of the work being done by the musicians.

(25.2X) Man, middle-aged, 1980s

A Monday evening, a visiting string quartet from Hungary, the Takács Quartet. The hall was of the smaller, more intimate type. The programme started with one of Haydn's great string quartets, Op. 76:5 D major, continued with Bartók's No. 6, finishing after the interval with Brahms's Op. 51:1 in C minor. We arrived with great, positive expectations and it became an unforgettable evening!

Because I myself play, it often happens during concerts—if the musicians show a certain hesitation—that I worry how it will go. You get tense and focus your listening on the technicalities of the playing. Here, it only needed a few minutes' listening to feel absolutely safe, lean back in the seat and let the music speak. The musicians gave evidence of total mastery of their instruments and the music and played with such self-evidence that you were amazed. The interplay and communication were total. The music affected you directly without you thinking about the reproductive factor, those who were doing the work, the musicians.

In large concert halls I am often distracted by the distance to the musicians and disturbing signals from other listeners. But not here! We were close to the podium—no disturbing audience between—and were all connoisseurs who could listen in concentration and thus not disturb others. A pin dropping would have been very disturbing! The preconditions were optimal for a great listening experience. Bartók's No. 6 has many brutal sections and often has a fairly difficult tonal language and is considered to be inaccessible and hard to interpret. Here, there were no difficulties—either for the player or the listener. A clear, translucent interpretation with nuances from brutal fortissimo to the most subtle. I have never heard Bartók's string quartet like that before. This piece as well as the following Brahms quartet were powerfully moving experiences of a celestial nature. We left the hall dazed and deeply affected, both by the music making and above all by the music's enormous power and message to us!

All the narrators in this section emphasize the technical skill of the artistes, their professionalism, and—above all—their insight, expressiveness, and personal interpretation of the music. The listeners' reactions are well known: shivers, tears, being lifted up from the seat, so to speak, or out of oneself, time and space cease to exist, one is moved by the music, merges with it, experiences absolute beauty, perfection, 'celestial' joy, feels elevated, strengthened, mirrored, and confirmed by the music, 'ready to meet the trivialities of everyday life'. It is a pleasure to remember the experience, and in stressful situations one can recall the feeling of absolute joy and regain one's balance—yet another example of how one uses music to influence one's mood (see Chapter 11, section 11.5). One looks for new opportunities to meet the artiste and buy records, and is inspired to play oneself.

The accounts in this section have been selected to illustrate as much as possible of the scope of listeners' reactions in strong experiences with music. The sample should, of course, absolutely not be understood as some form of 'ranking' of different artistes. Many other artistes are included in our complete material; they are listed later, in Chapter 30, section 30.3.2.

Finally, an account that I have taken from another source. It describes a bewildering experience of a charismatic musician in a situation that has suddenly arisen.

(25.2Y) Woman, middle-aged, 1980s

[Karl-Erik Welin has played at a concert during a festival in the county of Uppland. The following day, early in the morning, he phones the narrator, who lives in a forest, and wants to be fetched from the hotel.] He was waiting there, chirpy and happy beside the gate, soon in the car and then back to the forest. Karl-Erik was in a very good mood, a successful concert the previous evening, even a journalist who phoned was invited to come out to the forest for an interview and photographs. He repaired my son's bicycle with the broken gears, grilled food out in the open, walked in the forest. It was all peaceful, the silence hummed for him, he felt safe and secure.

Then my son came with a dead spotted flycatcher. Karl-Erik cried, ordered assistance for a funeral. Out to the shed to get a spade, then to a glade in the forest for the funeral. Together, we sang the hymn 'A mighty fortress is our God'. Karl-Erik held the funeral oration with a dignity that has never been known and never will be known again by such a congregation. After laying the wreath and putting up the hastily constructed cross and stones in a strict pattern on the grave, we returned to the house.

Now comes the music experience. Karl-Erik sits at the piano, playing while at the same time composing *Requiem for a Dead Bird*. At first it just roars, like a volcanic eruption without any preceding rumbling, like a raging snowstorm or thunder without forewarning. He plays not only on the keys but on the entire piano and he is in another world. He cries, laughs, is melancholy and happy, all in a mixture of tones in the major and minor modes. Me and my son sit absolutely silent and just wonder: What are we experiencing?

When it is at its worst and my brain has stabilized itself somewhat, a mean thought strikes me: Did he perhaps catch sight of the chainsaw in the shed when we fetched the spade? I am immediately ashamed of the reflection. After a while, he shuts the lid of the piano with a crash (afterwards, he explained that the bird then broke through the sound barrier on its way to heaven), and then there was lovely music with trills and beautiful painting in the upper registers; it all ended sacredly with a varied theme on '*Den blomstertid nu kommer*' ['Now comes the flowering season', a hymn about summer]. Afterwards, he was happy, had forgotten the dead bird and wanted to rest, which he did in the hammock, together with the cat (the bird's assassin?) curled at his feet.

How do you behave after such an experience? You keep quiet and try to get the fluid molecules in your body into balance, and you absolutely do not understand what you have just experienced. But nevertheless: to have been in the vicinity of a master when he was creating is in some way unreal and there will always be an image of Karl-Erik Welin in my heart.[2]

CHAPTER 26

MUSIC AT CONCERTS: JAZZ

WITHIN jazz music, prominence is usually given to the individual musicians—their image, skill, and expression—to a greater degree than is the case with classical music. Which musical pieces are played is mentioned more in passing, often not at all, and besides it is often a question of improvisation. The division between experience of the musical works and experience of the artistes that was applied in the previous chapter is thus not applicable here.

Here are a number of accounts of experiences at jazz concerts intended to illustrate different reactions and situations. In the first account, the main person is a gentleman in his sixties, who—when he lets himself go—makes the narrator experience '*music*' crossing all boundaries.

(26A) Man, middle-aged, 1970s

Stockholm Concert Hall: Benny Goodman and his Orchestra, my first chance to hear them. The usual murmur. Then the band—stout, not exactly young gentlemen—makes its entrance, accompanied by loud applause. Not a sound, then a clarinet trill is heard from back stage, and BG comes onto the bandstand, bows, goes up to the band and stamps or counts in his signature tune 'Let's dance'. Without any presentation, they go straight on with 'Bugle call rag'. The band sounds superb with lovely rhythmic bounce. The bandleader is in excellent spirits. Then he announces: 'Now, a few numbers with the quartet.' The 'quartet' turns out to consist of six musicians, including the clarinettist. They start with 'Poor butterfly', then, among others, 'Air mail special', which is a real hot number. With all due respect to the fine orchestra, it'd be nice to hear more of this.

After the interval, there is a new set with the 'quartet', including 'Sweet Georgia Brown', which becomes the *experience*! BG gets going, lets himself go, amuses himself and the audience by playing in a way that we haven't heard earlier in the evening. BG's playing is jazz in the best sense of the word, a raw yet flexible tone, spiced with growl. This is not a 60-year-old gentleman with glasses, grey hair, and a clarinet up on stage, but *music* crossing all boundaries as regards time, genre, and style. I don't, of course, think that at the time, I just listen and am part of it.

The awakening is almost brutal: through the thundering applause and whistling, a noise can be heard as if the ceiling is about to collapse. It is the audience higher up (I am in the stalls) who are stamping on the floor. BG looks up, seems (pretends to be?) surprised at the approval and says, with a little smile, that now perhaps it is time for 'a change of pace'. After three or four encores, it all ends with BG's sign-off, as always Gordon Jenkins's 'Goodbye'. The audience stands up and applauds.

In the next account, we find two more of the great names of jazz. The narrator is himself a jazz musician, which is evident in the description.

(26B) Man, middle-aged, 1960s

A concert with Coltrane and Miles Davis. Five men came onto the huge bandstand at the concert hall. The acoustics were dreadful. A glass sheet hung over it, meant to dampen the reverberation a bit but it didn't. I moved so that I'd be able to hear better, eventually finding a place where I heard well. It was in the days when there were no amplifiers for the basses, but there was an acoustic microphone in front of the bass, so that was what was heard least. I found a place where I could hear the bass, sat there and sank into the flow of music in some way.

Really, it is impossible to describe a musical experience in words, there aren't any such words, but if you have to compare it with anything, then it is like a deep meditation. You turn off the flow of thoughts that is always bothering you with its chatter inside your head, and sink into some sort . . . closer to God. That sounds a little high-flown, but that's what it feels like in some way. There was a tense atmosphere, completely silent, lots of people.

They played 'Autumn Leaves', a simple Edith Piaf tune, but of course Miles completely redid it. Logical chords for the improvisation, and the comp played during Miles's solo in a very unobtrusive way. The bass was only on 1 and 3, the drummer was using brushes, but then the performance sort of grew into a tenor solo. Coltrane played a wild solo, then the drummer started to play with drumsticks and really made the most of it. It was a fantastic feeling, it really moves you to tears, I'm almost in tears now when I think about it.

I had expectations that it would be good, but I didn't think it would be such an incredible shock. Coltrane played for a long time, it just got wilder and wilder . . . enormous, then it calmed down, the pianist took over. The tunes were long, about 20–25 minutes, but never boring. They had played together such a lot, they mastered the form, the tenor solo was the climax.

Here, two descriptions are alternated. On the one hand, the initiated listener's expert description of how the musicians played and how the music successively built up to a climax in Coltrane's solo, then calming down. On the other hand, the description of the experience: a tense atmosphere in the hall, he has been put in a state that is likened to a deep meditation, shutting out all thoughts and sinking into the flow of the music. The experience is a shock which exceeds his every expectation; he is moved to tears (both then and now).

Next we have another celebrity visit from the USA, also described by a jazz musician.

(26C) Woman, middle-aged, 1980s

Betty Carter and her Trio from the States were here and played at Fasching in Stockholm. There were a lot of people and I was sitting on a staircase backstage and listening. I didn't have any great expectations before, except that I knew they were damned good professional musicians and I realized that it couldn't be less than a certain level. So in that respect I did have certain expectations, I suppose. The mood at the place was good and positive, on the whole.

I got a really fantastic kick from the piano, the drums and bass, how they played, comped, and followed her. It was so divinely good that the tears came directly. Ah! This is how it should be! You rarely hear such good comp musicians. At the same time, it was weird because she was so diva-like. So she turned to the drummer and said: 'You're supposed to be professional now' loud in the microphone to the drummer. I thought that was goddam awful, even if he had played badly. But above all now when he played so divinely, it was totally out of place.

But it was an Aha! experience. What happens is that all the bits fall into place, there's a string inside you that gets into a spin in some way, a feeling deep inside that affects you. All the bits fall into place. This is what it must be like. This is what I want it to be like to be perfect. I didn't get such a kick from her as from her musicians. They played so that I started to cry with joy. Jeeeesus, so beautiful and it's just like it should be.

It is so difficult to express it in any other way. Partly, you've acquired knowledge of music that makes you think that it fits or not. But there is also a deeper, inner happiness that you feel when everything is in place. What's so nice is that you can't explain it in words, that's what's so wonderful about it. If we are out playing and we start talking too much about how we should do the music or perform it, you destroy the magic. You can't dissect and analyse this stuff too much, there must be something untouched in it all. That's what it's like for me, anyway, that's the magic.

In this account, too, one clearly notices the expert listener, but the emphasis in the description is on her own reaction: an Aha! experience, everything is absolutely perfect, this is just how it should be, all the bits fall into place, there is a sort of inner resonance—'a string inside you that gets into a spin'—it is beauty, deep inner happiness, tears of joy. And, really, it is impossible to describe in words, and that is what is so nice about it—one shouldn't analyse too much, because then one loses the magic.

There are some similar reactions in the next account. Overwhelming impressions of a well-known jazz drummer inspired the narrator to attempt to completely identify himself with him.

(26D) Man, young, 1980s

A music teacher at school gave me a record to listen to and it was an LP with the drummer Buddy Rich. I listened to it and just died on the sofa. Thought: 'Jesus, this really swings, it is just wild.' I played the same side four or five times straight off and just sat and bounced on the sofa. Then I listened to this for six months every evening, and then tried to be BR himself when I played the drums. It was just so bloody good, so incredibly good that I was completely . . .

Then I tried to go and see him when he was in Sweden. I finally got to see him in the summer of 1986, it was the last summer he was alive. I was sitting there ten metres in front of the guy. He was 69 years old and, man, the way he played. Then this experience got even stronger, he was as fit as a 30-year-old, dashing around on stage and playing for all he was worth. I felt as if all other thoughts, all activity, disappeared, I was somewhere else. Presumably I was in the midst of everyone who played, I was out of reach, I only know that I was terribly happy.

Then it ended with my not being able to sit still, but I stood up and danced in front of the stage, I mean I knew every single track on the LP, every single solo. I still do to this day. Every time I put the record on, it is still the same experience, it is so bloody good and in those days the only thing that counted was the big bands. It has influenced me afterwards, I mean I was him when I sat and practised, played like he did, and I'm sure I still play some things today like he did.

Next comes a meeting of musicians of a calmer type, between two well-known jazz musicians who had fun with music in a sincere and enchanting way. The strongest impression, however, was made by the one who conveyed his music in a totally open way, revealing his innermost self.

(26E) Man, middle-aged, 1980s

Chet Baker and Toots Thielemans, a cold and bleak day. It was mainly for Toots's sake that I was there. Chet was one of many jazz musicians from records, Toots I had experienced live previously. The evening was superb, on account of both—but Chet Baker was a dream! How superb and wonderful!

Together they had everyone in the room spellbound. I, who am sometimes irritated and disturbed in my experience by the drumming and stamping and humming of others, was able to feel total peace—the audience lived in the music but at the same time subordinated themselves to the discreet requirement of 'discipline' in relation to the message of the instruments and voices.

Together, they had fun with music—had fun themselves, and got us to laugh. I have seen/heard many others do that too, yet this meeting of musicians is what has left the clearest memory. Perhaps because I experienced them as so different—different characters, different styles, different charisma. This was a heartfelt meeting—occasional, as far as I know—where each one with respect and feeling for the other brought out the very best and most in each other—and in me as listener and fellow participant, with all of me, my circulatory system, and its pumping machine.

Nevertheless—most of all Chet, sometimes with his trumpet, his *unique* trumpet, sometimes with his equally unique voice. Loneliness, distance, and intimacy at the same time. Presumably he was a jazz legend already at that time, for me Chet Baker became one in that moment when he feverishly conveyed his music, revealing his innermost self, and without flattering the audience.

I shivered, got palpitations sometimes, was off dreaming the next second, wished it would never come to an end—but it did, and in doing so filled me with melancholia, warmth, and a lot of joy at the same time.

The next account features a trio of well-known Swedish jazz musicians. Their pregnant performance created a tense atmosphere and a feeling of total concentration and fellowship. The experience involved several senses—vision, hearing, touch—and was impossible to defend oneself against even if one had tried. The narrator rejoices, albeit in silence, and uses several images in his description.

(26F) Man, middle-aged, 1980s (from an edited interview)

I was present at a really enjoyable musical occasion with the Trio Con Tromba. Exceptionally competent musicians. They played a Russian folk tune that Jan Johansson had arranged. Bengt Hallberg kept the pedal down on the grand piano so that all the strings lay free, so that the echo of the trumpet came into the piano. It sounded incredibly beautiful, like church bells perhaps, an unexpected sound from the piano. Unusual and beautiful. Powerful. Carried out with enormous meaning, exactness, and colossal presence by the musicians, it was a signal—something is happening here.

The atmosphere became even more tense, there was absolute silence in the room. There was an unbelievable magnetic field between those who were on the stage and in the room, you could have cut the atmosphere into slices. It became one unit, the audience and the musicians, the boundaries between different roles merged together; we drank out of the same barrel. It was the music that counted, not who was doing what. 'Now we are all here and are involved in this!' The Trio Con Tromba were agents in the service of the audience.

I personally felt like I was just a big radio receiver. All channels tuned in to receive this particular music, and it could ravage my entire organism uninhibited—it was the only input just then. I sat absolutely still. It was almost a pity to breathe, it was something that irritated—you felt you didn't need any air. Time stopped, all my senses were concentrated—vision, hearing, and even touch too, because there were also vibrations, fully noticeable physical vibrations. It was a strong experience that took over, you couldn't prevent it from happening even if you'd wanted to, it came into you.

Unbelievable joy to be there and just receive this, that was all that mattered then. So you sat there and rejoiced, but silently. I was struck by the thought: how nice that I have the ability to appreciate, to receive, this! After the tune had been played, you were clearly affected, almost faint. I was happy and blissful, this was joy, an experience of bliss. The memory makes me warm, it's fun to think back to it.

But . . . we were recording and in the middle of the tune the tape came to an end . . . I asked them to do this tune again as an encore so that we could get a good recording. They did, they are after all three of Sweden's most experienced musicians, skilled and absolutely top class. So they played the same Russian folk tune in the same arrangement in the same room for the same audience, but just 15 minutes later, and this time it was nothing! This time there wasn't this electric atmosphere, this charge. It wasn't the same experience at all. I experienced it extremely clearly. The musicians too. Afterwards, Bengt Hallberg said: 'You should only play a tune once in a day.'

It was thus rather a disappointing, although in some ways instructive, ending to the experience. Usually, it doesn't become the same experience the next time. Absolutely everything must fit together—just this music in just this performance for just this listener in just this mood in just this situation and so on—for the result to be an especially great experience. More about this later in Chapter 32, section 32.1.

The artiste in the next account is from the blues scene. His playing and appearance gave rise to an immediate feeling of contact and provided an outlet for many different feelings.

(26G) Woman, young, 1980s

It was like a stroke of lightning. Already, after a few bars, I felt that this was 'my music' . . . The music engaged me, suited me. It was music that made me feel good, regardless of whether I was sad or happy . . .

It was a summer evening and some mates suggested we should go down to the pub and 'have a couple of beers and listen to some decent music'. First I was a bit hesitant, but it wasn't so hard to convince me, I was curious. We went. At first I wasn't so impressed. The pub was small and the tables were worn, wooden benches and chairs, there weren't so many people there either. It was pleasantly cool in any case, quite cosy really. We sat down at a table right next to the stage, ordered a beer each, started to talk. It was nice, all five of us were in a good mood. Meanwhile the pub filled with people, it wasn't half empty any longer. I liked it!

All of a sudden the taped music in the background silenced and there were some people standing on stage. Then lightning struck! It was an electric guitar that had broken out right in front of my eyes and ears. The volume was high and the music stirring. The artiste with the reverberating electric guitar was Roffe Wikström with his band Hjärtslag [Heartbeat], and that band got my heart beating for sure. I was totally fascinated by all the tones that whined out of that guitar. The guy must have been born with a guitar in his hands, I thought. The faces he made when he played were fascinating too.

After the concert I felt rather empty. I must have been pretty tired. If I'd had the energy I'd have wished they could play for a couple more hours (the concert was only three hours long, after all). What an evening. I had danced because I was happy, full of energy, but sometimes I sat down and felt almost melancholy when they played some really complaining and tragic blues. I had had an outlet for a load of feelings.

Sometimes, far too great expectations may lead to a certain disappointment. It doesn't become the same experience that it was that time in the past. But, instead, one is served a great experience that one hadn't expected, a total surprise.

(26H) Woman, middle-aged, 1990s

It was summer, and it was time for the Stockholm Jazz and Blues Festival. Me and my husband thought we would go on a nostalgia trip by listening to the idols of our youth, Blood, Sweat and Tears. It was with great expectation we went through the gates. The thing was, though, that it would be hours before our idols would be on stage. In the meantime, we would, however, be presented with other music. After a while, the MC comes forward and announces the next item on the programme, it would be big-band music: Louis Bellson with his double bass drums. That would be nice, we thought, and took a sandwich.

The members of the orchestra came in and took their seats. And started to play! They played with such zest, such commitment, such proficiency! The tenor saxophonists Scott Robinson and Louis Menza started to improvise together, respond to each other and even weave together their improvisations into a unison loop at the end. Incredible! A bit later, two elderly gentlemen were led on to the stage, a bassist and a trumpeter. You wondered what was going to happen. Anyhow, they pick up their instruments and start to play as if they have never done anything else. I find myself in an ocean of notes and sounds, pressure, impressions, everything at once, the music extremely tense and exact in the entrances. I found myself sitting there with my mouth open, literally as well as metaphorically. It felt almost as if it was too much to take in, at the same time as it was extremely delightful to listen to. The surprise was total. In some way, I forgot myself and just was in the music, which in some way enveloped all of me. This was—even though I have listened to a considerable amount of music in my day—something I'd never heard before. We sat there as though we had been nailed to the bench for the entire concert.

Afterwards there was a sort of 'audible' vacuum . . . But we were going to move on to the idols of our youth. The time passed, we waited a while. Expectations vibrated in the air. In they come at last. The vocalist starts to sing, but, hadn't his voice become a bit wobbly and unstable since the last time, and the musicians, well, I don't know, it didn't feel like in the old times. Everyone in the audience sings along and claps their hands. Myself, I feel in some way outside, presumably with far too high expectations. Strange how this and that can change.

Somewhat disappointed, we leave. It all felt rather watered down, wasn't the experience I thought I would be having. On the other hand I had been able to take part in something entirely different instead. The actual experience seemed to depend on both the expectations and moods in general but naturally also on the musicians' proficiency and insight. Perhaps it was an unfair order in which I had heard the different groups. Perhaps I would have experienced it completely differently if I'd heard them in the opposite order. Anyway, I was emotionally moved. It was a delightful experience, regardless.

First surprise, then disappointment. Would it have been different if she had heard her old idols first and then the big band afterwards? Impossible to know, but the question illustrates how such a 'peripheral' factor as the order in which artistes play can be decisive for the experience. (Something to bear in mind in connection with music competitions; judgements can be influenced by the order in which performers are presented.)

Two accounts follow that are about meeting the same group of musicians, the George Adams Quartet. In the first case, the outer circumstances are dreary, but the musicians gave everything and the narrator was totally thrilled by their commitment, intensity, and charisma. He forgot both the cold and the time and became so happy.

(26I) Man, middle-aged, 1980s (from an edited interview)

The greatest jazz experience I've had was at a jazz festival in Stockholm. Me and my mates were waiting for the George Adams Quartet. Unlucky with the weather. The band came last in the evening, the programme was behind time and the weather did its bit to ensure that you were hardly inclined to be enthusiastic—everybody froze and went home. There were only about 40 or 50 of us who remained, and we were like ice lollipops. But that seemed to vanish when the band started to play, I forgot that I was frozen and I believe I became warm, a warmth that crept in. You started to move too.

It was a visual as well as an aural experience. They really did a complete concert, they weren't downhearted at all, even though it was cold and a small audience, it didn't bother them. They themselves lived for music and they gave just everything. It was brave to give something—they wanted something with it, there was an intensity, an emotional transfer that completely grabbed me—the deepest of feelings. It could be both happiness and sadness at the same time. Since I remember it, it went in deeply. The time just flew. Yes, help, I was so happy!

It was musicians like George Adams, saxophonist, black Muslim I think, with a religious approach to music which was extremely powerful, super drummer Danny Richmond, Don Pullman, Cameron Brown—an ideal crew. They kept on for 45 minutes, but then they gave everything, they were professionals, they didn't give up, it was their job. An impression I got was just that religious approach, an attitude in it all. In his playing that was competent, direct, you could tell, in his concentration. His religious charisma was evident from his bearing, how he bowed, held his hands. He had a commanding presence.

It is difficult to pick out what makes an impression, when you watch live, it is the whole thing. I don't at all think that I would experience the same thing if I heard them on a record. I have never felt the need to get a recording of them. It was enough to hear them once. It is fairly common that it isn't the same thing at all to hear groups live and to hear them on a record. It is as if the spirit is lost, something happens in the contact with the audience.

This was during a time when my interest in jazz was really big, perhaps I had expected one of those peak experiences in some way, although it came when the conditions weren't optimal at all, you had heard music all day long, you can get so satiated with it, but it didn't matter—it just struck like lightning.

He makes a point of the one-off character of the experience and does not think it would be the same experience if he heard the music on a record. The visual impressions of the musicians' commitment and bearing meant a lot for the experience.

The same great admiration for the competent and committed musicians recurs with the other narrator, who is himself a jazz musician. His negative expectations were transformed into their complete opposite—to such a degree that he has an incredible experience in the middle of the concert.

(26J) Man, old, 1980s

A concert during a jazz festival with the George Adams Orchestra, an American jazz orchestra with an ad hoc constellation. It took place in a typical school hall, really dull with straight walls and simple chairs put out, lots of people. This is a group that plays avant-garde music, which I don't really like. I knew about them a bit from before, but really I had negative expectations when I came there and thought that it was going to be impossible to understand this. But they made a simplification you could say, because of the audience, presumably—they took it a bit calmer, it wasn't too wild you might say, but you could distinguish the melodies.

They started to play and I heard that the musicians had a delightful quality, absolutely superb. I can't distinguish whether it was in some solo or other, everything was good, the comp, and there was such an incredible feeling of togetherness between those who played, such a unity that you rarely come across but which occasionally happens when things really flare up. They were incredibly technical but at the same time very musical and never let the technique dominate but it was a purely musical experience, and besides it was in a fast tempo that I afterwards thought was a bit special.

After a while, when they played a tune it felt suddenly exactly as if the premises had disappeared, the surrounding almost disappeared like in a hallucination, the walls disappeared, it was sort of like in a dream. I could almost see how the ceiling opened up above the orchestra like when there are thunder clouds and there is a hole, an opening where the light comes through, the sun can be seen, that's exactly how I saw it, as if it was open up above and the orchestra sort of was raised up a bit in that hole. An incredible experience, afterwards I had to shake my head and I didn't understand what had happened. I was totally sober. The music was so superb, it penetrated in so deep and struck something so that it became like a hallucination. I have never experienced anything like it, either before or later.

Then, suddenly I descended into that boring room again. It's hard to express such an event, it probably only lasted a minute or so. I'll never forget it, I have never had any similar experience. I still don't understand what happened. If I'd taken LSD or something like that, then I could imagine something similar but that wasn't the case. You wonder afterwards if you were tired or something like that.

Then I bought some records by him but there I couldn't at all experience anything like that. It was the situation, the greatest live music I've ever heard.

'The greatest live music I've ever heard', a unique experience. A brief moment with another reality—like a hallucination, dream-like, the room disappears, the orchestra is raised up and surrounded by light—an example of transcendental elements in strong experiences with music (see Chapter 13, section 13.1). Returning to 'reality' afterwards doesn't feel so pleasant: 'Then, suddenly I descended into that boring room again.' It might suggest an out-of-body experience (see Chapter 8, section 8.2).

Finally, a young woman's enthusiastic and vivid description of her experience when she listened to four jazz musicians. Her already high expectations were surpassed, the interplay of the musicians, their energy and force called forth intense physical and mental reactions. It felt magical, total, ultimate.

(26K) Woman, young, 1980s (from an edited interview)

[She is listening to four well-known jazz musicians at her favourite club.] My highest expectations were fulfilled as to what I thought it could be like, and more besides! The best that I had heard from every musician in various contexts now merged together into something . . . really great! It was like a *force*, something that turns time inside out. Time doesn't exist. They create their own time. There was lots of energy, a force that is outstanding. That is . . . something religious.

It was four souls who created this at that moment, and then it becomes something that is much bigger than we ever can be as individual musicians. It becomes magic! When music really makes the leap, or whatever you should call it, something happens when the very thing that radiates out, the thing that sounds, becomes somewhat superior to what each person does.

The distinct feeling then was warmth, fellowship, happiness, and trust. Everybody was sitting, more or less jumping on the chairs and just *shouting* and more or less crazy. You sit and follow along, your body moves. It feels as if there is something that rushes around inside your body. A force that transmits itself into the tiniest little nerve you have!

I thought that this is the best I've heard. I might never get to experience this again. This is the total, the ultimate! Music can't get better than this.

Straight afterwards, it felt empty. It was a pity that it was over, at the same time it couldn't have gone on . . . I was tired in my soul, my head, everywhere, because you feel so much. It is a bit like being in love. It makes life bigger and gives a deeper picture of life. It's important. That life can be like this!

The 'ultimate', it can't get better than this, a deeper picture of life, 'That life can be like this!'—the account ends in reflections of an existential character.

The reactions that are described in this chapter are familiar from many earlier accounts and do not need to be listed again. The pieces that are performed are only mentioned as an exception. The emphasis lies entirely on the musicians themselves, their skill, commitment, interplay, and charisma. The visual impressions of the musicians and the communication between musicians and listeners play a great part; they are lacking when one listens to recordings.

The selection of accounts in this chapter should not be interpreted as some form of 'ranking' of different musicians. Several other jazz musicians are mentioned elsewhere in our material; they are listed together in Chapter 30, section 30.3.5.

CHAPTER 27

MUSIC AT CONCERTS: POP AND ROCK

THERE are a considerable number of accounts of strong experiences at pop and rock concerts in Chapter 5 on one's teenage years, especially in section 5.1. The reactions that are described there are also found to a great extent in the following accounts and are thus only commented upon sparingly below.

During teenage years, these concerts meant a longed-for and expectant meeting with an idol, with whom one had previously become acquainted on a record or in other media. The first account in this chapter is of this type. The idol is one of the absolutely biggest names within pop music, and his performance of well-known tunes gives rise to nostalgia, tears, and total joy. Sometimes it felt almost unreal.

(27A) Man, middle-aged, 1980s

My strongest musical experience took place when I was at a concert in Stockholm and saw Paul McCartney. The concert started with a film showing on three gigantic screens. The film was about The Beatles and major world events from 1963 to the present day. The atmosphere built up and you thought: 'Just imagine, I am soon going to hear and see one of the Beatles.'

When McCartney & Co started to play, you understood that this isn't an ordinary concert, and then I'm thinking mainly about the technical stuff, light and sound. After three tunes, McCartney started to play old Beatles tunes. When he played 'The long and winding road', which is a calm and very beautiful ballad, it really touched a nostalgia-feeling nerve in me, and the tears started to gush. The same thing happened two more times. During 'Can't buy me love', where he pulled out his old Höfner bass for the first time that evening, I shut my eyes and thought 'It sounds like The Beatles,' and when I look again, then I see Paul McCartney with his Höfner bass that you've seen so many times on record covers, idol pictures, TV, and so on.

The third time the tears gushed was during the song 'Fool on the hill', which is also an extremely beautiful tune. If I remember correctly, I was overwhelmed by feelings when the part with the flutes came, where he sings 'spinning around'. At the same time, McCartney and the grand piano were lifted up to the ceiling. Then I almost had to pinch myself in the arm to find out that it was for real. Talk of total joy!

Directly afterwards I felt extremely happy and exhilarated. I remember that I thought: 'I have seen The Beatles, I have seen The Beatles, I have seen The Beatles! (Almost!).'

The next narrator wanted most of all to hear his idol perform a certain piece but didn't really have any hopes that his wish would be fulfilled. So when the concert started with this particular piece, the experience became really exceptional.

(27B) Man, young, 1980s

My strongest musical experience took place at a concert with Mike Oldfield. In 1976, Mike Oldfield released an album with a number on it called 'Platinum' which for me is one of the best ever done. It is an old and long (25 minutes) tune so I didn't have any expectations of hearing that particular tune. After a long wait we finally got into the hall where some lovely expectant music was pouring out of the loudspeakers. I could immediately hear that it was Mike's music. We had our places in the seventh row from the stage, that is, the almost perfect place. The interval music already had me exhilarated and I felt really pleased.

Almost on time the MC came out onto the stage to check the mood of the audience and to present *Mike Oldfield* with his group. There was cheering when Mike finally came onto the stage but it was quietened by Mike himself when he said a few words in Swedish. The musicians got ready and the audience became quiet.

It is now that I get my music experience. The first notes almost made me faint. It was 'Platinum'! I felt that I disappeared for a moment and then woke up as if in a dream, but all the time aware of the music. In some way I was floating above the audience, which simply was there but I couldn't hear them and they didn't disturb me. It was like a dream, I was floating and the group was playing only for me. It is very hard to describe the feeling I had. I was totally gone—my friends noticed as they had tried to make contact with me during the number but failed. I came back to my senses again because of somebody hitting me on my shoulder several times and calling my name and wondering what was happening. My cheeks were wet and I had apparently been crying.

The concert continued with old and new tunes and it was simply super. What happened after the concert was for me a vacuum. That I was the one who drove home, I can't remember that. Nor what I did the next day. My friends have told me what we did and how I behaved. I had been very quiet and stand-offish. The only thing I remember of the day after is that I felt completely cleansed and empty inside, but pleased, incredibly pleased!

Fully conscious and unconscious at the same time: completely conscious of the music, unconscious of everything else—which nevertheless is there in some way, like in a dream. The feeling of floating freely is described in several other accounts (see Chapter 8, section 8.1). He felt chosen, confirmed: they were playing 'only for me' (see Chapter 16, section16.2).

In the next instance, the narrator had no expectations at all and his mood was subdued. Nevertheless, he was directly affected and imbibed every drop of the music.

(27C) Man, young, 1980s

Music, for me, is more than half of life—it is such an important point in this existence that without music I don't know if life would be worth living.

Had just got back from my first Roskilde trip. I was tired, unwashed, and generally whacked. A mate came and said that some unknown group was going to play in a little dive of a place in the Småland [southern Sweden] forests. So there we stood one warm evening in this little dive in Småland. I had no expectations at all, just felt worn out.

Whatever, we went into a little foyer in a theatre building. And then everybody suddenly started to pour into the actual theatre auditorium and once we were in there, on the stage there was a large piece of cloth hanging over almost all the stage. The cloth is painted with psychedelic colours and patterns. There were some instruments on the stage too. What I couldn't help looking at, and this went for a lot of other people too, was the guitar—the absolutely most beautiful guitar I've ever seen—can't do justice to it in a description.

Anyhow, then Danielle Dax comes onto the stage (didn't know then who it was) and it was now you gradually started to realize you'd be getting to see (and hear) something good. She had some pretty heavy make-up and long hair—but this hair was covered with some very fancy headgear. If you've ever seen the ceremonial headdress of an Indian medicine man—it was one of those! In leather complete with buffalo horns and everything.

And then they really got going—I'd never listened to such music before that time. But directly after the first note I just fell for it—largely because you had no expectations at all and it was so good. And then the entire concert went on in a mist, I sucked in every drop of it. When it was over, everybody stood up and applauded for at least five minutes—everybody.

The accounts are often about concerts with thousands of listeners. Apart from the actual music and the stage show, the atmosphere and the fellowship in the audience mean a great deal for the experience. One is usually familiar with the music before from records, TV or other media; one knows the tunes by heart and sings along. Here is a first example.

(27D) Man, young, 1980s

It was a concert in Stockholm with the group Saga. They play a perfectionist symphonic rock music with strong influences of classical scales in music. It builds a lot on drums, guitar, and various types of synths and keyboards. The music is extremely melodic and the arrangements are well done. There are both vocal and instrumental bits in the music, they are often integrated with each other in a very effective way.

It is an unbelievable experience to be in a well-filled arena together with several thousand other people who are all there for the same purpose, that is, to listen and to really devote yourself to music that is wonderful. To stand in the squash in front of the stage and sing along with the songs you have heard a long time ago on records, it makes you feel drunk, you feel happy quite simply, all your senses are directed towards one place, the stage. Your entire body takes part in the concert. When you see Saga live it isn't just about the music, but the stage show too, they've got a fantastic stage show with lots of lights on the stage. The music and the light show complement each other and increase the feeling of joy. You get high on music, that is exactly what it is about, you get feelings that can't be described in words.

Going to a concert is an experience, big style, even before you are there—you play old records to get in the mood, get the right feeling, a feeling that then just increases while the concert is going on. It's a total feeling that can't be described, you can only feel it on the spot. A very special feeling is when the group's hits come along, for example when Saga played the introductory bars of 'Don't be late (Chapter two)', a tune that the audience had called out for an hour before it came. A tune that starts calmly, and everybody flicks on their cigarette lighters—what an atmosphere. The entire arena illuminated with cigarette lighters, then the hair stands up on your skin.

When you go home from the concert you feel elevated, you walk around in raptures and hum the tunes and just enjoy yourself. A musical experience can remain with you quite a long time when you listen to records, but a good concert always gives the greatest experiences. A live concert has to be experienced, you can't describe it in words—it's another dimension of reality.

A well-known group that might be said to have had cosmic ambitions with its music and stage show was Pink Floyd. Something of that is reflected in the reactions of listeners in the following two accounts.

(27E) Man, middle-aged, 1990s

For me, the group Pink Floyd has always stood for mystery and emotional commitment, which has probably both helped me through my teenage years and given me many memorable musical experiences . . .

Wet with rain from top to toe we entered the arena to see a concert by my favourite artistes in the rock genre. The group has a reputation for being extremely visual, but this time the visual side presumably merged even more with the music in a total experience than ever before. I don't think I have ever been so moved by the totality in a rock concert. Some of the stronger things the group conveyed to me were these.

The guitarist David Gilmore played a bit of introduction on the guitar where strong impressions were given via auditory, visual, and even tactile perception. The guitar with its strong expression controlled two laser beams that projected their light through the sky and onto the clouds. Every time the guitar made a scraping, echoing sound slowly rising in pitch, I got the shivers all over and the lights reinforced the feeling. There was a synthetic bass sound all the time in the background and with powerful amplification this sound triggered the tactile perception to also influence the experience. Besides this primarily physiological reaction, there was also an inner feeling of well-being that arose, but I also got a frightened feeling from the composition of the notes. Somewhat mixed feelings, that is.

Right in the middle of the concert, I experience the entire situation with this gigantic lightshow and the magnificent music from the stage as almost unreal. I feel as though I have been moved to another planet and I suddenly have a distinct feeling of communication. Almost as if I have something supernatural before me that is desperately trying to catch my attention and make me understand something.

(27F) Woman, young, 1980s

It was a day in the late summer. We were going to go to a concert outside Copenhagen and get to listen to a group called Pink Floyd. They play music that has appealed to me since I was a teenager. They are very skilful musicians, you could say they play classical rock. They use a lot of effects. 'They play my feelings.'

When we had entered the enormous arena the clouds started to disperse and I could see the light blue sky. The stadium started to become filled and soon there were really a lot of people, there was room for about 30,000! Then this longed-for concert starts and I get goosepimples all over my body. They've got a fantastic technical set-up, you can hear every little detail in the music. The place we had chosen, right in the middle of the lawn, meant that we heard the music and the effects from everywhere, from behind, from the right, from the left. They had a big round film screen on the stage where they showed films from their videos to the music and sometimes colour effects. The films were incredibly beautiful and full of effects and fitted well with the music. The introduction of one of the tunes is such that you hear rippling water and somebody rowing a boat. The effect of this is that I very suddenly think I have the boat behind me. I turn round before I have time to think about it, and then discover that this is not the case. I smile a little to myself when I see that I am not alone in behaving in this slightly embarrassing way. Most people have turned round.

And then they played the good old tunes mixed with new but just as good ones, and I knew them so well and could stand there and sway and sing along. I felt at one with the music. I shivered.

When the group started to play again after the break, darkness had settled over the stadium and they had good use for the light effects which included laser beams that seemed to go out into the universe. Yes, that is actually what it felt like, everything became so infinite and I was one with it.

This is the first time I am so 'inside' the music. I feel how the bass comes from the ground into my body via the soles of my feet, goes up my calves, my thighs, backbone, and I am filled with the music. Borders are erased. I am at one with the universe. The music dissolves all boundaries in the way I've understood it means to be psychotic.

When they play my favourite tune, 'Learning to Fly', the tears start to fall. And I who have seen old films, for example The Beatles, where the girls cry, and thought 'How silly!'— now I'm in the same situation myself, although not as hysterical, no, I stand there very calmly and rock in time with the music and feel that I am whole and just let the tears run down my cheeks. That I got such strong experiences depends, I think, on that I had several senses that were satisfied rather than just hearing. Vision and touch got their bit too.

The concert starts to draw to a close, and I feel that I don't want that to happen, the way I always feel when everything is going well. I want to keep it. The finale becomes a climax when they set off one of the biggest firework displays I've ever seen. I stood there like a small child on Christmas Eve with my mouth open, and laughed and clapped my hands. What an experience!

Three hours of music have filled me. In the car on the way home, I felt both happy and elevated at the same time as I was sad that it was over. I dozed off with 'Learning to Fly' in my head and well-being in body and soul.

Besides aural and visual experiences, both narrators mention physical sensations as a result of the high sound level; the music literally enters the body. This can be a part of the feeling of merging with the music, 'becoming one with the music'. Both narrators also describe elements of a transcendent character: the feeling of something supernatural, messages from the cosmos, feeling of endlessness, being one with the universe.

The next account contrasts with the previous ones. A solitary musician on stage challenges the audience and presents a political message on an issue that was highly topical at that time. His commitment, his speech, and his music surprise and conquer everyone in the audience.

(27G) Man, middle-aged, 1980s

The place is the Roskilde Festival in Denmark. It is Saturday evening, about 10 o'clock. I am in the so-called Tuborg Tent together with another 15–20,000 people. The atmosphere inside the tent is fantastic. People are standing squashed together, many are probably a bit tipsy, most are elated and happy. The mass of people rock and sing as a sort of backwash from the intense concert that has just finished. We are all waiting for one of the evening's highlights, the intense British rock agitator Billy Bragg.

Suddenly the lights are turned off inside the tent and cheering comes from the audience in direct reply. The stage is in darkness. After a few minutes where the expectations from the audience almost get the tent canvas to flap, a spotlight is turned on and Billy Bragg makes his entrance. He is a fairly short, little man, a bit bony like Englishmen are, with his mop of slightly red hair cut short. He is wearing trainers, jeans, and a T-shirt with an African motif and a text about ANC and the struggle against apartheid. He is completely alone on the big stage. At first, he stands there completely silent in front of the microphone. The cheering from the audience has changed into a roar, which can be interpreted as a sign to start playing. Billy is still standing silently and looking right out into the crowd.

Then suddenly he starts talking, a really inflammatory speech. This one little man literally bawls out us 15–20,000 in the audience for about ten minutes. It is a speech that is charged with energy and is about our responsibility to commit ourselves in the struggle against apartheid. The angry little man's diatribe takes the audience by storm. The words are spat out and they fly like the flashes of a whip out in the tent. People just stand there with their mouths open. After a while, a sort of warm wave of sympathy comes from the crowd. The audience appreciates the courage of the little man—because you really do need courage to do something like this.

Suddenly he stops talking, hangs an electric guitar round his neck and starts to play. Very intense, charged with energy, and with his so characteristically distorted guitar. He is still on his own and plays without accompaniment. The tune is about the struggle in South Africa. It is so strong and charged. Suddenly the hairs on my neck start to rise, I get goosepimples all over my body and tears start to well up in my eyes. It feels so lovely and liberating in some way. I am not ashamed of it and don't try to hide it at all. Then I think: is it only me who is standing here crying or . . .? I turn round towards my companions nearby. They are all standing there drying their eyes!

The concert goes on for perhaps an hour. Billy Bragg, alone with his guitar. A furious tempo, enormous energy and masses of conviction and frankness in the lyrics.

After the concert I feel completely exhausted. The festival goes on many hours into the night, but I don't want to experience any more concerts this evening. I seek out my mates and talk about Bragg's concert. All of them had been just as moved as I had. My respect for Billy Bragg increased enormously. His courage and the upright manner in which he stands for his principles somehow also gave me courage.

In the next account, however, it is solely a question of the high class of the performance of a well-known rock musician and his fellow players. The listener recognizes himself in the music, is totally moved, almost shocked and completely exhausted at the end, can't manage to take in any more.

(27H) Man, young, 1990s

Recently I have understood that music is something much greater and more important to me than just a lot of sounds. Although I am fairly aware and find it easy to catch the 'right' music for the 'right' occasion, I have never experienced anything so totally embracing as I did this time at Eric Clapton's concert in Stockholm. Eric Clapton plays a form of blues-rock and has a fairly laid-back and harmonious style. Since I've always thought that some parts of what he does speak to me and give me something on every occasion I listen, I immediately decided to go along. When I arrived I managed to get a good ticket in the stalls. For once, they kept to the starting time, which doesn't often happen at rock concerts.

(Jesus, now comes the difficult bit. How can I verbally describe the following feelings?)

Eric Clapton makes his entrance onto the stage and together with a collection of extremely competent musicians they start off. First of all they seem to seek out each other on stage to capture a fellowship and a means of expression that suits them on this particular occasion. I was now sitting almost in the middle of the stalls where I'd found an empty seat, and it felt as if bits were finding their rightful place. The music and the tunes followed each other without lots of talk and pandering to the audience. I was fascinated by their incredible exactness without it sounding arranged and fixed in advance.

Then when the old classic 'Wonderful tonight' was played, all my barriers seemed to give way. A lump in my throat and tears pouring down my cheeks. I think that after that I cried, smiled, and held my breath in turn for the rest of the concert. It felt like an incredible togetherness, as if they were standing there painting a vision just like the picture I most of all wanted to see myself as and attempt to be like. I felt totally elated and a bit shocked and have no memory that I thought of anyone or anything beyond that feeling. That is, only the musicians, the music, and me existed in my thoughts.

The highlight during the concert was when the wonderful bassist, Nathan East, did a wonderfully airy solo, quietly and with few notes and chords on a five-stringed fretless base. The solo is really perfectly balanced and when the last note dies away completely, then there is a *total* silence in the 14,000-strong audience.

At that point, Eric Clapton steps in with his guitar and starts up 'Layla', a slightly more rocky tune. From the second before, having sat without a sound and held my breath, I now spontaneously stand up with an arm stretched out, fist clenched and cheering with tears streaming down my cheeks. Most of the people round about me in the stalls reacted in exactly the same way. It must have been the enormous change of nuance from total silence to full force that led to it feeling like the great highlight and total liberation.

Never before has any concert directly called forth such amounts of tears and spontaneous emotional reactions as this one. That's why it felt almost tense towards the end, and when they finished and were called back in for an encore, then I know that I thought: 'No, I can't take any more.' But, being curious, I was kept there and enjoyed a few more tunes that were performed really well. But if there had been a second encore, then I would probably have left, because I didn't want to push out the feeling of satisfaction, but continue to savour it a little while longer.

In the two final accounts it is a question of very enthusiastic, almost orgiastic experiences of music. The first narrator describes an ecstatic 'now' where there is total agreement between the band, the audience, and the setting. His body is governed completely by the music and no thoughts are released; it is like an orgasm. Everything is inexplicable and, essentially, indescribable.

(27I) Man, young, 1980s (from an edited interview)

[He is at a rock concert, knows about the group from before.] It was packed with folk, everybody felt good, no rowdy people. The group was sitting among the audience, which gives you an extra kick. There was contact with the audience directly.

Dancing, hot, sweaty, high volume, a hell of a pace. The band jumps out into the audience and give it all they've got, think it's really great. Then all of a sudden *it happens*! Which is inexplicable. Mass psychosis really, because that's what it's about. Everybody in the audience is so turned on and they all think it is so bloody good, so they just stand up and scream. The band can tame the audience and the opposite too. There's a sort of symbiosis between the group and the audience.

You are sucked into the rhythm. You become a part . . . The audience and the group and the place and all of that, it becomes a single living organism. Everything is so in agreement.

I couldn't have stood still. You had to move, that's just how it was. Your body wanted one thing. Your brain another. Then you must forget your head and just do what you feel. What your body wants. Your legs are just twitching!

There are no thoughts in your head. What should you be thinking about? There is nothing to think about! The only thing you can concentrate on is staying on your feet so you don't crash in your ecstasy.

You've just got to keep on going, accelerate, go right up to 190 [kmh]. There are no limits. You are just in raptures. You feel so bloody good, *incredible* well-being, it is like an orgasm!

It is a feeling that is so bloody hard to describe. You just can't do it, and if you try, then there's a risk that you butcher the experience totally. It just *is* there!

Directly afterwards you want it to keep on going, but it can't, of course. You do realize that. There is nothing that stays on inside your head afterwards. It is like an orgasm: nice as long as it lasts.

The next narrator is also overwhelmed by the music and overjoyed, but in a completely different way; it feels almost like a religious experience. The music and the message feel so honest and aimed at him personally that he is filled with energy and hope, a belief in life.

(27J) Man, young, 1980s (from an edited interview)

[A rock concert with a well-known American rock band] You sort of directly became a part of the concert. You were conquered directly, like a blow to the stomach. There was no going back. This is the total thing! You don't experience this sort of thing at many concerts. It was just such a hell of a force, such energy, such power in the performance. Such happiness, such intensity, such honesty. It felt so simple, so honest. It went right into your heart.

Then when the tempo slowed to calmer tunes it became almost even stronger. I suppose it is the nearest I have come to a religious experience. It was so genuine. A lot of music isn't but this type of music just is, it can't be distorted. I think the artiste means every bloody word he says, there is such conviction in the words and then you can't do otherwise than stand there and shudder. When you can feel 'He is singing for me, it is about me because I have experienced this in some way,' then you are filled with one hell of a joy. There is such a hell of a positive force in the melancholia. It fills you with joy and a belief in life. You become hopeful! You become filled with something—a huge *being*. This concerns me, my soul. It made me want to dance; I don't dance normally. You got such strength, such a kick, that you become filled with energy. It is like taking vitamins for three years and getting them all at once. You become positively converted!

Afterwards you are so incredibly happy and feel one hell of a joy and just want to dance on the streets. You get a *wow* feeling. I am a part of something just now! It took us six or seven hours to get over it.

Concerts like this are necessary. It isn't just a concert but a lifestyle, how you think. I suppose it's a sort of belief in something that the artiste is helping you to verbalize. If you have some dreams, perhaps you might believe in them a little longer. It becomes easier to live for a while!

The setting and the atmosphere at rock and pop concerts are very different from at concerts with classical music and many jazz concerts too. The surrounding arrangements are often extremely lavish, as is the stage show. The artistes often give full expression to their feelings and encourage or demand that the audience respond; they work up the mood among the listeners. The listeners don't usually sit or stand politely motionless in their places but move to the music, dance, sing along, egg each other on; you are sort of a part of the entire event, not just a listener. There is a strong feeling of fellowship in the audience, everyone has come for the same reason and they are all intent on the same thing: you only live for what is happening here and now, and you do what you feel like without thinking about it.

Just as the experience can be unrestrained, so sometimes can the language be. It is hard to imagine a classical concert described in the language that is used in the final accounts above. But they are undeniably vivid, very close to the actual experience and in agreement with the style and character usually associated with rock music. But as has been pointed out earlier (Chapter 18, section 18.1), several of these accounts are from interviews, that is, they are originally spoken language with a spontaneous choice of words and expressions in the interview situation with no thought of a 'neater' written linguistic presentation.

CHAPTER 28

METAPHORS AND SIMILES

It has often been said—by musicians, philosophers, writers, and others—that words do not suffice to describe how one experiences music, music goes beyond words, 'music starts where words come to an end'. That notion is also found among many of our narrators. They say that they can't find words that cover what they have experienced; the experience is—or certain parts of it are—indescribable.

One possibility is to make use of metaphors or similes, that is, one refers to other phenomena that in some way are similar to or mirror what one experienced. About 100 narrators (approximately 10% of our participants) have made use of metaphors or similes. Most of these cases are reproduced below in the form of short quotes from the accounts concerned. They are, thus, taken out of their context, but there is a reference to the corresponding complete account (if there is no reference, the quote is taken from accounts that have not been included in this book).

First we have metaphors and similes with regard to the actual music or performance (section 28.1), then metaphors and similes that concern experiences in connection with listening (28.2, 28.3), performance and composition (28.4). Finally there is a summary of the phenomena that have occurred in the metaphors and similes (28.5).

28.1 DESCRIPTIONS OF THE MUSIC OR THE PERFORMANCE

These metaphors and similes are mainly connected with works within classical music or their performance.

(About Bach's *Actus Tragicus* at a funeral) It was notes whirling around like snow-flakes, weightless. It was like angels playing the flute and the trumpet—notes that filled the room with happiness and hope. (Chapter 22, account 22C)

(About voices in a performance of the *St Matthew Passion*) The serious, wonderfully beautiful alto voice was gold, I thought . . . I was flying too, enjoying the light voices—like silver—of the boys' choir. (Chapter 25, account 25.1E)

(Mozart's *Eine kleine Nachtmusik*) The music is so 'exact'. I see before me endless rows of stone pillars with the same distance and space in between that never finishes.

(Mozart's Symphony No. 40) It was heaven; it was paradise; it was everything that was beautiful, pure, and deeply loving. (Chapter 13, account 13.4E)

(Mozart, Kyrie Eleison from the C minor mass) . . . where the tone foundation of the strings becomes like a catapult for the exultant flight of the solo voice, as if lifted by invisible wings towards the heights. A light, silver-glimmering voice that throws itself in dizzying intervals from low tones right up into the stratosphere . . . The solo voice is most of all reminiscent of the movements of a bird up and down in the air. (Chapter 25, account 25.2O)

(Beethoven's Symphony No. 9) . . .when I suddenly heard—heard!—the delightfully beautiful flower wind its way up as if from an incense holder in front of me, a bit into the slow movement in Beethoven's ninth. (Chapter 6, account 6.2D)

(The last movement in Beethoven's Symphony No. 9) The singing from the loud-speakers undulates and hisses, is carried along on high waves by the symphony orchestra's irrepressible music. (Chapter 14, account 14.3F)

(Beethoven's Violin Concerto in D major) The music's alternately tinny and strong silver-gleaming tones, from this solitary violin, in an almost unspeakable and unfath-omable beauty . . . Particularly evident in the gleaming, pure, and frail tones of the andante movement. (Chapter 25, account 25.2V)

(Wagner's opera *Parsifal*) . . . somewhere during the first act a new structure is exposed, the orchestra begins to be like one of those old toasters that we had when I was a child, it glows in the red-hot wires inside, the electricity increases in tension. (Chapter 18, account 18.1E)

(Tchaikovsky's *Pathétique* symphony) The third movement is strutting, almost humorous—it is the unconscious optimist who naively but proudly goes on and on. (Chapter 25, account 25.1Q)

(Dvořák symphony) When the orchestra tutti finally came, it was like a steam-roller—a will, an idea multiplied 80 times! (Chapter 18, account 18.1D)

(Grieg: '*Morgonstämning*' ['Morning mood']) I didn't think I had ever heard any-thing so beautiful in all my life, it was as if these tones were life itself.

(Sibelius's Symphony No. 4) Perhaps above all the emotional quality of desolation with strings of warmth, grey-brownness with reddish-yellow features (autumn colours!), the ascetic, unadorned, with oases of lushness (though that doesn't mean that the music is a desert!). Moving in a large space. (Chapter 9, account 9.3C)

(Rachmaninov, a piano concerto). It was so unbelievably beautiful and the music sort of came in waves roughly like a swell out at sea. (Chapter 6, account 6.1B)

(Ravel) They started to play with an unusual glow ... It was like a meltdown ... and the volume of the music must have bordered on a record high in art music contexts. (Chapter 25, account 25.1C)

Take Stravinsky's *Rite of Spring*, for example ... that's hard rock without electricity! So bloody big and powerful. There's such energy in it. (Chapter 11, account 11.2O)

Here are some other examples.

(About Felicity Lott) ... that an angel from the heavenly Lord had materialized and settled in the singer's chest ... the pianissimo comes without effort, like a veil that thinly covers the tone and gives it its silver gleam. (Chapter 25, account 25.2O)

(About music by Harold Budd) Timbre music—a minimum of notes, and between every note in–cred–ib–le pauses ... Raindrop music. 'Raindrops (notes) that quivered, gradually loosening their hold ...' (Chapter 20, account 20F)

(Boys' voices) Four boys about ten years old who sang a four-part arrangement of our most beautiful summer ballads ... They looked like cupids and their voices were like arrows of love fired at the large number of people that had gathered. (Chapter 6, account 6.1J)

(Tango) The music danced around like a whirlwind in the narrow room. (Chapter 17, account 17.2L)

28.2 DESCRIPTIONS OF BOTH THE MUSIC AND THE EXPERIENCE

In some of the accounts, there are metaphors or similes that concern both the music and the experience of it.

(Bach music in a cathedral) I heard the sound of the organ, sometimes gentle and sometimes majestic like a divine waterfall: Bach! (Chapter 11, account 11.2F)

(Mozart's 'Ave verum corpus') Quietly, gently as a warm summer breeze, the music reached me and went right in. I sat there without moving a muscle, leaning forward, and just sort of swallowed it ... every bit of me was filled with divine harmony. (Chapter 5, account 5.2H)

(The duet from Bellini's *Norma*) They gave us a coloratura bravura which was stunning. It was like going to the circus and I remember the feeling that 'this isn't true, I'm dreaming, you just can't do this'. (Chapter 25, account 25.2J)

(Mahler's Symphony No. 10) A super romantic (like early Schönberg) winding between different keys where the marked absence of beginning and end produces a somewhat hypnotic effect not unlike the feeling you experience when you lie in a boat moored by an island in the archipelago. (Chapter 11, account 11.3L)

('*En Vintersaga*' ['A Winter's Tale'] by Lars-Erik Larsson) A very good metaphor is the legend of the thorn bird which sings only once in its life, namely when it impales itself against a thorn and sings more beautifully than any other bird while it is dying. Just then, on these three occasions, for me the music was just so intense, so beautiful, so painfully wonderful. (Chapter 12, account 12.2H)

(A tango, '*Tanguero*', on guitar) I experienced it as 'unpredictable' and 'mischievous' ... The feeling I got was like when you meet a dear friend whom you haven't seen for a long time; you look carefully at each other, your eyes light up, you hug each other, and your hearts are filled with a feeling of togetherness and secret joy. There's also that lovely smell of skin and the sensation of soft hairs on their neck that tickle your nose. (Chapter 11, account 11.2B)

The group Sågskära who were ... playing ... so that the air was really glowing in the light from the candles ... you felt so elated, bubbling like all your body was filled with flowers. (Chapter 23, account 23E)

(Song in a musical) The lyrics went right into my heart, the hard armour around my emotions was pierced ... If you want to say it a bit poetically, you could say that the song broke the ice and after that there was a thaw! (Chapter 14, account 14.3D)

(Rock song) Springsteen played 'Cadillac Ranch', a tune that is like a steamroller that just flattens you. (Chapter 5, account 5.1D)

(Indian raga on sitar) In the half-dark room, notes were thrown out like silvered drops of rain. Everything seemed to be pervaded by them. Like carbon dioxide bubbles making their way through the liquid in a bottle of pop ... Unceasingly, as long as he played, I had a feeling of being lifted up and in some way purified. A sort of spiritual steam bath. (Chapter 24, account 24L)

28.3 LISTENERS' DESCRIPTIONS OF THE EXPERIENCE

The majority of metaphors and similes occur in descriptions of the actual experience. These can be grouped together in themes, as can be seen from the headings below.

Struck by music

(Beethoven's Serenade Op. 8 in D major) I was sort of touched by the fairy's wand and disappeared into a spell.

(Verdi's *Requiem*) All of my being was affected by an internal revolution ... But it was the Rex Tremendae Majestatis movement that was the definite knock-out for me. (Chapter 25, account 25.1G)

(George Adams Quartet) Perhaps I had expected one of those peak experiences in some way, although it came when the conditions weren't optimal at all, you had heard music all day long, you can get so satiated with it, but it didn't matter—it just struck like lightning. (Chapter 26, account 26.I)

(Blues singer Roffe Wikström) Then lightning struck! It was an electric guitar that had broken out right in front of my eyes and ears. The volume was high and the music stirring. The artiste with the reverberating electric guitar was Roffe Wikström with his band Hjärtslag [Heartbeat], and that music certainly got my heart beating. (Chapter 26, account 26.G)

(Singer Danielle Dax) But directly after the first note I just fell for it, largely because you had no expectations at all and it was so good. (Chapter 27, account 27C)

(Musicians Mikis Theodorakis and Manos Hadzidhakis) It happened when I played a record with music by Mikis Theodorakis and Manos Hadzidhakis ... A blow like being hit with a club wrapped in cotton wool. That was how I experienced it. (Chapter 15, account 15.2F)

(A section in Barber's Adagio) The harmony (dissonance) pierces deep into my heart like a knife. (Chapter 7, account 7.5F)

Twice, I have experienced that music has gone right into my heart like a piercing laser beam. Both times it has been very light, clear voices that have sung to an orchestra.

(Piano music) I was almost filled with dread and an enormously great respect ... I felt something of the smallness you can feel at the foot of a mountain when nature shows all of its scenery. (Chapter 14, account 14.4C)

Special susceptibility

(Bach's Piano Concerto in D minor) The music flowed and I felt that I experienced it with every tiny fibre in my body. Like when you drink or eat, it seemed to merge with my thoughts and feelings. (Chapter 25, account 25.2U)

(Wagner's *Das Rheingold*) It was a feeling of intense expectation with all my senses on full alert, wide open and susceptible, sucking in every note. (Chapter 13, account 13.3E)

(Prokofiev's *Romeo and Juliet*) The music caresses your ears and crawls into your brain and makes you understand what the composer felt when he wrote the piece. As if the brain was filled with music.

(About Sibelius) His entire tonal world suits my soul so that I think that every single pore on my body opens up. All my senses are turned on, even smell and taste.

(Classical music) I felt how I sucked in the music, I drank it, swallowed it, was being filled by it. Like a dry sponge which is reacquiring its shape ... it is a need—a nourishment ... like when somebody who is very thirsty is able to drink some water. (Chapter 5, account 5.2L)

(Singer Danielle Dax with comp) And then the entire concert went on in a mist, I sucked in every drop of it. (Chapter 27, account 27C)

I soak up music as if I were a dust rag, all music whatever it is, classical, rock, and pop, yeah, everything. (Chapter 5, account 5.3E)

(Trio Con Tromba) I personally felt like I was just a big radio receiver. All channels tuned in to receive this particular music, and it could ravage my entire organism uninhibited. (Chapter 26, account 26F)

(Listening to a tenor saxophonist from the 1930s or 1940s) ... a state of very strong identification with music that I have listened to ... I am at one with it. (Chapter 7, account 7.4C)

Atmosphere, mood, fellowship

(Wagner's *Das Rheingold*) The experience came gradually—started as a sort of charge or tension in the atmosphere, which gradually became all the more intense—roughly like a scent which you first get a hint of, rather than really feel, before it washes over you, inebriates you and takes you over. (Chapter 13, account 13.3E)

(Trio Con Tromba) The atmosphere became even more tense, there was absolute silence in the room. There was an unbelievable magnetic field between those who were on the stage and in the room, you could have cut the atmosphere into slices. It became one unit, the audience and the musicians, the boundaries between different roles merged together; we drank out of the same barrel. (Chapter 26, account 26F)

(Traditional Turkish music) I feel totally harmonious and free from the usual awareness of myself. A very pleasant sensation spreads across my chest and down to my solar plexus. It feels like fresh air. I feel contact with an inner ego, my soul. (Chapter 15, account 15.1C)

Discovery of something new

(Bach's Partita for solo violin) It was as if all the floodgates had opened.

(Handel's Concerto grosso) It was like a window that opened and this window is now always ajar. (Chapter 15, account 15.1E)

Mozart's 'Ave verum corpus' ... opened the door for me to a completely new world within music. (Chapter 5, account 5.2H)

(Beethoven's Serenade Op. 8) Opus 8 came to serve as a key to what until then had been a closed door for me, and open it wide.

(Paganini's Violin Concerto No. 1 in D major) The concert was an unprecedented experience for me—it was as though a curtain had been pulled away and the entire world of music opened up before me. (Chapter 5, account 5.2F)

Aha! experience, insight

(Listening to jazz singer Betty Carter) But it was an Aha! experience. What happens is that all the bits fall into place, there's a string inside you that gets into a spin in some way, a feeling deep inside that affects you. All the bits fall into place. This is what it must be like. (Chapter 26, account 26C)

(Listening to African Christian music in Assisi) It was such a radical experience to sit in an old church together with Christians from different countries and sing music from the Christians in Africa. It was as if all the preparations we had made led to this occasion during these few minutes. Like when you have just finished a jigsaw puzzle where every bit has been put in place to form a whole picture. (Chapter 14, account 14.2C)

(An inner hearing experience) I usually think of a strong experience with music as meaning that all brain cells, all nerves, are brought about by an outside force to bear in the same direction, like when a magnet arranges iron filings in a simple physics experiment. (Chapter 9, account 9.2E)

(Beethoven's Symphony No. 5 during a storm) I saw the power of music to evoke different emotions and to take me away from reality ... the night seemed to redefine my concept of music. I saw the forest, not just a clump of trees. (Chapter 23, account 23P)

Hovering, flying, floating

(Listening to Dizzy Gillespie's Big Band) I felt very happy and floated on small clouds a couple of days afterwards.

(Listened and sang along to the *Trio* album) It felt as if I was hovering and was lifted higher and higher up on the wings of music! (Chapter 5, account 5.3D)

('*En midvintersaga*' ['A Midwinter Saga'] by Ralph Lundsten) It was as if I was lifted up towards the stars and floated up there. (Chapter 21, account 21H)

('*En Vintersaga*' ['A Winter's Tale'] by Lars-Erik Larsson) In a way I wanted to fall down dead, just like that, in the middle of this fantastic music, to be absorbed by the music, to become a whole with it and just float there in the music for ever and ever. (Chapter 12, account 12.2H)

(Bach's *St Matthew Passion*) So I was flying too, enjoying the light voices . . . the solos, recitatives, and choir parts were like stations for me, but I kept on flying. (Chapter 25, account 25.1E)

(Adagietto in Mahler's Symphony No. 5) . . . then the music started again in a wonderful turn, I was completely sucked along as though I was carried, resting on the top of the waves.

(The same Adagietto) I thought it was the most gentle and beautiful I had ever heard. It was as if I myself was lifted up and floated off on the gentle waves.

(Shostakovich's String Quartet No. 8) I became absorbed in the music, and felt as if I was being carried along on waves. (Chapter 25, account 25.1I)

(Stravinsky's *Rite of Spring*) You could perhaps compare the overwhelming feeling with drowning in the enormous ocean's waves of sound, rich and innovative tones and pushing, robust rhythms.

Enclosed, screened off

(Saint-Saëns's *Samson and Delilah*) It seemed as though I was sitting in an enormous globe of light, filled with music. (Chapter 7, account 7.3A)

I felt as if I was living in a glass jar completely cut off from life. The only thing that reached into me was music. (Chapter 17, account 17.2E)

(Inner music) Every time I think about the event, I experience a weightless feeling of space at the same time that I seem to be shut inside an enormous soap bubble. (Chapter 14, account 14.4F)

(Traditional Turkish music) I feel love in the presence of this man . . . In some way, I am one with him. It is as if we together find ourselves in a room of our own which doesn't allow any disturbances to come in. (Chapter 15, account 15.1C)

Movements

(Philip Glass's *Satyagraha*) It felt as if my soul moved to the music. In certain parts of the music my soul was on a roller-coaster ride. In other parts zig-zagging.

(Listening to four jazz musicians) It felt like when you're on a big dipper. Extremely happy as if I was about to explode into bits.

(Listening to the singer Basia) . . . it made me dizzy, like going on the steepest part of a big dipper, my head felt like it would explode (Chapter 7, account 7.4D)

(Brahms's Symphony No. 4 in E minor, second movement) It felt like walking in an isolated hilly landscape on a night with melancholy light. (Chapter 21, account 21.I)

(Sibelius's Symphony No. 4) Moving in a large space . . .

The opposite, that is, immobility, is also described, as in the following examples.

(Bach's Piano Concerto in D minor) I sat there as if I was a part of the seat, as if I'd been glued to it. (Chapter 25, account 25.2U)

(Jazz concert) We sat there as though we had been nailed to the bench for the entire concert. (Chapter 26, account 26H)

Force, energy

(Listening to an American rock group) You got such strength, such a kick, that you become filled with energy. It is like taking vitamins for three years and getting them all at once. (Chapter 27, account 27J)

(Orff's *Carmina Burana*) There was such a force that I felt as if my soul was going to rise high up into the air . . . It felt as if I was alone in a sea of an incredible power that wanted to blow up the entire atmosphere. (Chapter 19, account 19.1C)

(Singing the 'Hallelujah' chorus in Handel's *Messiah*) Everybody sang, so the ceiling almost lifted.

Joy, ecstasy

(Bach's *St Matthew Passion*) Yes, and then I remember the feeling of happiness—how it gushed and bubbled within me. (Chapter 25, account 25.1E)

(Mozart's *Fantasie* K 475) An incredible joy, that you could compare to a musical orgasm, but of course a completely spiritual one. A spiritual experience when I saw suns and stars.

(Rock concert) You've just got to keep on going, accelerate, go right up to 190 [kph]. There are no limits. You are just in raptures . . . it is like an orgasm! (Chapter 27, account 27I)

The summer hymn has always been of great importance to me, but then everything that is nice and beautiful melted together into a warm ball of joy in my chest and stomach. (Chapter 19, account 19.1E)

Consolation, relief, cleansing, catharsis

I heard some music on the radio that reached deep into my innermost feelings. It felt as if a friendly voice spoke to me.

(At a funeral) . . . My father started to sing . . . It was like a door being opened . . . It felt so secure. (Chapter 22, account 22D)

I was in a deep depression, but as I continued to listen to the music my thoughts gradually became lighter . . . It lit up around me quite markedly. It was as if the sun shone right into my room, into my heart. (Chapter 17, account 17.2K)

I felt as if I was living in a glass jar completely cut off from life. The only thing that reached into me was music ... The music could penetrate through the walls and seep into me, and I think it was the music that meant that after a month or so I could start to fumble my way back out into life again. (Chapter 17, account 17.2E)

For me, however, the most important music was ... that which managed to open my mind totally and give me access to my innermost self ... Then came light, a feeling of consolation and hope. Afterwards came satisfaction and tranquillity. Something that led my thoughts to the consoling touch of a mother's hand. Balm for the soul. In short: catharsis. (Chapter 15, account 15.2F)

(Taizé religious service) It felt like showering to get clean, but on the inside ... All my blocks were breached and I just cried, a quiet crying—a bit like a summer rain. (Chapter 21, account 21E)

A couple of times, music has succeeded in untangling rather deep anxiety knots ... The experience is similar both times—sort of like a door that opens into a flooded bathroom. (Chapter 17, account 17.2C)

(While grieving) ... music can cause a storm of emotions that was more like a torrent in its sudden course and with the cleansing effect that it has. (Chapter 21, account 21J)

Feelings afterwards

(Bach's Piano Concerto in D minor.) Directly after the concert I felt as if I had been through a tough training session at the gym, spiritually. (Chapter 25, account 25.2U)

(Bach's Toccata and Fugue in D minor) Afterwards, I felt completely empty. It was as if the music had blown away all my thoughts. (Chapter 4, account 4.2D)

(Stravinsky's Rite of Spring) When the piece was finished, it was as if somebody had poured water over me. Was it finished?!

(Singing improvisation) It felt as if I had been present at a very hard job: giving birth and at the same time feeling joy, worry, and anguish. (Chapter 10, account 10.3A)

(Piazolla tango) After the concert I was silent but high, like I was drunk and completely whacked mentally. It felt as if a tractor had run over and mangled my brain and yet I felt incredibly inspired to go home and practise more on my accordion.

(After singing in a gigantic choir) When the last note had faded away, it was completely silent for a while and I dropped down to the ground again. I felt very overwhelmed and happy, but at the same time extremely confused, pulled down to the Earth and almost depressed at having to return to reality. (Chapter 19, account 19.3F)

28.4 PERFORMERS' AND COMPOSERS' DESCRIPTIONS OF THE EXPERIENCE

Being inside the music

(Orchestra musician) The total involvement in the music ... all that is there in a course of musical events. The closest you can get is to call it a state of trance, but keen and clear as crystal, without any thought of your own ego and your own life's circumstances, the focus is somewhere else, on a general human, or rather universal, plane. It is at just such a moment you could die calmly ... Just ascend ... I suppose that is my experience with music, the calm ... the eye of the hurricane—in the midst of life. (Chapter 18, account 18.1E)

(Singer in a choir) Can you imagine that you are standing up on a mountain, incredible views out across the city and over the sea? The wind is blowing and you are completely surrounded by it. That's exactly the feeling I have when I sing the song. I am completely surrounded by the music and the song, I am right in the middle of it. The feeling you get when you experience this totality, it is just wonder, you can just be completely filled by being in something whole and being a part of something great. It is enormous, it is like being taken out onto the great oceans.

(Improvisation) ... we 'just' played. This 'just' was an experience of inner balance and the music we played was like a sort of train that rushed along at full speed through and past inner stations, somewhere where you've not been able to reach rationally. (Chapter 18, account 18.3A)

(Improvisation) We ... get out and walk the tightrope. The music is composed and interpreted directly in the here and now, in front of the audience ... Suddenly there is a feeling of absolute concordance ... [everything is] just perfect, down to the micro-second ... You hardly know that you are playing—you simply 'are' in the music ... in a flow of function with the universe. (Chapter 18, account 18.3B)

Magic moments

... like walking the tightrope, sometimes you succeed, sometimes you fall down. When you succeed, it feels twice as good, then you're flying. (Chapter 18, account 18.6C)

... time suddenly stands still, the 'here and now' is everything and willpower is taken over by a self-driven accelerating spiral where transpiration makes up 0% and inspiration circa 110%! 'Feeling' takes charge while 'reason' is pushed aside and just stands there and looks on with a gaping mouth. The person who is playing experiences that an autopilot takes as regards technique over and perhaps even does things that the person concerned really doesn't master as regards technique. (Chapter 18, account 18.6A)

(Playing a Bach prelude) It was as if I was charged with some sort of high voltage, like a strong intoxication. The feeling made me ecstatic, inexplicably elated, everything concentrated to a single now. The music sort of flowed by itself. At that moment it felt to me as if I was filled with Bach's spirit: the music suddenly became so self-evident. (Chapter 18, account 18.6L)

(Playing together with Albert Ayler) I don't think I have ever experienced so much air under my wings! The whole thing was a dazzling adventure of swim or sink. Can we still touch ground? The form, will it hold? The periods? The harmonies? . . . Like being lifted high up and being able to discern endless possibilities! A spontaneous and resolute flood of inspiration, conscious and unconscious at the same time. Like a blessed gift from above—it isn't me who is playing—I am letting somebody play me. (Chapter 18, account 18.2B)

Relation to the audience

I feel like an aerial, a conveyor for something that sometimes reaches all the way to the audience. (Chapter 18, account 18.6C)

. . . when I played the first phrase, people started cheering . . . It was as if I was being blown up like an enormous balloon and everyone in the place was helping to blow up that balloon. (Chapter 18, account 18.4A)

(Playing in a rock group) You just hand out lots of happiness all at once. It is like scooping it out. It just pours out . . . more . . . here you are. Take it! . . . It is like opening the floodgates, everything just comes out. (Chapter 18, account 18.1L)

(Singing in a rock group) It's just so great to see that you can convey such a feeling of high spirits to people. People are going around and are happy. Roaring, rocking, completely letting everything go! It's like playing ping-pong with the audience, you get the ball back all the time; if they really get going, we get going even more. (Chapter 18, account 18.4B)

Feelings afterwards

(Orchestra member after a Dvořák symphony) Straight afterwards, I felt roughly like a euphoric dishcloth (one that has been wrung out) . . . (Chapter 18, account 18.1D)

(Conductor) After the concert, I felt tired, like a wrung-out dishcloth, more or less . . . (Chapter 18, account 18.1F)

Composing

In connection with pieces I have composed, at an early stage . . . it has felt like after a walk in a long tunnel suddenly to be standing before a majestic crystal hall, filled with previously unheard music. (Chapter 9, account 9.2F)

I'm sitting and working, working in a disciplined way without being satisfied with what I'm trying to create ... a melody pops up, a harmonic progression like a flash of lightning from a clear sky. (Chapter 9, account 9.2D)

The work with this was going very slowly, or not at all ... suddenly, creeping out from nowhere, it was there in my ears. It was as if you had ten holes in the ground around you, took ten balls, threw them at random up in the air and found that every ball had found its way to its own hole ... I got to experience what a teacher told me: 'Music writes itself, the composer is just an amanuensis who writes it down.' (Chapter 9, account 9.2C)

28.5 Summary

Certain phenomena recur in many metaphors and similes concerning either the music (section 28.5.1) or the experience (section 28.5.2)

28.5.1 The music

The music or performance is described as or likened to:

Water in movement

The music/notes are described as raindrops, raindrop music, rain drops that quiver, silver-coloured drops in a rain that flows through everything, carbon dioxide bubbles in a bottle of pop, a flow, a spring stream, a heavenly waterfall, a downpour, an ocean of incredible power; in frozen form like whirling weightless snowflakes.

Movements of various types

The music starts up and brakes, winds its way between different keys, penetrates through walls, seeps into the person (in a depression). A soprano solo is described as 'an exultant flight ... as if lifted by invisible wings towards the heights ... throws itself in dizzying intervals from low notes right up into the stratosphere ... most of all reminiscent of the movements of a bird up and down in the atmosphere.' Improvising music is likened to walking out onto a tightrope or like a train that rushes along at full speed through and past inner stations. In a successful performance one is flying, in an unsuccessful performance one is falling.

Colours, structures

Notes and voices are described as gold, silver-gleaming, as silvered drops of rain, as pure, brittle, delicate, glowing, as a flame. The structure in Mozart's *Eine kleine*

Nachtmusik is described as 'exact' like 'endless rows of stone pillars with the same distance and space in between that never finishes'. Sibelius's fourth symphony was experienced as 'desolation with strings of warmth, grey-brownness with reddish-yellow features (autumn colours!), the ascetic, unadorned, with oases of lushness'.

Natural phenomena: wind, flowers, trees, birdsong

Music is likened to a whirlwind, to a warm summer wind, to birdsong (thorn bird), a sequence of notes is described as a flower winding its way up from an incense holder, the sound of a choir as like 'how all the flowers on a meadow or all the trees in a forest create a whole where every part is unique'.

Power, electricity

The force and intensity in the music are described as a steamroller, as glowing electricity, as 'hard rock without electricity' (Stravinsky's *Rite of Spring*), as a meltdown, as an ice-breaker. A singer is described as a turbo-singer, and choir members sang so that the ceiling lifted or swelled.

Personality, character

A tango is described as 'unpredictable and mischievous', the third movement in Tchaikovsky's *Pathétique* is 'strutting, almost humorous—it is the unconscious optimist who naively but proudly goes on and on'.

Heaven, paradise, life

Music is described as heaven, paradise, as played or sung by angels, as if music and the notes were life itself. Boy singers 'looked like cupids and their voices were like arrows of love fired at the large number of people'.

28.5.2 The experience

The experience is described as, or is likened to:

Movements

Moving in a large space, like being lifted by the wings of music, getting air under one's wings, not feeling the ground any longer, being blown up like a balloon, lifted high up into the air, lifted up towards the stars and floating up there, floating among notes, floating on clouds, flying, as whirling round like a wheel, whirling like a speck of dust, walking a tightrope (sometimes you succeed, sometimes you fall down), like going to the circus, falling down flat, a roller-coaster ride.

The musicians pour out their music to the audience 'scoop after scoop' and play 'ping-pong with the audience, you get the ball back all the time; if they really get going, we get going even more'. After the experience it feels like landing on the ground again with a bump, being brought back to earth.

Immobility is likened to sitting as if petrified, as being fastened to the seat, nailed to the bench, as if one was sitting in glue.

Movements and water

One can feel as if one is in a stream, being carried by, resting, or floating in the waves or swell of the sea, taken out to great oceans, drowning in enormous waves, like being alone in an ocean of incredible power, feeling how it streams and bubbles in one's body, describing relief like when ice melts. Quiet crying is likened to a summer rain, an emotional storm to a downpour. After the experience: 'When the piece came to an end if was as if somebody had poured water over me.'

Landscape, nature

It feels like being up on or having a view from high mountains, feel surrounded by the wind, as if the music blows away all thoughts, like being in the eye of the hurricane (calm), like in a mist, like seeing suns and stars, like 'the feeling you experience when you lie in a boat moored by a island in the archipelago', like the littleness one can feel at the foot of a mountain when nature shows all its grandeur.

Movements in the landscape: like 'walking in an isolated hilly landscape on a night with melancholy light' or 'after a walk in a long tunnel suddenly to be standing before a majestic crystal hall, filled with previously unheard music' (when composing).

Atmosphere, smell

'The atmosphere became even more tense . . . There was an unbelievable magnetic field between those who were on the stage and in the room, you could have cut the atmosphere into slices.'

'The experience came gradually—started as a sort of charge or tension in the atmosphere, which gradually became all the more intense—roughly like a scent which you first get a hint of, rather than really feel, before it washes over you, inebriates you and takes you over.'

'A very pleasant sensation spreads across my chest and down to my solar plexus. It feels like fresh air. I feel contact with an inner ego, my soul.'

Light

It feels as if it is getting light, as if a door opens and light pours in, as if the sun shines right into my room, into my heart (these examples in connection with the relief of a depression). Like bathing in or being surrounded by light, as if the air glows, like being hit by a sharp laser beam right into one's heart.

Force, energy

Feeling as if an autopilot has taken over, like being in a sea of incredible power, like being charged with some sort of high tension, like being hit by lightning, a knife, a sharp laser ray, like 'taking vitamins for three years and getting them all at once'.

Discovery of something new, unknown

As if a closed door is opened wide, as if a door is opened into a flooded bathroom, as if a blind is pulled up, as if all the floodgates have been opened, as if a dam has been released, ice has melted, a bird has been let out of its cage, as 'descending into the ancient church, down into my own archaic rooms'.

Screening off

Feeling as if one is in a room of one's own which doesn't let disturbances enter, enclosed in a soap bubble, in a bubble of harmony and calmness, in an enormous globe of light filled with music, in a glass jar absolutely cut off from life.

Reception

Feeling like an antenna, a huge receiver with all the channels tuned to the music, like being on the same wavelength, being in tune, one's ears glued to the music, ears becoming like outstretched arms, all one's senses on full alert, wide open and susceptible, sucking in every note 'as a nourishment, as when somebody who is very thirsty gets to drink some water', the music 'could ravage my entire organism uninhibited'.

Bodily processes, phenomena

It feels like when one drinks, eats, swallows, sucks, slurps, is filled with the music ('like a sponge which is reacquiring its shape'), like taking vitamins and getting strength. The music seeps into one's body, is experienced with every tiny fibre in the body, every pore in one's body opens up, a stream of well-known notes passes through one's back, the music caresses one's eyes, goes right into one's heart, takes command of one's body, creeps into one's brain, one's brain is filled with music, one's head or body is blown to bits, the music gives one a heart attack, a knock-out, an internal revolution. One's whole body is filled with flowers, everything beautiful and lovely melts together into 'a warm ball of joy in my chest and stomach', it feels like a (spiritual) orgasm.

Afterwards: It felt 'as if a tractor had run over and mangled my brain', 'as if I had been present at a very hard job: giving birth and at the same time feeling joy, worry, and anguish'.

Aha! experience, sudden insight

It is as if all the pieces in a puzzle suddenly fall into place, like when the magnet arranges the iron filings in regular patterns, like 'a string inside you that gets into a spin', as if all one's brain cells and all one's nerves are going in the same direction. A musician described a new view of music as: 'I saw the forest, not just a clump of trees.'

When composing: a melody appears like a sudden stroke of lightning from a clear sky, as if 'you had ten holes in the ground around you, took ten balls, threw them at random up in the air and found that every ball had found its way to its own hole . . .'

Transcendence

It is like an intoxication, being spellbound, a hallucination, trance, like being in a flow of 'function with the universe', like being filled by the composer's (Bach's) spirit, like meeting or seeing angels, being in (seventh) heaven, in paradise.

Cleansing

It feels as if deep knots of anxiety become untangled, like being lifted and in some way cleansed, like having a shower to clean you but on the inside, like a spiritual steam bath, like balm for the soul, catharsis.

Encounters

The music felt like a blessed gift from above, like hearing a friendly voice, like a consoling touch of a mother's hand, like being hit by a club wrapped in cotton wool, like when you meet a dear friend you haven't met for a long time, like meeting someone in secret, being hit by the arrows of love, being touched by the fairy's wand.

Emptiness

Feeling as if the music has blown away all thoughts, feeling like a euphoric dishcloth, one that has been wrung out.

A few accounts also included poems rich in metaphors and similes. As they are very hard to translate in a way that does them full justice, they are omitted in this edition.

CHAPTER 29

SURVEY OF ALL REACTIONS

THE analysis of the content in all the 1,350 accounts has been a long and arduous process (see Chapter 2, section 2.2). It reveals a total of about 150 different reactions (aspects). These have been arranged in a scheme—a descriptive system—with three levels.

The top, fundamental level (level 1) comprises seven categories:

- General characteristics
- Physical reactions and behaviours
- Perception
- Cognition
- Feelings, emotion
- Existential and transcendental aspects
- Personal and social aspects.

Each of these comprises two to eight sub-categories (level 2), which in turn comprise a varying number of reactions (level 3).

It is thus a very comprehensive descriptive system that may seem difficult to survey and to take in. But strong experiences with music are an extremely complex and multifaceted phenomenon and necessitate a system that can include and illustrate this complexity and variety. There is a summarized presentation of the system in Appendix A. I recommend that you have a look at that now, before you read on. Then, after having read this chapter, you could also look at Appendix B, which provides an example of how the descriptive system can be used to analyse an account.

This chapter contains a description and examples of the various categories and reactions. Quite a lot will be familiar from the comments accompanying the accounts in the previous chapters. This will nevertheless be a long chapter, which can be read as one wishes—straight through and in its totality (which, of course, I would recommend) or selectively and in an order reflecting your own interests.[1]

29.1 General characteristics

The following two points may be said to be general characteristics for strong experiences with music:

a) The experience is described as fantastic, unforgettable, incredible, special, wonderful, unique, or with similar expressions.

b) The experience, or parts of it, is or are difficult or impossible to describe in words; the experience goes beyond what language can say. An illustrative quote: 'It was an experience that far exceeded my verbal and intellectual capacity, it includes things that I verbally can only touch upon.'

29.2 Physical reactions and behaviours

Within this category one finds physiological reactions, behaviours, and quasi-physical reactions.

There is usually information on how large a percentage of the participants have named the various reactions. To ascertain the approximate number of participants in absolute terms, one can multiply the percentage value by 10; for example, 5% of the participants equals roughly 50 people.

29.2.1 Physiological reactions

Strong music experiences often contain physiological reactions.

Tears, crying

The most common reaction is tears and crying. This occurs in about one quarter (24%) of all participants, more often among women (28%) than among men (18%); the least tears are to be found among young men. The tears can vary, ranging from eyes brimming with tears to gushing tears. They often occur when one has been strongly positively affected (touched, thrilled, captivated) by the music, and/or in situations in which one has been especially susceptible and expectant. It is for the greater part tears when one is moved and tears of joy. Tears can also appear in connection with negative feelings such as anxiety, sorrow, and despair.

Shivers, thrills, chills

Shivers and shudders are the next most common physiological reaction. They are reported by about 10% of all narrators, a little more among men (12%) than among women (9%). As is the case with tears, shivers occur in connection with one being strongly positively affected and/or having strong expectations (expectant shivers). Shivers rarely occur in connection with negative feelings. It can also be noted that shivers and tears are not usually reported together.

Gooseflesh, hair standing on end

Getting goosepimples or having one's hair stand on end is described by about 5% of the participants. It takes place in roughly the same situations as for tears and shivers, that is, when one is strongly affected and experiences strong positive feelings (happiness, joy, etc.).

Other physiological reactions

Other physiological reactions that are described to a lesser degree include a general bodily reaction ('a tingling sensation all over' and similar), a relaxation or tensioning of muscles, warmth (sweating, burning cheeks), changed breathing, heart palpitations, trembles/shakes, reactions in one's chest (feeling pressure on one's chest; feeling as if one's chest would explode; feeling relief in one's chest as if a burden had disappeared), in one's stomach (it tickles, tingles, there is a stabbing pain, butterflies in one's stomach), feel a lump in one's throat, dizziness, nausea, or pain.

One should remember that throughout it is a matter of self-experienced physiological reactions. Presumably, additional and more detailed reactions could be registered with special equipment to monitor, for example, muscular activity, electrodermal response (the skin's conductivity, perspiration), or activity in different places in the brain (brain imaging). Generally, such equipment is not available when a strong musical experience happens to take place. Recently, however, there have been attempts to study some reactions, primarily chills and thrills, when listening to music under experimental conditions.[2]

On the whole, these reactions show that the person/organism has been dislodged from its 'normal' state, has experienced something out of the ordinary—that, of course, is a criterion for especially strong experiences. The organism then often reacts with an activation, governed by the sympathetic branch of the autonomic nervous system, according to the principle of 'fight or flight', a prehistoric principle to ensure survival. Of course, the situation isn't so serious in connection with strong experiences with music, but several of the reactions that have been described—shivers, hair standing on end, pulse going up, breathing affected—have their origins in this prehistoric tendency to act. (It is, incidentally, the same phenomenon that occurs in connection with stage fright before a performance.) As regards 'flight', there are in fact a couple of examples of how a strong negative experience led to a person literally fleeing the field (Chapter 11, accounts 11.3P and 11.3R).

But the most common physiological reaction, tears and crying, involves instead the parasympathetic branch of the autonomic nervous system. In such cases, it is not a question of fighting or fleeing, but rather a sort of deactivation of the organism.

29.2.2 Behaviours, actions, activity

In behaviours, too, there is a clear distinction between activation and deactivation: on the one hand high activity and on the other, stillness and immobility.

Activities such as moving, jumping, dancing, clapping one's hands, clicking one's fingers, etc. are described by many narrators (11%), mainly young and middle-aged, especially when one is together with other people at concerts with folk music, jazz, rock, pop, or dance music. Other behaviours that occur to a slightly lesser degree are singing (along), laughing and shouting or screaming. Throughout, all these behaviours occur a little more in women than in men (screams or shouts, however, more often in men).

The opposite reaction—not to move at all, to sit still, to be completely silent, to break off all other activity—is also fairly common (9%). It occurs more in women than in men, more in middle-aged and old people, and often also with reproduced music and when one is alone. The music is for the greater part classical, sometimes with the focus on a particular artiste (e.g. Jussi Björling) or a special instrument (see also Chapter 30, section 30.4).

Other reactions are, for example, to smile, to shut one's eyes, or to not be able to speak, sing, or play because one is overwhelmed by feelings. A special reaction is—at whatever the cost—to try to not reveal one's feelings ('not to give the show away'), because one feels embarrassed or ashamed at having been so affected; one must 'behave properly' in public.

Sometimes the experience is so overwhelming that one can't cope with it ('I can't take any more, stop') and thus tries to get away from it, whether from a concert or by turning off the music on the radio or record player. Several people also describe how, after a strong experience at a concert, they hurry to sneak out of the way of others so that they can be left in peace with their thoughts and feelings.

29.2.3 Quasi-physical reactions

Quasi-physical reactions are reactions that are described in physical terms but which don't have any real physical equivalent: 'it feels as if . . .'. Several such reactions are described in Chapter 8: feeling light, weightless, one takes off from the ground, or rises up in the air and floats freely. Reactions such as these are described by about 9% of the participants, more often by women than by men. The most spectacular examples of quasi-physical experiences are so-called out-of-body experiences. There are about ten accounts of such experiences, most of them from women, in Chapter 8, section 8.2.

Other quasi-physical experiences are the feeling that one's body is filled with music. This is described by about 9% of the participants, more often by women than by men. A singer in a choir experienced that 'all my body is music', and a woman who was on work practice with an orchestra felt how 'the music filled all of me, squashed me to a little louse'. A couple of other examples:

(29.2.3A) Woman, middle-aged, 1980s (from Chapter 12, account 12.3B)

(Listening to a violin concerto) Suddenly it was as if all of me was filled with music and a light warmth. It filled my entire body and I 'grew', I expanded and filled the whole room. It felt as if my head 'bumped' into the ceiling.

(29.2.3.B) Woman, old, 1980s

[Listening to a performance of Sibelius's fifth symphony] I listened more intensely than I'd ever done before, with my eyes closed and my fists clenched, and it wasn't just with my ears I was listening—all of my body was listening. It was as if my body was perforated, the music went right through my body and I heard or experienced the music in my actual body . . . especially the strong trumpet tones made it sing in my body.

Yet another type of quasi-physical experiences is the feeling of being controlled, or being charged by or taken away by the music. Such descriptions are mentioned by just under 5% of the narrators. One woman listened to Finnish tango and felt how she 'was filled by a special feeling that the music began to take command of my body. I was charged in a way' (Chapter 17, account 17.2L). Another woman listened to the Adagietto from Mahler's fifth symphony and thought that 'it was as if I myself was lifted up and floated off on the gentle waves'. One man listened to Led Zeppelin's *Stairway to Heaven* and 'was carried along by the music as it intensified in power and majesty almost to a climax at the end' (Chapter 7, account 7.2D), and another man heard 'music (Coltrane) which completely blew me away, took me with gentle and urgent violence with volume and power that would not tolerate objections but rather kidnapped me on a secret journey'.

29.3 PERCEPTION

Perception concerns in general how our senses receive information from the world outside and also from the body itself.

Music and sound generally are in a physical sense vibrations that we can perceive with two senses: hearing (auditory perception) and touch (tactile perception).

29.3.1 Auditory perception

Certain aspects of the musical experience can be regarded as primarily auditory in character. The special timbre of a particular instrument, a singing voice, or a whole choir, is noticed by about 7% of the participants with some predominance of men.

Another aspect is high sound level, which is mentioned by 4%, again with some predominance of men, especially young men.

An important auditory aspect is 'the acoustics'. One usually means the reverberation in the room (not least in churches) and/or the diffusion of the sound. A choir singer described a concert in a monastery: 'the acoustics were fantastic. Everything sounded twice as good, whatever we did, and that, of course, gave the choir a lift' (Chapter 19, account 19.4B). An organist had the opportunity to play an organ in a large cathedral: 'It felt overwhelming to be able to fill the whole church, every corner, and every ear with tones, let the music gush out to a big crescendo' (Chapter 11, account 11.2N). One listener was impressed by a well-known singer: 'Ingvar Wixell. Without a microphone he filled every corner of the Concert Hall. Turbo-singer.'

Another strong experience is to feel embraced by the music, to find oneself in the midst of the field of sound. One listener wrote that 'the acoustics in the church gave space to the sound, and the fact that the music came from above and behind meant that I sort of was surrounded by it'. A choir singer got a strong feeling of pleasure from 'standing there in the middle of the choir and singing and hearing the other voices round about', and an instrumentalist who got to play in a large symphony orchestra for the first time wrote of 'a fantastic experience to sit enclosed in such a mighty body of sound'. The importance of these experiences—that the sound gets space, that it feels close, and that one feels surrounded by the sound—is stressed by about 7% of the participants and also includes cases where one has listened to music via high-quality sound-reproduction systems.

On the other hand, several participants (about 5%) have particularly mentioned that on certain occasions there was absolute silence—one could have heard 'a pin drop'—as, for example, in the tense wait before a longed-for performance, or between the movements in a long work, or just after the final note in a work which has made such a strong impression that nobody thinks of applauding until some time has passed (for example in Chapter 25, account 25.1P). Such an absence of applause can be just as significant as immediate thunderous applause.

29.3.2 Tactile perception

One can also literally feel the music in one's body—in one's head, chest, stomach, feet, legs, and so on. Such tactile perception is described by about 30 people (3%). A listener at a concert felt how 'My whole body was a part of the music, physical shock waves from the timpani hit me in my midriff' (Chapter 25, account 25.1C). Another listener felt how 'the bass comes from the ground into my body via the soles of my feet, goes up my calves, my thighs, backbone, and I am filled with the music' (Chapter 27, account 27F). The sound from a sitar 'seemed to penetrate into your pores, expand your skin and then penetrate out again' (Chapter 24, account 24L), and one man described how he experienced a fiddler's violin music 'as if the notes were real, that they were *real* notes that came and touched my face like balls of cotton wool'.

29.3.3 Visual perception

Visual impressions in connection with music are of great importance. Approximately half of all the participants describe some form of visual impressions. These concern primarily the appearance and actions of the musicians, their communication with each other and the audience, their commitment, joy in playing, and charisma. Often, too, there are comments on the composition of the audience and its reactions—whether the audience is big or small, quiet or noisy, concentrated or 'restless', whether there is a feeling of fellowship, and so on. For the musicians, the reactions of the audience mean a great deal for their commitment, which is evident in several accounts, such as in Chapter 18, accounts 18.1J, 18.4A ('as if I was being blown up like an enormous balloon'), 18.4B ('like playing ping-pong with the audience'). A somewhat different example of this follows.

(29.3.3A) Man, middle-aged

> A performance of Fauré's *Requiem* in a church. Then I played viola in the orchestra, but right in front of me in the audience sat a man who became more and more moved. Towards the end of the concert he was crying openly and he gave the conductor a resigned look as if he was thinking: 'No more now, I can't take any more!' I'll never forget that, and I found it hard to concentrate on my part!

Considerable space is often also devoted to describing the setting or situation around the experience, for example the size and appearance of the premises, what the stage looks like, sound effects, nature, the weather, the surroundings.

One can, of course, discuss whether visual impressions are at all a part of the music experience or whether they should rather be understood as a part of the conditions for the musical experience. This is partly a question of definition, but one can never really speak of a 'pure' music experience isolated from everything else. It is always in a context, and most people consider it natural to describe the experience in its 'totality' without caring about such questions of definition.

Besides, for most people vision represents the most concrete and reliable information about the world around them ('I have seen it with my own eyes'). Even if music is primarily a matter for hearing, it is thus not particularly surprising that one also stresses the visual impressions. The visual impressions of the musicians, the instruments, the setting, etc. can reinforce and clarify the content of the music, especially if one doesn't have much experience of music or when one is confronted with unfamiliar music—then it is to the highest degree natural and important to make use of *all* one's senses to interpret what is happening. That vision then has particularly great importance is sometimes evident in spontaneous characterizations such as 'It was the best concert I've seen.'[3]

29.3.4 Multimodal perception

Several people (about 3%) emphasize the importance of how the experience comprises several senses, that one both saw and heard, or saw, heard, and felt; for example: 'all my senses were concentrated—vision, hearing, and even touch too, because there were also vibrations, fully noticeable physical vibrations' (Chapter 26, account 26F).

29.3.5 Other senses

Some perception in other senses was mentioned in connection with physiological reactions, for example when one's body feels tense or, the opposite, totally relaxed (kinaesthetic perception, 'muscle sense'), that one feels warm or that one is cold, that one feels pain, etc. There are also occasional examples of sensations of smell, such as 'the theatre scent of newly ironed clothes, perfume, make-up and dust' (Chapter 5, account 5.2I).

29.3.6 Synaesthetic perception

There are a few examples of what is known as synaesthetic perception. Synaesthesia means 'together-sensation', that is, one also gets sensations in a sense other than the one which is stimulated. A common example is what is known as colour hearing, that is, one spontaneously experiences colours when one hears notes, sounds, chords, instruments, music of certain types, or music in general. Here are two examples from our material.

(29.3.6A) Woman, middle-aged

The beginning of Mozart's Symphony No. 40 in G minor gave me lovely visions of blue, long before I got to know Messiaen, for whom all notes have a colour.

(29.3.6B) Woman, old

I see colours inside my head. The sounds of different instruments have different colours. The sound of the violin is silvery white, sometimes with a bit of blue in it, the bassoon is coloured dark purple, and so on. Mahler's symphonies are blueish-black with silver edges, Mozart's are the opposite way round, that is, silver-grey with dark blue or black elements, occasionally pale pink. Green tones are uncommon in my head, with one major exception: Beethoven's fifth, which is dark green. The people that I have told about this think I am a bit 'nutty'. Perhaps I am? Letters of the alphabet and words have colours too!

That letters and words are associated with colours is another common example of synaesthesia; similarly, numbers, days of the week, and months can be associated with colours.[4]

One could, perhaps, under this heading also include examples of experiences of special light in connection with music. Several such experiences are described, for example: 'It seemed as though I was sitting in an enormous globe of light, filled with music' (Chapter 7, account 7.3A); 'then the earthly context disappeared and I experienced light' (Chapter 8, account 8.2E); 'In the fortissimo on the dominant in the last bars, it is like a light passes over my closed eyes, fading out more and more in the following diminuendo' (Chapter 14, account 14.1H); 'After the applause . . . I saw how the cellar roof broke up and a flood of light poured in' (Chapter 16, account 16.3G); 'I remember the seconds after the final cut-off like being in a sort of light' (Chapter 19, account 19.3A); 'The strong concentration that you are in . . . I feel it as a strong white, almost dazzling, light' (Chapter 19, account 19.3D); 'Suddenly, everything round about me became sunny, golden yellow . . . I just sort of floated in this sunny gold' (Chapter 24, account 24A); 'I was in some way entirely enveloped by a pleasant light that seemed to come from every side' (Chapter 25, account 25.1M).

These phenomena that are hard to explain one might also regard as transcendental. They are reminiscent of experiences of strong (intense, dazzling, white, yellow) light that are described in intensive religious experiences and also in near-death experiences.[5]

29.3.7 Intensified perception

Several narrators (4%) described intensified perception in the sense that one perceives the music as more intense than usual and notices every single detail. A woman who listened to Finnish tango 'swallowed all the notes that were streaming out in the air, not a single note, effect, or sequence missed my hungry ears. The music became so distinct. I was captivated by each of the instruments and what they had to offer me' (Chapter 17, account 17.2L). A man who listened to a Beethoven symphony explained that 'Most of the time when I listen, I can only follow the theme when it wanders between the different parts and the instruments, and the rest becomes like a carpet of notes in the background. This time, I could distinguish all the details, there was a blast from the trumpets, there was something contrapuntal in the cello part while the theme lay with the violas' (Chapter 7, account 7.1A). A man who listened to a requiem by Sven-David Sandström noted that 'this work etched itself into my consciousness note by note'.

Intensified perception can also be described through metaphors or similes, for example that one 'sucks in the music like a dry sponge' or experiences the music 'with every tiny fibre in the body' (see Chapter 28, section 28.3).

29.3.8 Musical perception-cognition

Many narrators describe or comment upon the actual music too, or the performance. If the description concerns objective or technical qualities (for example, genre, instrument, mode, tempo, melody, the structure of the music), it is placed in this category (see Chapter 31, sections 31.2 and 31.3).

If the description is given in 'subjective', that is, cognitive or emotional, terms, it is instead placed in section 29.4.7 below.

29.4 COGNITION

The boundary between perception and cognition is fluid, but on the whole one can say that perception is about how we receive information via our various senses, while cognition is about how the information is further processed. This can mean that one compares impressions from earlier experiences (for example: 'I have heard this music before'), one pays more attention ('I must listen to this closely'), expectations arise ('This is probably going to sound different'), memories ('When I was together with . . .'), associations ('This reminds me of . . .'), value judgements ('This sounds really nice'), reflections ('I ought to listen to more of this sort of music'), wishes ('Imagine if I could play like this'), inner images or fantasies ('I dream that I am . . .'), and so on. All of this, of course, is influenced by the person's earlier experiences, attitude, susceptibility, attention, expectations, preferences, etc.

Cognitive aspects of strong experiences with music are thus a large area. We have divided them into seven categories.

29.4.1 Expectations, receptivity, absorption

Many narrators (30%) say that they felt expectant, curious, open and susceptible, 'hungry for music'. One looks forward to hearing certain music, a certain artiste or ensemble, or music in general. Other narrators, however, say that they didn't have any special expectations at all but were entirely 'neutral', and some had, if anything, negative expectations.

Regardless of the circumstances, something happens—the music strikes the listener directly or sneaks up on them and captures all of their attention. One becomes totally absorbed by the music, nothing else is of any interest—no thoughts, no analyses, it is fully sufficient to just 'be' here and now. Some form of these types of reactions is described by about 20% of the participants, a little more among men than among women. Accounts of this kind are to be found in Chapter 6.

As far as performers are concerned, openness can also comprise putting oneself at the mercy of the audience and its reactions (see Chapter 18, section 18.7). Absorption can also refer to complete commitment to the task of performing the music—all that counts is giving everything in one's performance.

29.4.2 Altered experience of situation, body–mind, time–space, parts–wholeness

The absorption can manifest itself in many different ways. There is a different mood, a special atmosphere, particularly in a situation with live music. One's surroundings disappear, one is in a world of one's own, inaccessible to attempts by others to make contact. Time stands still, doesn't exist, the entire experience regardless of its duration seems to be contained in a single 'here and now'. One participant described this with the paradox 'a long moment'.

One loses consciousness of one's own body, and it feels as if one's ego is dissolved or is merged with something bigger. Everything feels unreal, like a dream, 'it can't be true'. One wishes that this state could last for ever, now one can die happy (or that is how one would like to die eventually if one could choose). It feels like a great disappointment to return to 'reality' afterwards.

One may get a feeling of that everything fits together. All impressions are united to a whole in which all the parts are in agreement—the music, the people, oneself, the mood, the time, the place, the setting, Nature, the weather and whatever else there might be—everything and everybody is 'on the same wavelength'. Everything can suddenly seem simple, natural and self-evident.

Some form of the above reactions is described by about 35% of the participants, a little more often among men than among women. There are examples in Chapter 7 and in many other places in this book.

29.4.3 Lose control, be surprised, moved, struck, overwhelmed

A strong experience means that, in some sense, one loses control. As a rule, one wants to know what is going on. A lack of control, not being able to influence the situation, is often a cause of stress. But in the situation that we are now discussing, it is rather the opposite: one gives up control and lets oneself be 'overpowered' by the music—sometimes deliberately and willingly, sometimes completely unplanned, and sometimes only after a certain opposition which does, however, turn out to be without effect; it is not possible to resist.

A relatively mild form of this is that one is surprised by the music or the performance, one is amazed, one loses one's head—what on earth is happening? Possibly, one is also surprised by one's own reaction, that is, surprised that one has been surprised, since one doesn't usually react so strongly.

A stronger form is that one becomes moved, thrilled, affected by the music, in even stronger form that one becomes struck, shaken, shocked, bewitched, overwhelmed. The music goes right through all cognitive barriers, 'straight in' to one's very core. Sometimes the reactions can be stronger than one can bear; it becomes too much: 'I can't stand it any longer, stop . . .'

Reactions of this type are described by 42% of the participants, somewhat more often among men than among women; with regard to experiences of the 'moved, thrilled, affected' type, both genders are more or less equally represented. Examples of these reactions are to be found in accounts in many different places in this book, starting as early as in childhood experiences (Chapter 4, section 4.2).

29.4.4 Special relation to the music

The preceding categories also mean a special relation to the music. This is expressed in many different ways: one feels (mentally) surrounded by, wrapped in, filled with the music, one lives the music, is sucked into the music, merges with the music, identifies oneself with the music: 'The music and me were one.' One feels directly addressed by the music, understands the music, what it wants to say, it seems simple, genuine, natural, timeless; for example: 'I understood the music. It was as if the music had always been there and that it always would be there' (Chapter 25, account 25.1L). Experiences of these types are described by about 20% of the participants and are illustrated by accounts in Chapter 7 and elsewhere.

For performers, it can feel as if everything goes by itself, one can surpass one's usual ability, it is as if 'somebody else is playing me'. One can devote oneself to being a listener rather than a performer: 'I just had to sit there and listen to what my fingers did.' Such experiences, often called 'magic moments', are described by about 6% of the music-playing participants, with a clear majority of men (see Chapter 18, section 18.6).

29.4.5 Associations, memories, thoughts

The music and the situation can arouse associations and memories (about 12% of the participants). They are, naturally, entirely individual and can concern the most varied things: people one has met, events one has been involved in, situations one has found oneself in, memories from journeys, etc., or memories of other music experiences.

The experience often (about 27% of the participants) also leads to thoughts and reflections about the music, for example whether one recognized the music or not, and what it was in the music or in oneself that caused the strong reaction. One draws comparisons with other music, reflects upon the importance of the music, asks oneself why one prefers certain music and why other people can think completely differently. The reflections can also concern completely different questions; for example, what sort of person one is, one's relation to other people and one's relation to strong experiences within other areas (see Chapter 33, section 33.3).

29.4.6 Inner images, inner music

The music can also arouse inner images or notions of, for example, landscape, nature, people, situations, and events; sometimes there are also auditory elements (notions of sounds, music). The notions are completely individual and vary considerably in length and richness of detail. Sometimes they are in the nature of pipedreams: yearning for another country, another life, something completely different and better—or that listeners imagine that it is they themselves who are standing there on the stage and performing the music. Inner images in some form are described by just over 10% of the participants: see Chapter 10. Inner images and associations or memories (29.4.5 above) can now and then overlap with each other.

Sometimes a strong experience of music can be generated by 'inner' music, that is, imagined music. One hears music, it comes without one knowing how or why. In some cases one is conscious that it is inner music, in other cases one tries to find out if there could have been music 'for real', but finds nothing. There are about ten accounts of this; see Chapter 9.

In some cases, the narrator can control the inner music; it thus comes close to a form of composing. There are also a few accounts of strong experiences in connection with deliberate composition of music. All these accounts come from men and primarily concern when, after a period of fruitless effort, one suddenly has a decisive idea about how the music should be shaped.

More common examples of inner music are that a melody 'hangs around', 'rings' or 'goes around' in one's head without one being able to do anything about it; it can sometimes be most irritating. Some people have also pointed out in passing that they nearly always have 'music in my head', music that they have heard or that is newly created.

29.4.7 Musical cognition-emotion

This concerns description of the music or the performance in 'subjective', cognitive-emotional terms (cf. 29.3.8 above), for example if the music is described as happy, serious, calm, dramatic, powerful, delightful, beautiful, wonderful, and so on, or if the performance is described as perfect, committed, exciting, expressive, and so on (see Chapter 31, section 31.1).

29.5 FEELINGS, EMOTION

The boundary between cognition and emotion is fluid. It is obvious that some of the reactions that are mentioned under cognition also concern feelings, for example when one is moved, touched, struck, or overwhelmed by the music. Associations, memories, and inner images can also be connected with different feelings. The relation between cognition and emotion is the subject of much discussion within psychology. Similarly, there is a lively discussion on the validity of various emotion theories and their relevance with regard to music.[6]

The analyses of our material concerning feelings/emotion leads to a division into four parts: strong, intense feelings (29.5.1), positive feelings (29.5.2), negative feelings (29.5.3), and different (mixed, contradictory, changed) feelings (29.5.4).

29.5.1 Strong, intense feelings

The first group concerns strong emotional reactions in general; for example 'They were great and powerful feelings', 'My feelings exceeded all bounds', 'It was an emotional charge that was blowing us up'. Thus one doesn't mention any specific feeling; what is stressed is the force or intensity of the feelings, the emotional commitment.

Descriptions of this type are mentioned by about 15% of the participants (see Chapter 11, section 11.1).

29.5.2 Positive feelings

The second group, positive feelings, is, as expected, the largest group, and these are described by 72% of the narrators, a little more among women (74%) than among men (70%).

The most commonly mentioned feelings are happiness, joy, pleasure, beauty, and delight or pleasure. There are, of course, degrees and nuances of these. One narrator, for example, carefully distinguished between on the one hand an immediate 'exultant and bubbling joy' and on the other a more low-key and calm yet still intense feeling of joy.

The next most common are, on the one hand, feelings like calm, harmony, peace and quiet, and, on the other hand, their opposites such as elation, tension, excitement, enthusiasm, euphoria, dizziness, enchantment, and ecstasy.

Some additional feelings are as follows (arranged in descending order of occurrence):

feeling satisfied, content, saturated, possessed

security, warmth, goodness

gratitude, love, perfection

feeling of greatness, pride, solemnity, wonder, reverence, respect, admiration

feeling little, insignificant, humble

sexual feelings, patriotism.

There are examples in Chapter 11, section 11.2 and in many other accounts; for example, perfection, pride, and euphoria are often mentioned in connection with successful performances as musicians.

According to a familiar theory of emotion, known as the valence-arousal model, most feelings can be described as a combination of valence (a continuum from negative to positive value) and activation level (from low to high activation). It is not entirely simple, however, to rank positive feelings according to activation level. It goes quite well concerning the most often mentioned feelings; they can be ranked in the following way according to ascending activation level:

calm, harmony, peace, quiet

security, warmth, goodness

satisfied, content, saturated, possessed

happiness, joy

elation, excitement, tension, enthusiasm

euphoria, intoxication, dizziness, rapture, ecstasy.

But beyond that, it is more difficult to find adequate placements. One might think that wonder, humility, feeling of insignificance or littleness, and reverence and respect would lie somewhere on the lower half of the continuum, perhaps also admiration, gratitude, and solemnity. The remainder—perfection, pride, patriotism, feeling of greatness, love, and sex—can lie on the upper half. A lot depends otherwise on the context.

The order of positive feelings in Appendix A (category 5.2) reflects this attempted ranking according to activation level.

Many narrators also mention emotional qualities in the actual music, for example that the music was happy, sad, calm, dramatic, mighty, delightful, beautiful, and so on, (cf. section 29.4.7 above). This can also involve an indirect description of one's own reaction. When, for example, one talks of 'pleasant', 'delightful', 'beautiful' music, this can also be interpreted as pleasure and approval. Sometimes it is difficult, almost impossible, to decide whether such expressions only allude to qualities in the music itself, or also to the person's reaction.

29.5.3 Negative feelings

Some sort of negative feeling occurs in 23% of the participants, a little more among women (25%) than among men (20%). Many of these negative experiences are not, however, so 'serious' and often they are not occasioned by the music but by other circumstances. There are examples in Chapter 11, section 11.3 and in other accounts, such as those of unhappy love (Chapter 20).

The most commonly mentioned feelings are feeling sad or depressed, melancholy or unhappy, and also feeling worn out, exhausted, tired, weak, and 'empty'. These feelings generally involve a low activation level. In addition, feelings of being worn out, of tiredness, weakness, and emptiness generally occur only after the end of the music. Listeners have had such a strong experience that they feel 'completely whacked', and performers feel totally 'washed out' after having put everything into their performance. It is thus a natural reaction to a preceding strong positive experience; one often describes oneself as 'tired and happy at the same time'.

Other negative feelings are as follows (listed in descending order of occurrence):

feeling nervous or uncertain, worried, confused

feeling fear, anxiety, despair, dread, broken-hearted, persecuted

feeling discomfort, (psychic) pain, jealousy or envy

fright or horror, panic, chaos, shock, unbearable

feeling frustrated, disappointed

embarrassed, ashamed

longing, (nostalgia)

anger, fury, hatred

feeling alone, abandoned, exposed to other person's mercy, little, insignificant.

Here, too, it is difficult to rank the feelings unambiguously according to activation level. This has been attempted in Appendix A, category 5.3.

Negative feelings with the highest activation level—anger, fury, hatred, fright, horror, shock, panic, chaos—fortunately occur in only a small percentage of the accounts. Nervousness or worry is mentioned especially by practising musicians in connection with performances (see Chapter 18, section 18.4). Embarrassment and shame are usually caused by one not being able to hide one's strong feelings from others; this applies particularly to men.

To feel alone, abandoned, little represents a low activation level, as is also usually the case with longing and nostalgia, which are fairly 'mildly' negative and can also have a positive aspect.

To feel little or insignificant is mentioned here as a negative feeling but was also mentioned under positive feelings in the previous section. When little/insignificant is placed under negative feelings, it is because these feelings occur together with expressions for loneliness and abandonment. When, however, little/insignificant is placed under positive feelings, they occur together with expressions for humility, which rather have a positive character (in any case, not negative).

In general, one should of course be aware of the closer circumstances to be able to understand what can lie behind the negative feelings. In Chapter 11, section 11.3, a distinction has therefore been made with regard to whether the negative feelings were primarily a result of factors outside the music, or of qualities in the music itself.

29.5.4 Mixed, contradictory, changed feelings

In many accounts, several feelings are mentioned that are sometimes closely related, in other cases completely different, as with mixed or contradictory feelings. Many also describe how the feelings changed during the course of the experience. Examples of some form of these reactions are found in about a fifth of the participants (21%), a little more often among women than among men.

Mixed feelings mean that positive and negative feelings occur side by side. One woman listened to the Dies Irae movement in Verdi's *Requiem* and 'felt shudders of both delight and horror' and another woman heard a boys' choir which 'sang so beautifully that it hurt'. Extremely contradictory feelings were experienced by a man who listened to Tchaikovsky's *Pathétique* symphony: 'a whole series of conflicting emotions: fright, sorrow, hate, love, anger, and last an internal peace that words cannot describe' (Chapter 6, account 6.2C). Further examples are to be found in Chapter 11, section 11.4, and changes between different feelings are described in accounts of music in love (Chapter 20).

The clearest examples of change in feelings are to be found in Chapter 17, Music as therapy. In such accounts there are descriptions of a change, successive or sudden, from negative to positive feelings—from pain, anxiety, sorrow, or depression, to calm, balance, hope, and new courage to face life. Other examples of changed emotional state—negative to positive—are found in accounts of music at funerals (Chapter 22) and of nervousness in musicians (Chapter 18, section 18.4).

29.6 EXISTENTIAL AND TRANSCENDENTAL ASPECTS

Many accounts concern questions of life and existence and experiences of transcendental character.

29.6.1 Existential aspects

Several accounts contain thoughts and reflections of an existential character. They might concern eternal questions about the meaning of life and existence, for man in general and/or the narrator in particular. The music can seem to express the content of what it means to be human and how one develops during different stages of life—which possibilities that are presented, which problems one is faced with and what multitude of feelings is included in these processes. It can lead to one acquiring a changed view of oneself, one's relation to other people, and of life in general, as well as leading to action.

There are concrete examples in Chapter 12. They show how music, of completely different types, can be perceived as a mirror of life, its greatness but also its transitoriness, its various phases, its mixing of different feelings—'pain, sorrow, passion, happiness'—indeed, 'everything, life, death, to exist as a human being'. They also illustrate how this can influence the joy of living and lead to changes in one's lifestyle. Some people emphasized the almost paradoxical fact that just a couple of minutes of listening to music radically changed their entire life.

Similar experiences can also be found in accounts of transcendental and religious experiences (Chapters 13 and 14) and of therapeutic effects of music (Chapter 17); the boundary between these different areas is often diffuse.

In the category of existential aspects, we also count experiences of special presence in life, an intense feeling of living—existing—here and now. On such rather rare occasions, the only thing that matters is quite simply 'just being', letting all one's worries and 'musts' subside, and enjoying the privilege of being able to exist, and receive what the world and life can offer; for example, 'To experience the beauty, the stillness, and existence without relation to knowledge and references, to just be there in this, was an overwhelming experience' (Chapter 23, account 23H).

A further category is experiences that are called 'ultimate', 'unsurpassable', or 'holy' moments in life. It is a question of an experience of such power and character that one cannot expect to experience the like ever again. It can take place in very different circumstances, but what is common to these experiences is the joy of having been able to be a part of this unique occasion: 'it can't get better than this', 'now I can die happy'; see further examples in Chapter 12, section 12.2.

Some form of the above existential aspects is found in about 8% of the participants.

29.6.2 Transcendental aspects

Transcendental experiences can be defined as experiences that go beyond (Latin *transcendo* = to exceed, to surpass) what are considered ordinary perception and experience. How this boundary between ordinary and extraordinary experiences should be drawn is, however, by no means self-evident but is a matter of judgement including a certain degree of arbitrariness. We have chosen a division into five somewhat overlapping groups.

(a) Experiences that are labelled as supernatural, magical, mysterious, occult, extraterrestrial, heavenly, or spiritual. All these expressions allude to something out of the ordinary, although the use of language is sometimes rather loose. Expressions such as 'heavenly' or 'spiritual' can also allude to religious experiences. They have, however, been placed here when it is evident that religious aspects are not being referred to, as in the following quote: 'It was a spiritual experience without having anything to do with religion' (Chapter 13, account 13.1D).

(b) Experiences described as ecstasy or trance. A clear distinction between these concepts cannot be made; the terms are used indiscriminately and in different ways by different people, even by experts in the field.

(c) 'Out-of-body' experiences or similar experiences are described by about ten people, most of them women. All the experiences took place in connection with live music and when one was together with other people, never on one's own. They can also be described as quasi-physical reactions (see Chapter 8, section 8.2)

(d) This group comprises experiences that are labelled 'total experiences' (with a rather diffuse content) and cosmic experiences. The latter mean experiences of endlessness, timelessness, and eternity, or an experience of being absorbed by something bigger, or merging with the universe; see the accounts in Chapter 13, section 13.3.

(e) An adjacent group comprises experiences of other worlds and existences; see Chapter 13, section13.4.

In all, some form of the above transcendental aspects is mentioned by almost 15% of the participants.

29.6.3 Religious experiences

Religious experiences can be regarded as a class of transcendental experiences with the special characteristic that they include a relation to a higher being usually called a god, in these accounts Christianity's God, or Jesus Christ, or the Holy Ghost. The music is for the greater part various types of religious music.

The analysis of all the accounts with religious content leads to a division into five groups. Accounts that exemplify these are to be found in Chapter 14.

(a) The first group contains statements of a very general or unspecified religious character without any further explanation; for example, 'I felt religious', 'It was a religious experience', or 'I can imagine that this is like a religious experience'.

(b) The next group contains descriptions of how the music gives rise to visions of heaven, life after death, paradise, or eternity.

(c) One group of statements involves feeling a special spiritual peace during the experience, a holy atmosphere, and/or Christian fellowship.

(d) The largest group, quantitatively, comprises accounts from just over 6% of the participants, who describe some form of religious communication: either that the music conveys a religious or Christian message to the listener, or that one is seeking or achieves contact with God in prayer or songs of praise. These aspects sometimes merge.

(e) The strongest expressions and the most detailed reports of religious experience in connection with music are found in descriptions of conversion or salvation and of meetings with the divine or the holy—God, Jesus Christ, the Holy Ghost.

In total, some form of religious experience occurs in connection with strong music experiences in just over 11% of the narrators, more often among women than among men (except as regards group (a) where men are in the majority).

29.7 Personal and social aspects

With almost half of all the narrators there are descriptions of what the experience has meant—what its consequences were—on a personal level. There are also many descriptions of the ability of music to create fellowship.

29.7.1 New insights, new possibilities

A strong experience with music can have considerable consequences for development and quality of life. Some form of new insights and new possibilities is mentioned by 41% of the participants, usually to a higher degree among women than among men. Accounts that illustrate such effects are found in many places, primarily in Chapters 15 and 17.

The effects can be divided into the following partly overlapping groups:

(a) An immediate and easily understandable effect is a wish that the music must go on, the wonderful experience must not be allowed to end, one wishes to hear or play the music over and over again.

(b) One feels a need to retain, confirm, reinforce, or change the feeling one had during the experience, either directly afterwards (for example, 'I didn't want to talk to anyone but keep this new, incredible emotional experience for myself') or more generally in the long term (for example, 'When I'm feeling depressed and low I usually listen to this tune so that my feelings will be confirmed in some way'). Examples of how one uses music to influence one's emotional state are found in Chapter 11, section 11.5.

(c) The music experience can lead to new insights about oneself, about other people, about life and much else. Thoughts and feelings that have been hidden can become evident, and one can feel as if one comes into contact with one's innermost core. Accounts that exemplify such effects are found in Chapters 12 and 15.

(d) The music experience can lead to the narrator feeling free, liberated, inspired, enlivened, invigorated, reborn, elevated, enriched, and to considering oneself to 'have grown or matured'.

(e) The music experience is described as an inner cleansing, a releasing of pent-up feelings, catharsis, or as a healing experience.

(f) Other effects often mentioned are that the experience gives consolation, hope, relaxation, alleviation, relief, strength, courage, a kick. Accounts that illustrate such effects are to be found in many places but especially Chapter 17.

(g) About ten people, almost all of them women, say that the experience has made them more open or unconditional, that they have relinquished previous defences and controls, that one 'dares to allow oneself to become immediately affected', or that one has learnt to 'meet or approach new experiences without prejudices'.

29.7.2 New insights, new possibilities, and new needs concerning music

Naturally, a strong experience with music also leaves its mark with regard to the person's attitude and relation to music. Almost half of the participants (44%) contribute with comments on this.

(a) Most comments involve the fact that one develops an interest in a particular piece of music, a certain type of music, a certain composer or artiste. One actively looks for possibilities to be able to hear the music concerned: for example, by buy records, buying a new stereo system, going to concerts, getting hold of the score, reading about the music, composer, or artiste, perhaps even joining a music circle or fan club.

(b) The interest can also be on a more general level, that one acquires an interest in and curiosity about music in general and, in particular, that one acquires a changed view of what music can mean and be used for. This is evident from many accounts, and a collection of illustrative quotes to this effect are included in Chapter 32, section 32.3.

(c) The experience leads to a wish to learn to play or sing or to continue to play or sing to an even greater degree than one has done before.

(d) About ten participants say that they have been inspired to do their own creative work, to compose music (most of them) or to write lyrics or a theatre script about music.

(e) For about ten other narrators, the experience led to the decision to devote themselves to music as a profession; five of these were still children at the time of the experience, four were teenagers.

(f) The music experience also meant that one wished that other people—preferably 'everyone'—would realize what fantastic experiences one can get through music. About 30 participants wanted to work in that direction, for example by talking about their own strong experiences, inspiring others to listen to particular music, playing or singing for listeners, or encouraging others to start to playing, singing, etc.

(g) Many participants became inspired to use music to influence their own mood or even to use music as their own therapy. This is mentioned spontaneously in accounts by about 10% of the participants, with a dominance of women. There are examples in Chapter 11, section 11.5 and also in Chapter 17.

Strong music experiences thus give rise to strong motivation to continue to be involved with music in various ways.[7]

29.7.3 Confirmation, self-actualization

To feel that one is confirmed—seen, accepted, understood, appreciated, needed, chosen—is a fundamental need and a foundation for developing good self-esteem and a stable identity. All this takes place in interplay with the people around us, but it can also take place in interplay with music. The music seems to reflect one's thoughts and feelings, and one can feel chosen to receive the music. To perform music oneself is a way to be seen and noticed, and it can also open new possibilities for expressing oneself.

Questions of these types are touched upon by almost 15% of participants. A division has been made into the following three groups:

(a) Most comments concern the fact that, through the experience, one got some form of confirmation and thus also increased self-confidence. In this group, men are slightly more represented than women (especially young men) and performers more represented than listeners. Common examples are musicians who receive appreciation and praise for their performance. There are several examples of this in Chapter 16, section 16.3 and Chapter 18, section 18.4.

(b) A second group of comments are about how the music mirrors the person concerned, their own thoughts and feelings; one recognizes oneself in the music. Such statements are most common with young women; accounts to this effect are to be found particularly in Chapter 16, section 16.1.

(c) A third group of statements are about feeling oneself to be especially chosen, addressed, that the music is directed 'just to me'. Such statements occur to a higher degree among women than among men; there are examples in Chapter 16, section 16.2.

29.7.4 Community

The ability of music to create a sense of fellowship between people is well known and often used in political and religious contexts—for example, think of national anthems, political anthems such as the *Internationale*, or of hymns and psalms that unite people with the same religion.

Comments about community, fellowship, and communication occurred with just over 18% of the narrators. Four groups can be distinguished:

(a) Fellowship among listeners. The typical example is the feeling of fellowship between listeners at a concert; for example, 'It was full of people. You were friends with everybody' (Chapter 5, account 5.1E), 'It is an enormous feeling, to be at a gigantic concert with your idols. Everybody who is there really loves what they are listening to, and there is an enormous sense of fellowship' (Chapter 5, account 5.1B).

(b) Fellowship between musicians/performers. Naturally, it is mainly performers who express themselves on this; for example, 'We got out our accordions and started to play. Some other accordionists came along and wanted to join in. We didn't know each other but the fellowship we felt was so great. We were like one big family' (Chapter 18, account 18.6I). But listeners, too, can observe such a feeling of fellowship among musicians: 'the musicians had a delightful quality, absolutely superb . . . there was such an incredible feeling of togetherness between those who played' (Chapter 26, account 26J).

(c) Fellowship between listeners and musicians; for example, 'It became one unit, the audience and the musicians, the boundaries between different roles merged together; we drank out of the same barrel. It was the music that counted, not who was doing what. "Now we are all here and are involved in this!"' (Chapter 26, account 26F), 'The band can tame the audience, and the opposite too. There's a sort of symbiosis between the group and the audience' (Chapter 27, account 27I).

(d) Some participants described an experience of boundless fellowship, fellowship with all people everywhere. To take a couple of examples:

(29.7.4A) Man, middle-aged, 1980s (excerpt from a long account)

Then a piece of music started to fill the room with loud powerful music. 'We are the world', and the experience was extremely powerful. The previous year, I had lived in a hut with a native family and one of the tunes there was this 'We are the world'. And just now, during these minutes, I experienced a strong feeling of fellowship with all people on our Earth and a colossal gratitude that these people exist and that I could live with them and be looked after despite their lack of material resources.

(29.7.4B) Woman, middle-aged (from 14.2D)

[Easter Sunday morning in Jerusalem] People of all nationalities were sitting everywhere . . . Then an orchestra started to play a song, which is called '*Han lever*' in Swedish ['He is alive'] . . . A song where everybody felt fellowship and could take part . . . All of me was filled with some holy meeting with all the world's humanity . . . We were united in a musical fellowship, where there was no feeling of being strangers, all of us were one. All ages, different races, man and woman, no difference. The music built a bridge to fellowship.

29.8 ANSWERS TO OTHER QUESTIONS

Apart from the summary of all the reactions, there are also other results to describe: questions of possible difference with regard to the gender and age of the participants (29.8.1), differences between performers and listeners (29.8.2), where and when the experience took place (29.8.3), whether it was live music or reproduced music (29.8.4), whether one had had the same strong experience before (29.8.5) or later (29.8.6), and how often strong experiences with music occur (29.8.7). There is also a short report on the results from the special questionnaire (29.8.8).

29.8.1 Gender and age

In comparison to men, women generally react more with tears or crying and say that they are more likely to use music to influence their mood. They describe, relatively more often, reactions such as being brought to immobility or stillness, feeling that one's body is filled with music or feeling enclosed in or surrounded by the music. They mention more positive feelings of low or moderate activation level—peace, tranquillity, humility, reverence, solemnity, pleasure, delight, beauty—and negative feelings such as sadness or sorrow. They also give more examples of mixed or changed feelings and of how the experience contributed to clarifying thoughts and feelings, that one recognizes oneself in the music and feels chosen to receive it. Women also describe different religious experiences to a greater degree than men—religious visions, that one feels spiritual peace or fellowship, that one is reached by a religious message, and that one meets divinity.

In comparison with women, men more often mention perceptual reactions (impressions of volume and loudness, tone colour or timbre, musicians' actions, audience reactions) and reactions such as total absorption, absence of other thoughts, experience of unreality and of a special wholeness, and also that they become surprised or shocked by the music. Among positive feelings, men mention gratitude and perfection to a higher degree than women, as they do embarrassment or shame among negative feelings. Men mention extraterrestrial or mysterious experiences and cosmic experiences relatively more often and more often describe the experience as a form of catharsis. They describe, somewhat more often than women, how the experience has given them increased self-confidence; this applies particularly to performers.

There are thus certain differences between the genders, but on the whole the similarities are greater than the differences. It is, for example, significant that with regard to the most common positive feelings—happiness and joy—there are no differences between the genders. In most cases, the difference between the genders is also linked to certain age groups, that is, there is a difference between the genders for two of the three age groups, but not for all three. As a couple of examples, one could mention that women's descriptions of how one's body is filled with music come from middle-aged and young women but not old women, and the likelihood of becoming completely immobile or still when listening applies to middle-aged and old women but not young women. There is a great deal to add about similar complicated interactions between gender and age which must, however, be set aside in this text.

It is thus difficult to see any completely general differences between different age groups. Young participants do, however, differ manifestly from middle-aged and old participants by being more likely to move to the music (dance, jump, clap one's hands, and so on). In comparison to middle-aged and old participants, young participants more often describe the experience as a 'kick', but this probably reflects differences in language rather than in the experience as such.

The above concerns how old the participants were when they told us about their SEM. It can be just as interesting to examine whether there are any differences depending on how old they were when the SEM took place. In order to study this, a division was made into five age intervals regarding when the SEM took place: 0–9 years of age (that is, as a child), 10–19 (youth), 20–29 (young adult), 30–59 (middle-aged) and 60–89 (old). Some of the clearest results are as follows.

The proportion of participants who reacted with tears increases successively with increased age at the time of the experience, from about 15% in the two youngest age groups to about 24% in middle-age and 34% among old people. Shivers seem to occur somewhat less during childhood (about 4%) than during all the other age intervals (7–10%).

Children, however, exhibit the highest frequency of singing along or shouting (11%); in the other age intervals, it occurs in 3% to 6% of cases, lowest among old people. Movements to music occur most with youths and young adults (9%), the opposite—becoming immobile—approximately the same (5% to 7%) in all age groups. The feeling of taking off or floating occurs in 6% to 7% of cases in all age intervals except for old (almost 2%). The feeling of being carried away/governed by the music is not described at all by children (0%).

As regards perception, one can note that the description of 'tone colour' or timbre occurs twice as often with children (11%) as with other ages (3% to 6%), which is in accordance with the notion that timbre in sound or music is the element that is observed earliest in one's musical development. The volume or loudness is commented upon relatively most within the three younger age intervals, while absolute silence ('could have heard a pin drop') is mentioned most by middle-aged and old.

Cognition variables such as openness or expectation, special atmosphere, unconsciousness of time or space, experience of unreality, and special wholeness are mentioned to a lesser extent during childhood years than during later age groups.

Feelings with low activation level such as peace, tranquillity, stillness occur to a greater degree during middle-age and old age (10% to 11%) than during childhood and youth (just over 5%), while the opposite situation applies for feelings of higher activation levels such as happiness, joy, elation; that is, they occur relatively more in the three younger age intervals (32% to 33%) than with middle-aged and old (27% to 28%). It can be noted that a feeling like wonder seems to occur somewhat more during childhood (4%) than in later age intervals (about 2%).

Reactions of existential, transcendental, or religious character are almost totally absent in accounts from childhood. Inner cleansing or catharsis are described by young adults and middle-aged (about 8%), considerably more than by children and youth (1% to 3%)

A newly aroused interest in music is described more often in childhood accounts (19%) than in the other age intervals (5% to 10%), as is the desire to learn to play (11% during childhood, 2% to 6% during the other age intervals). Most examples of the decisions to choose music as a career took place during childhood and youth (see section 29.7.2 above).

29.8.2 Listeners and performers

Most experiences, almost 81%, have taken place in connection with listening to music, the rest in connection with one's own playing of music (just under 19%) and composing of music (a few cases). There is a certain connection with the age of the participants: the greater their age, the more experiences as listener and the fewer as performer. For the old participants (60 years of age and older) the share of listener experiences was 88%, and as performer 11%. For middle-aged (30–59) the equivalent values were 81% and 18%; for the youngest participants 72% and 28%. Old participants have presumably had less opportunity to learn to play an instrument, and if they nevertheless have played any music themselves, this can have become less at an older age.

Experiences as a listener thus dominate greatly. This is valid even for the participants who perform themselves. For professional musicians, the proportion of experiences is 71% as listener, and thus 29% in connection with one's own performance. For amateur musicians, the equivalent values are 76% and 24%.

The participants also answered a direct question about whether they *usually* had SEM as listener or performer. The question was answered by 720 people (76% of the participants), of whom 70% said that they had SEM as a listener, 14% that they had SEM during their own performance or music making, and 15% said that they could have SEM both as a listener and as a performer. Here, too, there was a certain link with age. The listener alternative was most pronounced for old participants, 85%. For young and middle-aged participants, the equivalent value was 63% and

66% respectively. Not surprisingly, professional musicians showed a completely different distribution: SEM as listener 29%, as performer also 29%, and as listener or performer 39%. Among amateur musicians, the percentage of listener experiences was 66%, and for non-musicians it was of course 100%.

On the whole, there are no major differences between musicians and non-musicians in their descriptions of SEM other than that musicians sometimes use technical music terms and that their own experiences of performance can shine through. On the other hand, several musicians maintain that on the occasion of their SEM, they totally forgot any thought of technique and performance and 'just listened to the music' like any ordinary listener.

But there are, naturally, certain reactions that are special for performers, for example that one feels nervousness before a performance, that one sometimes cannot manage to sing or play because one is overwhelmed by feelings, that one on certain occasions surpasses oneself ('magic moments') and experiences total perfection in the music and performance, and that one can receive appreciation, confirmation, and increased self-confidence through a successful performance (see music performance generally in Chapter 18).

29.8.3 Where, when, and in what social situation did SEM occur?

The experiences have occurred in many different places: at home (20% of the cases), in church (16%), concert premises (15%), assembly hall (12%), outdoors in general (7%), at outdoor concerts (5%), at an opera, operetta, or musical (4%), in somebody else's home (3%), in a school context (3%), at a theatre (2%), and during a journey (car, bus, train, airplane, metro) (2%). In addition, the following places are represented: restaurant, sports hall, hospital, library, hotel/guesthouse, museum, studio, multipurpose hall, church ruin (Visby), shop, dancehall, practice room at a music school, office, children's home, circus tent, aircraft hangar, large country house, boarding school, club premises, military barracks, castle, exhibition premises, and a few more. Strong experiences with music seem to be able to take place almost anywhere. However, the five most common places (home, church, concert hall, assembly hall, outdoors) account for 70% of all cases.

As has been mentioned earlier (see Chapter 3), the experiences stretch over almost a hundred years, from 1908 to 2004. Of the just over 1,300 cases where it has been possible to establish the year for the experience (within a margin of error of one or two years), 13% have taken place before 1950, the remaining 87% thus after 1950 up until 2004. The largest number occurred in the 1980s (46%), which in part was certainly because the investigation started at the end of that decade, partly of course because there is a large proportion of young participants. Further information about dates is in Chapter 3.

For the most part, the experience took place when one was together with people one knows (68% of all the cases in which the social situation could be established), after that alone (19%) or together with other people one doesn't know (just over 12%). The values vary somewhat for different types of music. The largest proportion of experiences together with people one knows is for religious music, folk music, rock music and songs or tunes (75% to 78%), while the largest proportion of experiences alone was for classical (non-religious) music, pop music, and other popular music genres (27% to 29%). The proportion of experiences together with people one knows is also especially high (90%) for performers: they have played together with people they know, or have had them as listeners.

Furthermore, there is a difference between live music and reproduced music. With live music, experiences together with people one knows dominate (79%), but for reproduced music (records, radio, TV, etc.) it is the opposite, with experiences alone being the largest category (53%).

There are, of course, natural connections between the social situation and the place for the experience. The dominating social situation—being together with people one knows—takes place in churches, assembly halls, concert halls, schools, restaurants and at outdoor concerts, while the 'alone' situation almost exclusively involves one's own home and to a certain degree during journeys, for example in a car. Being together with people one doesn't know can also be in churches and concert halls and is the most common situation if the experience takes place during a hospital stay.

29.8.4 Live or reproduced music?

Most of the experiences have occurred with live music: just over 73%. Reproduced music (records, radio, TV, etc.) features in almost 27% of the cases. This distribution is similar for both genders and all three age groups.

All the experiences in which one is a performer are of course among the 'live' experiences. It is thus natural that the largest proportion of live experiences are with professional musicians (82%), after that with amateur musicians (75%), and the least with non-musicians (64%).

The largest proportion of live experiences is found in connection with folk music (90%), then with religious music and theatre music (80%). The largest proportion for reproduced music is in pop music (60%) and other adjacent genres (54%).

29.8.5 The first time?

The question 'Was it the first time you heard this music?' was answered in the affirmative in about 46% of the answers to this question (979 answers). In 54% of the cases, one had thus heard the music on some earlier occasion.

There were certain age differences here. The young participants (<30 years) had heard the music before in as many as 67% of the cases, while the equivalent value for the old participants (>60 years) was much lower, 41%. The first-time experience thus dominated for the old participants but not for the young ones.

For middle-aged participants, it was approximately an equal proportion (50/50) of the two alternatives.

The difference between young and old can in part reflect the difference in the selection of music available (a much greater selection towards the end of the twentieth century than earlier), and can in part also be a result of how reproduced music has become progressively more common.

It might also be connected with which music genre is preferred by old and young participants, respectively. There was clear dominance of first-time experience only in classical, non-religious music, (61%), that is, the music that appears most often in the accounts of the old participants (see more in this regard in Chapter 30). Clear dominance of the alternative, of having heard the music earlier, was true for rock music (71%), pop music (66%), religious music (65%), and songs, tunes, or hits (62%); of these, rock, pop, and to a certain degree songs, tunes, or hits occurred mostly with young participants. As can be seen from several accounts (for example in Chapter 5, section 5.1), young participants have often heard rock and pop tunes earlier on records before they hear the same music at live concerts of their favourite artistes.

29.8.6 The same strong experience next time?

Did the participants have the same strong experience on later occasions when they listened to the same music? This question is answered in only 597 cases (44% of all the cases; the question was not asked in all parts of the investigation, and even when the question was asked, it was not always answered).

The proportion of yes answers was 36%, no answers 64%. Most had thus not had the same strong experience when they encountered the same music again. The answers vary from 'It was still a strong experience but not as strong as that particular time' to 'It was not at all the same experience the next time'. Some people nuance their answer by referring to the memory of the experience; for example: 'When I heard the music the next time, I remembered what a strong experience I'd had the previous time, and it was nice to think back to it.'

Among those who had heard the music for the first time when they had their SEM, the proportion who had the same strong experience the next time was higher (42%) than among those who had already heard the same music earlier on some occasion (31%). But in both cases, the result was still such that the majority did not have the same strong experience on the next occasion.

The fact that the music ordinarily did not give the same SEM the next time shows that the experience was affected by factors other than the actual music. The situation can, of course, be entirely different, and one can oneself have changed in various ways. (A dramatic example of the experience not being at all the same, even if the next occasion takes place just a few minutes later, is described in Chapter 26, account 26G). The experience is always conditioned by an interplay between the music, the person, and the situation; this is treated thoroughly in Chapter 32.

29.8.7 How often does SEM occur?

This question was answered by 488 participants, just over half (51%) of all the participants. (Some questions did not fit in the available space when we looked for participants via newspaper articles. Further, several participants refrained from answering this question.) The answers have been divided into six categories as is shown in Table 29.8.7.

Naturally, this categorization necessitates a certain simplification of the answers. Many participants answer that, for example, how often they have had such experiences varies a great deal during different periods of their life—sometimes the experiences have been more often, sometimes more seldom, or they have taken place only during a limited period. Given this simplification, the answers nevertheless mean that strong experiences with music do not usually happen particularly often—once a year (44%) or a few times in a lifetime (32%). But for 16% (the total of the last three categories), SEM occur much more often.

Some participants have even had apprehensions about SEM occurring far too often: 'Just imagine if such strong experiences were to happen often, *goodness, how dreadful*' (Chapter 6, account 6.1E), and 'It's lucky you don't get such experiences too often because then you'd certainly become an alcoholic. You have to take something to help you wind down afterwards and then I think it's likely to be alcohol' (middle-aged woman).

29.8.8 Results of the questionnaire

As has been mentioned in Chapter 2, section 2.3, most of the participants also answered a questionnaire containing statements about strong experiences with music. For every statement, the participant was asked to judge how well it agreed with their own experience on a scale from 0 ('Does not agree at all') to 10 ('Agrees completely').

Table 29.8.7 Number and percentage of participants (*n* = 488) who estimated how often they have had an especially strong experience with music

Category	Number	%
Once in a lifetime	38	8
A few times in a lifetime	156	32
Once a year	215	44
Once a month	45	9
Once a week	29	6
Every day	5	1
Total	488	100

These judgements were subsequently analysed with various statistical methods, including factor analysis, for the purpose of finding a number of fundamental dimensions in strong music experiences. The factor analysis showed at least 14 dimensions—an unusually large number in the context of factor analysis—and thus confirmed in its way that strong experiences with music are very multifaceted. The content of the different dimensions was in most cases the same as that which was shown via the analysis of the accounts, such as tears or crying, shivers, quasi-physical experiences, changed perception of time and space, lost control, positive feelings, negative feelings, confirmation, existential, transcendental, and religious aspects.

In brief, one can thus say that the results from the qualitative and the quantitative parts of the investigation agree with each other. There is, however, no doubt that the qualitative part—the analysis of the participants' own accounts—has illustrated SEM with greater width as well as greater depth than an analysis of the questionnaire answers alone would offer.[8]

CHAPTER 30

MUSIC IN SEM

THERE are about 1,300 pieces of music or artistes mentioned in the material. To list all of these would be far too cumbersome and require too much space. What is important is to divide them into a limited number of categories which together can give a good overview.

30.1 DIVISION INTO CATEGORIES

Dividing music into different categories is an undertaking always fraught with difficulties, and some simplifications and compromises are inevitable. The system that I have chosen is adapted to the examples of music that occur in this particular material. It comprises 15 categories plus one extra category. Within each category there is a varying number of sub-categories, presented in the order of how often they are represented in the material.

(a) Classical, non-religious music. This category comprises mainly instrumental music. Most of the examples come from the Romantic period (35%), after that from the twentieth century (23%; late Romantic music from the twentieth century has, however, been placed under the Romantic period), Classicism (20%), and Baroque (8%). To these are added electronic and electro-acoustic music (3%) and a couple of examples of early music (pre-Baroque). The remaining 10% consist of unspecified classical music.

(b) Religious music. This category comprises an approximately equal amount of purely vocal music (singing) and singing and instrumental music together. The two biggest groups consist of hymns and songs of praise (26%) and of church music from the Baroque era (24%), then comes music from the Romantic period (17%), the twentieth century (8%), Classicism (5%) and early music (3%, for example Gregorian chant), then gospel songs (7%), Christian pop and rock songs and Christian musicals (6%), and others (4%).

(c) Theatre music. Half of the examples (50%) consist of operas from the Romantic period, then come musicals (18%), operas from Classicism (16%), operettas (11%), twentieth-century operas (2%), others (3%).

(d) Folk music. The greatest part is instrumental music but there is also some vocal music. Half of the examples come from Swedish and Scandinavian folk music, the rest is roughly equally divided into European and non-European folk music.

(e) Jazz music. Predominantly instrumental. Most of the examples belong to traditional jazz (27%) and 'modern' jazz (roughly from bebop to fusion and free-form jazz, 36%), then comes blues (9%), jazz rock and other hybrid forms, improvisation, and unspecified jazz.

(f) Rock music. Vocal and instrumental (mainly) or just instrumental. Most of the examples (56%) are described as rock music in general without further specification. Then comes hard rock (17%), symphonic rock (7%), rock ballads (6%), and diverse examples of synth-rock, punk rock, blues rock, and the like.

(g) Pop music. Almost exclusively vocal and instrumental. Is often mentioned as pop music in general (70%), but there is also synth-pop (15%), pop ballads (6%), and hybrids such as pop rock and pop jazz.

(h) Songs, tunes, melodies. This is a heterogeneous category containing Swedish songs (children's songs, Christmas songs, Evert Taube, Birger Sjöberg, Povel Ramel, Karin Liungman, Cornelis Vreeswijk, and so on) (41%), popular songs or hit songs (19%), Anglo-American songs and tunes (14%), European songs (for example, Theodorakis, Brel, 6%), non-European songs (African and others), other well-known melodies (for example, 'Säterjäntans söndag' ['The herds-maiden's Sunday']), evergreens, and diverse other examples.

(i) Entertainment music. Mainly instrumental; entertainment music in general (76%; for example, Lumbye's 'Champagne Galop', Jacob Gade's 'Tango Jalousie'), and marches (24%, for example Noack's 'The Brownies' guard parade').

(j) Other popular music. This is a provisional category to cover many different types of contemporary popular music that are represented in the material by a single or just a few cases each: 'ambient music', 'new age' music, funk, soul, disco, country, reggae, rap, techno, Latin-American music, synth music, and the like.

(k) Dance music. Dance music in general (44%), waltz (19%), tango (19%), salsa (12%), and samba (6%).

(l) Improvised music. About ten examples (jazz improvisation has, however, been put under jazz above).

(m) Artiste or ensemble. These include cases within classical music where the narrator primarily emphasizes the musician, singer, or ensemble, rather than the music that is performed (examples like those in Chapter 25, section 25.2).

(n) Art music in other cultures. This includes Indian ragas, Indonesian gamelan music, and flamenco.

(o) Instrument. In several accounts, it is primarily the experience of a certain instrument that is emphasized, for example a flute, trumpet, drums, or a certain singing voice, rather than the music that is played or sung.

(p) Several other unspecified types of music. This is a remainder category (about 1% of the entire material), which is not discussed further.

There is obvious overlap between different categories. Religious music and theatre music would equally well be called classical music by many people. The border between rock and pop is very fluid, as are the borders between songs and tunes, entertainment music and dance music, not to mention the many types of music gathered together in the category 'Other popular music'. There is generally quite a lot of uncertainty about suitable terminology among both our narrators and experts in the field.

30.2 Distribution across different categories

The number and percentage share of accounts in the different music categories are shown in Table 30.2A.

Classical, non-religious music is the single largest group, with just over 30% of the cases. Religious music comes next, with just over 15%, and almost 7% for theatre music. For the sake of simplicity, we can put the first three categories (classical, religious, and theatre) together in one group and call it art music, and this then comprises quite a good half of all the cases (52.8%). If one were to deduct gospel and Christian pop and rock, which are not normally counted as art music, one would end up with just over 50%.

Folk music, jazz, rock, pop, and other popular music each account for about 3% to 7% of the cases, together approximately 25%; if one adds gospel and Christian pop and rock music, they make up about 27%. Songs and tunes, the third largest category, account for almost 10% of the cases, entertainment and dance music together for almost 3%. The remaining 10% are distributed across the other categories; largest among these are Artiste and Instrument, while art music from other cultures and improvised music occur rarely.

If one wishes to further simplify the division, one can say that art music occurs in just over half the cases, 'popular music' (folk music, jazz, rock, pop, songs and tunes, entertainment music, dance music, other popular music) in just over 37% of the cases.

The distribution of different categories does, however, vary according to the participants' gender; see the columns on the right in Table 30.2A. Women show a higher percentage than men in the first three categories, especially for religious music, as well

Table 30.2A Distribution across different categories, across all narrators, and separately for women and men

Category	Number	%	Women	Men
Classical	415	30.6	32.1	29.7
Religious	211	15.6	19.2	10.4
Theatre	90	6.6	7.9	4.8
Folkmusic	77	5.7	5.2	6.6
Jazz	82	6.1	1.7	13.6
Rock	89	6.6	3.9	11.4
Pop	47	3.5	3.9	2.8
Songs and tunes	132	9.7	11.3	7.8
Entertainment	21	1.6	1.5	1.8
Other popular	41	3.0	2.3	4.2
Dance	16	1.2	1.1	1.4
Improvisation	10	0.7	0.8	0.6
Artiste	44	3.2	4.1	2.0
Other culture	7	0.5	0.4	0.8
Instrument	35	2.6	3.4	1.4
Others	37	2.8	1.3	0.6
All	1354	100	100	100

as for songs and tunes, also a little higher for experience of particular artiste or particular instrument. On the other hand, men show a considerably higher percentage than women regarding jazz and rock music, and a little higher for other popular music.

The picture becomes even more nuanced if we also include age in the calculation; see Table 30.2B.

The proportion of art music (classical, religious, theatre) generally increases with age for both genders. Folk music lies throughout within 5% and 7%, except for old women (1.7%). Jazz music occurs a lot more with men than with women, most of all with middle-aged men (19%). Rock music occurs most with young participants, especially young men, for whom rock music is the biggest category of all, with a share (29.7%) that is as large as for the three art music categories together (15.2% + 10.3% + 4.1% = 29.6%) for this group. Pop music has the largest share with young women, as do songs and tunes; the share of songs and tunes decreases with age for women, and for men it is highest in middle age. Other popular music occurs almost only in the youngest age group. Rock, pop, and other popular music are not represented at all among old men, and in only a few cases among old women.

Looking at all the combinations of gender and age, the difference is greatest between, on the one hand, old women and, on the other hand, young men. For old women, the

Table 30.2B Distribution (percentage) with regard to gender and age groups

	Women			Men		
Age	<30	30–59	≥60	<30	30–59	≥60
Classical	16.5	32.0	46.6	15.2	30.2	50.5
Religious	17.5	21.2	17.5	10.3	10.1	11.6
Theatre	5.2	7.1	10.3	4.1	3.6	6.3
Folkmusic	5.2	7.4	1.7	6.2	6.5	7.4
Jazz	2.4	2.3	0.4	8.3	19.0	8.4
Rock	12.7	1.1	0.0	29.7	5.6	0.0
Pop	11.8	1.7	0.4	4.1	3.2	0.0
Songs and tunes	13.7	11.3	9.4	6.2	10.1	3.2
Entertainment	0.5	1.4	2.6	1.4	0.4	6.3
Other popular	7.1	0.8	0.4	9.0	3.2	0.0
Dance music	1.9	0.8	0.9	1.4	1.6	1.1
Improvisation	0.9	0.8	0.9	1.4	0.4	0.0
Artiste	2.4	5.4	4.3	1.4	1.2	5.3
Other culture	0.0	0.6	0.4	0.0	1.6	0.0
Instrument	1.9	4.5	3.0	1.4	2.0	0.0

art music categories account for 74.4% together, as against only 29.6% for young men. The most common popular music categories (jazz, rock, pop, and other popular music) comprise 51.1% for young men but only 1.2% for old women. The difference between old men and young women is also considerable but not quite as large as between old women and young men.

These results must be seen in the light of how old the narrator was when the experience took place; see Table 30.2C. The % column shows the percentage of SEM that took place when the participants were under 10 years of age (first row), between 10 and 20 years (next row), and so on. In the next column, the accumulated percentage values are shown. The two columns on the right show the equivalent values for the older half of the participants, those who were older than 40 (median age = 40).

As can be seen in the column 'Accumulated %' (for All), just over one-third (35.3%) of all experiences have taken place before the narrator has reached the age of 20, and almost two-thirds (62.7%) have taken place before the age of 30. That these values are so high depends to a great extent on there being so many young participants in the investigation. If one looks separately at the participants who were older than 40, just over one-quarter (27.2%) of the experiences had taken place before 20 years of age and not far from half (44.3%) before 30 years of age. A very large part of the experiences have thus taken place already during the first decades of life. The age range 10–19 shows the highest percentage value (29.7 and 20.4 respectively) of all the

Table 30.2C Percentage and accumulated percentage SEM that took place at different ages, for all participants and for the older half of the participants (>40 years)

	All		Over 40 years	
Age	%	Accumulated %	%	Accumulated %
0–9	5.6	5.6	6.8	6.8
10–19	29.7	35.3	20.4	27.2
20–29	27.4	62.7	17.1	44.3
30–39	14.7	77.4	15.7	60.0
40–49	10.6	88.0	18.6	78.6
50–59	7.4	95.4	13.1	91.7
60–69	3.8	99.2	6.6	98.3
70–79	0.6	99.7	1.1	99.4
80–89	0.3	100	0.5	100

10-year intervals. There are other investigations that show that the autobiographical memories of adults for the greater part refer to youth and early adulthood, and that the preference for a certain type of music, literature, films, and so on, is developed during this period.[1]

One can further note that the number of very early experiences (before 10 years of age), expressed as a percentage, is larger for the older half of the participants (6.8%) than for the entire group (5.6%). For the very oldest participants, 60–91 years old, the share of early experiences is even higher, 8.7%—thus the older the participant, the more accounts of experiences during childhood. And for these oldest participants, too, the number of experiences was largest (22.6%) in the age range 10–19.

This data also shed light on a part of the big differences between different age groups that was evident in Table 30.2B. Since preferences for music seem to be established especially during youth and early adulthood, one must note which music was met with in Sweden at the time of the participants' experiences. During the early decades of the twentieth century, the opportunities to hear live music or to play music oneself were rather limited, especially in rural areas. This can be clearly seen in the accounts of several old participants, which also show what an almost revolutionary importance the radio and early gramophones had for the possibility of beginning to gain access to the world of music. Up until about the middle of the century, the music available was dominated by art music genres (classical, religious, and theatre music), some popular music (entertainment, songs and tunes, and so on), and early jazz music, which met with strong opposition in many places. After the middle of the century, the availability of music was generally widened, jazz got more room but was then pushed back by rock and pop, and during the last decades of the twentieth century the flora of popular music genres began to be almost limitless. On the whole, there has been a shift from dominance by art music to dominance by popular music.

The old participants in the investigation thus encountered, for the greater part, some form of art music during their youth, a little jazz and popular music, but this was long before the breakthrough of rock and popular music. For the young participants, the availability of music during their youth has been much greater, and also had much greater elements of popular music, especially rock and pop. The middle-aged participants (30–60 years) have found themselves between these two extremes, which can be clearly seen in Table 30.2B. An interesting detail is that jazz experiences occur most with middle-aged men. This is probably connected to the fact that, for many of them, their youth period occurred around the middle of the twentieth century, when jazz got more room in Sweden (but a little later was pushed back by rock and pop music).

An interesting question is whether the music in SEM belonged to the type of music that the narrator usually preferred. Most of the participants were asked a question about which music they preferred and/or usually listened to. A clear majority answered that they listened to (preferred) several different categories of music, and this was also connected to the age of the participants. Among the oldest participants (over 60 years), half said that they listened to several different types of music, among the middle-aged (30–60 years) it was two-thirds who did so, and among the youngest (up to 30 years) it was just over three-quarters. Thus, the younger the participants, the greater the spread across different categories of music; quite a lot of the participants even said that they listened to 'every sort of music'. This certainly reflects the fact that the selection of music available had become progressively larger and more diversified.

With music preferences being so widely spread across different categories, it is difficult to make comparisons between music in SEM and the music one usually listens to (prefers). On the whole, there is a positive connection in as much as the music in SEM is usually also represented among the respective participant's music preferences. The clearest connection is with regard to art music. The majority among those who had their SEM within art music usually also prefer art music; this applies especially for the relatively older participants. There is also a fairly clear tendency that those who have had SEM within jazz music and rock music usually prefer these genres.

On the other hand, one can find many accounts of a decisive—sometimes revolutionary or shocking—encounter with unknown music. Naturally, such encounters often take place during childhood or youth, which can be seen in many accounts in Chapters 4 and 5, particularly in Chapter 5, section 5.2. But they can also very well take place during later periods in life, which can be illustrated by the following examples of encounters with unknown music or artistes within different categories:

Art music: Tchaikovsky Symphony No. 6, *Pathétique* (6.2C), Beethoven Serenade Op. 8 in D major (6.2D), Handel Concerto Grosso, Op. 6, No. 6 (15.1E), Bartók *The Miraculous Mandarin* (17.2M), Arvo Pärt *Tabula rasa* (25.1H), Poulenc *Figure humaine* (25.1K).

Religious music: Gregorian chant (14.1D), Greek Orthodox mass (24A), gospel (24D).

Folk music: Turkish folk music (15.1C), Austrian folk music (23N).

Jazz: Albert Ayler (18.2B), George Adams (26I, 26J).

Rock and pop: Billy Bragg (27G), Danielle Dax (27C).

Music from another culture: flamenco (16.1I), African drums (24G, 24H, 24I), choir singing in Africa (24E), Indian sitar (24L), Chinese music (24N, 24O), gamelan music (24P).

Artistes: Felicity Lott (25.2O), Martin Best (25.2P), the Tapiola Children's Choir (25.1L).

30.3 EXAMPLES OF MUSIC IN SEM

This section contains registers of music that has occurred in the accounts (even in non-included accounts).

30.3.1 Art music, classical music

Table 30.3.1 shows composers and works of art music that are mentioned in the accounts, arranged in alphabetical order according to the composer's surname.

About 110 composers are listed here. Most of them have been mentioned in one or several accounts, but certain composers have occurred much more often: Bach, Bartók, Beethoven, Brahms, Chopin, Dvořák, Grieg, Handel, Larsson, Liszt, Lundsten, Mahler, Mendelssohn, Mozart, Orff (only *Carmina Burana*), Pärt, Rachmaninov, Ravel, Schubert, Schumann, Sibelius, Smetana (only *Moldau*), Shostakovich, Stravinsky (*Rite of Spring*), Tchaikovsky, Wagner, and Verdi. The works that are mentioned for each composer are in many cases regarded as the masterpieces in art music.

Besides the operas and operettas that are included in the list, there is also theatre music represented in the form of musicals such as Bernstein's *West Side Story*, Lloyd Webber's *Cats*, *The Phantom of the Opera* and *Les Misérables* as well as Benny Andersson and Björn Ulvaeus's *Chess* and *Kristina from Dufvemåla*.

30.3.2 Artistes and ensembles within art music

In many of the accounts, it is apparent that the strong experience is primarily dependent on the qualities of a particular artiste or ensemble.

Table 30.3.1 Composers and works in art music. The figure in brackets indicates the total number of accounts where the composer is mentioned

Adam: 'O holy night' ('*Le Cantique de Noël*')

Albinoni (3): Adagio

Alfvén, Hugo: '*Gryning vid havet*' ['Dawn by the sea'], chorus

Bach, J. S. (55): *St John Passion, St Matthew Passion*, Mass in B minor, Christmas Oratorio, cantatas, *Actus Tragicus*, Brandenburg Concerto No. 2, two concertos for violin (D minor, E major), Piano Concerto in D minor, Air (in Suite for Orchestra No. 3), partitas for violin and cello, preludes and fugues in *The Well-Tempered Clavier, Kunst der Fuge*; organ works: Toccata and Fugue in D minor, Organ Concerto in C major after Vivaldi, Trio Sonata in E-flat major

Barber: Adagio for Strings

Bartók (5): Piano Concerto No. 3, Violin Concerto, String Quartet No. 6, *The Miraculuos Mandarin, Duke Bluebeard's Castle*

Beethoven (50): Symphonies Nos. 3, 4, 5, 6, 7, and 9, Piano Concertos Nos. 3, 4, and 5, Violin Concerto, Triple Concerto, Leonore Overture No. 3, Serenade Op. 8 in D major, piano sonatas (especially '*Appassionata*', 'Moonlight' Sonata, *Pathétique*, and Op. 111 in C minor), the 'Archduke' trio, sonatas for cello and piano, *Fidelio* (opera)

Bellini: *Norma* (opera)

Berg (3): Violin concerto, *Wozzeck* (opera)

Berlioz (2): *Symphonie fantastique, L'Enfance du Christ* (oratorio)

Bizet (4): *Carmen, The Pearl Fishers*

Blomdahl, Karl-Birger (2): Symphony No. 3 ('*Facets*'), *Aniara* (opera)

Borodin: *Prince Igor* (opera), Polovtsian Dances (in *Prince Igor*)

Brahms (15) *Ein deutsches Requiem*, Symphonies Nos. 3 and 4, Double Concerto for Violin and Cello, Piano Sonata No. 3, Piano Quartet in C minor, Variations and Fugue on a theme by Handel, and 'Waltz in A-flat major' for piano

Britten: War Requiem

Bruch (5): Violin Concerto No. 1

Bruckner (4): Symphonies Nos. 7 and 8

Cage, John: 'Happening'

Chopin (14): Études, mazurkas, 'Nocturne No. 1 in B-flat minor', 'Scherzo No. 3', Prelude No. 15 'Raindrop', Fantaisie Impromptu in C-sharp minor Op. 66, Fantaisie in F minor Op. 49, 'Grande Valse brillante in E-flat major', 'Berceuse in D-flat major', 'Polonaise in A-flat major'

Cimarosa: Concerto for Two Flutes and Orchestra

Debussy: *Images*

Donizetti: *Mary Stuart, Daughter of the Regiment* (operas)

Dvořák (9): Symphony No. 8, Symphony No. 9 ('From the New World'), Cello Concerto, Serenade for Strings

Edlund, Swante: Organ Work in E-flat major Op. 8

Elgar (4): 'Pomp and circumstance', *The Dream of Gerontius* (oratorio), 'Carillon' (for organ)

Table 30.3.1 *(Continued)* Composers and works in art music. The figure in brackets indicates the total number of accounts where the composer is mentioned

de Falla: *The Three-Cornered Hat* (ballet)

Fanshawe: African Sanctus

Fauré (4): *Requiem*

Franck (2): Sonata for Violin and Piano in A major, '*Panis angelicus*'

de Frumerie, *Gunnar: Singoalla* (opera)

Gershwin: 'Rhapsody in blue'

Glass, Philip (2): *Satyagraha* (opera), an unspecified organ piece

Gluck: 'Dance of the blessed spirits' (in *Orpheus and Eurydice*, opera)

Górecki: Amen for Chorus Op. 35, Szeroka Woda [Broad Waters] op. 39

Gounod: *Messe Solennelle de Sainte Cécile*

Grieg (7): Piano Concerto in A minor, *Peer Gynt* incidental music ('Morning mood', 'Solveig's song'), piano pieces ('Last spring'), '*Landkjenning*' ['Land sighting', cantata], music in *Olav Trygvason* (opera, unfinished)

Handel (17): *Messiah* (oratorio, especially the 'Hallelujah' chorus), 'Water Music', Concerto Grosso, Op. 6, No. 6

Haydn (3): 'The Creation' (oratorio), Cello Concerto in C major, one string quartet

Honegger (2): *Pastorale d'été*, Symphony No. 2 for Strings and Trumpet

Hägg, Gustav: '*Bön F-dur*' ['Prayer F major'] in Op. 29 (organ)

Janáček: *Sinfonietta*

Khachaturian (2): 'Sabre dance' (in *Gayane*, ballet), Symphony No. 2

Kodály: *Psalmus Hungaricus*

Larsson, Lars-Erik (6): *Pastoralsvit* [Pastoral Suite], '*Förklädd gud*' ['God in disguise'], '*En vintersaga*' ['A Winter's Tale'], Concertino for Cello and String Orchestra

Lehár: *The Merry Widow*

Lindberg, Oskar (2): '*Gammal fäbodpsalm*' [Old pastoral hymn, organ], '*Pingst*' ['Pentecost', chorus]

Liszt (5): Hungarian Rhapsody No. 2', '*Liebestraum*', arrangement of Paganini's '*La Campanella*'

Lotti: Crucifixus (motet in eight voices, in Mass in F)

Lundsten, Ralph (8): *Nordisk natursymfoni* [Nordic Nature Symphonies] Nos. 1, 3 [Midwinter Saga], and 4, *Paradissymfoni* ['Paradise' Symphony], Tellus, *Vintermusik* [Winter Music], '*Fader Vår*' ['The Lord's Prayer'], Gustav III, '*Nattmara*' ['Nightmare']

Lutoslawski: Symphony No. 3

Mahler (18): Symphonies Nos. 1, 3, 4, 5 (especially the Adagietto), 6, 8, and 10, '*Das Lied von der Erde*', '*Kindertotenlieder*'

Martin: Mass for Double Choir

Massenet: Meditation (in *Thaïs*, opera)

Mehler, Friedrich (2): *Petrus de Dacia* incidental music

Mendelssohn (8): Violin Concerto in E minor, Symphony No. 4 ('Italian'), 'Hebrides', *A Midsummer Night's Dream*, String Quartet No. 6, Paulus (oratorio)

Table 30.3.1 *(Continued)* Composers and works in art music. The figure in brackets indicates the total number of accounts where the composer is mentioned

Mercadante: Rondo Russo in Flute Concerto in E minor

Mertens, Wim: 'Struggle for pleasure'

Messiaen (3): '*L'ápparition de l'église eternelle*', Turangalila Symphony

Morthenson, Jan (2): 'Neutron Star', Kyrie for children's choir

Mozart (41): Operas *Idomeneo, Così fan tutte, Don Giovanni, Le nozze di Figaro*, and *Die Zauberflöte; Requiem*, Mass in C minor, Exultate Jubilate, Ave verum corpus; Symphony No. 40, Sinfonia concertante in E-flat major, Concerto for Flute, Oboe and Orchestra in C major, piano concertos (e.g. No. 24), violin concertos (e.g. Concerto for Violin and Orchestra in G major); String Quintet in G minor, piano sonatas, Adagio for Piano in B minor (K 540); Fantasie in F minor for Organ; *Eine kleine Nachtmusik*

Musorgsky: *Pictures at an Exhibition*

Nielsen (2): 'The fog is lifting' (flute)

Nilsson, Torsten: *Jordens Natt [Night of the Earth]*, passion drama

Nordqvist. Gustaf (4): '*Till havs*' ['Out at sea']

Offenbach (3): '*La belle Hélène*', *Orpheus in the Underworld*, Barcarole in *The Tales of Hoffman*

Olsson, Otto: *Advent* (choir and organ)

Orff (6): *Carmina Burana*

Pachelbel: *Chaconne*

Paganini: *Il Palpiti* (variations on a theme by Rossini)

Pergolesi (2): Stabat Mater

Peterson-Berger, Wilhelm (2): '*Frösöblomster*' ['Flowers from Frösö Island', piano], '*I furuskogen*' ['In the fir wood', chorus]

Pettersson, Allan (3): Symphonies Nos. 7, 8, and 10; Violin Concerto No. 2

Piazzolla: '*Nuevo tango*'

Poulenc (2): *Figure Humaine*

Prokofiev: *Romeo and Juliet*

Puccini (2): *Bohème, Madame Butterfly, Tosca*

Pärt (6): *Johannes Passion, Berliner Messe, Spiegel im Spiegel, Tabula Rasa*

Rachmaninov (6): Piano Concertos Nos. 2 and 3, Symphonic Dances No. 1

Rameau: Gavotte in D major

Rangström, Ture: '*Kung Eriks visor*' ['King Erik's songs']

Ravel (5): *Boléro, Rapsodie espagnole*

Rehnqvist, Karin: '*Puksånger–Lockrop*' ['Timpanum songs–herding calls']

Reich, Steve: *Music for Mallets*

Respighi: 'The Pines of Rome'

Riley, Terry (2): Keyboard Studies, Untitled organ, Dorian Reeds

Roman, Johan Helmich: *Svenska mässan* [Swedish mass]

Table 30.3.1 *(Continued)* Composers and works in art music. The figure in brackets indicates the total number of accounts where the composer is mentioned

Rosenberg, Hilding (2): *Den heliga natten* [*The Holy Night*, Christmas oratorio], Symphony No. 4, '*Johannes uppenbarelse*' ['The Revelation of St John']

Rossini (3): *The Barber of Seville, The Thieving Magpie, William Tell*

Saint-Saëns: *Samson and Delilah* (opera)

Sandström, Sven-David (2): *Requiem 'De ur alla minnen fallna'* ['Mute the bereaved memories speak']; Agnus Dei (chorus)

Satie: Piano music (unspecified)

Scarlatti, Alessandro: Cantata (unspecified)

Schubert (25): Two symphonies, the 'Unfinished' in B minor and 'The Great' in C major, String Quintet in C major, Piano Quintet in A major ('The Trout'), String Quartet in D minor ('Death and the Maiden'), piano sonatas, piano pieces (e.g. Impromptu in A flat major Op. 142:2, Fantasia for piano in F minor Op. 103, the song cycle *Die schöne Müllerin*, lieder ('*Erlkönig*', '*Heidenröslein*'), *Rosamunde* incidental music, Ave Maria, Ständchen, and Military March Op. 51:1

Schumann (4): Piano Concerto in A minor, piano music: '*Träumerei*', Paganini études Op. 10, Nachtstücke Op. 23, Fugues Op. 72; lieder: '*Mondnacht*' (in Liederkreis Op. 39)

Shostakovich (10): String Quartet No. 8, Symphonies Nos. 5 and 7, Piano Trio No. 2 in E minor, Cello Sonata in D minor Op. 40

Sibelius (17): Symphonies Nos. 1, 2, 4, and 5; symphonic poems *Finlandia, En saga* [*A Fairy Tale*], string quartet '*Voces Intimae*'

Sinding (2): '*Frühlingsrauschen*' ['Rustle of spring']

Smetana (7): *Moldau*

Strauss, Johann II (4): '*An der schönen, blauen Donau*' ['Blue Danube waltz'], operettas *Der Zigeunerbaron* [*The Gypsy Baron*], *A Night in Venice*

Strauss, Richard (4): operas *Electra, Der Rosenkavalier, Salome*; '*Vier letzte Lieder*' ['Four last songs']

Stravinsky (11): *Rite of Spring* (10), Violin Concerto in D

Söderlundh, Lille Bror: '*Valsmelodi*' ('Waltz melody')

Tchaikovsky (13): Symphony No. 6 'Pathétique', Piano Concerto No. 1 in B minor, 1812 (overture), *Swan Lake* (ballet), Andante cantabile (in String Quartet No. 1)

Theodorakis (4): Songs

Verdi (17): *Requiem* (especially the Dies Irae movement); operas *Aida, Il Trovatore, La Traviata, Nabucco, Un Ballo in Maschera*

Villa Lobos: Prelude No. 1 (guitar)

Vivaldi (3): 'The Four Seasons', Piccolo Concerto in C major

Wagner (12): *Tannhäuser, Lohengrin, Die Meistersinger von Nürnberg, Das Rheingold, Die Walküre, Tristan und Isolde, Parsifal*

Webern: Six Pieces for Large Orchestra Op. 6

Wennerberg, Gunnar: '*Gören portarna höga*' [The Swedish version of '*Macht hoch die Tür*', a German Advent song]

Table 30.3.1 *(Continued)* Composers and works in art music. The figure in brackets indicates the total number of accounts where the composer is mentioned

Weyrauch, Johannes: Organ Sonata

Widor: Organ Symphony No. 5

Wikander, David: '*Kung Liljekonvalje*' ['King Lily of the Valley'], chorus

There are many singers here: Marian Anderson, Britt Marie Aruhn, Janet Baker, Martin Best, Jussi Björling, Sigurd Björling, José Carreras, Kathleen Ferrier, Birgit Finnilä, Dietrich Fischer-Dieskau, Nicolai Gedda, Håkan Hagegård, Barbara Hendricks, Tommy Körberg, Mario Lanza, Zarah Leander, Victoria de Los Angeles, Felicity Lott, Birgit Nilsson, Luciano Pavarotti, Doris Soffel, Frederica von Stade, Joan Sutherland, Set Svanholm, Elisabeth Söderström, Ingvar Wixell, Fred Åkerström.

Pianists and organists include Vladimir Ashkenazy, Greta Erikson, Annie Fischer, Clara Haskil, Gunnar Idenstam (piano, organ), Hans Leygraf, Sergei Rachmaninov (performed his own works), Svyatoslav Richter, Staffan Scheja, Per Thunarf (organ), Karl-Erik Welin (piano, organ).

Violinists include: Jascha Heifetz, Fritz Kreisler, Nathan Milstein, Anne-Sophie Mutter, David Oistrakh, Wolfgang Schneiderhahn, Isaac Stern, and Endre Wolf.

Cellists include Frans Helmersson and Guido Vecchi.

Guitarists include André Segovia and Göran Söllscher.

Conductors include Yuri Ahronovitch, Fritz Busch, Sergiu Celibidache, Sixten Ehrling, Charles Farncombe, Wilhelm Furtwängler, Carl Garaguly, Herbert von Karajan, Simon Rattle, and Georg Solti.

The ensembles include several Swedish choirs: the Swedish Radio Choir directed by Eric Ericson, the Adolf Fredrik Bach Choir directed by Anders Öhrwall, the Orphei Drängar male choir directed by Hugo Alfvén, the Amanda Choir, Gösta Ohlin's Vocal Ensemble and a children's choir from Finland, the Tapiola Choir. The instrumental ensembles include I Musici di Roma, the Fresk Quartet, the Takács Quartet, and several Swedish and foreign symphony orchestras.

30.3.3 Religious music

Most of the examples of religious music in our material also can be considered as art music, and have already been listed in Table 30.3.1: works by Bach, Berlioz, Brahms, Britten, Fauré, Franck, Gluck, Gounod, Handel, Haydn, Kodály, Lotti, Martin, Mendelssohn, Messiaen, Mozart, Pergolesi, Pärt, Roman, Rosenberg, Sandström, Verdi, and some other works such as *Missa Criolla* by Ariel Ramirez, 'The Lord's Prayer' by Albert Hay Malotte, Andrew Lloyd Webber's *Requiem* and the rock opera *Jesus Christ Superstar*, as well as the musical *Vildhonung* [*Wild Honey*] by Tomas Boström.

Furthermore, there are Gregorian chants, Greek Orthodox mass singing, Catholic and African choir singing, Taizé songs, some hymns, including two associated with end-of-term school assemblies and summer holidays: '*Den blomstertid nu kommer*' ['Now comes the flowering season'] and '*Sommarpsalm*' ['Summer hymn'], and the psalm and song of praise '*Helig, Helig, Helig, är Herren Sebaot*' ['Holy, Holy, Holy, Lord God Almighty'], Adam's well-known carol '*O helga natt*' ('*Le Cantique de Noël*') ['O holy night'], as well as 'Amazing grace', '*Kumbayah*', and other gospel songs performed by such singers as Mahalia Jackson and Cyndee Peters.

30.3.4 Folk music

Within the genres discussed below—folk music, jazz, pop and rock, other popular music—it is primarily the artistes who performed the music who are mentioned. When special pieces are mentioned, this is often more in passing.

Within Nordic folk music, Swedish, Norwegian, and Finnish musicians (who play violin, 'nyckelharpa' [keyed fiddle], mouth organ, cow horn, and bagpipe) are mentioned, including: Kalle Almlöf, Torleiv Bjørgum, Per Gudmundsson, Anton Jernberg, Olle Moraeus, Ale Möller, Påhl-Olle, Erik Sahlström, Skogsby Lasse, Jonny Soling, Ceylon Wallin, Erik Öst, and the folk music groups Filarfolket and Sågskära. Furthermore, singers such as Susanne Rosenberg and Lena Willemark with richly ornamented singing and elements of 'kulning', are also mentioned.

Folk music from other countries is represented by, among others, fado singers (Portugal), a Georgian male choir, Italian bagpipe (zampogna), launeddas players from Sardinia, Chinese tasima, West African drum virtuosi, and the group Fjedur, who performed African revolutionary and liberation songs.

30.3.5 Jazz

A large number of artistes from different fields within jazz are mentioned in the accounts:

Blues: B B King, Josh White, Rolf Wikström

Early jazz: Louis Armstrong, Sidney Bechet, Bunny Berigan

Swing era and later: Count Basie, Louis (Louie) Bellson, Duke Ellington, Benny Goodman, Don Redman

Bebop and later: Chet Baker, John Coltrane, Miles Davis, Gil Evans, Art Farmer, Dizzy Gillespie, Coleman Hawkins, Quincy Jones, Johnny Mandel, Charles Mingus, Modern Jazz Quartet, Gerry Mulligan, Horace Parlan, Buddy Rich, Toots Thielemans, Lester Young, Niels-Henning Ørsted-Pedersen

Free form, fusion, jazz-rock: George Adams, Albert Ayler, Blood, Sweat and Tears, Chick Corea, Keith Jarrett, Koinonia, John McLaughlin, Pat Metheny, Archie Shepp

Singers: Alice Babs, Betty Carter, Alma Cogan, Delta Rhythm Boys, Ella Fitzgerald, Carmen McRae, Frank Sinatra, Sarah Vaughan, Monica Zetterlund

Swedish jazz musicians: Arne Domnérus, Rune Gustafsson, Bengt Hallberg, Red Mitchell, Georg Riedel, Nisse Sandström.

30.3.6 Rock, pop, other popular music

The boundaries between different genres is very fluid here, and the division below should be regarded with considerable tolerance:

Mainstream rock: Alien, Dire Straits, Imperiet, Kinks, Elvis Presley, Rolling Stones, Smithereens, Bruce Springsteen, Supertramp, U2, Jerry Williams

Hard rock: Black Sabbath, Bon Jovi, Cult, Guns N' Roses, KISS, Led Zeppelin, Metallica, Motorhead, Scorpions, Thin Lizzy

Punk rock: Asta Kask

Symphonic rock: Genesis, Pink Floyd, Saga

Synth rock and pop: Depeche Mode, Duran Duran, Howard Jones, Malaria, Ratata

Synth music: Jean Michel Jarre

Pop: Animals, Beatles (14, including 'Hey Jude', 'If I Fell', 'Let It Be', 'She Loves You', 'Yesterday', the album *Sergeant Pepper's Lonely Hearts Club Band*), Carola Häggkvist, Phil Collins, Docenterna, Europe, Eurythmics, Marie Fredriksson, Gyllene Tider, Whitney Houston, Paul McCartney, Orup, Police, Lisa Stansfield, Magnus Uggla

Rock and pop: Chicago, Cock Robin, Cure, Hollies, Styx

Country, folk rock: Mary-Chapin Carpenter, Emmylou Harris, John Hiatt, Kebnekajse, Dolly Parton, Linda Ronstadt

Ambient music: Harold Budd, Brian Eno

New age: Kitaro, Andreas Vollenweider

Reggae: Bob Marley.

In addition to the above, there is a long number of other artists and groups who cannot be easily placed in some clearly limited category, but are found in different places and/or as 'mixed forms' (blues pop, jazz pop, ethno-pop, folk pop, pop jazz, pop soul, soul rock, and others). They comprise:

David Bowie, Billy Bragg, Eric Clapton, Phil Coulter, Danielle Dax, Georgie Fame, Merit Hemmingson, Joe Jackson, Michael Jackson, Mark Knopfler, Björn J:son Lindh, Miriam Makeba, Moondog, Gary Moore, Sinéad O'Connor, Mike Oldfield, Prince, Brenda Russell, Janne Schaffer, Sting, David Sylvian, Joakim Thåström, Sylvia Vrethammar, Stevie Wonder, Robert Wyatt, Frank Zappa.

30.3.7 Songs, tunes

This category comprises many different children's songs, Christmas songs, songs by Swedish composers or songwriters: Carl Michael Bellman, Evert Taube, Birger Sjöberg,

Povel Ramel, Karin Liungman, Ulf Lundell, Georg Riedel, Alice Tegnér, Cornelis Vreeswijk, Gabriel Jönsson, and Gunnar Turesson, and in addition Erna Tauro and Tove Jansson's '*Höstvisa*' ['Autumn song'], Ole Bull's '*Säterjäntans söndag*' ['The herdsmaiden's Sunday'], songs by Jaques Brel, Edith Piaf ('Exodus' and '*Je ne regrette rien*'), and Mikis Theodorakis, as well as several singer-songwriters (such as Basia, Leonard Cohen, Eva Dahlgren), non-European songs (African and others), some evergreens (such as Simon and Garfunkel's 'Bridge over Troubled Water') and some popular songs and hits, and a Swedish folk song '*Ack Värmeland du sköna*' ['Beautiful Värmland'].

30.3.8 Entertainment music, dance music

Examples of entertainment music are '*Tango Jalousie*' (J. Gade), '*Champagne Galop*' (Lumbye), 'In a monastery garden' and In a Persian market' (Albert Ketelbey), 'The Brownies' guard parade' (Kurt Noack), 'Harry Lime Theme' (Anton Karas), 'Ciribiribin' (Alberto Pestalozza), and 'Edelweiss' (from *The Sound of Music* by Rodgers and Hammerstein).

Within dance music, there is accordion music by Carl Jularbo and dance band music with the Flamingo Quartet and Ingmar Nordström's orchestra, as well as unspecified examples of tango (Argentinian, Finnish), salsa, and waltz.

30.3.9 Instruments, voices

Several narrators refer to the special timbre of a particular instrument or a particular voice.

The flute is mentioned in several accounts. It is for the main part played solo and often out in the open air; see, for example, accounts in Chapter 23. If there is any other instrument, it often tends to be overshadowed (see, for example, Chapter 22, account 22B). The trumpet has also often been played solo (for example, Chapter 14, account 14.1G, Chapter 23, account 23F); there was also an account, not included in this book, of a tattoo played by solo trumpet at a funeral.

Drums have given rise to special experiences (also dependent upon the rhythm) both when listening (for example, Chapter 13, account 13.4A about shaman drums, Chapter 15, account 15.1F about drums in a theatre performance, and Chapter 24, account 24I about West African drum virtuosi) and when dancing to drum rhythms (Chapter 24, accounts 24G and 24J).

Other instruments and voices that have been noted for their special timbre are the santor and sitar in Indian music, the Indonesian gamelan orchestra, the sound of an African girls' choir and a Gregorian male choir as well as the special technique and timbre in 'kulning' (herding calls). Children's choirs often give rise to strong feelings and gushing tears among listeners, not least among parents (but that certainly depends on more factors than the actual singing . . .).

The examples of music in SEM presented above should not, of course, be regarded as some form of order of preference of composers, artistes, or pieces of music. They reflect our participants' experiences and concepts. If the investigation were to be repeated with another sample of people—or in another country, another culture, at another time, etc.—the music could naturally be quite different.

30.4 CONNECTION BETWEEN CATEGORIES AND REACTIONS?

Is there any connection between certain SEM reactions and certain categories of music? If a certain reaction appears more often together with a certain category than the average across all categories, it could suggest a connection. If, for example, one looks at the reaction 'Movement' (dancing, jumping, clapping hands, etc.), one finds that it occurs much more often in folk music and rock music than average, and, on the other hand, less in classical music. For the reaction 'Being or becoming immobile' the exact opposite applies: more than average in classical music, and less in folk music and rock music.

A detailed treatment of all such results would take us much too far. One can, however, analyse this in a more condensed and easy-to-grasp manner by using factor analysis (previously mentioned in Chapter 29, section 29.8.8). In general, factor analysis is used to reduce data from a number of different variables to a smaller number of 'fundamental' factors. The detailed method of application is not described here. Instead, we will go directly to the results and concentrate on a solution with only two fundamental factors.

In the first factor, there is a contrast between on the one hand classical music, religious music and theatre music, and on the other hand categories such as folk music, jazz, rock, pop music, and songs and tunes. For the sake of simplicity, we can regard this as 'art music' versus 'popular music'. A closer examination of which reactions are associated with these two groups shows the following:

In comparison to popular-music genres, the following reactions occur to a greater extent within art-music genres:

Tears

Becoming or being immobile

Feeling of being lifted or floating

Feeling surrounded by the sounds or music (for example, in church acoustics)

Inner images

Positive feelings with a relatively low activation level (peace, tranquillity, wonder, reverence, solemnity, gratitude, pleasure, beauty, but also certain feelings with a high activation level, for example dizziness)

Thoughts about the meaning of life and existence

Trance or ecstasy, total experience, cosmic experiences, experiences of other worlds

Religious visions, spiritual peace, fellowship, meeting with the divine, reception of religious message

Feeling elevated and healed

New or increased interest in music generally, and in different respects

Feeling of being chosen.

Compared with art-music genres, popular-music genres have a greater occurrence of the following reactions (among others):

Laughing, singing along, shouting or screaming, moving (dancing, jumping, etc.)

Observations of the commitment of the musicians, their communication and charisma, and public reactions

No thoughts

Feeling a special atmosphere, a special wholeness

Being unaware of one's body

Recognizing the music

Positive feelings of a relatively high activation level such as elation, love, and perfection

Feeling of presence in the here and now, ultimate moments

Feeling free, inspired, catharsis, getting strength, a kick

The music mirroring one's own character or one's feelings

Fellowship between listeners, between performers, and between performers and listeners.

On the whole, this is perhaps what one in general usually associates with art music and popular music respectively. The more 'introverted' reactions of existential, transcendental, and religious character occur more often in connection with art music, as do feelings with a relatively low activation level, while more 'extrovert' reactions such as movements, singing along, contact between listeners, and between performers and listeners are more typical for popular music, as are feelings with a relatively higher activation level.

But, note that the above-mentioned reactions only concern *comparisons* between the two groups, not 'absolute' characteristics for them. Naturally, there are many examples of tears in connection with popular music; similarly one can become immobile, feel one is floating, end up in a trance, get cosmic experiences, feel chosen, etc. And naturally there are also examples that within art music, one observes the musicians' commitment and charisma, and can lose consciousness of one's body, experience ultimate moments, become inspired, feel fellowship with listeners and performers, etc. Besides, there are of course a lot of other SEM reactions apart from those above where (according to this analysis) there are no differences between 'classical' and 'popular'.

In the other factor, it is a contrast between on the one hand classical non-religious music and theatre music, and on the other hand religious music. This factor thus means a certain differentiation within the art-music genres; the popular-music genres were neutral in this factor.

Compared with classical non-religious and theatre music, religious music has a higher occurrence of the following reactions (among others):

Singing along (for example, in a hymn)

Feeling of being carried away by the music

Feeling of being surrounded by the sounds or music (for example, in church acoustics)

Positive feelings such as reverence, respect, and satisfaction

Religious visions, spiritual peace or fellowship, meeting with the divine, reception of religious messages

Feeling free, healed

Feeling fellowship between performers and between performer and listener.

Thus, one sees here that a part of the reactions that occurred for all the art-music genres together in the first factor are now primarily ascribed to religious music.

Since every attempt to categorize is problematic, attempts to find connections between categories and reactions also become very incomplete, which is the case in this attempt. Besides, one should observe that different categories can be associated with a certain gender or age group (see Table 30.2B). This can, for example, mean that a connection between a certain category and a certain reaction also reflects a connection between a certain category and a certain gender or age group, such as, for example, the connection between classical music—old women—or the connection between rock music—young men.

Finally: When our participants describe their experiences and what in the music they are influenced by, it is not at all the type of music that is emphasized, rather it is different qualities in the actual piece of music regardless of category. That is the subject of the next chapter.

CHAPTER 31

WHAT IN THE MUSIC ELICITED THE REACTIONS?

WHEN the participants tell about their experiences, they often also describe the expression in the music and which musical elements made a special impression. One can distinguish four types of such characterizations. The most common way is (a) to describe the emotional expression in the music generally (section 31.1). It is also fairly common that one (b) points out certain qualities in the music or the performance that were particularly important, for example the timbre, the rhythm, the melody, the harmony, the instrumentation, the voice, and so on (31.2). Some narrators have chosen (c) to specify certain sections or places in the music that were particularly important: certain phrases, certain themes, certain bars, sometimes even particular notes (31.3). Finally, it is evident in many accounts that the words (lyrics/libretto) have been of great importance for the experience (31.4).

31.1 EMOTIONAL EXPRESSION

The most common way of describing what it was in the music that made the greatest impression is to refer to its emotional character: the music is/sounds happy, easygoing, jolly; melancholy, serious, sad, dark, tragic; tranquil, calm, gentle, caressing; stimulating, passionate, dramatic; lively, vigorous, energetic, powerful, aggressive, violent; majestic, grand, solemn; charged, weird, devilish, as well as other characterizations. They are often combined with expressions for a positive evaluation: good, nice, lovely, delightful, beautiful, wonderful, fantastic, heavenly, grandiose, super, genial, etc. In a few cases, there are also negative evaluations, such as repulsive music. The boundary between describing and evaluating expressions is fluid. Examples of this type of descriptions can easily be found in many of the accounts that fill Chapters 4 to 27.

31.2 SPECIAL ELEMENTS IN THE MUSIC

A number of narrators refer to one or more specific qualities in the music that have been important for their reaction. The examples below are taken from accounts earlier in this book or accounts that have not occurred before.

First, are examples of the importance of the **timbre** of an instrument or a voice:

From account 4.5B

[The narrator was then six years old; it was at a Santa Claus parade outdoors, and they were playing 'The Brownies' guard parade' (Noack).] To start with, you could only hear the bass drum and that banged right through me. As the parade got closer, you could hear more and more instruments and the most beautiful of all was the glockenspiel. I was so amazed that the man who played it could know where he ought to hit so that it would sound so beautiful.

From account 26F

They played a Russian folk tune . . . Bengt Hallberg kept the pedal down on the grand piano so that all the strings lay free, so that the echo of the trumpet came into the piano. It sounded incredibly beautiful, like church bells perhaps . . . Powerful.

From account 25.1H

[The piece being played was *Tabula rasa* by Arvo Pärt.] All the time, the orchestra played pure and beautiful notes, the string soloists embroidered upon this and it was accompanied by the 'prepared piano' which brought forth sounds that were more like gongs or church bells.

From account 23C

It was at night. I delivered newspapers and was out working at 3.30 in the morning. Then somebody opened the window and played his flute. It was some classical piece, and included trills . . . I have heard many people play the flute and always think it is the most beautiful music but this was something unbelievably beautiful.

From account 23F

Bompa, bompa, bompa—there came the parade of the guards . . . The programme finally ended with a boy taking two steps forward and playing 'Memory' on solo trumpet and with some slightly muted accompaniment of drums at the end. The whole city stopped, and the goosepimples spread over your skin despite the heat. It was fantastically beautiful.

From account 25.1A

[*Sinfonietta* by Leoš Janáček] Already the urgent fanfares and the timpani entrances in the first movement of the sinfonietta completely enchanted me. What a timbre! . . . Then [in the final movement] the trumpet fanfares from the first movement came in again . . . but besides the brass and the timpani all the other voices in the strings and woodwinds played as well in big wonderful trills to back up the fanfares.

(31.2A) Woman, middle-aged, 1970s

It was the Leningrad Philharmonic who played a symphony by Tchaikovsky. I particularly remember a big brass place. The sound was so dense, so homogeneous, and the ensemble so perfect that I heard a big sound—like a body—not just the trumpet section, trombone section, and so on, a sound that filled the entire concert hall right into the smallest corner. I was completely convinced that the walls of the building would cave in. The intensity was enormous!! I felt I was little, so little, but not oppressed, I was possessed by this powerful music, happy, touched, stunned, elevated by this huge sound and all of the musical course, harmony, and melody. Never before had I been able to dream or imagine that brass instruments could sound like that together. I'll never forget it.

From account 24L

I had never previously heard or seen a sitar in real life, but I particularly noticed the instrument's unusual timbre. In the half-dark room, notes were thrown out like silvered drops of rain. Everything seemed to be pervaded by it. Like carbon dioxide bubbles making their way through the liquid in a bottle of pop.

From account 6.1D

It was on the radio that I heard Sinéad O'Connor's 'Nothing compares 2 U' . . . What affected me were exclusively the music and the voice, not the lyrics . . . The most characteristic [feature] is the singing voice. Sinéad really uses it as an instrument and 'plays' with it by in turn making it soft and hard and suddenly and unerringly going up in falsetto.

The timbre is greatly influenced by the **intonation**—perfect or special:

From account 6.1J

It was four boys about ten years old who sang a four-part arrangement of our most beautiful summer ballads . . . the music went right through me, my critical, well-trained ear for music couldn't find a false note, a weak voice, an uninspired expression . . . God it was beautiful! They are so sweet, I'll die! It really does hurt?! . . . There was nothing to criticize, it was perfect.

From account 25.1L

[The Tapiola Choir] They started the concert with an English madrigal for five voices . . . It was as clear as a bell! The phrasing was wonderful, every phrase was alive. Every note was tenderly cared for . . . During the 60 minutes the concert lasted, the children's choir managed to sing in eight different languages and in every imaginable style . . . All of it as clear as a bell! The intonation was perfect! The phrasing was wonderful!

From account 25.1M

[A choir from Riga] If my expectations as to the choir had been small, then my surprise was all the greater when the choir started to sing—they sang perfectly in tune from the first note to the last! During the entire concert, I didn't hear the slightest hesitation in the intonation anywhere, and all the time the choir showed an almost unbelievable capability of expression, flexibility . . . and precision . . .

From account 18.6M

I tried to tune the violin in a way I'd never done before: A–E–A–E. Then I lowered the A to a Baroque A as a G-sharp. I got a strange sort of tuning and tried it a little. Then, quite simply, there came a tune that was extremely clear straight away . . . After a while it turned rather nasty . . . I sort of couldn't stop playing, I was intoxicated by the sound that came from the violin. It sounded a different way, responded in a different way.

In the following examples, emphasis is upon the **loudness/dynamics**, often together with the timbre and/or tempo.

(31.2B) Man, middle-aged, 1980s (excerpt)

It was one morning in the cathedral in Chartres. It was quiet, nothing was happening there, and I was looking at some beautiful stained-glass windows. Suddenly, without any warning, the organist started to play an organ symphony by Widor. An extremely quick thing, a movement that starts straight off without forewarning and just charged along. Wow, what a boost! Incredible! Fantastic!

From account 25.1D

[Respighi's 'The pines of Rome'] I perceived a vibrating, pulsating, unobtrusive rhythm which slowly increased in loudness . . . The music became all the louder . . . Suddenly brass instruments could be heard 'as if by magic' in all directions on the balconies around the auditorium, and what had recently seemed to have reached its zenith further increased in force and intensity! The sound effect that arose gave me the feeling of being sucked into a heaving *ocean* of notes/music.

From account 12.1C

[Gustaf Mahler's Symphony No. 8, last movement] The choir started to sing, in a barely audible pianissimo, the Chorus mysticus, '*Alles Vergängliche ist nur ein Gleichnis*' . . . when the choir 'pulls along' the orchestra and soloists in a crescendo that accelerates right up to the last notes where the concert hall's magnificent organ joins them in a fortissimo, I am no longer in a concert hall, I am on Mount Tabor!

From account 6.1K

[Working outdoors, listening to the radio] The music starts: first fumblingly and weak, then all the stronger and more powerful. The structure is very clear and the power and magic invade me completely. I just stand still, leaning on my hoe, listening and filled with the magical atmosphere. In my numbed state, I hear the programme host say that it was Ravel's *Bolero*.

From account 7.2D

It was Led Zeppelin's 'Stairway to heaven' that was playing [on the car radio] . . . it starts gently and gets slowly stronger and more majestic the further you get in the tune. I was carried along by the music as it intensified in power and majesty almost to a climax at the end.

High sound level can have a deterrent effect.

From account 11.3R

[A Berlin girl band, Malaria] They played a hard, heavy fateful synth rock at top volume . . . The bass boomed out a heavy, numbing sound carpet, monotonous, which penetrated your body. The drummer too played with heavy and tired hits. Added to that was a howling saxophone that screamed in anguish, completely lacking melody and a definite key . . . This naked and ghastly death music . . . made me feel nauseous . . .

From account 11.3O

[A 'happening' with John Cage] Cage began to work the switches on his control table and hell broke loose! . . . the noise—recordings of street noise and compressors in various combinations—was let out and it pounced onto us defenceless listeners. The crashing and the din—it wasn't music—was so deafening that the mass of people started to get up and walk about . . . several went home . . .

From account 11.3P

[Organ concert] Sometimes it sounded as if the person playing laid his arms along the entire keyboard and his feet sideways across all the pedals—resulting in a roaring and a vibrating in the entire cathedral. The volume of the organ was very high and strong . . . This music and way of playing made me feel all the more ill . . . and I felt that most of all I'd like to run away from it all.

In other accounts, it is above all the **rhythm** that is the decisive factor. In the first two accounts below, there are well-known rhythmic motifs.

(31.2C) Man, old, 1940s (excerpt)

At the beginning of the war, about 1941 or 42, the Berlin Philharmonic with Furtwängler came on a visit. The great experience was Beethoven's fifth symphony, which moved me strongly, perhaps to start with mainly because of the rhythm but of course also for the powerful orchestration. I remember Furtwängler's almost ecstatic performance too.

(31.2D) Woman, middle-aged, 1980s (excerpt)

Stravinsky's *Rite of Spring*. I was slightly familiar with the piece already, but was totally unprepared when eight double basses started up with the rhythmic dá-da-da-dá-da-da. The music completely attacked me. I realized I was sitting and shaking in time with the double basses and with hands tightly gripping the edge of the balcony. The music grabbed hold of me quite physically. I lost time and space, caught up in dá-da-da-dá-da-da, and when the piece was finished, it was as if somebody had poured water over me. Was it finished? The rhythm pursued me all the way home, even when I was going to sleep.

(31.2E) Man, middle-aged, 1980s (excerpt)

It was salsa music, a fairly jazzy variety. The dance was soon in full swing. The special syncopation and the complete rhythmic carpet, I experienced those more intensely when my body could take part. It was particularly exciting in the rumba part when the comp played their repeated tumbao round and the loudness increased and the timbales player moved over to the big cow bell. The continuously repeated background that became more and more intensive almost put me into some sort of trance.

(31.2F) Woman, young, 1980s (excerpt)

What a divine drum solo! In front of us, a guy gets up by himself and starts to 'dance', claps his hands and is completely inside the music until the drum solo starts to die down. Then he looks up and notices that he is the only person who is standing up and 'digging'. He sits down, embarrassed. I thought it was a pity. I felt just the same as him, I felt this almost irresistible wish to get up, to dance, to rock, to dig away.

From account 6.1G

The music is complex as Latin American music often is. Various rhythms are played at the same time and make up a weave. Sometimes a guitar or a harp, for a few bars, makes a gliding journey from one rhythm to another . . . The tune is generous and playfully flowery and it hits me completely open and naked.

In the following cases, the **mode**, the **harmony**, and **formal aspects** come into the picture, besides the components mentioned in the previous accounts:

From account 13.3D

[In Oslo at the Edvard Munch museum] I looked at the works of art. Then in comes the pianist who is going to practise. They were going to have a concert in the evening, and he played Chopin, one of his mazurkas . . . It was in the minor mode. It was partly connected to the atmosphere in the room and perhaps how I was feeling myself. That was perhaps why it struck me as powerfully as it did . . .

From account 25.2U

[Bach's Piano Concerto in D minor] I personally experienced that it affected me so strongly because it was in the minor mode. I was absolutely not melancholy or sad that day, on the contrary, happy and satisfied. But sometimes I have noticed that the pieces in the minor mode can affect me emotionally on a deeper level than the ones in the major mode. Otherwise, I might have experienced them as being equally beautiful.

From account 11.4J

The piece was *Agnus Dei* by Sven-David Sandström . . . It almost created a feeling of anxiety, a sort of pressure in my chest, because it was so intense and extremely strong . . . you started to almost breathe heavily from the pressure you felt. It was a 16-part piece, atonal, without the common chords of three or four notes but still a bit romantic, sometimes with familiar chords. The piece ended in a long, weak 'pure' chord. The pressure relaxed, the feeling of security returned, and it became calm, and ended in the safe, pure F major chord.

(31.2G) Man, old, 1940s

I listened to Ravel's *Bolero* live for the first time. Both seeing and hearing an orchestra of this large format made me really enthusiastic, of course also the richness of instruments, the monotonous and incredibly suggestive rhythm underlined by the drums, the interplay between the different instruments and parts with special technical refinements—glissandi, pizzicato, and so on—as well how with every new variation the orchestra sound grew to an enormous crescendo. Towards the end of the piece, the key goes up one step, something that made us spontaneously get up from the bench—an irrepressible reaction and a purely physical influence that is unforgettable!

From account 26B

A concert with Coltrane and Miles Davis . . . They played 'Autumn Leaves', a simple Edith Piaf tune, but of course Miles completely redid it. Logical chords for the improvisation, and the comp played during Miles's solo in a very unobtrusive way. The bass was only on 1 and 3, the drummer was using brushes, but then the performance sort of grew into a tenor solo. Coltrane played a wild solo, then the drummer started to play with drumsticks and really made the most of it. It was a fantastic feeling, it really moves you to tears, I'm almost in tears now when I think about it.

(31.2H) Man, middle-aged, 1980s

It was at a bar and there was a bassist and a pianist who sort of amused themselves with the music. It was extremely atonal and beautiful at the same time; he was feeling his way for-wards—towards a theme and a rhythm. And just when that was replaced by him having got the theme, I think it was a cross between G minor and F major, switching between minor and then a major scale a whole tone lower. Incredibly good! Then came a rhythm up along-side which added to that. Ah! I thought it was fantastic! It gradually starts to swing and then the bass comes in and syncopates in some very strange way. It is roughly like in Keith Jarrett's 'Cologne concert', there's a thing there when he discovers a theme with the same feeling—ughh! he shouts and then he continues playing. It goes from something unstructured to then being dissolved and given a new structure.

31.3 CERTAIN PARTS OR PORTIONS OF
THE MUSIC

In the following examples, the narrator supplies very exact information of which moments in the music were especially important. It can be as little as **a single note** or **a few notes**.

From account 13.4E

Then they played Mozart's Symphony No. 40 . . . It was heaven; it was paradise; it was eve-rything that was beautiful, pure and deeply loving . . . It wasn't until the tenth note that I was, so to say, aroused. Don't know how I can explain this without a score, but the symphony starts one–two–three, one–two–three, one–two–three–four, which I found so brilliant (see the notation in account 13.4E, Fig. 13.1).

(31.3A) Woman, old, 1930s

It was New Year's Eve and a big family party. I was eight or nine years old and a bit tired of it all, I sat down beside the radio and switched it on. Somebody was singing Franck's 'Panis angelicus' (although I didn't know what it was then), and the first three sinking notes moved me so that tears started to run. I am still a little touched when I hear it, I have a weakness for that particular sequence of notes in other music too.

From account 4.5E

I could look at the fantastic deep-blue night sky which had always had an incredible effect on me, and in the hall outside our room the radio was playing Schubert's entr'acte music for *Rosamunda*. In some way I evidently experienced the child's awestruck littleness in the face of the majestic endlessness of the firmament coupled with a sense of complete security in experiencing myself as an infinitely little part of this whole, as well as the association with Schubert's music. In fact, it is only a very small part of the music that I clearly remember, the very beginning (see the notation in account 4.5E, Fig. 4.1):

(31.3B) Man, old (excerpt)

In Verdi's opera *La Traviata* at the end of the first act, Violetta has an aria where at first Alfredo stands out in the wings and sings against her and it ends with her singing some high C notes in her aria. This feeling of joy almost always comes there.

From account 25.2O

[About the aria '*Ruhe sanft*' from Mozart's unfinished opera *Zaide*, sung by Felicity Lott] When she reaches the peaks (an A in the fourth and fifth bars repeated in the twelfth and thirteenth), the pianissimo comes without effort like a veil that thinly covers the tone and gives it its silver gleam . . . she opens this note in pianissimo almost straight without vibrato, and with sort of a light sigh.

In the following examples, there is emphasis upon **particular chords** and **short themes**.

From account 4.2D

The first time I heard Bach's Toccata and Fugue in D minor, I was six years old and sat in church. My entire being was filled with the magnificent music. What I remember most is when note after note is added to a single large chord.

From account 11.3L

[Mahler's tenth symphony] A chord so heart-rending and hair-raising that I'd never experienced before. A single sound (trumpet, if I remember rightly) which is then built up with a large number of other instruments from the orchestra, not unlike an enormous organ where you pull out all the stops at random, a dissonance which pierces right into the very marrow of your bones . . . we were both filled with a horror so elementary and almost prehistoric that neither of us could utter a word.

From account 25.1P

[Mahler's tenth symphony, probably the same place] Towards the end of the first movement, the entire orchestra gathers together in a large, dreadful organ-like sound—a scream of pain and horror. It came as a shock after a fairly drawn-out pianissimo bit. I was completely overwhelmed by the violence in this horror before death.

From account 19.1D

[Singing Brahms's *Requiem*] When we came to 'Wie lieblich sind deine Wohnungen', bar 66, where the altos and basses sing in unison, I experienced an extremely strong feeling. I thought I was filled with a strong light, as if I became luminous! It has to do with the harmonies and the melody in the alto and bass voices in bar 66 and also 68.

Other narrators point out certain **themes**, **phrases**, or slightly **larger sections** in the music.

From account 4.2C

[Listened as a five-year-old to Mozart] When I had put on Mozart's *Eine kleine Nachtmusik*, it just 'clicked'. I listened over and over again to the first movement and what captivated me the most was the transition from the first theme to the second theme, and the reverse. This was really fantastic, like finding yourself in the music somehow.

(31.3C) Man, old, 1950s (excerpt)

I was at a concert where Hans Leygraf played Mozart's *Fantasie* and *Sonata*, among other pieces. I had great expectations about getting to hear the allegro part of the Fantasie which is extremely charged with an increase to the 29th bar, from where the musical tension increases to maximum. During these bars I experienced an extreme joy at the concert. A spiritual experience when I saw suns and stars, completely indescribable.

From account 18.1B

I have sometimes wondered why I get so 'turned on' by a part of Bach's Mass in B Minor, especially the 'Cum sancto spiritu' movement . . . Some bars, which I am more captivated by than others, go from the upbeat to bar 55 until half-bar 60, and the upbeat to bar 86 until half-bar 90. The upbeats start with a syncope feeling, which feels so nice and gentle to start with. It tickles my body gently and wonderfully when I start at these two places. I don't really know why, to be honest, but something in these upbeats makes it feel a bit special every time I sing them.

(31.3D) Man, middle-aged, 1970s (excerpt)

[Listening to Bach's Organ Concerto in C major after Vivaldi, the third movement, Allegro, just before the end] And then it starts, quavers or whatever they are. It goes round fast but just a foreboding. I wait patiently through a calm part. Of course it's nice here too but there's nothing special. Now it comes, descending scales, staccato. My ears are glued to the organ pipes. It goes fast but I can keep up. I am a whirling speck of dust in the organ. I start getting goosepimples on the skin in front of my ears. Now it's going round like a wheel, my soul has let go and is rotating upwards. Radiant joy in my head, a joy that borders upon sorrow, the tears come. Then the music stops with some slow rotations and I am back.

From account 7.2C

[Sibelius's Symphony No. 2, the finale] I was drawn into the endless repetitions of a sad and melancholy D minor theme, and got intoxicating kicks from the two surprising major resolutions; the first somewhere in the direction of a relative key, and the other, just before the end, to the parallel key D major which, of course, is a stronger effect . . . When the symphony was finished, I felt shaken and happy, a feeling almost like being newly in love.

From account 7.2B

[Shostakovich's 7th symphony, the 'Leningrad' Symphony, first movement] After a few minutes, this monotonous march started, at first extremely quiet, the same theme, again and again, while the music gets louder and louder. You think you can see, and above all hear, soldiers coming closer and closer. The music increased in intensity and becomes all the more creepy, and the grey apparitions just keep on marching. At the same time that you can feel that the music is cruel, you can't help but be fascinated by it. You're sitting on tenterhooks and waiting, because you know that soon the whole orchestra will explode and it feels as if something terrible is happening.

In the following quotes, the narrators describe their impressions of **certain parts of the piece** of music and/or **the work as a whole**. This means that they comment upon the work's musical form at the same time.

From account 4.4E

I was about eight to ten years old. The piece I heard was the overture to the third act of *Lohengrin* by Richard Wagner . . . The piece of music was in three parts with a euphoric introduction which was repeated at the end. The middle movement was gentle and melancholic. I think it was mainly the introductory fanfares with their violent outbursts, the heady triplets in the violin parts, and the overwhelming sound that caused the powerful sensations . . . But the gentle middle movement in the piece caused me to be moved to tears and then to be yet again slung up to the heights by the repeat of the A part.

(31.3E) Woman, old, 1980s

The strongest music experience I've had is Verdi's *Requiem* where especially the Dies Irae movement has etched itself into my memory and where I still feel the same shudders of both delight and horror, which I suppose is the intention of the composition. The Kyrie movement ends in pianissimo and the Dies Irae movement starts in fortissimo so you get pulled up out of the comfortable mood and feel the doomsday mood when the Day of Wrath will strike him who has dozed off in self-conceit. The trumpets that sound with a heavenly beauty in bar 93 are also somewhat deceptive when they—together with the timpani—again, in bar 111, make the sinner face his judgement. The entrance of the bass in bar 143 increases the mood of fateful destruction. But it is mainly the fortissimo entrances that give rise to the strong experience.

From account 5.2M

[Bach's Mass in B minor] I was especially struck by such places as Aria No. 5 with the violin solo in the introduction and the violin's duet with the soprano. Such rhythms as those in, for example, bar 3, really turn me on, as does the intensification heightening as in bars 5–6. Also rhythms as in bars 8–9–10 make me twitch, my legs and all my body. It really swings, Bach . . . Aria No. 9 provides another experience, perhaps more in depth, a feeling of hope, everything will be OK, worries disappear, it gives strength to deal with all sorts of difficulties, it builds you up inside, gives you power. In general, Bach's music lets me see the totality, not to get bogged down in details, of course he is a master at writing major works that stick together.

(31.3F) Woman, middle-aged, 1990s (excerpt)

[Bartók's Piano Concerto No. 3, second movement, Adagio religioso] The first movement has a melodic theme which is varied and stressed and which returns in the third movement's even more furious rage. The first movement ends sort of hanging there, then comes Adagio religioso with its dreamy breathing space. There I am out in nature, often beside a forest lake surrounded by smells and birds, like a source of strength for recovery, before the fury comes back, where also much sorrow is reflected. The end of the concerto, I perceive it as very strong and inexorable. If the second movement with its gentle address was rest and atonement, the end is more of an urge to break up. The multitude of feelings that this piano concerto arouses are not easy to sort out. And I suppose it is because I never finish it that it doesn't cease to fascinate me.

Longer examples of how the experience is connected to various parts of the musical course can be found in accounts of Barber's Adagio for Strings (7.5F), Mahler's tenth symphony (25.1P), Tchaikovsky's sixth symphony, *Pathétique* (25.1Q), Schumann's piano concerto (18.1F), and an Indian raga (24M).

31.4 THE IMPORTANCE OF TEXT (LYRICS, LIBRETTO)

In several accounts, there are clear statements about how much the text has meant for the experience. First, a short childhood account.

(31.4A) Woman, old, 1930s

One day when I was six years old, my father came home with a record that made an ineffaceable impression on me. The tune was '*Det var på Capri vi mötte varandra*' ['The Isle of Capri']. The melody was of course enormously beautiful, I thought, but the lyrics about Capri in the sunshine, full of romance . . . this fired my imagination and it was probably then that I felt my first longing to go out into big world. I wanted to see Capri! It wasn't until several decades later that this became a reality. I wasn't disappointed. Capri was even more beautiful than I had imagined. Still to this day when I hear that tune I again see these pictures from my childhood despite the fact that I nowadays think that the lyrics are rather banal. I do still, however, like the melody.

Some participants describe how they were influenced by the lyrics of certain artistes that they heard at concerts, for example the English songwriter and artiste Joe Jackson.

(31.4B) Man, middle-aged, 1980s (excerpt)

Wembly Arena was full. I have often felt that I have been filled with music, but the particular feeling of understanding what it is all about, a sort of deeper understanding, was extremely apparent. What got me most was probably the interpretation of Joe Jackson, the singer, his ability to give form to the words in such a way that I immediately understood what he was singing about. A simple and direct language with different themes that I could definitely identify with, for example the angry young man who has difficulties in contacts with the opposite gender in 'Is she really going out with him? Is she really gonna take him home tonight?'[a] Certain lyrics, for example in 'Home Town', contain reflections about how life has gone along and flashbacks like 'I just wanna go back to my home town, though I know it'll never be the same'.[b]

One young man got an enormous kick from the words from the singer in a rock group.

From account 27J

It felt so simple, so honest. It went right into your heart . . . I think the artiste means every bloody word he says, there is such conviction in the words . . . You feel: 'He is singing for me, it is about me because I have experienced this in some way', then you are filled with one hell of a joy . . . It fills you with joy and a belief in life . . . You become hopeful! . . . You got such strength, such a kick, that you become filled with energy. It is like taking vitamins for three years and getting them all at once.

In the next account, the emphasis is upon the importance both of the lyrics and that they are accompanied by good music.

From account 5.3C

The singer in Styx stood talking to the audience a very long time, it sounded exactly as if he himself had felt down a very long time, but had started to lift himself up out of the shit . . . that there was no point feeling down, that you should take one day at a time, etc., the usual

[a] 'Home Town' Joe Jackson Copyright 1986 Pokazuka Ltd. All rights administered by Sony/ATV Music Publishing LLC. All rights reserved. Used by permission.
[b] 'Is She Really Going Out With Him?' Joe Jackson. Copyright 1978 Pokazuka Ltd. All rights administered by Sony/ATV Music Publishing LLC. All rights reserved. Used by permission.

talk really, but incredibly more genuine . . . If I read the lyrics of a song that I'd never heard then it wouldn't really say much to me, you wouldn't be able to take any of it in. But on the other hand, if it is good and lovely music in just the right mood, then that has quite another effect . . . After the concert I felt so incredibly good when I left the place . . . afterwards everything got better, everything just went perfectly.

The importance of the text is particularly evident in accounts of religious SEM. This applies to the text in psalms, hymns and songs of praise—'How Great Thou Art' (14.1E), 'Holy, Holy, Holy, Lord God Almighty' (14.3C), 'Rest in Me' (21L), a text from the Book of Psalms, No. 40 (14.3G)—as well as text in large works like the Christmas Oratorio by Bach (14.3A), Handel's *Messiah* (14.1C) or Kodály's *Psalmus Hungaricus* (14.3E).

The importance of the text is also evident in several accounts of love experiences. The text said everything that was necessary in a passion that was just beginning.

From account 20E

It was in the beginning, when you are a bit shy about saying what you think, and those lyrics said *everything* in some way. We didn't have to say anything. The music sort of said what we were thinking, and because of that it became so strong for us. No words were needed. It spoke for us instead so we didn't need those unnecessary and embarrassing twists and turns round about.

Similarly, Phil Collins's 'Another day in Paradise' happened to fit perfectly in the mood when two people in love had a decisive meeting (20G).

Words can also arouse painful memories. One young woman told of how a ballad by Orup led to tears of sorrow as it reminded her of a friend who had not felt she was loved (20I), and a tune by Lisa Stansfield agreed with the feelings of a young woman who regretted that she had broken a relationship (20K). And in the following account, a few lines in the lyrics by Prince led to strong reactions after a separation from her boyfriend.

From account 20O

Well, I was sort of half-listening, but then suddenly it was there, the start of 'Purple Rain' (the last track on the album with the same name). Seemed to go right into my chest, then came the words [. . .] It felt 'Ouch!'—like a sudden pain in your stomach that makes you lose your breath for a moment. I literally gasped for breath, the music went right into me and stroked my insides. The words went on [. . .] Although I was still sitting on the floor, the volume seemed to increase, all the background sounds disappeared, there was only the voice and the melancholy guitar accompaniment. I started to shake and burst into tears. The feeling directly afterwards was an enormous feeling of emptiness and of loss.

There are also several accounts of how the lyrics have had a great effect when the narrator has experienced sickness and death at close hand.

From account 21F

One of my women friends died. The cause of death was a brain tumour that had led to a lot of suffering on several levels for several months. I visited her at the hospital. She was beyond reach then. When we drove in the car to the hospital I put the radio on and got to hear Erna Tauro's composition of Tove Jansson's '*Höstvisa*' ['Autumn song']. I don't know if it was the words or the music that moved me the most, I think perhaps it was the words. They include 'Hurry, beloved, hurry and love . . . soon the fleeing summer is over.' I felt so strongly, like at no other time during her illness, that it was all too late for her. I liked the autumn song before, but from this time on it acquired a special meaning for me, and I always remember this car journey and this hospital visit every time I hear it.

Finally, there is cause to remind readers of how the lyrics in a tune by the hard rock group KISS got a depressed young woman to divert her mind from the idea of suicide (5.3E).

31.5 COMMENTARY

Our investigation has primarily been intended to map out which reactions can be a part of strong experiences with music. Many narrators have, of course, also described various qualities in the music that have been important for their reactions. The examples referred to above show that the connections between the musical structure and the experience can be of a very varied character. They can be about the importance of many different musical elements (timbre, loudness, mode, rhythm, etc.), separately or in combination with each other, and can range from the importance of particular notes and themes to the impression of the work in its totality. Some of these questions are dealt with further in the following chapter.

CHAPTER 32

CAUSES, CONSEQUENCES, AND IMPORTANCE

PART of the purpose of the investigation was to examine, as far as was possible, which factors lie behind strong music experiences and what importance these experiences may have. The participants were therefore asked to answer questions about what they thought was the reason for the experience and what it had meant for them thereafter. There were many answers and they had a very varied content. In addition, quite a lot of causes and consequences can be seen directly in the actual accounts. Here is an overview concerning causes (section 32.1) and consequences (32.2).

32.1 Causes

Behind every music experience there is an interplay between three overall factors: the music, the person, and the situation. It is an illusion to believe that the music is the only causal factor. Every music experience—just like any experience at all—is connected to a certain person in a certain situation. The same piece of music can be experienced totally differently by different people. Similarly, one can oneself experience the same piece quite differently in different situations. As has previously been seen (Chapter 29, section 29.8.5), most of the narrators have heard the music on some earlier occasion but without then having had any strong experience. Similarly, most of them did not have the same strong experience when they heard the music the next time (Chapter 29, section 29.8.6). Not do strong experiences take place particularly often (Chapter 29, section 29.8.7). It would seem that there has to be a unique combination of the 'right music for the right person at the right time' in order for SEM to come about.

32.1.1 Music

Different factors in the music have been thoroughly treated in the previous chapter. A common way to 'explain' the strong experience was to refer to the emotional expression in the music. The music was perceived as being happy, easy-going, melancholy, sad, tranquil, gentle, vigorous, powerful, majestic, solemn, beautiful, delightful, heavenly, grandiose, genial, etc. (Chapter 31, section 31.1). Such wording is used even by participants who are very familiar with music analysis and music terminology, for example, professional musicians—they 'forgot' all their usual analysis of the music and the performance, and 'just listened to the music'.

Behind such expressions for feelings, there are in fact a number of different musical elements that are quite well charted within research in music psychology. Consider, for example, 'happy' and 'sad' music. Music that is perceived as happy is normally characterized by fast tempo, quite high volume, quite high pitch, light timbre, major mode, relatively simple melody and harmony, and an uncomplicated form. Expressions for sadness have, on the whole, the opposite qualities: slow tempo, lower volume and pitch than in happy music, darker timbre, minor mode, more legato, and more complex melody, harmony, and form than happy music. The equivalent connections with regard to other feelings (anger, fear, tenderness, etc.) are described in the specialist literature.[1]

Several participants specifically mentioned musical elements that contributed to their strong experience—timbre, intonation, volume, rhythm, mode, harmony, and formal aspects (Chapter 31, section 31.2)—or pointed out especially important sections in the music (Chapter 31, section 31.3). These might be particular tones or chords, themes, phrases, or entire movements. The experience can thus sometimes be very locally anchored to a certain part of the music, while all the rest is simply a background. And when one listens to the same music again, one waits for just 'that place' to come.[2]

In other cases, it is rather the impression of the work in its totality that is decisive. This applies not least to great works like Bach's passions, requiem masses by Mozart, Brahms, and Verdi, symphonies and concerts by the great masters (Beethoven, Brahms, Mahler, Mozart, Schubert, Sibelius, Tchaikovsky, and others), other orchestral works such as Stravinsky's *Rite of Spring*, operas by Wagner or musicals such as *Jesus Christ Superstar* and *The Phantom of the Opera*. One emphasizes partly certain sections of the work, partly also how the different sections complement each other in form and expression and together make a whole with a very strong effect, not least if there is a 'story' which the work is based on, as, for example, in Bach's passions or in an opera libretto.

Besides all this, one must also call attention to the importance of the *performance* of the music. In many accounts, the focus is rather upon the artistes and the performance (see Chapter 25, section 25.2 and Chapters 26 and 27). This might concern a singer's special timbre, the lovely tone of a violinist, a jazz trumpeter's virtuoso solo, the mastership of an Indian sitar player, the interplay between musicians in a string quartet, the 'go' of a rock group, the creativity of improvising musicians, and so on. In general, it concerns how musicians use the possibilities that are available to create a certain expression in the music—factors such as tempo, timing in rhythm and melody, articulation (legato, staccato), timbre of the instrument or voice, crescendo and diminuendo in loudness, expressive deviations in intonation, vibrato, and much else.[3]

Nor should one forget the visual impression of the artistes—their appearance and dress, body language, concentration, commitment, their joy in playing, charisma, internal communication, and contact with the audience—as well as the setting/surroundings, for example the stage decorations, lighting effects, the reactions of the audience, etc. Sometimes these factors would seem to be just as important as the music: 'It was the best concert I've seen' (see also the discussion on the role of visual perception in Chapter 29, section 29.3.3)

There is thus a large number of factors in the music and the performance that can contribute to SEM. However, the experience depends not only on the qualities of the music but also on the qualities of the receiving person and on the actual situation.

32.1.2 Person

Many participants expressly say that the cause of the experience must also be sought in themselves and mention a number of possible factors.

An obvious factor is the person's physical and mental condition on the occasion in question. On the whole, one can make a division into positive and negative states. Examples of positive states are that one was healthy, calm, relaxed, alert, happy, in love, etc.; negative states, that one was tired, stressed, unhappy, depressed, abandoned, ill, etc. What effect these factors have does, however, vary greatly depending on many other circumstances which can be studied in each particular case.

Another aspect that is emphasized concerns the attitude to the music in the actual situation. This can, for example, mean that one was especially open and susceptible to new impressions, curious, and expectant. One might have prepared oneself by reading about the composer or the artiste, one might have heard one's mother or father talking about the music, one listens to records before the event and looks forward to at last being able to hear the music 'live'.

But there are also examples of the opposite, that one doesn't have any special expectations, or that one even has negative expectations. All the greater, then, is the effect when one is suddenly 'struck' by music that one has never heard before, or that one has not expected much of. A special situation is the first-time experience of music in general, which is described by many old participants (Chapter 4, section 4.3) or encounters with unknown music (Chapter 5, section 5.2 and Chapter 30, section 30.2).

Further varieties of this are that one has been 'starved of music' and that a dammed-up need of music has now been satisfied. This might also have included a longing—perhaps unconscious—for music that should fit in with oneself, reflect one's own thoughts and feelings and lead to one being able to feel accepted and understood. One may have nourished a longing to be able to express oneself in music, to perform as a musician, receive appreciation and confirmation. One might have been entrusted to play with more advanced musicians, to be a soloist, to sing in a large choir, etc.—that is, to feel oneself especially chosen, privileged (Chapter 16 and Chapter 18, section 18.2).

As far as longer-term factors are concerned, many narrators point to the importance of earlier music experiences, knowledge of various types of music, and what attitude to music one has met with at home, at school, with friends, in mass media, and at other places. Several participants consider that a precondition for the strong music experience was that one had achieved a certain maturity, perhaps a necessary age: 'the time was ripe for me to be able to have such an experience'. Several participants also point out that they were particularly sensitive and easily influenced during their teens.

Something that in the highest degree can contribute to the experience is that the music can arouse memories of (associations with) certain events, people, situations, or other phenomena that have been important for that person, positively or negatively. They might, for example, be experiences of love, experiences in an exotic environment, experiences of war, sickness, death, and much more, and naturally all of this is completely individual.

Among the long-term factors are also, of course, the person's temperament, character, and personality and attitude to culture, religion, politics, and society. One characterizes oneself as, for example, curious, concentrated, optimistic, extrovert or introvert, sensitive, easily influenced, nervous, uncertain, gloomy, brooding, a religious believer, radical, conservative, etc., and considers that this can have contributed to the experience.[4]

Interestingly, it would seem that all these factors connected to the individual generally work in the same direction; they contribute to and strengthen the positive experience. It is easy to understand that 'positive' factors can contribute to a strong experience—that one is in good physical and mental shape, in a good mood, happy, relaxed, open, curious, expectant, prepared, etc. It is, however, more interesting that the strong experience to a great degree seems to be connected with factors that would normally be characterized as negative—that one is tired, worried, stressed, irritated, has pain, is ill, unhappy, depressed, suicidal: that is, some form of critical state. This is particularly evident in the accounts in Chapter 17. It is often in crises of some sort that music seems to have an especially strong effect, lead to new insights, give relief, consolation, strength, new hope, and zest for life, perhaps a feeling that 'I was sort of chosen to be able to have such an experience as this when I needed it the very most'.[5]

32.1.3 Situation

With regard to the situation, one can distinguish two categories: physical situation and social situation.

Physical situation usually means the time and place for the experience and the circumstances in connection with it. That the place can affect the experience is easy to imagine. There can be a considerable difference between listening to music in a church, a concert hall, out in nature, in the car, at a restaurant, in one's room at home, or in an exotic setting somewhere on Earth. The most common places were at home, in a church, a concert premises, an assembly hall, and outdoors (Chapter 29, section 29.8.3)

An important aspect is, of course, the acoustic conditions. Good acoustics in the form of clear audibility, suitable reverberation, and good diffusion of sound are generally favourable conditions, for live music as well as for reproduced music. That the music or sound fills the entire room and that one can feel oneself enveloped by music—find oneself in the midst of the sounding course—these are often described as a fantastic experience. But the absence of sound can also be important, for example the absolute silence of the audience waiting for the music to begin or while the music is being played.

Visual impressions can also mean a great deal for the experience. One often describes the size and form of the premises, the interior, colours, decorations, lighting, etc., as well as the composition of the audience (if there is one) and their reactions, in general all of the surrounding setting, indoors or outdoors.

The time at which the experience happened also has great, sometimes decisive, importance. The experiences range over almost a hundred years, from 1908 to 2004 (Chapter 29, section 29.8.3). They are affected to a considerable degree by which type of music that was prevalent during these different periods and how old the individual then was. This has been discussed at length in Chapter 30, section 30.2.

More limited aspects of the time at which the experience happened can concern the season of the year and everything connected with that (light, nature) as well as the time of day and the degree of wakefulness or tiredness associated with it. There are, for example, some instances of how tiredness and a situation on the border between wakefulness and sleep seem to pave the way for a particularly intense experience of the music. Most of the experiences (93%) have taken place in the daytime or in the evening, 5% have taken place at night, and 2% very early in the morning. Music at night on the radio has been an important support for several participants in difficult situations.

The social situation is usually one of three cases: that one is alone, together with other people one knows, or together with other people one doesn't know. In the 1,091 accounts where it has been possible to establish the situation, the most common has been that one is together with other people one knows (68% of the cases), then that one is alone (19%), or together with people one does not know (12%). This order is the same for both genders, for all three age groups and all the music genres that occur. The relative values, however, vary depending on the type of music, on whether one was a listener or performer, and whether the music was live or reproduced; details about this were given in Chapter 29, section 29.8.3.

Being on one's own means that one can be undisturbed, one can decide the volume oneself, and how long one wants to listen. One can give free rein to one's feelings and behave as one wishes, perhaps letting the tears come without being embarrassed in front of others, and so on. Being together with other people, people that one knows or not, does, however, always mean some form of influence, be it positive or negative. The behaviour of people around one can strengthen or restrict one's own feelings, increase or decrease one's attention, influence one's attitude to the music, etc., sometimes in very subtle ways. At a concert, the mood is very dependent upon the behaviour of the audience. A concentrated, silent, and expectant audience makes for a certain mood, a wild and noisy audience a different mood. And, of course, one may *feel* alone even though one is surrounded by many other people.

32.1.4 Interplay: music–person–situation

In summary: A potentially large number of different elements in music work together with a potentially large number of factors related to the individual and factors related to the situation. The number of possible combinations of music × person × situation seems to be practically endless. No wonder, then, that music experiences can be so varied and different.

It can be instructive to consider, in every individual case, how the three factors—music, person, situation—affect the experience and what their relative importance is. It is hardly possible to construct a theoretical model that could cover every imaginable combination of factors within them. Certain combinations are, however, more common than others and can thus be suitable as a starting point for model building. An interesting alternative is to take advantage of recent attempts to analyse the mechanisms through which music may arouse emotions—one of the fundamental categories in SEM—and use this as an element and heuristic device in attempting to construct a model that would comprise many other aspects/categories of SEM as well.[6]

32.2 CONSEQUENCES

This concerns how one felt after the experience and what the experience has meant in the long term.

32.2.1 Directly afterwards

The reactions directly afterwards can be summarized in a range of alternatives that are sometimes the opposite of one another:

(a) Directly after the last note one can feel a great disappointment that it is 'already finished'. One wants to remain in the fantastic experience and wishes that the music would go on or be played again.

(b) The experience has been so strong that one 'can't stand it any longer', one is completely exhausted, on the verge of a breakdown. The experience must be broken off so that one can get back into balance again.

(c) The experience has been felt so deeply that one has to be by oneself afterwards and contemplate it. The applause is just disturbing. One has absolutely no wish to talk with others, rather one avoids contact. The experience stays on in one's consciousness and can make it hard to sleep afterwards.

(d) One can't manage to deal with the strong experience oneself, but has to find an outlet for it by sharing it with others, talking about it, discussing.

The feelings afterwards are similar to those that are aroused during the actual listening or performing of the music, such as happiness, joy, elation, enthusiasm, delight, peace, calm, harmony, wonder, admiration, or gratitude. In a few cases, however, there are decidedly negative feelings such as fear, despair, anger, shock, or panic (examples in Chapter 11, section 11.3). Mixed feelings are also common. Musicians who have put everything into their performance and received response from the listeners are often exhausted afterwards, feeling completely empty inside but at the same time incredibly satisfied and happy.

Besides immediate emotional reactions, narrators also mention reactions of a more lasting character such as feeling relaxed, alert, free, elevated, purified, consoled, hopeful, filled with energy, or having had a kick. They point towards consequences in the long term.

32.2.2 Long-term perspective

Among effects in the long term, one can distinguish three different categories.

The memory of the experience

The experience lives on in one's memory. It is often described as unforgettable and provides an agreeable (nice, lovely, pleasant, amusing) memory, a jewel to enjoy now and then. If one gets to hear the music again—or simply think about it—one remembers what it felt like on that occasion, one relives the same feelings.

Several people mention that the memory of the experience works as a refuge if one is in a difficult situation. One tries to deliberately bring forth the memory of the experience since one knows that it makes one feel good. One can go a step further and make sure one gets to hear the music again. Here, thus, one is coming close to a form of self-therapy.

Some people mention that they were so strongly affected that they have not dared listen to the same music again, or that a very long time passed before that happened. Others avoided listening to the music because they were afraid that they might be disappointed when listening again; they didn't want to jeopardize the strong experience they had had.

Increased interest in music

The experience leads to new insights into what music can mean. One becomes interested in a certain type of music, a certain composer, a certain artiste, or in music in general. The experience can arouse a desire to learn to play or sing or to continue to do so even more than before. It can inspire one to do creative work and even lead to a decision to devote oneself to music as a profession. One wishes to spread to other people knowledge about what fantastic experiences music can give. Many narrators were inspired to use music to influence their own mood or to use music for self-therapy. There is more about these questions in Chapter 29, section 29.7.2.

Personal and social

A number of consequences on a personal and social level have been described earlier in Chapter 29, section 29.7 and in parts of Chapters 12 to 17. They can be briefly summarized as follows.

The experience can give the person new insights about himself or herself and about one's relation to other people. It can bring about a new view as to what life and existence mean, and arouse thought about one's own place in the world. Thoughts and feelings that have been hidden can manifest themselves, and one can think that one has reached into one's very core.

The experience has led to the person feeling free/liberated, inspired, refreshed, born again, elevated, enriched, and that one has grown or matured as a person.

The experience has meant an inner purification—catharsis—and/or had a healing effect. It has given consolation, help, hope, and fresh courage, relieved physical and mental pain, and provided a 'kick' to go on.

The experience has meant that one feels confirmed—accepted, understood, appreciated, needed, chosen—and has thus acquired greater self-confidence and a possibility to realize oneself. One has become more open and unreserved, learnt to meet new experiences without preconceived notions. The experience can also contribute to a strong feeling of belonging together and fellowship with others—listeners, performers, or 'everybody' in general.

There are also cases where one has broken away from one's accustomed environment to look for new possibilities, that one has changed one's political views or gone through a religious conversion.

Many of the above effects have involved or been parts of a therapeutic process (see Chapter 17).

Some strong music experiences have unfortunately been negative and also led to negative consequences (see examples in Chapter 11, section 11.3). Often, this is not on account of the music but is due to other circumstances which in some way have become associated with the music—illness, death, a broken love relationship, accidents, events during a war—so that the music arouses negative feelings. The result is that one is unable to appreciate the music concerned, it is 'spoilt', and one avoids encountering it again.

A negative attitude from parents, relations, or teachers has made some participants believe that they were unable to know anything about music or made them become especially nervous when performing music. In the worst case, they have stopped playing altogether, or refrained from all further contact with music, though they actually would like to have music.

In some cases, certain qualities in the music itself have led to a negative experience: music with a very high sound level, powerful dissonances, distorted timbre, 'noise', chaotic form, 'devilish expression', and similar. A common result of this is that one develops an aversion to the music concerned, and avoids coming into contact with it.

32.3 WHAT MUSIC CAN MEAN: QUOTATIONS

Much more can be said about what consequences strong music experiences can have, and naturally the effects should be seen in relation to the circumstances in each individual case. What has been said is, however, fully sufficient to have prompted the subtitle of this book, *Music is much more than just music*. Music offers a richness of human experiences, thoughts, and feelings that often will not allow themselves to be conveyed so concisely in any other way. It can satisfy fundamental personal and social needs and provide possibilities for individuals and groups to express and realize themselves.

To further illustrate this, I have gathered together a number of quotes taken from the participants' own accounts or reflections. They have been grouped under the following headings: Music is a vital part of life; Music interprets life and my own person; Music gives joy, strength, and help; What is unique about music. The following abbreviations are used: M = male, F = female; y = young (under 30), m = middle-aged (30—59) and o = old (60 and more). Thus F, m = middle-aged woman)

Music is a vital part of life

(F,m) To live without music is to be dead.

(F,y) Music is my life—I'd die without it!

(F,o) I must have my dose of music every day.

(M,o) I find it hard to imagine what life would be like without music.

(F,m) I think that I have found a spring that never dries up—the world of music.

(F,y) I have these experiences often, almost every day. Music is everything for me.

(F) What music does with me is that it strikes me directly! Music is indispensible, don't you think?

(F,m) Without music I'm just a half, for me music is just as important as the food I eat.

(F,o) Just as food is necessary for your body, music is necessary for your soul. That's how it's felt for me.

(F,y) Music is something that I have as a friend when you're sad and nobody can console you. Absolutely vital, that is!

(F,o) All the wonderful music experiences I've had over many years and still experience have enriched my life, yes, that is life for me.

(F,o) Music is and will remain a mystery—but at the same time a deep passion. I feel bad the day I don't even once listen to music! Or have not been able to practise.

(M,y) Music, for me, is more than half of life—it is such an important point in this existence, so without music I don't know if life would be worth living.

(F,m) Music is vitally important for me. It is an inexhaustible source of strength. I prepare myself with the help of music, I celebrate with music, and I let myself be consoled by music.

(F,m) After the concert I thought: If I wasn't able to experience music in this way, I would die! Or at any rate slowly fade away!

(M,o) I was born and brought up in an environment where there wasn't any music . . . So I have been starved of music. Now I experience this as a very great loss.

(F,y) Music means an awful lot to me, I wouldn't be able to live without it. I love a broad range of music, everything from hard rock, folk music, to classical music. All types of music affect me in different ways.

(F,y) What a great idea to research music experiences. I felt really enthusiastic, because music means an enormous amount to me. Without it, I doubt if I'd be able to live, perhaps I'd be like a joyless robot or zombie.

(M,m) Music experiences are a necessity for me, somewhat like eating, kissing my wife, or whatever. I can't live without art and music. For me it is connected with aesthetics. Music/art is food.

(M,m) Otherwise I think that my music listening is comparable to drug addiction or something like that. It's a need that must be satisfied. The need arose some time during childhood or youth out of some pleasure-filled experiences. Now I'm looking for the same kick.

(F,y) I'm a 20-year-old girl and am one of those people who always listen to music. I soak up music as if I was a dust rag, all music whatever it is, classical, rock and pop, yeah, everything, and all music is wonderful, if there hadn't been any music then I'd probably have invented it.

(M,o) I'm a 72-year-old man. To have favourites or to especially point out one composer or some music above others is naturally very difficult! Bach, Beethoven, Brahms, Sibelius—all of them are just as unique and brilliant. And Richard Strauss! Just think of waking to the strains of *Zarathustra*, brightening up life with *Der Rosenkavalier* and falling asleep to the third of his *Vier letzte Leider*, 'Beim Schlafengehn'! Then one hasn't lived in vain . . .

Finally, a quotation from an outsider, the philosopher Friedrich Nietzsche: 'Without music, life would be a mistake.'

Music interprets life and my own person

(F,o) To talk about music experiences, for me it is to talk about my life—very private.

(F,m) Music contains this seriousness: what takes life seriously, expresses what life is both in music and in words.

(M,y) Music can be a drug—but, handled correctly, I think it can lead to spiritual sensations that we as yet can't understand or master.

(F,m) I think that insight into, and experience of, music helps me to keep up my emotional life.

(F,o) Music has given me and my life all the excitement and content I have needed. It has always given a deeper dimension of life and the world around.

(F,y) There is something special about music which can hardly be explained with words. Often when it comes to strong experiences with music, the thing is that the music is some way expresses and makes situations and emotions clearer.

(M,m) As a teenager, I lived in music, my entire existence was interpreted with the help of music. All feelings of frustration, unhappy love, happy love, abandonment, fellowship, etc., were channelled into the music that I listened to.

(F,m) Music, for me, has been an enlarged part of reality, an extension. Through music, I can find myself, my identity, my strength, my soul. It always strengthens me, makes me feel fulfilled, bigger than myself. Gives me calm, peace, harmony, and balance.

(F,m) What is it in music when it is at its best? I have absolutely no answer, but it was a fantastic experience! And it has helped me to understand better others who often seem to experience music so much stronger than I do. They really experience something, it isn't just make-believe.

(F,y) I think all of us have experienced how music has helped us to spontaneously give full expression to various feelings. I am convinced that music is a good tool for increased self-knowledge. The idea that with the help of music you can help people to find themselves a bit more, I find that very attractive.

(F,y) Singing is a part of me. By singing, I can deal with emotions and impressions but also convey what is important for me or my moods to those who are listening. Through song and music I have the possibility to express what I feel, think, my imagination and my longing—a way of communicating with myself, with my heart.

(F) Music and my life have been woven together. [Music] has explained, supported, guided, consoled, relieved, helped me in my great despair, horror, distress, joy, hope, consolation. Most dreadful of all was a period when everything was silent—then too I was dying. Now I often wake with music—which talks to me and guides me.

Music gives joy, strength, and help

(F,m) Fantastic how nice music can influence one's mood, make one only see what is positive and joyful in life.

(F,m) Can't myself sing or play an instrument but am happy that I can appreciate music, which is a great source of joy in life.

(F,y) I think that you are extremely susceptible to strong experiences with music when you feel bad and weak. At least I was.

(F,o) The music can cry with me, it can laugh with me, it can make me happy, it can make me sad, and it can console me if I am sad.

(F,o) As soon as everything started to feel too difficult, I played my favourite record, which would help me persevere. I know that if I get into difficulties in the future, I shall seek help and relief in lovely music.

(F,o) Music gives me the strongest experiences; I listen to music loads of hours every week. Since I was widowed it has become even more important. Sad, gloomy, lonely, downhearted evenings I listen to quartets and jazz in turn.

(F,o) I am not musical. Can't sing, played the piano a bit in my childhood, don't understand how music is constructed and can't hear in which key the music is written. Anyway, I often go and hear our excellent symphony orchestra. I enjoy it, every bit of me from head to toe.

(M,m) As early as in the days of the ancient Greeks, music could speak to one's feelings, I have read. But even in our day, it is a force of nature . . . I think that now it is needed more than ever in a world of solitudes, conflicts, and anxiety-ridden needs!

(M,o) But above all I experience music as an incredible asset for me. Above all it helps me in the changeover from a depressed temperament to a normal one. Over the years I have had innumerable musical experiences that have got me into a normal understanding of what was happening after having looked at it bleakly in certain situations.

(F,m) I often need music when I feel I'm in poor mental or physical balance. The music works as some form of safety valve for me, a contrast to the stress and gloominess one meets in everyday life. When most things feel black and difficult, then I take the time to go to the opera or to a concert, and then I usually feel like a new person afterwards.

What is unique about music

(M,y) The experience has given me a faith in music that I don't have in anything else.

(M,y) These experiences have given me some sort of insight that is hard to define in words. Music is something more than just music.

(F,m) This was my very own experience that nobody could experience like I did just then. That is what is so unique about music. When writing, words, speech are unable to express what we people want to convey, then we can use music to help us.

(F,o) I don't think any other art form can give me the same joy and strong experiences as music, it is as if music always has a dimension more than everything else.

(F,y) The experience has made me better understand what an enormous resource and asset music is—it is not only something for entertainment but there is something else there that can hardly be explained.

(F,o) For me, music is an everlasting source of strong experiences. I brighten up my days with music, do the cleaning to Pavarotti, paint to Mahler, bake to Jussi, do copper etching to Maria Callas, draw to medieval music from Provence. Music is a language in which we can meet across the centuries.

(M) The best possibility to understand past generations' way of feeling and thinking is to listen to their music and learn from what the verses contain of feelings. So for me music is something of a time machine which immediately takes me back into the spiritual culture and life of a bygone age. Of all the ways to acquire knowledge of past times, I think music is the one that gives us the strongest experience and contact.

(M,y) After this experience [of music in China] I have formed a completely different view of music, listening as well as performing. Music has acquired a much more distinct place as an international means of communication. We sat there, two Swedes, and understood exactly what the musicians meant even though we spoke completely different languages and had completely different cultural backgrounds.

(M,m) My strongest and clearest music experiences are when I listen or compose. For me, those are the moments when music's own language speaks most distinctly and most undisturbed, and I, in the best and most open way, can be gripped by the enormous power and energy that is there. I would like to describe those moments as islands of an almost indescribable joy, comparable to nothing.

(F,m) Music is presumably something much greater than just music. Not being able to find answers, being humble in the face of greatness, to just let experiences and feelings happen—I think this too is something that is important for us today. Perhaps music, its importance and manifoldness, is precisely one of those areas where we won't find all answers and where the questions, instead, will come all the more.

(M,y) A magical power is inherent in certain music and it feels as if this can affect the environment around you . . . On certain occasions, the feeling has been particularly evident and this has been characterized by everything acquiring a stamp of something universal and comprehensive. It is as if the notes show meanings that are not noticeable in 'everyday' situations. But once you've sat down to listen and to give yourself time, these secrets are revealed.

CHAPTER 33

OVERVIEW, COMPARISONS, QUESTIONS, OUTLOOKS

IT is time to round off the presentation of what has emerged in this investigation of strong experiences with music.

33.1 BRIEF OVERVIEW/SUMMARY

The investigation can be very briefly summarized as follows. About 965 people have contributed accounts of strong experiences with music. Analysis of the content of the accounts has shown at least 150 different reactions/aspects of such experiences. They have been grouped in a descriptive system with three different levels shown in Appendix A and commented upon in Chapter 29.

The reactions are of many different kinds: physical, perceptual, cognitive, and emotional. They also concern existential, transcendental, and religious aspects as well as consequences—new insights, new possibilities—on personal and social planes.

The experiences range across almost a hundred years and have taken place in very varied circumstances. Most of them are experiences of listening to live music. The most common reactions are positive feelings (particularly happiness and joy), total absorption (the music is the only thing that matters, one is unconscious of one's body, of time, and space), lost control (one is surprised, deeply moved, struck, overwhelmed), a special relation to the music (one is pulled into the music, merges with the music), and that the experience leads to new insights and possibilities. There are certain gender and age differences as regards the extent and strength of different reactions (Chapter 29, section 29.8.1), but on the whole the similarities are greater than the differences. Strong music experiences do not usually take place so often, and when one encounters the same music on later occasions the reaction is often different. The cause of the experience thus cannot be sought only in the music, but also in factors associated with the individual and the situation.

Music that has featured in the experiences is of very varied types and to allow an overview these have been divided into 15 different categories (Chapter 30), ranging from classical music to contemporary forms of popular music and music from other cultures.

The participants in the investigation comprise both women and men (more of them women), from teenagers up to very old (80–90 years), performers as well as listeners. They have different levels of education, are active in many different fields and have music preferences in many different genres. The participants thus represent a wide selection with regard to gender, age, education, profession, experience of and preferences in music, so their accounts can be regarded as a representative sample of the population of possible strong experiences with music. Obvious reservations are naturally that the investigation took place at the end of the twentieth century and within the Western cultural sphere. If similar investigations were to be carried out with people in other countries, cultures, and at other times, the music would certainly be different from that in this investigation. However, the reactions as such might to a large extent be similar. For instance, there is no reason to believe that 'automatic' physiological reactions (shivers, gooseflesh, heart palpitations, etc.) would be any different, nor basic perceptual reactions (auditory, tactile, visual), or emotional reactions such as happiness, sadness, anger, and fear (so-called 'basic emotions'). Furthermore, many features associated with trance or ecstasy in different cultures seem related to categories in our descriptive system—in fact, Judith Becker considers strong experiences with music, 'deep listening', as 'a kind of secular trancing, divorced from religious practice but often carrying religious sentiments such as feelings of transcendence or a sense of communication with a power beyond oneself' (see Chapter 13, note 1). However, it is also apparent that people's reactions in strong experiences may be modelled according to customs, norms, and values in different cultural settings.

I regard the descriptive system in Appendix A as a step in the charting of which reactions can be a part of SEM, not as a final product. It is, of course, open for amendments and modifications as new observations are made, and can probably never acquire a final form—who would dare to claim that they had exhausted everything that can be embraced in strong music experiences? The scheme shows the breadth and manifoldness of reactions in SEM, but much remains to be done with regard to deepening and further exemplification of various aspects. It is also important to realize that all the reactions that are listed in Appendix A are the cumulative result of more than 1,300 accounts. It thus shows which reactions *can* be a part of strong music experiences in general, not what is a part of every individual experience. Every single account contains only a limited part of all the reactions mentioned.

The descriptive system can be used as a reference for comparisons with music experiences in other contexts, for instance, in everyday listening to music; I have recently made such a comparison.[1] And, naturally, every reader can compare their own music experiences with those described in this investigation and judge how they can fit in in different places in the descriptive system. One can recognize one's own reactions in certain accounts, perhaps be surprised by or question other accounts. Whatever the case, the accounts demonstrate the manifoldness of reactions that can be elicited by music and how many factors can lie behind every individual case. It provides food for thought as well as a feeling of humility and enthusiasm before everything that music can offer.

33.2 COMPARISONS WITH EARLIER STUDIES

The results of this investigation are in many ways similar to the results from a few earlier studies (Chapter 1, section 1.3). Maslow's characteristics for 'peak experience'—that one is completely absorbed, forgets time and space, merges together with the phenomenon, feels joy, happiness, ecstasy, and that the experience can lead to a new view of life and serve as therapy—are found in our results too. Similarly, one finds several examples of Panzarella's four factors, namely 'renewal ecstasy' (altered perception of the world), 'motor-sensory ecstasy' (shivers, palpitations, movements, floating, etc.), 'withdrawal ecstasy' (total absorption, no contact with one's surroundings) and 'fusion-emotional ecstasy' (one merges with the music). Partly the same reactions were also included in Laski's categories, and she added the feeling of 'ineffability', that is, the experience is indescribable, something that our participants also emphasize. Most of these reactions are also briefly described in a much later study, in which the participants listened to selected pieces of music and with the push of a button should indicate occasions when they felt 'deep and profound pleasure or joy'. It was thus an attempt to study strong experiences under experimentally controlled conditions.[2] Concerning strong experiences while one plays music oneself, our musicians' accounts of 'magic moments' are directly reminiscent of what has been called 'peak performance' (Privette) or 'flow' (Csikszentmihalyi). Similar magic moments have been described in interviews with musicians in different branches of popular music (see Chapter 1, note 11).

The description and summary of reactions presented in this investigation are, however, far more comprehensive and detailed than in any of these earlier studies as well as being concretized with a large number of accounts in a way that doesn't have any earlier equivalent either.

However, the purpose of the studies has been partly different. Maslow intended to study 'peak experiences' regardless of which area they came in, while our investigation concerns only music experiences. Nor would all the strong experiences in this book fulfil all of Maslow's criteria for 'peak experience'. Maslow did, however, find that the two easiest ways to get 'peak experiences' were through music, especially classical music, or sex. Laski, similarly, found that such experiences were primarily generated by classical music but also by poetry, art, literature, drama, ballet, and film. This raises the question of whether there are common characteristics in strong experiences within different fields.

33.3 SIMILARITIES WITH OTHER STRONG EXPERIENCES

About half of all the participants (473 people) were asked in an open question whether they had had similar strong experiences in circumstances other than with music. The majority (70%) of them answered that they had had similar strong experiences within other fields and named one or more such fields. Fifty-eight participants (12%) answered 'No' and 86 participants (18%) did not answer the question.

Among all the examples given, nature experiences were the most common (20% of the cases), followed by love (13%), literature (10%), art (8%), theatre, religion, sex, and films, these last four being 5% each. Further examples were meetings or being together with other people (for example, family members, close friends), experiences in connection with children's birth, dance (as performer or spectator), one's own creative activity, sport, and meditation, each of these being represented with small percentages. There were also solitary examples of strong experiences of children, animals, space, journeys, riding, mountain climbing, parachute jumping, car driving, weddings, psychotherapy, historic events (such as VE day 1945, Olof Palme's death, the fall of the Berlin Wall), death, funerals, experiences in connection with war, Aha! experiences of some sort, occasions when one has been praised for, or felt proud of, an achievement, and a few other special events.

Strong nature experiences can concern the beauty of nature, its magnificence, stillness, or agitation, qualities that also have equivalents in SEM. Most often the sea and mountains are mentioned: the grandeur of the sea, its endlessness and continually changing surface, the sea when calm or rough, sailing out at sea; the immenseness of mountains, their beauty, desolation, sunlit mountain tops, mountain walking in solitude, skiing in brilliant sunshine. Other examples are early summer mornings when nature slowly wakes up to a new day, sunrise, dead calm water as smooth as a mirror, droning insects, bird song, and nature's own music.

SEM are likened by many participants to being in love. They are similar in intensity—time stands still, one lives intensely in the here and now, thinks one sees and hears everything in a new and clearer way, and can cope with any difficulties at all. One is possessed by music or love, enveloped by them, both of them 'feel right', one is filled with joy and in raptures. One has been seen by somebody else, one abandons oneself to love or music and is always longing for the next encounter. One may equate SEM and love: 'Strong and lovely music experiences—I rather like to see them as fine and beautiful moments of love' and associate both with religious feelings: 'Both love and music can have a sort of religious effect on me. Like a force that grabs hold of you and makes you take off.'

SEM are also described as being like intense sexual experiences, like an orgasm during intercourse, or like a 'spiritual orgasm', linked with feelings of strong joy and fellowship, an 'incredible well-being'.

Some participants think that SEM can have similarities to experiences under the influence of drugs but emphasize at the same time that they themselves were not influenced by drugs in any way. The number of SEM accounts with elements of drugs or alcohol is very small. Possible influence of drugs (marijuana, psychopharmacological drugs) is mentioned only obliquely in a couple of accounts, mild influence of alcohol (beer, wine) in about 15 accounts.

In the examples of strong experiences of literature there is mention of works by poets (for example, Karin Boye, Gunnar Ekelöf, Gösta Oswald, Edith Södergran, Tomas Tranströmer, Paul Valéry) and novelists (for example, Dostoyevsky, Selma Lagerlöf, Sara Lidman, Torgny Lindgren). As regards poetry, one participant says: 'Music and poetry have quite a lot in common. Music or poetry that reaches me doesn't do so via my head, rather, first the totality/experience, then the analysis.' When reading a novel, one can, as with SEM, become totally absorbed, 'devoured' by the plot, find oneself inside the novel together with its characters, even long after one has finished reading. The same applies to films: 'You become enveloped by impressions in a film and even more in music. You can't defend yourself, you become absorbed by what is happening in front of you so that you become a part of it.'

Within art, there is mention of paintings (for example, Giotto's frescos in Assisi, the Impressionists), sculptures (for example at Millesgården, Stockholm) and architectonic masterpieces (for example the pyramids, the Sphinx, the Parthenon, the cathedral in Chartres, St Peter's in Rome, the Temple church in Helsinki) which render the observer speechless and give rise to wonder and gratitude for being able to encounter something so perfect. Some participants are artists and paint to the accompaniment of music.

Dance can give strong experiences to spectators—'I saw Anneli Alhanko dance solo in *Swan Lake*, a totally spiritual experience of pure, infinite beauty'—as well as to dancers, for example when 'you just flow, bounce along, your feet just do it right, everything goes perfectly and the music swings'.

Within our project, there were also two studies of strong dance and art experiences respectively, each of them comprising just over 60 participants. It transpired that the accounts of dance and art experiences could be analysed and described according to the same principles as for SEM. Most of the aspects that are included in SEM are thus also found in these accounts, with some minor modifications. This can be illustrated by the following extracts from the studies:

> Summing up, one could say that strong dance experiences can have different forms, but that most of them are characterized by a strong feeling of joy, a changed perception of time and space, a state of trance, intense concentration, being one with the dance, feeling alive ... For most of the participants, the experience has become a vivid and positive memory, for many of them it has meant a

great deal for their personal development and for others again it has had profound consequences—for example, given rise to a strong and lasting interest in dance, influenced their choice of career and inspired them to do creative work themselves.[3]

About strong art experiences:

> The following are common: feelings of amazement, astonishment, the person feels taken by surprise, what is around them disappears, one is absorbed by the work of art, there is a change in the experience, it intensifies and becomes stronger than usual, the state is sufficient in itself, moments of total presence. When the experience goes over into a sort of finishing phase, the person is filled with happiness, joy, calm, gratitude, new opportunities open up, new insights take shape. Sometimes, the experience leads to deep lasting changes and re-evaluations of what is important in one's life, for others it can provide a generally enhanced quality of life, inspire them to create things themselves, it gives self-confidence and strength or power and courage when winter feels too grey, some people become more open in their attitudes and some are influenced in their choice of career.[4]

SEM are often compared to religious experiences, either that one refers to one's own religious experiences or that one supposes that SEM can resemble a religious experience as one has heard it described by others. Some people mention religious experiences they have had in connection with a religious service, christening, confirmation, or prayers. One experiences a special atmosphere, 'a powerful stillness, the air seems to become saturated in some way' and one senses 'a strong feeling of the presence of something higher'.

One participant got a strong music experience when he listened to a children's choir (Chapter 25, account 25.1L) and compared this experience to earlier experiences of God: 'In experiences of God I often feel completely broken-hearted and at the same time eternally grateful to God who wants to come so close to me. So it was shocking to experience the same feelings but from a totally different cause, namely music. The music was not sacral but it gave me the same feeling as in the meeting with God. This is, of course, very perplexing since I thought that the strong feelings were a direct proof of God's existence. At the same time, it gives rise to a lot of interesting questions about both music and my faith in God.' In his opinion, experiences of God and strong music experiences are both characterized by a lost feeling of time and feelings of a broken heart, being in raptures, love, and consensus. The experience of God also includes forgiveness and a feeling of weightlessness (he doesn't, however, mention weightlessness in connection with his music experience, but it is described by many other participants). 'There are thus several feelings/experiences in both cases. Is it that music can replace God or is it that God is in music? . . . Music can thus produce the same effect as the meeting with God. Can it be explained in psychological ways? I don't know . . .'

Within the psychology of religion there have long been thorough studies of intense religious experiences. A pioneer was philosopher and psychologist William James who as early as the beginning of the twentieth century pronounced four criteria for a 'mystical experience', namely 'ineffability' (the experience cannot be formulated in words), 'noetic quality' (from the Greek *noesis* = sensation, thinking, reason; the experience gives new knowledge, new insights), 'transiency' (the experience is comparatively short-lived), and 'passivity' (one's own will is put out of action, one is gripped by the experience). James further emphasized the connection with music: 'not conceptual speech, but music rather, is the element through which we are best spoken to by mystical truth'. Philosopher Walter Terence Stace also named several characteristics for 'mystical experience', including 'ineffability', a changed experience of time and space, a feeling of something holy or divine, and above all an experience of 'unity' with the universe or with 'everything'. All these characteristics are also represented in our material about strong music experiences. Other researchers have carried out comprehensive empirical studies concerning prevalence and content of religious experiences. Their results display many parallels to what is usually described in strong music experiences. A full summary of these studies is given in a thesis by Siv Lindström Wik, my colleague for large parts of the SEM project.[5]

In Sweden, religion psychologist Antoon Geels has published thorough analyses of religious visions described by about a hundred people.[6] They too display many elements that are found in SEM, for example focused attention, feeling of weightlessness, experience of special light, feelings of joy, happiness, peace, security, and love, feeling directly addressed, and of merging with something bigger. The vision leads, in turn, to a new view of life. The persons concerned have found themselves in a difficult situation in their lives, and the vision comes as a solution to this; the vision creates order in a chaotic psyche. This reminds us of several accounts in our material where the participant was in a crisis that was resolved through a strong music experience; the experience seems to come when one needs it most (Chapter 17).

33.4 CAN ONE TRUST MEMORY AND LANGUAGE?

The 1,350 accounts upon which the investigation is based are of course accounts of events in the past (retrospective reports), that is, they represent the participants' memories of the actual experience. The experience itself took place several years, or even several decades, earlier. One may ask oneself how reliable these memories are, that is, how well they reflect what 'really' happened.

One way to study this could be to—after a certain time—ask the participants to tell about their experience once more to see if the account is the same or not. It would undoubtedly be of interest, but would still not provide a proper solution to the question. It is possible, for example, that one can fall back upon the memory of what one has already told, or that it becomes a mixture of the memory of the original experience and the memory of what one has told about it. Naturally, various personal circumstances on the different occasions for the two accounts can also influence in ways that are hard to ascertain. Moreover, a new round of accounts would demand even more work, both for the researchers and for the narrators. Several participants have said that they have devoted many hours, some of them even several days, to the task, and they would presumably not be so inclined to do this once more. A request to tell the story again could also be interpreted as a vote of no confidence, that we didn't trust their accounts.

The general impression is that our narrators have been very thorough and open—and why would they otherwise put so much time into the task? Some of them are also aware that one's memory is not always reliable and make allowances such as 'I think that what I felt was . . .' Interestingly, there are also some accounts where the narrator has been able to make use of notes made in connection with the experience (see, for example, Chapter 10, accounts 10.2A and 10.3B, and Chapter 18, account 18.6L).

Memories of this type are called autobiographical memories, and there has been a great deal of research and discussion about the degree to which autobiographical memories are true 'copies' of the original event or rather reconstructions of it; they are probably a mixture of both. They are perhaps never completely faithful to the original, but can nevertheless be said to be accurate in the sense that they represent the meaning that the experience had for the person concerned. One has also been able to show that events of a strong emotional character and of great importance for the person result in memories that are very detailed, easy to retrieve, and very resistant to forgetfulness. Most SEM evidently belong to this category of events.[7]

One may also ask oneself how reliable language is to describe strong music experiences. People differ greatly as regards vocabulary, the meaning they assign to different words and concepts, and in their ability and willingness to describe experiences in words. Many participants emphasize that it is difficult for them to find words for what they experienced; the experience seems to be 'indescribable'. This problem was commented upon already in the introduction to the book (Chapter 1, section 1.2), where there is a discussion of the possibility of using physiological and neurological measurements as an indication of the experience. After we have studied hundreds of accounts of strong music experiences, it is now even more apparent that such 'objective' measurements can never replace the person's own description of their experience. It is impossible for such measurements to do justice to all the perceptions, cognitive processes, feelings, and much else that can be a part of the experience and which have been collected in the descriptive system for SEM. On the other hand, such measurements can, of course, be important complements and contribute to the understanding of, and further research into, such experiences.

Many participants have expressed their enthusiasm for the research project and said that it is welcome and urgent. One has found it inspiring to think through and try to formulate one's experience. One participant emphasized that 'This particular aspect—strong music experiences—seems, I think, to be among the least known, least talked about, least valued in all contexts where music is commented upon. A paradox since it is at the same time the most interesting and deepest aspect.' Several participants express their gratitude that they have now had the chance—and even been asked—to share an experience that they have carried within them a long time and not told anyone else: 'It was nice to write this, it feels like it has been some sort of confession'; 'Since my strongest music experience is so infinitely more strong than all others in that line, it is wonderful that you ask about it'; 'It feels good to have written about this experience and the catharsis feeling is still associated with that particular music'. An old woman told of a shocking experience during her childhood and added: 'Will never forget it. Ought to have had the chance to talk about it then.' Another participant wrote: 'I have never dared tell this to anybody, people would think I was crazy.'

33.5 SOME OUTLOOKS AND RELATIONS TO OTHER TOPICS

As has been previously seen, the descriptive system has shown itself to be applicable also in adjacent areas such as strong dance and art experiences. Recently, it has also been successfully used in a doctoral thesis in pedagogy by Johanna Ray.[8] The purpose of her research was to study what strong experiences can mean for pupils and music teachers in secondary school, and to see whether there was room for such experiences within music teaching in school. The study was carried out in Swedish-speaking Finland. She analysed 166 15-year-olds' written accounts of strong music experiences (originally collected by Leif Finnäs) and interviewed 28 music teachers about their strong music experiences and how they see the purpose of music teaching in school. Furthermore, she analysed different curriculum texts with regard to what they say about music experience. It transpired that the pupils' strong music experiences usually took place in leisure contexts and almost never in the classroom setting. Similar results are found in other studies,[9] and in our own investigation SEM rarely occur in a school context (3% of the cases; see Chapter 29, section 29.8.3).

In a comprehensive study in Swedish-speaking Finland, Leif Finnäs has collected descriptions of 'significant experiences' within different aesthetic areas—music, drama, literature, art, dance, and also nature experiences—among pupils aged 15–16 years, in all about 760 participants. Most examples of such experiences concerned music, especially among pupils in urbanized districts; next came nature experiences; these dominated among pupils in rural districts. Other areas were drama, literature, art, and dance, in that order. Similar to our results, the music experiences took place more often when listening to music (about 75% of the cases) than when performing music, but contrary to our results the listener experiences for the greater part concerned reproduced music (about two-thirds of the cases). The music in the experiences was mainly pop and rock music.[10]

Studies of strong music experiences can generally be of great interest in the context of music pedagogy. Describing and discussing one's own music experiences, and those of others, can have a strong motivating effect and provide a broader perspective on daily and arduous practice with the instrument. There is considerable scope here for innovative music teachers. Studies of SEM are evidently also highly relevant for music therapists and are also very close to certain varieties of music therapy, for example in *Guided Imagery with Music* (see Chapter 10, note 1).

Our investigation is of a descriptive character, a mapping of which reactions can be a part of strong music experiences. It would, of course, be satisfactory if this could be complemented by a comprehensive theory of SEM. But given at least 150 different aspects of the experience and an indefinitely large number of underlying factors, one cannot expect any comprehensive theory other than in the long term. The great number of reactions and underlying factors must, in some way, be reduced to manageable quantities to enable them to be subjected to one or more testable theories. This question is left open here, but some connections to other areas shall be suggested.

SEM can, in certain respects, be regarded as examples of altered state of consciousness. This is a collective term for many different phenomena, for example, hypnagogic states (between wakefulness and sleep), dreams, meditation, hypnosis, ecstasy, trance, guided imagery, shamanism, and various drug-induced states. Suggestions for definitions of altered state of consciousness include several phenomena that are described in SEM accounts: for example, 'States of consciousness where we lose our sense of identity with the body or with our perceptions are altered states of consciousness.' As a characteristic, there is mention of 'alterations in thinking, disturbed time sense, loss of control, change in emotional expression and body image, perceptual distortions, change in meaning or significance, a sense of the ineffable, feelings of rejuvenation and hypersuggestibility'.[11] It is perfectly obvious that there are connections between certain elements in SEM and altered states of consciousness without one necessarily for that reason having to equate the two phenomena.

Music as a means to achieve a state of trance occurs in many different cultures and is thoroughly described and discussed in works by Gilbert Rouget and Judith Becker.[12] Several of our narrators also mention trance as a result of the music. A common idea is that monotonous repetition can lead to an altered state of consciousness, not least while listening to, or performing, drum rhythms. A study that supports this notion has recently been carried out. Subjects in the study were instructed to imagine a hike down through a hole in the ground and then walking around down there, and note their experiences. One group did this while listening to drum rhythms (210 beats per minute for half an hour), while another group did the same under silence. The people who listened to drum rhythms described changes in their body perception, it felt as if one's body expanded, time went more slowly or faster than usual, their perception of the surrounding world and themselves was altered, their self-awareness became more diffuse, the border between the self and the world around became vague, the meaning of different phenomena was changed, and one felt as if one was governed by the drumming in some way (the drums decided where one could or couldn't go). These phenomena didn't occur in the group that only imagined the hike, that is, without drum rhythms.[13] Experiences of a similar nature are also found in several SEM accounts regardless of with which type of music they occurred. There are also examples with drum rhythms (Chapter 7, account 7.5C; Chapter 13, account 13.4A; Chapter 15, account 15.1F; Chapter 24, account 24G) and with repetitive instrumental music (Chapter 13, accounts 13.4J and 13.4K; Chapter 31, account 31.2G).

In a large overview of different factors behind altered states of consciousness, trance caused by drum rhythms is mentioned as an example of psychologically induced altered state of consciousness.[14] Rhythmic body movements during performance of drum rhythms can also contribute to inducing trance, as can dance. The physiological and neurological background is still little researched, but in one study it was found that monotonous drumming (3–8 beats per second) could trigger brainwaves (EEG) with the equivalent frequency, and in another study, listening to monotonous rhythms was associated with theta activity, that is, brainwaves with a frequency of 4–8Hz, which, for example, occurs during meditation and in a state of drowsiness. It is also pointed out that certain personality traits can play a part in the induction of trance, especially a trait called absorption. This means a disposition to be in a state of intense concentration on the phenomenon (for example, music) concerned and is linked to susceptibility to hypnotic suggestion.[15] Absorption is, of course, an important aspect in the descriptive system for SEM.

Brain research concerning music is a very active area and there are many reports of how different musical aspects—pitch, timbre, consonance/dissonance, rhythm, etc.—are processed in the brain. To my knowledge there is no direct investigation of what happens in the brain during SEM, and considering how many aspects SEM can contain, one can hardly expect any all-inclusive study of this. In connection with accounts of quasi-physical experiences, such as feeling that one is floating or leaving one's body, there was a description of some neurological research about such experiences (Chapter 8, section 8.3). As regards positive feelings—the most commonly mentioned aspect of SEM—it has recently been shown that music which triggers strong positive feelings involves areas in the brain associated with experienced reward and affect and that also can be activated by other stimuli that bring euphoria, such as food, sex, and certain drugs. This opens new perspectives on the connection between music and emotions, and its biological background. There are further exciting attempts to integrate insights of phenomenology (subjective experience) with observations and theories in contemporary biology, and Judith Becker has outlined a theory of trance consciousness, relating phenomena in trance states to current neurophysiological models for consciousness.[16]

Philosophers often refer to strong experiences as 'sublime'. This concept has a long tradition in philosophy and may in the present context refer both to a musical work—'a sublime piece of music'—and to listeners' experience. With regard to the latter, definitions vary. Sublime experience may mean a feeling of awe, to feel overwhelmed, insignificant, before something great; the experience may be mainly positive, however, with a touch of discomfort or pain, that is, mixed feelings. There are some accounts in our material that seem to agree with such characteristics. The best examples may be some of the accounts on religious experiences in Chapter 14, sections 14.3 and 14.4, for example, account 14.3E on a shocking yet positive experience of Kodàly's *Psalmus Hungaricus*, account 14.4C (listening to music in a religious setting, 'I wasn't afraid, but I felt something of the smallness you can feel at the foot of a mountain when nature shows all of its scenery, but this was nevertheless different, much stronger. I automatically bowed my head and did not dare, did not want to and could not move, and it wasn't the pianist I felt small before, it was God. I felt broken-hearted, not floored but like I said extremely small'), a further account in Chapter 4,

4.5E relating a young child's 'awestruck littleness in the face of the majestic endlessness of the firmament coupled with a sense of complete security in experiencing myself as an infinitely little part of this whole, as well as the association with Schubert's music'; see further the comments on similarities between music experience and religious experience in Chapter 33, section 33.3. Still other definitions include more reactions—tears, chills, absorption, strong emotions, trance, ecstasy—in their understanding of sublime experience. Regardless of which definition, there are obvious connections to many categories of SEM. However, the term 'sublime' practically never appears in the accounts of our participants—maybe mainly due to a difference in vocabulary between philosophers and lay people.[17]

This outlook to other disciplines is just a sketch that ought to be supplemented by studies of how SEM or similar phenomena may be touched upon in still other areas, such as music aesthetics, music sociology, music anthropology, theories of evolution regarding music, etc. It is also tempting to study fictional descriptions of music experiences and compare them to the results of the present study.[18] These are just suggestions and pointers for some further means of progressing the study of strong or extraordinary experiences.[19]

33.6 Personal final comments

I have lived with these SEM accounts on and off for many years. It has been a great privilege to have been allowed to share these personal testimonies about music. It has taught me a great deal, both about music and about people, and I believe the reader will also come to learn quite a lot. I never cease to be surprised at how well many of our narrators—none of them authors, as far as I know—manage to convey their experiences, even though they complain of the difficulty of formulating them in words.

Just the very act of reading these accounts has given me many strong experiences: now and then I have become totally absorbed and very moved, felt shivers, tears welling in my eyes, and recognized reactions in myself. I have reflected at length upon the importance of music for mankind, felt confirmed that my strong commitment to music is shared by so many others, and inspired to continue studying this remarkable phenomenon—music—in practice as well as in theory. Not least, I have felt great gratitude for everything that music can give—without music, life would indeed be much the poorer.

When I have talked about this investigation in various contexts, I have often been asked about my own strong music experiences. While the investigation was still ongoing, I have for the most part declined to answer that question, well aware that what I would then describe could influence what other people would want to tell.

But now that the investigation has been completed, I can allow myself to say something. I have had strong experiences when, as a youth, I played the organ in Varnhem's monastery church with its wonderful acoustics, sometimes at Christmas morning services with candles and a full church, sometimes on light summer evenings when all the tourists had finally left the church and I had the organ and church all to myself. I have experienced those 'magic moments' when everything in the playing goes by itself, when one is completely inside the music and can feel that one is flying with it, for example in Bach's great Prelude and Fugue in B minor or in the Dorian toccata that I practised intensely for the entrance examination to the Royal College of Music in Stockholm. The feeling of being in the midst of the music, of being enveloped by it, drowning in it—I have experienced this when I have sung the *St Matthew Passion* or when, late one evening, somewhere on the radio I heard one of the masterpieces of vocal polyphony and felt as if I flowed along in this mass of notes which never seemed to end and which I didn't want to end either. Messiaen's music, completely unique and separated from all other music, can make me disappear from the world and glimpse other realities, at the same time as in other pieces it can also be very concrete and down to earth.

I remember when my father one day at home discovered that I (then 6–7 years old) had absolute pitch, how he trained my organ playing every day and supervised my debut as organist at a church morning service when I was nine. I remember the Aha! experience in my youth when my big brother explained the form of the fugue and sonata to me, and much later how a teacher at the music college pointed out how Bach had made his 'simple' two-part inventions that I had played so many times without having given them a thought. I remember the strong impressions of Honegger's *Symphonie Liturgique* that he composed at the end of the Second World War and which I heard in Salzburg in 1957 when traces of the war could still be seen. I remember how organ professor Franz Sauer, while he was my teacher, smuggled me in backstage at the Festspielhaus in Salzburg, where we then could study at close range how Rafael Kubelik conducted Brahms's first symphony. And I remember the partly scandalous audience reactions ('*Schwein!*') that Ligeti met with after the premiere of his *Apparitions* at the ISCM festival in Cologne in 1960. Further musical highlights now and then are big band jazz, jazz piano, the swing of the Swedish nyckelharpa [keyed fiddle], African rhythms and voices, Latin American rhythms, tango (Argentine as well as Finnish), Indian ragas, and Roma Balkan music.

But, nevertheless, mostly the great masters whose music holds its own over the centuries. Just to mention two of them, Schubert and Bach. Schubert is indeed a miracle—how did he have time to create all these lieder, piano sonatas, string quartets, and symphonies during his short life of just 31 years?

And Bach . . . A good friend of mine called him 'the greatest therapist in history'. Nobel Prize laureate J. M. Coetzee has written that Bach's music 'comes as a gift, unearned, unmerited, for free'. He would like to speak to Bach and tell him 'how we still play your music, how we revere and love it, how we are absorbed and moved and fortified and made joyful by it. I would say: In the name of all mankind, please accept these words of tribute'.[20] I agree.

A DESCRIPTIVE SYSTEM FOR STRONG EXPERIENCES WITH MUSIC

1 GENERAL CHARACTERISTICS

1.1 Unique/fantastic/incredible/unforgettable experience
1.2 Hard-to-describe experience, words insufficient

2 PHYSICAL REACTIONS, BEHAVIOURS

2.1 Physiological reactions

General physical reaction in the body
Muscular tension/relaxation
Gooseflesh, piloerection, hair stands on end
Shivers, chills, thrills
Trembling, twitching, shaking
Palpitation of the heart, feel blood pulsating
Become warm, perspire, cheeks flushing
Changed breathing
Chest: feeling of pressure/burst/expansion/relief
Stomach: jitters/stabs/butterflies
Tears, crying
Lump in the throat
Feel dizzy, as if intoxicated
Feel sick, pain

2.2 Behaviours/actions

Close one's eyes
Open one's eyes/mouth wide
Smile, laugh, shout with joy
Sing, shout, scream
(Feel need to) Move, jump, swing, dance, clap one's hands
Become still, silent, immovable, interrupt other activities
Not give the show away, pretend to be unaffected
Withdraw, leave, feel need to be alone
Various others: rise, clench one's hand, keep hold of armrest
Performers (sometimes): Have difficulty in breathing, speaking, singing, playing

2.3 Quasi-physical reactions

Feel as if one's body is filled by/dissolved into music, rhythm, light, feelings
Feel light, weightless, as if the body is lifting/floating
Feel as if leaving one's body/the soul is leaving the body
Feel as if one's body expands/grows/shrinks
Feel as if being charged/led/controlled/carried away by the music

3 PERCEPTION

3.1 Auditory

Quality of sound, timbre
Loudness
Not a sound, complete silence
Acoustics: reverberation, diffusion of sound/music
Feeling surrounded by/enveloped by sound/music

3.2 Visual

General importance of visual impressions
Visual impressions of:
Musicians' appearance, behaviour, body language, instruments
Musicians' concentration, 'presence', commitment, joy in playing, charisma
Communication between musicians, between musicians and audience
The audience's behaviour and reactions
The premises, surroundings, nature, light effects, etc.

3.3 Tactile

Tactile sensations:
Generally in chest, midriff, on skin, in feet, legs, hands, arms, etc.

3.4 Kinaesthetic

Muscle tension/relaxation

3.5 Other senses

Sensations of smell, warmth, cold, etc.

3.6 Synaesthetic

Colour hearing
Other synaesthetic or synaesthetic-like sensations, e.g. light

3.7 Intensified perception, multimodal perception

Generally intensified perception
Intensified perception of sounds/notes/music/light/touch
Emphasis on importance of multimodal perception

3.8 Musical perception-cognition

Description of objective/technical qualities of the music
Description of objective/technical qualities of the performance

4 COGNITION

4.1 Changed/special attitude

Special openness, receptivity, expectancy, curiosity
(Performers: openness = expose oneself to the listeners' judgement)
Focused attention, complete absorption
(Performers: total focus on performance, 'give everything')
No thoughts, abandon analytical attitude
Strong feeling of just being/living here and now

4.2 Changed experience of situation, body–mind, time–space, parts–wholeness

Feeling of special atmosphere/mood
Lose consciousness of one's body/oneself, dissolution of ego
The surroundings disappear, be in one's own world
Changed experience of time and space
Experience of unreality, 'this is not true', like a dream
Experience of wholeness, everything fits together, seems simple, natural, self-evident
(Performers: Take on another ego, become another person on stage)

4.3 Loss of control

Be surprised, amazed
Be moved, touched, captivated
Be hit/struck, shaken, shocked, spellbound, paralysed, fascinated, as if intoxicated, 'mad', overwhelmed, on the verge of a breakdown
The music goes straight in, breaks through cognitive barriers, all resistance broken

4.4 Changed relation/attitude to the music

Feel (psychologically) surrounded by/enveloped by the music
Live the music, be drawn into the music, become one with the music, merge with the music (Performers: 'The music is inside me')
Feel directly addressed by the music, understand the music, the music feels simple, genuine, natural, self-evident
Performers surpass their usual capacity, 'somebody is playing me', feel oneself as listener rather than as performer

4.5 Associations, memories, thoughts, reflections, wishes

Relating to earlier experiences, people, situations, life, nature, etc.
Relating to the music: expectations, recognition (or not), reflections, wishes, etc.

4.6 Imagery

Inner images of landscape, nature, persons, situations, etc.
Dream oneself away
Imagine oneself as/identify oneself with the performer
Inner music afterwards
SEM elicited by imagined/inner music
SEM during composing of music

4.7 Musical cognition-emotion

Description of the music in cognitive/emotional terms
Description of the performance in cognitive/emotional terms

5 Feelings/emotions

5.1 Intense/powerful emotions

5.2 Positive feelings/emotions

Calm, harmony, peace, quiet
Security, warmth/goodness
Feeling little, insignificant, humble
Wonder, admiration, reverence, respect
Solemnity, patriotism
Feeling satisfied, content, saturated, possessed, grateful
Enjoyment, delight, sweetness, beauty
Joy, happiness, bliss, honour
Elation, excitement, (positive) tension, enthusiasm
Love, sexual feelings
Feeling of perfection, pride, greatness
Euphoria, as if intoxicated, rapture, ecstasy

5.3 Negative feelings/emotions

Feeling tired, faint, exhausted, 'empty'
Feeling lonely, abandoned, little, insignificant
Longing, (nostalgia)
Unhappiness, melancholy, sadness, depression
Confusion, nervousness, worry
Frustration, disappointment
Embarrassment, shame
Discomfort, (psychic) pain, jealousy, envy
Anxiety, fear, dread, despair, feeling broken-hearted, attacked, persecuted
Anger, fury/rage, hatred
Shock, horror, terror
Chaos, panic, unbearable

5.4 Different feelings/emotions

Many feelings, mixed feelings, conflicting feelings, changed feelings

6 EXISTENTIAL AND TRANSCENDENTAL ASPECTS

6.1 Existence

Meaning of human life/existence
Meaning of one's own life/existence
Intense feeling of life/living
Pure being
Feeling of unsurpassable/optimal/ultimate/holy moments in life
Changed view of life/existence

6.2 Transcendence

Magical/mysterious/supernatural/heavenly/spiritual experiences
Trance, ecstasy
Out-of-body experience
Experience of totality, e.g. the experience includes 'everything'
Cosmic experience, merge with something greater/endlessness/eternity
Experience of other worlds, other existences

6.3 Religious experience

General religious experience
Vision of heaven/life after this/paradise
Spiritual peace/harmony/fellowship
Holy/devout atmosphere/mood
Be addressed by religious/Christian message
Seeking/getting in contact with God in prayer, songs of praise
Contact/meeting with the divine/sacred, religious confirmation

7 PERSONAL AND SOCIAL ASPECTS

7.1 New possibilities, insights, needs

Become open/unreserved, defences/resistances broken
Reach new insights
One's own thoughts and feelings become clear
Reach one's innermost core/self
Feeling free, liberated, relaxed, inspired, enlivened, invigorated, reborn
Feeling uplifted, enriched, 'having grown/matured'
Internal cleansing, catharsis
Healing experience
Get consolation, help, hope, alleviation, relief, strength, courage, a kick
Feel need to keep/confirm/elicit/change feelings
Reluctant to break the experience, want to listen/play more/again

7.2 Music: new possibilities, insights, needs

Need for/interest in/changed view of music, generally
Need for/interest in certain type of music, certain music, certain composer,
certain performer, etc.
Want to learn or continue performing music
Get inspiration for own creativity
Choose music as a profession
Want to disseminate knowledge of music's benefits
Use music to affect one's mood, as therapy

7.3 Confirmation of identity, self-actualization

Feel need for/obtain confirmation
Feel chosen/directly addressed, 'they play solely for me'
The music reflects one's person, thoughts, and feelings
Increased self-confidence

7.4 Community, communication

Among listeners
Among performers
Between performers and listeners
With 'everybody', the whole of mankind

APPENDIX B

AN EXAMPLE OF ANALYSIS OF AN ACCOUNT

CHAPTER 17, ACCOUNT 17.2L

I looked forward curiously (4.1) to my first meeting with a band playing Finnish tango. It was in a pub crowded with people (3.2). There was no stage, so the band was standing at the same level as all the others and this gave another kind of community between musicians and audience (7.4). The band started and let their instruments whirl in fervent dramatic tango rhythms (4.7). Even then I was filled by a special feeling that the music began to take command of my body (2.3; 4.2). I was charged in a way (2.3). A tremendous feeling of harmony (5.2) which made me really enjoy the music (5.2), and I found it difficult to stand still (2.2).

But it was not until the second half of the performance that the mystery and the power (4.7) really gripped me (4.3). I was filled by an enormous warmth and heat (2.1). I really swallowed all the notes that were streaming out in the air, not a single note, effect or sequence missed my hungry ears (3.7). The music became so distinct (3.7). I was captivated by each of the instruments and what they had to offer me (3.7; 4.3). Nothing else existed! (4.1)

I was dancing, whirling (2.2), and really gave myself up to the music and the rhythms (4.4), overjoyed (5.2)—laughing (2.2). Tears came into my eyes (2.1)—however strange that may seem—and it was as a further sign, some kind of liberation. The music set me free from my sober everyday life (7.1). Now I could let my body parts dance as freely as they wanted (2.2)— just let them follow the rhythms and totally lose control (4.3).

The music danced around like a whirlwind (4.7) in the narrow room and all the dramatic sentiment that it conveyed (4.7) reflected my own situation in life (7.3)—but in a new way that I liked (5.2). I went hand in hand with the music (4.4). Afterwards I remained standing flushed with joy (5.2), as if intoxicated (5.2), and it was a real kick for me (7.1). I felt religious (6.3)— and the music was my god.

Before I was in a very bad state. Depressed (5.3). It was during the most critical time ever in my life. I found it hard to get on with people and had to really exert myself to be able to get to grips with things. Afterwards I was bouncy, giggling (2.2), lively and filled with deep joy (5.2).

It was really about a life-kick (7.1). There was also a kind of religious feeling. It was so bewildering that it almost felt as a salvation (6.3). It was as if I was selected to take part in such an experience when I needed it the most (7.3). I was filled by zest for life and suddenly had quite another view of the grey tomorrow (6.1, 7.1).

I think that you are extremely susceptible to strong experiences with music when you feel bad and weak (4.5). At least I was. This event became a kind of turning point in my life (6.1; 7.1). During the period after the experience it was very important. It helped to loosen all knots that I had within me so that instead of going even further into my depression I started to climb out of it (5.4; 7.1).

NOTES

CHAPTER 1 Introduction

(1) Recent surveys of music psychology are:

Thompson, W. F. (2009). *Music, thought, and feeling. Understanding the psychology of music.* Oxford: Oxford University Press.

Hallam, S., Cross, I., & Thaut, M. (eds) (2009). *The Oxford handbook of music psychology.* Oxford: Oxford University Press.

(2) Some studies of music in daily life are:

Clarke, E., Dibben, N., & Pitts, S. (2010). *Music and mind in everyday life.* Oxford: Oxford University Press.

DeNora, T. (2000). *Music in everyday life.* Cambridge, UK: Cambridge University Press.

Juslin, P. N., & Laukka, P. (2004). Expression, perception, and induction of musical emotions: A review and a questionnaire study of everyday listening. *Journal of New Music Research, 33,* 217–38.

Laukka, P. (2007). Uses of music and psychological well-being among the elderly. *Journal of Happiness Studies, 8,* 215–41.

North, A. C., Hargreaves, D. J., & Hargreaves, J. J. (2004). Uses of music in everyday life. *Music Perception, 22,* 41–77.

Sloboda, J. A., Lamont, A., & Greasley, A. (2009). Choosing to hear music. Motivation, process, and affect. In S. Hallam, I. Cross, & M. Thaut (eds), *The Oxford handbook of music psychology* (pp. 431–40). Oxford: Oxford University Press.

Sloboda, J. A., O'Neill, S. A., & Ivaldi, A. (2001). Functions of music in everyday life. An exploratory study using the Experience Sampling Method. *Musicae Scientiae, 5,* 9–32.

(3) James, W. (1902/1985). *The varieties of religious experience* (p. 39). Middlesex, UK: Penguin Books.

(4) Maslow, A. H. (1968). *Toward a psychology of being* (2nd edn, p. 71). New York: Van Nostrand Reinhold.

(5) Maslow, A. H. (1976). *The farther reaches of human nature* (p. 169). New York: Penguin Books.

(6) Maslow, A. H. (1968). *Toward a psychology of being* (2nd edn, Chapter 6, 'Cognition of being in peak experiences'). New York: Van Nostrand Reinhold.

(7) 'I think that the arts . . . are so close to our psychological and biological core . . . that rather than think of these courses as a sort of whipped cream or luxury, they must become

basic experiences in education. I mean that this kind of education can be a glimpse into the infinite, into ultimate values. This intrinsic education may very well have art education, music education, and dancing education as its core.' In Maslow, A. H. (1976), *The farther reaches of human nature* (p. 172).

(8) Panzarella, R. (1980). The phenomenology of aesthetic peak experiences. *Journal of Humanistic Psychology, 20,* 69–85.

The analysis of the individuals' accounts was made according to a division into 11 different response categories, such as attentional responses, sensations, motor responses, emotions, aesthetic judgements, and other cognitive reactions. These were then analysed using a statistical technique known as factor analysis, which makes it possible to find a number of fundamental dimensions in complex phenomena, in this case dimensions in 'intense joyous experience of listening to music'. 'Motor-sensory ecstasy' and 'fusion-emotional ecstasy' were salient in experiences with music, 'renewal ecstasy' was more salient in experiences with visual art, and 'withdrawal ecstasy' was about equally salient with both music and visual art.

(9) Laski, M. (1961). *Ecstasy: A study of some secular and religious experiences.* London: Cresset Press.

(10) Sloboda, J. A. (1990). Music as a language. In F. R. Wilson & F. L. Roehmann (eds), *Music and child development* (pp. 28–43). St Louis, Missouri: MMB Music. Reprinted in Sloboda, J. A. (2005), *Exploring the musical mind* (pp. 175–89). Oxford: Oxford University Press.

(11) See, for example, interviews with musicians in different genres of popular music in Boyd, J., & George-Warren, H. (1992). *Musicians in tune.* New York: Simon & Schuster.

(12) Privette, G. (1983). Peak experience, peak performance, and flow: A comparative analysis of positive human experiences. *Journal of Personality and Social Psychology, 45,* 1361–8.

Privette, G. (2001). Defining moments of self-actualization. Peak performance and peak experience. In K. J. Schneider, J. F. T. Bugental, & J. F. Pierson (eds), *The handbook of humanistic psychology* (pp. 161–80). London: Sage Publications.

Privette, G., & Landsman, T. (1983). Factor analysis of peak performance: the full use of potential. *Journal of Personality and Social Psychology, 44,* 195–200.

(13) Csikszentmihalyi, M. (1990). *Flow: The psychology of optimal experience.* New York: Harper & Row.

(14) Some studies focus on 'chills' or 'thrills' in strong experiences with music:

Goldstein, A. (1980). Thrills in response to music and other stimuli. *Physiological Psychology, 8,* 126–9.

Panksepp, J. (1995). The emotional sources of 'chills' induced by music. *Music Perception, 13,* 171–207.

Sloboda, J. A. (1991). Music structure and emotional response: Some empirical findings. *Psychology of Music, 19,* 110–20.

Further papers on 'chills/thrills' appear in Chapter 29, note 2.

(15) Discussion and examples of different types of relationship between perceived and felt emotion are given in the following papers:

Evans, P., & Schubert, E. (2008). Relationships between expressed and felt emotion in music. *Musicae Scientiae, 12,* 75–99.

Gabrielsson, A. (2001–2002). Emotion perceived and emotion felt: same or different? *Musicae Scientiae, Special Issue: Current Trends in the Study of Music and Emotion,* 123–47.

Kallinen, K., & Ravaja, N. (2006). Emotion perceived and emotion felt: Same and different. *Musicae Scientiae, 10,* 191–213.

CHAPTER 2 How the investigation was carried out

(1) Published articles, chapters, and theses in the SEM project are:

Antonsson, G., & Nilsson, K. (1991). *Starka musikupplevelser hos ungdomar i gymnasieåldern* [Strong experiences with music in high-school students]. Uppsala University: Department of Applied Psychology.

Berggren, S. (2001). *Starka musikupplevelser genom livet* [Strong experiences with music through life]. Uppsala University: Department of Psychology.

Boman, H. (1991). *Sång i kör. Stimulerande stämningsfull samhörighet* [Singing in choir. Stimulating moving togetherness]. Uppsala University: Department of Applied Psychology.

Gabrielsson, A. (1989). Intense emotional experiences of music. *Proceedings of The First International Conference on Music Perception and Cognition,* Kyoto, Japan, 17–19 October 1989 (pp. 371–6).

Gabrielsson, A. (1991). Experiencing music. *Canadian Music Educator, Research Edition, 33,* 21–6.

Gabrielsson, A. (1995). The study of music experience in music psychology. In M. Manturzewska, K. Miklaszewski, & A. Bialkowski (eds), *Psychology of music today* (pp. 25–8). Warsaw: Frederic Chopin Academy of Music.

Gabrielsson, A. (2001). Emotions in strong experiences with music. In P. N. Juslin and J. A. Sloboda (eds), *Music and emotion: Theory and research* (pp. 431–49). Oxford: Oxford University Press.

Gabrielsson, A. (2002). Old people's remembrance of strong experiences related to music. *Psychomusicology, 18,* 103–22.

Gabrielsson, A. (2006). Strong experiences elicited by music—What music? In P. Locher, C. Martindale, & L. Dorfman (eds), *New directions in aesthetics, creativity, and the psychology of art* (pp. 251–67). Amityville, NY: Baywood Publishing Company.

Gabrielsson, A. (2006). *Individuella starka musikupplevelser* [Individual strong experiences with music]. In G. Hermerén (ed.), *Konsterna och själen. Estetik ur ett humanvetenskapligt perspektiv* [The arts and the mind. Aesthetics from a humanistic perspective] (pp. 107–17). Stockholm: Kungliga Vitterhets, Historie och Antikvitets Akademien, Konferenser 61.

Gabrielsson, A. (2010). Strong experiences with music. In P. N. Juslin, & J. A. Sloboda (eds), *Handbook of music and emotion: Theory, research, applications* (pp. 547–74). Oxford: Oxford University Press.

Gabrielsson, A., & Lindström, S. (1992). *Esperienze musicali intense e loro implicazioni nello sviluppo personale* [Strong experiences with music and their implications for personal development]. In L. R. Pritoni (ed.) *La musicoterapia nelle sue implicazioni cliniche e psicopedagogiche* (pp. 11–18). Pisa, Italia: Edizioni del Cerro.

Gabrielsson, A. & Lindström, S. (1993). On strong experiences of music. *Jahrbuch der Deutschen Gesellschaft für Musikpsychologie, 10*, 118–39.

Gabrielsson, A. & Lindström, S. (1995). Can strong experiences of music have therapeutic implications? In R. Steinberg (ed.), *Music and the mind machine. The psychophysiology and psychopathology of the sense of music* (pp. 195–202). Berlin: Springer-Verlag.

Gabrielsson, A. & Lindström Wik, S. (2000). Strong experiences of and with music. In D. Greer (ed.), *Musicology and sister disciplines: Past, present and future* (pp. 100–8). Oxford: Oxford University Press.

Gabrielsson, A. & Lindström Wik, S. (2003). Strong experiences related to music: A descriptive system. *Musicae Scientiae, 7*, 157–217.

Grill, M. (1991). *Folkmusic—World music.* Uppsala University: Department of Applied Psychology.

Jansson, I. (2000). *Tidiga musikupplevelser* [Early experiences with music]. Uppsala University: Department of Psychology.

Lindström, S. (1989). *Sanslös sinnesnärvaro i tid och o-tid. En uppsats om starka musikupplevelser* [Senseless presence of mind in time and un-time]. Uppsala University: Department of Applied Psychology.

Lindström Wik, S. (2001). *Strong experiences related to music and their connection to religious experience.* Uppsala University: Department of Psychology.

Lundahl, M., & Sanner, I. (1990). *That's why I go for that rock 'n' roll music.* Uppsala University: Department of Psychology.

Löfstedt, A. C. (1999). *Upprymd, Omtumlad, Berörd. En uppsats om starka konstupplevelser* [Elated, bewildered, affected. An essay on strong experiences of visual art]. Uppsala University: Department of Psychology.

Ray, J. (1999). *Musikupplevelse—En kvalitativ studie* [The experience of music—A qualitative study]. Uppsala University: Department of Psychology.

Tchotoklieva, M. (1999). *Starka dansupplevelser* [Strong experiences with dance]. Uppsala University: Department of Psychology.

(2) Further descriptions of different parts in the analysis are given in

Gabrielsson, A., & Lindström Wik, S. (2003), Strong experiences related to music: A descriptive system. *Musicae Scientiae, 7*, 157–217.

CHAPTER 7   Merging with the music

(1) Stern, D. N. (1985). *The interpersonal world of the infant: A view from psychoanalysis and developmental psychology.* New York: Basic Books.

Stern, D. N. (2010). *Forms of vitality: Exploring dynamic experience in psychology, the arts, psychotherapy, and development.* Oxford: Oxford University Press.

CHAPTER 8   Feeling light, floating, leaving one's body

(1) After very careful examination of these six patients, the researchers speculated that out-of-body experiences and autoscopy (the experience of seeing one's own body in

extra-personal space) 'are related to a failure to integrate proprioceptive, tactile, and visual information with respect to one's own body (disintegration in personal space) and by a vestibular dysfunction leading to an additional disintegration between personal (vestibular) and extrapersonal (visual) space'. Both disintegrations 'are due to a paroxysmal cerebral dysfunction of the temporo-parietal junction in a state of partially and briefly impaired consciousness'. The quotations are from the following article:

Blanke, O., Landis, T., Spinelli, L., & Seeck, M. (2004). Out-of-body experience and autoscopy of neurological origin. *Brain, 127*, 243–58.

See further the following papers:

Blanke, O., Mohr, C., Michel, C. M., Pascual-Leone, A., Brugger, P., Seeck, M., Landis, T., & Thut, G. (2005). Linking out-of-body experience and self-processing to mental own-body imagery at the temporoparietal junction. *Journal of Neuroscience, 25*(3), 550–7.

Blanke, O., & Arzy, S. (2005). The out-of-body experience: Disturbed self-processing at the temporo-parietal junction. *The Neuroscientist, 11*(1), 16–24.

Tong, F. (2003). Out-of-body experiences: from Penfield to present. *Trends in Cognitive Sciences, 7:3*, 104–6.

Recently researchers have been able to induce out-of-body experiences in laboratory experiments by using certain combinations of simultaneous visual and tactile stimulation:

Ehrsson, H. H. (2007). The experimental induction of out-of-body experiences. *Science, 317*, 1048.

Petkova, V. I., & Ehrsson, H. H. (2008). If I were you: Perceptual illusion of body swapping. *PLoS ONE 3(12)*: e3832.

Lenggenhager, B., Tadi, T., Metzinger, T., & Blanke, O. (2007). Video ergo sum: Manipulating bodily self-consciousness. *Science, 317*, 1096–9.

Miller, G. (2007). Out-of-body experiences enter the laboratory. *Science, 317*, 1020–1.

CHAPTER 9 Inner music

(1) The proposal of four different stages in the creative process appeared in Graham Wallas (1926), *The art of thought* (London: Watts). The stages are: (a) preparation, (b) incubation, (c) illumination, and (d) verification. Wallas's proposal refers to creative activity in general and seems to fit quite well for the examples of composition that are found in our material. However, each creative process has its own special features that don't fit into one and the same pattern. A survey of different approaches in research on creativity, including discussion of the above-mentioned stages, appears in

Sawyer, R. K. (2006), *Explaining creativity. The science of human innovation*. Oxford: Oxford University Press.

Composing music is often associated with imagery of different kinds, above all auditory imagery of how the composed music may sound, sometimes also with visual and kinaesthetic/motoric imagery. Examples and discussion of this appear in the following paper:

Mountain, R. (2001). Composers and imagery: Myths and realities. In R. I. Godøy & H. Jørgensen (eds), *Musical imagery* (pp. 271–88). Lisse, The Netherlands: Swets & Zeitlinger.

Visual and kinaesthetic/motoric imagery appear occasionally in some accounts, for example: 'What is typical of such an inner hearing experience is that I think I can hear the entire piece—say it is ten minutes—in one minute. Together with the memory of the music, there is a visual memory. Much later I used this memory as the starting point for a movement in an orchestral piece' (in Chapter 9, account 9.2E); 'In connection with pieces I have composed, at an early stage (long before the ideas have reached the music paper) it has felt like after a walk in a long tunnel suddenly to be standing before a majestic crystal hall, filled with previously unheard music' (in Chapter 9, account 9.2F).

CHAPTER 10 Inner images

(1) Guided imagery with music (GIM) was proposed by Helen Bonny, American musician and music therapist, around 1970 and has since attracted much international attention in music therapy practice and theory.

Bonny, H. L., & Savary, L. M. (1973). *Music and your mind.* Barrytown, NY: Station Hill Press.

Bruscia, K. E., & Grocke, D. E. (eds) (2002). *Guided imagery and music: the Bonny method and beyond.* Gilsum, NH: Barcelona Publishers.

Körlin, D. (2005). *Creative arts therapies in psychiatric treatment: A clinical application of the Bonny method of guided imagery and music (BMGIM) and creative arts groups.* Stockholm: Karolinska Institute.

Summer, L. (ed.) (2002). *Music and consciousness: The evolution of guided imagery and music.* Gilsum, NH: Barcelona Publishers.

An attempt at finding possible relationships between factors in the musical structure and images coming up in a GIM session is described in Aksnes, H., & Ruud, E. (2008), Body-based schemata in receptive music therapy. *Musicae Scientiae, 12,* 49–74.

CHAPTER 11 Feelings and emotion

(1) I have described this chord in:

Gabrielsson, A. (2001), Emotions in strong experiences with music. In P. N. Juslin & J. A. Sloboda (eds), *Music and emotion: Theory and research* (pp. 431–49). Oxford: Oxford University Press.

(2) DeNora, T. (2000). *Music in everyday life.* Cambridge, UK: Cambridge University Press.

Laukka, P. (2007). Uses of music and psychological well-being among the elderly. *Journal of Happiness Studies, 8,* 215–41.

North, A. C., Hargreaves, D. J., & O'Neill, S. A. (2000). The importance of music to adolescents. *British Journal of Educational Psychology, 70,* 255–72.

Saarikallio, S., & Erkkilä, J. (2007). The role of music in adolescents' mood regulation. *Psychology of Music, 35,* 88–109.

Öblad, C. (2000). *Att använda musik—om bilen som konsertlokal* [Using music—The car as concert hall]. Publications from Department of Musicology, Gothenburg University, no. 63.

For a recent survey, see Sloboda, J., Lamont, A. & Greasly, A. (2009). Choosing to hear music. Motivation, process, and effect. In S. Hallam, I. Cross, & M. Thaut (eds), *The Oxford handbook of music psychology* (pp. 431–40). Oxford: Oxford University Press.

CHAPTER 13 Music and transcendence

(1) The meaning and use of the concepts 'trance' and 'ecstasy' vary between different languages and different authors. A thorough analysis of this is made in Rouget, G. (1985), *Music and trance: A theory of the relations between music and possession*, University of Chicago Press. Rouget regarded ecstasy and trance as opposite poles on a continuum with many levels in between. Some of his keywords for ecstasy were immobility, silence, solitude, and sensory deprivation, while the corresponding keywords for trance were movement, noise, in company, and sensory overstimulation. 'Whereas trance . . . is very frequently and very closely associated with music, ecstasy, as it has just been defined, never makes use of it at all . . . immobility, silence, and sensorial deprivation are incompatible with music' (pp. 11–12). According to Rouget, then, ecstasy does not occur in connection with music. However, many other authors discuss ecstasy in musical contexts and often with the meaning that Rouget associates with trance. In daily language it seems that both concepts are used in varying ways and without clear distinction.

Rouget provides a broad survey of the relation between music and trance in different cultures and during different epochs. This is also thoroughly discussed in Becker, J. (2004), *Deep listeners: Music, emotion and trancing*, Bloomington: Indiana University Press, with special reference to 'religious institutionalized trancing'. 'Deep listeners' are 'persons who are profoundly moved, perhaps even to tears, by simply listening to a piece of music' (p. 2). She quotes examples from our earlier published accounts of strong experiences with music (pp. 54–5) and claims that 'deep listening is a kind of secular trancing, divorced from religious practice but often carrying religious sentiments such as feelings of transcendence or a sense of communion with a power beyond oneself' (p. 2).

(2) The programme 'Ingmar Bergman and music' was broadcast by Swedish Television on Christmas Day 2000.

CHAPTER 16 Confirmation through music

(1) Different aspects of the relation between music and identity are discussed in:

MacDonald, R. A. R., Hargreaves, D. J., & Miell, D. (eds) (2002), *Musical identities*. Oxford: Oxford University Press.

MacDonald, R. A. R., Hargreaves, D. J., & Miell, D. (2009). Musical identities. In S. Hallam, I. Cross, & Thaut, M. (eds), *The Oxford handbook of music psychology* (pp. 462–70). Oxford: Oxford University Press.

Ruud, E. (1997) *Musikk og identitet* [Music and identity]. Oslo: Universitetsforlaget.

CHAPTER 17 Music as therapy

(1) A survey of investigations on how music listening may reduce physical pain is:

Standley, J. (1995). Music as a therapeutic intervention in medical and dental treatment: Research and clinical applications, in T. Wigram, B. Saperston, & R. West (eds), *The art and science of music therapy: A handbook* (pp. 3–22). Chur: Harwood Academic Publishers.

Music listening in connection with surgery is exemplified in:

Nilsson, U. (2003). The effect of music and music in combination with therapeutic suggestions on postoperative recovery. Linköping, Sweden: Linköping University.

(2) This piano concerto meant a relief for Rachmaninov himself. His first symphony was badly received (probably mainly due to a bad conductor), which made him very depressed. He asked for help from Dr Nikolay Dahl, who used hypnosis and gave Rachmaninov repeated suggestions to compose a piano concerto. Rachmaninov regained his creative joy and the result was his second piano concerto, perhaps his best known work and dedicated to Dr Dahl.

(3) Part of these explanations of the positive effects of music are also found in cancer patients' accounts of how they used music, especially spiritual music, during their illness, see

Ahmadi, F. (2006), *Culture, religion and spirituality in coping. The example of cancer patients in Sweden.* Uppsala: Acta Universitatis Upsaliensis, Studio Sociologica Upsaliensa 53.

CHAPTER 18 When performing music oneself

(1) This account was conveyed to me by Dr Bengt Ahlbeck.

(2) Performance anxiety in musicians—prevalence, symptoms, causes and ways of coping—is treated in:

Kenny, D. T. (2010). The role of negative emotions in performance anxiety. In P. N. Juslin & J. A. Sloboda (eds), *Handbook of music and emotion: Theory, research, applications* (pp. 425–51). Oxford: Oxford University Press.

Steptoe, A. (2001). Negative emotions in music making: the problem of performance anxiety. In P. N. Juslin & J. A. Sloboda (eds), *Music and emotion: Theory and research* (pp. 291–307). Oxford: Oxford University Press.

Valentine, E. (2002). The fear of performance. In J. Rink (ed.), *Musical performance: A guide to understanding* (pp. 168–82). Cambridge, UK: Cambridge University Press.

Wilson, G. D., & Roland, D. (2002). Performance anxiety. In R. Parncutt & G. E. McPherson (eds), *The science and psychology of music performance* (pp. 47–61). Oxford: Oxford University Press.

(3) This account appears in:

Wallner, B. (1988). 'Uppleva–Iaktta–Beskriva–Förmedla' [Experience–Observe–Describe–Convey] in F. V. Nielsen & O. Vinther (eds), *Musik—oplevelse, analyse og formidling* [Music—experience, analysis, and mediation] (pp. 173–92), Denmark: Egtved Edition.

(4) Similar accounts of magic moments with musicians performing popular music appear in:

Boyd, J., & George-Warren, H. (1992). *Musicians in tune*, New York: Simon & Schuster.

CHAPTER 19 Singing in a choir

(1) Several recent studies demonstrate physiological, psychological, and social benefits of choral singing:

Bailey, B. A., & Davidson, J. W. (2005). Effects of group singing and performance for marginalized and middle-class singers. *Psychology of Music, 33,* 269–303.

Chorus America (2009). *The Chorus Impact Study. How children, adults and communities benefit from choruses.* Washington, DC: Chorus America.

Clift, S., Hancox, G., Morrison, I., Hess, B., Kreutz, G., & Stewart, D. (2010). Choral singing and psychological well-being: Quantitative and qualitative findings from English choirs in a cross-national survey. *Journal of Applied Arts and Health, 1*(1), 19–34.

Cohen, G. (2009). New theories and research findings on the positive influence of music and art on health with ageing. *Arts & Health, 1* (1), 48–62.

Cohen, G. D., Perlstein, S., Chapline, J., Kelly, J., Firth, K. M., & Simmens, S. (2006). The impact of professionally conducted cultural programs on the physical health, mental health, and social functioning of older adults, *The Gerontologist, 46* (6), 726–34.

Grape, C., Theorell, T., Wikström, B. M., & Ekman, R. (2009). Choir singing and fibrinogen, VEGF, cholecystokinin and motilin in IBS patients. *Medical Hypotheses, 72,* 223–5.

Grape, C., Wikström, B. M., Hasson, D., Ekman, R., & Theorell, T. (2009). Saliva testosterone increases in choir singer beginners. *Psychotherapy and Psychosomatics, 79,* 196–8.

Kreutz, G., Bongard, S., Rohrmann, S., Hodapp, V., & Grebe, D. (2004). Effects of choir singing or listening on secretory immunoglobulin A, cortisol, and emotional state. *Journal of Behavioral Medicine, 27,* 623–35.

Chapter 24 Music from and in other cultures

(1) The question about musical universals is complicated for several reasons. Ultimately it depends on how you choose to define music—what should be considered music and what should not be considered music?

Proposals of plausible musical universals are, among others, that most music makes use of discrete pitch levels (rather than, say, glissando or microtones); that the octave constitutes a frame for construction of different scales; that the number of pitches within the octave usually is 7±2 (that is, 5–9); that melodies are dominated by small intervals; that you can perceive a regular pulse and metre (although to a varying degree); that there are rhythm patterns of varying length and complexity; and that melody contours and/or rhythm patterns are used as organizing principles (through repeating or varying these patterns at different pitch levels, in different tempos, etc).

It is, however, easy to find exceptions to these proposals, not least in a lot of art music from the twentieth century and nowadays. Furthermore, the above proposals only deal with factors regarding the musical structure. An interesting but still little investigated question is whether there are emotional universals, that is, whether there are general ways of expressing certain emotions (joy, sadness, anger, fear, etc.) in music regardless of culture.

For further discussion of musical universals, see:

Thompson, W. F., & Balkwill, L.-L. (2010), Cross-cultural similarities and differences. In P. N. Juslin, & J. A. Sloboda (eds), *Handbook of music and emotion: Theory, research, applications* (pp. 755–88). Oxford: Oxford University Press.

CHAPTER 25   Music at concerts: classical music

(1) The narrator says: 'When the orchestra had silenced, we in the audience sat quietly a long while. How long, I don't know.' Since I happened to record this concert on a cassette, from the radio broadcast, I know that the silence lasted 22 seconds before somebody dared to break it and start the applause.

(2) This account is taken from the article 'Musik för en fågel' [Music for a bird] by Naomi Lindh in the local newspaper *Upsala Nya Tidning*, 5 July 1996. Karl-Erik Welin, 1934–1992, was an internationally renowned composer, pianist, and organist, perhaps best known for his performances of avant-garde music as well as of instrumental theatre and happenings.

CHAPTER 29   Survey of all reactions

(1) The development of the descriptive system is briefly related in section 2.2 and in more detail in

Gabrielsson, A., & Lindström Wik, S. (2003). Strong experiences related to music: A descriptive system. *Musicae Scientiae, 7,* 157–217.

The disposition of the categories in Appendix A, and in this chapter, may look like a classification. However, I call it a descriptive system since the requirements for a classification cannot be fulfilled. A classification should preferably be exhaustive, that is, comprise all phenomena within the domain concerned, and its categories should be mutually exclusive, independent of each other. Neither of these requirements can be regarded as fulfilled. Although we have identified a large number of reactions, about 150 in all, there may, of course, be still other reactions in SEM that did not appear in the present investigation. Nor can the categories be regarded as mutually exclusive. As noted at several points in the text, the borders between different categories are fluid and some overlap may occur.

There are certain similarities between the categories in SEM and concepts used by the Danish musicologist and pedagogue Frede V. Nielsen. He discerns different layers of meaning in the musical object and their counterparts in listening experience. The layers extend from a superficial/acoustical layer to successively deeper layers associated with structure, kinaesthetic/motoric reactions, tension, emotion and spiritual-existential experience. Most of them can be said to have correspondences in the SEM descriptive system. His model and its possible consequences for musical education are discussed in:

Nielsen, F. V. (1998). *Almen musikdidaktik* [*General music didactics*]. Copenhagen: Akademisk Forlag.

(2) Craig, D. G. (2005). An exploratory study of physiological changes during chills induced by music. *Musicae Scientiae, 9,* 273–87.

Grewe, O., Nagel, F., Kopiez, R., & Altenmüller, E. (2007). Listening to music as a recreative process: Physiological, psychological and psychoacoustical correlates of chills and strong emotions. *Music Perception, 24,* 297–314.

Guhn, M., Hamm, A., & Zentner, M. (2007). Physiological and musico-acoustic correlates of the chill response. *Music Perception, 24,* 473–83.

Kone˘cni, V. J., Wanic, R. A., & Brown, A. (2007). Emotional and aesthetic antecedents and consequences of music-induced thrills. *American Journal of Psychology*, *120*, 619–43.

Nagel, F., Kopiez, R., Grewe, O., & Altenmüller, E. (2008). Psychoacoustical correlates of musically induced chills. *Musicae Scientiae*, *12*, 101–13.

Theories of music-induced chills/thrills are discussed in:

Huron, D. & Margulis, E. H. (2009), Musical expectancy and thrills, in P. N. Juslin & J. A. Sloboda (eds), *Handbook of music and emotion: Theory, research, applications* (pp. 575–604). Oxford: Oxford University Press.

(3) Visual impressions of musicians' commitment, joy in playing, and charisma have positive effects on listeners. Alternatively, if a musician seems 'absent' or uncommitted this has a negative influence: 'I hate listening to musicians who stand somewhere far away and poke at their instrument with an introverted expression on their faces' (in Chapter 7, account 7.5A). Performers who appear nervous or not fully competent may make the listeners feel worried: 'It often happens during concerts—if the musicians show a certain hesitation—that I worry how it will go. You get tense and focus your listening on the technicalities of the playing' (in Chapter 25, account 25.2X). Similar comments appear in Thompson, S. (2007), Determinants of listeners' enjoyment of a performance, *Psychology of Music*, *35*, 20–36.

Investigations into the role of vision in connection with live music and with audio-visually reproduced music (music videos, music programmes on television) have shown mixed outcomes, and many other factors have to be considered, such as the type of music, the listeners' familiarity with and attitude to the music. A survey of such studies and discussion of related topics appears in Finnäs, L. (2001), Presenting music live, audio-visually or aurally—does it affect listeners' experiences differently? *British Journal of Music Education*, *1ö*, 55–78.

(4) There is a rich literature on synesthesia of various types, its prevalence and possible background; for example:

Baron-Cohen, S., Burt, L., Smith-Laittan, F., Harrison, J., & Bolton, P. (1996). Synaesthesia: Prevalence and familiarity. *Perception* 25(9): 1073–9.

Cytowic, R. E. (2002). *Synesthesia: A Union of the Senses* (2nd edn). Cambridge, MA: MIT Press.

Cytowic, R. E., & Eagleman, D. M. (2009). *Wednesday is indigo blue: Discovering the brain of synesthesia*. Cambridge, MA: MIT Press.

Harrison, J. E., & Baron-Cohen, S. (1996). *Synaesthesia: Classic and contemporary readings*. Oxford: Blackwell Publishing.

Robertson, L., & Sagiv, N. (eds) (2005). *Synesthesia: Perspectives from cognitive neuroscience*. Oxford: Oxford University Press.

Ward, J. (2008). *The frog who croaked blue: Synesthesia and the mixing of the senses*. Oxford: Routledge.

(5) Experiences of light in intense religious experiences are related in several works; for instance:

Paper, J. D. (2004). *The mystic experience: a descriptive and comparative analysis*. Albany: State University of New York Press.

Geels, A. (1991). *Att möta Gud i kaos. Religiösa visioner i dagens Sverige* [*Meeting God in chaos. Religious visions in today's Sweden*]. Stockholm: Norstedts.

Experiences of light in near-death experiences are discussed in Blackmore, S. (1993), *Dying to live: Science and the near-death experience*, London: Grafton.

(6) The relationship between music and emotion is extensively treated in

P. N. Juslin & J. A. Sloboda (eds) (2010), *Handbook of music and emotion: Theory, research, applications*, Oxford: Oxford University Press.

Two chapters in this volume of special relevance in the present context are:

Sloboda, J. A., & Juslin, P. N., At the interface between the inner and outer world—psychological perspectives (ibid., pp. 73–97).

Juslin, P. N., Liljeström, S., Västfjäll, D., & Lundqvist, L.-O., How does music evoke emotions? Exploring the underlying mechanisms (ibid., pp. 605–42).

A related work is Juslin, P. N. & Västfjäll, D. (2008), Emotional responses to music: The need to consider underlying mechanisms, *Behavioral and Brain Sciences*, *31*, 559–75.

Questions about musical emotions are also much discussed in Becker, J. (2004), *Deep listeners. Music, emotion and trancing*, Bloomington, Indiana: Indiana University Press.

(7) Similar results—positive experiences increase the willingness to occupy oneself with music in the future, whereas negative experiences have the opposite effect—are reported in

Sloboda, J. (2005), *Exploring the musical mind* (Chapter 9, pp. 175–89), Oxford: Oxford University Press.

In a comprehensive Polish study— Manturzewska, M. (1990), A biographical study of the lifespan development of professional musicians, *Psychology of Music*, *18*, 112–39 — prominent musicians told that they remembered intense experiences of music during childhood and spoke in great detail about the music and how it was performed, memories that remained for their whole lives.

(8) The results of the questionnaire are reported in Gabrielsson, A. & Lindström Wik, S. (2003), Strong experiences related to music: A descriptive system, *Musicae Scientiae*, *7*, 157–217. It includes a comparison between the results based on the narrators' accounts and the results of the questionnaire.

CHAPTER 30   Music in SEM

(1) Conway, M. A., & Holmes, A. (2004). Psychosocial stages and the accessibility of autobiographical memories across the life cycle. *Journal of Personality*, *72*, 461–80.

Rubin, D. C., Rahhal, T. A., & Poon, L. W. (1998). Things learned in early adulthood are remembered best. *Memory & Cognition*, *26*, 3–19.

Schulkind, M. D., Hennis, L. K., & Rubin, D. C. (1999). Music, emotion, and autobiographical memory: They're playing your song. *Memory & Cognition*, 27, 948–55.

CHAPTER 32   Causes, consequences, and importance

(1) Gabrielsson, A., & Lindström, E. (2010). The role of structure in the musical expression of emotions. In P. N. Juslin & J. A. Sloboda (eds), *Handbook of music and emotion: Theory, research, applications* (pp. 367–400). Oxford: Oxford University Press.

(2) That the experience may be especially strong at a certain passage in the music can probably be confirmed by many listeners. A recent study—Rozin, A., Rozin, P., & Goldberg, E. (2004) The feeling of music past: How listeners remember musical affect, *Music Perception*, 22, 15–39—showed that the emotional impression (memory) of the music was related to (a) the passage in the piece that had highest emotional intensity, further to (b) how the piece ended, and to (c) passages of high emotional intensity that came after passages of low emotional intensity (contrast effect).

(3) Gabrielsson, A., & Juslin P. N. (2003). Emotional expression in music. In R. J. Davidson, K. R. Scherer, & H. H. Goldsmith (eds), *Handbook of affective sciences* (pp. 503–34). New York: Oxford University Press.

Juslin, P. N., & Timmers, R. (2010). Expression and communication of emotion in music performance. In P. N. Juslin & J. A. Sloboda (eds), *Handbook of music and emotion: Theory, research, applications* (pp. 453–89). Oxford: Oxford University Press.

(4) Little is known about how different traits of personality may affect strong experiences with music. Some comments are found in the following works:

Whaley, J., Sloboda, J. A. & Gabrielsson, A. (2009). Peak experience in music. In S. Hallam, I. Cross, & M. Thaut (eds), *The Oxford handbook of music psychology* (pp. 452–61). Oxford: Oxford University Press.

Fachner, J. (2007). Music and altered states of consciousness: An overview. In D. Alridge & J. Fachner (eds), *Music and altered states: Consciousness, transcendence, therapy and addictions* (pp. 15–37), London: Jessica Kingsley Publishers.

(5) An interesting parallel is that religious visions often occur when the individual is in a difficult situation of life. Religion psychologist Antoon Geels has proposed a model for the relationship between crises and visions meaning that the vision creates order in a chaotic psychological system; see Geels, A. & Wikström, O. (1999), *Den religiösa människan. En introduktion till religionspsykologin [The religious man. An introduction to the psychology of religion]* (Chapter 5), Stockholm: Natur och Kultur. It seems that a strong experience with music may work in a similar way, for instance, elicit new insights and new possibilities in somehow critical situations (cf. Chapters 16 and 17).

(6) Juslin, P. N., Liljeström, S., Västfjäll, D., & Lundqvist, L.-O. (2010). How does music evoke emotions? Exploring the underlying mechanisms. In P. N. Juslin & J. A. Sloboda (eds), *Handbook of music and emotion: Theory, research, applications* (pp. 605–42). Oxford: Oxford University Press.

Juslin, P. N., & Västfjäll, D. (2008). Emotional responses to music: The need to consider underlying mechanisms. *Behavioral and Brain Sciences*, 31, 559–75.

CHAPTER 33 Overview, comparisons, questions, outlooks

(1) Such a comparison appears in Gabrielsson, A. (2011). How do strong experiences with music relate to experiences in everyday listening to music? In I. Deliège & J. Davidson (eds), *Music and the mind: Essays in honour of John Sloboda* (Chapter 6). Oxford: Oxford University Press.

(2) The experiment is described in Lowis, M. J. (1998). Music and peak experiences: An empirical study, *The Mankind Quarterly*, *39*, 203–24. It showed that listeners indicated more 'peaks' in listening to 'upbeat music' than when listening to 'gentle music'. Various problems with investigating peak experience under experimental conditions are discussed.

(3) Tchotoklieva, M. (1999). *Starka dansupplevelser* [*Strong experiences with dance*]. Uppsala University: Department of Psychology.

(4) Löfstedt, A. C. (1999). *Upprymd, Omtumlad, Berörd. En uppsats om starka konstupplevelser* [Elated, bewildered, affected: An essay on strong experiences of visual art]. Uppsala University: Department of Psychology.

(5) Lindström Wik, S. (2001). *Strong experiences related to music and their connection to religious experience.* Uppsala University: Department of Psychology. References in this thesis include, among others, the following works:

Argyle, M. (1990). The psychological explanation of religious experience. *Psyke & Logos, 11,* 267–74.

Hardy, A. (1980). *The spiritual nature of man.* New York: Oxford University Press.

Hay, D. (1990). *Religious experience today. Studying the facts.* London: Mowbray.

Hills, P., & Argyle, M. (1998). Musical and religious experiences and their relationship to happiness. *Personality and Individual Differences, 25,* 91–102.

James, W. (1902/1985). *The varieties of religious experience.* Harmondsworth, Middlesex, England: Penguin Books.

Laski, M. (1961). *Ecstasy. A study of some secular and religious experiences.* London: Cresset Press.

Stace, W. T. (1960). *Mysticism and philosophy.* New York: Lippincott.

Similarities between religious-mystical and aesthetic experiences are also discussed and investigated in Stange, K., & Taylor, S. (2008).Relationship of personal cognitive schemas to the labeling of a profound emotional experience as religious-mystical or aesthetic, *Empirical Studies of the Arts, 26,* 37–49. The authors claim that when strong emotional experiences are described as religious/mystical or as aesthetic, this reflects the person's own religious or artistic/aesthetic commitment.

(6) Geels, A. (1991). *Att möta Gud i kaos. Religiösa visioner i dagens Sverige* [*Meeting God in chaos. Religious visions in today's Sweden*]. Stockholm: Norstedts.

Geels, A. (2008). The night is the mother of day. In J. A. Belzen & A. Geels (eds), *Autobiography and the psychological study of religious lives* (pp. 95–114). Amsterdam–New York: Rodopi.

(7) Further discussion of autobiographical memories and SEM appears in Gabrielsson, A. & Lindström Wik, S. (2003), Strong experiences related to music: A descriptive system. *Musicae Scientiae, 7,* 157–217.

(8) Ray, J. (2004). *Musikaliska möten man minns. Om musikundervisningen i årskurserna sju till nio som en arena för starka musikupplevelser* [*Memorable musical encounters. About music education for teenage pupils in compulsory school as an arena for strong experiences related to music*]. Åbo: Åbo Akademis Förlag. (with English summary)

(9) Sloboda, J. (2005). *Exploring the musical mind* (Chapter 9, pp. 175–89). Oxford: Oxford University Press.

Low prevalence of music experiences in school settings is also reported by Finnäs (see note 10 below).

(10) Finnäs, L. (2006). Ninth-grade pupils' significant experiences in aesthetic areas: the role of music and of different basic modes of confronting music. *British Journal of Music Education, 23*, 315–31.

(11) These quotes are taken from D. Alridge & J. Fachner (eds) (2007). *Music and altered states. Consciousness, transcendence, therapy and addictions* (pp. 12 and 16). London: Jessica Kingsley Publishers.

(12) Rouget, G. (1985). *Music and trance: A theory of the relations between music and possession.* Chicago: Chicago University Press.
Becker, J. (2004). *Deep listeners: Music, emotion and trancing.* Bloomington, IN: Indiana University Press.

(13) Szabó, C. (2007). The effects of listening to monotonous drumming on subjective experiences. In D. Alridge & J. Fachner (eds) (2007). *Music and altered states: Consciousness, transcendence, therapy and addictions* (pp. 51–9). London: Jessica Kingsley Publishers.

When interpreting these results, one should perhaps notice the fairly widespread notion that monotonous drumming leads to some kind of altered consciousness. The subjects in the group that listened to drum rhythms may have had or felt certain expectations that they would react in a special manner. Judith Becker emphasizes that trance behaviour is often learned in a way that is special/acceptable within the culture in question; see Becker, J. (2004). *Deep listeners—Music, emotion and trancing* (pp. 41–3), Bloomington: Indiana University Press.

(14) Vaitl, D., Bierbaumer, J., Gruzelier, J., Jamieson, G.A, Kotchoubey, B., Kübler, A., et al. (2005). Psychobiology of altered states of consciousness. *Psychological Bulletin, 131*, 98–127.

(15) A basic paper on absorption as a personality trait is Tellegen, A., & Atkinson, G. (1974). Openness to absorbing and self-altering experiences ('absorption'), a trait related to hypnotic susceptibility, *Journal of Abnormal Psychology, 83*, 268–77.

Some later works on absorption are discussed in D. Alridge & J. Fachner (eds) (2007). *Music and altered states. Consciousness, transcendence, therapy and addictions* (pp. 23–7), London: Jessica Kingsley Publishers.

(16) Becker, J. (2004). *Deep listeners. Music, emotion and trancing.* Bloomington, IN: Indiana University Press.
Blood, A. J., & Zatorre, R. J. (2001). Intense pleasurable responses to music correlate with activity in brain regions implicated in reward and emotion. *Proceedings of the National Academy of Sciences of the United States of America 98* (20): 11818–23.
Menon, V., & Levitin, D. J. (2005). The rewards of music listening: Response and physiological connectivity of the mesolimbic system. *NeuroImage, 28*, 175–84.
Patel, A. P. (2008). *Music, language, and the brain.* Oxford: Oxford University Press.
Peretz, I., & Zatorre, R. J. (eds) (2003). *The cognitive neuroscience of music.* New York: Oxford University Press.
Peretz, I., & Zatorre, R. J. (2005). Brain organization for music processing. *Annual Review of Psychology, 56*, 89–114.

Sacks, O. (2007). *Musicophilia. Tales of music and the brain,* New York: Alfred A. Knopf.

It may also be interesting to follow the development of two recently appearing disciplines, neuroaesthetics and neurotheology, aimed at investigating the possible neurological background of aesthetic experience and of spiritual/religious experience.

(17) A condensed and critical survey of the concept of sublime and its relations to findings in empirical research is given in Bicknell, J. (2009). *Why music moves us,* Basingstoke, UK: Palgrave Macmillan.

For further discussion see, for example:

Keltner, D., & Haidt, J. (2003). Approaching awe, a moral, spiritual, and aesthetic emotion. *Cognition and Emotion, 17,* 297–314.

Kone˘cni, V. J. (2005). The aesthetic trinity: Awe, being moved, thrills. *Bulletin of Psychology and the Arts, 5,* 27–44.

(18) Some suggestions for further reading:

Becker, J. (2004). *Deep listeners. Music, emotion and trancing.* Bloomington, IN: Indiana University Press.

Becker, J. (2009). Exploring the habitus of listening. Anthropological perspectives. In P. N. Juslin & J. A. Sloboda (eds), *Handbook of music and emotion: Theory, research, applications* (pp. 127–57). Oxford: Oxford University Press.

Bicknell, J. (2009). *Why music moves us.* Basingstoke, UK: Palgrave Macmillan.

Brown, S. & Volgsten, U. (eds) (2006). *Music and manipulation. On the social uses and social control of music.* New York: Berghahn Books.

Davies, S. (1994). *Musical meaning and expression.* Ithaca, NY: Cornell University Press.

DeNora, T. (2000). *Music in everyday life.* Cambridge, UK: Cambridge University Press.

Patel, A. P. (2008). *Music, language, and the brain.* Oxford: Oxford University Press.

Stern, D. N. (2010). *Forms of vitality. Exploring dynamic experience in psychology, the arts, psychotherapy, and development.* Oxford: Oxford University Press.

Stock, K. (ed) (2007). *Philosophers on music. Experience, meaning, and work.* Oxford: Oxford University Press.

Wallin, N., Merker, B., & Brown, S. (eds) (2000). *The origins of music.* Cambridge, MA: MIT Press.

(19) For psychologists SEM offers many interesting possibilities to study phenomena in different areas, such as:

mood management and different theories in emotion psychology

autobiographical memories, their relation to emotions and their importance for shaping of personal identity

different kinds of altered states of consciousness, including their relation to personality traits as absorption and sensation seeking

communication, audience reactions, 'mass psychosis', etc. within social psychology

different kinds of (psycho)therapy that may include music and other arts

generally, studies of strong experiences and their importance for the individual.

(20) Coetzee, J. M. (2007). *Diary of a bad year* (p. 221). London: Penguin Books.

INDEX

Note: This index contains the names of artistes, ensembles (in italics), researchers, and other persons mentioned in the main text. Those persons mentioned only in the Notes are not included.

Adam, Adolphe 29, 411, 416
Adams, George 342, 410, 416
Adolf Fredrik Bach Choir 89, 415
Ahronovitch, Yuri 79, 85, 151, 152, 313, 415
Åkerström, Fred 415
Albinoni, Tomaso 216, 281, 411
Alfvén, Hugo 411, 415
Alhanko, Anneli 453
Alien 417
Almeido, Laurindo 123
Almlöf, Kalle 416
Althén, Ragnar 323
Amanda Choir 415
Anderson, Marian 44, 203, 415
Andersson, Benny 410
Andersson, Micke 124
Animals 417
Armstrong, Louis 33, 46, 49, 416
Aruhn, Britt Marie 326, 415
Ashkenazy, Vladimir 332, 415
Asta Kask 55, 417
Attenborough, David 52
Ayler, Albert 234–235, 366, 410, 416

Babs, Alice 24, 141, 416
Bach Choir (London) 256
Bach, J. S. 17, 18, 19, 50, 52–53, 78, 89, 96,
   124, 126, 132, 155, 160, 162, 163, 168,
   170, 172, 178, 216, 223, 227–228, 241,
   247, 255–256, 276, 279, 299, 309, 332,
   356, 357, 359, 360, 362, 363, 364, 366,
   371, 410, 411, 415, 427, 429, 430, 432,
   434, 437, 445, 461
Backhaus, Wilhelm 214
Baker, Chet 339, 416
Baker, Janet 415
Bamberger, Carl 276
Barber, Samuel 89, 359, 411, 432
Barere, Simon 45
Bartók, Bela 50, 67, 220, 334, 409, 410, 411, 432
Basia 85, 362, 418
Basie, Count 416
Beatles, The 26, 65, 69, 264, 346–347, 350, 417
Bechet, Sidney 196, 416
Becker, Judith 450, 458, 459, 477, 482, 485, 486

Beethoven, Ludwig van 16, 20, 21, 44, 70, 76, 77,
   85, 93, 94, 130, 163, 166, 181, 200, 214, 216,
   240, 290–291, 292, 306, 333, 356, 358, 361,
   380, 381, 409, 410, 411, 426, 437, 445
Bellini, Vincenzo 126, 327, 357, 411
Bellman, Carl Michael 417
Bellson, Louis (Louie) 341, 416
Berg, Alban 220, 411
Bergman, Ingmar 168, 170, 175, 477
Berigan, Bunny 48, 416
Berlin Philharmonic 277, 426
Berlioz, Hector 178, 320, 321, 411
Bernstein, Leonard 410
Best, Martin 330–331, 410, 415
Bird, Charlie 123
Bizet, Georges 126, 272, 317, 411
Bjørgum, Torleiv 416
Björling, Jussi 26, 216, 287, 322–324, 376, 415
Björling, Sigurd 204, 287, 415
Black Sabbath 417
Blomdahl, Karl-Birger 411
Blood, Sweat and Tears 341, 416
Bon Jovi 417
Bonny, Helen 119, 476
Bono 182
Borodin, Alexander 324, 411
Boström, Tomas 179, 415
Bowie, David 194, 239, 417
Boye, Karin 453
Bragg, Billy 351, 410, 417
Brahms, Johannes 14, 16, 63, 83, 86, 129, 163, 201,
   241, 245, 252, 275–276, 306, 324, 328, 334,
   362, 410, 411, 415, 430, 437, 445, 461
Brel, Jaques 404, 418
Britten, Benjamin 411, 415
Brown, Cameron 342
Bruch, Max 18, 156, 162, 411
Bruckner, Anton 411
Budd, Harold 266, 357
Bull, Ole 34, 35, 418
Bumbry, Grace 126
Busch, Fritz 415

Cage, John 137, 138, 411, 426
Callas, Maria 448

Carpenter, Mary Chapin 33, 417
Carreras, José 329, 415
Carter, Betty 337, 361, 416
Celibidache, Sergiu 306, 415
Chicago 417
Chicago Symphony Orchestra 175
Chopin, Frédéric 16–17, 45, 63, 108, 141, 164,
    210, 214, 291, 332, 410, 411, 427
Chung, Kyung-Wha 162
Cimarosa, Domenico 411
Clapton, Eric 351–352, 417
Clooney, Rosemary 52
Cock Robin 271, 417
Coetzee, J. M. 461, 486
Cogan, Alma 416
Cohen, Leonard 418
Collins, Phil 267, 417, 434
Coltrane, John 138, 337, 377, 416, 428
Como, Perry 52
Corea, Chick 416
Corelli, Arcangelo 195
Coulter, Phil 417
Csikszentmihalyi, Mihaly 5, 107,
    225, 451, 472
Cult 417
Cure 417

Dahlgren, Eva 418
Dahlin, Jacob 142
Davis, Miles 138, 337, 416, 428
Dax, Danielle 348, 359, 360, 410, 417
de Falla, Manuel 412
de Frumerie, Gunnar 412
de Los Angeles, Victoria 415
Debussy, Claude 411
Delirious 178–179
Delta Rhythm Boys 416
Depeche Mode 37, 417
di Bondone, Giotto 453
Dire Straits 201, 269, 417
Dizzy Gillespie's Big Band 361
Docenterna 417
Domnérus, Arne 417
Donizetti, Gaetano 411
Dostoyevsky, Fyodor 453
Driscoll, Phil 175
Duran Duran 141, 417
Dvořák, Antonín 145, 195, 201, 224, 306,
    356, 366, 410, 411

E Street Band 39, 154
East, Nathan 352
Edlund, Swante 117, 411
Egebjer, Lars 216
Ehrling, Sixten 291, 415
Ehrling, Thore 49
Ekelöf, Gunnar 453

Elgar, Edward 127, 253, 411
Eliasberg, Karl 313
Ellegaard, France 291
Ellington, Duke 416
Éluard, Paul 314
Eno, Brian 169, 170, 194, 417
Ericson, Eric 309, 415
Erikson, Greta 85–86, 415
E-type 65, 234
Europe 417
Eurythmics 334
Evans, Gil 416

Fame, Georgie 417
Fanshawe, David 80, 412
Farmer, Art 286, 416
Farncombe, Charles 415
Fauré, Gabriel 96, 152, 379, 412, 415
Feidman, Giora 147
Ferrier, Kathleen 161, 415
Filarfolket 416
Finnäs, Leif 457, 481, 485
Finnilä, Birgit 415
Fischer, Annie 21, 415
Fischer-Dieskau, Dietrich 78, 168, 415
Fitzgerald, Ella 416
Fjedur 416
Flamingo Quartet 418
Flotow, Friedrich von 324
Flynn, Errol 49
Franck, César 86, 412, 415, 429
Fredriksson, Marie 57, 417
Fresk Quartet 53–54, 415
Fröding, Gustaf 327
Frykberg, Sten 47
Furtwängler, Wilhelm 163, 415, 426

Gabrielsson, Alf 473–474, 476, 480,
    482, 483, 484
Gade, Jacob 404, 418
Garaguly, Carl 108, 131, 415
Garfunkel, Art 108–109, 418
Garner, Erroll 75, 143
Gävleborg County Orchestra Society 24, 25
Gävleborg Symphony Orchestra 310
Gedda, Nicolai 317, 415
Geels, Antoon 455, 481, 483, 484
Geldof, Bob 141
Genesis 156, 214, 417
George Adams Quartet 342–343, 359
Gershwin, George 412
Gillespie, Dizzy 50, 416
Gilmore, David 349
Giordano, Umberto 324
Glass, Philip 130, 362, 412
Gluck, Christoph Willibald 412, 415
Goodman, Benny 49, 336, 416

Górecki, Henryk Mikołaj 261, 262, 412
Gösta Ohlin's Vocal Ensemble 415
Gothenburg Radio Orchestra 47
Gothenburg Symphony Orchestra 53, 291
Gounod, Charles 412, 415
Grieg, Edvard 23, 281, 356, 410, 412
Grimes, Peter 49
Grünewald, Isaac 81
Gudmundsson, Per 416
Gullberg, Hjalmar 251, 257
Guns N' Roses 38, 200, 417
Gustafsson, Rune 417
Gyllene Tider 417

Hadzidhakis, Manos 197, 359
Hagegård, Håkan 317, 327, 415
Hägg, Gustav 216, 412
Häggkvist, Carola 37, 417
Haitto, Heimo 47
Hallberg, Bengt 340, 417, 423
Hammarskjöld, Dag 278
Hammerstein II, Oscar 418
Handel, George Frideric 16, 19, 89, 123, 172,
        173, 192, 254, 278, 360, 363, 409, 410,
        411, 412, 415, 434
Handy, W.C. 50
Harnoncourt, Nikolaus 172
Harris, Emmylou 59, 417
Haskil, Clara 331, 415
Hawkins, Coleman 84, 416
Haydn, Franz Joseph 333–334, 412, 415
Heifetz, Jascha 48, 76, 415
Helmersson, Frans 19, 333, 415
Hemmingson, Merit 197, 417
Hendricks, Barbara 129, 216, 328, 415
Hiatt, John 417
Hitler, Adolf 125
Hjärtslag [Heartbeat] band 55, 341, 359
Holgersson, Nils 117
Hollies 26, 417
Honegger, Arthur 220, 412, 461
Houston, Whitney 42, 417
Howard, Leslie 49

I Musici di Roma 114, 415
Idenstam, Gunnar 126, 415
Ikeda, Carlotta 152
Imperiet 417

Jackson, Joe 417, 433
Jackson, Mahalia 416
Jackson, Michael 41–42, 417
James, William 2, 454–455, 471, 484
Janáček, Leoš 306, 424
Jansson, Tove 274, 418, 435
Jarre, Jean Michel 417
Jarrett, Keith 428

Järvi, Neeme 333
Jenkins, Gordon 337
Jernberg, Anton 416
Johansson, Jan 340
Jones, Howard 417
Jones, Quincy 416
Jönsson, Gabriel 418
Jularbo, Carl 418

Karas, Anton 418
Katchen, Julius 16
Kebnekajse 417
Ketelbey, Albert 24, 418
Khachaturian, Aram 412
Khan, Imrat 299
King, B. B. 416
Kinks, The 26–27, 417
KISS 59–60, 150, 417, 435
Kitaro 112, 417
Knopfler, Mark 417
Kodály, Zoltán 148, 180, 412, 415, 434, 459
Koinonia 416
Körberg, Tommy 415
Kreisler, Fritz 23, 48, 415
Kubelik, Rafael 135, 461

Lagerlöf, Selma 118, 453
Lanza, Mario 415
Larsson, Lars-Erik 154, 155, 166, 287, 358,
        361, 410, 412
Laski, Marghanita 4, 451, 472, 484
Leander, Zarah 142, 415
Led Zeppelin 80, 377, 417, 426
Lehár, Franz 412
Leningrad Philharmonic 313, 424
Leygraf, Hans 415, 430
Lidman, Sara 453
Ligeti, György 220, 461
Lindberg, Oskar 412
Lindgren, Torgny 453
Lindh, Björn J:son 269, 417
Lindman, Erik 116–117
Lindström Wik, Siv 455, 473–474, 480, 482, 484
Liszt, Franz 294, 320, 321, 324, 410, 412
Liungman, Karin 275, 404, 417
Lloyd Webber, Andrew 135, 167, 170,
        183, 410, 415
London Philharmonic Orchestra 256
Lott, Felicity 330, 357, 410, 415, 429
Lotti, Antonio 412, 415
Lucena, Carmen 202
Lumbye, H. C. 92, 210, 404, 418
Lundell, Ulf 417
Lundsten, Ralph 167, 170, 275, 286, 361, 410
Lupu, Radu 318
Lutoslawski, Witold 412
Lynn, Vera 49

McCartney, Paul 346–347, 417
McLaughlin, John 416
McRae, Carmen 416
Mahler, Gustav 135, 136, 140, 151, 152, 161, 175,
     204, 240, 241–242, 317, 319, 357, 362, 377,
     380, 410, 412, 425, 429, 430, 432, 437, 448
Makeba, Miriam 417
Malaria 138, 139, 417, 426
Malmö Symphony Orchestra 46
Malotte, Albert Hay 240, 415
Mandel, Johnny 153, 286, 416
Marley, Bob 88, 417
Martin, Frank 412, 415
Maslow, Abraham 3, 4, 5, 451, 471–472
Massenet, Jules 268, 329, 412
Matt Bianco 85
Mehler, Friedrich 79, 412
Mendelssohn, Felix 57, 195, 216, 220, 410, 412, 415
Menza, Louis 341
Mercadante, Saverio 413
Mertens, Wim 194, 413
Messiaen, Oliver 380, 413, 415, 461
Metallica 417
Metheny, Pat 416
Miller, Glenn 49
Milstein, Nathan 415
Mingus, Charles 416
Mitchell, Red 287, 417
Modern Jazz Quartet 416
Möller, Ale 416
Möller, Eva 153, 202
Moondog 417
Moore, Gary 417
Moraeus, Olle 416
Morthenson, Jan 128, 315, 413
Motorhead 417
Mouskori, Nana 197
Mozart, Wolfgang Amadeus 19, 47, 48, 129, 132,
     147, 157, 165, 166, 170, 192, 197, 210, 214, 216,
     226, 241, 265, 324, 328, 329, 331, 356, 357,
     360, 363, 367, 380, 410, 413, 415, 428, 429,
     430, 437
Mulligan, Gerry 286, 416
Munch, Edvard 164
Musorgsky, Modest 413
Mutter, Anne-Sophie 333, 415

Nielsen, Carl 132, 279, 413
Nietzsche, Friedrich 445
Nilsson, Birgit 93, 324, 325, 326, 415
Nilsson, Torsten 185, 413
Nirvana 148
Noack, Kurt 28, 404, 418, 423
Nordqvist, Gustaf 173, 204, 287, 323, 413
Nordström, Bengt 'Frippe', 234
Nordström, Ingmar 69, 418
Nyvall, Jacob 173

O'Connor, Sinéad 68, 270, 417, 424
Offenbach, Jacques 142, 413
Öhrwall, Anders 415
Oistrakh, David 78, 415
Oldfield, Mike 92, 203, 347, 417
Olsson, Otto 413
Orff, Carl 239, 251, 363, 410, 413
Orphei Drängar male choir 415
Ørsted-Pedersen, Niels-Henning 416
Orup 267, 417, 434
Öst, Erik 111, 416
Oswald, Gösta 453

Pachelbel, Johann 413
Paganini, Niccolò 47, 361, 412, 413, 414
Page, Elaine 20
Påhl-Olle 416
Palestrina, Giovanni Pierluigi 128, 315
Palme, Olof 72, 452
Panzarella, Robert 4, 5, 451, 472
Parlan, Horace 416
Parker, Charlie 50
Pärt, Arvo 169, 170, 311, 409, 410, 413, 415, 423
Parton, Dolly 59, 144, 417
Pavarotti, Luciano 415, 448
Penfield, Wilder 97
Perahia, Murray 318
Pergolesi, Giovanni Battista 126, 197, 326,
     327, 413, 415
Pestalozza, Alberto 418
Peters, Cyndee 416
Peterson-Berger, Wilhelm 413
Peterson, Oscar 75, 143
Pettersson, Allan 144, 220, 413
Piaf, Edith 43, 44, 337, 418, 428
Piatigorsky, Gregor 76
Piazzolla, Astor 413
Pink Floyd 160, 165, 349–350, 417
Pleijel, Agneta 261
Police, The 417
Ponsay, Mr 303–304
Poulenc, Francis 314, 409, 413
Power, Tyrone 49
Presley, Elvis 417
Primrose, William 76
Prince 40–41, 270, 417, 434
Privette, Gayle 5, 451, 472
Prokofiev, Sergei 359, 413
Puccini, Giacomo 84, 167, 170, 329, 413
Pullman, Don 342

Quincy Jones Big Band 234

Rachmaninov, Sergei 68, 148, 214, 218, 331,
     332, 357, 410, 413, 415, 478
Radiohead 178
Raimondi, Ruggero 216

Rameau, Jean-Philippe 223, 413
Ramel, Povel 404, 417
Ramirez, Ariel 415
Rangström, Ture 413
Ratata 273, 417
Rattle, Simon 318, 415
Ravel, Maurice 72, 80, 307, 357, 410,
    413, 425, 428
Ray, Johanna 457, 474, 484
Redman, Don 416
Rehnqvist, Karin 413
Reich, Steve 220, 413
Respighi, Ottorino 308, 413, 425
Rice, Tim 183
Rich, Buddy 338, 416
Richmond, Danny 342
Richter, Svyatoslav 415
Riedel, Georg 417
Riley, Terry 220, 413
Rimsky-Korsakov, Nikolai 324
Robinson, Scott 341
Rodgers, Richard 418
Rolling Stones, The 417
Roman, Johan Helmich 260, 413, 415
Ronstadt, Linda 59, 417
Rosenberg, Hilding 251, 257, 414, 415
Rosenberg, Susanne 416
Rossini, Gioachino 15, 68, 413, 414
Roth, Emerich 261
Rouget, Gilbert 458, 477, 485
Russell, Brenda 417

Saedén, Erik 124, 309
Saga 348, 417
Sågskära 285, 358, 416
Sahlström, Erik 416
Saint-Saëns, Charles-Camille 81, 362, 414
Sandberg, Sven Olof 23
Sandström, Nisse 417
Sandström, Sven-David 144, 381, 414, 415, 427
Satie, Erik 414
Sauer, Franz 461
Savage Rose 197
Scarlatti, Alessandro 176, 414
Schaffer, Janne 417
Schauwecker, Frederick 324
Scheja, Staffan 68, 269, 415
Schneiderhahn, Wolfgang 415
Schubert, Franz 23, 24–25, 26, 29, 30, 44, 46–47,
    78, 142–143, 145, 165, 166, 216, 245, 317,
    318, 410, 414, 429, 437, 460, 461
Schumann, Robert 159, 223, 226–227, 245, 319,
    410, 414, 432
Schwarzkopf, Elisabeth 330
Scorpions 417
Second Chapter of Acts 179
Segovia, André 415

Shakespeare, William 299
Sharma, Shiv Kumar 300–301
Shepp, Archie 416
Shostakovich, Dmitri 53, 73, 74, 79, 86, 111, 217,
    295, 312, 313, 314, 362, 410, 414, 431
Sibelius, Jean 24, 25, 44, 50–51, 53, 79, 80, 108,
    113, 114, 131, 132, 356, 359, 362, 368, 377, 410,
    414, 431, 437, 445
Simon, Paul 108–109, 418
Sinatra, Frank 416
Sinding, Cristian 285, 414
Sjöberg, Birger 404, 417
Skoglund, Annika 179–180
Skogsby, Lasse 416
Slash 38
Sloboda, John 4, 471, 472, 476, 482, 483, 484
Smetana, Bedřich 15, 113, 121, 145, 410, 414
Smithereens 87, 417
Södergran, Edith 453
Söderlundh, Lille Bror 414
Söderman, August 216
Söderström, Elisabeth 278, 415
Soffel, Doris 326–327, 415
Soling, Jonny 416
Söllscher, Göran 415
Solti, Georg 175, 306, 415
Springsteen, Bruce 39, 149, 154, 239, 358, 417
Stace, Walter Terence 455, 484
Stalin, Josef 313
Stanley, Paul 60, 150
Stansfield, Lisa 268, 417, 434
Stenberg, Birgit 309
Stern, Daniel 84, 474, 486
Stern, Isaac 415
Sting 417
Stockhausen, Karlheinz 220
Stockholm Concert Society Orchestra 108
Stockholm Philharmonic Orchestra 79, 151,
    201, 313
Stradella, Alessandro 329
Strauss, Johann 414
Strauss, Richard 276, 320, 321, 324, 414, 445
Stravinsky, Igor 22, 114–116, 128, 131, 198,
    241, 357, 362, 364, 368, 410, 414, 426, 437
Strindberg, August 95
Styx 58, 417, 433–434
Supertramp 417
Sutherland, Joan 415
Svanholm, Set 49, 50, 415
Swedish Radio Choir 415
Swedish Radio Symphony Orchestra 172–173, 306
Sylvian, David 194, 417

Takács Quartet 334, 415
Tapiola Children's Choir 128, 315, 410, 415, 424
Taube, Evert 404, 417
Tauro, Erna 274, 418, 435

Tchaikovsky, Peter 32, 46, 53, 74, 75, 143, 166,
    170, 200, 204, 277, 294, 295, 317, 320–321,
    356, 368, 388, 409, 410, 414, 424, 432, 437
Te Kanawa, Kiri 216
Tegnér, Alice 417
Thallaug, Edith 79
Thåström, Joakim 127, 417
Theodorakis, Mikis 122, 197, 359, 404, 414, 418
Theodore, Michael 197
Thielemans, Toots 339, 416
Thin Lizzy 121, 417
Thunarf, Per 216, 415
Tidblad, Inga 95
Tosti, Paolo 329
Tranströmer, Tomas 453
Trio Con Tromba 340, 360
Turesson, Gunnar 418

U2, 178, 182, 417
Uggla, Magnus 417
Ulvaeus, Björn 410
Umeå Sinfonietta 333

Valéry, Paul 453
van Kesteren, Jon 309
Vaughan, Sarah 416
Vecchi, Guido 195, 415
Verdi, Giuseppe 92, 205, 216, 309, 310, 326,
    359, 388, 410, 414, 415, 429, 431, 437
Vienna Philharmonic 290, 306
Villa-Lobos, Heitor 162
Vivaldi, Antonio 15, 114, 195, 284, 411, 414, 430
Vollenweider, Andreas 288, 417
von Karajan, Herbert 52, 126, 192, 277, 415

von Koch, Erland 216
von Stade, Fredrica 328, 415
Vreeswijk, Cornelis 404, 418
Vrethammar, Sylvia 417

Wadenberg, Anders 166
Wagner, Cosima 94
Wagner, Richard 27, 49, 50, 94, 164, 165,
    225, 325, 326, 356, 359, 360, 410,
    414, 431, 437
Walcha, Helmut 17
Wallin, Ceylon 416
Wasa Music 22
Webern, Anton 414
Welin, Karl-Erik 185, 335, 415
Wennerberg, Gunnar 92, 173, 414
Weyrauch, Johannes 415
White, Josh 43, 416
Widor, Charles-Marie 415, 425
Wikander, David 415
Wikström, Roffe 55, 341, 359, 416
Willcocks, David 256
Willemark, Lena 416
Williams, Jerry 275, 417
Wixell, Ingvar 378, 415
Wolf, Endre 415
Wolf, Hugo 245, 324
Wonder, Stevie 417
Wyatt, Robert 194, 417

Young, Lester 416

Zappa, Frank 19–20, 417
Zetterlund, Monica 416